T0189551

# Lecture Notes in Computer Science 12783

More information about this subseries at http://www.springer.com/series/7409

Fiona Fui-Hoon Nah · Keng Siau (Eds.)

# HCI in Business, Government and Organizations

8th International Conference, HCIBGO 2021
Held as Part of the 23rd HCI International Conference, HCII 2021
Virtual Event, July 24–29, 2021
Proceedings

 Springer

*Editors*
Fiona Fui-Hoon Nah
Missouri University of Science
and Technology
Rolla, MO, USA

Keng Siau
Missouri University of Science
and Technology
Rolla, MO, USA

ISSN 0302-9743               ISSN 1611-3349  (electronic)
Lecture Notes in Computer Science
ISBN 978-3-030-77749-4      ISBN 978-3-030-77750-0  (eBook)
https://doi.org/10.1007/978-3-030-77750-0

LNCS Sublibrary: SL3 – Information Systems and Applications, incl. Internet/Web, and HCI

This Springer imprint is published by the registered company Springer Nature Switzerland AG
The registered company address is: Gewerbestrasse 11, 6330 Cham, Switzerland

# Foreword

Human-Computer Interaction (HCI) is acquiring an ever-increasing scientific and industrial importance, and having more impact on people's everyday life, as an ever-growing number of human activities are progressively moving from the physical to the digital world. This process, which has been ongoing for some time now, has been dramatically accelerated by the COVID-19 pandemic. The HCI International (HCII) conference series, held yearly, aims to respond to the compelling need to advance the exchange of knowledge and research and development efforts on the human aspects of design and use of computing systems.

The 23rd International Conference on Human-Computer Interaction, HCI International 2021 (HCII 2021), was planned to be held at the Washington Hilton Hotel, Washington DC, USA, during July 24–29, 2021. Due to the COVID-19 pandemic and with everyone's health and safety in mind, HCII 2021 was organized and run as a virtual conference. It incorporated the 21 thematic areas and affiliated conferences listed on the following page.

A total of 5222 individuals from academia, research institutes, industry, and governmental agencies from 81 countries submitted contributions, and 1276 papers and 241 posters were included in the proceedings to appear just before the start of the conference. The contributions thoroughly cover the entire field of HCI, addressing major advances in knowledge and effective use of computers in a variety of application areas. These papers provide academics, researchers, engineers, scientists, practitioners, and students with state-of-the-art information on the most recent advances in HCI. The volumes constituting the set of proceedings to appear before the start of the conference are listed in the following pages.

The HCI International (HCII) conference also offers the option of 'Late Breaking Work' which applies both for papers and posters, and the corresponding volume(s) of the proceedings will appear after the conference. Full papers will be included in the 'HCII 2021 - Late Breaking Papers' volumes of the proceedings to be published in the Springer LNCS series, while 'Poster Extended Abstracts' will be included as short research papers in the 'HCII 2021 - Late Breaking Posters' volumes to be published in the Springer CCIS series.

The present volume contains papers submitted and presented in the context of the 8th International Conference on HCI in Business, Government and Organizations (HCIBGO 2021), an affiliated conference to HCII 2021. I would like to thank the Co-chairs, Fiona Fui-Hoon Nah and Keng Siau, for their invaluable contribution to its organization and the preparation of the proceedings, as well as the members of the Program Board for their contributions and support. This year, the HCIBGO affiliated conference has focused on topics related to electronic, mobile and ubiquitous commerce, work and business operations, HCI in finance and industry, innovation, collaboration, and knowledge sharing, as well as artificial intelligence in digital transformation.

I would also like to thank the Program Board Chairs and the members of the Program Boards of all thematic areas and affiliated conferences for their contribution towards the highest scientific quality and overall success of the HCI International 2021 conference.

This conference would not have been possible without the continuous and unwavering support and advice of Gavriel Salvendy, founder, General Chair Emeritus, and Scientific Advisor. For his outstanding efforts, I would like to express my appreciation to Abbas Moallem, Communications Chair and Editor of HCI International News.

July 2021                                                    Constantine Stephanidis

# HCI International 2021 Thematic Areas
# and Affiliated Conferences

**Thematic Areas**

- HCI: Human-Computer Interaction
- HIMI: Human Interface and the Management of Information

**Affiliated Conferences**

- EPCE: 18th International Conference on Engineering Psychology and Cognitive Ergonomics
- UAHCI: 15th International Conference on Universal Access in Human-Computer Interaction
- VAMR: 13th International Conference on Virtual, Augmented and Mixed Reality
- CCD: 13th International Conference on Cross-Cultural Design
- SCSM: 13th International Conference on Social Computing and Social Media
- AC: 15th International Conference on Augmented Cognition
- DHM: 12th International Conference on Digital Human Modeling and Applications in Health, Safety, Ergonomics and Risk Management
- DUXU: 10th International Conference on Design, User Experience, and Usability
- DAPI: 9th International Conference on Distributed, Ambient and Pervasive Interactions
- HCIBGO: 8th International Conference on HCI in Business, Government and Organizations
- LCT: 8th International Conference on Learning and Collaboration Technologies
- ITAP: 7th International Conference on Human Aspects of IT for the Aged Population
- HCI-CPT: 3rd International Conference on HCI for Cybersecurity, Privacy and Trust
- HCI-Games: 3rd International Conference on HCI in Games
- MobiTAS: 3rd International Conference on HCI in Mobility, Transport and Automotive Systems
- AIS: 3rd International Conference on Adaptive Instructional Systems
- C&C: 9th International Conference on Culture and Computing
- MOBILE: 2nd International Conference on Design, Operation and Evaluation of Mobile Communications
- AI-HCI: 2nd International Conference on Artificial Intelligence in HCI

# List of Conference Proceedings Volumes Appearing Before the Conference

1. LNCS 12762, Human-Computer Interaction: Theory, Methods and Tools (Part I), edited by Masaaki Kurosu
2. LNCS 12763, Human-Computer Interaction: Interaction Techniques and Novel Applications (Part II), edited by Masaaki Kurosu
3. LNCS 12764, Human-Computer Interaction: Design and User Experience Case Studies (Part III), edited by Masaaki Kurosu
4. LNCS 12765, Human Interface and the Management of Information: Information Presentation and Visualization (Part I), edited by Sakae Yamamoto and Hirohiko Mori
5. LNCS 12766, Human Interface and the Management of Information: Information-rich and Intelligent Environments (Part II), edited by Sakae Yamamoto and Hirohiko Mori
6. LNAI 12767, Engineering Psychology and Cognitive Ergonomics, edited by Don Harris and Wen-Chin Li
7. LNCS 12768, Universal Access in Human-Computer Interaction: Design Methods and User Experience (Part I), edited by Margherita Antona and Constantine Stephanidis
8. LNCS 12769, Universal Access in Human-Computer Interaction: Access to Media, Learning and Assistive Environments (Part II), edited by Margherita Antona and Constantine Stephanidis
9. LNCS 12770, Virtual, Augmented and Mixed Reality, edited by Jessie Y. C. Chen and Gino Fragomeni
10. LNCS 12771, Cross-Cultural Design: Experience and Product Design Across Cultures (Part I), edited by P. L. Patrick Rau
11. LNCS 12772, Cross-Cultural Design: Applications in Arts, Learning, Well-being, and Social Development (Part II), edited by P. L. Patrick Rau
12. LNCS 12773, Cross-Cultural Design: Applications in Cultural Heritage, Tourism, Autonomous Vehicles, and Intelligent Agents (Part III), edited by P. L. Patrick Rau
13. LNCS 12774, Social Computing and Social Media: Experience Design and Social Network Analysis (Part I), edited by Gabriele Meiselwitz
14. LNCS 12775, Social Computing and Social Media: Applications in Marketing, Learning, and Health (Part II), edited by Gabriele Meiselwitz
15. LNAI 12776, Augmented Cognition, edited by Dylan D. Schmorrow and Cali M. Fidopiastis
16. LNCS 12777, Digital Human Modeling and Applications in Health, Safety, Ergonomics and Risk Management: Human Body, Motion and Behavior (Part I), edited by Vincent G. Duffy
17. LNCS 12778, Digital Human Modeling and Applications in Health, Safety, Ergonomics and Risk Management: AI, Product and Service (Part II), edited by Vincent G. Duffy

**http://2021.hci.international/proceedings**

# 8th International Conference on HCI in Business, Government and Organizations (HCIBGO 2021)

Program Board Chairs: **Fiona Fui-Hoon Nah and Keng Siau,** *Missouri University of Science and Technology, USA*

- Kaveh Abhari, USA
- Andreas Auinger, Austria
- Michel Avital, Denmark
- Denise Baker, USA
- Valerie Bartelt, USA
- Kaveh Bazargan, Iran
- Langtao Chen, USA
- Constantinos Coursaris, Canada
- Brenda Eschenbrenner, USA
- JM Goh, Canada
- Netta Iivari, Finland
- Qiqi Jiang, Denmark
- Yi-Cheng Ku, Taiwan
- Murad Moqbel, USA
- Norman Shaw, Canada
- Martin Stabauer, Austria
- Chee-Wee Tan, Denmark
- Werner Wetzlinger, Austria
- I-Chin Wu, Taiwan
- Dezhi Wu, USA
- Dezhi Yin, USA
- Jie Yu, China

The full list with the Program Board Chairs and the members of the Program Boards of all thematic areas and affiliated conferences is available online at:

http://www.hci.international/board-members-2021.php

# 8th International Conference on ICT in Business, Government and Organizations (ICTBGO 2021)

Program Board Chairs: Fiona Fui-Hoon Nah and Keng Siau, Missouri University of Science and Technology, USA

- Karen Abuni, USA
- Andreas Auinger, Austria
- Michel Avital, Denmark
- Denise Baker, USA
- Valerie Bartelt, USA
- Kaveh Bazargan, Iran
- Langtao Chen, USA
- Constantinos Coursaris, Canada
- Brenda Eschenbrenner, USA
- JM Goh, Canada
- Neha Ihyan, Finland

- Onji Jiang, Denmark
- Yu-Cheng Kin, Taiwan
- Murad Moeini, USA
- Norman Shaw, Canada
- Marlie Stabauer, Austria
- Chee-Wee Tan, Denmark
- Werner Wetzlinger, Austria
- I-Chin Wu, Taiwan
- Dezhi Wu, USA
- Dezhi Yin, USA
- Jie Yu, China

The full list with the Program Board Chairs and the members of the Program Board of all thematic areas and affiliated conferences is available online at:

http://www.held.org/international-board-members-2021.php

# HCI International 2022

The 24th International Conference on Human-Computer Interaction, HCI International 2022, will be held jointly with the affiliated conferences at the Gothia Towers Hotel and Swedish Exhibition & Congress Centre, Gothenburg, Sweden, June 26 – July 1, 2022. It will cover a broad spectrum of themes related to Human-Computer Interaction, including theoretical issues, methods, tools, processes, and case studies in HCI design, as well as novel interaction techniques, interfaces, and applications. The proceedings will be published by Springer. More information will be available on the conference website: http://2022.hci.international/:

General Chair
Prof. Constantine Stephanidis
University of Crete and ICS-FORTH
Heraklion, Crete, Greece
Email: general_chair@hcii2022.org

**http://2022.hci.international/**

# Contents

## HCI in Finance and Industry

## Work and Business Operations

## Innovation, Collaboration, and Knowledge Sharing

## Digital Transformation and Artificial Intelligence

# Electronic, Mobile and Ubiquitous Commerce

# Consumers' Acceptance of a Voice Commerce Application in FMCG in Germany, U.S. and U.K.

Elena Adolphs and Silvia Zaharia[✉]

University of Applied Sciences Niederrhein, Krefeld, Germany
silvia.zaharia@hs-niederrhein.de

**Abstract.** Shopping-related voice assistant applications are on the rise, but their acceptance differs depending on the country. This paper examines customers' acceptance of a voice commerce application developed by a global fast moving consumer goods company based on a survey of online shoppers (n = 824) conducted in Germany, U.K. and the U.S. The main objective of the study is to identify which factors influence the acceptance of the voice commerce application, and whether there are differences between Germany, the U.S. and U.K. An integrated explanatory model was developed based on the Unified Theory of Acceptance and Use of Technology 2 (UTAUT2) with the antecedents: hedonic motivation, performance expectancy, effort expectancy and social influence. The original model was expanded to include the construct of perceived risk with the dimensions privacy and functional risk. The main result is that there are differences between the three countries regarding the factors that influence the acceptance of the voice commerce application. Only two factors have a significant influence in all three countries: performance expectancy and social influence, with performance expectancy demonstrating the strongest effect. From the perceived risks, only privacy risk has a negative influence on the intention to use the voice application in Germany. This study indicates that researches on the consumers' acceptance from one country should not be applied readily to another. It is rather advisable to consider the unique circumstances of each country.

**Keywords:** Voice commerce · Voice application · Voice assistant · Hedonic motivation · Performance expectancy · Effort expectancy · Social influence · Privacy risk · Functional risk · Intention to use · Smart speaker

## 1 Introduction

Many consider voice commerce a revolution in online retailing. It enables new types of services to emerge and offers companies the opportunity to establish an exclusive and personal relationship with their customers [19]. Driven by mobile commerce, the usage of smart speakers, digital assistants and the ongoing implementation of the "Internet of things", this topic has become of significant relevance [11]. Voice commerce is a special form of e-commerce. It describes the interaction between users and commercial platforms and applications that utilize natural language speech recognition to enable self-service transactions over connected devices [18]. The devices used are equipped with

© Springer Nature Switzerland AG 2021
F. F.-H. Nah and K. Siau (Eds.): HCII 2021, LNCS 12783, pp. 3–21, 2021.
https://doi.org/10.1007/978-3-030-77750-0_1

conversational communication interfaces and intelligent software programs and are oper-ated by the user using natural language [26]. The devices can be so-called smart speakers (such as Amazon Echo, Google Home or HomePod from Apple), but also computers or smartphones into which the software application of a voice assistant such as Alexa (Amazon), Google Assistant, Siri (Apple) or AliGenie (Alibaba) is integrated. Compared to previous voice-controlled human-computer interactions, the communication skills of artificial intelligence (AI) empowered voice assistants are far more advanced. Natural language processing enables people to talk to a computer/device like to a person and to receive contextual answers from them [6]. The two voice assistants covering commerce the most (in the western world) are Alexa and Google Assistant. Companies looking to sell their products using either of the voice assistants (VA) must develop a so-called shopping solution (for Alexa, these are called "skills" and for Google, "actions").

For the consumer, the main benefits of using voice assistants are: convenience (they allow personalized, hands and eyes free usage [10] and are easy to use [12]), efficiency (less mental effort) and usage enjoyment [24]. The interaction and conversation with the artificial voice while shopping can be fun for the user. Over time, users can develop an emotional closeness to the devices and build a sense of a social relationship, similar to when interacting with people [7]. Consumers are also fascinated by the ability of the voice application to learn (due to the artificial intelligence of the voice assistant software) [9]. Alongside the benefits of using voice assistance, consumers hold several concerns regarding a lack of trust in the technology and a fear of losing privacy. The main barriers include: concerns about personal data (refusing to be actively recorded or personal data to be used) [10, 16], concerns about the functionality of the voice assistants (e.g. voice-only voice assistants don't allow users to visualize information/choices or they do not understand the user and his/her reactions) [12]. Further concerns relate to the utility of voice assistants as well as the quality of the information provided [10].

Online retailers and consumer brands manufacturers expect the convenience and user experience offered by the voice assistants to have great potential in electronic commerce [19]. Over 60% of consumers in the U.S. who have an intelligent voice assistant have already used it for purchases. For the year 2022, revenue in the area of voice commerce for the U.S. market is estimated at over \$ 40 billion [18]. Looking at the relevance of different branches in voice commerce, FMCG is a favorite product range for voice-assisted purchases [25].

Voice commerce applications can be used for more than simply purchasing prod-ucts or services. Rather, they are relevant to all phases of the customer journey. Activ-ities like "making a shopping list", "researching a product/service", "searching for a product/service", "comparing products/services" and "price comparison for prod-ucts/services" are the most important reasons for using voice assistance in an e-commerce context [17]. However, this "market mediation" function may also jeopardize brand man-ufacturers by changing their relationship to consumers. Voice assistants become "gate keepers", whose built-in AI recommends specific brands to consumers based on their known preferences and purchasing behavior. Consumer brands fear a reduction in brand visibility via organic search results and in turn the rise of retailers' private labels [13].

Despite the attention given to voice commerce from practitioners and industry reports, there is little academic research on the topic. There are some papers on the acceptance of voice assistants in general, but few empirical researches that relate to shopping (voice commerce). Most of these studies were merely carried out in one country, usually with a sample of students or university employees. The extent to which the results would differ between countries due to local peculiarities was not examined. Closing this research gap is the aim of this study.

The research object for this study is a German fast moving consumer goods (FMCG) manufacturer. The company in question is globally successful, with Germany, U.S. and the U.K. among its most important markets for beauty care products. The manufacturer pursues indirect distribution, does not have its own online shop and sells its products exclusively through offline and online retailers (e.g. Amazon). For this reason, the company does not aim to sell products via voice commerce. Instead, its goal is to develop a voice commerce application that calls consumers attention to its products early on in the customer journey to raise the visibility of the brand. For the purposes of this study, a prototype of a voice application was developed (use case) that dialogues with the user to suggest tailored beauty care solutions. With the help of Amazon skills or Google actions, the products can then be purchased through an associated online retailer. The present paper aims to answer the following research questions:

(1)  Is there an intent to use the voice application?
(2)  Which factors influence the intention to use the voice application and to what extent?
(3)  Are there differences between the studied countries Germany, U.S. and U.K.?

## 2  Conceptual Framework

### 2.1  Technology Acceptance and Perceived Risk

Studies on the acceptance of voice assistants are based in part on the *Technology Acceptance Model* (TAM) by Davis et al. [4] as well as the *Unified Theory of Acceptance and Use of Technology* (UTAUT) and UTAUT2 by Venkatesh et al. [27, 28]. The UTAUT2 is the evolution of the UTAUT. It integrates eight established behavioral models of psychology and technology: The Theory of Reasoned Action, the Technology Acceptance Model, the Motivational Model, the Theory of Planned Behavior, the Combined TAM and TPB, the Model of PC Utilization, the Innovation Diffusion Theory and the Social Cognitive Theory [28]. The UTAUT2 represents an improved version of the UTAUT used to investigate use intentions (behavioral intention), thus better predicting the adoption (use behavior) of a technology [14]. The four determinants of UTAUT performance expectancy, effort expectancy, social influence and facilitating conditions were extended by hedonic motivation, price value and habit. The effect of performance expectancy on behavioral intention are moderated by the variables of age and gender. The effects of all other predictors (effort expectancy, social influence, facilitating conditions, hedonic motivation, price value and habit) on behavioral intention are moderated through the variables age, gender and experience [28].

When it comes to technology acceptance research, perceived risk has proven to be an important barrier. Featherman/Pavlou [5] used seven risk dimensions in their model and integrated the TAM in their study to find out how important perceived risk is for the decision to introduce e-services. The seven risk dimensions are: performance, financial, time, psychological, social, privacy and overall risk. Martins et al. [14] applied the model of Featherman/Pavlou [5] to the UTAUT of Venkatesh et al. [28] and developed a *Unified Theory of Acceptance and Use of Technology and Perceived Risk Application.*

## 2.2 Literature Review

Most studies on the acceptance/adoption of voice assistants do not relate explicitly to voice commerce [3, 7, 8, 10], or are of a qualitative nature [9, 16, 24]. Some current quantitative studies from the U.S., U.K. and Germany are presented below.

Liao et al. [10] conducted a survey with 1.178 users and non-users of voice-controlled intelligent personal assistants (IPAs) in the U.S. to investigate (1) the motivations and barriers to adopting IPAs and (2) how concerns about data privacy and trust in company compliance with social contract related to IPA data affect acceptance and use of IPAs. The adoption (or rejection) decisions are influenced by classical constructs in TAM and UTAUT: *perceived usefulness, performance expectancy* and *effort expectancy* associated with IPA use. Respondents who refused to consider purchasing a Home IPA (i.e. smart speaker) had significantly higher concerns about the use of data and a significantly lower confidence that the data is sufficiently secure.

McLean/Osei-Frimpong [15] take a Uses and Gratification Theory (U&GT) approach to explain the use of in-home voice assistant with a sample of 724 users in the U.K. The results from a structural equation model illustrate that individuals are motivated by the *utilitarian benefits, symbolic benefits* and *social benefits* provided by voice assistants. The *hedonic benefits* do not motivate the use of in-home voice assistants. Additionally, the research establishes a moderating role of *perceived privacy risks* in dampening and negatively influencing the use of in-home voice assistants.

Wagner et al. [30] investigated (1) the role of anthropomorphism in the context of digital voice assistants and (2) the determinants of the UTAUT2 for digital voice assistants by conducting an online survey with 283 users. The results of the structural equation modelling show (1) that anthropomorphism in general plays a role concerning the behavioral intention for voice assistants with a *humanlike-fit* having the highest impact on a human driven likeability. (2) The relevant drivers of the intention to use voice assistants (referring to the UTAUT2 model) are *performance expectancy, hedonic motivation* and *habit. Facilitating conditions, effort expectancy* and *social influence* had no significant influence on the intention to use voice assistants.

Two relevant voice commerce studies based on UTAUT2 were conducted at the University of Applied Sciences Niederrhein in Germany. Puschmann et al. [22] used multiple regression analysis to study the acceptance of voice assistants in e-commerce (n = 429). The key findings of the analysis are that *performance expectancy* and *hedonic motivation* have the strongest influence on the intention to use voice assistants for purchases (*behavioral intention*). Meanwhile, *effort expectancy* and *social influence* only have a low influence on purchasing intentions. *Facilitating conditions* had no significant influence on the intention to use, while *perceived risk* had a weak negative effect on it. The influence of the moderators (age, gender and experience) on the relationship between predictors and behavioral intention proved significant for only two predictors (performance expectancy and hedonic motivation): The older a person is, the weaker the influence of performance expectancy on behavioral intention. Meanwhile, the effect of performance expectancy and hedonic motivation on behavioral intention is weaker for women than for men.

By means of a representative online survey of German online shoppers (n = 684), Zaharia/Würfel [33] studied the factors influencing the acceptance of smart speakers throughout the customer journey. The explanatory model developed for the study was based on UTAUT2 and expanded to include the construct of perceived risk. The examined structural equation model revealed *performance expectancy* and *hedonic motivation* as the strongest factors influencing the willingness of online shoppers to use smart speakers (*behavioral intention*). Prior *experience* and the perceived *price value* of smart speakers had little effect on the intention to use them in voice commerce. *Effort expectancy* had no direct effect on behavioral intention, while *perceived risk* had a negative effect on the intention to use. Furthermore, the intention to use smart speakers was shown to be higher during the information phase than in the purchasing phase.

## 2.3 Model and Hypotheses

The present study builds on the results of Zaharia/Würfel [33] and Puschmann et al. [22]. The basic model is the UTAUT2, extended to include the construct perceived risk. Ideally, the acceptance of voice commerce applications would be measured on the basis of actual use behavior. However, the application in question exists only as a prototype shown to respondents for the first time in the context of the study. Instead, the dependent variable for measuring acceptance is *behavioral intention* (BI). Users are meant to utilize the selected voice commerce application during the pre-sales phase.

In developing the model for this study, three independent variables were eliminated from the UTAUT2 model (facilitating conditions, price value and habit): According to Puschmann et al. [22] and Wagner et al. [30], the variable facilitating conditions is a not significant factor. Price value as an independent variable is not relevant to this study because the software is free of charge, and a consumer need not buy a smart speaker to use the voice commerce application. Furthermore, the actual voice application (the use case) cannot be related to habit, as it was not used by the consumer prior to the study. The model developed can be seen in Fig. 1. *Perceived risk* (*functional* and *privacy*) is assumed to have a negative effect on the intention to use the presented voice application (*behavioral intention*). The factors *performance expectancy* (PE), *effort expectancy* (EE), *social influence* (SI) and *hedonic motivation* (HM) have a positive influence on the *behavioral intention* (BI). *Age* and *gender* moderate the influence of PE, EE, SI and HM on BI.

*Perceived risk* is defined as the degree to which a user thinks that using a technology will have negative implications for him or her and has a negative impact on the intention to use a technology [14]. Consumers have been shown to hold several concerns about the usage of voice assistants. Liao et al. [10] found that perceptions of whether IPA providers adhere to privacy and security rules affects users' likelihood of using IPAs, even if only 7% of respondents cited privacy concerns as the main reason for not using IPAs. An exploratory German study names the following negative beliefs toward voice commerce [24]:

- limited transparency (no visual representation, no comparison function, limited product information)

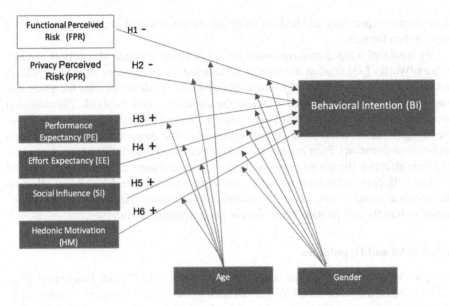

**Fig. 1.** Explanatory model for the acceptance of a voice commerce application

- low technical maturity (limited interactivity, speech recognition errors)
- limited control (potential misuse by strangers, no manual input modality, risk of misunderstanding)
- lack of trust (vendor's competence/benevolence, technology reliability).

The different facets of perceived risk can be summarized by the two dimensions of *functional perceived risk (FPR)* and *privacy perceived risk* (PPR). For the moderators age and gender, it is found that the major demographic using voice assistants is 33–45 years old [2] and male [23]. Ipso facto, it is assumed that this group perceives less functional and privacy risk than older people and women. This leads to the following hypotheses:

**H1:** The influence of FPR on BI is negative.
**H1a:** The influence of FPR on BI is weaker for younger people.
**H1b:** The influence of FPR on BI is stronger for women.
**H2:** The influence of PPR on BI is negative.
**H2a:** The influence of PPR on BI is weaker for younger people.
**H2b:** The influence of PPR on BI is stronger for women.

*Performance expectancy (PE)* means the degree to which a consumer expects to experience a performance advantage (utility) from using a voice commerce application. Consumers expect an advantage in terms of convenience and time savings by using voice assistants [33]. Furthermore, the available functions of the voice assistants have a positive influence on the adoption of the technology [9]. This leads to the assumption that a positive PE increases the usage intention of the use case. For the moderators age and gender, studies demonstrate that women are less task-oriented than men. This suggests that it is less important for them to implement a task in a targeted way. For age it is mentioned that younger people tend to attach greater importance to extrinsic rewards [28]. This leads to the following hypotheses:

**H3:** The influence of PE on BI is positive.
**H3a:** The influence of PE on BI is stronger for younger people.
**H3b:** The influence of PE on BI is weaker for women than men.

*Effort Expectancy (EE)* refers to the amount of effort expected when using a technology. In the voice commerce context, it is defined as the degree to which a consumer considers an application easy to learn and operate [29, 33]. According to UTAUT2 the assumption is that a high usability of the voice commerce application will have a positive influence on BI. For the moderator gender it was found that there is a gender difference and that ease of learning a technology is more important for women than for men [31]. For age it can be detained that younger people have a higher cognitive capacity for innovation [9]. This leads to the following hypotheses:

**H4:** The influence of EE on BI is positive.
**H4a:** The influence of EE on BI is stronger for younger people.
**H4b:** The influence of EE on BI is stronger for women.

*Social influence (SI)* means the degree to which a consumer experiences important people (family and friends) recommending the voice assistant application [22]. Yang et al. [32] explain that four social influenced indicators affect the individual's intention to use a technology: subjective norm, image, visibility and voluntariness. The presented use case cannot refer to image, visibility or voluntariness effects, but it can refer to subjective norms. Subjective norms means that individuals are influenced by other people and prefer them as a source for information and guidance [32]. People mention an increased interest in voice assistants, if a friend has told them about it [9]. This leads to the assumption that BI towards the use case is increased by SI. This effect is moderated by age and gender because women and older people tend to attach greater importance to the opinions of others [27]. This leads to the following hypotheses:

**H5:** The influence of SI on BI is positive.
**H5a:** The influence of SI on BI is stronger for older people.
**H5b:** The influence of SI on BI is stronger for women.

*Hedonic motivation (HM)* refers to the perceived pleasure an individual experience from using a technology [9]. In the voice commerce context, HM is defined as the degree to which a consumer considers using voice commerce applications as fun, entertaining, exciting and pleasant [33]. According to previous research, it is assumed that a high degree of fun and satisfaction while using the voice application will lead to a higher intention to use it (BI). Age and gender moderate the fun and enjoyment arising from new technology use. It tends to be stronger for men, as men have a greater interest in innovative systems and are more open-minded to integrating them [1]. This is emphasized by studies showing that voice assistants are used by a majority of men [23]. Furthermore, younger people are more curious about discovering new technologies and older people are more skeptical of technological innovation [21]. This leads to the following hypotheses:

**H6:** The influence of HM on BI is positive.
**H6a:** The influence of HM on BI is stronger for younger people.
**H6b:** The influence of HM on BI is weaker for women.

## 3 Research Design

### 3.1 Presenting the Use Case

In order to develop a voice commerce application for this study, a qualitative survey was conducted as a first step. Researchers studied voice commerce applications already on the market (from competitors, retailers or best practices from other industries) and interviewed experts. This resulted in a mockup voice application (use case) that recommends tailored product solutions by dialoging with users. The voice application is a hair advisor based on visual content that targets consumers looking for new hair styles and hair trends. Users will use it in the bathroom or in favorite spaces like the living room or kitchen on display devices like smartphones, Google Nest Hub and Amazon Echo Show. The skill was launched for both the voice assistants Alexa and Google Assistant. The user contacts the skill or action by name and call to action i.e. "Alexa/Google open the Hair Application". The skill can also be found by asking "Alexa/Google show me the newest hairstyle", "Alexa/Google, I want to color my hair", "Alexa/Google how can I braid/curl/straighten my hair?". The aim is to attract customers by identifying their preferred looks before they begin searching for products. The products linked to each look (e.g. hair color) are then suggested to the user. The user can look up product information for each product and put items on their shopping list if using the Amazon voice assistant. In Google's case the phrase "put it on a shopping list" will advise the user on where to purchase the product by showing and redirecting the customer to the top three online retail shops where the product is available.

### 3.2 Data Collection

The quantitative data of the research was obtained from a sample of 824 participants in an online survey conducted in September 2019. The studied countries were Germany (DE; n = 281), United Kingdom (U.K.; n = 286) and the United States (U.S.; n = 257). The sample represents the FMCG company's target group: men and women from each country ages 16–65 years who are open to new technologies (e.g. voice commerce/voice assistants) and who have a basic interest in hair styling. Quotas were set in order to reach a sufficient case number within each gender and age group. For age it was equally 33% through the main age groups 16–29, 30–49 and 50–65 years. For gender the quotas were 90% women and 10% men to cover the target group.

The survey starts with presenting the use case (mockup) to the respondent followed by questions on the actual use of voice assistance and voice skills. Further questions target each individual construct. The constructs were measured using multi-item scales on a 5-point Likert Scale (1 = "I strongly disagree"/5 = "I strongly agree"). The operationalization of the constructs can be seen in Appendix A.

## 4   Results

The descriptive evaluation answered the first research question "Is there an intent to use the voice application?". The top-two analysis shows that, in total, 54% of consumers agree with the statement "I intend to use the application in the future". However, responses differ at a country level. The highest share of people who state intentions to use the application are in the U.S. (70%) followed by U.K. (51%). Germans seem to be the most hesitant with only 41%. To learn more about the general usage, two additional questions were stated in the survey asking the respondents for the actual use of voice assistance and voice skills. Most respondents do not yet use voice assistance (36%) nor voice skills (40%).

To verify the constructs, a confirmatory factor analysis (CFA) was performed on the total database. A data quality check and testing of univariate exploratory factor analysis (EFA) was done in advance [34]. The total result can be summarized as very good, having used basically proven operational questions from existing models. The following test results are valid (see Table 1):

1. Cronbach's Alpha refers to the joint consideration of the Item-to-Total-Correlation (ITC). Depending on the number of items $\alpha$ limits are between $\geq 0.5$–$\geq 0.7$ (2 items $\alpha \geq 0.5$; 3 items $\alpha \geq 0.6$; more than 4 items $\alpha \geq 0.7$.) The limit values are maintained for all constructs.
2. By using exploratory factor analysis, the constructs are tested for reliability and validity. The factor loadings should show a correlation between item and factor of at least 0.7. The indicator reliability should be above the value of 0.5 in the form of communalities. The test by univariate EFA is positive for all items.
3. By performing CFA (AMOS), the significance of the factor loads and the standardized factor loads are determined. From this the quality criteria of the average variance extracted (AVE $\geq 0.5$) and the factor reliability (FR $\geq 0.6$) are calculated and tested. All factor loads could be tested as significant.
4. The Fornell-Larcker criterion determines the discriminant validity of the construct to the other constructs, thus demonstrating the quality of the factor. To substantiate this, the average variance of a factor must be higher than the factors squared correlation and other measured factors. This can be supported for all factors used in the model.

The hypotheses were tested using multiple regression analysis. Multiple regression is linked to a number of assumptions about the nature of the data [34]. These assumptions were fulfilled for all three countries. Testing the model revealed that the variance of BI (the probability to use the voice application) can be explained by 67.8% (DE), 74.4% (U.K.) and 65.8% (US) of the variance of the predictors. At a 0.01% level, the model contributes to explaining the regressor for all countries (ANOVA).

The results of the regression analysis (see Table 2) answer the second research question: "Which factors influence the intended use?" Appendix B shows the effect model for each country. Germany is the only country showing an effect (negative) from perceived risk. In all three countries, the effects of the predictors are weak to moderate.

- For Germany, *the intention to use the voice application* is significantly influenced by *performance expectancy, social influence* and *hedonic motivation*. Meanwhile, *perceived privacy risk* has a weak negative effect.
- In the U.K. only *performance expectancy, social influence* and *hedonic motivation* have a significant effect on the *intention to use the voice application*.
- The results from the U.S. differ. *Performance expectancy, effort expectancy* and *social influence* have a significant effect on the *intention to use the voice application*.

The analysis shows that all main hypotheses, with the exception of H1, could be supported for nearly all cases across the three countries (see Table 3).

The effect of the moderators age and gender on respective predictor-criterion relationships was examined using multiple group regression analysis. For gender, the moderating effect was not assessed by country since, after data cleaning, fewer than 30 men per country remained (D: n = 24 and U.K.: n = 28). In reviewing the requirements for the regression analysis, a problem arose in the VIF value for HM (5.571), meaning the moderator effect of age and gender for the influence of HM on BI could not be assessed. The hypotheses involving moderating effects could not be supported in most cases (see Appendix C).

The third research question "Are there differences between the studied countries Germany, U.S. and U.K.?", can be answered affirmatively. Differences arise both in the use intention as well as the triggers and barriers for the intention to use the voice commerce application.

## 5  Discussion, Recommendations and Limitations

The present study has shown that there are differences between Germany, the U.S. and the U.K. when it comes to acceptance of the voice commerce application. The highest intention to use was seen in the U.S. (70%) followed by the U.K. (51%). In Germany, only 41% stated an intention to use the voice commerce application. From the UTAUT2 antecedents only two were shown to have an influence in all three countries, namely performance expectancy and social influence.

- Performance expectancy has the strongest effect in all countries and was shown to be higher for men.
- The effect of social influence on the intention to use the voice commerce application is higher in DE and the U.K. than in the U.S. For age differentiation, the influence of social influence was shown to be stronger for older people in Germany. The social influence effect is in all three countries higher for women.
- Effort expectancy has an influence only in the U.S. where it demonstrated the second strongest effect.
- Hedonic motivation only has an influence in Germany and the U.K.
- Privacy risk has a negative influence only in Germany. For all other countries, the risk predictors are not significant.

**Table 1.** Confirmatory factor analysis results including quality criteria

| Construct | α ≥ 0.5-0.7 | Average variance (AVE) ≥ 0.5 | FR ≥ 0.6 | 1-factorial solution | Explained variance in % | Indicator | ITC ≥ 0.3-0.5 | α if Item is deleted | Sign. Factor loading | Factor loading ≥ 0.7 | Commonalities ≥ 0.5 |
|---|---|---|---|---|---|---|---|---|---|---|---|
| *Functional Perceived Risk* | 0.912 | 0.812 | 0.945 | yes | 79.124 | FPR_1 | 0.785 | 0.891 | *** | 0.880 | 0.775 |
| | | | | | | FPR_2 | 0.781 | 0.892 | *** | 0.878 | 0.770 |
| | | | | | | FPR_3 | 0.823 | 0.878 | *** | 0.904 | 0.817 |
| | | | | | | FPR_4 | 0.810 | 0.883 | *** | 0.896 | 0.803 |
| *Privacy Perceived Risk* | 0.796 | 0.657 | 0.847 | yes | 71.009 | PPR_1 | 0.556 | 0.804 | *** | 0.784 | 0.614 |
| | | | | | | PPR_2 | 0.703 | 0.65 | *** | 0.880 | 0.775 |
| | | | | | | PPR_3 | 0.669 | 0.69 | *** | 0.861 | 0.741 |
| *Performance Expectancy* | 0.875 | 0.784 | 0.916 | yes | 80.199 | PE_1 | 0.787 | 0.799 | *** | 0.909 | 0.827 |
| | | | | | | PE_2 | 0.752 | 0.834 | *** | 0.890 | 0.792 |
| | | | | | | PE_3 | 0.748 | 0.835 | *** | 0.887 | 0.787 |
| *Hedonic Motivation* | 0.875 | 0.797 | 0.921 | yes | 80.135 | HM_1 | 0.807 | 0.78 | *** | 0.922 | 0.849 |
| | | | | | | HM_2 | 0.813 | 0.774 | *** | 0.925 | 0.855 |
| | | | | | | HM_3 | 0.665 | 0.906 | *** | 0.836 | 0.699 |
| *Effort Expectancy* | 0.900 | 0.780 | 0.934 | yes | 77.078 | EE_1 | 0.714 | 0.894 | *** | 0.833 | 0.694 |
| | | | | | | EE_2 | 0.811 | 0.859 | *** | 0.899 | 0.809 |
| | | | | | | EE_3 | 0.809 | 0.86 | *** | 0.898 | 0.807 |
| | | | | | | EE_4 | 0.777 | 0.871 | *** | 0.879 | 0.773 |
| *Social Influence* | 0.868 | 0.745 | 0.921 | yes | 71.634 | SI_1 | 0.651 | 0.857 | *** | 0.799 | 0.638 |
| | | | | | | SI_2 | 0.733 | 0.826 | *** | 0.855 | 0.731 |
| | | | | | | SI_3 | 0.756 | 0.815 | *** | 0.869 | 0.756 |
| | | | | | | SI_4 | 0.739 | 0.823 | *** | 0.860 | 0.740 |
| *Behavioral Intention* | 0.942 | 0.899 | 0.964 | yes | 89.588 | BI_1 | 0.877 | 0.917 | *** | 0.946 | 0.895 |
| | | | | | | BI_2 | 0.846 | 0.941 | *** | 0.930 | 0.864 |

(ns) = not significant/ *significance on 5% level/ ** high significance on 1% level/ *** highly significance on 0.1% level

**Table 2.** Results of the regression analysis

| Construct | Dimension | B | | | (Beta) | | | Significance | | | adjR² | | |
|---|---|---|---|---|---|---|---|---|---|---|---|---|---|
| | | DE | U.S. | U.K. | DE | US | U.K. | DE | | U.S. | | U.K. | | DE | U.S. | U.K. |
| | (Constant) | 0.060 | -0.377 | -0.497 | | | | 0.816 | (ns) | 0.122 | (ns) | 0.043 | (ns) | | | |
| | (FPR) Functional Perceived Risk | 0.121 | 0.030 | 0.053 | 0.097 | 0.039 | 0.044 | 0.016 | * | 0.379 | (ns) | 0.271 | (ns) | | | |
| | (PPR) Privacy Perceived Risk | -0.150 | 0.004 | -0.094 | -0.139 | 0.005 | -0.072 | 0.001 | *** | 0.908 | (ns) | 0.068 | (ns) | | | |
| Behavioral Intention | (PE) Performance Expectancy | 0.423 | 0.540 | 0.464 | 0.391 | 0.487 | 0.400 | 0.000 | *** | 0.000 | *** | 0.000 | *** | 0.678 | 0.658 | 0.744 |
| | (HM) Hedonic Motivation | 0.208 | 0.009 | 0.252 | 0.187 | 0.007 | 0.206 | 0.007 | ** | 0.919 | (ns) | 0.001 | * | | | |
| | (EE) Effort Expectancy | 0.004 | 0.312 | 0.031 | 0.003 | 0.252 | 0.022 | 0.950 | (ns) | 0.000 | ** | 0.685 | (ns) | | | |
| | (SI) Social Influence | 0.390 | 0.203 | 0.361 | 0.348 | 0.241 | 0.345 | 0.000 | *** | 0.000 | *** | 0.000 | *** | | | |

(ns) = not significant/ *significance on 5%-level/ ** high significance on 1% level/ *** highly significance on 0.1% level

medium effect (> 0.3)     weak effect (> 0.1)

**Table 3.** Test result of the main hypotheses

| Hypothesis | | Assessment | | |
|---|---|---|---|---|
| | | *DE* | *U.S* | *U.K* |
| H1 | The influence of FPR on BI is negative | x | x | x |
| H2 | The influence of PPR on BI is negative | Supported | x | x |
| H3 | The influence of PE on BI is positive | Supported | Supported | Supported |
| H4 | The influence of EE on BI is positive | x | Supported | x |
| H5 | The influence of SI on BI is positive | Supported | Supported | Supported |
| H6 | The influence of HM on BI is positive | Supported | x | Supported |

x = not supported

This raises the question if, and to what degree, studies from one country can be applied readily to another. This study shows that it is advisable to consider the specific circumstances of each country when developing and implementing the application. Since users' performance expectancy (i.e. the perceived benefit to him or her from using the voice commerce application) has the strongest effect on acceptance in all countries, success hinges on the ability to ensure performance of the voice commerce application. The user will rate the voice application primarily according to how well it helps him/her to find the right product. This means that the intelligent software should make the right product suggestions based on the input from the consumer and provide the desired information.

Social influence is in all three countries very important for implementing the application, especially for women. This key trigger should be pushed in all three countries. This can be done by using a recommendation function in the app. The intention to use the application can for example be influenced by sweepstakes on social media where people are asked to test the application and tell about it.

Due to the differences between the three countries, the following country-specific measures are recommended: In the U.S., the effortlessness (easy to understand and operate) of the application should be underlined. For the U.K. and Germany, where hedonic motivation plays a role in acceptance, communication should focus on the fun experienced while using the application. In order to guarantee the perceived enjoyment of use and to avoid frustration, companies should ensure the integration of the voice channel with internal processes. In Germany in particular, the perceived privacy risk must be taken into account. Companies should be proactive to build trust and ensure and communicate the privacy and security of customer data.

There is a number of limitations in our research study that should be addressed in future research. The first limitation pertains to the research object: the results of the study are relevant for FMCG manufacturers in the area of beauty care products and their voice commerce application. Results for a different voice commerce application in another industry could turn out quite differently. The second limitation pertains to the countries included in the study. To generate the most relevant findings, the study focused on the three selected countries because they are the most important for e-commerce for the

FMCG manufacturer. Still, other relevant markets should be considered for future study. China is an interesting option since it is indicated as open minded for new technologies.

# 6 Conclusion

Voice commerce applications carry opportunities and risks for consumers, but they are weighed differently depending on the country. This study examined customers' acceptance of a voice commerce application developed by a global FMCG Company based on an online survey of online shoppers (n = 824) conducted in Germany, U.K. and the U.S. An integrated explanatory model was developed based on the UTAUT2. The original model was expanded to include the construct of perceived risk with the dimensions privacy and functional risk. The proposed conceptualization and operationalization of the constructs was analyzed by means of exploratory and confirmatory factor analysis and found to be very good (based on generally recognized quality criteria). The hypothesized relationships were examined with the help of regression analysis. The present study has shown that there are differences between the three countries regarding the factors that influence the intention to use the voice commerce application. Performance expectancy and social influence have a significant influence in all three countries, with performance expectancy demonstrating the strongest effect in all countries. The influence of performance expectancy is higher for men while social influence is higher for women. From the perceived risks, only privacy risk has a weak but highly significant negative influence on the intent to use the voice application in Germany. Perceived functional risk has no significant effect. Effort expectancy has an influence only in the U.S. where it has the second strongest effect. Hedonic motivation only has an influence in Germany and the U.K. This study shows that it is advisable to consider the specific circumstances of each country when developing and implementing voice commerce applications.

# Appendix A: Operationalization of the Constructs

| | |
|---|---|
| **Functional Perceived Risk** | |
| FPR_1 | *I suspect the voice application (VA) could...* <br> ...not perform well and create problems with my devices. |
| FPR_2 | ...highly probably not provide desired results. |
| FPR_3 | ...advise me wrong, because of malfunction. |
| FPR_4 | ...advise me wrong, because the assistant will not understand me. |
| **Privacy Perceived Risk** | |
| PPR_1 | Using the VA with my voice assistant will cause my conversations to be over-heard. |
| PPR_2 | Signing up for and using the application would lead to a loss of privacy because my personal information would be used without my knowledge. |
| PPR_3 | Internet hackers (criminals) might take control of my checking account if I use the VA. |
| **Performance Expectancy** | |
| PE_1 | *When I think of the VA, I would assume...* <br> ...that I would find it useful in my daily life. |
| PE_2 | ...it to enable me to answer my questions about hair styling and hair products more quickly. |
| PE_3 | ...it to increase my productivity because I can do several things at once. |
| **Effort Expectancy** | |
| EE_1 | The interaction with the application is clear and understandable. |
| EE_2 | It is easy for me to become skillful at using the application. |
| EE_3 | I find the application easy to use. |
| EE_4 | Learning how to use the application would be easy for me. |
| **Social Influence** | |
| SI_1 | *Whether I will use the VA in the future could be influenced by...* <br> ...friends or family members recommending it to me. |
| SI_2 | ...Influencers recommending it to me via social media (e.g. Facebook or Instagram). |
| SI_3 | ...very important people recommending it to me via advertising. |
| SI_4 | ...colleagues and superiors whose opinion I value recommending it to me. |
| **Hedonic Motivation** | |
| HM_1 | Using the application is fun. |
| HM_2 | Using the application is entertaining. |
| HM_3 | The VA supports me in the shopping process (e.g. suggest products to me and put them in the shopping cart). |
| **Behavioral Intention** | |
| BI_1 | I intend to use the application in the future. |
| BI_2 | I will always try to use the application in my daily life. |
| BI_3 | I plan to use the application frequently. |

## Appendix B: The Effect Model for Each Country

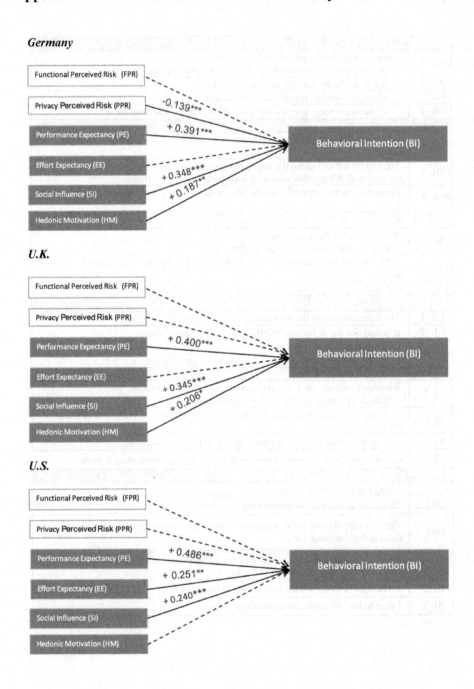

*Germany*

Functional Perceived Risk (FPR)
Privacy Perceived Risk (PPR)    −0.139***
Performance Expectancy (PE)    + 0.391***
Effort Expectancy (EE)
Social Influence (SI)    + 0.348***
Hedonic Motivation (HM)    + 0.187**

Behavioral Intention (BI)

*U.K.*

Functional Perceived Risk (FPR)
Privacy Perceived Risk (PPR)
Performance Expectancy (PE)    + 0.400***
Effort Expectancy (EE)
Social Influence (SI)    + 0.345***
Hedonic Motivation (HM)    + 0.206*

Behavioral Intention (BI)

*U.S.*

Functional Perceived Risk (FPR)
Privacy Perceived Risk (PPR)
Performance Expectancy (PE)    + 0.486***
Effort Expectancy (EE)    + 0.251**
Social Influence (SI)    + 0.240***
Hedonic Motivation (HM)

Behavioral Intention (BI)

## Appendix C: Test Result of Hypotheses for Moderating Effects

| Hypothesis | DE | U.S | U.K |
|---|---|---|---|
| H1a: The influence of FPR on BI is weaker for younger people | x | x | x |
| H1b: The influence of FPR on BI is stronger for women | x | | |
| H2a: The influence of PPR on BI is weaker for younger people | x | x | x |
| H2b: The influence of PPR on BI is stronger for women | x | | |
| H3a: The influence from PE on BI is stronger for younger people | x | x | x |
| H3b: The influence of PE on BI is weaker for women than men | Supported | | |
| H4a: The influence of EE on BI stronger for younger people | x | x | x |
| H4b: The influence of EE on BI is stronger for women | x | | |
| H5a: The influence of SI on BI is stronger for older people | Supported | x | x |
| H5b: The influence of SI on BI is stronger for women | Supported | | |

x = not supported

## References

1. Burke, R.R.: Technology and the customer interface: what consumers want in the physical and virtual store. J. Acad. Mark. Sci. **30**(4), 411–432 (2002)
2. Capgemini: Conversational Commerce: Why Consumers Are Embracing Voice Assistants (2018). https://www.capgemini.com/resources/conversational-commerce-dti-report/
3. Coskun-Setirek, A., Mardikyan, S.: Understanding the adoption of voice activated personal assistants. Int. J. E-Serv. Mob. Appl. **9**(3), 1–21 (2017). https://doi.org/10.4018/IJESMA.201 7070101
4. Davis, F.D., Bagozzi, R.P., Warshaw, P.R.: User acceptance of computer technology: a comparison of two theoretical models. Manag. Sci. **35**(8), 982–1003 (1989)
5. Featherman, M.S., Pavlou, P.A.: Predicting e-services adoption: a perceived risk facets perspective. Int. J. Hum. Comput. Stud. **59**(4), 451–474 (2003)
6. Guzman, A.: Voices in and of the machine: source orientation toward mobile virtual assistants. Comput. Hum. Behav. **90**, 343–350 (2019). https://doi.org/10.1016/j.chb.2018.08.009
7. Han, S., Yang, H.: Understanding adoption of intelligent personal assistants. Ind. Manag. Data Syst. **118**(3), 618–636 (2018)
8. Kääriä, A.: Technology acceptance of voice assistants: Anthropomorphism as a factor – Master thesis; Jyväskylä: University of Jyväskylä (2017)
9. Kessler, S.K., Martin, M.: How do potential users perceive the adoption of new technologies within the field of Artificial Intelligence and Internet-of-Things? - A revision of the UTAUT2 model using Voice Assistants - Master thesis Lund University, Sweden (2017)
10. Liao, Y., Vitak, J., Kumar, P., Zimmer, M., Kritikos, K.: Understanding the role of privacy and trust in intelligent personal assistant adoption. In: Taylor, N.G., Christian-Lamb, C., Martin, M.H., Nardi, B. (eds.) iConference 2019. LNCS, vol. 11420, pp. 102–113. Springer, Cham (2019). https://doi.org/10.1007/978-3-030-15742-5_9
11. Loweg, R.: Sprachassistenten vermehren sich rasant (2019). https://www.wiso-net.de/doc ument/CID_155452

12. Luger, E., Sellen, A.: Like having a really bad PA: the gulf between user expectation and experience of conversational agents. In: Proceedings of the CHI Conference on Human Factors in Computing System, pp. 5286–5297 (2016)
13. Mari, A., Mandelli, A., Algesheimer, R.: The evolution of marketing in the context of voice commerce: a managerial perspective. In: Nah, F.-H., Siau, K. (eds.) HCII 2020. LNCS, vol. 12204, pp. 405–425. Springer, Cham (2020). https://doi.org/10.1007/978-3-030-50341-3_32
14. Martins, C., Oliveira, T., Popovič, A.: Understanding the Internet banking adoption: a unified theory of acceptance and use of technology and perceived risk application. Int. J. Inf. Manag. **34**(1), 1–13 (2014)
15. McLean, G., Osei-Frimpong, K.: Hey Alexa … examine the variables influencing the use of artificial intelligent in-home voice assistants. Comput. Hum. Behav. **99**, 28–37 (2019). https://doi.org/10.1016/j.chb.2019.05.009
16. Moorthy, A.E., Vu, K.-P.L.: Privacy concerns for use of voice activated personal assistant in the public space. Int. J. Hum.-Comput. Interact. **31**(4), 307–335 (2015)
17. Olson, C., Kemery, K.: Voice report: from answers to action: customer adoption of voice technology and digital assistants (2019). https://printkr.hs-niederrhein.de:2069/study/63323/digital-assistant-and-voice-assistant-adoption-2019
18. Paluch, S., Wittkop, T.: Voice marketing – Die Stimme der Zukunft? In: Bruhn, M., Burmann, C., Kirchgeorg, M. (eds.) Marketing Weiterdenken: Zukunftspfade für eine marktorientierte Unternehmensführung, pp. 509–520. Springer, Wiesbaden (2020). https://doi.org/10.1007/978-3-658-31563-4_26
19. Piacenza, B., Kress, R., Klämt, M.: Voice Search Engine Optimization: Guidebook (2018)
20. Pohlgeers, M.: Voice-Commerce ist die größte Revolution im Online-Handel seit dem Smartphone (2019). https://www.onlinehaendler-news.de/digital-tech/innovationen/131110-voice-commerce-groesste-revolution-online-handel-seit-smartphone?utm_source=newsletter&utm_medium=email&utm_campaign=expertsnl%20(accessed%2005/06/2019)
21. Prein, J.: Akzeptanz mobiler Kundenkartenprogramme bei Konsumenten. Diss. Univ. Kassel. Gabler Verlag, Wiesbaden (2011)
22. Puschmann, T., von der Bank, K., Winterwerber, T., Dürbaum, A., Birven, L.: Akzeptanz von Voice Technologien im E-Commerce. Hochschule Niederrhein, Krefeld (2019)
23. Riaz, N.: Im Redeschwall (2018). https://www.lead-digital.de/im-redeschwall/
24. Rzepka, C., Berger, B., Hess, T.: Why another customer channel? consumers' perceived benefits and costs of voice commerce. In: Proceedings of the 53rd Hawaii International Conference on System Sciences (HICSS 2020), Wailea, Hawaii, USA, 7–10 January (2020)
25. Statista: Voice commerce in the United States (2019). https://www.statista.com/study/60607/voice-commerce-in-the-united-states/
26. Tuzovic, S., Paluch, S.: Conversational commerce – a new era for service business development? In: Bruhn, M., Hadwich, K. (eds.) Service Business Development, pp. 81–100. Springer, Wiesbaden (2018). https://doi.org/10.1007/978-3-658-22426-4_4
27. Venkatesh, M., Davis, D.: User acceptance of information technology: toward a unified view. MIS Q. **27**(3), 425–478 (2003). https://doi.org/10.2307/30036540
28. Venkatesh, V., Thong, J.Y.L., Xu, X.: Consumer acceptance and use of information technology: extending the unified theory of acceptance and use of technology. MIS Q. **36**(1), 157–178 (2012). https://doi.org/10.2307/41410412
29. Wagner, M.: Entwicklung und Überprüfung eines konsolidierten Akzeptanzmodells für Lernmanagementsysteme lmu]. EndNote Tagged Import Format (2016)
30. Wagner, K., Nimmermann, F., Schramm-Klein, H.: Is it human? The role of anthropomorphism as a driver for the successful acceptance of digital voice assistants. In: Proceedings of the 52nd Hawaii International Conference on System Sciences (2019)

31. Wang, H.-Y., Wang, S.-H.: User acceptance of mobile internet based on the unified theory of acceptance and use of technology: investigating the determinants and gender differences. Soc. Behav. Personal. Int. J. **38**(3), 415–426 (2010)
32. Yang, H.-D., Moon, Y.J., Rowley, C.: Social influence on knowledge worker's adoption of innovative information technology. J. Comput. Inf. Syst. **50**(1), 25–36 (2009)
33. Zaharia, S., Würfel, M.: Voice commerce - studying the acceptance of smart speakers. In: Ahram, T., Taiar, R., Langlois, K., Choplin, A. (eds.) IHIET 2020. AISC, vol. 1253, pp. 449–454. Springer, Cham (2021). https://doi.org/10.1007/978-3-030-55307-4_68
34. Zinnbauer, M., Eberl, M.: Die Überprüfung von Spezifikation und Güte von Strukturgleichungsmodellen: Verfahren und Anwendung, München (2004)

# A Survey Study on Successful Marketing Factors for Douyin (Tik-Tok)

Zining Chen[1] and Qiping Zhang[2(✉)]

[1] Portledge School, Locust Valley, NY 11560, USA
[2] Long Island University, Brookville, NY 11548, USA
Qiping.Zhang@liu.edu

**Abstract.** With the recent worldwide emergence of short video firms, these new platforms offer a unique opportunity for Businesses and creators to market their products through short advertisements. The aim of this study is to identify controllable factors that contribute to a successful short video advertisement, i.e., increasing the purchase intention of potential customers. The data of the study is collected through an online survey and user posting analysis. Based on the previous models [13], a new theoretical consumer purchase intention model was proposed and fully supported, given the correlation analysis of our survey results. We found that among all video characteristics, taste and content contributed most towards consumer purchase intention. The findings of this study would provide guidance to small business owners in their using short video platforms as well as researchers in their further study regarding purchase intention on other short video platforms.

**Keywords:** Short video advertising · Marketing · Douyin/TikTok

## 1 Background and Aim

### 1.1 History Short Video Apps and Douyin

The emergence of short videos started around 2011, along with the accelerating growth of internet users and technology development. Short length-wise, these videos quickly attracted users with their constantly refreshing content and AI mechanisms that recommended videos targeting each user's preference. Today's most iconic and representative short video app today would be Bytedance's Douyin (also known as Tik Tok as its international version).

Since its founding in 2016, the short video app Douyin has grown rapidly at an unimaginable pace. Up to 2019, its daily active users have already surpassed 0.4 billion in China alone, with 0.8 billion monthly active users worldwide. Thanks to its strategic and well-refined AI algorithms and by appealing to the younger generation. It took over market shares and quickly exceeded the influence of Kuaishou, securing its leadership in the newly emerged short film industry. Today, Douyin (Tik Tok) is available in 155

© Springer Nature Switzerland AG 2021
F. F.-H. Nah and K. Siau (Eds.): HCII 2021, LNCS 12783, pp. 22–42, 2021.
https://doi.org/10.1007/978-3-030-77750-0_2

countries, 70+ languages, and has gained a large portion of users in many of those countries around the world, such as the U.S, Egypt, Japan, making it the most representative sample to study regarding the short video firms [2, 3].

The Douyin app allows users to create short videos, usually around 15 s and less than 2 min. The short videos are essentially composed of four parts: the video itself, video description, likes, and comments; most videos featuring music in the background. In addition, users can edit and share such short videos as well as Livestream [1].

## 1.2 Decreased Short Visual Attention in Advertisement

For the past decade, a booming variety of media and information gave the new generations limitless choices to spend their time on. Such development caused the shortening of consumer attention span, from 12 s in 2000 to 8 s in 2015 [4]. Such a trend is not only beneficial to short video platforms that rely on constant refreshing of new information to keep its users, but also has an implication to advertisers and commercials who need to grab their audience's attention within the first few seconds with interesting videos [5].

## 1.3 Aim of the Study

Given the rapid decrease in visual attention and the growth of short video app users worldwide, these short video platforms offer a great opportunity for businesses to quickly and effectively advertise their product to the target audience. The goal of this study is to identify the factors that contribute to the success of a short video advertisement. Our study focuses particularly on the community of Douyin (Tik-Tok), as we find it to be the fastest growing and most representative short video platform in China and worldwide. In addition, there is a lack of research on the newly emerged short video platforms in the field of web advertisement effectiveness. The findings of our study will provide implications to small startup business owners for using short video platforms to enlarge their market and consumer base.

There are many types of user comments for each Douyin advertisement video. However, this study only focuses on those regarding video characteristics. It will address the following three research questions:

*RQ1: What video characteristics influence the perception and purchase intention of a short advertisement video?*
*RQ2: What types of comments regarding video characteristics correlate to the number of likes of a short advertisement video?*
*RQ3: Will types of comments regarding video characteristics be varied by categories of advertisement videos?*

RQ1 will be answered by the survey data, while RQ2 and RQ3 will be answered by the content analysis of user comments.

## 2  Related Work

### 2.1  Informativeness, Credibility, Entertainment, and Irritation

According to [19], Informativeness is defined as an advertisement's ability to supply relevant and truthful information. It is derived from the User Gratification theory, which considers the informativeness as "one of the need-satisfying functions derived from media communications." [19] **Informativeness** of an advertisement acts as one of the most prominent factors for consumers to accept the ad in the first place. According to the research of [13, 19], informativeness enhances the advertisement value and therefore positively influences the purchase intention of a consumer.

**Credibility** is defined as the reliability and trustworthiness of the advertisement [13]. It has a direct positive relationship with both advertisement value and attitude.

**Entertainment** is described as the advertisement's ability to offer enjoyment and pleasantness to the target customer. it is a characteristic that consumers look for and expect of today's advertisement [13]. As suggested by the work of [19], entertainment has a positive and direct relationship with Advertising value and brand awareness.

According to [19], **irritation** is the main cause of a consumer's dislike for an advertisement. It occurs when an Ad "employs techniques that annoy, offend, insult, or are overly manipulative." [19] It is shown in both [13, 20] that irritation has a negative relationship with the Advertising value.

### 2.2  Incentives

According to [13], the term incentive is described as something that offers monetary gains, such as discount, gifts, lotteries, etc. Such financial benefit is said to increase consumer attention upon the received Advertisement, therefore causing Incentives to have a positive relationship with advertisement values [13].

### 2.3  Social Influence

Social influence is described as the degree to which an individual's behavior is influenced by important others. According to [14], "social influence is a direct determinant of behavioral intention" and that "individuals tend to comply with the social influence." Based on [20], this compliance is caused by the "tendency to learn about products through seeking information from others, conforming to others' expectations to receive rewards or avoid punishments, and identifying one's image with others through the acquisition of certain products or brands" Therefore, social influence is likely to play an important role in impacting the perception and purchase intention of an advertised product.

## 2.4 Brand Awareness

Brand awareness is defined as the customer's familiarity of a brand. According to [13], brand awareness is "reflected by consumers' ability to recall or recognize the brand under different conditions." Today's social media has made brand awareness easier to achieve, offering many chances for businesses to interact with their consumers and gain recognition [12]. Brand awareness plays an important factor in determining purchase intention, as customers have shown to consider the brand itself when deciding on a purchase, and the brand with higher brand awareness will more likely be favored by the consumer [13].

## 2.5 Ad Value and Attitude

According to [19], Ad value is "a subjective evaluation of the relative worth or utility of advertising to consumers," reflecting the degree of satisfaction of the consumers. It is a subjective factor that has been shown to positively correlate with informativeness, entertainment, and credibility, negatively correlates with irritation, and heavily influences a consumer's purchase intention.

According to [13, 15], Attitude towards online advertisement is the "aggregation of weighted evaluations of perceived attributes and consequences of products." it is a subjective factor just like Ad value, and it shares the same correlations as Ad value as well, heavily impacting the purchase intention of a consumer.

# 3 Theoretical Framework

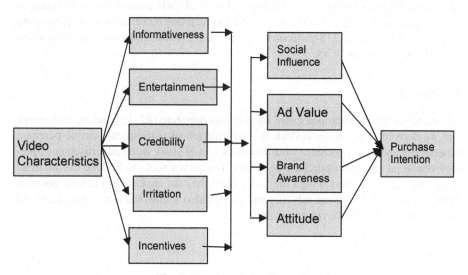

**Fig. 1.** Framework for this study

To answer above research questions, a conceptual framework is developed to predict factors influencing the purchase intention to Douyin advertisement videos. The framework is based on related work including Ducoffe (1995)'s advertising value model [19], and Bracket and Carr (2003)'s advertising attitude model [13], along with the works of Yang [15], Martin [13], Dehghani [12] and some aspects of the Vekentash (2012)'s UTAUT2 model [14] (Fig. 1).

In the framework above, there are three layers of factors that influence the purchase intention. The first layer as an input to the framework is video characteristics. The second layer, directly influenced by the video characteristics, consists of five factors (informativeness, entertainment, credibility, irritation, and incentives). They influence the factors in the third layer [12–15, 19], and influence purchase intention indirectly. The third layer, directly influencing the consumers' purchase intention, an output of the framework, includes four factors (social influence, Ad value, brand awareness, and attitude).

## 4   Method

This study uses a combination of online survey and social media data analysis method.

### 4.1   Participants

Upon LIU IRB approval, participants were recruited through Wenjuanxing, the largest survey platform in china. There are two screening criterias for our survey, the first one requires the participants to be existing users of Douyin, in order to ensure the validity of their responses regarding their Douyin experience. The second screening criteria ensures that the participant must be age 18 or above. A total of 230+ participants participated in our survey, and due to the effectiveness of the wenjuanxing recruitment system, we were able to collect a total of 218 valid survey responses. Upon completion, each participant was offered a payment of ¥5.

### 4.2   Survey

An online survey is developed based on previous literature [12–15] and the framework that we derived. The survey collects the information of participants' online purchase experiences and the importance of different factors of short video advertisement's persuasiveness on consumer purchase decisions. The survey seeks to find the overall trend of factors that consumers weigh the most when they are making a purchase decision through short video platform advertisements, and also studies the user's perceptions of advertisements in the Douyin community.

The survey has 48 questions, including 5 demographic information (age, gender, education, residence, income), 3 Douyin usage behavior (frequency of Douyin usage, frequency of Douyin purchase, reading comments or not), 10 video characteristic questions, and 30 construct questions with three questions for each survey construct. It takes approximately 10–15 min to complete the survey.

The survey data are collected via WenJuanXing (https://www.wjx.cn). Since founding, Wenjuanxing has had 81.67 million users that completed 6.427 billion surveys on its website. It offers quick user recruitment, precise criteria scan, and many forms and templates of questionnaires to choose from. Its large user base and profound service makes it the best candidate for this study focusing on China's Dou Yin.

### 4.3 Social Media Data Analysis

The social media data analysis aims to find the characteristics of successful short video advertisements through content analysis of video comments. It is predicted that the Descriptive analysis of metric data and content analysis of user postings reveals the attention grabbing characteristics of the video. By coding the content of the comments, we would be able to gather which characteristics of the video contributed to the majority of the discussion, signifying the importance of those characteristics in influencing the customers. Another benefit of finding such characteristics is that the finding may be applied to future videos, where creators could possibly add such characteristics to stimulate comments and discussion. Given the AI filtering mechanism of Douyin, more comments would lead to AI pushing the video to a greater audience for more views, thus contributing to the success of a short video advertisement.

We picked four most popular categories for ecommerce merchandise, as listed and categorized by China's largest ecommerce app, Taobao's front page. These categories include clothing, makeup, food, and digital devices. For each of those categories, we chose related keywords listed as Douyin's most popular tag [11], and filtered the top five most liked videos (with a shopping cart link attached, to ensure that we are analyzing an advertisement) within the tags for each of the four categories. We then crawled the basic data for the 20 videos we picked, including 500 comments (user postings) for each, profile of creator, url of the video, number of likes, video description, and merchandise that the video was advertising for.

Our analysis is derived from the data collected above, and a table of codes is pasted below as an explanation of each characteristic that we explored.

Out of the 500 comments, we only coded the ones that are relevant or semi relevant to the content (i.e. what the creator could manipulate) (Table 1).

Overall, we believe that the triangulation of survey methods with social media data analysis provides a better understanding of factors influencing user's purchase intention on Douyin.

## 5  Results

In the following, we will present the results from the survey data and coding analyses of video comments.

**Table 1.** Coding categories for Douyin advertisement videos

| N | Category | Codes | Definition |
|---|----------|-------|------------|
| 1 | Advertiser | Fame | Statements regarding the fame of the advertiser in the video |
| 2 | Artistic | BGM | Statements regarding a fitting background music |
| 3 | Artistic | General Praise | Statements with general praise to the Douyin video (such as a smiling emoji) |
| 4 | Artistic | Humor | Statements regarding the video's good sense of humor |
| 5 | Artistic | Taste | Statements regarding the good aesthetic tastes of a video |
| 6 | Content | Content | Statements regarding the interesting content/plot of a video |
| 7 | Content | Description | Statements regarding the video description |
| 8 | Content | Clarification | Statements with questions related to the video |
| 9 | Content | Criticism | Negative comments on the video or the product that is being advertised |
| 10 | Marketing | Product Review | Any statements containing a positive review of the product that is being advertised |
| 11 | Marketing | Price | Statements about the price |
| 12 | Marketing | Purchase intention | Statements regarding a direct purchase intention expressed towards the merchandise that is being advertised |

## 5.1 Survey Results

**Demographic Results**
(See Table 2).

**Survey Reliability Result.** As shown in Table 3, reliability of all survey constructs reached an acceptable level (>.65).

**Survey Construct Results.** As shown in Fig. 2, in terms of user's rating of video characteristics, taste(in pink) was rated as highest, followed by content(in blue), marketing(in orange), and advertiser(in green) (Table 4).

**Correlation Analysis**
(See Table 5).

**Table 2.** Results of demographic information

| Measure | Item | # | % | Graph |
|---------|------|---|---|-------|
| Age | 18-25<br>26-35<br>36-40<br>above 40 | 71<br>118<br>26<br>17 | 31%<br>51%<br>11%<br>7% | |
| Gender | Male<br>Female<br>Prefer not to say | 82<br>150<br>0 | 35%<br>65%<br>0% | |
| Education | High School<br>Bachelor<br>Master<br>Ph.D.<br>None of above | 8<br>198<br>25<br>0<br>1 | 3%<br>85%<br>11%<br>0%<br>0% | |
| Monthly Income | under ¥1,000<br>¥1,001- ¥3,000<br>¥3,001- ¥6,000<br>¥6,001- ¥10,000<br>¥10,000-¥20,000<br>above ¥20,000 | 17<br>22<br>43<br>93<br>47<br>10 | 7%<br>9%<br>19%<br>40%<br>20%<br>4% | |

(*continued*)

**Table 2.** (*continued*)

| | | | | |
|---|---|---|---|---|
| Frequency of Douyin Usage | Several times a day | 194 | 84% | |
| | About once a day | 27 | 12% | |
| | Several times a week | 11 | 5% | |
| | About once a week | 0 | 0% | |
| | < once a week | 0 | 0% | |
| Frequency of Douyin Purchase | Daily | 6 | 3% | |
| | Weekly | 87 | 38% | |
| | Monthly | 99 | 43% | |
| | Annually | 15 | 6% | |
| | Never | 25 | 11% | |
| Read Reviews in Douyin | Yes | 208 | 90% | |
| | No | 24 | 10% | |

**ANOVA Analysis Results.** 1) Age effect: significant on all constructs ($p < .01$). Posthoc Tukey showed Group 1 (18–25) was significantly lower than Group 2 (26–35) ($p < .01$) on all constructs (Tables 6, 7 and 8).

**Table 3.** Reliability results of all survey constructs

| Construct | Crobach's Alpha |
|---|---|
| Video characteristic | 0.67 |
| Social influence | 0.71 |
| Informativeness | 0.61 |
| Entertainment | 0.77 |
| Credibility | 0.85 |
| Irritation | 0.84 |
| Incentives | 0.82 |
| Ad value | 0.85 |
| Attitude | 0.90 |
| Brand awareness | 0.70 |
| Purchase intention | 0.79 |

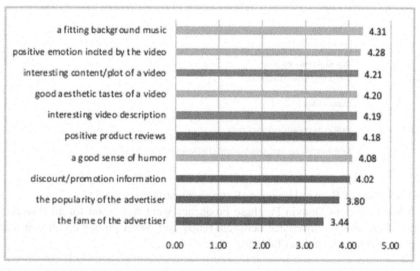

**Fig. 2.** Result of video characteristics rating (1 = not important at all; 2 = not important; 3 = neutral; 4 = important; 5 = very important) (Color figure online)

2) Gender Effect

Main effect of gender was only significant on Credibility, which showed that male (mean = 3.62, std. = .79) was significantly higher than female (mean = 3.33, std. = .74) (t(230) = 2.82, $p < .01$).

3) Education Effect

4) Income Effect

**Table 4.** Average rating to Douyin advertisement video (1 = not important at all; 2 = not important; 3 = neutral; 4 = important; 5 = very important)

|  | Douyin advertisement is … | Mean | Overall mean |
|---|---|---|---|
| Informativeness | … is a good source of product information | 3.76 | 3.92 |
|  | … supplies relevant product information | 4.14 |  |
|  | … provides timely information | 3.85 |  |
| Entertainment | … entertaining | 3.80 | 3.77 |
|  | … enjoyable | 3.63 |  |
|  | … pleasing | 3.88 |  |
| Credibility | … credible | 3.47 | 3.43 |
|  | … trustworthy | 3.41 |  |
|  | … believable | 3.43 |  |
| Irritation | … annoying | 2.52 | 2.36 |
|  | … irritating | 2.09 |  |
|  | … intrusive | 2.46 |  |
| Incentives | I am satisfied to get Douyin advertisements that offer rewards | 3.72 | 3.69 |
|  | I take action to get Douyin advertisements that offer rewards | 3.71 |  |
|  | I respond to Douyin advertisement to obtain incentives | 3.65 |  |
| Social Influence | People who are important to me think that I should buy the item | 3.64 | 3.66 |
|  | People who influence my behavior think that I should buy the item | 3.69 |  |
|  | People whose opinion that I value prefer that I buy the item | 3.66 |  |
| Ad Value | I feel that Douyin advertisement are… |  |  |
|  | … useful | 3.58 | 3.50 |
|  | … valuable | 3.61 |  |
|  | … important | 3.31 |  |
| Brand Awareness | I have heard of this brand | 4.01 | 3.82 |
|  | This brand is what I first thought of | 3.46 |  |
|  | Most people know this brand | 4.00 |  |
| Attitude | Overall Impression of Douyin Ad |  |  |
|  | Bad – Good | 5.22 |  |
|  | Dislike – Like | 5.03 |  |
|  | Unfavorable – Favorable | 4.84 |  |
| Purchase Intention | I will try the products shown on Douyin | 4.00 | 3.71 |
|  | I intend to consider the products shown on Douyin in my future purchase | 3.88 |  |
|  | I will frequently purchase products advertised in Douyin in the future | 3.23 |  |

5) No effect of Douyin Usage on all survey constructs ($p > .05$).

6) Main effect of Douyin Purchase Frequency were significant for all constructs. Overall, there was no difference between Yearly and Never groups on all constructs except on purchase intention (Table 9).

### 5.2 Result of Content Analysis of Video Comments

In the following, analyses of codlings to review comments of chosen Douyin videos are presented.

First, the results of successful video measures (total number of likes and comments) by video categories is summarized in Table 10.

Overall total number of comments was positively correlated with total number of likes (Pearson Correlation = .69 **).

ONEWAY ANOVA showed that the main effect of video category was significant on total number of likes (F(3,46) = 5.84, p < .05), Both Food and Makeup categories received significantly more Likes than Digital Device category ($p < .01$).

**Table 5.** Confirmation of our framework

| Pairs | Pearson (*$p < .05$; **$p < .01$) |
|---|---|
| *Correlation between Video Characteristic and 2nd layer construct* | |
| Video characteristic - Informativeness | .35** |
| Video characteristic - Entertainment | .52** |
| Video characteristic - Credibility | .43** |
| Video characteristic - Irritation | −.37** |
| Video characteristic - Incentives | .32** |
| *Correlation between 2nd and 3rd layers* | |
| Informativeness - Social Influence | .39** |
| Entertainment - Social Influence | .48** |
| Credibility - Social Influence | .47** |
| Irritation - Social Influence | −.41** |
| Incentives - Social Influence | .48** |
| Informativeness - Ad Value | .58** |
| Entertainment - Ad Value | .66** |
| Credibility - Ad Value | .68** |
| Irritation - Ad Value | −.65** |
| Incentives - Ad Value | .59** |
| Informativeness - Brand Awareness | .37** |
| Entertainment - Brand Awareness | .43** |
| Credibility - Brand Awareness | .47** |
| Irritation - Brand Awareness | −.39** |
| Incentives - Brand Awareness | .38** |
| Informativeness - Attitude | .59** |
| Entertainment - Attitude | .70** |
| Credibility - Attitude | .62** |
| Irritation - Attitude | −.69** |
| Incentives - Attitude | .65** |
| *Correlation between 3rd layer and Purchase Intention* | |
| Social Influence - Purchase Intention | .54** |
| Ad Value - Purchase Intention | .65** |
| Brand Awareness - Purchase Intention | .55** |
| Attitude - Purchase Intention | .64** |

**Table 6.** ANOVA results of age effect on survey constructs (G1: 18–25; G2: 26–35; G3: 36–40; G4: 40+)

| Construct | F | p | Posthoc Tukey p | Means Plot |
|---|---|---|---|---|
| Informativeness | 5.17 | .002 | 18-25 < 26-35 (.001) | |
| Entertainment | 6.43 | .000 | 18-25 < 26-35 (.000) | |
| Credibility | 6.53 | .000 | 18-25 < 26-35 (.002)<br>18-25 < 36-40 (.001) | |
| Irritation | 6.16 | .000 | 18-25 > 26-35 (.001)<br>18-25 > 36-40 (.046)<br>18-25 > 40+   (.049) | |
| Incentives | 5.19 | .002 | 18-25 < 26-35 (.001) | |
| Social Influence | 3.24 | .023 | 18-25 < 26-35 (.017) | 18-25: 4.17 (.62)<br>26-35: 2.34 (.70)<br> |
| Ad Value | 6.38 | .000 | 18-25 < 26-35 (.000) | |

*(continued)*

**Table 6.** (*continued*)

| Brand Awareness | 5.11 | .002 | 18-25 < 26-35 (.011)<br>40+ < 26-35 (.046) | |
|---|---|---|---|---|
| Attitude | 4.60 | .004 | 18-25 < 26-35 (.003) | |
| Purchase Intention | 8.23 | .000 | 18-25 < 26-35 (.000)<br>18-25 < 36-40 (.043)<br>18-25 < 40+  (.039) | |

The main effect of video category on the number of total comments was not significant. All four categories of video received a large number of comments (average = 22,209).

Second, codings to successful advertisement videos by video category are summarized in Table 11.

Among 12 codes, only Content and Taste showed significant differences among four video categories.

- For Content, *Food* category was significantly lower than other three categories (Clothing, Makeup, Digital Device); *Makeup* category was also significantly higher than *Clothing* category.
- For Taste, *Clothing* category was significantly higher than *Food* and *Digital Device* category.

## 6 Discussion and Conclusion

### 6.1 Survey Results

For demographic information, our survey mainly featured people of ages below 35. The gender of the participants is female-skewed, as 65% of the respondents are female. As for education, most of the participants earned the highest of a bachelor's degree, and the monthly income reveals that they earn mostly medium to high-end salaries. Our demographic information corresponds to various market research regarding Douyin, which reveals that Douyin has a larger portion of female users; it also corresponds to

**Table 7.** ANOVA results of education effect on survey constructs (1 = High School, 2 = Bachelor, 3 = Master)

| Construct | F | p | Posthoc Tukey | Means Plot |
|---|---|---|---|---|
| Social Influence | 4.35 | .014 | HS<BS (.041)<br>HS<MS (.010) | |
| Credibility | 3.34 | .037 | HS-BS (.059)<br>BS-MS (.086) | |
| Irritation | 2.85 | .060 | HS-BS (.082)<br>HS-MS (.048) | |
| Ad Value | 3.80 | .024 | HS-BS (.082)<br>HS-MS (.018) | |
| Purchase Intention | 2.62 | .075 | HS-BS (.093)<br>HS-MS (.062) | |

the market impression that Douyin has gained more of the younger generation and the higher end when it comes to education and income, compared to other short video apps in China such as Kuaishou.

Regarding the Douyin Usage behavior, most (83%) participants reported using Douyin several times per day, and the majority will make a purchase weekly or monthly. The survey also shows that almost all (90%) participants will search for reviews and relative information on Douyin if they are interested in a specific product. This data indicates that Douyin platform offers a substantial amount of exposure for advertisers and businesses to market their products.

Overall, for video characteristics, Taste related characteristics (fitting BGM, Positive emotions incited, good aesthetic taste, and a good sense of humor) contribute the most to consumer purchase intention, followed by content-related characteristics (interesting content/plot and interesting video description), promotional related characteristics (promotional/discount information and positive product review), and lastly advertiser related characteristics (fame of the advertiser and popularity of the advertiser.

**Table 8.** ANOVA results of income effect on survey constructs (G1: ¥1,000; G2: ¥1,001–¥3,000; G3: ¥3,001–¥6,000; G4: ¥6,001–¥10,000; G5: ¥10,000–¥20,000; G6: ¥20,000+)

| Construct | F | $p$ | Posthoc Tukey $p$ | Means Plot |
|---|---|---|---|---|
| Informativeness | 5.20 | 0.000 | G1<G3 (.043)<br>G1<G4 (.001)<br>G1<G6 (.001)<br>G2<G6 (.030) | |
| Entertainment | 6.75 | 0.000 | G1<G3 (.052)<br>G1<G4 (.000)<br>G1<G5 (.009)<br>G1<G6 (.000)<br>G2<G4 (.015)<br>G2<G6 (.002) | |
| Credibility | 5.17 | 0.000 | G1<G4 (.049)<br>G1<G5 (.024)<br>G1<G6 (.002)<br>G2<G6 (.021)<br>G3<G6 (.007) | |
| Irritation | 6.27 | 0.000 | G1<G4 (.035)<br>G2<G4 (.000)<br>G2<G5 (.023)<br>G2<G6 (.029)<br>G3<G4 (.007) | |
| Incentives | 4.06 | 0.001 | G1<G4 (.005)<br>G1<G5 (.008)<br>G1<G6 (.067) | |
| Ad Value | 6.61 | 0.000 | G1<G4 (.012)<br>G1<G5 (.048)<br>G1<G6 (.000)<br>G2<G6 (.001)<br>G3<G6 (.001)<br>G4<G6 (.067)<br>G5<G6 (.056) | |
| Brand Awareness | 3.16 | 0.009 | G1<G4 (.024)<br>G1<G5 (.042)<br>G1<G6 (.041) | |

(*continued*)

**Table 8.** (*continued*)

| Attitude | 3.87 | 0.002 | G1<G6 (.024)<br>G2<G4 (.035)<br>G2<G6 (.012) | |
|---|---|---|---|---|
| Purchase Intention | 8.75 | 0.000 | G1<G3 (.018)<br>G1<G4 (.000)<br>G1<G5 (.000)<br>G1<G6 (.005)<br>G2<G4 (.001)<br>G2<G5 (.001)<br>G2<G6 (.062) | |

According to the ANOVA analysis (the graphs are shown above), the age effect is significant on all constructs. The general trend is that the younger generation (ages 18–25) has a more negative impression of the Douyin advertisements than the older age group.

The gender effect is only significant towards the perception of credibility. Our results show that males rate the credibility of Douyin advertisements higher compared to females.

The education effect is significant for social influence, credibility, irritation, Ad value, and Purchase intention. Groups with a higher degree tend to be more affected by social influence, and the general trend is that Groups with higher degrees hold a more positive view of Douyin advertisements than the group with a lower degree.

The income effect is very similar to the education effect. The general trend indicates that higher income groups have a more positive view of Douyin advertisements than the Lower income group.

The purchase frequency effect also yielded a fascinating result. The general trend indicates that a significantly more positive impression towards Ads on Douyin is strongly correlated with a more frequent purchase of goods through Douyin, and vice versa.

## 6.2   Coding Results

Overall all our chosen successful Douyin advertisement videos received both high number of likes (average = 841,980) and high number of comments (average = 21,209). There was a positive correlation between total number of video comments with total number of video likes.

Different categories of advertisement video demonstrated different characteristics. First, certain categories of advertisement video (such as food and makeup) tend to receive more likes than other (digital device). Second, in terms of video characteristics, food category was unique. It attracted least content codes and taste codes. Clothing and

**Table 9.** ANOVA results of effect of Douyin purchase frequency on survey constructs (D-daily; W-weekly, M-monthly, Y-yearly, N-never).

| Construct | F | $p$ | Posthoc Tukey $p$ | Means Plot |
|---|---|---|---|---|
| Informativeness | 5.74 | 0.000 | W>Y (.024)<br>W>N (.000)<br>M>N (.018) | |
| Entertainment | 4.34 | .002 | W>N (.002) | |
| Credibility | 10.11 | 0.000 | D>N (.004)<br>W>N (.000)<br>M>N (.002)<br>W>M (.017)<br>W>Y (.019) | |
| Irritation | 5.63 | 0.000 | W<N (.000)<br>M<N (.004) | |
| Incentives | 5.84 | 0.000 | D>N (.014)<br>W>N (.000)<br>M>N (.034) | |
| Social Influence | 6.50 | 0.000 | D>N (.008)<br>W>N (.000)<br>M>N (.003) | |
| Ad Value | 7.40 | 0.000 | D>N (.020)<br>W>M (.049)<br>W>N (.000)<br>M>N (.015) | |
| Brand Awareness | 8.55 | 0.000 | D>N (.028)<br>W>N (.000)<br>M>N (.000) | |

*(continued)*

**Table 9.** (*continued*)

| Attitude | 6.17 | 0.000 | D>N (.027)<br>W>M (.030)<br>W>N (.000) | |
|---|---|---|---|---|
| Purchase intention | 29.23 | 0.000 | D>Y (.006)<br>D>N (.000)<br>W>Y (.001)<br>W>N (.000)<br>M>Y (.026)<br>M>N (.000)<br>Y>N (.004) | |

**Table 10.** Total number of likes and comments by video categories

| Category | Total # of like | | Total # of comments | |
|---|---|---|---|---|
| | Mean | Std | Mean | Std |
| Clothing | 896,300 | 427,642 | 22,162 | 23,743 |
| Food | 1,305,100 | 720,353 | 28,230 | 27,429 |
| Makeup | 950,133 | 605,826 | 22,795 | 18,179 |
| Digital device | 388,867 | 447,842 | 17,639 | 20,437 |
| Average | 841,980 | 633,934 | 22,209 | 21,665 |

makeup categories received relative more discussion on their video contents and aesthetic taste aspect.

### 6.3 Douyin Community Perception Towards Advertising

As stated above, our individual survey question reveals that participants overall lean positive regarding informativeness, entertainment, credibility, value, and purchase intention, while having a below-average value for irritation. The data also indicated a positive overall attitude regarding Douyin Ad. These results indicate that users of the Douyin community generally have a good impression of the advertisements posted, and again shows that the platform works in favor of creators looking to use Douyin for advertising.

### 6.4 Theoretical/Practical Implication

According to the correlation analysis, our model is fully supported. The video characteristics are strongly correlated with the second layer construct (informativeness, entertainment, credibility, irritation, and incentives), all second layer construct is strongly

**Table 11.** ANOVA results of video category on comment codes (Clothing, Food, Makeup, Digital)

| Codes | F (3,15) | p | Posthoc Tukey p | Means Plot |
|---|---|---|---|---|
| Content | 11.34 | .000 | Food < Clothing *<br>Food < Makeup **<br>Food < Digital *<br>Clothing < Makeup * | |
| Taste | 5.76 | .010 | Clothing > Food *<br>Clothing > Digital * | |

correlated with the third layer construct (social influence, Ad value, Brand awareness, and attitude), and all third layer construct correlates with our final layer – Purchase intention. Therefore, all relationships within the theoretical framework are validated and strongly support our proposed model.

Many previous works have studied consumer attitude and purchase intention, such as the renowned works of [19] and [13], or the more recent works of [12] and [15]. However, these studies are mainly focused on the earlier social media and internet environments; a few, if any, have examined the newly emerged short video platforms (especially Tik-Tok and Douyin). This paper combined old theoretical models and added new elements to the framework to develop a new consumer purchase intention model. This study hopes to provide context and possible applicational information to help more businesses and creators seeking to market on short video platforms, particularly Douyin.

### 6.5 Limitation and Future Research

This study has a few limitations that could be addressed with future research. The first limitation is choosing Douyin as our only platform. To gain a more comprehensive knowledge of consumer purchase intention on short video platforms, future studies could benefit from selecting different platforms such as Kuaishou or Instagram reels. The second limitation is data collection. For the Coding analysis, we were only able to cover five videos and 2500 comments per category. To find a more distinct and reliable pattern, it would be better to cover 10–15 videos for each category. The third limit is language. Because the survey and framework derived from previous studies were English, and our study was conducted within a Chinese environment, some aspects may be lost through translation.

# References

1. Hussain, A., Mkpojiogu, E.O., Mohmad Kamal, F.: Mobile video streaming applications: a systematic review of test metrics in usability evaluation. J. Telecommun. Electron. Comput. Eng. **8**(10), 35–39 (2016)
2. Iqbal, M.: TikTok revenue and usage statistics. Business of Apps, 30 October 2020. https://www.businessofapps.com/data/tik-tok-statistics/#1
3. Xu, S., Li, Y., Sun, B., Xiao, X., Li, S.: Research on business model innovation of short video enterprises from the perspective of community economy. In 2019 3rd International Conference on Education, Economics and Management Research (ICEEMR 2019), pp. 324–330. Atlantis Press, January 2020. https://doi.org/10.2991/assehr.k.191221.077
4. Gausby, A.: Attention Spans. Consumer Insights, Microsoft Canada (2015)
5. Chen, Z., He, Q., Mao, Z., Chung, H.M., Maharjan, S.: A study on the characteristics of Douyin short videos and implications for edge caching. In: Proceedings of the ACM Turing Celebration Conference-China, pp. 1–6, May 2019
6. Abu-El-Haija, S., et al.: Youtube-8m: a large-scale video classification benchmark. arXiv preprint arXiv:1609.08675 (2016)
7. Ji, X.: The impact of brand awareness on consumer purchase intention: the mediating effect of perceived quality and brand loyalty. J. Int. Manag. Stud. **4**(1), 135–144 (2009)
8. Konuk, F.A.: The role of store image, perceived quality, trust and perceived value in predicting consumers' purchase intentions towards organic private label food. J. Retail. Consum. Serv. **43**, 304–310 (2018)
9. Xiao, Y., Wang, L., Wang, P.: Research on the influence of content features of short video marketing on consumer purchase intentions. In: 4th International Conference on Modern Management, Education Technology and Social Science (MMETSS 2019). Atlantis Press, October 2019
10. Zhou, Q.: Understanding User Behaviors of Creative Practice on Short Video Sharing Platforms–A Case Study of TikTok and Bilibili (Doctoral dissertation, University of Cincinnati) (2019)
11. Common tags and categories of Douyin conten ( 抖音内容常见标签及分类). https://wenku.baidu.com/view/98c1bb13031ca300a6c30c22590102020640f23e.html. Accessed 14 Jan 2021
12. Dehghani, M., Niaki, M.K., Ramezani, I., Sali, R.: Evaluating the influence of YouTube advertising for attraction of young customers. Comput. Hum. Behav. **59**, 165–172 (2016)
13. Brackett, L., Carr, B.: Cyberspace advertising vs. other media: consumer vs. mature student attitudes. J. Advertising Res. **41**(5), 23–32 (2001). https://doi.org/10.2501/JAR-41-5-23-32
14. Martins, J., Costa, C., Oliveira, T., Gonçalves, R., Branco, F.: How smartphone advertising influences consumers' purchase intention. J. Bus. Res. **94**, 378–387 (2019)
15. Venkatesh, V., Thong, J.Y., Xu, X.: Consumer acceptance and use of information technology: extending the unified theory of acceptance and use of technology. MIS Q. **36**(1), 157–178 (2012). https://doi.org/10.2307/41410412
16. Yang, K.C., Huang, C.H., Yang, C., Yang, S.Y.: Consumer attitudes toward online video advertisement: YouTube as a platform. Kybernetes (2017)
17. Kanchan, U., Kumar, N., Gupta, A.: A study of online purchase behaviour of customers in India. ICTACT J. Manag. Stud. **1**(3), 136–142 (2015)
18. Punj, G.: Effect of consumer beliefs on online purchase behavior: the influence of demographic characteristics and consumption values. J. Interact. Mark. **25**(3), 134–144 (2011)
19. Srinivasan, S.R.: Impact of education on purchase behaviour of luxury brands. Bus. Manag. Rev. **5**(4), 66 (2015)
20. Ducoffe, R.H.: How consumers assess the value of advertising. J. Curr. Issues Res. Advertising **17**(1), 1–18 (1995)

# Research on Experience Evaluation of Taobao Shopping Platform Service

Tianhong Fang[✉] and Hongyu Sun

School of Art Design and Media, East China University of Science and Technology,
Shanghai, China
thfang@ecust.edu.cn

**Abstract.** In China, the user base of Online shopping platforms is huge and increasing year by year. In order to provide users with a better service experience, it is increasingly important for online shopping platforms to take the user's evaluation of service experience as an important standard to evaluate their own service quality and to provide user centered service design. From the perspective of service design, taking Taobao, the largest shopping platform in China, as an example, this article analyzes and summarizes the online shopping service process, touch point, and the service indicator, and after that, uses Semantic Difference (SD) to analyze the main stakeholders – consumers' subjective feeling on service indicators, and gets the perceptual evaluation on each indicator of online shopping service. At the same time, Factor analysis is used to construct a service experience evaluation model of shopping platform with 23 specific indicators. Besides, Analytic hierarchy process (AHP) is used to analyze the weight of the score of each service indicator to provide suggestions for future service improvement. At last, it is also found that there is little difference in the overall perception of service indicators among consumers with different genders and ages, but the difference is significant between the users with different between shopping frequencies. In conclusion, this article constructs an experience evaluation model of online shopping service by studying the relevant indicators that affect online shopping customer experience, which would provide some reference for service designers and decision makers to improve online shopping service experience.

**Keywords:** Shopping platform service · Service experience · Evaluation model · Semantic difference method · Analytic hierarchy process

## 1 Introduction

With the continuous development and improvement of the smart phone industry and network technology, the number of Chinese netizens keeps increasing. By June 2019, the number of mobile internet users in China had reached 847 million, with 99.1% of them using mobile phones to surf the Internet. Online shopping has also entered people's lives gradually. Data show that the online shopping penetration rate of 2015H1–2019H1 in China is on the rise, and the online shopping penetration rate of 2019H1 is 74.8%. From the above data, it can be concluded that online shopping is increasingly becoming

© Springer Nature Switzerland AG 2021
F. F.-H. Nah and K. Siau (Eds.): HCII 2021, LNCS 12783, pp. 43–54, 2021.
https://doi.org/10.1007/978-3-030-77750-0_3

an indispensable part of daily behaviors. Therefore, it is essential to study, evaluate and improve the quality of online shopping service.

Currently, most scholars study on the visual features of online shopping platform products [1], the color design of the homepage [2], search function [3], platform interface design [4], product packaging design [5], logistics service [6], after-sales service [7] these kinds of single service link. Besides, some scholars, taking SERVQUAL model [8], cloud model [9], service design concept [10] and other methods as the theoretical basis, carry out systematic research on related factors of online shopping platforms in terms of service quality and satisfaction evaluation. However, the researches based on the concept of service design mainly aim at the process of shopping platform, interaction and interface. However, not only shopping platform, but the business service, payment service, logistics service and some other services can affect the user's use experience. In this article, the touch points of online shopping service are further completed and perfected, and a comprehensive evaluation index system of three levels, namely, target level, criterion level and indicator level, is constructed.

From the perspective of service design, taking Taobao, the largest shopping platform in China, as an example, this article analyzes and summarizes the service process, touch point, and the service indicator during online shopping process, and discusses the experience evaluation and improvement of online shopping service.

## 2   The Preliminary Construction of Experience Evaluation System of Online Shopping Service by Semantic Differential Method

Semantic Differential (SD), also known as SD method, is a psychological research method proposed by Osgood (1957). It is easy to operate and can be used for objective quantitative analysis of the research object. In fact, SD method has been adopted in many research fields at home and abroad, and it is mostly combined with other statistical methods [11]. In this article, semantic difference method is used to construct a seven-level semantic difference scale to get the perceptual evaluation of experience service of Taobao platform.

### 2.1   Online Shopping Service Process Analyzing and Touch Point Identification

Service touch point is the direct source of service experience and the core of the whole service system [12], and the identification of touch points is the first step to improve the service experience, and it also provides a reference for the collection and selection of service indicators and perceptual words in the application of semantic difference method [13]. According to order of action, the shopping process is divided into three stages, namely "pre-transaction", "in transaction" and "post-transaction", to draw a flow chart of shopping behavior (Fig. 1), and on the basis of the behavioral process, the touch points are summarized. The details of general process and touch points are as follows (Table 1).

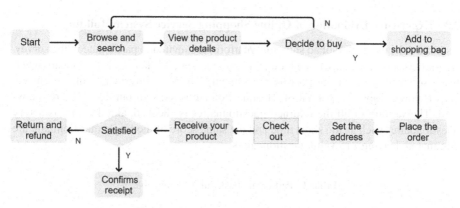

**Fig. 1.** Flow chart of shopping behavior

**Table 1.** General process and touch points of online shopping service

| Item | Pre-transaction | In transaction | Post-transaction |
|---|---|---|---|
| Process | Start | Search, browse, enter product details page, add to shopping bag, confirm the delivery address, place the order, check out | Logistics transportation, receiving, return and refund |
| Touch-point | App icon | Homepage, searching box, search results display page, the order of search results, filter function, product customer satisfaction, store information, consumer reviews, production recommendation, customer service, store page, shopping bag adding, shopping bag viewing, address setting, order placing, payment method selecting, checking out | Logistics transportation, products receiving, receiving confirming, comment making, return and refund applying, product posting |

## 2.2 Collection and Selection of Service Indicators and Perceptual Words

100 online shopping service indicators and their corresponding perceptual word pairs are found by literature searching and selecting. After 4 rounds of group discussion and selection with 3 graduate students of industrial design engineering, 23 service indicators and corresponding pairs of perceptual words are finally selected for further investigation and evaluation. In order to avoid the wrong understanding of service indicators by the subjects, some indicators are interpreted accordingly.

## 2.3  Experience Evaluation of Online Shopping Service System Building

In this article, users of Taobao shopping platform are invited to participate in the survey. All participants score 23 service indicators using a 7-point Likert scale (−3 means negative assessment and 3 means positive assessment). The basic information of participants is as follows (Table 2). A total of 218 questionnaires are sent out and 218 are recovered. The validity of all the returned questionnaires is checked, and the unsatisfactory questionnaires such as too short time and the same score of the single questionnaire are eliminated, leaving 215 valid questionnaires.

**Table 2.** Participant basic information table

| Variable | Description |
| --- | --- |
| N | 215 |
| Male/female | 75/140 |

The effective questionnaire results obtained in this study show that males account for 34.9% and females account for 65.1%. Most of them are aged between 18 and 40. Since females are the main shopping population, the gender distribution is reasonable. The number of people who shop online more than 10 times a year via Taobao platform accounts for 89.3%, among which the number of people who shop online more than 20 times a year via Taobao platform accounts for 68.8%. It means that, they have a high degree of familiarity with the Taobao platform and its service process, which meets the requirements of this study.

Data graph of evaluation score of service indicator questionnaire (Fig. 2). In the figure, the horizontal axis shows 23 service indicators and the vertical axis shows the average score of each service indicator.

**The Reliability Analysis.** In this study, participants' subjective feelings are investigated in the form of questionnaires, so reliability and validity analysis of the questionnaire data are needed [14]. Cronbach's Alpha is the most commonly used reliability coefficient at present [15]. In this article, SPSS is used to analyze the data, and the results are as follows (Table 3).

It can be seen from the above table that the Cronbach's Alpha is 0.907, greater than 0.6, which indicates that the reliability quality of the research data is high and can be used for factor analysis.

**Validity Analysis.** Before the correlation analysis, the validity analysis of the measurement results of the questionnaire is also needed, and the higher the validity, the higher the accuracy of the data [14]. The test results of KMO and Bartlett's are as follows (Table 4).

It can be seen from the above table that KMO is 0.888, greater than 0.6, and the data passed Bartlett sphericity test ($P < 0.05$), indicating that the research data are suitable for factor analysis.

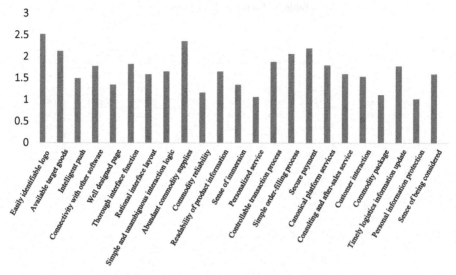

**Fig. 2.** Evaluation score of service indicator

**Table 3.** Cronbach reliability analysis table

| Reliability statistics | | |
| --- | --- | --- |
| No. of items | N | Cronbach's Alpha |
| 23 | 215 | 0.907 |

**Table 4.** Variable KMO and Bartlett sphere tests

| KMO and Bartlett's Test | | |
| --- | --- | --- |
| KMO measure of sampling adequacy | | 0.888 |
| Bartlett's test of sphericity | Approx. Chi-Square | 1910.333 |
| | df | 253 |
| | p | 0.000 |

**Factor Analysis.** Principal component analysis is used for factor analysis, and a total of 5 factors are extracted, and the eigenvalues are all greater than 1. The rotation sums of squared loadingsof these 5 factors are 15.806%, 13.247%, 12.395%, 9.877% and 5.920%, respectively, and the cumulative rotation sums of squared loadings is 57.245% (Table 5). The rotated component matrix is shown in Table 6. It can be seen that under the condition of extracting 5 factors, 23 evaluation indicators can be explained well.

**Table 5.** Factor analysis table

Total variance explained

| Component | Initial eigenvalues | | | Extraction sums of squared loadings | | | Rotation sums of squared loadings | | |
|---|---|---|---|---|---|---|---|---|---|
| | Total | % of variance | Cumulative % | Total | % of variance | Cumulative % | Total | % of variance | Cumulative % |
| 1 | 7.852 | 34.141 | 34.141 | 57.245 | 57.245 | 57.245 | 3.635 | 15.806 | 15.806 |
| 2 | 1.863 | 8.102 | 42.243 | 57.245 | 57.245 | 57.245 | 3.047 | 13.247 | 29.053 |
| 3 | 1.293 | 5.623 | 47.866 | 57.245 | 57.245 | 57.245 | 2.851 | 12.395 | 41.449 |
| 4 | 1.121 | 4.873 | 52.739 | 57.245 | 57.245 | 57.245 | 2.272 | 9.877 | 51.326 |
| 5 | 1.036 | 4.506 | 57.245 | 57.245 | 57.245 | 57.245 | 1.362 | 5.920 | 57.245 |
| 6 | .965 | 4.194 | 61.439 | | | | | | |
| 7 | .872 | 3.792 | 65.231 | | | | | | |
| 8 | .811 | 3.528 | 68.758 | | | | | | |
| 9 | .773 | 3.363 | 72.121 | | | | | | |
| 10 | .746 | 3.242 | 75.363 | | | | | | |
| 11 | .670 | 2.915 | 78.279 | | | | | | |
| 12 | .634 | 2.757 | 81.035 | | | | | | |
| 13 | .555 | 2.414 | 83.450 | | | | | | |
| 14 | .525 | 2.284 | 85.734 | | | | | | |
| 15 | .506 | 2.199 | 87.933 | | | | | | |
| 16 | .458 | 1.993 | 89.926 | | | | | | |
| 17 | .431 | 1.874 | 91.800 | | | | | | |
| 18 | .413 | 1.794 | 93.594 | | | | | | |
| 19 | .356 | 1.548 | 95.142 | | | | | | |
| 20 | .327 | 1.424 | 96.566 | | | | | | |
| 21 | .299 | 1.302 | 97.867 | | | | | | |
| 22 | .272 | 1.183 | 99.051 | | | | | | |
| 23 | .218 | .949 | 100.000 | | | | | | |

It can be seen from the above table that the communalities of all the items are higher than 0.5 or close to 0.5, which means that there is a strong correlation between the research items and the factors, and the factors can effectively extract information.

**Hierarchy Partitioning and Naming.** The five extracted factors are interpreted as "Satisfaction of basic function", "Satisfaction of psychological need", "Rational design", "Service and Security" and "Sense of convenience" respectively, and taken as the criterion layer, thus establishing the online shopping service experience evaluation system (Table 7).

Generally, the comprehensive evaluation index system is divided into three levels: the target layer, the criterion layer and the indicator layer. The analysis results of the semantic difference method are used as the hierarchical structure model [13]. The hierarchical model of online shopping service is shown in the following figure (Fig. 3):

**Index Layer Item Score Weight Analysis.** In this study, the CI is 0.000, and the RI is 1.659, so the CR is 0.000 < 0.1. It means the weight analysis is consistent (Table 8).

The AHP result of the indicator layer are as follows (Table 9).

The AHP results of the weight of the indicator are arranged from the highest to the lowest in terms of the weight, which means that the higher the indicator is, the higher the score of the indicator is.

**Table 6.** Rotating component matrix

| | Component | | | | |
|---|---|---|---|---|---|
| | 1 | 2 | 3 | 4 | 5 |
| Commodity reliability | 0.718 | | | | |
| Sense of immersion | 0.667 | | | | |
| Readability of product information | 0.649 | | | | |
| Personalized service | 0.636 | | | | |
| Commodity package | 0.634 | | | | |
| Well designed page | 0.512 | | | | |
| Timely logistics information update | 0.467 | | | | |
| Simple order-filling process | | 0.654 | | | |
| Canonical platform services | | 0.632 | | | |
| Abundant commodity supplies | | 0.605 | | | |
| Easily identifiable logo | | 0.601 | | | |
| Secure payment | | 0.561 | | | |
| Controllable transaction process | | 0.473 | | | |
| Rational interface layout | | | 0.682 | | |
| Thorough interface function | | | 0.644 | | |
| Simple and unambiguous interaction logic | | | 0.597 | | |
| Sense of being considered | | | 0.499 | | |
| Accurate search function | | | 0.480 | | |
| Consulting and after-sales service | | | | 0.684 | |
| Customer interaction | | | | 0.638 | |
| Personal information protection | | | | 0.543 | |
| Intelligent push | | | | | 0.752 |
| Connectivity with other software | | | | | 0.461 |

The scores of "Easily identifiable logo", "Abundant commodity supplies", "Secure payment", "Accurate search function", "Simple order-filling process", "Controllable transaction process", "Thorough interface function", "Canonical platform services", "Connectivity with other software", "Timely logistics information" are relatively high, indicating that the users are more satisfied with the 10 kinds of service of Taobao platform. On the other hand, the scores of "Simple and unambiguous interaction logic", "Readability of product information", "Consulting and after-sales service", "Sense of being considered", "Rational interface layout", "Customer interaction", "Intelligent push", "Well-designed page", "Sense of immersion", "Commodity reliability", "Commodity package", "Personalized service", "Personal information protection" are relatively low,

**Table 7.** Hierarchical division and coding of experience evaluation of online shopping service

| Criterion layer | Indicator layer |
| --- | --- |
| Satisfaction of basic function | Simple order-filling process |
| | Canonical platform services |
| | Abundant commodity supplies |
| | Easily identifiable logo |
| | Secure payment |
| | Controllable transaction process |
| Satisfaction of psychological need | Commodity reliability |
| | Sense of immersion |
| | Readability of product information |
| | Personalized service |
| | Commodity package |
| | Well-designed page |
| | Timely logistics information update |
| Rational design | Rational interface layout |
| | Thorough interface function |
| | Simple and unambiguous interaction logic |
| | Sense of being considered |
| | Accurate search function |
| Service and Security | Consulting and after-sales service |
| | Customer interaction |
| | Personal information protection |
| Sense of convenience | Intelligent push |
| | Connectivity with other software |

indicating that the users are more unsatisfied with the 13 kinds of services of Taobao platform.

Contrasting the result of AHP with the experience evaluation of online shopping service system, 80% of the high score indicators are from the criterion layer of Satisfaction of basic function and the criterion layer of Rational design. It's also worth noting that 90% of the indicators of the criterion layer of Satisfaction of psychological need and the criterion layer of Service and Security are with the low scores. It means that Taobao platform has a good performance in basic function and rational design, and it need to pay more attention to the user's inner feeling, service feeling and other deeper needs.

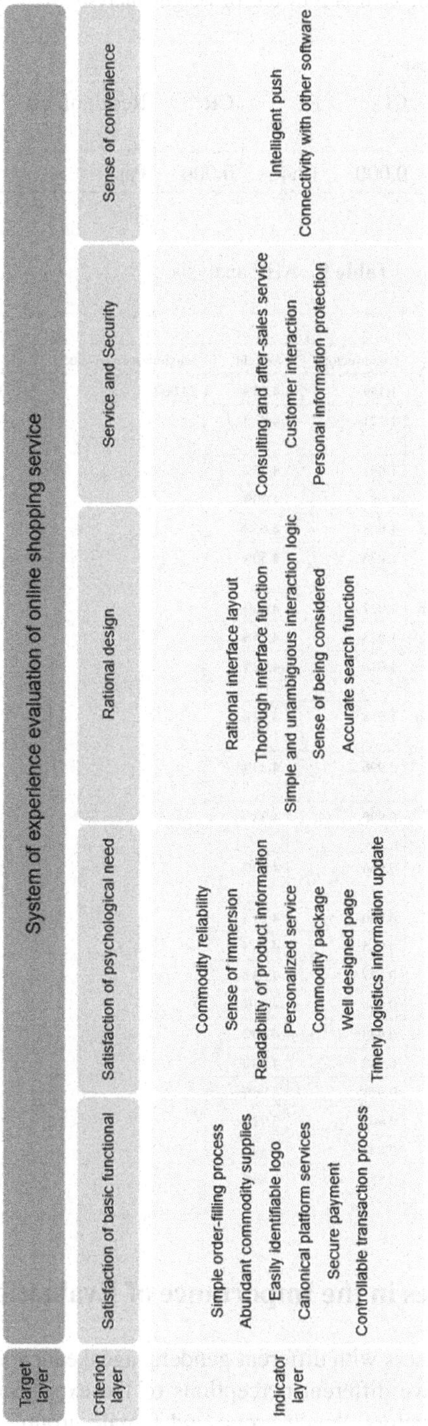

**Fig. 3.** Experience evaluation of online shopping service system

**Table 8.** Consistency test of weight analysis

| Consistency test | | | | |
|---|---|---|---|---|
| Maximum eigenvalue | CI | RI | CR | Result of test |
| 23.000 | 0.000 | 1.646 | 0.000 | Pass |

**Table 9.** AHP analysis

| AHP Analyze | | | | |
|---|---|---|---|---|
| Items | Eigenvectors | Weight | Maximum eigenvalue | CI |
| Easily identifiable logo | 1.149 | 4.99% | 23.000 | 0.000 |
| Abundant commodity supplies | 1.121 | 4.87% | | |
| Secure payment | 1.091 | 4.75% | | |
| Accurate search function | 1.08 | 4.70% | | |
| Simple order-filling process | 1.068 | 4.65% | | |
| Controllable transaction process | 1.036 | 4.50% | | |
| Thorough interface function | 1.027 | 4.46% | | |
| Canonical platform services | 1.023 | 4.45% | | |
| Connectivity with other software | 1.018 | 4.42% | | |
| Timely logistics information update | 1.018 | 4.42% | | |
| Simple and unambiguous interaction logic | 0.996 | 4.33% | | |
| Readability of product information | 0.996 | 4.33% | | |
| Consulting and after-sales service | 0.986 | 4.29% | | |
| Sense of being considered | 0.986 | 4.29% | | |
| Rational interface layout | 0.985 | 4.28% | | |
| Customer interaction | 0.977 | 4.25% | | |
| Intelligent push | 0.968 | 4.21% | | |
| Well-designed page | 0.943 | 4.10% | | |
| Sense of immersion | 0.943 | 4.10% | | |
| Commodity reliability | 0.911 | 3.96% | | |
| Commodity package | 0.902 | 3.92% | | |
| Personalized service | 0.894 | 3.89% | | |
| Personal information protection | 0.884 | 3.84% | | |

# 3   Perceived Differences in the Importance of Evaluation Indicators

In order to explore whether users with different genders, ages, education backgrounds, and shopping frequencies have different perceptions of the experience evaluation of online shopping service indicators, "male group and female group", "low-frequency shopping Taobao use group and high-frequency Taobao use group", "old user group and young user group" are set up respectively, and independent T-test is used to analyze the data. The results are as follows.

High-frequency Taobao use group (Users with shopping frequency of more than 20 times per year)and low-frequency shopping Taobao use group(Users with shopping frequency of less than 20 times per year) have significant differences in the evaluation of many indicators ($P < 0.05$), such as "Well-designed page", "Simple and unambiguous interaction logic", "Commodity reliability" "Readability of product "information Sense of immersion", "Controllable transaction process", "Simple order-filling process", "Secure payment", "Canonical platform services", "Consulting and after-sales service", "Timely logistics information update", and "Easily identifiable logo". High-frequency Taobao users are apparently give more points to these indicators than low-frequency Taobao users, meaning that they more satisfied with above services, and that's also the reason why they use Taobao with such a high frequency. However, in terms of the indicator of "Easily identifiable logo", the users who shop more think the logo is not easily identifiable compared with the users who less.

There is no significant difference between different genders ($P > 0.05$).

For the "old user group and young user group", In order to reduce the differences caused by different age classification criteria, the "old user" and the "young user" are divided in three different ways (Group1 – under 18 years old and over 50 years old, Group2 – under 25 years old &over 40 years old, Group3 – under30 years old & over 30 years old). From the results of the T-test, we can know get the conclusion that there is only 1 indicator (Personal information protection) of Group2 and Group3 shows the significant differences($P < 0.05$), There is no significant difference in the other 22 indicators($P > 0.05$). Therefore, it can be concluded that gender and age have little influence on the importance perception of evaluation indicator. Therefore, it is not necessary to further subdivide the user group, and a general model of experience evaluation of online shopping platform can be built directly for all users.

## 4 Summary

Online shopping platforms occupies an important place in our daily life. Users' experience evaluation of service is an important standard for evaluating service quality. Based on the experience evaluation of Taobao platform service, this article constructs a basic evaluation system of the experience of online shopping service by semantic difference method and factor analysis. Besides it also gives weight to each evaluation index score according to the analytic hierarchy process to clarify the service indicators to be improved in the current online shopping process. In general, this article can help related service designers and decision makers understand the users' concerns and subjective feelings in the process of experience more, thus optimizing online shopping services and improve user service experience.

## References

1. Ye, X., Han, F., Weng, T.: Research on the influence of visual features of online shopping platform products. J. Ind. Eng. Eng. Manag. **33**(02), 84–91 (2019)

2. Xu, B., Lu, Z., Li, M.: Study on the color design elements of the homepage of online shopping APP for middle-aged and elderly users. Packag. Eng. 1–8

3. Chen, H., Tao, C., Wen, W.: Research on quality evaluation approaches for search function of online shopping platforms. Comput. Sci. **44**(11), 125–133 (2017)

4. Wang, J., Yang, C., Zhou, Y.: Shopping APP interface optimization design. Packag. Eng. **40**(18), 207–213+226 (2019)

5. Yu, S.: Product packaging design in the age of online shopping. Packag. Eng. **40**(12), 309–312 (2019)

6. Liu, Z., Yin, L., Yuan, L.: Research on the impact of logistics service factors on consumers' online shopping intention based on structural equation modeling. Math. Pract. Theory **49**(04), 34–42 (2019)

7. Zeng, Y., Zhu, Z., Zhu, J., et al.: Investigation and research on after-sale service of college students' online shopping. Consum. Econ. **28**(05), 86–88 (2012)

8. Qi, M.: An empirical study of SERVQUAL model on service quality evaluation of C2C E-commerce. China Bus. Trade (03), 110–111 (2011)

9. Guo, X., Luo, Z., Shi, C.: Comprehensive evaluation of online shopping satisfaction based on cloud model. Stat. Decis. **34**(23), 60–62 (2018)

10. Yao, Y.: Research on B2C E-commerce website design based on service design concept. Digit. Technol. Appl. (02), 153 (2016)

11. Wang, J., Wei, S., Yao, R., et al.: Quantitative evaluation of landscape perception features and classification of garden space. J. Northwest Forestry Univ. **27**(02), 221–225+229 (2012)

12. Cha, S.: Research on Service Design Touch Points. Research of Industrial Design (3rd series)

13. Zhang, Y., Wang, X.: Research on experience evaluation of community health service. Packag. Eng. 1–10

14. Zhou, M., Chao, L., Ru, S.: A service design model of cross-border E-commerce based on trust. Packag. Eng. **40**(16), 101–107 (2019)

15. Liu, Z., Liu, Z.: Questionnaire design strategy based on improving Cronbach's coefficient of judgment. Contemp. Educ. Pract. Teach. Res.: Electron. Ed. (4), 173–174 (2016)

# Enhanced Product Presentation with Augmented Reality: The Role of Affective Reactions and Authenticity

Joschka C. Firnkes, Christopher Zerres$^{(\boxtimes)}$, and Kai Israel

Offenburg University, Badstraße 24, 77652 Offenburg, Germany
`christopher.zerres@hs-offenburg.de`

**Abstract.** When shopping online, it is usually not possible to view products in the same way as you are used to when shopping offline. With augmented reality (AR), it is not only possible to view the product in detail, but also to view it at home in the real environment. Such an AR application sets stimuli that can affect the users and their purchase decision and Word-of-mouth intention. In this work, we assume that when viewing a product in AR, not only affective internal states but also cognitive perception processes have an impact on purchase decision and Word-of-mouth intention. While positive affective reactions have already been studied in the context of AR, this paper will also describe inner cognitive perception processes, using the construct of AR authenticity. To test these assumptions, a study was conducted with 155 participants. The results show that both the purchase intention and the Word-of-mouth intention are influenced by the constructs of positive affective reactions and AR authenticity.

**Keywords:** Augmented reality · Purchase intention · Positive affective reaction · S-O-R model · AR authenticity · Word-of-mouth intention

## 1 Introduction

A consumer's buying intention is often influenced by product information found on search engines and company websites [31]. In addition to existing product information on the website, some companies offer users the opportunity to use an augmented reality (AR) application to obtain further product information. Also, Google now shows three dimensional (3D) models under the search results, which can be accessed using an AR application. These embedded 3D models allow users to get more detailed information about the product by using a mobile device such as a smartphone or tablet. For example, a person is looking for some new furniture for the living room and is searching the web for further information. On the search results page the user sees the opportunity to use an AR application. This AR application allows the virtual presentation of the new furniture in the form of a 3D model on the mobile device, showing it in the physical environment of the user. The live image of the environment from the device's camera is used. The experience provides important and helpful information but is also entertaining

© Springer Nature Switzerland AG 2021
F. F.-H. Nah and K. Siau (Eds.): HCII 2021, LNCS 12783, pp. 55–70, 2021.
https://doi.org/10.1007/978-3-030-77750-0_4

and unique. AR therefore represents a very innovative and helpful opportunity to present products [47]. However, in order to successfully use this new technology, it is important to understand what users are expecting from such a technology and what is important for them. Since AR represents an opportunity for online retailers to present their products in a more attractive way and possibly even increase customers' behavioral decisions, it is important to know what influences these decisions. In our research we investigate the role of positive affective reactions and the perceived authenticity of AR experiences and their influence on purchase intention and Word-of-mouth intention. We assume that an enjoyable experience and a highly perceived authenticity of the AR experience positively influence these behavioral intentions.

## 2  Augmented Reality

### 2.1  Definition of AR

In previous research, especially in the fields of computer technology and human computer interaction [8, 27, 28, 41, 47], AR is defined following Azuma et al. [2, p. 34]: "An AR system supplements the real world with virtual (computer-generated) objects that appear to coexist in the same space as the real world." Furthermore, an AR system is attributed with the following characteristics: 1. combining real and virtual objects in a real environment, 2. working interactively and in real time, 3. aligning real and virtual objects with each other [2].

AR is understood as the connection of virtual elements and real content. Virtual objects are synchronized with reality [28] and integrated into a real environment [41]. Even though very realistic results are achieved with current applications, many of them still create the impression described by Javornik [28] that the real environment is only overlaid by the virtual objects. Thus, according to Azuma et al.'s [2] definition, AR aims to make this overlay invisible to the user and to create the impression that real and virtual objects coexist in the same space. However, whether all AR applications will meet this claim depends on further technological developments.

Whether the application is like a mere overlay of the real environment or an actual embedding of the virtual object into the real environment, in both cases the augmentation must not be time-delayed. This is another major factor that should be considered here: the embedding of the virtual objects in the real environment must happen in real time [2, 25, 28, 32].

The definition proposed by Azuma et al. [2] describes virtual, computer-generated objects. According to other studies, these virtual objects may include images, videos, or other virtual elements [41, 47]. Accordingly, the term *other virtual elements* should include 3D models, text, etc.

AR is thus the integration of virtual objects (consisting of images, videos, or other virtual elements) into a real environment in real time.

### 2.2  AR in E-Commerce

AR received increased attention within computer science in the 1990s [28]. The fact that this technology was first used in advertising only in 2008 is probably due to its lack of accessibility to the general population [47]. Due to the ubiquity of smartphones and their rapid technological advancement an increased interest in AR applications for mobile devices is emerging [8, 41].

Research has long been dedicated only to the acceptance of AR technologies [41]. The full potential of AR for marketing purposes is only gradually being recognized in scientific studies [8, 9, 15, 41]. For example, Dacko [8] describes virtual try-ons for clothing and make-up as an opportunity to improve conversion and return rates. Rese et al. [41] investigated the possibility of using AR to present additional product information and thus support the purchase decision.

Online retailers are also recognizing the great potential of AR and are increasingly offering the opportunity for users to view products in AR applications. Yet the use of AR still varies widely. In addition to virtual try-ons of make-up, glasses or clothing, 3D models of furniture or other products are also offered. However, such applications require the product to be mapped as a 3D model, and also entail increased technical effort compared to the usual image gallery, which can be an obstacle for online retailers. With service providers offering complete solutions for the use of AR, the technical effort required to integrate AR applications on an online retailer's own website is eased. Thus, it can be assumed that with more providers for AR applications, the hurdles will also be removed for more and more online retailers and AR will be offered more frequently in the future.

It is likely that AR technologies will support consumers in their purchasing activities. In the context of fashion products, research shows that AR applications can have a positive influence on purchasing decisions [47]. However, there have been only a few studies dealing with AR applications and their effects on purchasing behavior [27, 40, 47].

## 3 Theoretical Framework

To examine the impact of AR on customer behavior, this study uses the Stimulus-Organism-Response (SOR) model of Mehrabian and Russel [36]. The traditional model assumes that when individuals are presented with a stimulus (S), they develop internal states (O), which in turn cause responses (R). Since its application to the retail environment by Donovan and Rossiter [10], a number of studies have also used the SOR model to examine consumer behavior in e-commerce [11, 24, 33, 37].

### 3.1 Stimulus

In e-commerce, the SOR model has already been used in some studies to investigate relationships between e-commerce characteristics and customers' internal states or purchase intentions [4, 24, 34, 37, 47]. The stimulus in our study is an AR application with which users can perceive the 3D model of a product in their real environment. Therefore, this study aims to investigate the impact of an AR application on consumers' internal states and behavior.

## 3.2 Organism

**Positive Affective Reactions.** An important component of the organism, in addition to cognitive aspects, are affective reaction. In this context, various studies have been able to prove that innovative e-commerce applications can elicit positive emotional states in the user [22, 39, 47]. According to Chang et al. [4] positive affective reactions are understood as emotional states such as excitement, enthusiasm, enjoyment, entertainment, happiness, and inspiration. In the study by Watson et al. [47], a positive effect of an AR application on positive affective reactions of users was found. This relationship between positive affective reactions and AR applications is also supported by characteristics of the AR technology described by Javornik [28]. Studies have shown that such characteristics have an effect on positive affective reactions [7, 24, 44, 46].

**AR Authenticity.** Stimuli (e.g. an AR application) are processed in the organism and transformed into meaningful information that leads to an altered cognitive or emotional state. (Mehrabian and Russel [36]) Most studies of AR applications in e-commerce have so far focused on affective reactions [42]. Thus, in addition to affective aspects, the cognitive perception of the stimulus also plays an important role. Cognition, although a very broad term, can be broadly summarized as an interplay of internal mental processes and states that include subjective attitude, perception, understanding, and prior knowledge, among others [11]. How an AR application is perceived and processed thus also depends on these internal processes.

The perceived augmentation of 3D models in an AR environment has been studied by Javornik [27]. The results of the study show that AR applications are perceived differently by users [27]. Two aspects in particular are relevant: the realism of the 3D model and the realistic placement of the object in real time in the real environment. Whether users perceive an AR application to be realistic or not depends on an interplay of the general perception of the components of the AR application, prior knowledge, and the understanding of a realistic representation. The dimensions 'realism of the 3D model' and 'realism of the spatial embedding' proposed by Javornik [27] are used as the basis for the construct of perceived authenticity of the AR application in our study.

In order to explain the internal states triggered by the perception of a 3D model, Algharabat and Dennis [1] propose the construct of 3D authenticity in distinction to the concept of telepresence (or presence). Especially in the context of product presentation, where the represented 3D model has a real counterpart (i.e. a product), the concept of authenticity is more appropriate than the concept of presence, since it does not imply any form of illusion [1]. 3D authenticity is defined as a "psychological state in which virtual objects presented in 3D in a computer-mediated environment are perceived as actual objects in a sensory way" [1, p. 76]. In addition to the authentic perception of the 3D model, however, its realistic placement in the user's real environment is also relevant for the authentic perception of the AR application [27]. This spatial dimension is not addressed in 3D authenticity according to Algharabat and Dennis [1]. However, it should be considered in the context of an AR application [1, 27]. Therefore, 3D authenticity should be complemented by spatial presence adapted for AR by Hilken et al. [20]. Spatial presence describes a mental state in which the used technology is no longer perceived by the user, resulting in the feeling of being there [35]. If users do not perceive the superimposition of their real environment with virtual elements as such, this also means they have an authentic AR experience, since the virtual elements seem to coexist with the real elements. In this respect, spatial presence is suitable for mapping the authenticity of the spatial representation of an AR application. However, since AR does not simulate a virtual change of location, but adds virtual elements to the real environment, the construct of spatial presence has to be adapted accordingly. According to Hilken et al. [20, p. 890], this requires the exchange of "a person's feeling of 'self-location' with a feeling of 'object-location' in the physical reality". With this adaptation, the construct can then be applied to AR [20].

Based on the two terms '3D authenticity' and 'spatial presence', this study proposes the construct of AR authenticity. AR authenticity takes into account both the perception of the 3D model and its integration into the real environment and, within the framework of this model, is intended to describe the internal processes stimulated by the AR application as a stimulus. In summary, AR authenticity is understood as: the mental state in which virtual objects presented in 3D in an AR environment are perceived as real objects.

Studies have shown the effect of AR applications on positive affective reactions [27, 47]. Furthermore, in the context of 3D product presentations, it has also been found that the authentic perception of 3D models has a positive influence on hedonic internal states [1]. Similarly, as 3D authenticity has an influence on affective internal states when using a 3D model, it is suggested that by having high AR authenticity, the overall AR experience will be perceived more positively, and consequently, positive affective reactions will be stronger. Therefore, the following hypothesis will be proposed:

$H_1$: AR authenticity enhances positive affective reactions.

### 3.3 Response

**Word-of-Mouth Intention.** The Word-of-mouth intention generally describes the intention to make a statement about a product [3]. In accordance with Heller et al. [17], this statement is specifically defined in this paper as a recommendation of the product from the AR experience. The construct of the Word-of-mouth intention is thus intended to measure whether participants would recommend the product perceived in the AR application. Studies have shown that the positively perceived spatial presence of a product when using an AR application can increase the willingness to recommend a product to others [20]. This effect will also be investigated in this study in relation to the construct of AR authenticity. Since the construct of AR authenticity describes a state in which virtual objects are perceived authentically in the real environment, we assume that this state influences the Word-of-mouth intention. Positive affective reactions also affect behavioral intentions [11, 47, 48].

Taking into account the findings of these previous studies, we suggest that a positive affective reaction also has a positive effect on Word-of-mouth intention. Therefore, the following hypotheses will be proposed:

$H_2$: *The positive affective reaction of the users has a positive effect on the Word-of-mouth intention.*

$H_3$: *The perceived AR authenticity has a positive effect on the Word-of-mouth intention.*

**Purchase Intention.** The effects of positive affective reactions in e-commerce have been widely studied [11, 24, 30, 34, 37, 47]. Studies have shown that positive affective reactions such as enthusiasm, enjoyment, positive emotion, and positive mood can increase purchase intention. The purchase intention represents the consumers' interest and possibility to buy a product and can be used for the estimation of the future purchase behavior of consumers [47]. In addition to positive affective reactions, research on the concepts of 3D authenticity and spatial presence, on which the construct of AR authenticity is based, also suggest that AR authenticity has a positive influence on purchase intention [1, 20]. The positive effect of 3D authenticity on purchase intention has already been observed [1]. Also the perception of spatial presence has an effect on purchase intention [20]. Thus, an authentic perception of the displayed product is proposed to have an influence on the purchase decision, and we assume that this is also the case in the context of an AR application. Our assumption is that the customer has a better understanding of the product thanks to the authentic presentation, and therefore the purchase decision is influenced. Therefore, in summary, the following hypotheses will be proposed:

$H_4$: *The positive affective reaction of the users has a positive effect on the purchase intention.*

$H_5$: *The perceived AR authenticity has a positive effect on the purchase intention.*

In addition, the effect of Word-of-mouth intention on purchase intention will be considered. The decisions to recommend a product and to buy a product are probably very similar and subject to similar criteria. A person who recommends a product evaluates this product positively. This positive evaluation of the product is also an important criterion affecting the purchase decision [49]. For these reasons, the following hypothesis is proposed:

$H_6$: *Word-of-mouth intention influences purchase intention.*

Figure 1 summarizes the proposed model and the hypotheses (Fig. 1).

## 4 Study

### 4.1 Study Participants

A total of 155 people participated in the study. As the characteristics of the respondents (Table 1) indicate, 55.5% of the participants were female, 42.6% male, and 1.3% diverse. At 74.8%, a majority of respondents were between the ages of 20 and 29. Furthermore, 61.3% students participated in the survey. Many participants were already familiar with

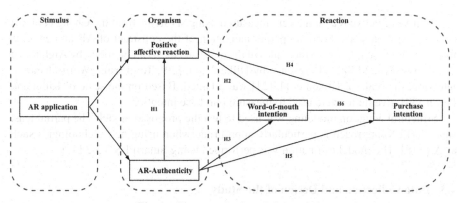

**Fig. 1.** Conceptual research framework

the term AR before taking part in the study (81.9%). Nearly 60% of all participants had used an AR application before the study.

## 4.2 Measurement of Constructs

All constructs of the model were measured using seven-point Likert scales, ranging from "strongly disagree" (1) to "strongly agree" (7).

**Table 1.** Characteristics of respondents (n = 155)

| Characteristics | | Frequency | Percentage (%) |
|---|---|---|---|
| Gender | Female | 86 | 55.5 |
| | Male | 66 | 42.6 |
| | Divers | 2 | 1.3 |
| | Not specified | 1 | 0.6 |
| Age | Under 20 | 9 | 5.8 |
| | 20-29 | 116 | 74.8 |
| | 30-39 | 21 | 13.6 |
| | 40+ | 6 | 3.9 |
| | Not specified | 3 | 1.9 |
| Profession | Student | 95 | 61.3 |
| | Employee | 39 | 25.2 |
| | Others | 19 | 12.2 |
| | Not specified | 2 | 1.3 |
| Familiar with term "augmented reality" | Yes | 127 | 81.9 |
| | No | 28 | 18.1 |
| Augmented reality used | Yes | 95 | 61.3 |
| | No | 60 | 38.7 |

Positive affective reactions were measured using six items from the Chang et al. [4] positive emotion scale. For the operationalization of the construct of AR authenticity, five items were adapted from the scales of the construct of 3D authenticity by Algharabat and Dennis [1] and Spatial Presence by Hilken et al. [20]. To measure Word-of-mouth intention, the scale of Hilken et al. [21] was adapted. Based on the scale of Kühn and Petzer [34], five items were used to measure purchase intention.

Structural equation modeling was used to test the proposed model. The partial least squares (PLS) approach is particularly appropriate when using new technologies such as AR [18]. The model estimation was performed using SmartPLS 3.3.2 [43].

### 4.3 Data Collection and Design of the Study

The participants in the study were invited to take part via e-mail distribution lists of three German universities. In the e-mail a link to a website created especially for this study was provided. The website contained a brief explanation of the study procedure, an embedded AR application, and a direct link to the questionnaire. In the first step, participants were asked to run the AR application and view a 3D model of a chair in their surrounding environment. The 3D model of the chair could be viewed in AR after tapping on the application using a smartphone or tablet. Participants who participated via a computer were asked to scan a quick response (QR) code with a smartphone or tablet after opening the AR application. This QR code then also led to the study's AR application. The participants were able to decide how long they would use the AR application. After viewing the AR application, the participants were asked to complete the online questionnaire. At the beginning of the questionnaire, the participants were informed about the data use and anonymity of the study. To ensure that the participants went through the steps of the study in the correct order, the use of the AR application was queried at the beginning of the questionnaire. If this question was negatively answered, the participant was directed back to the AR application.

**Fig. 2.** Example of an AR product presentation

# 5  Results

## 5.1  Assessment of the Measurement Model

In a first step the measurement model was assessed. According to Hair et al. [16] an analysis of the internal consistency reliability, convergence validity, and discriminant validity should be made. For the assessment of the internal consistency reliability, Cronbach's alpha coefficient (α) and the composite reliability (ρc) [18] were analyzed. The minimum requirement for the Cronbach's alpha coefficient (α) and the composite reliability (ρc) was in both cases 0.7 [38]. This criterion was met by all constructs, so that the internal consistency reliability could be confirmed (Table 2).

The convergence validity of the measurement model was evaluated by outer loadings, indicator reliability, and average variance extracted (AVE). A significant outer loading above 0.7 was considered as an acceptable value [16]. Therefore, we analyzed whether the individual indicators had a high outer loading on the assigned construct. As shown in Table 2 all indicators met this requirement. To assess the indicator reliability, the squared factor loadings were analyzed. The squared factor loadings should exceed the value 0.5 [16]. All squared factor loadings were above this requirement. Finally, the convergence validity was verified by determining the AVE, which should also exceed the value of 0.5 [18]. The AVE is the result of the mean value of all squared factor loadings assigned to a construct. In our study all constructs met the required value for AVE. Therefore, the convergence validity could be confirmed (Table 2).

The last step in assessing the measurement model is the evaluation of the discriminant validity. To analyze the discriminant validity, the Fornell-Larcker criterion and the heterotrait-monotrait (HTMT) ratio of correlations were used. The Fornell-Larcker criterion requires that the AVE of a latent variable must be greater than the squared correlation with the other latent variable [12]. Regarding the heterotrait-monotrait ratio of correlations (HTMT), a limit value of 0.85 should not be exceeded [19]. The Fornell-Larcker criterion was met by all constructs and the limit value of 0.85 of the HTMT ratio was not exceeded, so that the discriminant validity could also be confirmed (Table 3).

## 5.2  Assessment of the Structural Model

In a second step the results of the structural model were evaluated. The analysis was based on the coefficient of determination ($R^2$), the predictive relevance ($Q^2$), the standardized root mean square residual (SRMR), and the strength and the significance of the path coefficients. The explained variance of an endogenous variable ($R^2$) is considered high if the value is above 0.26 [6]. The two endogenous variables Word-of-mouth intention and purchase intention both have higher values than 0.26. Only the value of the endogenous variable positive affective reaction is slightly below this limit value ($R^2 = 0.198$). However, the model still has a high quality of explanation (Fig. 3). The SMRR is "…the square root of the sum of the squared differences between the model-implied and the empirical correlation matrix" [18, p. 9]. Hu and Bentler [23] recommend a cut-off value of 0.08. With 0.062 the SRMR was below the recommended limit value, so that a high quality of adaptation could be ascertained for the overall model.

**Table 2.** Validity and reliability of the constructs

| Construct and items | α | ρA | ρc | AVE | Loading |
|---|---|---|---|---|---|
| Criteria | >0.7 | >0.7 | >0.7 | >0.5 | >0.7 |
| **AR authenticity (AUTH)** | **0.857** | **0.861** | **0.898** | **0.639** | |
| When using the AR application, I had the impression that the chair was in the real environment | | | | | 0.855 |
| The AR application allowed me to look at the chair as if it was a real object | | | | | 0.867 |
| The chair made me feel like I could sit in it | | | | | 0.717 |
| When using the AR application, it felt like I could move the chair with my fingers in my real environment | | | | | 0.789 |
| When using the AR application, I felt like the chair was a part of my real environment | | | | | 0.758 |
| **Positive affective reaction (PAR)** | **0.900** | **0.902** | **0.923** | **0.669** | |
| It was exciting to use the AR application | | | | | 0.850 |
| I felt entertained while using the AR application | | | | | 0.882 |
| I enjoyed using the AR application | | | | | 0.841 |
| Using the AR application inspired me | | | | | 0.760 |
| I was excited while using the AR application | | | | | 0.796 |
| Using the AR application made me happy | | | | | 0.770 |
| **Word-of-mouth intention (WOM)** | **0.865** | **0.876** | **0.918** | **0.789** | |
| I would recommend the chair I interacted with to my friends | | | | | 0.927 |
| I would recommend my friends to view the chair in augmented reality | | | | | 0.828 |
| If a friend of mine were looking for a new chair I would recommend this one | | | | | 0.906 |
| **Purchase intention (PI)** | **0.911** | **0.915** | **0.934** | **0.739** | |
| I would consider buying the chair shown in the AR application | | | | | 0.840 |
| There is a high probability that I will buy the chair | | | | | 0.900 |
| If I were looking for a chair, I would choose the chair shown in the AR application | | | | | 0.874 |
| I would buy the chair shown in the AR application | | | | | 0.877 |
| I intend to purchase the chair shown in the AR application in the future | | | | | 0.805 |

Furthermore, the predictive relevance of the structural model must be verified. An appropriate assessment is the cross-validated redundancy approach (Stone-Geisser criterion) [5, 13, 45]. "This technique represents a synthesis of cross-validation and function fitting with the perspective that 'the prediction of observables or potential observables is of much greater relevance than the estimation of what are often artificial construct-parameters'" [14, p. 320]. In PLS the predictive relevance is calculated on the basis of

**Table 3.** Squared-inter-correlations between constructs (AVE shown in bold on diagonal) and HTMT$_{.85}$ criterion (gray).

|       | AUTH  | PAR   | WOM   | PI    |
|-------|-------|-------|-------|-------|
| AUTH  | **0.639** | 0.503 | 0.455 | 0.521 |
| PAR   | 0.198 | **0.669** | 0.551 | 0.552 |
| WOM   | 0.153 | 0.234 | **0.789** | 0.759 |
| PI    | 0.213 | 0.255 | 0.464 | **0.739** |

the blind-folding procedure. For all endogenous variables the predictive relevance ($Q^2 > 0$) could be confirmed (Fig. 3). Therefore, the predictive capability of the structural model was proved.

**Table 4.** Results of hypothesis testing.

|     | Relationships | Path coefficient | CI (Bias Corrected) | t-Value | p-Value | Supported |
|-----|---------------|------------------|---------------------|---------|---------|-----------|
| H1  | AUTH → PAR    | 0.445***         | [0.289, 0.559]      | 6.500   | 0.000   | Yes       |
| H2  | PAR → WOM     | 0.387***         | [0.207, 0.540]      | 4.568   | 0.000   | Yes       |
| H3  | AUTH → WOM    | 0.219*           | [0.050, 0.381]      | 2.519   | 0.012   | Yes       |
| H4  | PAR → PI      | 0.169*           | [0.032, 0.305]      | 2.445   | 0.015   | Yes       |
| H5  | AUTH → PI     | 0.180**          | [0.051, 0.313]      | 2.722   | 0.007   | Yes       |
| H6  | WOM → PI      | 0.529***         | [0.372, 0.667]      | 7.033   | 0.000   | Yes       |

Note: *** $p < 0.001$, ** $p < 0.01$, * $p < 0.05$.

To examine the research hypotheses, the path coefficients were analyzed to verify the research hypotheses. We used a PLS algorithm to determine the strength of the path coefficients and a bootstrapping method (5,000 subsamples) to determine the significance of the respective paths. The results are presented in Table 4. All six proposed relationships were significant, so all hypotheses were supported. As predicted, the factors AR authenticity ($\beta = 0.219*$) and positive affective reaction ($\beta = 0.387***$) both had a positive influence on the Word-of-mouth intention. Both factors also had an influence on the purchase intention ($\beta = 0.169*$; $\beta = 0.180**$). In addition, we found a significant effect of AR authenticity on the positive affective reaction ($\beta = 0.445***$). Finally, the factor Word-of-mouth intention had a strong positive effect on purchase intention ($\beta = 0.529***$).

## 6   Implications

The study examined how internal states that emerge when using an AR application influence consumer behavior. Regarding product rotation or virtual make-up try-ons in

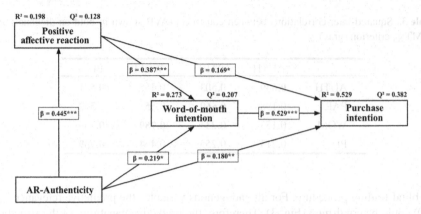

**Fig. 3.** PLS results of the structural model.

e-commerce, the effect of positive affective reactions on consumer behavior has already been studied [39, 47]. This work can confirm the impact of positive affective reactions on Word-of-mouth intention and purchase intention also in the context of an AR application that displays 3D models in the user's environment.

Most studies of AR applications in e-commerce have so far focused on affective responses [42]. Moreover, the cognitive view of AR has mostly been based on the Perceived Ease of Use and Perceived Usefulness variables, which can be explained by the use of the Technology Acceptance Model [40, 41]. However, according to Riar et al. [42] this view is not enough to describe the perception of AR on a cognitive level. Other studies have also questioned the relevance of cognitive responses in the perception of AR applications, calling for further research [28, 47]. Our study shows that the cognitive perception of AR applications in e-commerce also needs to be addressed. AR authenticity describes a mental state in which the user authentically perceives a product from an AR application. The results of the present study show that this mental state has a direct influence on purchase intention and Word-of-mouth intention. In addition, it also affects the positive affective reactions of users. The processing of the AR application and its visual stimuli in terms of authenticity is a relevant cognitive aspect of the description of the inner processes taking place. AR authenticity is therefore recommended as a construct to study AR product presentations in which a real product is virtually represented.

The results of this work can be used to derive important recommendations for e-commerce companies. The influence of positive affective reactions on consumer behavior shows that eliciting positive affective reactions can also promote sales in the context of AR. In this context, studies suggest that these affective reactions can be triggered by active control over the application [24]. Based on these studies, retailers should ensure that their AR applications elicit these positive affective reactions through a high level of active control.

In addition to positive affective reactions, AR authenticity is also relevant to e-commerce, due to its positive influence on Word-of-mouth intention and purchase intention but also on positive affective reactions. AR authenticity has two dimensions: the perceived authenticity of the 3D model and the authentic integration of the product into the user's real environment. This leads to two practical recommendations for the design and development of AR applications for product presentation: 1. The 3D models used should be of high quality and should represent the product as realistically as possible. 2. The integration of this 3D model using the AR application should be as authentic as possible and should create the impression that the product is in the user's real environment. For most online retailers the first recommendation should be the main step toward an authentic AR experience. The implementation of 3D models in AR, however, is comparatively easy to accomplish with online providers offering corresponding AR applications.

## 7  Limitations and Further Research

Most of the respondents were students between the ages of 20 and 29. This population group is particularly familiar with technology and was therefore suitable for participation in this study in which an AR application had to be used independently. Further studies could investigate the extent to which the present results also apply to other, especially older, population groups.

The representation of a product as a 3D model in the real environment investigated here is only one possible application of AR. There are also other forms of AR applications, such as virtual try-ons, where the product is displayed on the users themselves rather than in the surrounding environment. Depending on the product, different forms of application are suitable. For fashion and accessories, it is suggested that the embedding of the virtual product is done with a virtual try-on application [29]. The product used in this study, a chair, on the other hand, is an example of a product that should be presented in the user's environment. Besides the form of application, the choice of product can also be varied. In addition to furniture, kitchen appliances could also be interesting viewing objects. Future studies could therefore examine whether the findings can be transferred to other application forms and product types.

This study does not make a comparison to other virtual technologies. The effect of virtual reality (VR) applications on consumer behavior has already been addressed [26]. Additionally, there could be an investigation of whether the perceived authenticity of the displayed products is important in VR applications.

It was confirmed that the authenticity with which products are perceived in AR applications has an impact on the user's purchase and Word-of-mouth intention. Furthermore, an authentic perception of the product means that the user can easily access information about the product that is close to reality. As a result, customer satisfaction after purchase could also be increased. The influence of AR authenticity on customer satisfaction could thus be the subject of further research efforts.

## References

1. Algharabat, R., Dennis, C.: Modelling the impact of 3D authenticity and 3D telepresence on behavioural intention for an online retailer. In: Morschett, D., Rudolph, T., Schnedlitz, P., Schramm-Klein, H., Swoboda, B. (eds.) European Retail Research, pp. 93–109. Gabler Verlag, Wiesbaden (2011). https://doi.org/10.1007/978-3-8349-6147-1_4

2. Azuma, R., Baillot, Y., Behringer, R., Feiner, S., Julier, S., MacIntyre, B.: Recent advances in augmented reality. IEEE Comput. Graph. Appl. **21**, 34–47 (2001). https://doi.org/10.1109/38.963459
3. Brown, T.J.: Spreading the word: investigating antecedents of consumers' positive word-of-mouth intentions and behaviors in a retailing context. J. Acad. Mark. Sci. **33**, 123–138 (2005). https://doi.org/10.1177/0092070304268417
4. Chang, H.-J., Eckman, M., Yan, R.-N.: Application of the Stimulus-Organism-Response model to the retail environment: the role of hedonic motivation in impulse buying behavior. Int. Rev. Retail Distrib. Consum. Res. **21**, 233–249 (2011). https://doi.org/10.1080/09593969.2011.578798
5. Chin, W.W.: The partial least squares approach for structural equation modeling. In: Marcoulides, G.A. (ed.) Modern Methods for Business Research, pp. 295–336. Lawrence Erlbaum Associates Publishers, Mahwah (1998)
6. Cohen, J.: Statistical Power Analysis for the Behavioral Sciences. Lawrence Erlbaum Associates Publishers, Hillsdale (1988)
7. Cyr, D., Head, M., Ivanov, A.: Perceived interactivity leading to e-loyalty: development of a model for cognitive–affective user responses. Int. J. Hum Comput Stud. **67**, 850–869 (2009). https://doi.org/10.1016/j.ijhcs.2009.07.004
8. Dacko, S.G.: Enabling smart retail settings via mobile augmented reality shopping apps. Technol. Forecast. Soc. Chang. **124**, 243–256 (2017). https://doi.org/10.1016/j.techfore.2016.09.032
9. de Ruyter, K., Heller, J., Hilken, T., Chylinski, M., Keeling, D.I., Mahr, D.: Seeing with the customer's eye: exploring the challenges and opportunities of AR advertising. J. Advert. **49**, 109–124 (2020). https://doi.org/10.1080/00913367.2020.1740123
10. Donovan, R., Rossiter, J.: Store atmosphere: an environmental psychology approach. J. Retail. **58**, 34–57 (1982)
11. Eroglu, S.A., Machleit, K.A., Davis, L.M.: Atmospheric qualities of online retailing a conceptual model and implications. J. Bus. Res. **54**, 177–184 (2001)
12. Fornell, C., Larcker, D.F.: Evaluating structural equation models with unobservable variables and measurement error. J. Mark. Res. **18**(1), 39 (1981). https://doi.org/10.2307/3151312
13. Geisser, S.: A predictive approach to the random effect model. Biometrika **61**(1), 101 (1974). https://doi.org/10.2307/2334290
14. Geisser, S.: The predictive sample reuse method with applications. J. Am. Stat. Assoc. **70**(350), 320–328 (1975)
15. Gervautz, M., Schmalstieg, D.: Anywhere interfaces using handheld augmented reality. Computer **45**, 26–31 (2012). https://doi.org/10.1109/MC.2012.72
16. Hair, J.F., Hult, T.M., Ringle, C.M., Sarstedt, M.: A Primer on Partial Least Squares Structural Equation Modeling (PLS-SEM). SAGE Publications, Inc, Thousand Oaks (2017)
17. Heller, J., Chylinski, M., de Ruyter, K., Mahr, D., Keeling, D.I.: Let me imagine that for you: transforming the retail frontline through augmenting customer mental imagery ability. J. Retail. **95**, 94–114 (2019). https://doi.org/10.1016/j.jretai.2019.03.005
18. Henseler, J., Hubona, G., Ray, P.A.: Using PLS path modeling in new technology re-search: updated guidelines. Ind. Manag. Data Syst. **116**(1), 2–20 (2016)
19. Henseler, J., Ringle, C.M., Sarstedt, M.: A new criterion for assessing discriminant validity in variance-based structural equation modeling. J. Acad. Mark. Sci. **43**(1), 115–135 (2014). https://doi.org/10.1007/s11747-014-0403-8
20. Hilken, T., de Ruyter, K., Chylinski, M., Mahr, D., Keeling, D.I.: Augmenting the eye of the beholder: exploring the strategic potential of augmented reality to enhance online service experiences. J. Acad. Mark. Sci. **45**(6), 884–905 (2017). https://doi.org/10.1007/s11747-017-0541-x

21. Hilken, T., Keeling, D.I., de Ruyter, K., Mahr, D., Chylinski, M.: Seeing eye to eye: social augmented reality and shared decision making in the marketplace. J. Acad. Mark. Sci. **48**(2), 143–164 (2019). https://doi.org/10.1007/s11747-019-00688-0

22. Hoffman, D.L., Novak, T.P.: Flow online: lessons learned and future prospects. J. Interact. Mark. **23**, 23–34 (2009). https://doi.org/10.1016/j.intmar.2008.10.003

23. Hu, L.-T., Bentler, P.M.: Cutoff criteria for fit indexes in covariance structure analysis: conventional criteria versus new alternatives. Struct. Equ. Model. **6**(1), 1–55 (1999)

24. Huang, E.: Online experiences and virtual goods purchase intention. Internet Res. **22**, 252–274 (2012). https://doi.org/10.1108/10662241211235644

25. Huang, T.-L., Liao, S.: A model of acceptance of augmented-reality interactive technology: the moderating role of cognitive innovativeness. Electron. Commer. Res. **15**(2), 269–295 (2014). https://doi.org/10.1007/s10660-014-9163-2

26. Israel, K., Zerres, C., Tscheulin, D.K.: Presenting hotels in virtual reality: does it influence the booking intention? J. Hosp. Tour. Technol. **10**, 443–463 (2019). https://doi.org/10.1108/JHTT-03-2018-0020

27. Javornik, A.: Augmented reality: research agenda for studying the impact of its media characteristics on consumer behaviour. J. Retail. Consum. Serv. **30**, 252–261 (2016). https://doi.org/10.1016/j.jretconser.2016.02.004

28. Javornik, A.: 'It's an illusion, but it looks real!' consumer affective, cognitive and behavioural responses to augmented reality applications. J. Mark. Manag. **32**, 987–1011 (2016). https://doi.org/10.1080/0267257X.2016.1174726

29. Javornik, A., Rogers, Y., Moutinho, A.M., Freeman, R.: Revealing the shopper experience of using a 'magic mirror' augmented reality make-up application. In: Proceedings of the 2016 ACM Conference on Designing Interactive Systems, DIS 2016, Brisbane, QLD, Australia, pp. 871–882 (2016)

30. Jiang, Z., Chan, J., Tan, B., Chua, W.: Effects of interactivity on website involvement and purchase intention. J. Assoc. Inf. Syst. **11**(1), 34–59 (2010). https://doi.org/10.17705/1jais.00218

31. Katawetawaraks, C., Wang, C.L.: Online shopper behavior: influences of online shopping decision. Asian J. Bus. Res. **1** (2011). https://doi.org/10.14707/ajbr.110012

32. Kim, H.-C., Hyun, M.Y.: Predicting the use of smartphone-based Augmented Reality (AR): does telepresence really help? Comput. Hum. Behav. **59**, 28–38 (2016). https://doi.org/10.1016/j.chb.2016.01.001

33. Kim, J., Lennon, S.J.: Effects of reputation and website quality on online consumers' emotion, perceived risk and purchase intention: based on the stimulus-organism-response model. J. Res. Interact. Mark. **7**, 33–56 (2013). https://doi.org/10.1108/17505931311316734

34. Kühn, S.W., Petzer, D.J.: Fostering purchase intentions toward online retailer websites in an emerging market: an S-O-R perspective. J. Internet Commer. **17**, 255–282 (2018). https://doi.org/10.1080/15332861.2018.1463799

35. Lombard, M., Snyder-Duch, J.: Interactive advertising and presence: a framework. J. Interact. Advert. **1**, 56–65 (2001)

36. Mehrabian, A., Russell, J.A.: An approach to environmental psychology. MIT Press (1974)

37. Menon, S., Kahn, B.: Cross-category effects of induced arousal and pleasure on the internet shopping experience. J. Retail. **78**, 31–40 (2002). https://doi.org/10.1016/S0022-4359(01)00064-1

38. Nunnally, J.C.: Psychometric Theory. McGraw-Hill, New York (1978)

39. Park, J., Stoel, L., Lennon, S.J.: Cognitive, affective and conative responses to visual simulation: the effects of rotation in online product presentation. J. Consum. Behav. **7**, 72–87 (2008). https://doi.org/10.1002/cb.237

40. Park, M., Yoo, J.: Effects of perceived interactivity of augmented reality on consumer responses: a mental imagery perspective. J. Retail. Consum. Serv. **52** (2020). https://doi.org/10.1016/j.jretconser.2019.101912

41. Rese, A., Baier, D., Geyer-Schulz, A., Schreiber, S.: How augmented reality apps are accepted by consumers: a comparative analysis using scales and opinions. Technol. Forecast. Soc. Chang. **124**, 306–319 (2017). https://doi.org/10.1016/j.techfore.2016.10.010

42. Riar, M., Korbel, J.J., Xi, N., Zarnekow, R., Hamari, J.: The use of augmented reality in retail: a review of literature. In: Proceedings of the 54th Hawaii International Conference (2021)

43. Ringle, C.M., Wende, S., Becker, J.-M.: SmartPLS 3. Boenningstedt: SmartPLS GmbH (2015)

44. Song, J.H., Zinkhan, G.M.: Determinants of perceived web site interactivity. J. Mark. **72**, 99–113 (2008). https://doi.org/10.1509/jmkg.72.2.99

45. Stone, M.: Cross-validatory choice and assessment of statistical predictions. J. R. Stat. Soc. Ser. B (Methodol.) **36**(2), 111–147 (1974)

46. van Noort, G., Voorveld, H.A.M., van Reijmersdal, E.A.: Interactivity in brand web sites: cognitive, affective, and behavioral responses explained by consumers' online flow experience. J. Interact. Mark. **26**, 223–234 (2012). https://doi.org/10.1016/j.intmar.2011.11.002

47. Watson, A., Alexander, B., Salavati, L.: The impact of experiential augmented reality applications on fashion purchase intention. IJRDM **48**, 433–451 (2018). https://doi.org/10.1108/IJRDM-06-2017-0117

48. Yoo, J., Kim, M.: The effects of online product presentation on consumer responses: a mental imagery perspective. J. Bus. Res. **67**, 2464–2472 (2014). https://doi.org/10.1016/j.jbusres.2014.03.006

49. Yusuf, A., Che Hussin, A., Busalim, A.: Influence of e-WOM engagement on consumer purchase intention in social commerce. J. Serv. Mark. **32**, 493–504 (2018). https://doi.org/10.1108/JSM-01-2017-0031

# Dimensions of Retail Customer Experience and Its Outcomes: A Literature Review and Directions for Future Research

Anna Hermes[1]([✉])(iD) and René Riedl[1,2]

[1] Institute of Business Informatics–Information Engineering,
Johannes Kepler University Linz, Linz, Austria
anna.hermes@jku.at

[2] University of Applied Sciences Upper Austria, Steyr, Austria
rene.riedl@fh-steyr.at

**Abstract.** Due to changes in customers' shopping habits and increasing omnichannel behavior (i.e., use of both online and offline channels), a seamless customer experience (CX) with a retailer extends beyond the online shop. CX is a broad construct and researchers have used various measures to capture this construct. Consequently, it is difficult to compare CX outcomes. Against this background, this literature review analyzes CX dimensions, measures, and outcomes in a human-computer interaction context and beyond. Our results indicate that both affective and cognitive CX have been studied intensively. While affective CX has mostly been measured using the PAD (pleasure, arousal, dominance) scale, cognitive CX has largely been studied based on the flow concept. A few researchers have studied CX holistically, or as a social and sensorial phenomenon. Major outcomes studied in the extant literature include engagement, purchase intention, loyalty, commitment, word-of-mouth, satisfaction, and trust. Based on our findings, we discuss managerial implications as well as directions for future research.

**Keywords:** Customer experience · Retail environment · Literature analysis

## 1 Introduction

How and where customers shop has fundamentally changed in the last decade [1]. Today customers can make use of an enormous offering of online and offline shopping channels, resulting in a fragmented customer journey [2]. Hence, it is important for retailers to provide a unified and integrated customer experience (CX) across different retail channels, referred to as an omnichannel experience [2, 3].

Beginning with the work of Holbrook and Hirschman [4], a rich body of research has found that not only logical reasoning and thought processes, but also emotions, can shape consumer behavior [5–7]. An influential definition by Lemon and Verhoef [2] described CX as "a multidimensional construct focusing on a customer's cognitive, emotional, behavioral, sensorial, and social responses to a firm's offerings during the customer's entire purchase journey" (p. 71). Further, how a customer perceives a channel

© Springer Nature Switzerland AG 2021
F. F.-H. Nah and K. Siau (Eds.): HCII 2021, LNCS 12783, pp. 71–89, 2021.
https://doi.org/10.1007/978-3-030-77750-0_5

and makes the decision to buy strongly depends on individual psychological factors such as emotions and cognition [4, 5, 8–11]. As a result, researchers and practitioners alike have investigated how customers experience various channels and how these experiences affect company and marketing outcomes [2, 3]. It follows that while this paper focuses on human-computer interactions (HCI) on e-commerce websites, as well as mobile shopping apps, it is nowadays not reasonable to look at those channels in an isolated fashion (e.g., [12]). Thus, in this paper we review retail CX along with its measurements and outcomes from a cross-disciplinary view, also including non-HCI-channels.

Despite this large body of research and its growing importance, the literature on retail CX scales and outcomes of specific CX dimensions is still fragmented [13]. Previous literature reviews have focused on the determinants and antecedents of experiential value in general, but have not considered specific CX dimensions such as emotion and cognition [13]. Some researchers have also mainly focused on single retail channels such as online shopping [14] or retail store experiences [15]. Further, De Keyser et al. [11], Mahr et al. [16], and Becker and Jaakkola [17] conducted literature reviews including CX dimensions such as cognitive and sensorial CX. Yet, these papers did neither provide insights into specific CX scales used nor did these papers examine the relationship between specific CX dimensions and marketing outcomes.

In the current paper, we go beyond the existing insights in the literature and review a highly fragmented research field. Specifically, we (i) provide an overview of retail CX dimensions and scales in an HCI-context and beyond, and (ii) shed light on those dimensions of retail CX that have been found to influence specific marketing goals. Therefore, this study aims to synthesize CX dimensions and scales and their outcomes to then provide managerial implications that can help retailers enhance CX. We purposely reviewed findings from online as well as offline CX. In doing so we want to encourage e-commerce retailers and researchers to broaden their view on CX, considering the omnichannel perspective in which a customer crosses a wide range of company touchpoints, both online and offline. Finally, we propose future research directions. To achieve these goals, we conducted a systematic literature review based on the framework by vom Brocke et al. [18] to search for, identify, and analyze the relevant retail CX literature. This review included high-quality, peer-reviewed, English-language journal papers, and excluded papers that did not meet the defined quality criteria as well as conference papers and books. The guiding research questions for our literature review were as follows:

RQ1: Which dimensions and scales are used to measure CX?
RQ2: What are the outcomes of specific CX dimensions?

## 2 Literature Review Methodology

We used the literature review guidelines provided by vom Brocke et al. [18]. Figure 1 visualizes the search process. The scope of this literature review included empirical CX studies. We reviewed the used CX scales and methodologies as well as research findings. This review is conceptualized as a neutral summary of relevant studies. Further, the scope of this research is the customer side of CX and its outcomes (e.g., a customer's satisfaction) rather than CX from a firm perspective (e.g., improvement of

CX management and quality, see also [19]). To search relevant journals, we consulted the databases EBSCOhost and Web of Science. These databases contain a wide range of relevant research papers in the fields of business, information science, information systems, psychology, and marketing, among others. We used the search term ("customer experience*" AND "retail") to identify papers. The initial search queries returned a vast number of indexed articles (EBSCOhost and Web of Science returned a total of 5,160 hits). We then filtered for English-language, peer-reviewed journal articles published in 2007 or later. We chose 2007 due to the introduction of the iPhone, which prompted a major shift in smartphone technology that allowed for mobile shopping and made the Internet more accessible as a shopping channel. After removing duplicates, 312 papers matched our query (last accessed November 2020). In the first step, we reviewed the title and abstract of each paper to identify relevant literature. We eliminated a total of 56 papers that did not focus on retail shopping environments. For example, we excluded studies from the financial sector [20] because corresponding findings can hardly be compared with traditional shopping experiences (due to the high risk and security requirements involved). Further, 118 papers did not focus on CX in a retail context (e.g., studies focusing purely on product experiences). The focus of this paper is the customer side of CX (i.e., customers' perceptions during the shopping process). As such, we excluded 56 papers that focused on business processes, for example, business quality, customer relationship management, or innovation management. We included the top 400 journals in the fields of business, computer science, and psychology (according to the 2019 Scimago Institutions Rankings, sorted by journal rank indicator). A total of 26 articles did not meet this quality criterion and were thus eliminated.

At this stage, a total of 56 articles remained and were assessed for full-text eligibility. Since the scope of this study included only empirical studies, we eliminated nine conceptual papers, four literature reviews, and eight scale development papers. Of the 35 empirical papers, 13 had researched CX as a dependent variable or as a moderator and, hence, lacked findings on the outcomes of CX. Moreover, Khan et al.'s [21] study was excluded because they included service providers like travel agencies as well as restaurants, hence, did not purely focus on retailing. For the final set of 21 papers, we focused on CX measurements and their outcomes, reviewing the theoretical framework and findings sections. Six papers were published between 2012 and 2017, and 15 were published between 2018 and 2020. Seven papers used a mixed-methods approach (a combination of experiments and surveys), while 14 used surveys. The dominance of surveys is consistent with the results of previous literature reviews in the CX field (e.g., [11]).

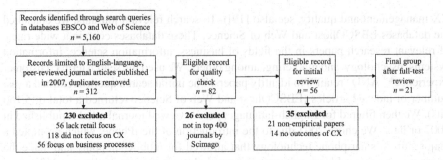

**Fig. 1.** Search strategy and selection process.

# 3 Findings

The next chapter gives an overview of CX scales that have been used to measure CX and CX dimensions and its outcomes. In line with our research questions, we included only direct relationships between CX and its outcomes (e.g., purchase intentions) in our analysis. This chapter concludes with the section *Summary of Major Results*, which answers RQ1 and RQ2. Figure 2 and Table 1 provide an overview of CX dimensions and their outcomes.

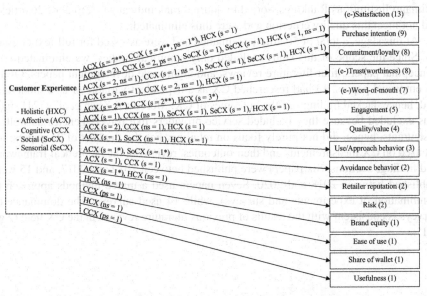

**Fig. 2.** Empirical findings regarding CX dimensions and their outcomes. S = significant, ns = not significant, ps = partially significant (study count). *[22, 23], and [24] found negative relationships; **[25] found that negative CX positively influenced dissatisfaction and negative WOM, positive affective CX positively influenced satisfaction and positive WOM; all other findings identify positive CX and positive effects with the outcome.

**Holistic CX and Its Outcomes.** Eight papers considered CX as a holistic construct rather than measuring single CX dimensions. Krasonikolakis et al. [22] measured shopping CX through a combination of Mehrabian and Russell's [26] pleasure, arousal, and dominance (PAD) scale and Novak et al.'s [27] flow scale (for more information on PAD, please refer to the *Affective CX and Its Outcomes* section; the concept of flow is explained in the *Cognitive CX and Its Outcomes* section). In their experiment and survey ($n = 59$; Southern Europe), the researchers found that CX negatively influenced word-of-mouth (WOM) intentions in 3D online shops. Moreover, online shopping CX was not linked with purchase intention. McLean et al. [28] adapted Watson et al.'s [29] Positive and Negative Affect Schedule (PANAS) scale, which Kuhlthau [30] used to measure positive emotions, and combined it with a measurement of mobile shopping app satisfaction used by Song and Zinkhan [31]. They concluded that CX impacted how frequently customers used a retailer's mobile apps (survey; $n = 1,024$; UK). Terblanche [32] also considered satisfaction in his research of in-store CX and found that the internal shop environment and in-store emotions drove satisfaction (in-store survey and focus group; $n = 329$). Mohd-Ramly and Omar [33] measured CX using the brand experience scale by Brakus et al. [34] and concluded that CX positively influenced customer engagement (survey; $n = 484$; Malaysia). Applying a brand experience scale developed by Schmitt [35], Srivastava and Kaul [36] found a positive influence of CX on attitudinal and behavioral loyalty, yet no impact on a customer's spent (survey; $n = 840$; India).

Mainardes et al. [37] compared the scores of customers shopping at a single-branded store (they refer to it as "franchise customers") and customers who shop at multi-branded shops (in their reference "non-franchise customers") on Klaus and Maklan's [38] customer service experience (EXQ) scale (survey; $n = 1,097$; Brazil). The EXQ breaks CX down into four subcomponents: product experience; outcome focus (a goal-oriented experience); moments of truth (coping with service failure, service recovery); and peace of mind (customer's emotional benefits during and after the shopping encounter) [38]. For franchise customers, EXQ showed a significantly greater positive influence on the perceived product and service quality, brand trustworthiness, and purchase intention. However, no differences were found between the two groups in terms of the relationship between brand equity (i.e., the brand adding value for the customer) and perceived risk. Siqueira et al. [39] examined in-store CX (survey; $n = 390$; Colombia) and found that CX positively influenced online and offline WOM. This link was confirmed in a later study, where Siqueira et al. [40] found that CX positively influenced offline WOM behavior ($n = 293$; survey; Colombia).

**Affective CX and Its Outcomes.** As highlighted by Bleier et al. [41] "[c]ustomer interactions with products online can evoke affective responses and might be enjoyed for their own sake" (p. 99). Accordingly, the affective CX dimension focuses less on functional shopping perspectives, it rather highlights the customer's affective state or individual emotions when shopping [42]. A total of 12 papers considered affective CX. The preceding section presents the findings of Krasonikolakis et al. [22] (who combined PAD and flow), McLean et al. [28] (who combined the PANAS and satisfaction), and Terblanche [32] (who combined in-store emotions with in-store environments to measure CX holistically). While we are aware of the distinct meanings of the terms "emotion," "affect," and "feeling" ([43]; see also [44]), most of the reviewed literature used these words interchangeably (nine papers considered affective CX, two papers considered emotional CX, and one paper considered single emotions). Five papers adopted Mehrabian and Russell's [26] PAD to measure affective CX. Moreover, two papers applied Voss et al.'s [45] hedonic dimension scale, and one paper used Watson et al.'s [29] PANAS. Lastly, four papers implemented additional scales to measure affective CX (see *Additional Scales* section in this chapter).

*PAD.* In our literature review, Rose et al. [42] were the first to use PAD to measure affective CX. Rose et al. [42] conducted a survey ($n = 220$; the US and Europe) and found that affective CX influenced a customer's online shopping satisfaction but not the level of trust in online shopping. Re-examining Rose et al.'s [42] research design, Martin et al. [24] surveyed 555 Australian online shoppers and concluded that affective CX influenced satisfaction positively, perceived risk negatively, and trust positively. Moreover, Molinillo et al. [46] surveyed 393 participants in Spain and found that a customer's affective CX with a retailer's app had a positive influence on their satisfaction and trust. Micu et al. [47] conducted an online survey ($n = 400$; 200 Tunisian, 200 Romanian) and found an impact of the customer's affective experiential state on perceived value, e-satisfaction, and e-trust. Lastly, Anninou and Foxall [23] found that a customer's level of pleasure positively determined the approach behavior of grocery and technology retail experiences. Further, customers' avoidance behaviors were negatively determined by high levels of pleasure and arousal (survey, $n = 260$, UK).

*Hedonic Dimensions to Measure Consumer Attitudes.* Voss et al. [45] developed a hedonic and utilitarian scale to measure consumer attitudes. The hedonic scale measures affective customer involvement (e.g., having fun), while the utilitarian scale measures aspects such as functionality and helpfulness. Two papers applied the hedonic dimensions of this scale to measure affective CX. Barari et al. [25] investigated the influence of negative and positive online shopping encounters on affective CX (two experiments and surveys; study 1 $n = 201$, study 2 $n = 200$; USA). They found that customers with a negative affective experience showed higher engagement in negative WOM and were more likely to be dissatisfied. In addition, shoppers reported more positive affective experiences in a successful shopping encounter. Finally, a customer's affective experiences showed a greater influence on positive WOM in a successful online shopping encounter. Considering the effects of affective CX in in-store grocery shopping environments, Roy et al. [51] found that affective CX positively influenced customer commitment and engagement behavior (i.e., compliance, cooperation, helping other customers, and positive WOM; survey; $n = 187$; Australia).

*PANAS.* First developed by Watson et al. [29], the PANAS lists a total of 20 affective states (e.g., active, distressed) to measure positive and negative affect. Högberg et al. [49] applied Thompson's [54] version of the PANAS scale to measure only positive emotions (survey and field experiment; $n = 378$, Europe). The researchers found that people with higher positive affect (caused by gamified in-store elements) perceived higher hedonic value (i.e., more enjoyable interactions with the retailer) and gave higher ratings of the satisfying effects of rewards (e.g., a coupon).

*Additional Scales.* Bleier et al. [41] applied Hausman and Siekpe's [55] entertainment scale and found that entertainment (as affective CX) had the greatest influence on purchase intention (experiment and survey; $n = 10{,}470$). Affective CX was especially important if a product was best to be physically experienced ("experience product") or if the brand was perceived to be less trustworthy. Additionally, Foroudi et al. [48] measured affective CX with a brand experience scale designed by Dennis et al. [56] (survey; $n = 606$; UK). The findings revealed that affective CX influenced loyalty as well as the customer's perception of the retailer's reputation. Additionally, Tyrväinen et al. [52] applied Brakus et al.'s [34] affective brand experience scale to measure affect in omnichannel CX (survey; $n = 4{,}418$; Sweden and Finland). The researchers found a positive effect on WOM and repeat purchase intentions in online and in-store environments. Pandey and Chawla [50] found that customers who enjoyed online shopping showed a higher level of satisfaction (two surveys; study 1 $n = 217$, study 2 $n = 615$; India). In addition to enjoyment, the researchers included other factors to measure CX (e.g., logistic ease); however, to report all factors would be outside the scope of this review.

**Cognitive CX and Its Outcomes.** The cognitive CX dimension highlights the website or in-store capabilities in supporting customers during their pending purchase decisions, as such, it concerns a customer's mental processing and thought processes [8, 41]. Various papers measured cognitive CX (total of 10), frequently using the flow construct (four papers) but also through a range of other scales (six papers; for details, see the *Additional Scales* section of this chapter).

*Flow.* Novak et al. [27] further shaped this field of research, which was first introduced by Csikszentmihalyi [57], and described flow as the state in which a customer is so involved in a task that their thoughts and perceptions are irrelevant and/or screened out. In our review, Rose et al. [42] were the first to measure cognitive CX using the concept of flow. They found that flow could impact the degree of a customer's satisfaction but did not influence trust in online shopping. Molinillo et al. [46] concluded that experiencing flow while using a retailer's app influenced both customer satisfaction and trust in the app. Additionally, Martin et al. [24] found that flow negatively influenced online shopping satisfaction for infrequent shoppers. Micu et al. [47], further found that cognitive experiential flow states positively impacted e-satisfaction and e-trust but did not influence the perceived customer value.

*Additional Scales.* In a study examining negative CX, Barari et al. [25] applied Voss et al.'s [45] utilitarian scale to measure cognitive CX. They found that customers who had a negative cognitive experience due to retailer failure were more likely to be dissatisfied and to engage in negative WOM. Moreover, when comparing affective and cognitive CX, the latter showed a greater impact on the degree of a customer's dissatisfaction in an unsuccessful online shopping encounter. Further, cognitive CX (measured using the informativeness scale developed by Luo [58]) significantly influenced purchase intention in a study by Bleier et. al [41]. This effect was strongest if a brand was perceived to be trustworthy as well as for "search products" (i.e., those evaluated based on hard facts, rather than by physical touch).

Roy et al. [51] applied Bhattacherjee's [59] confirmation scale to measure cognitive CX. Their results indicated that neither customer commitment nor customer engagement

**Table 1.** Overview of studies, dimensions, and findings. CX = Customer Experience; (e-) WOM = (electronic-) Word-of-Mouth; EXQ = Customer Service Experience; HED/UT = Hedonic/Utilitarian scale; PAD = Pleasure, Arousal, Dominance; PANAS = Positive and Negative Affect Schedule. Findings significant at least at $p > 0.05$, unless otherwise noted as not significant (ns), or partially significant (ps). *considers negative CX

| [Paper] Context (sorted alphabetically by author) | CX component | | | | | Scale | Outcome |
|---|---|---|---|---|---|---|---|
| | Holistic | Affect | Cognition | Social | Sensorial | | |
| [23] General | | x | | | | PAD | Approach (+), avoidance behavior (−) |
| | | | x | | | PAD | Approach (ns), avoidance behavior (−) |
| [25] Online* | | | x | | | HED/UT | Dissatisfaction (+), negative WOM (+) |
| | | x | | | | HED/UT | Dissatisfaction (+), negative WOM (+) |
| [41] Online | | | x | | | Informativeness | Purchase intention (+) |
| | | x | | | | Entertainment | Purchase intention (+) |
| | | | | x | | Social presence | Purchase intention (+) |
| | | | | | x | Sensory appeal | Purchase intention (+) |
| [48] General | | | x | | | Brand experience | Loyalty (+), retailer's reputation (+) |
| | | x | | | | Brand experience | Loyalty (+), retailer's reputation (+) |
| [49] Store | | x | | | | PANAS | Hedonic value (+), Satisfaction (+) |
| [22] Online | x | | | | | PAD, flow | Purchase intention (ns), WOM (−) |
| [37] Store | x | | | | | EXQ | Single-brand store customers reported higher perceived quality (+), brand trustworthiness (+), purchase intention (+) (vs. multi-brand store customers); no difference found for perceived risk (ns) and perceived brand equity (ns) |
| [24] Online | | x | | | | PAD | Risk (−), trust (+), satisfaction (+) |
| | | | x | | | Flow | Satisfaction (-/ps, only for infrequent shoppers) |
| [28] Mobile | x | | | | | PANAS, satisfaction | Frequency of use (+) |
| [47] Online | | x | | | | PAD | Value (+), e-satisfaction (+), e-trust (+) |
| | | | x | | | Flow | Value (ns), e-satisfaction (+), e-trust (+) |
| [33] Store | x | | | | | Brand experience | Customer engagement (+) |
| [46] Mobile | | x | | | | PAD | Satisfaction (+), trust (+) |
| | | | x | | | Flow | Satisfaction (+), trust (+) |
| [50] Online | | x | | | | E-enjoyment | Satisfaction (+), loyalty (ns) |
| [42] Online | | x | | | | PAD | Satisfaction (+), trust (ns) |

(continued)

**Table 1.** (*continued*)

| [Paper] Context (sorted alphabetically by author) | CX component | | | | | Scale | Outcome |
|---|---|---|---|---|---|---|---|
| | Holistic | Affect | Cognition | Social | Sensorial | | |
| | | | x | | | Flow | Satisfaction (+), trust (ns) |
| [51] Online | | | x | | | Confirmation | Customer commitment (ns), customer engagement behavior (ns) |
| | | x | | | | HED/UT | Customer commitment (+), customer engagement behavior (+) |
| | | | | | x | Servicescape | Customer commitment (+), customer engagement behavior (+) |
| | | | | x | | Social | Customer commitment (+), customer engagement behavior (+) |
| [39] General | x | | | | | CX | WOM (+), eWOM (+) |
| [40] General | x | | | | | CX quality | WOM (+) |
| [36] Store | x | | | | | Brand experience | Attitudinal loyalty (+), behavioral loyalty (+), share of wallet (ns) |
| [32] Store | x | | | | | In-store emotions and environment | Satisfaction (+) |
| [52] Online and store | | | x | | | Brand experience | Repeat purchase intention (+), WOM (+) |
| | | x | | | | Brand experience | Repeat purchase intention (+), WOM (+) |
| [53] Online | | | x | | | Cognitive absorption | Purchase intention (+/ps), usefulness (+/ps), ease of use (+/ps) |
| Total | 8 | 12 | 10 | 3 | 2 | | |

behavior was influenced by a customer's cognitive CX. Foroudi et al. [48] found that intellectual CX (measured via Dennis et al.'s [56] intellectual brand experience scale) modified loyalty and retailer reputation. Lastly, Visinescu et al. [53] compared 2D and 3D web designs and used Agarwal and Karahanna's [60] cognitive absorption scale which includes various factors, namely curiosity, temporal dissociation, focused immersion, and heightened enjoyment (experiment and survey; $n = 348$; US). The researchers found several implications, e.g., for customers with previous online shopping experiences, curiosity, temporal dissociation, and focused immersion positively influenced purchase intention. However, for customers without previous online shopping experiences, heightened enjoyment showed a positive effect on a customer's purchase intention. Temporal dissociation influenced perceived usefulness for experienced customers, while curiosity and heightened enjoyment influenced perceived usefulness for inexperienced customers. Moreover, temporal dissociation, curiosity, and heightened enjoyment influenced perceived ease of use. Lastly, Tyrväinen et al. [52] applied Brakus et al.'s [34] cognitive brand experience scale and found a positive direct effect of cognitive CX on WOM and repeat purchase intentions.

**Social CX and Its Outcomes.** Three papers considered social CX and its outcomes. Social CX refers to a CX element—for example, on a website—that creates a socially connected and warm feeling which allows customers to connect with retailers on a human level [41, 61]. A study by Bleier et al. [41] found that social CX significantly influenced purchase intentions, yet its effect was weaker than that of affective or cognitive CX. Applying Reimer and Kuehn's [62] Servicescape to measure social CX, Roy et al. [51] found that social CX impacted a customer's commitment and engagement. Lastly, Anninou and Foxall [23] used PAD to measure social CX (for thematic reasons, these findings are presented in section *Affective CX and its Outcomes* under PAD).

**Sensory CX and Its Outcomes.** Two papers considered sensory CX and its outcomes. Sensory CX includes CX elements that can stimulate a customer's senses, such as smell, touch, taste, or sight [8, 41]. Bleier et al. [41] found that, although sensory appeal significantly influenced purchase intention in online shopping, yet other CX dimensions (e.g., affective, cognitive, and social CX) had a greater influence on purchase intention. Further, Roy et al. [51] concluded that there was a relationship between customers' sensory CX and their commitment and engagement behavior.

**CX Dimensions in HCI Contexts and Beyond.** The majority of the reviewed studies researched CX in a HCI context (nine papers researched online CX [22, 24, 25, 41, 47, 50, 51, 53, 63] and two studies mobile CX [28, 46]). Moreover, five studies were conducted in in-store shopping settings [32, 33, 36, 37, 49]. One paper researched online and in-store omnichannel experiences [52]. Lastly, four papers examined CX with regard to shopping or retailers in general without focusing on a particular channel [23, 39, 40, 48]. In summary, we found that PAD was used to measure CX across all channels. However, brand experience scales and the PANAS were mainly used to measure in-store experiences or general retailer and brand experiences. In particular, the flow scale was applied in an HCI context to measure CX with online shops or mobile apps. In addition to these scales, a wide range of additional scales has been used to measure dimensions such as cognitive absorption, informativeness, entertainment, or enjoyment. In an online and mobile context, three studies examined relationships between the CX dimensions of affective and cognitive CX. Rose et al. [42] found that the affective CX of online shoppers influenced their cognitive experiential state, and Molinillo et al. [46] found that affective CX positively influenced cognitive CX. Moreover, Barari et al. [25] found that when the shopping experience was positive, affective CX showed a greater impact on positive WOM as well as satisfaction than cognitive CX.

**Summary of Major Results.** Regarding RQ1 ("Which dimensions and scales are used to measure CX?") we summarize the findings as follows: Most of the reviewed studies (12 papers) researched affective CX and its outcomes, followed by cognitive CX (10 papers), holistic CX (eight papers), social CX (three papers), and sensory CX (two papers). The dominance of emotion research in the CX community is consistent with the findings of other researchers (e.g., [11]). Additionally, eight papers combined established scales such as PAD, flow scales, or the PANAS to measure CX holistically. The 12 papers that measured affective CX mostly used PAD. Researchers also used the PANAS or hedonic measurements such as entertainment or enjoyment to measure affective CX. With regard to cognitive CX, a total of 10 papers applied the flow concept or scales that measured utilitarian dimensions such as informativeness or cognitive absorption. Three papers also measured social CX through, for example, social presence or the Servicescape scale. Additionally, two papers measured sensory CX (e.g., through measuring sensory appeal; see Table 1 for an overview of all scales used).

Regarding RQ2 ("What are the outcomes of specific CX dimensions?") we summarize the findings as follows: Researchers have not only found that holistic CX can influence marketing outcomes such as (e-)satisfaction and purchase intention. Rather, especially affective CX is highly researched and has been found to impact outcomes such as (e-)satisfaction, perceptions of product quality and shopping value, purchase intention, loyalty/commitment, (e-)trust, and (e-)WOM. Further, cognitive CX influences customers' level of (e-)satisfaction, perceived ease of use and usefulness, purchase intentions, commitment/loyalty, (e-)trust, and (e-)WOM. In our review, social CX and sensorial CX were researched the least. Both social CX and sensorial CX affected purchase intention, commitment/loyalty, and engagement. Additionally, social CX influenced customers' shopping approach behavior (see Fig. 2 and Table 1 for an overview of all CX dimensions and their outcomes). We conclude that some CX dimensions (e.g., affective CX), as well as some outcomes (e.g., satisfaction, loyalty/commitment, and purchase intention) have been heavily researched, but others have hardly been investigated (e.g., CX and its influences on actual money spent). Finally, some researchers have concluded that affective CX can influence cognitive CX and that affective CX in general shows a stronger influence on, for example, satisfaction and purchase intention [24, 41, 42].

## 4 Research Agenda and Managerial Implications

This section presents a detailed research agenda to advance the current understanding of CX. By framing the research agenda to reflect the unanswered research questions and underrepresented topics (as identified in the literature review), the structure herein presents three major domains: (1) examination of future moderators in the CX–outcome relationship; (2) study of additional CX outcomes; and (3) integration of Neuro-Information-Systems (NeuroIS) methods with traditional CX methods and a comparison of the findings. Figure 3 presents an overview of possible future research actions. Additionally, we provide managerial implications based on the review's findings.

**Examination of Future Moderators in the CX–Outcome Relationship.** This paper highlights the importance of emotions in CX research. However, although affective CX has already been heavily researched, we still see research opportunities concerning this dimension of CX. Researchers have argued that there are two types of emotions: incidental (task-unrelated) and integral (task-related) [64]. While the reviewed papers considered outcomes of integral emotions (e.g., measurements of enjoyment of a shopping process), we call future researchers to examine how CX is influenced by incidental emotions. Incidental emotions are affected by a customer's personality and may influence consumer decision-making [9]. Hence, we encourage future researchers to consider the role that personality may play in influencing affective CX and its outcomes, as measured by scales like Costa and McCrae's [65] Big Five, HEXACO (e.g., [66]), or Davis et al.'s [67] Affective Neuroscience Personality Scale (ANPS). Further, more research is needed to examine moderating effects from channel-specific factors (e.g., channel type, store environment). Each shopping channel has certain advantages and potentials; for example, trust is an important factor in online shopping [68]. Hence, the effects of CX on its outcomes might vary depending on the channel a customer is using. Additionally, other personal factors (e.g., goals, mood) might influence the relationship between CX and its outcomes.

**Study of Additional Outcomes of CX.** While some factors, such as satisfaction (e.g., [24, 32, 42, 47]) and purchase intention (e.g., [22, 37, 41]), have been highly researched as outcomes of CX, other outcomes were hardly or not at all examined in the extant literature, including perceived usefulness, perceived ease of use, attention, time spent shopping, brand awareness, and retailer or channel preferences. Examining these outcomes could thus be a fruitful addition to the current CX literature. In addition, it is valuable to learn more about the relationship between different CX dimensions and actual money spent, especially from a company's point of view. Surprisingly, Srivastava and Kaul [36] did not find a relationship between holistic CX and customer spending, although other researchers have found evidence that CX can impact various customer behaviors such as purchase intention (e.g., [41]) and shopping approach behavior (e.g., [23]). As such, we call for future research examining CX and its dimensions and their impact on actual sales data. Further, most of the reviewed studies researched online environments, with only one comparing the outcomes of CX across multiple channels. Accordingly, we call for additional research examining more than one channel and comparing CX in different channels.

**Integration of NeuroIS Methods With Traditional CX Methods.** Researchers have claimed that the field lacks a strong and robust scale to measure CX [2]. In a very recent paper, De Keyser et al. [11] concluded that "[i]t is time to move beyond the dominant focus on survey research" (p. 447). This is consistent with the finding of this review that there is no one dominant scale directly measuring CX. It follows that the CX research community has begun to use established scales such as PAD and the PANAS or the concept of flow. While PAD has been highly researched in this context, we still see research opportunities for other scales. The PANAS, for example, has only been used to measure the impact of positive affective CX on customers' value perceptions, satisfaction, and frequency of usage of mobile shopping apps. Future researchers could use the PANAS to measure both positive and negative affective CX and its influences. Additionally, Roy et al. [51] did not find a significant effect of cognitive CX on customer engagement. While they measured cognitive CX using Bhattacherjee's [59] confirmation scale, future researchers could reexamine this relationship—for example, measuring cognitive CX using flow. Moreover, HCI researchers might consider scales that seem to be typically used to measure in-store CX, such as brand-experience scales.

Moreover, all reviewed papers used structured questionnaires to measure CX. However, there has been a longstanding discussion in research regarding how to accurately measure emotions that are felt in the body through cognitive processes such as questioning or other self-report methods [43]. As Caruelle et al. [69] have also pointed out, the use of self-reports to measure consumer emotions can pose various risks, including biased data due to respondents' unwillingness or inability to correctly identify, capture, and communicate their own emotions. Hence, using a self-report methodology to measure consumer emotions and affective states, in general, can have various pitfalls.

An alternative to self-report methods in consumer research can be found in the field of NeuroIS research (e.g., [70]). This field of research applies neuroscience theories and tools to measure neurophysiological responses in the context of information systems (IS) research [71]. NeuroIS research has been expanded from pure IS research to other areas, such as customer behaviors in HCI contexts (e.g., [72]; for an overview, see [70]). Researchers have also specifically called for the expansion of NeuroIS research into the realm of emotions research [44]. While a handful of studies have used NeuroIS tools to research customer emotions in general, there is a growing need for additional insights from future research [69, 73, 74]. Studies applying neurophysiological methods in the context of CX are still scarce, and researchers have made an explicit call to advance research in this realm [2, 11, 75]. Hence, we encourage researchers to apply NeuroIS tools (e.g., measurements of skin conductance, facial expression recognition, eye-tracking) to identify different dimensions of CX during a shopping encounter [71]. A possible RQ could involve how affective CX can be measured using tools such as facial expression recognition and how cognitive CX can be measured with NeuroIS tools that examine cognitive load (e.g., EEG [76]). Moreover, HCI researchers have called for a comparison of findings from traditional self-report methods, such as surveys, with findings from studies employing NeuroIS tools [44]. Since various studies have already examined CX and its outcomes through self-report methods, researchers could compare findings from "traditional studies" (e.g., CX effects on purchase intention, or satisfaction) with findings from studies with NeuroIS methods. Against this background, we call for more research comparing results from studies applying various methods (including NeuroIS tools) with those from traditional methods (i.e., surveys).

Figure 3 provides an overview of possible future research areas.

**Summary of Future Research Directions.** Based on the insights from our review and the discussion in this chapter, we broadly formulated future research opportunities. The following research questions were identified (see also Fig. 3):

- Additional CX Moderators: How do incidental (task-unrelated) emotions, as well as a customer's personality, influence the relationship between CX and its outcomes? How do channel-specific, or individual factors (e.g., mood, shopping goals) influence the relationship between CX and its outcomes?
- Additional CX Outcomes: What is the influence of single CX dimensions on less researched CX outcomes (e.g., the influence of cognitive CX on risk; the influence of affective CX on ease of use and perceived usefulness)? What is the influence of less or not yet examined CX outcomes such as retailer and channel preference, brand awareness, and actual money or time spent? How can the CX of different channels be compared (e.g., online vs. mobile vs. in-store)? How does the effect on CX outcomes depend and differ based on the method used to measure CX?

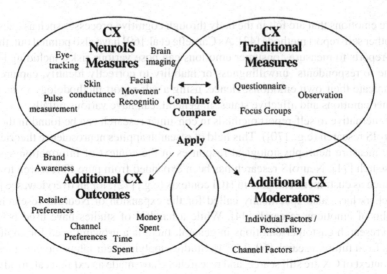

**Fig. 3.** Possible future research areas.

- Measurement of CX: Which self-report scales are best suited to examine the various dimensions of CX? How can self-report and neurophysiological methods be combined or compared to measure CX?

**Managerial Implications.** This paper provided an overview of the various CX dimensions and their measurements and outcomes. These findings are important for a company's CX researchers and digital retail professionals. First, we reviewed possible CX measurements and offered suggestions for future CX research, such as the use of NeuroIS tools. This information can be used by CX or marketing professionals to plan, conduct, and interpret their CX studies. Further, we provided an overview of the possible outcomes of CX. We documented that affective CX, in particular, has been heavily researched and has an overarching impact on marketing outcomes such as satisfaction and purchase intention. Hence, retailers are advised to emphasize differentiating and managing customer emotions in their retailing environments (see also [77]).

## 5   Conclusion

This study presented a systematic literature review with a focus on CX scales, as well as CX dimensions and its outcomes, and made several contributions. First, it added to the knowledge on dimensions of CX and its measurements. We want to encourage HCI researchers to consider CX beyond online shopping environments and mobile websites, and hence we reviewed HCI *and* in-store CX studies in a cross-disciplinary manner. We found that affective CX in particular—but also cognitive, social, and sensory CX—has been considered when measuring CX. Additionally, researchers can consider CX holistically, without identifying specific dimensions. Further, this research revealed that in our sample only self-report measures have been used to measure CX. Some researchers have used established measurements such as PAD, the PANAS, or the flow scale, while others have used CX-specific scales such as the EXQ or various brand experience scales. Consistent with previous researchers, such as Lemon and Verhoef [2], we thus conclude that there is no one CX scale; rather, different researchers have applied different measures. Understanding the wide range of CX dimensions and scales can help researchers and retail managers to interpret their CX studies as well as those conducted by other researchers.

Second, due to the extremely broad measurements of CX, it is difficult to draw conclusions regarding specific outcomes of CX. Hence, we provided an overview of outcomes organized by each CX dimension. While some outcomes have been researched for various dimensions (especially customer engagement, purchase intention, loyalty, commitment, (e-)WOM, satisfaction, and trust, see Table 1 for an overview), others have yet to be further explored. This overview can help academic researchers obtain an overview of possible research gaps. Practitioners can achieve valuable insights into which CX dimensions (e.g., affect) showed an effect on marketing goals such as satisfaction or purchase intention. However, generalizations should be drawn with caution. The vast amount of CX scales that are used to measure each CX dimension might also affect CX outcomes, hence, it might be useful to also consider the CX scale when interpreting outcomes of specific CX dimensions.

The limitations of this study are mostly related to the review and categorization processes. Although we believe that the findings of this paper are comprehensive, it cannot be completely ruled out that relevant papers on CX and its outcomes using different keywords were not identified and hence not considered. To increase validity, we used particularly broad keywords to secure a large pool of possible papers. Additionally, in line with the research question, we purposely only searched for papers with a CX customer focus (e.g., not a business process perspective). We also focused on the retail context and eliminated papers from (for example) the finance sector. Despite these limitations, however, this literature review comprises a wide variety of retail CX literature and highlights its outcomes for academia and marketing professionals alike. It is hoped that the present review will prompt future studies in this important domain.

**Acknowledgments.** This study has been conducted within the training network project PERFORM funded by the European Union's Horizon 2020 research and innovation program under the Marie Skłodowska-Curie grant agreement No. 765395. Note: This research reflects only the authors' views. The Agency is not responsible for any use that may be made of the information it contains.

# References

1. Verhoef, P.C., Kannan, P.K., Inman, J.J.: From multi-channel retailing to omni-channel retailing. J. Retail. **91**, 174–181 (2015)
2. Lemon, K.N., Verhoef, P.C.: Understanding customer experience throughout the customer journey. J. Mark. **80**, 69–96 (2016)
3. von Briel, F.: The future of omnichannel retail: a four-stage Delphi study. Technol. Forecast. Soc. Chang. **132**, 217–229 (2018)

4. Holbrook, M.B., Hirschman, E.C.: The experiential aspects of consumption: consumer fantasies, feelings, and fun. J. Consum. Res. **9**, 132–140 (1982)
5. Laros, F.J.M., Steenkamp, J.B.E.M.: Emotions in consumer behavior: a hierarchical approach. J. Bus. Res. **58**, 1437–1445 (2005)
6. Richins, M.L.: Measuring emotions in the consumption experience. J. Consum. Res. **24**, 127–146 (1997)
7. Babin, B.J., Darden, W.R., Griffin, M.: Work and/or fun: measuring hedonic and utilitarian shopping value. J. Consum. Res. **20**, 644–656 (1994)
8. Gentile, C., Spiller, N., Noci, G.: How to sustain the customer experience: an overview of experience components that co-create value with the customer. Eur. Manag. J. **25**, 395–410 (2007)
9. Achar, C., So, J., Agrawal, N., Duhachek, A.: What we feel and why we buy: the influence of emotions on consumer decision-making. Curr. Opin. Psychol. **10**, 166–170 (2016)
10. Puccinelli, N.M., Goodstein, R.C., Grewal, D., Price, R., Raghubir, P., Stewart, D.: Customer experience management in retailing: understanding the buying process. J. Retail. **85**, 15–30 (2009)
11. De Keyser, A., Verleye, K., Lemon, K.N., Keiningham, T.L., Klaus, P.: Moving the customer experience field forward: introducing the touchpoints, context, qualities (TCQ) nomenclature. J. Serv. Res. **23**, 433–455 (2020)
12. Petre, M., Minocha, S., Roberts, D.: Usability beyond the website: an empirically-grounded e-commerce evaluation instrument for the total customer experience. Behav. Inf. Technol. **25**, 189–203 (2006)
13. Varshneya, G., Das, G., Khare, A.: Experiential value: a review and future research directions. Mark. Intell. Plan. **35**, 339–357 (2017)
14. Izogo, E.E., Jayawardhena, C.: Online shopping experience in an emerging e-retailing market: towards a conceptual model. J. Consum. Behav. **17**, 379–392 (2018)
15. Sachdeva, I., Goel, S.: Retail store environment and customer experience: a paradigm. J. Fash. Mark. Manag. **19**, 290–298 (2015)
16. Mahr, D., Stead, S., Odekerken-Schröder, G.: Making sense of customer service experiences: a text mining review. J. Serv. Mark. **33**, 88–103 (2019)
17. Becker, L., Jaakkola, E.: Customer experience: fundamental premises and implications for research. J. Acad. Mark. Sci. **48**(4), 630–648 (2020). https://doi.org/10.1007/s11747-019-007 18-x
18. vom Brocke, J., Simons, A., Niehaves, B., Niehaves, B., Reimer, K.: Reconstructing the giant: on the importance of rigour in documenting the literature search process. In: Proceedings of the European Conference on Information Systems (ECIS), pp. 2206–2217. Academic Conferences International Limited, Reading (2009)
19. Kranzbühler, A.-M., Kleijnen, M.H.P., Morgan, R.E., Teerling, M.: The multilevel nature of customer experience research: an integrative review and research agenda. Int. J. Manag. Rev. **20**, 433–456 (2018)
20. Yoon, H.S., Barker Steege, L.M.: Development of a quantitative model of the impact of customers' personality and perceptions on Internet banking use. Comput. Human Behav. **29**, 1133–1141 (2013)
21. Khan, I., Hollebeek, L.D., Fatma, M., Islam, J.U., Riivits-Arkonsuo, I.: Customer experience and commitment in retailing: does customer age matter? J. Retail. Consum. Serv. **57**, 102219 (2020)
22. Krasonikolakis, I., Vrechopoulos, A., Pouloudi, A., Dimitriadis, S.: Store layout effects on consumer behavior in 3D online stores. Eur. J. Mark. **52**, 1223–1256 (2018)
23. Anninou, I., Foxall, G.R.: The reinforcing and aversive consequences of customer experience. The role of consumer confusion. J. Retail. Consum. Serv. **51**, 139–151 (2019)

24. Martin, J., Mortimer, G., Andrews, L.: Re-examining online customer experience to include purchase frequency and perceived risk. J. Retail. Consum. Serv. **25**, 81–95 (2015)
25. Barari, M., Ross, M., Surachartkumtonkun, J.: Negative and positive customer shopping experience in an online context. J. Retail. Consum. Serv. **53**, 101985 (2020)
26. Mehrabian, A., Russell, J.A.: An Approach to Environmental Psychology. The MIT Press, Cambridge (1974)
27. Novak, T.P., Hoffman, D.L., Yung, Y.-F.: Measuring the customer experience in online environments: a structural modeling approach. Mark. Sci. **19**, 22–42 (2000)
28. McLean, G., Al-Nabhani, K., Wilson, A.: Developing a mobile applications customer experience model (MACE)-implications for retailers. J. Bus. Res. **85**, 325–336 (2018)
29. Watson, D., Clark, L.A., Tellegen, A.: Development and validation of brief measures of positive and negative affect: the PANAS scales. J. Pers. Soc. Psychol. **54**, 1063–1070 (1988)
30. Kuhlthau, C.C.: Seeking Meaning: A Process Approach to Library and Information Services. Libraries Limited, Westport (2004)
31. Song, J.H., Zinkhan, G.M.: Determinants of perceived web site interactivity. J. Mark. **72**, 99–113 (2008)
32. Terblanche, N.S.: Revisiting the supermarket in-store customer shopping experience. J. Retail. Consum. Serv. **40**, 48–59 (2018)
33. Mohd-Ramly, S., Omar, N.A.: Exploring the influence of store attributes on customer experience and customer engagement. Int. J. Retail Distrib. Manag. **45**, 1138–1158 (2017)
34. Brakus, J.J., Schmitt, B.H., Zarantonello, L.: Brand experience: what is it? How is it measured? Does it affect loyalty? J. Mark. **73**, 52–68 (2009)
35. Schmitt, B.: Experiential marketing. J. Mark. Manag. **15**, 53–67 (1999)
36. Srivastava, M., Kaul, D.: Exploring the link between customer experience-loyalty-consumer spend. J. Retail. Consum. Serv. **31**, 277–286 (2016)
37. Mainardes, E.W., Gomes, V.C.A., Marchiori, D., Correa, L.E., Guss, V.: Consequences of customer experience quality on franchises and non-franchises models. Int. J. Retail Distrib. Manag. **47**, 311–330 (2019)
38. Klaus, P., Maklan, S.: EXQ: a multiple-item scale for assessing service experience. J. Serv. Manag. **23**, 5–33 (2012)
39. Siqueira, J.R., Peña, N.G., ter Horst, E., Molina, G.: Spreading the word: how customer experience in a traditional retail setting influences consumer traditional and electronic word-of-mouth intention. Electron. Commer. Res. Appl. **37**, 100870 (2019)
40. Siqueira, J.R., ter Horst, E., Molina, G., Losada, M., Mateus, M.A.: A Bayesian examination of the relationship of internal and external touchpoints in the customer experience process across various service environments. J. Retail. Consum. Serv. **53**, 102009 (2020)
41. Bleier, A., Harmeling, C.M., Palmatier, R.W.: Creating effective online customer experiences. J. Mark. **83**, 98–119 (2019)
42. Rose, S., Clark, M., Samouel, P., Hair, N.: Online customer experience in e-retailing: an empirical model of antecedents and outcomes. J. Retail. **88**, 308–322 (2012)
43. Walla, P.: Affective processing guides behavior and emotions communicate feelings: towards a guideline for the NeuroIS community. In: Davis, F.D., Riedl, R., vom Brocke, J., Léger, P.-M., Randolph, A.B. (eds.) Information Systems and Neuroscience. LNISO, vol. 25, pp. 141–150. Springer, Cham (2018). https://doi.org/10.1007/978-3-319-67431-5_16
44. vom Brocke, J., Hevner, A., Léger, P.M., Walla, P., Riedl, R.: Advancing a NeuroIS research agenda with four areas of societal contributions. Eur. J. Inf. Syst. **29**, 9–24 (2020)
45. Voss, K.E., Spangenberg, E.R., Grohmann, B.: Measuring the hedonic and utilitarian dimensions of consumer attitude. J. Mark. Res. **40**, 310–320 (2003)
46. Molinillo, S., Navarro-García, A., Anaya-Sánchez, R., Japutra, A.: The impact of affective and cognitive app experiences on loyalty towards retailers. J. Retail. Consum. Serv. **54**, 101948 (2020)

47. Micu, A.E., Bouzaabia, O., Bouzaabia, R., Micu, A., Capatina, A.: Online customer experience in e-retailing: implications for web entrepreneurship. Int. Entrepreneurship Manag. J. **15**(2), 651–675 (2019). https://doi.org/10.1007/s11365-019-00564-x
48. Foroudi, P., Jin, Z., Gupta, S., Melewar, T.C., Foroudi, M.M.: Influence of innovation capability and customer experience on reputation and loyalty. J. Bus. Res. **69**, 4882–4889 (2016)
49. Högberg, J., Ramberg, M.O., Gustafsson, A., Wästlund, E.: Creating brand engagement through in-store gamified customer experiences. J. Retail. Consum. Serv. **50**, 122–130 (2019)
50. Pandey, S., Chawla, D.: Online customer experience (OCE) in clothing e-retail. Int. J. Retail Distrib. Manag. **46**, 323–346 (2018)
51. Roy, S.K., Gruner, R.L., Guo, J.: Exploring customer experience, commitment, and engagement behaviours. J. Strateg. Mark. 1–24 (2020)
52. Tyrväinen, O., Karjaluoto, H., Saarijärvi, H.: Personalization and hedonic motivation in creating customer experiences and loyalty in omnichannel retail. J. Retail. Consum. Serv. **57**, 102233 (2020)
53. Visinescu, L.L., Sidorova, A., Jones, M.C., Prybutok, V.R.: The influence of website dimensionality on customer experiences, perceptions and behavioral intentions: an exploration of 2D vs. 3D web design. Inf. Manag. **52**, 1–17 (2015)
54. Thompson, E.R.: Development and validation of an internationally reliable short-form of the positive and negative affect schedule (PANAS). J. Cross. Cult. Psychol. **38**, 227–242 (2007)
55. Hausman, A.V., Siekpe, J.S.: The effect of web interface features on consumer online purchase intentions. J. Bus. Res. **62**, 5–13 (2009)
56. Dennis, C., Joško Brakus, J., Gupta, S., Alamanos, E.: The effect of digital signage on shoppers' behavior: the role of the evoked experience. J. Bus. Res. **67**, 2250–2257 (2014)
57. Csikszentmihalyi, M.: Beyond Boredom and Anxiety. Jossey-Bass, San Francisco (1975)
58. Luo, X.: Uses and gratifications theory and e-consumer behaviors: a structural equation modeling study. J. Interact. Advert. **2**, 34–41 (2002)
59. Bhattacherjee, A.: Understanding information systems continuance: an expectation-confirmation model. MIS Q. **25**, 351–370 (2001)
60. Agarwal, R., Karahanna, E.: Time flies when you're having fun: cognitive absorption and beliefs about information technology usage. MIS Q. **24**, 665–694 (2000)
61. Gefen, D., Straub, D.: Managing user trust in B2C e-Services. e-Service J. **2**, 7–24 (2003)
62. Reimer, A., Kuehn, R.: The impact of servicescape on quality perception. Eur. J. Mark. **39**, 785–808 (2005)
63. Novak, T.P., Hoffman, D.L., Duhachek, A.: The influence of goal-directed and experiential activities on online flow experiences. J. Consum. Psychol. **13**, 3–16 (2004)
64. Pham, M.T.: Emotion and rationality: a critical review and interpretation of empirical evidence. Rev. Gen. Psychol. **11**, 155–178 (2007)
65. Costa, P.T., McCrae, R.R.: Normal personality assessment in clinical practice: the NEO personality inventory. Psychol. Assess. **4**, 5–13 (1992)
66. Lee, K., Ashton, M.C.: Psychometric properties of the HEXACO-100. Assessment **25**, 543–556 (2018)
67. Davis, K.L., Panksepp, J., Normansell, L.: The affective neuroscience personality scales: normative data and implications. Neuropsychoanalysis **5**, 57–69 (2003)
68. Gefen, D.: E-commerce: the role of familiarity and trust. Omega **28**, 725–737 (2000)
69. Caruelle, D., Gustafsson, A., Shams, P., Lervik-Olsen, L.: The use of electrodermal activity (EDA) measurement to understand consumer emotions – a literature review and a call for action. J. Bus. Res. **104**, 146–160 (2019)
70. Verhulst, N., De Keyser, A., Gustafsson, A., Shams, P., Van Vaerenbergh, Y.: Neuroscience in service research: an overview and discussion of its possibilities. J. Serv. Manag. **30**, 621–649 (2019)

71. Riedl, R., Léger, P.-M.: Fundamentals of NeuroIS: Information Systems and the Brain. Springer , Berlin (2016)
72. Veilleux, M., et al.: Visualizing a user's cognitive and emotional journeys: a fintech case. In: Marcus, A., Rosenzweig, E. (eds.) HCII 2020. LNCS, vol. 12200, pp. 549–566. Springer, Cham (2020). https://doi.org/10.1007/978-3-030-49713-2_38
73. Hermes, A., Riedl, R.: The nature of customer experience and its determinants in the retail context: literature review. In: Gronau, N., Heine, M., Krasnova, H., Pousttchi, K. (eds.) WI2020 Zentrale Tracks, pp. 1738–1749. GITO Verlag, Potsdam (2020)
74. Hermes, A., Riedl, R.: How to measure customers' emotional experience? A short review of current methods and a call for neurophysiological approaches. In: Davis, F.D., Riedl, R., vom Brocke, J., Léger, P.-M., Randolph, A.B., Fischer, T. (eds.) NeuroIS 2020. LNISO, vol. 43, pp. 211–219. Springer, Cham (2020). https://doi.org/10.1007/978-3-030-60073-0_25
75. Phelps, E.A.: Emotion and cognition: insights from studies of the human amygdala. Annu. Rev. Psychol. **57**, 27–53 (2006)
76. Müller-Putz, G.R., Riedl, R., Wriessnegger, S.C.: Electroencephalography (EEG) as a research tool in the information systems discipline: foundations, measurement, and applications. Commun. Assoc. Inf. Syst. **37**, 911–948 (2015)
77. Kim, S., Park, G., Lee, Y., Choi, S.: Customer emotions and their triggers in luxury retail: understanding the effects of customer emotions before and after entering a luxury shop. J. Bus. Res. **69**, 5809–5818 (2016)

# Users' Reception of Product Recommendations: Analyses Based on Eye Tracking Data

Feiyan Jia[1,2(✉)], Yani Shi[3], Choon Ling Sia[1,4], Chuan-Hoo Tan[5],
Fiona Fui-Hoon Nah[6], and Keng Siau[6]

[1] City University of Hong Kong, Hong Kong, China
feiyanjia2-c@my.cityu.edu.hk, iscl@cityu.edu.hk
[2] University of Science and Technology of China, Hefei, People's Republic of China
[3] Southeast University, Nanjing, People's Republic of China
yanishi@seu.edu.cn
[4] National Taiwan University, Taipei, Taiwan
[5] National University of Singapore, Singapore, Singapore
tancho@comp.nus.edu.sg
[6] Missouri University of Science and Technology, Rolla, USA
{nahf,siauk}@mst.edu

**Abstract.** Based on eye tracking technology, we study consumers' overall attention to recommendations appearing at different time settings (i.e., early, mid, and late) and their attention to different information contained in each recommendation, such as recommendation signs, product descriptions, and reviews. By investigating consumers' eye movement patterns and attention distributions on recommendations, we open the "black box" of why consumers' reception to recommendations appearing at different time settings varies. The product preference construction literature and mindset theory help to explain why the early recommendations receive the most attention. The need for justification helps to explain why the late recommendations should receive more attention than the mid recommendations. Besides, the fact that not all information appearing in recommendations will receive every customer's attention inspires a more efficient recommendation page design. By exploring the patterns of consumers' attention to recommendations, we contribute to the accumulation of recommendation literature and provide guidance for the practice.

**Keywords:** Recommendation agents · Eye tracking · Attention distributions

## 1 Introduction

Recommendation agents have been widely used in various kinds of digital platforms, especially in e-commerce. During the past decades, recommendation agents act as a powerful tool to drive profits for companies such as Netflix, Amazon, and so on. During

© Springer Nature Switzerland AG 2021
F. F.-H. Nah and K. Siau (Eds.): HCII 2021, LNCS 12783, pp. 90–104, 2021.
https://doi.org/10.1007/978-3-030-77750-0_6

the last quarter of 2020, Amazon generated total net sales of approximately 125.56 billion U.S. dollars, surpassing the 87.44 billion U.S. dollars in the same quarter of 2019.[1] Mckinsey estimated that 35 percent of consumer purchases on Amazon come from product recommendations.[2] Recommendation agents also attract attention from academia besides practitioners. There are numerous academic research works on recommendation agents. However, most of these research works focus on the recommendation agents themselves such as changing recommendation sources or recommendation algorithms (Ghoshal et al. 2015; Lee and Benbasat 2011; Zhang et al. 2011), leaving consumers' cognitive processes and psychological activities less investigated. Consumers' cognitive processes and psychological activities play a key role in consumer behaviors. Having a better understanding of consumers' cognitive processes can help practitioners appreciate consumers' behavior better (Just and Carpenter 1976) and such knowledge can assist practitioners to design better e-commerce systems and recommendation agents.

Consumers' online shopping typically consists of two stages, i.e., the searching stage and the evaluation stage (Ho and Tam 2005; Moe 2006). During the searching stage, consumers search for products and form their consideration sets. During the evaluation stage, consumers make their final choices from their consideration sets. Ho and Tam (2005) investigate the effects of different timing on consumers' choice and they find that consumers' acceptance of recommended products diminishes as recommendation timing is delayed. Furthermore, the interaction effect of recommendation timing and recommendation type is investigated in Ho et al. (2011). They show that there is a tradeoff between recommendation timing and recommendation accuracy because although the recommendation accuracy can be improved at later stages, consumers are less willing to accept recommendations at later stages. However, consumers' real cognitive processing of recommendations appearing at different time settings is less investigated. Therefore, our first research question is what leads to the decreasing acceptance of recommendations at later stages.

Reviews and recommendations are previously treated as separate elements in consumer research and investigated in different research. More and more researchers start to realize the relating role of reviews and recommendations. Lee and Hosanagar (2020) find that reviews and recommendations are complementary in the searching stage and they are replaceable in the final purchase stage. However, consumers' real information processing of the reviews and recommendations is seldom investigated. Besides, some research works treat recommendation signals, such as "Other consumers recommend this to you" as an important base for generating attention from consumers. Whether these signals really attract attention is also rarely studied. The cognitive processing is not necessarily synchronized with the time at which the stimulus appears and not all the features of the stimulus will attract attention (Léger et al. 2014). Thus, our second

---

[1] Tugba Sabanoglu, "Net revenue of Amazon from 1st quarter 2007 to 4th quarter 2020," Statista, February 11, 2021, accessed March 9, 2021 www.statista.com/statistics/273963/quarterly-rev enue-of-amazoncom/

[2] Daniel Faggella, "The ROI of recommendation engines for marketing," Martech, October 30, 2017, accessed January 19, 2021, https://martechtoday.com/roi-recommendation-engines-mar keting-205787

research question is what information is taken into consideration when consumers are evaluating recommendations.

There is a call in IS area to adopt advanced technology such as eye-tracking to gain a better knowledge of consumers (Buettner et al. 2018; Dimoka et al. 2012a; Dimoka et al. 2011). Just and Carpenter (1976) demonstrate that traces and durations of eye fixations can be closely related to the human's cognitive processing activities. With the maturity and advancement of devices, eye-tracking has been used to investigate the cognitive process in IS given its strength in objectively, accurately, and unobtrusively measuring the tracks of eye movements. Shi et al. (2013) build a hierarchical hidden Markov (HMM) model to investigate information acquisition during online shopping based on eye-tracking data. The HMM model consists of three layers and it shows the inter-relationship among eye-tracking data, information acquisition type, and strategy switching. Bera et al. (2019) investigate mental processes involved when readers use conceptual modeling scripts to handle tasks based on attention data, demonstrating that eye-tracking can be used to understand the cognitive processes. Pfeiffer et al. (2020) train and test prediction models to predict consumers' shopping motives (goal-directed VS. exploratory) based on eye-tracking measures, demonstrating that eye tracking can also be used in prediction. Therefore, we take advantage of the eye-tracking technology to study the research questions mentioned above.

Based on eye-tracking technology, we investigate consumers' attention to recommendations appearing at different time settings (i.e., early, mid, and late) and their attention to different recommendation information, i.e., area of interest (AOI) such as recommendation signs. We look at consumers' eye movement patterns and the distributions of their attention on recommendation signs, product descriptions, and reviews. By investigating the patterns of consumers' attention to recommendations, this research contributes to the accumulation of recommendation literature and guide the practice.

## 2   Literature Review and Hypotheses

### 2.1   Product Preference Construction

Although the goal of recommendations is consumers' acceptance, studies show that recommendations can still affect consumer decision-making even if they fail to persuade consumers to choose the recommended products. For example, Häubl and Murray (2003) show that the inclusion of an attribute in a recommendation will make consumers feel that this attribute is more important to their decision-making. Marketing literature has shown that most consumers' product preferences are not well-defined at the beginning of shopping, contrary to most recommendation literature that assumes user preference is static during the shopping process. The notion that consumers' product preferences are often constructed or evolved when decisions are being made rather than retrieved from memory has gained more acceptance (Carpenter and Nakamoto 1989; Yoon and Simonson 2008). Adomavicius et al. (2013) show the anchoring effect of recommendations on consumers' product preference construction by analyzing the music piece rating data. Köcher et al. (2019) show the attribute-level anchoring effect of recommendations on consumers' product preferences. From the above literature, we can see that recommendations can help consumers construct their product preferences.

Consumers' mindsets also vary in different shopping stages (Gollwitzer et al. 1990; Ho and Tam 2005). The recommendation time settings are operationalized as early, mid, and late recommendations in this study. Early recommendation timing means recommending immediately after a user enters into the website. Mid recommendation timing means recommending after a user adds one product into the shopping cart. Late recommendation timing means recommending after a user decides which one to purchase but before making confirmation. At the very beginning of shopping, consumers are going to inspect available alternatives, thus they are most open-minded. In the searching stage, consumers are developing a consideration set from the entire available choices. Although they may have constructed a relatively concrete product preference during the searching process, they are still open to alternative products. However, when they come to the evaluation stage, consumers are working to make their final decisions, thus they are least open to alternative products.

Therefore, we propose the following hypotheses:

*H1a: Compared with mid recommendations and late recommendations, early recommendations will receive the most attention.*
*H1b: Compared with early recommendations and mid recommendations, late Recommendations will receive the least attention.*

## 2.2 Product Preference Uncertainty

Consumer product preference uncertainty is mainly due to the following two reasons -- product quality uncertainty and product fit uncertainty (Hong and Pavlou 2014). A recommendation contains different kinds of information. To process these different kinds of information, consumers may use different routes. According to the elaboration likelihood model, consumers tend to carefully and thoughtfully consider the true merits of information when using the central route. On the contrary, consumers tend to rely on positive or negative cues when using the peripheral route.

To reduce the product quality uncertainty, consumers can acquire more product information. Product recommendation signs can be signals of high product quality and the product recommendation signs can be especially useful when consumers use the peripheral route to make decisions. Also, product descriptions can help consumers reduce product quality uncertainty because they provides details about product attributes, which are particularly informative for search product. And it is useful for consumers that are utilizing the central route. Reviews not only provide additional information about the product itself but also provide valuable after-use information, which assists in reducing product fit uncertainty by showing the actual use consequences.

Although recommendation signs can only provide peripheral cues, they can assist a consumer in decision-making. Given the rich information provided by product descriptions and product reviews, they will also attract attention. Therefore, we expect that the three kinds of information in each recommendation will attract attention and we propose our second hypothesis:

*H2: Recommendation signs, product descriptions, and reviews in each recommendation will receive attention.*

Because the recommendation signs are quite standardized and easy to be processed compared to product descriptions and product reviews, we expect the recommendation signs will receive a similar amount of attention at different recommendation time settings. Although product descriptions and reviews are relatively standardized, they contain much richer information. Based on the preference construction theory and mindset theory, we expect that the attention patterns for the product descriptions and reviews will be similar to the overall recommendations, thus we propose the following hypotheses:

*H3a: The recommendation signs in different recommendation time settings will receive a similar amount of attention.*
*H3b: The product descriptions in early recommendations will receive the most attention.*
*H3c: The product descriptions in late recommendations will receive the least attention.*
*H3d: The reviews in early recommendations will receive the most attention.*
*H3e: The reviews in late recommendations will receive the least attention.*

## 3 Data

The data are collected from a lab experiment, and Shi, Zeng et al. (2017) have used the data in their research to explore the timing effect of recommendation agents and compare the effects of consumer reviews and expert reviews. We use part of the data in this research and we will describe the data used in this research in the following section.

The experiment was conducted in the Laboratory for Information Evaluation at an institution in the Midwest of the US. Self-developed websites were used in a 3*2 experimental design. The first factor is the time settings that recommendations are offered, i.e., recommend immediately after a user enters into the website, recommend after a user adds one product into the shopping cart, and recommend after a user decides which one to purchase but before making confirmation. The second factor refers to product types, i.e., mobile phone and laptop. The first factor is a between-subject factor whereas the second factor is a within-subject factor. The design is counter-balanced. Participants' eye movements were recorded by Tobii T60 eye-trackers, which were used as the computer monitor displays for the experiment. We utilized three Tobii eye-trackers, which enabled us to conduct three concurrent experimental sessions.

Participants were presented with a consent form to sign when they arrived for the study. The experimenters were given a standardized moderator script to follow to avoid moderator biases. Participants first went through a training session to get familiar with the websites designed for the experiment. Then they were asked to carry out two shopping tasks for two types of products. Undergraduate students from the institution participated in the experiment. Each participant was given extra credits for their class and provided with a souvenir after the experiment. Due to technical problems, we failed to record the eye movements of several participants. Our data set consists of around ten observations in each recommendation setting. Each observation includes two shopping tasks and the sequence of these two tasks was counterbalanced as mentioned earlier.

## 4 Data Analysis

We first analyzed participants' overall attention to recommendations appearing at different time settings. Previous studies show that eye visits and fixations indicate information processing (Ahn et al. 2018; Just and Carpenter 1976). Processing more information will induce more fixation counts and longer total fixation duration (Ahn et al. 2018; Cheung et al. 2017; Pfeiffer et al. 2020; Vance et al. 2018) (see Table 1 for the definitions of the eye-tracking measures used in this study). Visit duration, fixation count, fixation duration, and total fixation duration on each recommendation page are used to measure the attention to the overall recommendations.

### 4.1 Analysis of the Overall Attention to the Recommendations

To analyze the fixation data on the recommendation pages, we first labeled the timestamps of each recommendation, i.e., the starting time of each recommendation and the end time of each recommendation, in the file exported from Tobii Studio. After labeling the timestamps, we checked the details of fixation data during each recommendation appearing period and we found several failure cases.

**Table 1.** Definition of eye-tracking measures used in this study

| Measures | Definition |
| --- | --- |
| Visit duration | The duration of each individual visit within a certain area |
| Visit count | The number of visits within a certain area |
| Total visit duration | The sum of all visit durations |
| Fixation count | The number of times the participant fixates |
| Fixation duration | The duration of each individual fixation |
| Total fixation duration | The sum of all fixation durations |
| Time to first fixation (TFF) | How long it takes before a test participant fixates on a certain area for the first time |
| Percentage fixated | The number of recordings in which the participant has fixated at least once within an AOI. This is expressed as a fraction of the total number of recordings |

In the early recommendation group, the eye movements of one participant were not collected when the participant was shopping for a laptop. In the mid recommendation group, the eye movements of one participant were not collected in both shopping tasks. In the late recommendation group, there were two failures in the collection of eye movements when shopping for mobile phones and two failures in the collection of eye movements when shopping for laptops. We have a total of 63 observations of shopping left after excluding the failure cases (see Table 2 for the details of observations in each treatment group).

After data cleaning, we analyzed the overall attention during each recommendation appearing period based on eye-tracking measures. Table 2 shows the descriptive data analysis. We first analyzed the mobile phone recommendation group. Analysis of variance (ANOVA) reveals that the average total visit duration, average total fixation duration, and fixation count of different recommendation time settings differ significantly in the mobile phone recommendation group at the 0.10 level of significance ($p < 0.0482$, $p < 0.0320$, $p < 0.0546$, correspondingly), suggesting that there are significant attention differences among different recommendation time settings. There is no significant difference among the average fixation duration ($p < 0.3374$), suggesting that each information processing unit is relatively stable.

From the analysis result of the mobile phone recommendation group (see Table 2), we can see that the early recommendation group receives the most attention (i.e., longest average visit duration, largest fixation counts, and longest average total fixation duration), supporting H1a. The mid recommendation group has the least attention (i.e., shortest average visit duration, smallest fixation counts, and shortest average total fixation duration), not supporting H1b. The significance testing and attention distribution patterns of the laptop recommendation group show a similar result.

Then, we conducted Tukey's test to compare attention differences between paired recommendation time setting groups. The results show that the visit duration, total fixation duration, fixation count of the mobile phone early recommendation group are statistically larger than those of the mobile phone mid recommendation group at the 0.10 level of significance ($p < 0.065$, $p < 0.044$, $p < 0.065$, correspondingly). The total fixation duration of the mobile phone early recommendation is statistically larger than that in the mobile late recommendation group at the 0.10 level of significance ($p < 0.090$). The differences of other paired comparisons of eye tracking measures are not statistically significant. The Tuckey's test of the laptop recommendation group shows a similar result.

It is consistent with prior findings and logical arguments that the early recommendation group has more attention than the mid and late recommendation groups. However, it is interesting that the late recommendation group receives more attention (see Table 2: longer average total visit duration, more fixation counts, and longer average total fixation duration) than the mid recommendation group, but the differences are not statistically significant. The non-significant results are different from past literature. Based on prior studies (Chiou and Ting 2011; Okada 2005; Xu and Schwarz 2009), late recommendations may receive more attention than mid recommendations because of the need for justification. Consumers have a higher degree of need for justification in the final decision stage due to the risk of unwanted decision consequences in the future. To make a justified decision, consumers need to base their decisions on reasons, which need to be carefully constructed. The salience effect of recommendations will make consumers pay special attention to the recommendations, which may facilitate the consumers to treat the recommendations as anchors. According to the preference construction literature, consumers make decisions highly contingent on the environment and there is an attraction effect, i.e., the existence of an inferior alternative will make consumers have more confidence in their initial choice (Huber et al. 1982). According to the attraction effect, a recommendation may switch consumer choice to the recommended product if it is superior to the consumer's initial choice. Otherwise, the recommended product may make the consumer feel more confident about the initial choice if it is superior to the recommended one. In both cases, the need for justification will make consumers treat the recommendations seriously and spend time processing the recommendations, which should result in more attention to the late recommendations than the mid recommendations. One possible reason for the non-significant results may be the small sample size. We aim to verify the results in future studies.

**Table 2.** Visit duration and fixation analyses of the recommendation pages

| Recommendation Timing | Observation | Average total visit duration | Product Type | Average fixation count | Average fixation duration | Average total fixation duration |
|---|---|---|---|---|---|---|
| Early | 12 | 70141.4 | Mobile phone | 235 | 209.705 | 54390.833 |
| | 11 | 58621.3 | Laptop | 206 | 221.292 | 47834.182 |
| Mid | 10 | 28888.4 | Mobile phone | 97 | 181.727 | 18232.502 |
| | 10 | 32941.8 | Laptop | 74 | 173.915 | 12794.700 |
| Late | 10 | 34000.7 | Mobile phone | 121 | 198.758 | 23067.998 |
| | 10 | 54667.5 | Laptop | 168 | 198.103 | 35535.000 |

Notes: Total visit duration (seconds), fixation duration (seconds), total fixation duration (seconds)

## 4.2  Analysis of Attention to Different AOIs

Tobii studio provides several visualization tools to vividly show the attention sequence (such as gaze plot) and distribution (such as heat map). In Fig. 1, we depict one visualization figure as an example.

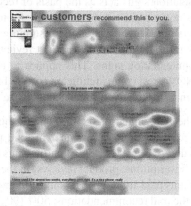

**Fig. 1.** Heat map of one recommendation

From Fig. 1, we can see that the product description area and the review information area attract lots of participants' attention. To investigate which one matters more when consumers evaluate recommendations, we labeled the product description information area as AOI-product description and product review area as AOI-product review. Because prior studies also looked at recommendation signs as justification for recommendations but earlier studies seldom tracked whether consumers pay attention to these signs or not, we also studied the recommendation sign area in this research and labeled it as AOI-recommendation sign.

**Analysis of the Eye Movement Sequence.** We first looked at the time to first fixation (TFF) for different AOIs (see Table 3). From Table 2, we see that there is no significant attention difference between mobile phone recommendation group and laptop recommendation group. To increase the sample size, we combined the mobile phone recommendations and laptop recommendations to do the data analysis. From Table 3, we can see that the TFF for the recommendation sign is much larger than the TFF for product description and product review. Take the early recommendation group as an example, 16.68 s is much larger than 6.34 s and 9.40 s. It shows that when a recommendation appears, consumers are more likely to first pay attention to the product description information, i.e., the product attributes, indicating that the recommended products themselves are pre-requisites for further processing of recommendations.

**Table 3.** Mean times to first fixation (TFF) for different AOIs (seconds)

| Recommendation timing | Recommendation sign | Product Description | Product Review |
|---|---|---|---|
| Early | 15.68 | 6.34 | 9.40 |
| Mid | 4.51 | 2.46 | 3.97 |
| Late | 15.86 | 10.90 | 11.54 |

Although previous research uses recommendation signs to label their recommendations and the recommendation signs acts as the basis of recommendations, a recommendation sign itself does not contain too much meaningful information. Our analysis results show that consumers allocate their attention first to the meaningful information, i.e., the product attributes information and the product review information, instead of the less meaningful recommendation signs. This applies to all recommendation time settings. However, the ANOVA test is not significant ($p < 0.1465$). This may be due to the relatively small differences or relatively small sample size.

**Analysis of Fixations.** The percentage of fixation shows the ratio of the number of participants fixating on certain areas to the number of total participants. From Panel A of Table 4, we can see that 57% (100%, 86%) participants paid attention to recommendation signs (product descriptions, product reviews) in the early recommendations. 80% (100%, 80%) participants paid attention to recommendation signs (product descriptions, product reviews) in the mid recommendations. 50% (90%, 90%) participants paid attention to recommendation signs (product descriptions, product reviews) in the late recommendations. The result shows that not all recommendation signs, product descriptions, or product reviews in recommendations will attract every participant's attention, not supporting H2.

**Table 4.** Fixation statistics of different AOIs

Panel A Percentage of fixation on different AOIs

| Recommendation timing | Recommendation sign | Product description | Product review |
| --- | --- | --- | --- |
| Early | 57% | 100% | 86% |
| Mid | 80% | 100% | 80% |
| Late | 50% | 90% | 90% |

Panel B Mean total fixation duration for different AOIs (seconds)

| Recommendation timing | Recommendation sign | Product description | Product review |
| --- | --- | --- | --- |
| Early | 0.600 | 4.970 | 25.493 |
| Mid | 0.563 | 2.249 | 5.781 |
| Late | 0.756 | 3.569 | 10.999 |

Panel C Mean fixation count for different AOIs

| Recommendation timing | Recommendation sign | Product description | Product review |
| --- | --- | --- | --- |
| Early | 3.250 | 21.429 | 101.667 |
| Mid | 3.250 | 13.100 | 35.625 |
| Late | 4.000 | 16.000 | 55.111 |

Notes: Total fixation duration (seconds)

From Panel B and Panel C of Table 4, we can see that attention to recommendation signs does not vary too much in different recommendation time settings. The ANOVA results show that the mean total fixation duration and mean fixation count for recommendation sign do not differ significantly among different recommendation time settings ($p < 0.8116$, $p < 0.8794$), supporting H3a. The product description of the early recommendation group receives the most attention, while the product descriptions of the mid and late settings receive a similar amount of attention (i.e., 2.249 s is comparable to 3.569 s and 13.1 is comparable to 16). However, the ANOVA results show that the mean total fixation duration and mean fixation count for product description do not differ significantly among different recommendation time settings ($p < 0.2215$, $p < 0.4025$), not supporting H3b and H3c. The product review of the early recommendation group receives the most attention and the product review of the mid recommendation group receives the least attention. However, the ANOVA results show that the mean total fixation duration and mean fixation count for product description do not differ significantly among different recommendation time settings ($p < 0.2177$, $p < 0.3599$), not supporting H3d and H3e. Although there are attention differences on the same AOI in different recommendation time settings, the ANOVA results show that none of the differences is statistically significant. Again, this may be due to the relatively small sample size.

Although the descriptive statistics are in line with our earlier discussion, the differences are not statistically significant. However, based on prior studies, consumers at the beginning of searching are most open to new choices because of the exploratory mindset, which corresponds to why the early recommendation time setting receives the most attention. From the habituation literature (Brinton Anderson et al. 2016; Vance et al. 2018), consumers will become familiar with the same interface as exposure to it increases. Thus, the product description of the early recommendation group tends to require more attention than the mid and late recommendations. The results also show that the main attention difference of product review between the mid setting and late setting corresponds to our discussion of the need for justification. The higher degree of need for justification in the final stage results in late recommendations receiving more attention than mid recommendations, which can be explained by the product preference uncertainty theory. Although the consumers almost achieve a decision when arriving at the end of the evaluation stage, they still face product preference uncertainty.

Previous literature suggests that there are two causes of product preference uncertainty, i.e., uncertainty about own evaluation criteria and uncertainty about product quality (Dimoka et al. 2012b; Hong and Pavlou 2014; Lee and Hosanagar 2020). Although consumers may have relatively clear evaluation criteria about the products, there is still uncertainty about product quality when shopping. Both product description information and reviews can help to alleviate product quality uncertainty. Product description helps reduce concerns about pre-purchase quality uncertainty. Reviews help reduce both pre-purchase and post-purchase product quality uncertainty because experience information is provided in the review. Therefore, even for consumers in the almost purchase stage, they are still in need of additional information to reduce their post-purchase uncertainty. Although reviews of other products may not be directly relevant to their initial choices, it may help them imagine their post-purchase states and thus be more able to evaluate their choices thoroughly.

**Analysis of Visits.** From Panel A and Panel B of Table 5, we can see that the attention to different AOIs in different time settings is similar to that of the analysis of fixation, validating our above attention distribution patterns. We also notice that the average visit duration of recommendation signs is much smaller than that of product descriptions, which is much smaller than that of product review and the ANOVA shows that the difference is statistically significant ($p < 0.0001$). The same trend applies to average total visit duration and average visit count (see Panel B and Panel C of Table 4) and the ANOVA shows that the difference is statistically significant ($p < 0.0019, p < 0.0086$, correspondingly).

The differences among average visit duration and average total visit duration may be due to the different information contained in different AOIs. As we can see from Fig. 1, the information contained in a recommendation sign is less and standardized. On the contrary, the information contained in a product review is much richer and varies a lot.

All the average visit counts of different AOIs are larger than one, showing that consumers iterate among the information, which is consistent with the eye movement-based memory literature (Althoff and Cohen 1999). The eye movement-based memory literature states that consumers' memory will not fade away immediately after seeing certain information, i.e., they will remember such information for a short time. However, they will not be able to remember all the information after one look. Thus, they will need to go back to the information to recall or strengthen their memory of such information.

**Table 5.** Visit statistics of different AOIs

| Panel A Average visit duration for different AOIs (seconds) | | | |
|---|---|---|---|
| Recommendation timing | Recommendation sign | Product Description | Product Review |
| Early | 0.295 | 1.078 | 4.554 |
| Mid | 0.223 | 0.650 | 2.026 |
| Late | 0.282 | 0.736 | 3.289 |
| Panel B Average total visit duration for different AOIs per recommendation (seconds) | | | |
| Recommendation timing | Recommendation sign | Product Description | Product Review |
| Early | 0.643 | 7.194 | 38.378 |
| Mid | 0.619 | 3.360 | 8.965 |
| Late | 0.804 | 4.240 | 15.506 |
| Panel C Average visit count for different AOIs per recommendation | | | |
| Recommendation timing | Recommendation sign | Product Description | Product Review |
| Early | 2.0 | 6.0 | 6.2 |
| Mid | 2.6 | 4.2 | 3.6 |
| Late | 3.0 | 5.3 | 3.7 |

Notes: Visit duration (seconds), total visit duration (seconds)

## 5   Discussions and Limitations

From this research, we have the following observations. First, consumers pay most attention to the early recommendations. The late recommendations attract more attention than the mid recommendations. The product preference construction literature and mindset theory support the fact that the early recommendations attract the most attention. The higher need for justification in the decision stage supports the fact the late recommendations receive more attention than the mid recommendations.

Second, although there are several information elements contained in the recommendation page, consumers weigh them differently when processing different pieces of information. For example, consumers tend to first pay attention to product descriptions instead of recommendation signs or reviews. Besides, the attention to recommendation signs does not vary too much in different recommendation time settings, whilst the attention to product descriptions and reviews varies a lot in different recommendation time settings but the differences are not statistically significant. There is another interesting finding, that is, not all the information in the recommendation page will attract every consumers' attention. And consumers always iterate among different information to recall or strengthen their memory of these pieces of information.

Our study has the following limitations. First, our sample size is relatively small. Although most eye-tracking research works are based on small sample sizes due to the availability of devices, it is still worthy to increase the sample size to achieve higher generalizability. One possible reason that some of the hypotheses are not supported is because of the small sample size. Second, our study only uses the utilitarian and search products. Although this is applicable for the purpose of replicating findings, using hedonic and experience products to verify and generalize the findings is also desirable. Third, although primacy and recency effect do not quite applicable to our research context because final choice is made from a consideration set and there is little reliance on memory, additional studies should be conducted to consider these two effects. Future research can expand our research in the following directions. First, future research can increase the sample size when resources are available. Second, future research can use other product categories to test the findings. Third, additional studies can be conducted to test alternative explanations.

## 6  Conclusions and Implications

Our study contributes to the accumulation of recommendation literature by opening the black box of cognitive information processing when consumers encounter recommendations. This research also demonstrate another eye-tracking application in academic research. The practice can also benefit from this research. For example, contrary to "the early, the better" belief, our study shows that late recommendations also play a vital role. Thus, the practice should take the advantage of the late recommendations to drive consumers' purchases. The finding that consumers first pay attention to the product description information suggests that practitioners should place the most attractive production description information in the recommendation page to increase the possibility of deeper recommendation information processing. Consumers reliance on reviews to make justification can also inspire practitioners to motive other consumers to write reviews in more detail.

**Acknowledgment.** This research is partially supported by the Hong Kong Research Grants Council and City University of Hong Kong (Project No. CityU 11504417/11507619/9360147), a Taiwan Yushan Scholar grant NTU-109V0701, and the National Natural Science Foundation of China (NSFC No. 71701043).

## References

Adomavicius, G., Bockstedt, J.C., Curley, S.P., Zhang, J.: Do recommender systems manipulate consumer preferences? A study of anchoring effects. Inf. Syst. Res. **24**(4), 956–975 (2013)
Ahn, J.-H., Bae, Y.-S., Ju, J., Oh, W.: Attention adjustment, renewal, and equilibrium seeking in online search: an eye-tracking approach. J. Manag. Inf. Syst. **35**(4), 1218–1250 (2018)
Althoff, R.R., Cohen, N.J.: Eye-movement-based memory effect: a reprocessing effect in face perception. J. Exp. Psychol. Learn. Mem. Cogn. **25**(4), 997 (1999)
Bera, P., Soffer, P., Parsons, J.: Using eye tracking to expose cognitive processes in understanding conceptual models. MIS Q. **43**(4), 1105–1126 (2019)
Brinton Anderson, B., Vance, A., Kirwan, C.B., Eargle, D., Jenkins, J.L.: How users perceive and respond to security messages: a neurois research agenda and empirical study. Eur. J. Inf. Syst. **25**(4), 364–390 (2016)
Buettner, R., Sauer, S., Maier, C., Eckhardt, A.: Real-time prediction of user performance based on pupillary assessment via eye tracking. AIS Trans. Hum. Comput. Interact. **10**(1), 26–56 (2018)

Carpenter, G.S., Nakamoto, K.: Consumer preference formation and pioneering advantage. J. Mark. Res. **26**(3), 285–298 (1989)

Cheung, M.Y., Hong, W., Thong, J.Y.: Effects of animation on attentional resources of online consumers. J. Assoc. Inf. Syst. **18**(8), 605–632 (2017)

Chiou, J.-S., Ting, C.-C.: Will you spend more money and time on internet shopping when the product and situation are right? Comput. Hum. Behav. **27**(1), 203–208 (2011)

Dimoka, A., et al.: On the use of neurophysiological tools in is research: developing a research agenda for NeuroIS. MIS Q. **36**(3), 679–702 (2012a)

Dimoka, A., Hong, Y., Pavlou, P.A.: On product uncertainty in online markets: theory and evidence. MIS Q. **36**(3), 395–426 (2012b)

Dimoka, A., Pavlou, P.A., Davis, F.D.: Research commentary—neurois: the potential of cognitive neuroscience for information systems research. Inf. Syst. Res. **22**(4), 687–702 (2011)

Ghoshal, A., Menon, S., Sarkar, S.: Recommendations using information from multiple association rules: a probabilistic approach. Inf. Syst. Res. **26**(3), 532–551 (2015)

Gollwitzer, P.M., Heckhausen, H., Steller, B.: Deliberative and implemental mind-sets: cognitive tuning toward congruous thoughts and information. J. Pers. Soc. Psychol. **59**(6), 1119 (1990)

Häubl, G., Murray, K.B.: Preference construction and persistence in digital marketplaces: the role of electronic recommendation agents. J. Consum. Psychol. **13**(1–2), 75–91 (2003)

Ho, S.Y., Bodoff, D., Tam, K.Y.: Timing of adaptive web personalization and its effects on online consumer behavior. Inf. Syst. Res. **22**(3), 660–679 (2011)

Ho, S.Y., Tam, K.Y.: An empirical examination of the effects of web personalization at different stages of decision making. Int. J. Hum. Comput. Interact. **19**(1), 95–112 (2005)

Hong, Y., Pavlou, P.A.: Product fit uncertainty in online markets: nature, effects, and antecedents. Inf. Syst. Res. **25**(2), 328–344 (2014)

Huber, J., Payne, J.W., Puto, C.: Adding asymmetrically dominated alternatives: violations of regularity and the similarity hypothesis. J. Consum. Res. **9**(1), 90–98 (1982)

Just, M.A., Carpenter, P.A.: Eye fixations and cognitive processes. Cogn. Psychol. **8**(4), 441–480 (1976)

Köcher, S., Jugovac, M., Jannach, D., Holzmüller, H.H.: New hidden persuaders: an investigation of attribute-level anchoring effects of product recommendations. J. Retail. **95**(1), 24–41 (2019)

Lee, D., Hosanagar, K.: How do product attributes and reviews moderate the impact of recommender systems through purchase stages? Manag. Sci. **67**, 524–546 (2020)

Lee, Y.E., Benbasat, I.: Research note—the influence of trade-off difficulty caused by preference elicitation methods on user acceptance of recommendation agents across loss and gain conditions. Inf. Syst. Res. **22**(4), 867–884 (2011)

Léger, P.M., Sénecal, S., Courtemanche, F., de Guinea, A.O., Titah, R., Fredette, M., Labonte-LeMoyne, É.: Precision is in the eye of the beholder: application of eye fixation-related potentials to information systems research. In: Association for Information Systems (2014)

Moe, W.W.: An empirical two-stage choice model with varying decision rules applied to internet clickstream data. J. Mark. Res. **43**(4), 680–692 (2006)

Okada, E.M.: Justification effects on consumer choice of hedonic and utilitarian goods. J. Mark. Res. **42**(1), 43–53 (2005)

Pfeiffer, J., Pfeiffer, T., Meißner, M., Weiß, E.: Eye-tracking-based classification of information search behavior using machine learning: evidence from experiments in physical shops and virtual reality shopping environments. Inf. Syst. Res. **31**(3), 675–691 (2020)

Shi, S.W., Wedel, M., Pieters, F.: Information acquisition during online decision making: a model-based exploration using eye-tracking data. Manage. Sci. **59**(5), 1009–1026 (2013)

Vance, A., Jenkins, J.L., Anderson, B.B., Bjornn, D.K., Kirwan, C.B.: Tuning out security warnings: a longitudinal examination of habituation through fMRI, eye tracking, and field experiments. MIS Q. **42**(2), 355–380 (2018)

Xu, J., Schwarz, N.: Do we really need a reason to indulge? J. Mark. Res. **46**(1), 25–36 (2009)

Yoon, S.-O., Simonson, I.: Choice set configuration as a determinant of preference attribution and strength. J. Consum. Res. **35**(2), 324–336 (2008)

Zhang, T., Agarwal, R., Lucas, H.C., Jr.: The value of it-enabled retailer learning: personalized product recommendations and customer store loyalty in electronic markets. MIS Q. **35**(4), 859–881 (2011)

# Augmented Reality: Does It Encourage Customer Loyalty?

Aboli Lele[✉] and Norman Shaw

Ryerson University, Toronto, Canada
{aboli.lele,norman.shaw}@ryerson.ca

**Abstract.** As mobile shopping becomes more popular, mobile app developers and marketers are continually looking for innovative options to provide consumers with unique shopping experiences. One such area popular in recent times is an augmented reality (AR) virtual try-on feature. This study extends the electronic service quality model (ES-QUAL) with two additional constructs of Hedonic Motivation and Perceived Value and seeks to explain the factors influencing consumer loyalty intentions in AR beauty apps. Sephora is a popular and leading brand in the cosmetic industry and has a virtual try-on feature known as Virtual Artist. An online survey was conducted with 251 university students. PLS-SEM analysis suggests that Hedonic Motivation and Efficiency significantly impact loyalty intentions, while Perceived value, Perceived Privacy Risks, System Availability and Fulfilment were not significant. This study contributes to the existing literature on consumer loyalty and AR shopping apps. Retail practitioners will be able to use the results to boost consumer loyalty and further predict purchase intention using the app.

**Keywords:** Virtual try-on · AR beauty apps · Service quality · Loyalty · PLS-SEM

## 1 Introduction

The Internet has created a global market for exchanging goods and services because it is available around the clock. E-commerce platforms use this interactive approach to attract consumers to electronically buy and sell products online. The Internet helps businesses establish new channels for marketing and improving the brand image [1]. With the growing penetration of smartphones, other mobile devices and Internet services, e-commerce has emerged as a powerful shopping platform worldwide [2]. Consumers have turned to online shopping for its convenience and time saving [3]. Sales of online retailers in Canada amounted to approximately CAD$615 billion in 2019 [4].

Augmented Reality (AR) aligns real and virtual objects with each other [5] and due to its potential to capture consumers' attention and influence their purchasing decision, some retailers are incorporating AR into their marketing adding smart mirrors in stores and developing apps for mobile devices [6]. An AR app can add a new dimension to the shopping experience by creating a more realistic and personalized experience [7].

© Springer Nature Switzerland AG 2021
F. F.-H. Nah and K. Siau (Eds.): HCII 2021, LNCS 12783, pp. 105–119, 2021.
https://doi.org/10.1007/978-3-030-77750-0_7

Kumar [8] mentioned that the cosmetics and personal care sector depend a lot on face-to-face consultation, with promotions on the Internet aimed to drive users to beauty counters for makeovers and samples. Deciding between beauty products can be a daunting experience as traditionally the process consists of applying and removing different shades, repeating the process until the desired results are achieved [9]. AR apps enable a 'try before you buy' experience and bridge the gap between an online and offline shopping experience [10, 11]. AR apps can show consumers, through their smartphone's camera, how the makeup will look on their faces [12].

Researchers have explored AR apps in different ways: applying the experimental method [13], looking at technology adoption [14] and analyzing the results of qualitative studies in a domestic setting [15]. There has been limited research in the context of beauty apps. This study fills this gap by asking the question: how does the use of an AR beauty app influence consumer loyalty? More specifically, this study looks at the influence of privacy concerns and perceived value on consumer loyalty.

This study evaluates the use of Sephora's Virtual Artist app, which is an AR tool that allows consumers to try on thousands of lipstick shades, eyeshadows, false lashes, and many other makeup products. It also lets users go through beauty tutorials on their face digitally to learn how to achieve particular looks [16]. Virtual Artist is available in the Sephora app and in select retail outlets in the form of smart mirrors. The app was launched in early 2016 and had 1.6 million visits in the first eight weeks, with 45 million makeup products being tried by consumers [17].

This paper is structured as follows. We begin with the literature review, which includes the theoretical foundation, followed by the methodology and results from the data analysis. The final sections are the discussion and conclusions, including limitations and suggestions for future research.

## 2    Literature Review

### 2.1    Service Quality

Service quality is defined as 'the difference between expected service and perceived service' [18, 19]. Just as service quality is vital to various service locations, such as retail stores [20] and hotels [21], service quality is critical for e-commerce websites too [22]. E-service quality is defined as 'the extent to which a website facilitates efficient and effective shopping, purchasing and delivery of products and services' [23]. E-commerce consumers often expect equal or higher service quality levels than from traditional channels [24].

Parasuraman et al. [18] developed SERVQUAL to measure consumers' perception of service quality over five dimensions: tangibility, reliability, responsiveness, assurance and empathy. Parasuraman et al. [25] adapted the dimensions of SERVQUAL to websites, naming the new model Electronic Service Quality (ES-QUAL). The ES-QUAL scale consists of 22 items on four constructs: Efficiency, Fulfilment, System Availability and Privacy, developed based on the shopping experiences of actual web site users of two online stores, Amazon and Walmart [25]. We use ES-QUAL as the foundational model of this study.

A study done by T. Kuo, Tsai, Lu, & Chang [26] used the ES-QUAL model to understand mobile apps service quality for social networking sites like Facebook and Line. Efficiency and Usability indicators are already part of the existing ES-QUAL model and relatable to a retail shopping AR app. In this empirical study, we extend the ES-QUAL model with the constructs of Hedonic Motivation and Perceived Value.

## 2.2 Efficiency

Efficiency is defined as 'the ease and speed of accessing and using the site' [25]. Efficiency is always considered essential in e-commerce since convenience and saving time is generally regarded as the main reasons for shopping online [27]. Studies of m-commerce apps have found that functional elements like Efficiency and convenience are the most important motivators for consumer engagement [28]. Researchers have highlighted Efficiency as a critical motivator for mobile shopping [29].

A user-friendly app interface affords this Efficiency and generally commands universal acceptance by users, regardless of the type of goods or services offered [30]. Efficiency is desired for mobile shopping, as the restrictive visual interface is considered a significant barrier [31].

Thus, Efficiency is identified as an essential construct in any retail shopping platform, whether in-store or through a website or via an AR app like Sephora. Studies have found that Efficiency is rated highly by respondents [32]. In the ES-QUAL model developed by Parasuraman et al. [25], Efficiency has a positive effect on consumer loyalty. Therefore, the first hypothesis is as follows:

**H1:** There is a positive and direct impact of Efficiency on consumers' Loyalty Intentions in AR beauty apps.

## 2.3 Fulfilment

Parasuraman et al. [25] define Fulfilment as 'the extent to which the website's promises about order delivery and item availability are fulfilled. Parasuraman et al. [25] mention that Efficiency and Fulfilment are the most critical facets of web site service quality. It is argued that order fulfilment is the most critical operation for Internet retailers and that those online retailers who outperform the competition in this regard have much to gain [33, 34]. Researchers also mention that, given the virtual nature of mobile commerce, potential users would be concerned about the quality of product and unjustifiable delay in product delivery [35].

This is applicable for the Sephora app where consumers use it to choose a particular product, place an order for the same, and then their loyalty will be dependent upon how the order is fulfilled. The ES-QUAL model [25] supports Fulfilment's positive effect on consumer loyalty intentions. Therefore, the second hypothesis is as follows:

**H2:** There is a positive and direct impact of Fulfilment on consumers' Loyalty Intentions in AR beauty apps.

## 2.4  System Availability

System Availability is defined as 'The correct technical functioning of the site' [25]. Santos [36] has mentioned that this factor's importance has proved to be critical in e-service. Service availability and app stability are the two features that determine the service quality of an app [37]. Loss of information, app failure or crashing of an app are concerns [37]. Hence, the third hypothesis is as follows:

**H3:** There is a positive and direct impact of System Availability on consumers' Loyalty Intentions in AR beauty apps.

## 2.5  Perceived Privacy Risks

Privacy in the ES-QUAL model is defined as the degree to which the site is safe and protects consumer information [25]. Instead of taking the Privacy construct from the ES-QUAL study, we have replaced it with Perceived Privacy Risk [38]. Smartphone apps often request personal private information, resulting in a higher evaluation of the risks associated with mobile commerce [39, 40]. Perceived privacy risk is significant in consumer intention to use technology [41]. With the combination of AR and gesture recognition technology, the consumer can try on different products using the Sephora app. The apps' integration with the camera, location, and other personal information increases risk to privacy. Perceived privacy risk is the uncertainty associated with the negative consequences of using a particular product or service that involves any potential losses resulting from disclosing personal information [42]. Hence, perceived privacy risks negatively impact consumer loyalty and we propose the fourth hypothesis as:

**H4:** There is a negative impact of Perceived Privacy Risks on consumers' Loyalty Intentions in AR beauty apps.

## 2.6  Perceived Value

In an E-commerce setting, not only the product, website and the Internet channel add value to consumers but the processes of finding, ordering and receiving product also contribute value [43]. In this study, perceived value is defined as a consumer's perception of the net benefits gained based on the trade-off between relevant benefits and sacrifices derived from the online shopping process [44]. A consumer may perceive value in a product or technology based on its social value, emotional value or convenience [45]. In marketing research, perceived value is an important concept in influencing preferences, satisfaction and loyalty outcomes [44, 46]. Engagement in mobile technology and its omnipresent service leads to perceived value and satisfaction, which in turn leads to consumer loyalty [47]. In a study done on mobile apps, perceived value was found to have a significant impact on satisfaction and behavioural engagement [48]. Hence, the fifth hypothesis is as follows:

**H5:** There is a positive and direct impact of Perceived Value on consumers' Loyalty Intentions in AR beauty apps.

## 2.7  Hedonic Motivation

Hedonic motivation is defined as the fun or pleasure derived from using technology [49]. Hedonic motivation also plays an essential role in determining technology acceptance, and, thus, directly influences behavioural intentions [49]. Both hedonic and utilitarian elements are essential in the retail experience [50, 51]. The pleasurable and fun experiences evoke favourable and positive feelings that will lead to a higher degree of satisfaction and continued usage intention in social apps [52]. Rauschnabel et al. [53] found that hedonic benefits and perceived AR quality (i.e., high levels of perceived realism and integration) increase inspiration for branded AR apps. One of the main features of AR technology is providing additional information on products and services by stimulating pleasant experiences [54]. Hedonic motivation is an added construct to this study and for any technology to be adopted enjoyment, fun and pleasure in using that technology is important. This will lead to positive consumer loyalty and, hence, the sixth hypothesis is as follows:

**H6:** There is a positive and direct impact of Hedonic motivation on consumers' Loyalty Intentions in AR beauty apps.

## 2.8  Consumers' Loyalty Intentions

In this study, we are using the definition of consumer loyalty as explained by Srinivasan et al. [55] who define e-loyalty as a consumer's favourable attitude toward the e-retailer, resulting in repeat buying behaviour. With the boom of e-commerce, consumer loyalty has become a metric to judge a company's performance. With so many options available with just a click of a mouse or swipe of a thumb, consumer retention is critical. Several studies have stressed the importance of various operational factors in determining consumer retention and loyalty and, ultimately, a firms' success [56]. Consumer loyalty is generally very strongly related to the profitability and long-term growth of a firm [57]. Although it is challenging to gain loyal consumers on the Internet [58], customers are loyal when there are high switching barriers and lack of real alternatives.

## 2.9  Research Model

The research model is illustrated in Fig. 1.

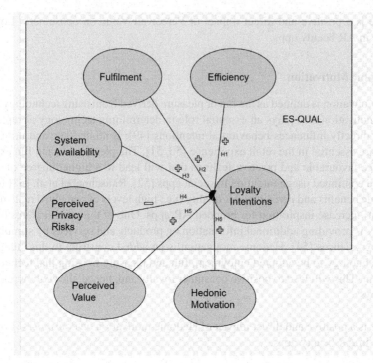

**Fig. 1.** Proposed research model

# 3 Methodology

The proposed research model was evaluated using a quantitative survey research method. The constructs were measured with indicators from existing literature (see Table 1) and using a 5-point Likert scale with 1 being strongly disagree and 5 being strongly agree.

**Table 1.** Source of indicators

| Construct | Indicators adapted from |
|---|---|
| Efficiency | [25] |
| Fulfilment | |
| System availability | |
| Perceived privacy risks | [59, 60] |
| Perceived value | |
| Hedonic motivation | [49] |
| Loyalty intentions | [25] |

A questionnaire was developed and, after a pilot test, was sent to a sample of university students. The questionnaire was administered via Qualtrics, a US company specializing in quantitative surveys. The response rate was 64%, resulting in 160 usable surveys out of 251 participants. The survey also captured gender and age (see Table 2). The age groups were 18 to 20, 21 to 23, and 24 and over.

**Table 2.** Gender and age groups

|  | Male | Female | Prefer not to answer | Skip | Total |
|---|---|---|---|---|---|
| Age Group 1 (18–20) | 31 | 67 | 1 |  | 99 |
| Age Group 2 (21–23) | 10 | 34 |  | 1 | 45 |
| Age Group 3 (24 +) | 7 | 5 | 1 | 3 | 16 |
| **Grand Total** | **48** | **106** | **2** | **4** | **160** |

The statistical tool employed was Partial Least Squares (PLS), which is a variance-based technique that is capable of testing complex models and non-normal data [49, 61]. PLS is a two-step systematic evaluation process, where the first step is the assessment of the measurement model and the second step is the assessment of the structural model [62]. Specifically, we used SmartPLS [63]. We computed the goodness of fit and tested each construct for internal consistency, convergent validity and discriminant validity [62]. For the structural model, the path coefficients and $R^2$ were calculated. Bootstrapping with 5,000 replacement determined the significance of the paths.

## 4 Results

### 4.1 The Measurement Model

The measurement model was based on 33 indicators measuring the six independent constructs of Efficiency (EFF), Fulfilment (FUL), System Availability (SYS), Perceived Privacy Risks (PPR), Perceived value (PEV) and Hedonic Motivation (HM). The dependent variable of Consumer Loyalty (Loyalty Intentions, LI) was measured by five indicators. To assess internal consistency, Cronbach's alpha was calculated: the values were greater than 0.7 indicating internal consistency [62].

To confirm convergent validity, AVE and outer loadings were calculated. AVE values were greater than 0.5 and the outer loadings were greater than 0.7 [64].

In order to assess discriminant validity, Fornell-Larcker criterion was used [62]. The square root of each construct's AVE was greater than its highest correlation with any other construct [62]. Table 3 shows that the criterion was established.

**Table 3.** Fornell-Larcker criterion

|      | SYS    | EFF    | FUL    | HM     | LI     | PPR    | PEV    |
|------|--------|--------|--------|--------|--------|--------|--------|
| SYS  | **0.888** |        |        |        |        |        |        |
| EFF  | 0.315  | **0.765** |        |        |        |        |        |
| FUL  | 0.222  | 0.300  | **0.827** |        |        |        |        |
| HM   | 0.264  | 0.522  | 0.320  | **0.904** |        |        |        |
| LOY  | 0.064  | 0.533  | 0.191  | 0.515  | **0.793** |        |        |
| PPR  | −0.230 | −0.110 | −0.090 | −0.108 | −0.061 | **0.899** |        |
| PEV  | 0.277  | 0.303  | 0.128  | 0.253  | 0.237  | −0.193 | **0.831** |

A second discriminant test is the heterotrait-monotrait ratio (HTMT), which is a measure of similarity between variables. This test is more sensitive than Fornell-Larcker [65]. HTMT is the ratio of the between-trait correlations to the within-trait correlations and discriminant validity is established if all values are less than 0.85 [62]. In this study, all values were less than 0.85, thereby confirming discriminant validity. See Table 4.

**Table 4.** HTMT Ratio

|      | SYS   | EFF   | FUL   | HM    | LI    | PPR   | PEV |
|------|-------|-------|-------|-------|-------|-------|-----|
| SYS  |       |       |       |       |       |       |     |
| EFF  | 0.413 |       |       |       |       |       |     |
| FUL  | 0.281 | 0.381 |       |       |       |       |     |
| HM   | 0.326 | 0.594 | 0.369 |       |       |       |     |
| LI   | 0.101 | 0.618 | 0.217 | 0.601 |       |       |     |
| PPR  | 0.266 | 0.127 | 0.148 | 0.117 | 0.076 |       |     |
| PEV  | 0.377 | 0.313 | 0.182 | 0.287 | 0.250 | 0.218 |     |

## 4.2  The Structural Model

The analysis of the structural model included calculation of the path coefficients, followed by bootstrapping with 5000 sub-groups to find the significance of the paths. The coefficient of determination ($R^2$) represents the percent of variance explained from the independent variables [66]. The $R^2$ was 0.388 and the results (see Table 5) suggest that Efficiency and Hedonic Motivation constructs had a significant impact on loyalty.

**Table 5.** Path coefficients

| | Whole Population | | | Females | | |
|---|---|---|---|---|---|---|
| | Path coeff | T statistic | P Values | Path coeff | T statistic | P Values |
| EFF -> LI | 0.386 | 4.781 | 0*** | 0.385 | 4.667 | 0*** |
| FUL -> LI | −0.007 | 0.088 | 0.929 | −0.016 | 0.165 | 0.869 |
| AVA -> LI | −0.170 | 1.817 | 0.062 | − 0.095 | 1.059 | 0.290 |
| PPR -> LI | −0.006 | 0.081 | 0.936 | − 0.038 | 0.448 | 0.654 |
| PEV -> LI | 0.081 | 1.076 | 0.285 | 0.145 | 1.536 | 0.125 |
| HM -> LI | 0.340 | 4.754 | 0*** | 0.342 | 4.580 | 0*** |
| R squared | 0.388 | | | 0.444 | | |
| Sample size | 160 | | | 106 | | |

***$p < 0.001$

### 4.3 Summary of Results

Table 6 is a summary of results. Efficiency and Hedonic Motivation have a significant impact on consumers' loyalty intentions.

**Table 6.** Summary of results

| Hypothesis | Path | Result |
|---|---|---|
| H1 | EFF -> LI | ✓ |
| H2 | FUL -> LI | Not Supported |
| H3 | AVA -> LI | Not Supported |
| H4 | PPR -> LI | Not Supported |
| H5 | PEV -> LI | Not Supported |
| H6 | HM -> LI | ✓ |

## 5   Discussion

This study provides an understanding of the factors that influence consumer loyalty. This research was quantitative and used a non-experimental survey approach. From a survey of 251 participants, the results indicate that the current AR beauty apps are most influenced by Efficiency (EFF) and Hedonic Motivation (HM). Constructs like Perceived Privacy Risks (PPR), Perceived Value (PEV), Fulfilment (FUL) and System Availability (SYS) did not have a significant influence on consumers Loyalty Intentions.

Efficiency and Hedonic Motivation are the two factors that have a positive and direct impact on consumer's loyalty intentions in AR apps. The results are consistent with the findings from prior studies. AR apps unique attributes are likely to enhance the practical usefulness and enjoyment of the consumer's shopping experience [67]. Researchers also believe that using technology quickly has a considerable effect on brand interaction with its mobile apps through the AR features. The usefulness of the technology, with the novelty, interactivity and the sharpness of the AR features', increases consumers' commitment to the brand [68]. Prior studies have also suggested that utilitarian benefits in the form of perceived usefulness drive brand satisfaction [69]. Efficiency is explored as a utilitarian motivator for mobile shopping retail apps [28]. Chen et al. [70] found that both utilitarian and hedonic benefits, based on perceived usefulness and perceived enjoyment, positively impacted app loyalty.

Perceived Privacy risks (H4) did not have a significant impact on loyalty intentions. This may be because consumers' share their personal details on various social media platforms and hence they are less concerned about privacy data being misused. Also, consumers may place their trust in Sephora, which is a well know brand with a clear privacy policy, stating that information collected is private [71].

Perceived Value (H5) was not significant. In this survey, around 66.88% of participants were first time Sephora users, which means they had to download the app for this study. It might be the case that they will not use the app again in the near future and hence they do not perceive a value in the app.

### 5.1 Theoretical Contribution

This study contributes to the existing knowledge of consumer loyalty in retail. The ES-QUAL model is extended with two constructs, Perceived Value and Hedonic Motivation. The model is robust and can be applied to mobile apps in general and to AR apps in particular.

### 5.2 Implication for Practitioners

This study provides an insight for AR-app developers and supports the fact that a retail shopping app should be fun, efficient and entertaining. Along with that, it should be easy to use and well organized. Online marketers and app developers should keep up with advancing technologies to provide consumers with efficient, fast and more convenient features. A study done by Google in 2016 shows that we live in a mobile-first world, with an average of three hours per day spent on smartphones [72]. Online marketers and app developers should therefore develop an easy and well-organized smartphone interface. Human beings are social creatures; they need to talk, share, discuss and interact with each other. AR games such as Pokémon Go have shown emotional, hedonic and social benefits as factors that impact consumer attitude [15, 73]. Since both utilitarian and hedonic factors had significant impact on consumer loyalty, practitioners should aim for higher levels of engagement and enjoyment which will lead to increased consumer loyalty.

### 5.3  Limitations and Future Research

As with any study, this study has several limitations. First and foremost, this study was limited to one particular AR beauty app, Sephora. Apart from the beauty industry, various other retail sectors like clothing, furniture, and apparel have AR-enabled technology advancement, but our results may not be transferable. This study followed a non-experimental design approach and the majority of participants were undergraduate students. A further limitation was that only opinions about loyalty intentions were collected rather than observation of actual purchases. This study was conducted in Toronto, Canada and did not include any other regions. There was an unequal distribution of males and females, with differences between males and females could not be analyzed due to an insufficient number of males.

Future research could follow a longitudinal approach. This will help in understanding the actual usage of AR apps in day-to-day life. Taking an inductive study approach might identify some constructs that would otherwise be unnoticed in a survey-based study. Online shoppers have surged in the year 2020 and comparative studies using technology acceptance models to access significant differences between online and offline channels usage intentions could be another area to explore. This model can also be further extended to study Purchase Intention with the general population.

## 6  Conclusion

The beauty industry started taking advantage of the AR technology to boost sales of digital platforms and gain an edge over competitors. During the Covid-19 pandemic, the beauty brands had a huge setback mainly for two reasons: first, the physical stores were closed with lifestyle changing to work from home; and, second, there is less need to wear make-up when half the face is covered with masks [74]. This was the unfortunate timing when most of the beauty brands upgraded their Virtual Try-on experience to give consumers an online experience of various make-up products.

This study used a widely tested and robust research model developed primarily for website service quality. The model was extended with Perceived Value and Hedonic Motivation. This approach is applicable for understanding service quality in the mobile apps domain. Future research can be extended to various other retail industry sectors. Efficiency (EFF) and Hedonic Motivation (HM) are the two constructs that significantly influenced consumers' Loyalty Intentions. Thus fun, play, enjoyment, ease of navigation, well organized and pleasing visual appeal are valued aspects of user experience for a beauty app. Olsson et al. [54] and Scholz & Duffy [15] found similar results: intrinsic benefits like entertaining and app efficiency were valued more than the extrinsic benefit of shopping efficiency.

## References

1. Wells, J.D., Valacich, J.S., Hess, T.J.: What signal are you sending? How website quality influences perceptions of product quality and purchase intentions. MIS Q. **35**(2), 373–396 (2011)

2. Mordor Intelligence: Retail industry - growth, trends (2019). https://www.mordorintellige nce.com/industry-reports/retail-industry
3. Szymanski, D.M., Hise, R.T.: E-satisfaction: an initial examination. J. Retail. **76**(3), 309–322 (2000)
4. Statista: Sales of retail trade in Canada from 2012 to 2019 (in billion Canadian dollars) (2019). https://www-statista-com.ezproxy.lib.ryerson.ca/statistics/431661/sales-of-ret ail-trade-in-canada/
5. Azuma, R., et al.: Recent advances in augmented reality. IEEE Comput. Graph. Appl. **21**(6), 34–47 (2001)
6. Pantano, E.: Innovation drivers in retail industry. Int. J. Inf. Manag. **34**(3), 344–350 (2014)
7. Smink, A.R., et al.: Try online before you buy: How does shopping with augmented reality affect brand responses and personal data disclosure. Electron. Commer. Res. Appl. **35**, 100854 (2019)
8. Kumar, S.: Exploratory analysis of global cosmetic industry: major players, technology and market trends. Technovation **25**(11), 1263–1272 (2005)
9. Saettler, M.: Sephora augmented reality mirror reflects sales potential of digital sampling. https://www.retaildive.com/ex/mobilecommercedaily/sephora-reflects-on-cos metic-sampling-trend-with-augmented-reality-mirror. Accessed 25 Dec 2020
10. Baek, T.H., Yoo, C.Y., Yoon, S.: Augment yourself through virtual mirror: the impact of self-viewing and narcissism on consumer responses. Int. J. Advert. **37**(3), 421–439 (2018)
11. Scholz, J., Smith, A.N.: Augmented reality: designing immersive experiences that maximize consumer engagement. Bus. Horiz. **59**(2), 149–161 (2016)
12. Hilken, T., de Ruyter, K., Chylinski, M., Mahr, D., Keeling, D.I.: Augmenting the eye of the beholder: exploring the strategic potential of augmented reality to enhance online service experiences. J. Acad. Mark. Sci. **45**(6), 884–905 (2017). https://doi.org/10.1007/s11747-017-0541-x
13. Hofmann, S., Mosemghvdlishvili, L.: Perceiving spaces through digital augmentation: an exploratory study of navigational augmented reality apps. Mob. Media Commun. **2**(3), 265–280 (2014)
14. Rese, A., et al.: How augmented reality apps are accepted by consumers: a comparative analysis using scales and opinions. Technol. Forecast. Soc. Chang. **124**, 306–319 (2017)
15. Scholz, J., Duffy, K.: We are at home: how augmented reality reshapes mobile marketing and consumer-brand relationships. J. Retail. Consum. Serv. **44**, 11–23 (2018)
16. Rayome, D.A.: How Sephora is leveraging AR and AI to transform retail and help customers buy cosmetics (2018). https://www.techrepublic.com/article/how-sephora-is-leveraging-ar-and-ai-to-transform-retail-and-help-customers-buy-cosmetics/. Accessed 15 Feb 2018
17. Milnes, H.: Makeup brands are testing augmented reality to drive conversions (2016). https:// digiday.com/marketing/makeup-brands-testing-augmented-reality-drive-conversions/
18. Parasuraman, A., Zeithaml, V.A., Berry, L.L.: SERVQUAL: a multiple-item scale for measuring consumer perceptions of service quality. J. Retail. **64**(1), 12 (1988)
19. Parasuraman, A., Berry, L.L., Zeithaml, V.A.: Understanding customer expectations of service. Sloan Manag. Rev. **32**(3), 39–48 (1991)
20. Gaur, S.S., Agrawal, R.: Service quality measurement in retail store context: a review of advances made using SERVQUAL and RSQS. Mark. Rev. **6**(4), 317–330 (2006)
21. Chaturvedi, R.K.: Mapping service quality in hospitality industry: a case through SERVQUAL. Asian J. Manag. **8**(3), 413 (2017)
22. Kuan, H.-H., Bock, G.-W., Vathanophas, V.: Comparing the effects of website quality on customer initial purchase and continued purchase at e-commerce websites. Behav. Inf. Technol. **27**(1), 3–16 (2008)
23. Zeithaml, V.A., Parasuraman, A., Malhotra, A.: Service quality delivery through web sites: a critical review of extant knowledge. J. Acad. Mark. Sci. **30**(4), 362–375 (2002)

24. Lee, T.: The impact of perceptions of interactivity on customer trust and transaction intentions in mobile commerce. J. Electron. Commer. Res. **6**(3), 165 (2005)
25. Parasuraman, A., Zeithaml, V.A., Malhotra, A.: ES-QUAL: a multiple-item scale for assessing electronic service quality. J. Serv. Res. **7**(3), 213–233 (2005)
26. Kuo, T., et al.: Relationships among service quality, customer satisfaction and customer loyalty: a case study on mobile shopping apps. In: Proceedings, The 17th Asia Pacific Industrial Engineering and Management System Conference (2016)
27. Ranganathan, C., Ganapathy, S.: Key dimensions of business-to-consumer web sites. Inf. Manag. **39**(6), 457–465 (2002)
28. Parker, C., Wang, H.: Examining hedonic and utilitarian motivations for m-commerce fashion retail app engagement. J. Fashion Mark. Manag. Int. J. **20**(4), 487–506 (2016)
29. Yang, K., Kim, H.-Y.: Mobile shopping motivation: an application of multiple discriminant analysis. Int. J. Retail Distrib. Manag. **40**(10), 778–789 (2012)
30. Newman, C., Wachter, K., White, A.: Bricks or clicks? Understanding consumer usage of retail mobile apps. J. Serv. Mark. **32**(2), 211–222 (2018)
31. Lee, W., Benbasat, I.: Designing an electronic commerce interface: attention and product memory as elicited by web design. Electron. Commer. Res. Appl. **2**(3), 240–253 (2003)
32. Herington, C., Weaven, S.: Can banks improve customer relationships with high quality online services? Manag. Serv. Qual. Int. J. **17**(4), 404–427 (2007)
33. De Koster, R.B.: Distribution strategies for online retailers. IEEE Trans. Eng. Manag. **50**(4), 448–457 (2003)
34. Grewal, D., Iyer, G.R., Levy, M.: Internet retailing: enablers, limiters and market consequences. J. Bus. Res. **57**(7), 703–713 (2004)
35. Chung, K.C.: Mobile (shopping) commerce intention in central Asia: The impact of culture, innovation characteristics and concerns about order fulfilment. Asia-Pacific J. Bus. Adm. **11**, 251–266 (2019)
36. Santos, J.: E-service quality: a model of virtual service quality dimensions. Manag. Serv. Qual. Int. J. **13**(3), 233–246 (2003)
37. Knote, R., Söllner, M.: Towards design excellence for context-aware services-the case of mobile navigation apps (2017)
38. Dinev, T., Hart, P.: An extended privacy calculus model for e-commerce transactions. Inf. Syst. Res. **17**(1), 61–80 (2006)
39. Yang, K., Forney, J.C.: The moderating role of consumer technology anxiety in mobile shopping adoption: differential effects of facilitating conditions and social influences. J. Electron. Commer. Res. **14**(4), 334 (2013)
40. Slade, E., et al.: Exploring consumer adoption of proximity mobile payments. J. Strateg. Mark. **23**(3), 209–223 (2015)
41. Huang, N., Qin, G.: A study of online virtual fitting room adoption based on UTAUT. In: 2011 International Conference on E-Business and E-Government (ICEE). IEEE (2011)
42. Zhou, T.: Examining location-based services usage form the perspective of unified theory of acceptance and use of technology and privacy risks. J. Electron. Commer. Res. **13**(2), 135–144 (2012)
43. Keeney, R.L.: The value of Internet commerce to the customer. Manag. Sci. **45**(4), 533–542 (1999)
44. Chang, H.H., Wang, H.W.: The moderating effect of customer perceived value on online shopping behaviour. Online Inf. Rev. **35**(3), 333–359 (2011)
45. Zhou, T.: The impact of privacy concern on user adoption of location-based services. Ind. Manag. Data Syst. **111**(2), 212–226 (2011)
46. Joseph Cronin, J., Brady, M., Tomas, G., Hult, M.: Assessing the effects of quality, value, and customer satisfaction on consumer behavioral intentions in service environments. J. Retail. **76**(2), 193–218 (2000)

47. Kim, Y.H., Kim, D.J., Wachter, K.: A study of mobile user engagement (MoEN): engagement motivations, perceived value, satisfaction, and continued engagement intention. Decis. Supp. Syst. **56**, 361–370 (2013)
48. Dovaliene, A., Masiulyte, A., Piligrimiene, Z.: The relations between customer engagement, perceived value and satisfaction: the case of mobile applications. Procedia Soc. Behav. Sci. **213**, 659–664 (2015)
49. Venkatesh, V., Thong, J., Xu, X.: Consumer acceptance and use of information technology: extending the unified theory of acceptance and use of technology. MIS Q. **36**(1), 157–178 (2012)
50. Carpenter, J., Moore, M., Fairhurst, A.: Consumer shopping value for retail brands. J. Fashion Mark. Manag. Int. J. **9**(1), 43–53 (2005)
51. Childers, T.L., et al.: Hedonic and utilitarian motivations for online retail shopping behavior. J. Retail. **77**(4), 511–535 (2001)
52. Hsiao, C.-H., Chang, J.-J., Tang, K.-Y.: Exploring the influential factors in continuance usage of mobile social apps: satisfaction, habit, and customer value perspectives. Telematics Inform. **33**(2), 342–355 (2016)
53. Rauschnabel, P.A., Felix, R., Hinsch, C.: Augmented reality marketing: how mobile AR-apps can improve brands through inspiration. J. Retail. Consum. Serv. **49**, 43–53 (2019)
54. Olsson, T., et al.: Expected user experience of mobile augmented reality services: a user study in the context of shopping centres. Pers. Ubiquit. Comput. **17**(2), 287–304 (2013)
55. Srinivasan, S.S., Anderson, R., Ponnavolu, K.: Customer loyalty in e-commerce: an exploration of its antecedents and consequences. J. Retail. **78**(1), 41–50 (2002)
56. Collier, J.E., Bienstock, C.C.: Measuring service quality in e-retailing. J. Serv. Res. **8**(3), 260–275 (2006)
57. Reichheld, F.F., Teal, T.: The loyalty Effect: The Hidden Force Behind Growth, Profits, and Lasting Value. Harvard Business School Press, Boston (1996)
58. Gommans, M., Krishman, K.S., Scheffold, K.B.: From brand loyalty to e-loyalty: a conceptual framework. J. Econ. Soc. Res. **3**(1), 43–58 (2001)
59. Yang, Y., et al.: Understanding perceived risks in mobile payment acceptance. Ind. Manag. Data Syst. **115**(2), 253–269 (2015)
60. Shaw, N., Sergueeva, K.: Convenient or useful? Consumer adoption of smartphones for mobile commerce. In: 26th Annual DIGIT Workshop, Dublin, Ireland (2016)
61. Martins, C., Oliveira, T., Popovič, A.: Understanding the Internet banking adoption: a unified theory of acceptance and use of technology and perceived risk application. Int. J. Inf. Manag. **34**(1), 1–13 (2014)
62. Hair, J.F., et al.: A Primer on Partial Least Squares Structural Equation Modeling (PLS-SEM). Sage Publications, Thousand Oaks (2016)
63. Ringle, C.M., Wende, S., Becker, J.-M.: SmartPLS3 (2015). Bönningstedt: SmartPLS. http://www.smartpls.com
64. Henseler, J., Ringle, C.M., Sinkovics, R.R.: The use of partial least squares path modeling in international marketing. Adv. Int. Mark. **20**, 277–319 (2009)
65. Henseler, J., Ringle, C.M., Sarstedt, M.: A new criterion for assessing discriminant validity in variance-based structural equation modeling. J. Acad. Mark. Sci. **43**(1), 115–135 (2014). https://doi.org/10.1007/s11747-014-0403-8
66. Hair, J.F.: Multivariate data analysis. 6th ed, vol. xxiv, 899 p. Pearson Prentice Hall, Upper Saddle River (2006)
67. Park, M., Yoo, J.: Effects of perceived interactivity of augmented reality on consumer responses: a mental imagery perspective. J. Retail. Consum. Serv. **52**, 101912 (2020)
68. McLean, G., Wilson, A.: Shopping in the digital world: examining customer engagement through augmented reality mobile applications. Comput. Hum. Behav. **101**, 210–224 (2019)

69. Li, C.-Y., Fang, Y.-H.: Predicting continuance intention toward mobile branded apps through satisfaction and attachment. Telematics Inform. **43**, 101248 (2019)
70. Chen, C.-C., Hsiao, K.-L., Li, W.-C.: Exploring the determinants of usage continuance willingness for location-based apps: a case study of bicycle-based exercise apps. J. Retail. Consum. Serv. **55**, 102097 (2020)
71. SephoraUSA: Sephora's Privacy Policy (2021). https://www.sephora.com/ca/en/beauty/privacy-policy. Accessed 8 Jan 2021
72. Google: How People Use Their Devices (2016)
73. Rauschnabel, P.A.: Virtually enhancing the real world with holograms: an exploration of expected gratifications of using augmented reality smart glasses. Psychol. Mark. **35**(8), 557–572 (2018)
74. Perez, S.: Google now lets you virtually try on makeup using AR, shop from influencer videos (2020). https://techcrunch.com/2020/12/17/google-now-lets-you-virtually-try-on-makeup-using-ar-shop-from-influencer-videos/. Accessed 17 Dec 2020

# Application of User Research in E-commerce App Design

Cong Mu(✉)

East China University of Science and Technology, Shanghai 200237, People's Republic of China

**Abstract.** With the rise of online sales platform, e-commerce App has swept the sales market in the 21st century, and impacted the offline sales of many physical stores to a great extent. Combined with the current economic factors, the real economy that New Coronavirus has caused has become increasingly sluggish, and the online economy may usher in some new development opportunities on the existing basis. Therefore, in this market background, e-commerce economy has a good momentum of development, and the competition of e-commerce app is becoming more and more fierce. More and more enterprises will focus on considering users' habits and preferences when using products in the design and development process, positioning the use logic of their app products based on users' needs, designing the visual and interactive framework of product interface and other important functions of APP products Constituent elements.

This paper aims to explore the position of user needs in the design of e-commerce app, how to carry out the research of user needs, and how to apply user research results in the design process of e-commerce app. How to really consider the user needs in the design of e-commerce app and apply the importance of user needs in the design. In this paper, the research method of user needs is Kano model user needs research method, and the specific application of user research in the process of pinduoduo App Design and development is analyzed. Kano model, invented by Noriaki Kano, a professor of Tokyo Polytechnic University, is a useful tool for classifying and prioritizing user requirements. Based on the analysis of the impact of user requirements on user satisfaction, it reflects the nonlinear relationship between product performance and user satisfaction. It divides the demand characteristics of products and services into five categories: (1) Basic Quality, (2) Performance Quality, (3) Attractive Quality, (4) Neutral Quality, (5) Reverse Quality. This paper uses Kano model to study the nonlinear relationship between product performance and user satisfaction, takes the importance of user demand as the iterative basis for the design of e-commerce app, demonstrates the competitive advantage of user demand research for the design of e-commerce app, and discusses the role and significance of user research in the design of e-commerce app from the whole product operation level.

**Keywords:** User research · E-commerce app · KANO model · Interaction design

© Springer Nature Switzerland AG 2021
F. F.-H. Nah and K. Siau (Eds.): HCII 2021, LNCS 12783, pp. 120–130, 2021.
https://doi.org/10.1007/978-3-030-77750-0_8

# 1    Overview of E-commerce App Design

## 1.1    E-commerce App

E-commerce, refers to the electronic transaction activities and related service activities on the Internet, intranet and value-added network, which makes the traditional business activities Electronic and networked. China's e-commerce started in the 1990s. In March 1998, China's first Internet transaction was successful. From 2000 to 2009, e-commerce gradually took B2B as the main body of traditional industry, marking that e-commerce has entered a stable period of sustainable development [1].

With the vigorous development of e-commerce, e-commerce app has entered thousands of households with smart phones. As an enterprise product, it directly faces and serves users. E-commerce app is more used as a consumer platform between users and enterprises. Through this shopping platform, enterprises can build a user-friendly consumption system, and users can meet their shopping needs through online transactions through app.

E-commerce app is mainly divided into comprehensive category, vertical domain category and social group category. Taobao and Jingdong belong to comprehensive e-commerce mall app. Businesses can enter the app platform and sell a variety of goods, and users can quickly find the products they want on the app. Vertical field mainly refers to focusing on a certain vertical field, such as maternal and infant e-commerce app, pet e-commerce app, new energy automobile mall app, etc. Attracting users by providing more detailed and professional services in a certain vertical field. Pinduoduo belongs to the last category of social e-commerce. It mainly encourages users to share and spread through the functions of distribution, and makes commission through promotion. In three years, its market value reaches 100 billion, surpassing that of Jingdong.

## 1.2    Current Situation of E-commerce App Design

With the development of different operating systems of smart phones, the design of e-commerce app has derived many design styles. Generally, it needs to comply with the design specifications of IOS system and Android system, and the design style has changed from the initial three-dimensional to flat and extremely simplified. In terms of color matching, it is best to use brand color to match various festivals or promotional activities to attract users' attention. The purpose of design.

The advantage of this design trend is that it can attract users' attention, create a lively atmosphere for shopping, and stimulate users' consumption. On the other hand, there are a series of use problems based on this kind of design status, such as redundant visual experience caused by too many design elements, inappropriate interaction and UI design caused by not deep mining of user needs, increased misuse rate in the process of user use, and reduced user experience. Therefore, the research on user needs has always been one of the most important links in the design of e-commerce app. Through user research, the user needs are sorted according to certain rules, and the requirements are arranged from high to low frequency. Based on the sorting results, the design framework of app is summarized in the design, and the function distribution of the first, second and third level interface of app is sorted out, so as to make the product more meet the needs of users and the use logic more clear.

## 2  Research and Analysis Methods of User Requirements

### 2.1  User Demand Research

If e-commerce products want to achieve the expected effect, they must meet the needs of users as much as possible. In order to design products that meet the needs of users, it is necessary to integrate the user needs research into the whole design. User needs research refers to some research methods, such as questionnaire survey, interview, card classification, focus group interview, etc. to investigate users, so as to get their actual needs and use feedback for the product [2].

### 2.2  Analysis of User Demand

User needs analysis refers to the analysis and classification of user needs obtained from user research. Because the same level of requirements can not be divided into priority or important levels, these requirements can not be directly applied to the design. In order to digitize user needs and make them more convenient and intuitive for comparison and analysis, it is necessary to choose appropriate needs analysis methods, such as Maslow hierarchy needs theory, Kano model, censydiam user motivation analysis model and Boston matrix.

The specific contents of Maslow's hierarchical needs theory are: physiological needs, security needs, social needs, respect needs, cognitive needs, aesthetic needs and self realization needs. This theory helps to grasp the needs of users from a macro level and the user needs that the product itself may meet, such as physical needs, such as shopping, takeaway products, etc. most of the APP providers first meet these needs; security needs such as financial products, Alipay, and social needs such as social networking products, WeChat, unfamiliar street, etc. This Maslow's different levels of requirements are not suitable for user research scenarios of e-commerce App Design.

Kano model is not a quantitative tool to directly measure user satisfaction, but to distinguish the different needs of users. According to the principle of Kano model, it can help us to understand the needs of different levels of users to the greatest extent. It is a crucial entry point to identify user needs and design product functions. Through in-depth understanding of users and active control of products, we can comprehensively improve the user experience of products. In the design of e-commerce app, users' needs can be classified by Kano model, so as to optimize the interfaces of different levels of products and sort out the framework structure of the whole product.

Censydiam user motivation analysis model is mainly used to study the motivation behind user behavior, attitude or goal. The basic logic of the model is: the needs of users exist in both social and individual levels. In the face of different levels of needs, users will have different demand solving strategies. By studying the demand coping strategies adopted by users, we can see the intrinsic motivation of users. Boston matrix thinks that there are two basic factors that generally determine the product structure: market attraction and enterprise strength. Through the interaction of the above two factors, there will be four different types of products: Star products, thin dog products, problem products and Taurus products, forming different product development prospects. Therefore,

Boston matrix is suitable for analyzing the market Analysis of market management trend and enterprise investment direction.

The application scenarios of the above four requirements analysis methods are shown in Table 1.

**Table 1.** Applicable scenarios of requirement analysis method

| Analysis method | Applicable scenarios | Select or not |
|---|---|---|
| Maslow's hierarchy demand theory | It's suitable for the demand analysis of different products | No |
| Kano Model | Multiple requirements analysis for the same product | Yes |
| Censydiam user motivation analysis model | It's more suitable for the analysis of user needs in the process of brand building | No |
| Boston matrix | Market operation trend analysis for different products | No |

Through the discussion of the above four methods and the analysis of Table 1, this paper will select Kano model for the corresponding experimental user needs analysis.

## 3 User Demand Analysis of E-commerce App Based on Kano Model

### 3.1 Attributes of User Requirement

According to the relationship between user requirements and product quality characteristics, in order to identify different levels of user requirements, Kano model divides user requirements attributes into five categories:

(1) Basic quality: the attribute that the user thinks the product must have. When meeting this requirement, it will not significantly improve the user's satisfaction. However, if this demand is not met, user satisfaction will be greatly reduced. (2) Performance quality: also known as the itch and pain point of user needs, user satisfaction is positively correlated with the optimization degree of such needs. (3) Attractive quality: it is a demand that will not be over expected by users. Once such demand is met, it will dramatically improve user satisfaction and bring surprise to users. If it is missing, it will not reduce user satisfaction. (4) Neutral quality: no matter whether this requirement is provided or not, it will not affect the user experience or interfere with the user satisfaction. (5) Reverse quality: a requirement attribute that can cause users' strong dissatisfaction will reduce users' satisfaction; when it does not have such a requirement attribute, it will increase users' satisfaction [3].

The non-linear relationship between user demand and user satisfaction of Kano model is shown in Fig. 1.

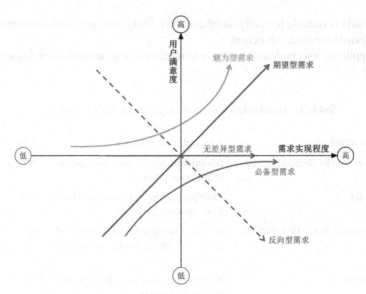

**Fig. 1.** Kano model

## 3.2 Target Population and Demand Extraction

In order to make the survey more targeted, this paper focuses on the target group of 18–55 years old with online shopping needs, uses the user interview method and on-site observation method to obtain the explicit and implicit needs of users, transforms the original description of users into clear user needs, and selects and refines 20 main functional demand points of pinduoduo, Taobao and Jingdong e-commerce app. Finally, the demand elements are integrated according to the functional types, which are divided into shopping, social, entertainment and other four categories and numbered, as shown in Table 2.

**Table 2.** Users' functional requirements for e-commerce app

| Demand classification | Demand |
|---|---|
| Shopping | 1. Popular new products |
| | 2. Clothing accessories |
| | 3. Food products |
| | 4. Cosmetics |
| | 5. Electrical products |
| | 6. Pharmaceutical products |

*(continued)*

**Table 2.** (*continued*)

| Demand classification | Demand |
|---|---|
| | 7. Household products |
| Social contact | 8. Add friends |
| | 9. Recommend friends |
| | 10. Share with friends (via app, wechat, etc.) |
| | 11. Help pay |
| | 12. Bargaining (Pinduoduo bargaining function) |
| Entertainment | 13. Shopping Carnival |
| | 14. Cloud pets |
| Other | 15. With search function |
| | 16. Personalized recommendation |
| | 17. Watch the live broadcast of products with goods |
| | 18. Can be added to my shopping cart |
| | 19. Can be added to my favorites |
| | 20. There are customer service feedback channels |

### 3.3  Making Kano Questionnaire

Firstly, according to the 20 user demand points in Table 2, the Kano questionnaire is made. 100 e-commerce app users aged 18–55 were investigated. Each functional attribute in Kano questionnaire is set with two positive and negative questions to measure the attitude of users when they have or don't have a certain functional attribute. The answers are five level options, namely "like", "it should be", "indifferent", "can stand it" and "dislike", as shown in Table 3,

**Table 3.** Kano questionnaire topic setting mode

| Question | Like | It should be | indifferent | can stand it | Dislike |
|---|---|---|---|---|---|
| If it has the function | O | O | O | O | O |
| If it doesn't have the function | O | O | O | O | O |

100 sample questionnaires were collected and the results were sorted out. The results corresponding to Kano evaluation results are shown in Table 4.

**Table 4.** Comparison of Kano evaluation results

| User demand | | Doesn't have this function | | | | | Remarks |
|---|---|---|---|---|---|---|---|
| | | Like | It should be | indifferent | can stand it | Dislike | |
| | Like | Q | A | A | A | O | M: Basic Quality |
| | It should be | R | I | I | I | M | O: Performance Quality |
| has this function | indifferent | R | I | I | I | M | A: Attractive Quality |
| | can stand it | R | I | I | I | M | I: Neutral Quality |
| | Dislike | R | R | R | R | Q | R: Reverse Quality |

### 3.4 Data Analysis

Firstly, the data obtained from the corresponding evaluation table are summarized, and then the user requirements in Table 1 are classified by the method of "taking the maximum value", that is, the highest quality characteristic corresponding to a certain demand number is regarded as the product function quality characteristic corresponding to the demand. [4]. For example, 88 people think that the search function is a necessary attribute, and the number accounts for the largest proportion, so the search function is a necessary requirement (m). Berger, a foreign scholar, proposed that the importance of the demand can be obtained by calculating the relative satisfaction Si and the relative dissatisfaction Di: [5]

$$Si = \frac{(Ai + Oi)}{(Ai + Oi + Mi + Ii)} \tag{1}$$

$$Di = -1 * \frac{(Mi + Oi)}{(Ai + Oi + Mi + Ii)} \tag{2}$$

According to this method, the questionnaire data are collected, and the demand attribute classification and satisfaction coefficient of various functions of e-commerce app (Table 2) are obtained, as shown in Table 5.

**Table 5.** Functional requirement attribute classification and satisfaction coefficient of e-commerce app

| | Demand | Number | | | | | | Classification | Si | Di |
|---|---|---|---|---|---|---|---|---|---|---|
| | | M | O | A | I | R | Q | | | |
| Shopping | 1 | 16 | 32 | 27 | 12 | 13 | 0 | O | 0.68 | −0.55 |
| | 2 | 73 | 13 | 8 | 6 | 0 | 0 | M | 0.21 | −0.86 |
| | 3 | 78 | 11 | 6 | 5 | 0 | 0 | M | 0.17 | −0.89 |
| | 4 | 66 | 8 | 15 | 10 | 1 | 0 | M | 0.23 | −0.747 |
| | 5 | 60 | 15 | 17 | 8 | 0 | 0 | M | 0.32 | −0.75 |

*(continued)*

**Table 5.** (*continued*)

|  | Demand | Number | | | | | | Classification | Si | Di |
|---|---|---|---|---|---|---|---|---|---|---|
|  |  | M | O | A | I | R | Q |  |  |  |
|  | 6 | 63 | 14 | 18 | 3 | 2 | 0 | M | 0.33 | −0.79 |
|  | 7 | 70 | 15 | 12 | 3 | 0 | 0 | M | 0.27 | −0.85 |
| Social contact | 8 | 30 | 18 | 38 | 12 | 2 | 0 | A | 0.57 | −0.49 |
|  | 9 | 14 | 12 | 16 | 51 | 7 | 0 | I | 0.30 | −0.28 |
|  | 10 | 46 | 19 | 22 | 12 | 1 | 0 | M | 0.41 | −0.66 |
|  | 11 | 22 | 21 | 41 | 10 | 6 | 0 | A | 0.659 | −0.46 |
|  | 12 | 13 | 20 | 36 | 22 | 9 | 0 | A | 0.62 | −0.36 |
| Entertainment | 13 | 12 | 14 | 49 | 21 | 4 | 0 | A | 0.656 | −0.27 |
|  | 14 | 6 | 20 | 14 | 58 | 2 | 0 | I | 0.35 | −0.27 |
| Other | 15 | 88 | 4 | 5 | 3 | 0 | 0 | M | 0.09 | −0.92 |
|  | 16 | 21 | 18 | 47 | 13 | 1 | 0 | A | 0.656 | −0.40 |
|  | 17 | 5 | 58 | 10 | 19 | 8 | 0 | O | 0.74 | −0.68 |
|  | 18 | 72 | 10 | 16 | 2 | 0 | 0 | M | 0.26 | −0.82 |
|  | 19 | 82 | 8 | 4 | 5 | 1 | 0 | M | 0.12 | −0.91 |
|  | 20 | 90 | 7 | 2 | 1 | 0 | 0 | M | 0.09 | −0.97 |

According to the data statistics in Table 5, it can be found that there is no reverse attribute in the 20 user requirements in Table 1. Among them, the recommended friend and cloud pet requirements are undifferentiated attributes. That is to say, whether the two requirements are provided or not, they will not affect the user satisfaction and need to be eliminated because they are not concerned by users. Among them, the requirements of essential attributes, expectation attributes and charm attributes should be met in the design [6].

### 3.5 Kano Model Requirement Analysis

After eliminating the requirements of reverse attributes and indifference attributes, according to Si coefficient and Di coefficient, the demand importance of essential attributes, expectation attributes and charm attributes is ranked.

1. The essential attribute is a characteristic of the product. When the product provides this requirement, the user satisfaction will not be improved. When the product does not provide this requirement, the user satisfaction will be greatly reduced. According to table 5, there are 11 essential attributes in shopping demand, including clothing accessories, food, cosmetics, electrical appliances, medicine and home furnishings; sharing function in social demand and search function, shopping cart, favorites and customer service feedback in other demand. The order of their demand importance

**Table 6.** Essential attribute requirements of e-commerce app

| Demand | Demand classification | Relative dissatisfaction(Di) |
|---|---|---|
| 20. There are customer service feedback channels | Other | −0.97 |
| 15. With search function | Other | −0.92 |
| 19. Can be added to my favorites | Other | −0.91 |
| 3. Food products | Shopping | −0.89 |
| 2. Clothing accessories | Shopping | −0.86 |
| 7. Household products | Shopping | −0.85 |
| 18. Can be added to my shopping cart | Other | −0.82 |
| 6. Pharmaceutical products | Shopping | −0.79 |
| 5. Electrical products | Shopping | −0.75 |
| 4. Cosmetics | Shopping | −0.747 |
| 10. Share with friends (via app, wechat, etc.) | Social contact | −0.66 |

is shown in Table 6, and customer service feedback is the most needed. As these requirements have been fully met and mature in Taobao app, we should continue to provide these requirements in the design. Pinduoduo lacks the function of shopping cart, so we should consider adding this module in the design.

2. Expectation attribute is the quality that users expect the product to have. When the demand is provided, user satisfaction will be improved. When the demand is not provided, user satisfaction will be reduced. According to the survey, there are two demands that belong to the expectation attribute (see Table 7). The highest expectation is that you can watch the live broadcast of the products with goods, followed by the new popular products. Because these two demands in Taobao app have been met, and pinduoduo and Jingdong lack the demand of new popular products, the App Design of new popular products should be given priority.

3. Charm attribute is generally an unexpected demand of users. When the product does not provide this demand, user satisfaction will not decrease. Once the demand is provided, user satisfaction will be greatly improved. According to the survey, five needs belong to the charm attribute (see Table 8), among which the most needed charm attribute is to help friends pay, so the experience needs should be given priority in the charm attribute. Most of the charm attributes are innovative needs, which should be met as much as possible in the design, which can help e-commerce app highlight the differentiation in the market competition and bring surprise to users.

**Table 7.** Expected attribute requirements of e-commerce app

| Demand | Demand classification | Relative satisfaction (Si) |
|---|---|---|
| 17. Watch the live broadcast of products with goods | Other | 0.74 |
| 1. Popular new products | Shopping | 0.68 |

**Table 8.** Charismatic attribute demand of e-commerce app

| Demand | Demand classification | Relative satisfaction (Si) |
|---|---|---|
| 11. Help pay | Social contact | 0.659 |
| 16. Personalized recommendation | Other | 0.656 |
| 13. Shopping Carnival | Entertainment | 0.656 |
| 12.Bargaining (Pinduoduo bargaining function) | Social contact | 0.62 |
| 8. Add friends | Social contact | 0.57 |

## 4   Application of E-commerce App Design

Based on the ranking of the importance of user needs in the design of e-commerce app obtained from the analysis of Kano model, it can be concluded that shopping needs and some types of needs of search and customer service feedback are the essential needs of e-commerce app. E-commerce app can not give up such basic needs in the process of innovative design [7]. If it is given up, user satisfaction will decline rapidly, and the basic needs of users can not be guaranteed.

For some social and entertainment needs, e-commerce app, especially pinduoduo, has sprung up in recent years. It mainly takes advantage of the advantages of multi person cooperative shopping, such as price bargaining and bill making, to obtain discounts, and is welcomed by a large number of users. However, its essential demand is temporarily short of a shopping cart. Although it takes advantage of consumers' rush to buy and stimulate consumers' desire to buy, it is still very popular When consumers shop in bulk and in the shopping carnival, the shopping cart function can well meet the needs of users.

At the same time, some innovative e-commerce app designs, such as charming attribute function, personalized recommendation plate based on user's collection and purchase records, interactive shopping link similar to pinduoduo bargaining, payment function for family and friends, can attract users, so that users can obtain more convenient and comprehensive experience when using this kind of e-commerce app.

## References

1. Lin, Z., Qi, Z.: Difficulties and solutions of e-commerce app economic development from the perspective of Internet green consumption. Econ. Res. Guid. **24**, 118–119 (2020)

2. Chen, C.: User requirements of short video platform under the perspective of use and satisfaction tiktok App as an example. Technol. Commun. **12**(16), 156–157 (2020)
3. Lin, Y.L., Qian, C.: Research on improved design of desk function based on Kano model. Packag. Eng. 1–12 (2021)
4. Lu, C., Xiao, Z., Fu, X.: User experience design of household integrated cooker based on Kano model. Packag. Eng. **41**(20), 91–96 (2020)
5. Tang, Z., Long, Y.: Research on method of acquiring individual demand based on Kano model. Soft Sci. **26**(2), 127–131 (2012)
6. Kano, N.: Attractive quality and must-be quality. J. Jpn. Soc. Qual. Control **41**(2), 39–48 (1984)
7. Xu, Y., Li, Y., Zhu, L.: Research on app user interface design for elderly smart phones based on Kano model. Packag. Eng. **38**(16), 63–167 (2017)

# Social Commerce: The Mediating Effects of Trust and Value Co-creation on Social Sharing and Shopping Intentions

Bo-chiuan Su[1], Li-Wei Wu[2(✉)], and Ju-Ching Hsu[2]

[1] Department of Information Management, National Dong Hwa University, Hualien, Taiwan
bsu@gms.ndhu.edu.tw
[2] Department of International Business, Tunghai University, Taichung, Taiwan
lwwu@thu.edu.tw

**Abstract.** As social media developed rapidly all over the world, online customers tend to seek advices before making purchase decisions. Yet little known is about how social media community members would influence each other and in what ways that lead to social commerce, especially social sharing intention and social shopping intention. This study argues the more social media participation the more consumers' interaction favors of experience sharing, and the better consumer engagement in social shopping. This study proposes the quantitative models and collects data through sending email survey to the social media users, reporting data collected from 286 respondents. Eight of the ten research hypotheses are supported. The results of the analysis of structured equation modeling show that indicate that three social factors, social presence, social support, and social commerce construct, have significantly and positively affected consumers' trust and value co-creation. Furthermore, the results indicate that consumers' cognition, trust, value co-creation have positive impacts on two social commerce intentions, social shopping intention and social sharing intention, referring that cognitive variables have significant mediation effects between social factors and social intention variables. Theoretical and practical implications are provided.

**Keywords:** Social media · Social commerce · Trust · Value co-creation · Social support

## 1 Introduction

### 1.1 Research Background and Motivation

Social commerce was introduced by Yahoo in 2005, and quickly became a means for adding value to commercial services through the use of customer engagement by major web companies, such as Amazon, Groupon and eBay [1]. While IBM also defined social commerce as "the concept of word of mouth marketing applying on e-commerce" [2]. Nowadays, social commerce is mostly selling goods or services through online social platforms. At the same time, because of the elements of social platforms (people

© Springer Nature Switzerland AG 2021
F. F.-H. Nah and K. Siau (Eds.): HCII 2021, LNCS 12783, pp. 131–142, 2021.
https://doi.org/10.1007/978-3-030-77750-0_9

gathering, two-way communication, and information sharing), social e-commerce sales make users feel like trading with "people".

We believe social media have created a new communication paradigm in the marketplace because they enable customers to communicate between themselves and allows business to reach customers [3]. As social media become very easy to access, a tremendous number of customers prefer to use social media as a reliable source for information on products, services, and brands [4]. Therefore, by combining social media with e-commerce, social commerce has emerged as the latest innovation in e-commerce [5].

Social factors, which represent unique characteristics of social commerce, can play important roles in the facilitation of trust [6]. Accordingly, social presence and social support are important social factors considered in this proposal because customers can have a sense of intimacy with each other via supportive interactions [7]. Ellahi and Bokhari [8] have make a point that thanks to the social networking developed techniques, social commerce provides user-generated content functions like reviews, ratings, recommendations, referrals to encourage customers to share personal experiences after use products or services. This study, therefore, will adopt ratings, reviews, recommendations, and referrals as social commerce constructs mainly features that the platform provided.

Therefore, the research objectives will be:

1. To recognize how social presence, social support and social commerce constructs affect consumers trust and value co-creation to a company.
2. To understand how consumers trust and value co-creation to a company will positively affect social shopping intention and social sharing intention.
3. To examine whether consumers trust and value co-creation to a company have mediating effect between antecedents and consequences.

## 2 Literature Review and Hypotheses

### 2.1 Social Presence and Trust

Social presence is defined as the extent to which a medium allows a customer to experience other people as being psychologically present [9]. The concept of social presence is grounded in social presence theory that elaborates the ability of a communication medium to transmit social cues [10]. Research has shown that increased sense of social presence can be achieved by stimulating imagined interaction with other humans or by providing means for actual interaction with other humans [11].

Park and Cameron [12] proposed that levels of social presence increase as interpersonal interactions are perceived in an online context. Social commerce is a combination of commercial and social activities [13]. Social commerce marketplace is not only a transactional space, but also a social presence where social cues, experiences, and previous actions can be observed [14].

Social presence develops through the observation of cues during communication, and the media provide differing levels of social presence [15]. During communication, customers relate to each other and naturally develop trust toward those they communicate with [16]. Essentially, social presence is derived from media capabilities and increases trust in e-commerce contexts [12, 17]. When a social commerce platform has social presence, customers feel more secure and consequently have more confidence in it [18]. Cyr, Hassanein, Head, and Ivanov [19], Gefen and Straub [20], and Hassanein and Head [21] all confirmed the significant, positive relationship between social presence and trust. Thus, it is hypothesized that:

H1: Social presence will have a positive effect on trust.

### 2.2 Social Presence and Value Co-creation

If there is social presence, participants feel that they are communicating with real people, even though the communication is mediated by communication technologies [22]. That of Gunawardena and Zittle [23] expresses the idea clearly and succinctly: the degree to which a person is perceived as "real" in mediated communication. Tools embedded in social media, such as message boxes, icon boxes, audio or video chats, facial expressions, gestures, and other non-verbal prompts, enable participants to bridge distances through instant communication and interaction, evoking people to socialize in social being aware of media.

Because the value of communication is usually established through continuous interaction between the two parties, a high level of social presence may be a prerequisite for individuals to perceive the value co-creation on social commerce. Past research has also confirmed this [21], and value co-creation is an important psychological consequence of social existence. In marketing activities on social media, a higher degree of personal and intimate interaction between participants helps participants to have a more favorable impact on the activity, such as perceived value co-creation. When participants were able to chat, make fun, and play with friends during the event on social commerce, they were more likely to find the event valued. Thus, it is hypothesized that:

H2: Social presence will have a positive effect on value co-creation.

### 2.3 Social Support and Trust

Social support is defined as the social resources that persons perceive to be available or are provided to them in the context of both formal support groups and informal helping relationships [24]. Yan and Tan [25] highlighted two types of social support, informational and emotional, which are considered measures of how customers experience feelings of being cared for, responded to, and facilitated by their social groups.

Yan and Tan [25] defined emotional support from the psychological perspective, the disbursement of empathy, intimacy, encouragement and care belong to emotional support. Hajli [26] confirmed informational support is the provision of advice, guidance, suggestions, or useful information that users could gather from the community member. Since customers are usually intangible in an online environment, social support is considered as the exchange of verbal and nonverbal messages to communicate emotional and informational messages thereby reduce the searcher's stress [27].

When customers obtain valuable information and advice from their social groups, they may be willing to increase interaction frequency and maintain a close relationship with these social groups [25]. They may build trust in these social groups as the information and advice that social groups provide demonstrate the ability and integrity to offer support [28]. Informational support may also enhance confidence because it may help improve customers' understanding of social groups' ideas and form a shared language. Strong social support makes a customer feel connected to friends while building trust toward them. Liang et al. [24] suggested that better social support leads to better relationships, which can strengthen customers' trust. Thus, it is hypothesized that:

H3: Social support will have a positive effect on trust.

### 2.4 Social Support and Value Co-creation

The concept of social support is derived from the theory of social support [29] which was introduced to explain how social relationships affect cognition, emotion and communion behavior [30, 31]. Based on our analysis above, a number of studies have used social support as an antecedent to examine the customer's continued use, participation in and engagement with the social commerce context. Hajli, Shanmugam, Powell, and Love [32] adopted the planned behavior theory to study continuance participation in social commerce online communities.

The determination of the value of customer is a subjective, personal, and free-conscious judgment for the participants. There is a large amount of research has been used to convert customer value into value co-creation, and to define consumer value as the overall evaluation of the utility provided by the users based on the perception of giving and receiving, and the preference experience after interaction [33]. This study believes that consumers who have value co-creation refers to the feelings obtained after participating in the experience, and if the process of participating in the activity is supported by the previous experience or the positive and negative opinions of the outside world and the support of relatives and friends, will it affect the overall feelings of consumers. Thus, it is hypothesized that:

H4: Social support will have a positive effect on value co-creation.

### 2.5 Social Commerce Constructs and Trust

We have acknowledged social commerce constructs provides user-generated content features, such as comments, reviews, ratings, and recommendation list to encourage platform users to share personal experiences after using a product or service [8]. These features enhance user participation and facilitate social interaction [13, 16]. Another study stated that the social business structure includes the following aspects: suggestions and recommendations; ratings and reviews [34]. Ratings and reviews are defined as toolsets provided by social commerce sites that enable customers to exchange product feedback and inform each other in their choices [35].

In general, ratings, reviews, referrals, and recommendations are user-generated content conveying positive or negative information related to sellers and products disseminated and communicated within social commerce [36]. In other words, social commerce constructs are stimuli that online vendors can use to influence customers' affective and cognitive evaluations.

On the other hand, social commerce constructs that produce textual information tend to affect customers' attitudes [26]. When customers browse ratings, reviews, and recommendation systems, they access valuable information resulting from direct or indirect friends on social networking sites and information from friends differs from promotions or persuasive messages from e-commerce. Furthermore, customers regard information from friends as impartial, and thus, customers can easily make trust decisions based on the ratings, reviews, referrals, or recommendations. As a result, customers like to interact in real-time with businesses to ask questions and share their opinion on social commerce. This two-way communication is an important driver of customers' trust [37]. Thus, it is hypothesized that:

H5: Social commerce constructs will have a positive effect on trust.

### 2.6 Social Commerce Constructs and Value Co-creation

Social commerce emphasizes customers' active roles in value co-creation [38]. Knowledge sharing consistently emerge as critical for the success of value co-creation, because they constitute sources of operant resources and enable the integration of operant with operand resources [39]. Social commerce platforms are no longer the channels that simply convey information or sell products and services to customers because they have become the transformed platforms for dialogue and value co-creation between firms and customers [40].

In essence, solicited and unsolicited feedback of customers to the business is one feature of social commerce reflecting the active role of customers [26]. Customers can offer suggestions to businesses to help improve product quality, which is a form of value co-creation [5, 41]. Accordingly, social commerce constructs are a primary antecedent of value co-creation [42, 43]. Thus, it is hypothesized that:

H6: Social commerce constructs will have a positive effect on value co-creation.

### 2.7 Trust and Social Shopping Intention

Trust drives trust-related behaviors in online marketplaces, such as sharing information or making purchases [44]. A trusted social commerce website can also be expected to take steps to reduce buyer risk, such as identifying and removing problematic sellers or taking legal action against fraudulent sellers on behalf of customers [45]. Kim, Ferrin, and Rao [46] verified empirically the effects of trust on customers' purchase intention in online shopping contexts. Therefore, customer trust is considered a predictor of repurchase intention in social commerce [47, 48]. Furthermore, if people trust the marketplace, they will more likely disseminate the features and benefits of the marketplace [49]. Users in s-commerce are generally eager to find out whether or not particular online services are trustworthy prior to any purchase. Thus, it is hypothesized that:

H7: Trust will have a positive effect on social shopping intention.

### 2.8 Trust and Social Sharing Intention

Recent studies have empirically demonstrated the central role of trust in social commerce settings. Trust is an antecedent of purchase intentions and word of mouth intentions over social media [16], and it should be used to interpret social behavior in social commerce research [13]. For example, when a person uses an online forum or social network to find information about a product or a seller, he or she is more likely to trust the information and the medium if a reputable member or a friend has provided that information [50].

Institutional based trust here refers to customers' trust in online shopping in general, it affects their online behavior, and may influence the use of social media as a shopping channel as well. Trusting beliefs describe the beliefs that when customers use social media to purchase, the firms care and are interested about their well-being. These beliefs are influenced by both dispositions to trust and institutional trust, and in turn influence behavioral intentions. Online retailers employ different tools to increase customers' trusting beliefs and sustain a good relationship with them, such as chat plug-ins in their websites or direct support through social network sites. In other words, trust will make customers believe that what others share in the social commerce is of good quality, and therefore they are willing to spread and share information to connected friends. This implies that trust in social commerce also has an influence on social sharing intention [28]. Thus, it is hypothesized that:

H8: Trust will have a positive effect on social sharing intention.

### 2.9    Value Co-creation and Social Shopping Intention

Social commerce businesses should make great efforts to improve the quality of customer value co-creation experience and behaviors, as these can largely improve customer retention and growth in terms of customer commitment, participation, and recommendations in the service [51]. Sawhney, Verona, and Prandelli [52] indicated that purchase intention may be affected by associated service value creation behaviors.

As a result, value co-creation between customers and companies through collaboration can influence the final purchase decisions made by customers. See-To and Ho [53] indicated that co-creation experiences during online purchase positively influences customers' purchase intention. Specifically, in social commerce, customers with high value co-creation have more effective ways to make purchasing decision on the social commerce business [54]. Thus, it is hypothesized that:

H9: Value co-creation will have a positive effect on social shopping intention.

### 2.10    Value Co-creation and Social Sharing Intention

Values are created when customers shift from a passive audience to an active partner working with suppliers [55, 56]. Customers become good value co-creators when they engage in dialogue and interaction with suppliers. The previous study also refers that value perceiving from social commerce provider have significant effects on sharing attitude [57]. After getting value co-creation by interact with brands/enterprises, it motivates customers' willingness to share the information and enlarge the scope that their information can reach.

In other words, social commerce underscores the influence of engaged customers in constructing social context, which promotes iteration and dynamics of service exchanges manifested in continuing value co-creation with social sharing intention. Thus, it is hypothesized that:

H10: Value co-creation will have a positive effect on social sharing intention.

## 3 Research Methodology

### 3.1 Conceptual Framework

This study develops a framework that links social presence, social support, social commerce constructs, trust, value co-creation to social sharing intention and social shopping intentions (Fig. 1). This framework has two main features. First, it examines the direct effects of social presence, social support and social commerce constructs on trust and value co-creation (H1-H6). Second, it examines the direct effects of trust and value co-creation on social sharing and social shopping intentions (H7-H10). These relationships can be summarized in the conceptual framework as shown in the diagram below:

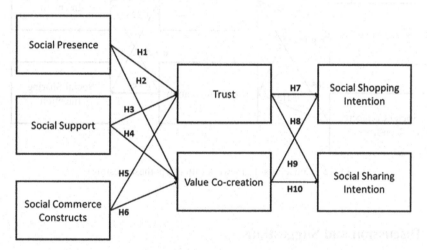

**Fig. 1.** Conceptual framework

### 3.2 Sample and Data Collection

This study conducted survey of social commerce using experience in Taiwan through online survey. The questionnaires are collected from 2020/3/9 to 2020/4/7. In total, 248 were returned in the way of online form. All the returned 248 questionnaires were valid.

## 4   Data Analysis and Empirical Results

### 4.1   Hypotheses Testing

This study adopted AMOS 24 to test 248 valid data and estimates the suitability of theoretical model. To test the construct validity of each scale, a confirmatory factor analysis (CFA) was conducted. The fit statistics of reputation and intention model ($X^2$ = 1001.897; $X^2$/df = 2.973; goodness-of-fix index [GFI] = 0.754; adjusted goodness of fit index [AGFI] = 0.704; comparative fix index [CFI] = 0.959; root mean square error of approximation [RMSEA] = 0.0973) filled the requirements suggested by the literature.Using Amos 24 to test the p-value of the paths in this study, we found all the p-value are smaller than 0.05, it means all the effects are significant, as shown in Fig. 2.

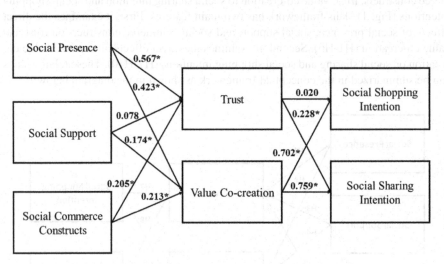

**Fig. 2.**   Conceptual framework (after hypotheses testing)

## 5   Discussion and Suggestions

### 5.1   Discussion and Conclusions

The motivation of this study was targeted on investigating the phenomenon of customer's reaction while using social commerce. Thus, this research examined the antecedents that may influence customer feeling of trust and value co-creation; moreover, discussed whether trust and value co-creation would cause the effect of customer intention of shopping as well as sharing. Extant literature has many studies on this field, but only few have composed them into a whole to probe. Furthermore, previous studies focused on the western countries for their research background, whereas this study focused on the emerging market social commerce environment in Taiwan. Future studiers and practitioners in s-commerce industry could benefit from this study of customer social interaction to adapt values for use no matter in Asian countries around Taiwan.

Analyzing the data collected from online questionnaires, this study found out that social presence, social support and social commerce constructs can positively affect customer's trust and value co-creation (except Hypothesis 3) in social commerce service providers. Moreover, trust and value co-creation influence and strengthen the level of customer agreement which lead them to make decision towards social commerce such as shopping and sharing (except Hypothesis 7) among a group of people.

## 5.2 Managerial Implications

The way of providing service nowadays has changed from the past, the participation of the customers in the service has become more and more frequent and prevalent. Customers are invited to participate in social commerce service procedure together, composing their idea or plan with the service provider, wishing that their astonishing or crazy pop thought would come up into reality someday and had an exceptional outcome.

According to the research results, social presence and social commerce constructs increase customers' trust and value co-creation on social commerce service providers. Which means if you want to win consumers' favorable impression, those are the conditions you need to have. To put it differently, the participation of the customer to join in structuring the business is influenced by the gentle, friendly, and private environment offered by service providers, the warm and endorsing communication with other members from social commerce community, and the self-decorate space consumer could express freely companies gave. By applying and strengthening these two elements for the customers may have great potential to increase the sensibility of trust and value co-creation while employing service process.

Furthermore, as the analysis of this study shows, value co-creation would enhance the level of social shopping intention and social sharing intention, meaning that it may lead to customers' new purchasing and once repurchasing if companies have customers credence value-added. Companies committed on social commerce could focus on this phenomenon in order to increase the customer's contented feelings on the service they received.

The relationships between the customer and provider of service has always been an issue widely discussed, with this above information of this study, social commerce service companies in Taiwan or even around the world can figure out what factors are relatively vital in the service procedures; moreover, discover how to catch on customers' eyes tightly as the marketplace is really competitive. By identifying what aspects in the service might increase customers' participation throughout the whole circulation, the service suppliers would finally develop customer favor to the firm and keep them stay in place.

## 5.3 Limitations and Suggestions for Future Research

This study has some limitations. First of all, the research collected the questionnaires non-randomly when the respondents were predominantly recruited from particular university and most of them went to business school. Second, the customers we met mainly reside in western Taiwan, it represents that there are scarce feedbacks from the eastern regions in Taiwan. Third, the designed questionnaire was delivered to participants throughout the Internet. The respondents who could not understand question item are not able to get real-time explanation while filling out the online survey. Due to the limitations above, the discoveries of this study may not generalize into a completed interpretation of customer sense and intention phenomenon.

For further research, the situation of customer participation in different cultures may be an interesting topic to study on. Distinctive cultures might not be similar to the results of this study, especially for those western countries that have already step ahead in the field of social commerce. Besides, factors that may influence and strengthen the degree of customer sense and intention in service environment among different cultures might be dissimilar.

# References

1. Han, H., Xu, H., Chen, H.: Social commerce: a systematic review and data synthesis. Electron. Commer. Res. Appl. **30**, 38–50 (2018)
2. Turban, E., Strauss, J., Lai, L.: Social Commerce. Prentice Hall, Upper Saddle River (2015)
3. Gatautis, R., Medziausiene, A.: Factors affecting social commerce acceptance in Lithuania. Procedia Soc. Behav. Sci. **110**, 1235–1242 (2014)
4. Zhou, L., Zhang, P., Zimmermann, H.D.: Social commerce research: an integrated view. Electron. Commer. Res. Appl. **12**(2), 61–68 (2013)
5. Huang, Z., Benyoucef, M.: User preferences of social features on social commerce websites: an empirical study. Technol. Forecast. Soc. Change **95**, 57–72 (2015)
6. Ogonowski, A., Montandon, A., Botha, E., Reyneke, M.: Should new online stores invest in social presence elements? The effect of social presence on initial trust formation. J. Retail. Consum. Serv. **21**(4), 482–491 (2014)
7. Qiu, L., Benbasat, I.: Online consumer trust and live help interfaces: the effects of text-to-speech voice and three-dimensional avatars. Int. J. Human-Comput. Interact. **19**(1), 75–94 (2005)
8. Ellahi, A., Bokhari, R.H.: Key quality factors affecting users' perception of social networking websites. J. Retail. Consum. Serv. **20**(1), 120–129 (2013)
9. Fulk, J., Steinfield, C.W., Schmitz, J., Power, J.G.: A social information processing model of media use in organizations. Commun. Res. **14**(5), 529–552 (1987)
10. Lu, B., Fan, W., Zhou, M.: Social presence, trust, and social commerce purchase intention: an empirical research. Comput. Hum. Behav. **56**, 225–237 (2016)
11. Hassanein, K., Head, M., Ju, C.: A cross-cultural comparison of the impact of social presence on website trust, usefulness and enjoyment. Int. J. Electron. Bus. **7**(6), 625–641 (2009)
12. Park, H., Cameron, G.T.: Keeping it real: exploring the roles of conversational human voice and source credibility in crisis communication via blogs. Journal. Mass Commun. Q. **91**(3), 487–507 (2014)
13. Liang, T.P., Turban, E.: Introduction to the special issue social commerce: a research framework for social commerce. Int. J. Electron. Commer. **16**(2), 5–14 (2011)
14. Lu, B., Zeng, Q., Fan, W.: Examining macro-sources of institution-based trust in social commerce marketplaces: an empirical study. Electron. Commer. Res. Appl. **20**, 116–131 (2016)
15. Carlson, J., George, J., Burgoon, J., Adkins, M., White, C.: Deception in computer-mediated communication. Group Decis. Negot. **13**(1), 5–28 (2004). https://doi.org/10.1023/B:GRUP.0000011942.31158.d8

16. Kim, K.J., Park, E., Sundar, S.S.: Caregiving role in human–robot interaction: a study of the mediating effects of perceived benefit and social presence. Comput. Hum. Behav. **29**(4), 1799–1806 (2013)
17. Hess, T.J., Fuller, M., Campbell, D.E.: Designing interfaces with social presence: using vividness and extraversion to create social recommendation agents. J. Assoc. Inf. Syst. **10**(12), 889–919 (2009)
18. Weisberg, J., Te'eni, D., Arman, L.: Past purchase and intention to purchase in e-commerce. Internet Res. **21**(1), 82–96 (2011)
19. Cyr, D., Hassanein, K., Head, M., Ivanov, A.: The role of social presence in establishing loyalty in e-service environments. Interact. Comput. **19**(1), 43–56 (2007)
20. Gefen, D., Straub, D.W.: Consumer trust in B2C e-Commerce and the importance of social presence: experiments in e-Products and e-Services. Omega **32**(6), 407–424 (2004)
21. Hassanein, K., Head, M.: Manipulating perceived social presence through the web interface and its impact on attitude towards online shopping. Int. J. Hum. Comput. Stud. **65**(8), 689–708 (2007)
22. Lombard, M., Ditton, T.: At the heart of it all: the concept of presence. J. Comput.-Mediated Commun. **3**(2), JCMC321 (1997)
23. Gunawardena, C.N., Zittle, F.J.: Social presence as a predictor of satisfaction within a computer-mediated conferencing environment. Am. J. Dist. Educ. **11**(3), 8–26 (1997)
24. Liang, T.P., Ho, Y.T., Li, Y.W., Turban, E.: What drives social commerce: the role of social support and relationship quality. Int. J. Electron. Commer. **16**(2), 69–90 (2011)
25. Yan, L., Tan, Y.: Feeling blue? Go online: an empirical study of social support among patients. Inf. Syst. Res. **25**(4), 690–709 (2014)
26. Hajli, M.N.: The role of social support on relationship quality and social commerce. Technol. Forecast. Soc. Change **87**, 17–27 (2014)
27. Reychav, I., Weisberg, J.: Bridging intention and behavior of knowledge sharing. J. Knowl. Manag. **14**(2), 285–300 (2010)
28. Chen, J., Shen, X.L.: Consumers' decisions in social commerce context: an empirical investigation. Decis. Support Syst. **79**, 55–64 (2015)
29. Lakey, B., Cohen, S.: Social Support and Theory. Social Support Measurement and Intervention: A Guide for Health and Social Scientists, p. 29 (2000)
30. Gottlieb, B.H., Bergen, A.E.: Social support concepts and measures. J. Psychosom. Res. **69**(5), 511–520 (2010)
31. Hajli, N., Lin, X., Featherman, M., Wang, Y.: Social word of mouth: How trust develops in the market. Int. J. Mark. Res. **56**(5), 673–689 (2014)
32. Hajli, N., Shanmugam, M., Powell, P., Love, P.E.: A study on the continuance participation in on-line communities with social commerce perspective. Technol. Forecast. Soc. Change **96**, 232–241 (2015)
33. Holbrook Moris, B.: Customer value-a framework for analysis and research. Adv. Consum. Res. **23**(1), 138–142 (1996)
34. Hajli, N.: Social commerce constructs and consumer's intention to buy. Int. J. Inf. Manag. **35**(2), 183–191 (2014)
35. Kim, S., Park, H.: Effects of various characteristics of social commerce (s-commerce) on consumers' trust and trust performance. Int. J. Inf. Manag. **33**(2), 318–332 (2013)
36. Bansal, H.S., Voyer, P.A.: Word-of-mouth processes within a services purchase decision context. J. Serv. Res. **3**(2), 166–177 (2000)
37. Hollebeek, L.: Exploring customer brand engagement: definition and themes. J. Strateg. Mark. **19**(7), 555–573 (2011)
38. Baghdadi, Y.: A framework for social commerce design. Inf. Syst. **60**, 95–113 (2016)
39. Vargo, S.L., Lush, R.F.: Evolving a services dominant logic. J. Mark. **68**(1), 1–17 (2004)

40. Zhang, M., Guo, L., Hu, M., Liu, W.: Influence of customer engagement with company social networks on stickiness: mediating effect of customer value creation. Int. J. Inf. Manag. **37**(3), 229–240 (2017)

41. Curty, R.G., Zhang, P.: Website features that gave rise to social commerce: a historical analysis. Electron. Commer. Res. Appl. **12**(4), 260–279 (2013)

42. Bolton, R., Saxena-Iyer, S.: Interactive services: a framework, synthesis and research directions. J. Interact. Mark. **23**(1), 91–104 (2009)

43. Gillin, P.: Secrets of social media marketing. Bus. Horiz. **52**(4), 357–365 (2009)

44. McKnight, D.H., Choudhury, V., Kacmar, C.: Developing and validating trust measures for e-commerce: An integrative typology. Inf. Syst. Res. **13**(3), 334–359 (2002)

45. Pavlou, P.A., Gefen, D.: Building effective online marketplaces with institution-based trust. Inf. Syst. Res. **15**(1), 37–59 (2004)

46. Kim, D.J., Ferrin, D.L., Rao, H.R.: A trust-based consumer decision-making model in electronic commerce: The role of trust, perceived risk, and their antecedents. Decis. Supp. Syst. **44**(2), 544–564 (2008)

47. Chong, A.Y.L., Lacka, E., Boying, L., Chan, H.K.: The role of social media in enhancing guanxi and perceived effectiveness of E-commerce institutional mechanisms in online marketplace. Inf. Manag. **55**(5), 621–632 (2018)

48. Hong, I., Cho, H.: The impact of consumer trust on attitudinal loyalty and purchase intentions in B2C e-marketplaces: Intermediary trust vs. seller trust. Int. J. Inf. Manag. **31**(5), 469–479 (2011). https://doi.org/10.1016/j.ijinfomgt.2011.02.001

49. Laroche, M., Habibi, M.R., Richard, M.O., Sankaranarayanan, R.: The effects of social media based brand communities on brand community markers, value creation practices, brand trust and brand loyalty. Comput. Hum. Behav. **28**(5), 1755–1767 (2012)

50. Lu, Y., Zhao, L., Wang, B.: From virtual community members to C2C e-commerce buyers: Trust in virtual communities and its effect on consumers' purchase intention. Electron. Commer. Res. Appl. **9**(4), 346–360 (2010)

51. Pentina, I., Gammoh, B.S., Zhang, L., Mallin, M.: Drivers and outcomes of brand relationship quality in the context of online social networks. Int. J. Electron. Commer. **17**(3), 63–86 (2013)

52. Sawhney, M., Verona, G., Prandelli, E.: Collaborating to create: the Internet as a platform for customer engagement in product innovation. J. Interact. Mark. **19**(4), 4–17 (2005)

53. See-To, E.W., Ho, K.K.: Value co-creation and purchase intention in social network sites: the role of electronic Word-of-Mouth and trust–A theoretical analysis. Comput. Hum. Behav. **31**, 182–189 (2014)

54. Saenger, C., Thomas, V.L., Johnson, J.W.: Consumption-focused self-expression word of mouth: A new scale and its role in consumer research. Psychol. Mark. **30**(11), 959–970 (2013)

55. Prahalad, C.K., Ramaswamy, V.: Co-creation experiences: the next practice in value creation. J. Interact. Mark. **18**(3), 5–14 (2004)

56. Vargo, S.L., Lusch, R.F.: Service-dominant logic: continuing the evolution. J. Acad. Mark. Sci. **36**(1), 1–10 (2004). https://doi.org/10.1007/s11747-007-0069-6

57. Yang, S.C., Chang, W.T., Hsiao, Y.T., Chen, B.Y.: The effects of perceived value on Facebook post sharing intention. In: Proceedings of the 12th International Conference on Advances in Mobile Computing and Multimedia, pp. 444–450 (2014)

# Dark Patterns in Online Shopping: of Sneaky Tricks, Perceived Annoyance and Respective Brand Trust

Christian Voigt, Stephan Schlögl$^{(\boxtimes)}$ ⓘ, and Aleksander Groth

MCI – The Entrepreneurial School, Innsbruck, Austria
stephan.schloegl@mci.edu
https://www.mci.edu

**Abstract.** Dark patterns utilize interface elements to trick users into performing unwanted actions. Online shopping websites often employ these manipulative mechanisms so as to increase their potential customer base, to boost their sales, or to optimize their advertising efforts. Although dark patterns are often successful, they clearly inhibit positive user experiences. Particularly, with respect to customers' perceived annoyance and trust put into a given brand, they may have negative effects. To investigate respective connections between the use of dark patterns, users' perceived level of annoyance and their expressed brand trust, we conducted an experiment-based survey. We implemented two versions of a fictitious online shop; i.e. one which used five different types of dark patterns and a similar one without such manipulative user interface elements. A total of $n = 204$ participants were then forwarded to one of the two shops (approx. 2/3 to the shop which used the dark patterns) and asked to buy a specific product. Subsequently, we measured participants' perceived annoyance level, their expressed brand trust and their affinity for technology. Results show a higher level of perceived annoyance with those who used the dark pattern version of the online shop. Also, we found a significant connection between perceived annoyance and participants' expressed brand trust. A connection between participants' affinity for technology and their ability to recognize and consequently counter dark patterns, however, is not supported by our data.

**Keywords:** Dark patterns · Online shopping · Perceived annoyance · Brand trust scale · Affinity for technology

## 1 Introduction

Design patterns have the ability to significantly affect the way people interact with user interfaces and consequently how such interactions are perceived. Hence, there is a connection between design elements and whether or not they help users reach desired outcomes [18]. To this end, online shops increasingly utilize techniques which help trigger subconscious or potentially unintended customer

© Springer Nature Switzerland AG 2021
F. F.-H. Nah and K. Siau (Eds.): HCII 2021, LNCS 12783, pp. 143–155, 2021.
https://doi.org/10.1007/978-3-030-77750-0_10

behavior to support e-commerce goals (e.g., increase customer reach, boost sales numbers, optimize advertising efforts, etc.). These so-called *dark patterns* aim at tricking users into unintended actions, such as for example the unwilling subscription to a newsletter or the accidental clicking on an ad[1].

A detailed analysis of 680 out of the 10.000 most viewed websites in the United Kingdom, showed that over 88% of them use at least some sort of dark patterns [15]. Given, that on average an Internet user (between 16 and 64 years) spends approx. 6 h and 40 min online per day, the superfluous use of dark patterns may be considered a common, although somewhat unethical, business practice. A practice not only to be found on e-commerce websites but also on smartphone apps (Note: a random selection of 240 apps available in the Google Play Store showed that 95% of them use dark patterns). While the impact of dark patterns on brand trust (i.e., how and how much dark patterns potentially harm perceived trust in a brand) has not yet been fully investigated, a negative impact on app ratings as well as usage has been identified [5]. In order to increase our understanding within this field, our study aims to explore the use of dark patterns in a simulated e-commerce setting and how these are connected to peoples' perceived level of annoyance as well as the respective trust they put into brands when shopping online. Respective analyses were guided by the following research question:

*"What is the connection between dark patterns, perceived level of annoyance and brand trust when shopping online?"*

We will begin with a brief discussion describing the emergence of software patterns and the accompanying rise of dark patterns highlighted by Sect. 2. In Sect. 3 we outline our research design and respective methodology. Section 4 presents our results and Sect. 5 discusses their relevance and limitations. Finally, Sect. 6 concludes and proposes future research directions.

## 2   The Rise of Dark Patterns

Originally applied in structural engineering and architecture [1], design patterns were popularized within software development in the early 1990s [9]. Ever since, their goal has been to improve overall software quality and to offer template solutions to reoccurring architectural problems. However, the proliferation of these 'good design practices' was accompanied by a similar strong appearance of *anti-patterns* (i.e., bad design practices), as well as *dark patterns* which are described as *"[...] instances where designers use their knowledge of human behavior (e.g. psychology) and the desires of end users to implement deceptive functionality that is not in the user's best interest"* [10, p. 1] [2]. As for the latter, three fields of application are identified, which have seen a particularly high level of respective adoption [14]. First, in retail, where customers are being increasingly exposed to deceptive practices such as *psychological pricing* or *false advertising*. Second,

---

[1] Online: https://darkpatterns.org [accessed: November 2nd 2020].

in sales management, where through *growth hacking* companies have been using a combination of big data analysis, marketing and deceiving design practices to increase product adoption. And third, in consumer research and public policy, where *nudging* has become the de facto standard for affecting and consequently changing people's behaviour. From a user (or customer) perspective those practices may be deemed unethical, and with respect to the processing of personal data even unlawful. Ever since the introduction of the General Data Protection Regulation (GDPR) by the European Union in April 2016, the processing of personal data has been legally restricted. Outlining that the consent to process data regards:

> *"[...] any freely given, specific, informed and unambiguous indication of the data subject's wishes by which he or she, by a statement or by a clear affirmative action, signifies agreement to the processing of personal data relating to him or her."* [19, Article 4(8)]

the GDPR regulates e.g. the implementation and utilization of so-called cookies on websites, pushing for particularized user consent. Yet, a recent study in the UK clearly shows that respective compliance is often missing: Out of 680 investigated websites only 11.8% offered (1) **explicit consent** where (2) **accepting all** is **as easy as rejecting all**, and (3) selection **boxes** are **not pre-ticked** [13]. To this end, the concepts *privacy dark patterns* and *privacy dark strategies* are of particular interest, as they describe strategies which focus exclusively on the exploitation of personal data, thereby underlining the great relevance such unethical practices still have in e-commerce [2].

Previous work has outlined various concepts on how to integrate ethical considerations into the design of and consequent interaction with modern user interfaces. These practices usually center around value approaches such as Value Sensitive Design (VSD) [7] or Value Levers [17]. All of them have in common that they aim for human values to be prioritized in the (technical) design processes [8,17]. While the use of dark patterns clearly violates such values, and thus may be considered unethical, one might argue that it is not only ethical concerns which are at play here. Although companies might increase their benefits by tricking customers into unwilling behavior, these practices often lead to a negative user experiences. Additionally, they may affect the trust customers put into a given brand, which eventually might harm an organization's reputation. E-commerce companies may thus be willing to refrain from using dark patterns if it can be shown that the negative consequences regarding long-term brand trust outweigh respective gains in short-term sales.

## 3   Methodology

In order to investigate a potential connection between brand trust and the use of dark patterns, we used an experiment based on a between-subject design in which two versions of a fictitious online shop served as stimuli. One shop (i.e., DARK) used five different dark patterns based on the categorization by Gray and colleagues [10], the other (i.e., CLEAN) was free of such manipulative interface elements (cf. Sect. 3.1).

## 3.1  Stimuli

As outlined above, we used two different versions of the same online shop to investigate upon perception differences connected to the appearance of dark patterns. Following, we describe the patterns implemented by the DARK version of our shop and compare them to the respective interface elements used by the CLEAN version:

***Forced Action:*** Forced action is one of the first and most commonly dark patterns users will encounter when visiting a website. According to Gray et al., *forced action* describes a situation where *"users are required to perform a specific action to access (or continue to access) a specific functionality."* [10]. When encountering such a pattern, users are given little choice but to follow a pre-set path. An often implemented type of forced action is referred to as *Privacy Zuckering* and is found in cookie consent banners. The goal is to make users share their information in ways they do not mean to. This is achieved by making mandatory privacy settings intentionally complicated and/or incomprehensible to use [2, 10]. For example, the DARK version of our online shop uses a banner to outline cookie and privacy settings. It appeared in the center of the website and blocked all further access to the other navigational elements. In order to close it, users were visually drawn towards the already and only pre-selected "Accept" button (note: the accept button was the most prominent visual interface element due to its black background), thereby agreeing to activate all cookies and so accepting full user tracking (cf. Fig. 1).

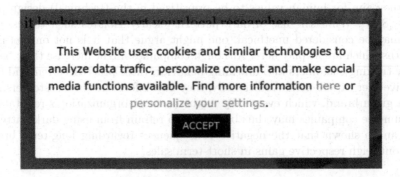

**Fig. 1.** Cookie consent banner using the *Forced Action* pattern

To adjust these settings and reject all unnecessary tracking, users had to select the "personalize your settings" option presented as a text-link (note: we used light blue colored text with intentionally low contrast so that this option would be significantly less obvious than the accept button). It should be noted that this type of cookie banner is not compliant with GDPR rules, yet still found on many websites. The CLEAN version of our online shop showed a cookie banner which did not push users towards accepting unwanted settings, and thus may be considered GDPR compliant (cf. Fig. 2).

**Fig. 2.** GDPR compliant cookie consent banner }

*Nagging:* Nagging uses scheduled intrusions such as pop-ups to repeatedly disrupt normal interaction workflows [3]. Users may develop militant feeling against these nagging elements, which may go as far as to trigger a purchase for the sole purpose of skipping forward [10,12]. Following this approach, the DARK version of our online shop presented pop-ups on every single product page, inviting users to visit the sales section. One had to either close the pop up or visit the sales section in order to proceed. All other navigation elements were blocked (cf. Fig. 3). Additionally, a similar pop-up was triggered when users reviewed the shopping cart, inviting them once more to visit the shop's sales section. On the other hand, the CLEAN version of our online shop was completely free of such pop-ups.

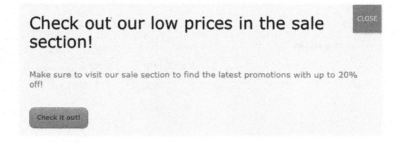

**Fig. 3.** Advertisement Pop-up representing *Nagging*

*Confirmshaming:* When users of the DARK version of our online shop eventually proceeded to the checkout, they were asked to enter their name and shipping address. Here we implemented the so-called confirmshaming pattern, which in our case was represented by a pop-up window trying to convince users to "Be cool" (cf. Fig. 4).

**Fig. 4.** Pop-up representing *Confirmshaming*

The respective button opened a new browser tab, showing our school's Instagram page. According to Gray [10], the goal of the confirmshaming pattern is to use dedicated interface elements such as specific language, sound, color or style to convey emotions and consequently incite users to perform an originally unintended action.

**Sneaking:** In addition to a confirmshaming pattern, our DARK shopping cart embedded a sneaking pattern; a hidden action which is accompanied by potentially undesired effects or unexpected costs. In other words, if the user would be aware of the hidden procedure or recognize it, he/she would object [10]. In our case, the DARK version of our online shop automatically added a Vinyl Record for € 1.00 to a user's shopping basked (cf. Fig. 5) whereas the CLEAN version did not.

Shopping Cart

| | | Product | Price | Quantity | Subtotal |
|---|---|---|---|---|---|
| × | | Vinyl Record from Team Tata | €1,00 | 1 8 | €1,00 |
| × | | Hoodie with Zipper | €45,00 | 1 8 | €45,00 |
| Coupon code | Apply coupon | | | | Update cart |

**Fig. 5.** *Sneak* into basket approach

**Double Negative:** Concluding, our DARK online shop also implemented a double negative pattern. During the check-out process users had to consent to terms and conditions as well as to the shops privacy policy. By doing this, we also asked for a potential newsletter subscription (cf. Fig. 6). The used double negative formulation, as described by Gray et al.'s [10] as aesthetic manipulation, asked users to tick the box in order to NOT receive the newsletter. The CLEAN version of the online shop asked them to tick the box in case he/she wanted to receive future marketing communication.

☐  Please tick here if you do not wish to receive future e-mail marketing communications from Lowkey Clothing.

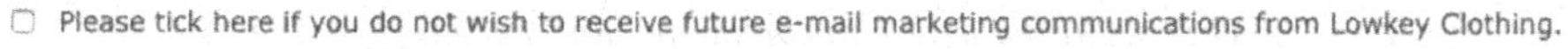

**Fig. 6.** *Double Negative* checkbox used for the newsletter subscription

## 3.2  Questionnaires

After completing their interaction with either the CLEAN or the DARK version of the online shop, participants were asked to fill in a questionnaire survey. Survey items focused on users' perceived annoyance level and respective brand trust. The level of perceived annoyance was measured overall ( *"Please rate your overall level of annoyance during your visit of the Lowkey Clothing webshop"*) and for each respective dark pattern ( *"Please rate your level of annoyance regarding pattern XX"*) on a 5-point Likert scale ranging from *1 = "not annoyed at all"* to *5 = "very annoyed"*.

As for brand trust, we used the Brand Trust Scale (BTS) by Delgado-Ballester and colleagues [4], which allows for quantitative measures based on two dimensions, i.e. *fiability* and *intentionality*. *Fiability* focuses on need satisfaction and is thus related to a brand's (company's) value promise and whether a customer believes in it; i.e. whether the company sticks to its promises. *Intentionality* focuses on hypothetical, unexpected problems with a product or brand and evaluates how a brand (company) deals with consumer interests. In other words, it represents the customer's emotional security towards a brand's (company's) problem-solving behaviour. Both dimensions consist of four questions, each measured on a 5-point Likert scale ranging from *1 = "completely disagree"* to *5 = "completely agree"* (cf. Table 1).

In order to investigate potential experience effects, we used the *Affinity Towards Technological Interaction* (ATI) scale [6]. It acts as an indicator for effective interaction with technology and thus helps characterize user diversity. The ATI is grounded in the NFC (i.e., Need For Cognition) construct and consists of nine items, each measured on a 6-point Likert scale ranging from *1 = "completely disagree"* to *6 = "completely agree"* (cf. Table 2).

Finally, we collected basic demographic data (i.e., *Gender, Age, Country of Residence* and *Level of Education*) in order to validate our sample (cf. Sect. 3.3).

**Table 1.** Question items on brand trust according to Delgado-Ballester et al.'s BTS scale [4].

| *Fiability* |
| --- |
| BTS-F1 – *With Lowkey Clothing I did obtain what I looked for in an online shop* |
| BTS-F2 – *Lowkey Clothing was always at my consumption expectations level* |
| BTS-F3 – *Lowkey Clothing gave me confidence and certainty in the consumption of clothes* |
| BTS-F4 – *Lowkey Clothing never disappointed me so far* |
| *Intentionality* |
| BTS-I1 – *Lowkey Clothing seemed honest and sincere in its explanations* |
| BTS-I2 – *I could rely on Lowkey Clothing* |
| BTS-I3 – *Lowkey Clothing would make any effort to make me be satisfied* |
| BTS-I4 – *Lowkey Clothing would repay me in some way for a problem with the hoodie* |

**Table 2.** Question items on technology affinity according to Franke et al.'s ATI scale [6].

| |
| --- |
| ATI1 – *I like to occupy myself in greater detail with technical systems* |
| ATI2 – *I like testing the functions of new technical systems* |
| ATI3 – *I predominantly deal with technical systems because I have to* |
| ATI4 – *When I have a new technical system in front of me, I try it out intensively* |
| ATI5 – *I enjoy spending time becoming acquainted with a new technical system* |
| ATI6 – *It is enough for me that a technical system works; I don't care how or why* |
| ATI7 – *I try to understand how a technical system exactly works* |
| ATI8 – *It is enough for me to know the basic functions of a technical system* |
| ATI9 – *I try to make full use of the capabilities of a technical system* |

## 3.3   Ethics, Sampling and Study Period

The study followed common ethical considerations concerning research with human participation. Respective approval was obtained from the school's Ethics Commission in May 2020. Study sampling focused on representatives from Generation Y, i.e. so-called *digital natives* who were born between 1980 and 2000 (note: we are aware that the PEW Research Institute defines different age brackets for Generation $Y^2$, yet did not consider this slight variation relevant with respect to our target group). Most of them have been growing up with technology and are thus accustomed to shopping online [11, 16]. We reached out to potential participants via social media, direct messaging, as well as face-to-face contact. The two versions of our online shop (i.e., DARK and CLEAN) as well as the above described questionnaires were available from May 20th to July 6th 2020, which amounts to a total study period of 47 days.

### 3.4    Study Procedure

Participants were first given some background information on the study goals (i.e., investigation of behaviour in online shopping) and then asked to consent to data processing (note: they were not told about the potential use of dark patterns). Next, they were given the task to buy a distinct product (i.e., a hoodie with a zipper) via the online shop version they were forwarded to (cf. Fig. 7).

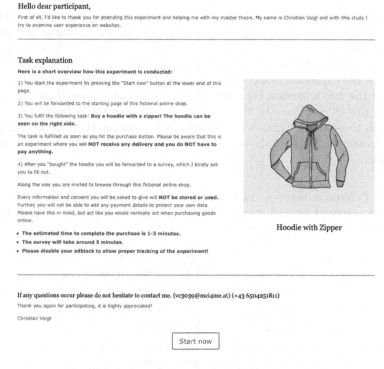

**Fig. 7.** Introduction and task description

As mentioned earlier, approx. 2/3 of respondents were forwarded to the DARK version of the shop and 1/3 to the CLEAN one. Both versions were designed to

---

2 Online: https://www.pewresearch.org/fact-tank/2019/01/17/where-millennials-end -and-generation-z-begins/ [accessed: February 12th 2021].

appear as realistic as possible, without asking users to provide any payment details. After participants successfully completed the check-out process (sans payment), they were forwarded to the questionnaire survey. Its purpose was scientifically reasoned, yet its connection to our key survey components, i.e. *perceived level of annoyance*, *expressed brand trust* and *affinity for technology*, was not further explained so as to inhibit bias. Still, our survey introduced participants to dark patterns and asked them to rate the level of annoyance they perceived with each of the patterns they were exposed to, before moving on to the questions on brand trust and affinity for technology. Note: with respect to the used *Double Negative* and *Sneaking* patterns, participants were first asked whether they noticed the pattern during their preceding shopping task. Only if they noticed the pattern, they were then asked to rate their perceived level of annoyance.

## 4    Results

A total of $n = 204$ participants (48.53% female) completed the study, of whom $n_{dark} = 134$ used the DARK and $n_{clean} = 70$ the CLEAN version of our online shop. For the analyses we used a 95% confidence level. Results show significant differences between the two versions of the online shop regarding both perceived annoyance and expressed brand trust (cf. Table 3). On the one hand, participants who used the DARK version reported a higher annoyance level than those who used the CLEAN version. On the other hand, the expressed brand trust was lower with those participants who used the DARK version than those who used the CLEAN version. Such applied to both the *fiability* as well as the *intentionality* dimension.

**Table 3.** Differences between the DARK and the CLEAN version of the online shop concerning perceived level of annoyance and expressed brand trust; cf. Sect. 3.2 for further details on the used BTS scale.

|  | DARK | CLEAN | $p$ |
|---|---|---|---|
| $Mean_{Annoyance}$ | 3.44 | 2.34 | 0.000 |
| $SD_{Annoyance}$ | 1.173 | 1.178 | |
| $Mean_{Fiability}$ | 3.26 | 3.55 | 0.011 |
| $SD_{Fiability}$ | 0.789 | 0.727 | |
| $Mean_{Intentionality}$ | 3.07 | 3.42 | 0.003 |
| $SD_{Intentionality}$ | 0.838 | 0.679 | |

In addition, only 24% of users from the CLEAN version reported negative experiences, whereas more than 70% of users from the DARK version highlighted unintended or negative effects. When asking participants what triggered these negative experience, over 75% recalled the returning advertisement pop-ups (i.e.,

*Nagging*) as being particularly annoying. The data furthermore shows a connection between participants' overall level of annoyance and their brand trust. It points to a statistically significant correlation between the overall level of annoyance and the fiability dimension ($r_s = -.457; r^2 = .2970; p = .000$), as well as the intentionality dimension ($r_s = -.545; r^2 = .2088; p = .000$). A connection between participants' affinity for technology use and their ability to detect dark patterns, however, is not supported by the collected data (recognition of *Double Negative*: $p = 0.215$; recognition of *Sneaking*: $p = 0.232$), which may underline the often rather subconscious nature of these interface elements. Finally, regarding the annoyance level of perceived dark patterns our data shows that participants found *Sneaking* to be most displeasing, followed by *Confirmshaming* and *Nagging* (cf. Table 4).

**Table 4.** Perceived level of annoyance regarding each of the experienced dark patterns; Scale: *"1 = not annoyed at all"* to *15 = "very annoyed"*

|       | Forced Action | Nagging | Confirmshaming | Sneaking | Double Negative |
|-------|---------------|---------|----------------|----------|-----------------|
| *Mean* | 3.16          | 4.02    | 4.28           | 4.53     | 3.53            |
| *SD*   | 1.268         | 1.007   | 1.127          | 0.822    | 0.492           |

## 5 Discussion and Limitations

Our study results indicate that dark patterns do harm brand trust and that they are connected to an increased level of annoyance perceived by customers when shopping online. Yet, the results also show that dark patterns do work. The aesthetic manipulation via *Double Negative* used by the DARK version of our online shop increased newsletter subscriptions by 12% compared to the CLEAN version. Surprisingly, those 60% of participants who did recognize the manipulation, rated its level of annoyance rather low (i.e., $Mean = 3.53$). Also the *Sneaking* pattern worked in 38 out of 134 cases. This means, that over 11% of our study participant accidentally purchased an additional product; even though this dark pattern was rated as highly annoying by over 68% of all the participants who were exposed to the DARK version of the shop.

Considering our results, we need to highlight that respective ratings only apply to those five distinct patterns applied in our study. They may not generalise to other instances, that potentially use very different forms and appearances. For example, the annoyance of *Forced Action* was rated rather low in our study. This may be caused by the implementation via a cookie banner when first entering the website. Today, users face cookie banners on nearly every website and may thus be more forgiving. On the other hand, *Sneaking* is a less commonly used pattern, for which it may have triggered higher annoyance ratings in our study.

As for the measured *brand trust*, our results may also be considered limited, as our setup used a fictional brand: *Lowkey Clothing*. The BTS scale aims to measure trust in brands that are already known to a consumer [4]. In our study however, participants rated trust based solely on the experience gained from this one-off shopping task, which may certainly be too little time to build up a sufficient trust level.

Finally, our data does not point to a connection between participants' ATI scores and their ability to recognize dark patterns. This is unexpected, since one would assume that through a higher affinity towards technological interaction, one would be more aware of malicious design and therefore recognize dark patterns more often. Furthermore, the data does not support a connection between participants' ATI scores and their perceived level of annoyance. One would assume at least a weak link, since users with a higher affinity towards technological interaction tend to spend more time online, and may thus be confronted more often with dark pattern. The empirical lack thereof underlines the importance of our study and shows that more research is necessary in order to increase our understanding of the effects dark patterns have on users.

## 6    Conclusion and Future Outlook

We conducted an experiment-based survey to understand a potential connection between the use of dark patterns in online shopping, users' level of perceived annoyances, and their expressed brand trust. While results support connections to both (i.e., perceived annoyance and expressed brand trust), its impact is not yet fully understood. Hence, future work should aim to model these connections so that we may be able to identify a threshold at which the negative effects with respect to annoyance and brand trust outweigh the gains resulting from the use of dark patterns. In addition, we see a need for targeted information and user education. Although the results of our study rejected the assumption that affinity for technology yields a higher level of dark pattern recognition, we do believe that more targeted awareness raising programs may still help users recognize hidden tricks and consequently prevent unintended actions.

To our knowledge, there has been no empirical analysis investigating the connection between dark patterns and brand trust so far. And although our results are still preliminary and require further validation, they underline the negative side effects of dark patterns. Hence, companies may reflect on the use of dark pattern or at least counterbalance its value against the detrimental effects it could bring to ones' perceived brand value.

## References

1. Alexander, C.: A Pattern Language: Towns, Buildings, Construction. Oxford University Press, Oxford (1977)
2. Bösch, C., Erb, B., Kargl, F., Kopp, H., Pfattheicher, S.: Tales from the dark side: Privacy dark strategies and privacy dark patterns. In: Proceedings on Privacy Enhancing Technologies, vol. 2016, no. 4, pp. 237–254 (2016)

3. Chromik, M., Eiband, M., Völkel, S.T., Buschek, D.: Dark patterns of explainability, transparency, and user control for intelligent systems. In: IUI Workshops, vol. 2327 (2019)
4. Delgado-Ballester, E., Munuera-Aleman, J.L., Yague-Guillen, M.J.: Development and validation of a brand trust scale. Int. J. Mark. Res. **45**(1), 35–54 (2003)
5. Di Geronimo, L., Braz, L., Fregnan, E., Palomba, F., Bacchelli, A.: UI dark patterns and where to find them: a study on mobile applications and user perception. In: Proceedings of the 2020 CHI Conference on Human Factors in Computing Systems, pp. 1–14 (2020)
6. Franke, T., Attig, C., Wessel, D.: A personal resource for technology interaction: development and validation of the affinity for technology interaction (ATI) scale. Int. J. Human-Comput. Interact. **35**(6), 456–467 (2019)
7. Friedman, B.: Value-sensitive design. Interactions **3**(6), 16–23 (1996)
8. Friedman, B., Hendry, D.G.: Value Sensitive Design: Shaping Technology with Moral Imagination. MIT Press, Cambridge (2019)
9. Gamma, E.: Design Patterns: Elements of Reusable Object-oriented Software. Pearson Education India, Chennai (1995)
10. Gray, C.M., Kou, Y., Battles, B., Hoggatt, J., Toombs, A.L.: The dark (patterns) side of UX design. In: Proceedings of the 2018 CHI Conference on Human Factors in Computing Systems, pp. 1–14 (2018)
11. Jones, V., Jo, J., Martin, P.: Future schools and how technology can be used to support millennial and generation-z students. In: ICUT 2007 (Proc. B), 1st International Conference on Ubiquitous Information Technology, pp. 886–891. Citeseer (2007)
12. Lewis, C.: Irresistible Apps: Motivational Design Patterns for Apps, Games, and Web-Based Communities. Springer, Heidelberg (2014). https://doi.org/10.1007/978-1-4302-6422-4
13. Mohan, J., Wasserman, M., Chidambaram, V.: Analyzing GDPR compliance through the lens of privacy policy. In: Gadepally, V., et al. (eds.) DMAH/Poly-2019. LNCS, vol. 11721, pp. 82–95. Springer, Cham (2019). https://doi.org/10.1007/978-3-030-33752-0_6
14. Narayanan, A., Mathur, A., Chetty, M., Kshirsagar, M.: Dark patterns: past, present, and future. Queue **18**(2), 67–92 (2020)
15. Nouwens, M., Liccardi, I., Veale, M., Karger, D., Kagal, L.: Dark patterns after the GDPR: scraping consent pop-ups and demonstrating their influence. In: Proceedings of the 2020 CHI Conference on Human Factors in Computing Systems, pp. 1–13 (2020)
16. Prensky, M.: Digital natives, digital immigrants part 1. Horizon **9**(5), 1–6 (2001). https://doi.org/10.1108/10748120110424816
17. Shilton, K.: Values levers: building ethics into design. Sci. Technol. Human Values **38**(3), 374–397 (2013)
18. Sommerer, C., Mignonneau, L.: The Art and Science of Interface and Interaction Design (Vol. 1), vol. 141. Springer, Heidelberg (2008). https://doi.org/10.1007/978-3-540-79870-5
19. European Union: Regulation (EU) no 2016/679 of the European parliament and of the council n the protection of natural persons with regard to the processing of personal data and on the free movement of such data (general data protection regulation – GDPR). OJ (2018)

# Methodical Framework and Case Study for Empowering Customer-Centricity in an E-Commerce Agency–The Experience Logic as Key Component of User Experience Practices Within Agile IT Project Teams

Beatrice Weber[1(✉)], Andrea Müller[2], and Christina Miclau[2]

[1] Flagbit GmbH und Co. KG, Griesbachstraße 10, 76185 Karlsruhe, Germany
Beatrice.weber@flagbit.de, beatrice.weber93@web.de
[2] Offenburg University, Badstrasse 24, 77652 Offenburg, Germany

**Abstract.** In an experience economy market competition in software branches is becoming more and more intense. Technical innovations, global retail practices and the multidimensional conception of experiences provide both opportunities and challenges for companies worldwide. Retailers strive for an optimized conversion rate, but poor UX still abound. Particularly Germany-based companies are less evolved in an international comparison of industrialized economies. The value of integrating users in the development process is recognized, but methodologies must carefully be incorporated into existing agile workflows. The goal of this study is to bridge the gaps between internal agency and external client and user interests. The contribution is four-fold: an overview of the current status of customer centricity in the E-Commerce branch of trade is provided (I). Based on this corpus, a methodical framework, aiming to incorporate the experience logic in UX practices within an agile project team, is presented (II). The framework is applied by a single case study - the shop relaunch of a motorbike accessory store (III). Finally, all interest groups (UX, development and project management) are incorporated in the qualitative content analysis (IV).

**Keywords:** E commerce · Customer centricity · User experience · Agility

## 1 Introduction

The 'World Wide Web' changed the way people communicate, exchange goods, buy products and gather information in an unpredictable way. Nowadays approximately 4,39 billion people regularly use the internet worldwide. 94 million of those live in Germany, Austria and Switzerland, which is 91% of the local population with an average usage time of 4,4 h daily (Germany). Mobile devices enhance the evolution by simplifying product information search, communication and more. E-Commerce (EC) market revenue is expected to grow by 11,7% in 2021, currently amounting to approximately 2.3 million US Dollar [1].

© Springer Nature Switzerland AG 2021
F. F.-H. Nah and K. Siau (Eds.): HCII 2021, LNCS 12783, pp. 156–177, 2021.
https://doi.org/10.1007/978-3-030-77750-0_11

The experience economy describes an economic era in which businesses operate as experience creators, staging an event for their customers. EC agencies are bound to incorporate both client and user interests as consumers seek more than functional attributes. They claim comprehensive experiences. This results in a demand for higher productivity and flexibility in user experience (UX) practices [2, 3].

Nevertheless, technology-focused companies often rely on functionality as differentiation tool. Issues trace back to engineering dominated cultures, a lack of UX expertise and customer understanding. Profitability of human-centered design is underestimated, the capability of the experience logic not yet taken. A methodological guidance for systematic inclusion of needs is required [4, 5].

Therefore, the EC agency FLAGBIT GmbH und Co. KG and OFFENBURG UNIVERSITY conduct a unique research project: Aligning customer-centric business activities with human-centered design as part of agile IT software development.

A four-phase methodical framework has been developed in order to provide a valuable guidance. Key components are to understand, convey, capture and manage experiences. Experience thinking provides an approach for pursuing value-creating activities regardless of the industry.

The framework is applied by a single case study. As user integration in all project phases, particularly the realization workflow (Scrum), is of central interest, quantitative and qualitative research methods are performed. This includes a UX testing.

Results and insights of the expert interviews and interactive case study polls serve as basis for evaluating strengths and weaknesses of proposed methods and phases. The overall aim of this study is to answer the following research questions:

1. How is customer centricity adding value to the business activities of an EC agency?
2. How can the experience logic be holistically incorporated into UX practices?
3. How can the UX workflow be optimally united with an agile project workflow?

The first research question reflects the current challenge of meeting customer expectation and is supposed to determine value-adding opportunities in the agency context. Hence, it is important to bridge the gap between the interest of agency clients that are paying for the projects and users of the online shop – the client's customers. For creating an online shop with individual solutions based on preferences and needs, user integration is of central interest.

The second research question aims to find ways of integrating an experience mindset into interdisciplinary UX practices. The experience logic as a holistic approach is realized by conducting profound research and performing a customer experience (CX) tracking (5-s and moderated usability test). The framework is based on both the company's and the customer's abilities and needs.

The third process-focused research question reflects the challenge of efficiently aligning agile project operations with the UX workflow that is advocating for user interests as compatible parts. The framework aims to enhance interdisciplinary exchange, strengthen creativity, openness to new ideas and an innovative spirit.

## 2 Current State of Customer Centricity in E-Commerce

### 2.1 Specifications of the Agency Perspective in E-Commerce

The evolution of E-Commerce (EC) is affecting all parts of the customer journey in almost all kinds of businesses. Making purchases online is possible for everyone with access to the internet able to handle a computer. This, in turn, affects customer loyalty and competitor differentiation [6]. Consumers are testing new opportunities through various online traders [7]. The more engaging a purchase process, the more specialized services and the more flexible network configurations are, the smarter a marketplace is [8].

Global growth rates of users and increasing average usage time are related to the importance of EC in our society, proved by rising revenues [9]. Considering shopping as leisure activity, the competition shifts from products to entertainment, the so-called 'entertailing' [10]. Online and traditional shopping differ in the number of presentable products and the virtual or physical environment [11]. The evolution of the market is characterized by simultaneous entrance of new players and an ongoing interplay between concentrations [8].

A key feature of EC is to permit businesses to overcome geographic barriers in the context of globalization [12]. The capability in terms of sales, customer orientation (data mining), time and cost savings, efficiency, competitive positioning and realization of new business models is unlimited [13]. From a customer perspective advantages of EC are price transparency, location independence, product variety, convenience, lower risk due to review availability. Drawbacks can be missing product haptic, information overflow, filesharing, lack of service fulfillment and knowledge to evaluate supplier reliability [14].

EC agencies as part of the EC service industry subdivision, have arisen by the lack of expertise and operational competence of traditional manufacturers [15]. They partner with businesses to solve problems and help them achieving goals. Such agencies perform in the fields of consultation, conception, UX design, EC improvement, technical implementation, interfaces, conversion optimization and support [16]. Risks in EC emerge from cybercrime, data manipulation, lack of frameworks, distorted identities and rising IT infrastructure costs traced back to online shop integration [14]. Those risks as well as complex requirements like product and target group specifications and various order types are handled by the agency.

### 2.2 Exploiting the Layers of Customer Centricity

The roots of customer centricity trace back to the idea of customers determining business activities in the 1960s, when direct marketing and the concept of keeping records of customer habits became popular [17, 18]. Nowadays it is regarded as basic requirement for online retailing but many firms strive for a successful realization [19, 20]. The strategic term encompasses various issues:

- holistic implementation (organizational, inter-department and inter-firm dynamics);
- the important role of organizational commitment and a process-based view;

- consideration of company-specific aspects e.g. exogenous variables;
- customer value maximization;
- the endless learning scope and the need for continuous improvements[17, 18, 21].

Some companies dress themselves for being customer-oriented and do not make use of the potential two-way communication between the company and the customer [22]. Creating positive CX implies inspirational leadership, empathetic people and an empowering culture- both on a broader agency and a narrow team perspective [23].

Customer *orientation* is conceptualized as individual emotional cognitive attitude, whereas user friendliness of software is estimated as one of its most important factors [24]. Customer *participation* can be conceptualized as a spectrum starting at passive observation, ending at customers playing an active role in creating the experience [2]. The interactions within the experience imply customer *involvement* at different levels, such as thoughts, acts, values [25]. Involvement basically changes the way a service is perceived and is determined by the degree of interaction and intensity (felt strengths of the involvement) [26]. Customer *engagement* determines the overall experience, can lead to value creation for companies (positive reviews, users generating ideas and concepts) and customers (appealed senses, cognition, emotions, performance and context) [27, 28]. Customer *satisfaction* is a standard performance measure, a variable that determines the outcome of process quality, the gap between expectation and actual experience [29].

## 2.3  Creating Value Adding Customer Experiences

The concept of selling valued experiences, originated in the business of selling entertaining theatre performances, is forwarded by emerging technologies. It is not only relevant in consumer industries, but also applicable in the B2B context [2]. 'Experience' as complex, dynamic and empirical phenomenon engage individuals in an inherently personal way, are anamorphic constructs and consequently are a result of a real offering such as any service, good, or commodity [30]. Consensus in the experience literature can be found in the holistic conceptualization and multidimensional structure [31]. Table 1 provides a comparison of experience logic approaches.

CX can be described as a broader perspective of the experience. The term also considers the internal process, such as employee's adaption of customer-centric mindset [33]. It can be described as the subjective response to (in)direct customer-company contact [34]. It includes search, purchase, consumption, after-sales and multiple retail channels [31]. Not every customer automatically is a user (multichannel retail) and not every user automatically turns into a customer (transaction needed).

Value addition does not reside in the object consumption but additionally lies in the experience consumption, changing over the course of lifetime [35]. It is evidenced that value is linked to experiential features and the desire for positive experiences [25]. Additional value gives customers confidence in the choices they make by confirming attributes, aspiration satisfaction, joint vision of associations and social contribution [36].

**Table 1.** Comparison of literary experience logic approaches

| Six experiential components [25] | Strategic Experiential Modules (SEMs) [28] | Model-based system [32] | In this study: |
|---|---|---|---|
| 'sensorial': stimulation of human senses | 'sense' = sensory; sight, sound, touch, taste, smell | Dopaminergic system, able to reinforce experience anticipation | Multisensorial |
| 'emotional': generation of moods and feelings | 'feel' = affective reaction; feelings and emotions through stimuli | Emotional evaluation, before, during and after the experience | Emotions |
| 'cognitive': thinking and conscious mental process | 'think' = creative cognitive; appeals to intellect, surprise and provocation | Cognitive evaluation of the process and the outcomes | Cognition |
| 'pragmatic': practical act of doing something | 'act' = physical; appeals to behaviors | Affective evaluation, before, during and after the experience | Performance |
| 'lifestyle': approval of values and beliefs 'relational': social context and relationships | 'relate' = social identity; Individual's desire for self-improvement (interaction with reverence group) | Dopaminergic system, able to reinforce experience anticipation | Context |

## 2.4 User Experience: From User- to Human-Centered Design

The base of users is growing and changing, positive experiences are desired and new interactive design opportunities are available [37]. Consumers are eager to optimize their own experience [38]. Defined by the ISO-Norm 9241–210 human-centered design for interactive systems is characterized by a profound understanding of users, tasks and context [39]. The term 'human-centered' replaced 'user-centered' due to its limitation to digital products [4]. End-user are integrated in all project stages. It addresses end-user integration in all project stages, collaborative and co-design methods [40].

UX can be defined as evaluative, variable and subjective feeling shifting the attention from product to human senses while interacting [41]. Also, internal state (motivation, expectation, mood), post-use phase (reflection), design system characteristics (usability, purpose) and context (environment)are relevant for determining the overall experience [4, 37]. A fundamental research about the target groups is desperately needed for designing an experience that matches their needs and wants [42]. Theme and design must fit brand personality and appeal to the target audience.

Often used for measuring an experience, usability can be described as "appropriate-ness to a purpose of any particular artefact" [43, 44]. It covers effectiveness, efficiency and satisfaction. Usability is considered a valid predictor of user's buying intention and purchase decision, followed by shop size and trust [45]. Quantitative research as main type of empirical evaluation in the field of UX is predominant. However, the number of qualitative methods is rising [46]. Cause of the imbalance could the simple, neat and precise characteristics of numerical values be.

The value of UX lies in the comprehensive approach emphasizing all aspects of the user interaction with the product or service [47]. Research in the context of agile software development reveals its value over time and can prevent failure due to unapproved ideas [48]. Less retroactive development work is required due to customer involvement in the process [3]. Positive UX promotes the creation of an emotional tie which in turn enhances customer loyalty [25]. Positive sales, credibility, exposure and performance impacts can be observed. Shop design and usability influence conversion rate as important columns for differentiating and competitive positioning. It can further reduce resource burden and customer support activities due to error reduction. Studies show the degree of satisfaction positively affects consumer spending in EC.Nevertheless user involvement, particularly in large-scale IT projects, is not a common practice [49, 50].

The value of user's participation is not controversial, but the realization and implementation are [51]. The degree of involvement and user's role in development process is being discussed due to the need of balancing several interests and issues arising in practice [52]. Also, the topic is a central concern of HCI as the importance of integrating human factors in software engineering environment is acknowledged broadly [53].

Reasons and prejudices against UX are prioritization of quality, cost and delivery times, missing innovative spirit, ideas and expertise. UX regarded as worthless or even obstructive to reach project goals [54]. Communication barriers may arise, and users are regarded untalented or a disturbing factor [24]. Poor UX performances can be traced back to a lack of management support or missing recognition of human factor benefits. UX is often considered as optional component in software development. Apart from that, some organizational structures are too complex to be fundamentally redesigned [47].

### 2.5   Agility and Interdisciplinarity in IT Project Management

Agile means to be ready for motion at any time answering to query of the business community for fast and 'light' processes in a rapidly growing internet software industry [55]. "A core principle of agile development is to satisfy the customer by providing valuable products on an early and continuous basis." [56]. Key principles of the agile manifesto cover collaboration between motivated and self-organized team individuals, narrow customers integration, face-to-face interactions, sustainable development and efficiency reflection, transparency, flexibility, etc. [57].

A popular agile development methodology is Scrum – focusing on narrow feedback-cycles and short iterations ('sprints') based on a vision that is built on values, needs and behavior of the target group in the usage context [39]. Different roles such as Product Owner (PO), Scrum Master and (development) team are pre-defined [58]. Sprints can last from seven to thirty days, phases are pre-planned in a meeting based on the product backlog (uncompleted tasks) and short daily stand-ups ('Daily Scrum') serve as opportunity for continuous exchange [59].

Organizations often customize roles and internal processes by combining agile components with traditional practices [58]. When incorporating agile principles, efficient project management is of remarkable importance as suitable approaches must be chosen and aligned with daily rhythms. Used methods in agile product development must be considered from a vertical (level of detail) and horizontal perspective (coverage of development phases) for not to be too generalized or too restricted [55].

Mutual awareness is considered as necessary element for cooperative work and interdisciplinarity is regarded as imperative for agile processes [60]. 'Interdisciplinary' describes disciplines working closely together in order to produce new knowledge and engage with each other [61]. Collaboration, open mindsets and curiosity are key factors of success and should be highlighted as common ways of thinking. Interdisciplinary teams are able to consider issues and solutions from different perspectives.

A barrier to successful interdisciplinary work can be knowledge integration across different disciplines [62]. This can be traced back to different goals, processes, commercial pressures and skills among team members [60]. In an IT working environment, engineering culture focusing on the production of bug-free codes on time and budget can broadly be observed with a lack of tolerance for human factors and creativity [63]. Communication between developers (technical focus) and UX designers (conceptual and design focus) is affected by independencies and an inherent conflict of interests.

Guo [3] emphasizes that both software engineering and UX Design approaches start by defining a problem, followed by solution generation. UX often takes the role of cross-functional facilitator as the input of all team members is important in the context of generating solutions that solve user difficulties. UX professionals are not supposed to become change professionals, but to be enabled to spread experience thinking and design practices among the entire organization [64]. With effective communication and collaboration project success and a good UX can be reached [47].

"As groups collaborate together over a number of projects, they develop substantial shared problem models, transactive memory, and skill at working together." A balance between proven and new team members is recommended due to the need for diverse perspectives mental models in order to enhance idea generation [62].

## 3   Four-Phase Methodical Framework

The purpose of UX research as recently established scientific area is to define the scope, operationalize experiential qualities, meet or even surpass user expectations and effectively guide users based on their needs [43]. In order to meet those challenges, the multidimensional structure of experiences serves as basis (multisensorial, emotions, cognition, performance and context).

The examination of related theory and evolved insights serve as a fundament for the development of a new methodical framework that is evaluated subsequently. Based on the theoretical considerations, the following hypotheses in accordance to the research questions can be formulated:

- EC agencies command online shop related expertise that enables their clients to ensure against risks and exploit the potential of trading good and services online.
- If customer-centricity is adapted company-specifically, realized holistically and continuously improved, it serves as differentiator by maximizing customer and company value.

- The multidimensional structure and complex perception of experiences serves as foundation for understanding and incorporating them into UX practice of an agile project team.
- If online shopping experiences are designed according to human-centered design principles and therefore co-created by users, they are likely to meet customer needs and expectations.
- Agile project management enables interdisciplinary teams to collaborate efficiently and develop sustainable solutions by promoting flexibility, personal interaction and speed.
- If cross-functional exchange and mutual appreciation become key elements of a project workflow, all team members can broaden their level of knowledge and benefit long-term.

The implementation is regarded as a strategic alignment of customer and user interests. EC agencies can increase user and customer satisfaction by understanding, capturing, displaying and managing their experiences. Companies can create most excellent experiences, but if they do not match target audience's dreams and desires, business goals will not be achieved.

All four phases are regarded iteratively with fluent transition. The methodology and its tools are supposed to be appropriate for interdisciplinary teams as customer-centric business activities that provide value. Therefore, the current UX workflow and feedback of the UX team members is taken into account.All subcategories are displayed with associated methodologies and experience logic components.

**Phase 1.** The first phase of the framework aims to basically understand the (current and/or future) UX. The design opportunities for the relaunch of an old or the launch of a new online shop are commonly partly predefined by the client but technological advances such as new features are proposed. A profound understanding of the experience is based on an analysis of the current state and the potential (the experience logic aspects within the existing and the desired experience). As starting point serves the given initial situation. Online Shops differ in the kind of offering (products vs. services) and online business activity (B2B vs. B2C). Therefore, the expertise of the UX designer is enhanced by project specific aspects. The goal is to gain a better understanding of the project scope and requirements, defined in collaboration with the clients. A profound UX research and user classification is needed. Competitors (online retailers) are analyzed, and suitable trends integrated in the considerations. This phase can be described by the keywords: *insight(s) and user classification.* The better the team knows the user, which kinds of interactions take place and what the experience is like for the user and the client, the better it can develop a product based on customer needs, values and behavior. Therefore, research data and user classifications should be stored on an easily accessible site, allowing all team members to refer to it. Key questions are:

- What is the current experience offering and what could it be offering in the future?
- Who is the user and what are his needs?

**Table 2.** Phase 1 of the four-phase methodical framework

| Subcategory | Methodology, approach | Experience logic |
| --- | --- | --- |
| Understand the experience | • identify value adding factors<br>• co-create memorable experiences | Potentially each aspect |
| Define the baseline and project scope | • infrastructure, KPIs, setup, etc<br>• project 'Job to be done'<br>• Sailboat Exercise | Cognition, performance, context |
| Conduct research and ascertain benchmarks | • technical research<br>• qualitative and quantitative user research tools<br>• competitive analysis, benchmarking | Potentially each aspect |
| Classify the user by experiential qualities | • Limbic Map<br>• Empathy Map | Multisensorial, emotions, cognition |

**Phase 2.** The second phase of the framework is supposed to convey the (current and/or future) user experience to the whole team, including stakeholders such as clients. It can be regarded as extension of the first phase and builds on its insights (experience and user understanding). Every project team member ought to recognize the capability of user centric values and principles by producing *appropriate products* based on customer needs/expectations besides producing *products appropriately* [65]. *Empathy* and *tangibility* are keywords of this phase as the knowledge gained, is given to project actors. This process can be reiterated if new insights are gained, the context has changed, or the experience differs. Conveying who the user is, is regarded essentially in the interdisciplinary context and for incorporating stakeholders in the development process. The task is to impart the experience logic aspects project-specifically. Besides exploiting existing personas and research results, the goal is to develop an authentic image of the user in order to create a customer-centric development process. This can be reiterated accordingly if different or new findings are captured in phase 3. Key questions are:

• How can the information gained in phase 1 be conveyed to all stakeholders?
• What journey(s) is the user going through in which context(s)?

**Phase 3.** The third phase of the framework aims to capture the (current and/or future) user experience and expands on the results and insights of the first two phases. The perceptions of the current experience, defined requirements suitable capabilities (competitor analysis and benchmarking) and evoked user empathy within the whole team and the client function as fundament for the further process. *User involvement* and *feasibility* can be regarded as keywords of this phase as the experience is firstly prototyped and secondly testes with customers and users. This is intended to be rapid and iterative process. The opportunity for gathering targeted feedback on specific shop aspects is regarded essentially for incorporating the user in the development process. Besides exploiting

**Table 3.** Phase 2 of the four-phase methodical framework

| Subcategory | Methodology, Approach | Experience Logic |
|---|---|---|
| Convey the experience | • logical to emotional component<br>• utilize visualization tools | Emotions, cognition |
| Give your target group a face and specific attributes | • Persona | Emotions, cognition, Context |
| Map the customer journey and devise scenarios | • Customer (User) Journey Map<br>• (believable) Scenario | Potentially each aspect |
| Display design ideas visually | • Moodboard<br>• Storyboard | Emotions, performance |
| Evoke empathy by telling a Story | • Data-based Storytelling<br>• evoke empathy | Multisensorial, emotions |

existing designs and features, the goal is to develop an authentic individual selling position for the shop in order to improve the conversion rate. Therefore, human-centered design and user responses are indispensable. Use cases and user stories transform the knowledge gained in phase 1 (conveyed in phase 2) and transfer into technical aspects. The task is to make the experience tangible, put it in practice and integrate solutions for identified difficulties and pain points in wireframes and sketches. Tools for prototyping can be individually chosen by the UX designer and in accordance with the project team rules. Key questions are:

• How can the design intention be adjusted to technical specification?
• How can the potential of a new (prototyped) experience be exploited, taking user feedback into account?

**Phase 4.** The fourth as last phase of the methodical framework can be considered as complementing part that focuses on holistic approaches. It enhances UX by promoting the topic as integrated part of the project workflow. Knowledge gained by research and user classification in phase 1 has been conveyed to the team by visual, emotional and memorable tools in phase 2 and enriched by tangible elements such as prototypes in phase 3. Furthermore, user orientation and involvement play a key role in all phases due to the benefits of iterative processes and early testing. Phase 4 is inspired by that of Heinemann [20]as it describes the establishment of organizational prerequisites such as structures and processes.If a holistic concept realization is targeted, the promotors and challenges should be considered in order to prepare change management process. *Holistic implementation* and *dynamic long-term process* can be regarded as keywords in this phase. The task is to disseminate the user-centric mindset within the team, while

**Table 4.** Phase 3 of the four-phase methodical framework

| Subcategory | Methodology, Approach | Experience Logic |
|---|---|---|
| Capture the experience | • beware of problematic topics (cognitive biases, solving the wrong problem and missed opportunities)<br>• innovate by human-centered design | Potentially each aspect |
| Formulate user stories and estimate effort | • Use cases, user stories<br>• User story map<br>• Planning poker | Cognition, performance, context |
| Prioritize ideas, tasks and other issues | • Prioritization matrix<br>• Impact/effort matrix | Emotions, cognition, performance |
| Sketch and prototype the experience | • Wireframing (Mockups)<br>• (Experience) prototyping | Multisensorial, cognition |
| Involve users by testing the experience | • 5-s test<br>• (Un)moderated usability test<br>• Usability (cognitive) walkthrough<br>• Card sorting, eye tracking, etc | Emotions, cognition, performance |

paying attention to customer (client) needs. Considering the framework from a long-range perspective, performance measurement for investigating strengths and weaknesses of the approach and the methods is indispensable. Key questions are:

- What is essential for establishing a customer and user-centric mindset?
- How can the approach be holistically implemented considering the environment?

## 4   Qualitative Methodical User Experience Study

The described framework is applied to a concrete case that is fulfilling predefined requirements: Both client and project team are willing to participate, informative customer research data is available, and the target group is accessible for participating in the UX testing. As object of investigation a German motorbike accessory shop project is adducted. The initial online shops, created in 2018/2019 and operating in around 25 countries, are currently relaunched by Flagbit based on the template of a new version of a popular shop system.

Founded in 2007, the German EC agency Flagbit is now employing fifty people, mostly divided into interdisciplinary project teams. The company, based in Karlsruhe, is creating individual EC solutions industry independent (B2C and B2B market). Flagbit originally started as agency for web development and transformed to a comprehensive

**Table 5.** Phase 4 of the four-phase methodical framework

| Subcategory | Methodology, approach | Experience logic |
| --- | --- | --- |
| Manage the experience | • strategic alignment and interpretable guidelines<br>• ensure shop consistency (Atomic Design System) | Performance, context |
| Regard all team members as equal partners | • align methods and tools<br>• Code of conduct<br>• Low-tech social network | Multisensorial, emotions, cognition |
| Share knowledge interdisciplinary | • expand individual expertise<br>• facilitate cooperation (communication modes/principles) | Cognition, context |
| Measure and review project and product performance | • Sprint reviews (predefined Scrum values)<br>• Speed car retrospective | Cognition, performance, context |
| Integrate the experience logic holistically within the organization | • Service design clues and customer-experience management<br>• degree of UX maturity | Potentially each aspect |

EC partner. They are operating in the fields of consulting (technologies, systems and strategy), conception (UX), development, implementation (e.g. Product-Information-Management) as well as maintenance and support [16].

The starting point for new projects is the determination of general conditions, requirements and expectations. A detailed plan covering all aspects of the venture is established in order to overview the scope and estimate timeframes. Workshops help to determine concrete project goals, status quo, potential obstacle, etc., e.g. by performing the sailboat exercise. Flagbit is using Scrum as project management method, teams are therefore working with agile sprints. The former central (project independent) UX team has been divided to project teams in 2019 in accordance with agile principles.

### 4.1 Empirical Single Case Study Design

The investigation encompasses feedback of the interdisciplinary team concerning all methods and individual expert interviews. Interactive polls, integrated in the case study, offer valuable clues to the assessment of every single method. They are answered independently in preparation of the expert interviews. The five interviewees are regarded as representatives of their interest groups due to their expertise in a specific research related field (UX, development and project management) [66]. Interview questions are based on hypothesis, derived from theoretical considerations.

Guideline-based expert interviews are chosen as they allow in-depth topic comprehension by reviewing individual issues and enabling spontaneous interaction. The question of what qualifies someone to be an expert is controversially discussed in research

[67]. In this study experts are employees of the EC agency Flagbit working in an agile project team and commanding expertise from working experience.

Data collection is followed by data preparation, leaning on a category system (Tables 2, 3, 4 and 5) [68]. Transliterated data is listed in a table for the explorative process of analyzing and interpreting. Qualitative research is utilizing exemplary generalization by interpreting a single representative case study. Information is summarized and paraphrased in order to reduce the data content [66]. Similarities and contrastive statements are accentuated according to quality criteria of data interpretation (validity and reliability) [69]. This study can be classified as descriptive analysis.

As user involvement is one of the key components of the framework, a usability test in cooperation with Offenburg University is conducted as part of phase three of the framework. Precisely, a 5-s test and a moderated usability testing were carried out. According to the experience logic, this is using a multi-indicator sensor-system combining mimic analysis, qualitative user interviews and think-aloud [70]. The quality of answers is essential both in usability testing and study evaluation context [71].

## 4.2  Results and Findings

This chapter concentrates on summarizing results of introductive named research questions. Particularly, relations between the different components experience logic, UX, project workflow and customer centricity in the EC (agency) context are pointed out and conclusions are drawn.

**How is Customer Centricity Adding Value to Business Activities of an EC Agency?**
For examining the term 'customer-centricity' in the context of the EC agency Flagbit, two different perspectives have been considered: the 'macroenvironment', with regard to the agency perspective (predominance of client interest) and the 'micro-environment', with regard to the team perspective (gap between client and user interests).

Further, a differentiation between user (shop) and customer experience (agency) is basically needed. Both are crucial for project success and correlate with each other. On one hand, unanswered service requests from clients during project realization might result in unwillingness to effort user research and therefore influence the UX. On the other hand, a positive UX can boost conversion rate and therefore satisfies clients fairly long-term. Value adding impacts of a positive UX, stated by the interviewees, are:

- users turn into customer due to ease and joy of use – 'entertailing' is realized;
- UX is decisive for (quality) assessment – rising turnover (returning customers);
- users recommend their preferred shops to others – word-of-mouth advertising;
- well-structured shops and consistent experience – competitive positioning;
- intuitive shop navigation – decreases support issues and increases loyalty.

Both client and user require fast loading time, system stability and a simple buying process. Clients primary for boosting conversion rate. Users enjoy 24/7 availability and a convenient timesaving busing process. Technical aspect such as fast development and shop maintenance (backend) are not relevant for users. Instead, they are interested in the products itself with the goal to look around or buy something specific.

The interviewees are not in complete agreement concerning the term 'customer'. The perception is equal, but the context differs. Some associate it with shop users, others with agency clients. Neglecting the agency perspective 'customer-centricity' refers to solving user problems and user-centered processes instead of focusing on other project stakeholder's interests. The perceived high level of client-centricity is in contrast to the expandable level of user-centricity at Flagbit. Latter is progressing as UX is now representing user needs and product owner takes care of client needs.

Interests in the interdisciplinary project team are varying. This is valuable on one hand, as various viewpoints ensure shop components are considered from all relevant instances and challenging on the other hand, as the focus during project realization is on different aspects. Value can be realized by incorporating all perspectives in the project planning, research, effort estimation and prioritization process.

As unexpected technical challenges often arise and exhaust budget allowance, the consequences of poor UX must be conveyed to clients from beginning on. Separate budget approvals and monetary autonomy ensure the end result is in line with user interests. UX is acting as 'agent for users' and mutual translator. This is valuable on one hand as technical constraints of the shop system are explained to clients and solution concepts/designs are collectively established. On the other hand, interests are transformed into tangible elements by creating prototypes (basis for development).

By integrating users in the project workflow, the team's expertise can be enhanced by insights about the shop software and knowledge regarding general behavior patterns. Realistic findings are not discussable and further reusable for other template (re)launches (standardized components). The more insights are gained, the better the shop meets user needs. If optimization ideas and UX methods such as expert reviews are offered appositely (customer bonding), UX can be regarded as additional revenue stream. It can further be realized as project independent activity.

UX should be incorporated in sales as the range of services requires additional explanation and expert advice. Uncertainties can be clarified from beginning on and the agency is experienced positively regarding customer support expertise. Individual Flagbit case studies and figures that prove arguments can be represented to (potential) clients and exhibit persuasive power.

**How can the Experience Logic be Incorporated Holistically into UX Practices?**
Experiences are a product of human consolidation with sensory information - the 'takeaway' impression of customer's interaction with a product, service and business. Therefore, it is essential to analyze the experiential world of the customer. This research question is addressing the internal methodology - UX tasks and responsibilities during sales, consultation, conception, project realization and shop monitoring phases.

UX potential can be exploited by holistically incorporating it in business processes. Starting at the acquisition phase, the value of approaches can be conveyed, and the range of methodologies can be examined according to project requirements before the conception starts and the project workflow is determined. This prevents UX from being perceived as "nice-to-have" project component.

In consultation and conception phase qualitative and quantitative data is collected. Demographic characteristics, click behavior, used devices and browsers are enriched by authentic user statements from integrated surveys. Content like heatmaps, insights from recordings, surveys and polls provide user-centered data. Access to suitable tools and accounts is indispensable. Responsibility for initialization, configuration and monitoring of the tools needs to be specified.

The conceptual project scope analysis is enhanced by collective workshops (e.g. sailboat exercise). Also, this provides an opportunity for project stakeholders to become acquainted with each other. Research knowledge and workshop results are transformed into technical aspects by considering user and client perspective in user stories.

User needs, values and behavior must be conveyed to the team and to clients. Appropriate methods (in line with project and company characteristics) must be identified: Personas, Limbic Maps, Empathy Maps and Customer Journey Maps as well as Moodboards, Storyboards and Storytelling should be regarded as experience facilitators. Instead of simply showing and explaining results, a story makes content memorable and enjoyable for all project stakeholders. Willingness, budget and time for applying the methods must therefore be given. The goal is to progress from logical to emotional engagement by visualizing data and communicating emotions.

UX consultant activity can proceed in excess of project realization as innovation is continuously needed in the field of human-computer-interaction. Performing additional usability tests is regarded particularly valuable in an MVP (minimum viable product) approach, as shop potential is exploited iteratively. Optimization ideas, methods and concept drafts based on new findings or features should be communicated proactively.

The internal user focus and empathy is progressing since the UX team members have been divided among project teams. Interviewees state the rising importance of UX within the last couple of years. The experience topic should actively be promoted within the organization by sharing knowledge within and among teams. User interests should play a key role within all project phases due to the positive impacts of UX.

The first part of UX working practice within a team is to identify gaps that can be filled by suitable tools and to contrast subjective opinions with objective research results. UX responsibility is to question decisions based on user interests (value/effort). During project organization and realization UX presence enables the team to keep in mind who they are creating a shop for. UX specialist as part of an agile project team points out to experience consequences such as clerical errors in client documentations (CX) and missing consistency (UX).

**How can the UX Workflow be Optimally United with Agile Project Workflows?**
Project workflows become more efficient by aligning timeline and budget with the external perspectives (CX and UX) and the internal team perspective. This research question is examining how UX practices can be aligned with an agile EC project workflow.

Currently, the main challenge for project management is to find a balance and cope with external (client) and internal (team) interests. A concrete solution proposal is to divide the project management instance into regular scrum functions. Responsibilities and terms can be adjusted to Flagbit specifications.

The product owner should focus on ensuring the end result quality: functionality, in accordance with requirements, usability (in cooperation with UX instance). Also, professional collaboration with clients that requires technical expertise is required. Another task is to keep track of project budget and timeline (controlling) by managing the product backlog and reviewing progress.

Scrum Master instance is taking care of an efficient (internal) project workflow and moderates internal meetings. He or she ensure fast feedback loops by strengthening direct communication between team members and clients (customer-developer links) and coordinates tasks within the team.

During consultation and conception phase collaboration is of central interest. UX, project management and technical expertise are incorporated for defining project scope and requirements with clients. Target group specific knowledge is gained by performing research methods and benchmarking the experience. Content (qualitative and quantitative results) must be stored availably for clients and the team.

Conception phase aims to collectively create a 'product backlog' by formulating and prioritizing (Impact/Effort Matrix) user stories. The User story map as artefact provides an overview about the project baseline. The goal is to create a shared vision by incorporating all perspectives. The holistic Design System (style guide) serves as conceptual frontend specification that ensures a consistent shop experience.

Wireframes and Screendesigns make the future UX more tangible for all project stakeholders. Their creation starts in project organization phase. Periodic problems (e.g. handing screen designs off) require distinct definition and mutual agreement. Responsibilities and tasks for identifying bugs by testing developed instances (before forwarding to clients) should be distributed among team members.

Collective effort estimation (Planning Poker) during sprint planning results in a 'sprint backlog' (artefact). 'Versions' further predefine sprint increments and take care of the CX. An adjustable template (project specifically) must be developed by ensuring UX components are coordinated with technical aspects. Starting with initialization (infrastructure, databases) and configuration (shop system adaption), further versions are user flow based: Home page, category and product site, cart, checkout, account, etc.

By optimizing the internal workflow and integrating design sprints into scrum sprints, additional timeslots could be enabled. Project realization and therefore development can start earlier, which indeed saves time for unexpected (technical) circumstances. Sprints are realized as iterative process (duration between 2–4 weeks).

'Dailys' ensure interdisciplinary collaboration and up-to-date information sharing. Therefore, states of knowledge and skills of all team members are enriched. Mutual understanding and sympathy as preconditions should be realized in communication. Team independent scrum values can be predefined as reference point.

In a 'sprint review' project progress and current status (finalized versions) are evaluated. Sprints further strengthen motivation by creating tangible increments that help imagining the end result (for the team and clients). 'Sprint retrospective' ensures the product and performance is reviewed: Documented 'lessons learned' serve as artefact. Insights help team members to improve individually. Solution documentation (e.g. integrating a new feature) should be shared among teams and communicated actively.

### 4.3 Recommended Course of Action for the E-Commerce Agency Flagbit

The complexity of the term 'customer' in the agency context spawns challenges for all functions, striving to bridge gaps. Defining the baseline as well as conducting research in Phase 1 is fundamentally needed for the whole project team to understand scope and context. Therefore, e.g. information concerning the sailboat exercise (requirements) should be given to clients ahead of project start. Time and resources for performing collective workshops should be calculated in budget and timeframe. In order to exploit project management potential, clear contact persons and decision makers on client's side (in general or topic-specifically) must be defined from beginning on.

If clients are informed and engaged with UX from project beginning on, their user empathy is likely to be enriched and UX project components can be sold. Indeed, methodologies from phase 2 should be regarded as optional. They seem more relevant for shop launches than relaunches. When launching a new shop user needs and interests basically need to be discovered. Data is needed for creating concepts that are built on facts instead of assumptions. Therefore, particularly qualitative and quantitative research tools should be predefined components of an EC project.

As the EC agency Flagbit is operating industry and branch independent, benchmarking the shop experience and creating a knowledge base is considered indispensably because the end result is forced to be competitive. All information should be referable, explained to the team and stored on an accessible platform. Appropriate methods should be applied by project manager and UX specialist reasonably.

Usability test preparation and evaluation should include all team members. This ensures appropriate test items (shop components, features, etc.) and empathy towards users is evoked by authentic statements, issues and proposals. The availability of qualitative and quantitative research results further enables the project team to reach decisions based on non-discussable user needs and behavior.

Collaboration within and among interdisciplinary teams is key drivers of innovation and building an experience mindset. Communication modes should be evaluated critically on a continuous basis. Employees can refer to team workspaces and knowledge base, but responsibilities must be defined for managing and updating information.

It is recommended to introduce "lessons learned" workshops function-specifically for avoiding repetitive mistakes, sharing innovative solutions and building a network. The results of sprint reviews and retros can be utilized for that purpose, enriched by individual insights and findings. Everyone needs to do their part as reviewing experiences and sharing knowledge is valuable for all participants. This is further a suitable opportunity for new employees to connect with one's interest group. Workshops can be performed remotely, and a moderator as symbolic "head of function" is needed who can further encourage news sharing within specific communication channels.

## 5    Conclusion

This academic study covers the methodical part of content-related scientific goals. A relatively unexplored topic in a comparably young field of research (HCI) is examined.

The value of theoretically proposed methods (usefulness and value) is acknowledged by case study participants in practice. Indeed, the impact of individual methods varies according to the project context (client's and user's role, requirements, scope, etc.).

Organizations such as Google and Apple perceive customer-centricity as key factor for success. The research reveals insights that value adding factors such as increased loyalty, competitive positioning and word-of-mouth-advertising can be realized by considering the (external) agency perspective with predominant client interests and the (internal) team perspective. As service provider in the field of EC, all employees should be aware of the gap between client and user interests as equally important aspects.

In the past years, interest in UX has risen and its proven adoption as a strategic advantage turned out to be a driving force. UX is acting as intersection between users, clients (external) and developers (internal coordination). Tasks and responsibilities encompass sales, consultation, conception, project realization and shop monitoring phase.

In relation the complexity of meeting rising customer expectations, the 'extra mile' must be stressed. The process-focused component of this study reflects the challenge of efficiently aligning UX practices with agile project operations. Incorporating design sprints into scrum sprints is one of the suggested solutions.

The goal is to collectively manage methods and processes with UX, project management and technical instances. All interest groups should be involved, solutions shared with the whole team and compliance with agreements supervised. If project starts are realized collaboratively, goals and expectations can be adapted collectively. The better the team is informed about requirements and goals, the lower is the probability for misunderstandings and faulty implementations.

## 6  Limitations and Future Perspective

Reflecting on research results and study approach is inevitable as validity is regarded an important quality criterion.

Limitations concern the fleeting nature of experiences, that UX methods strive to capture. UX test results must be reviewed critically with clients and the team. Solution proposals are prioritized according to effort/impact ratio and components should be monitored after implementation. Additional A/B tests with controversial elements ensure they are in line the target group's needs and interests.

Internal UX progress (holistic approach) and potential can be identified by the UX maturity framework. The goal is to overcome (internal agency) barriers and to create a positive shop experiences as key driver for (external client) success.

Clients must be sensitized about UX to reflect digital touchpoints as part of the whole CX. The more positive all components are perceived, the higher the likelihood users return to a shop and tell others about it. This is particularly important in an experience economy as described introductorily.

A prioritization of methods per phase – indispensable and optional ones – should further be conducted. Additionally, concrete guidance and specific requirements for each method would facilitate execution. A classification of which method fits which type of agency client could be executed in the future.

As the scope of this study is limited, solely the internal perspective (team members) is examined. Client's experience with the agency would also be of note. Further, the single case study could prospectively be enlarged by multiple case studies within Flagbit as all teams represent various experiences and expertise. By reviewing research results in different contexts, validity and reliability is ensured. Contrasting the results with external organizations (agile IT project teams that incorporate UX) would exploit the potential of the topic examined in this study.

# References

1. Statista: eCommerce – worldwide (2020). https://www.statista.com/outlook/243/100/eco mmerce/worldwide?currency=eur. Accessed 12 Nov 2020
2. Pine, B.J., Gilmore, J.H.: Welcome to the experience economy. Harv. Bus. Rev. **76**, 97–105 (1998)
3. Guo, H.: Lean but not mean UX: towards a spiral ux design model. In: Marcus, A. (ed.) DUXU 2016. LNCS, vol. 9746, pp. 25–33. Springer, Cham (2016). https://doi.org/10.1007/ 978-3-319-40409-7_3
4. Weichert, S., Quint, G., Bartel, T.: Quick Guide UX Management, So verankern Sie Usability und User Experience im Unternehmen. Springer Gabler, Wiesbaden (2018). https://doi.org/ 10.1007/978-3-658-22595-7
5. Duczman, M., Brangier, E., Thévenin, A.: Criteria based approach to assess the user experi-ence of driving information proactive system: integration of guidelines, heuristic mapping and case study. In: Rebelo, F., Soares, M. (eds.) Advances in Ergonomics in Design, pp. 79–90. Springer, Cham (2016). https://doi.org/10.1007/978-3-319-41983-1_8
6. Tekin, M., İnce, H., Etlioğlu, M., Koyuncuoğlu, Ö., Tekin, E.: A study about affecting factors of development of E-commerce. In: Durakbasa, N.M., Gencyilmaz, M.G. (eds.) ISPR 2018, pp. 625–642. Springer, Cham (2019). https://doi.org/10.1007/978-3-319-92267-6_52
7. Riekhof, H.C.: E-Branding-Strategien. Gabler Verlag, Wiesbaden (2001)
8. Werthner, H., Ricci, F.: E-commerce and tourism. Commun. ACM **47**(12), 101–105 (2004). https://doi.org/10.1145/1035134.1035141
9. Heinemann, G.: Der neue Online-Handel. Geschäftsmodelle, Geschäftssysteme und Bench-marks in E-Commerce. 11th edn. (2020)
10. Stephan, P.F.: Handel und Wandel. In: Stephan, P.F. (ed.) Events und E-Commerce, pp. 207–214. Springer, Heidelberg (2000). https://doi.org/10.1007/978-3-642-45779-1_16
11. y Monsuwé, T.P., Dellaert, B.G.C., de Ruyter, K.: What drives consumers to shop online? A literature review. Int. J. Serv. Ind. Manage. **15**, 102–121(2004)
12. Ho, S.-C., Kauffman, R.J., Liang, T.-P.: Internet-based selling technology and e-commerce growth: a hybrid growth theory approach with cross-model inference. Inf. Technol. Manage. **12**(4), 409–429 (2011). https://doi.org/10.1007/s10799-010-0078-x
13. Turban, E., King, D., Lee, J.K., Liang, T.-P., Turban, D.C.: Electronic Commerce. A Man-agerial and Social Networks Perspective. 8th edn. Springer, Switzerland (2015).https://doi. org/10.1007/978-3-662-46327-7_2
14. Deges, F.: Grundlagen des E-Commerce. Strategien, Modelle, Instrumente. Springer Gabler (Lehrbuch), Wiesbaden (2020). https://doi.org/10.1007/978-3-658-26320-1
15. Cai, S., Li, L.: Quality contingent pricing under asymmetric information in electronic markets. In: 4th IEEE International Conference on Industrial Informatics, Piscataway, NJ, pp. 1307–1311 (2006)
16. Flagbit GmbH & Co. Kg: E-Commerce Leistungen. https://www.flagbit.de/leistungen.html. Accessed 08 June 2020
17. Fader, P.: Customer Centricity: Focus on the Right Customers for Strategic Advantage. Focus on the Right Customers for Strategic Advantage, 2nd edn. Wharton digital press, Philadelphia (2020)
18. Shah, D., Rust, R.T., Parasuraman, A., Staelin, R., Day, G.S.: The path to customer centricity. J. Serv. Res. **9**(2), 113–124 (2006)
19. Ulaga, W.: The journey towards customer centricity and service growth in B2B: a commentary and research directions. AMS Rev. **8**(1–2), 80–83 (2018). https://doi.org/10.1007/s13162-018-0119-x

20. Heinemann, G.: B2B eCommerce. Grundlagen, Geschäftsmodelle und Best Practices im Business-to-Business Online-Handel. Springer Gabler, Wiesbaden (2020). https://doi.org/10. 1007/978-3-658-27367-5_1
21. Lamberti, L.: Customer centricity: the construct and the operational antecedents. J. Strateg. Mark. 21(7), 588–612 (2013)
22. Kaur, G.: The importance of digital marketing. Int. J. Res. - Granthaalayah 5(6), 72–77 (2017). https://doi.org/10.5281/ZENODO.815854
23. Shaw, C., Ivens, J.: Building Great Customer Experiences. Houndmills Basingstoke Hampshire. Palgrave, New York (2002)
24. Heinbokel, T., Sonnentag, S., Frese, M., Stolte, W., Brodbeck, F.C.: Don't underestimate the problems of user centredness in software development projects there are many! Behav. Inf. Technol. 15(4), 226–236 (1996). https://doi.org/10.1080/014492996120157
25. Gentile, C., Spiller, N., Noci, G.: How to sustain the customer experience: an overview of experience components that co-create value with the customer. Eur. Manage. J. 25(5), 395–410 (2007). https://doi.org/10.1016/j.emj.2007.08.005
26. Atwal, G., Williams, A.: Luxury brand marketing – The experience is everything! J. Brand Manage. 16(5–6), 338–346 (2009). https://doi.org/10.1057/bm.2008.48
27. Adikari, S., Keighran, H., Sarbazhosseini, H.: Embed design thinking in co-design for rapid innovation of design solutions. In: Marcus, A. (ed.) DUXU 2016. LNCS, vol. 9746, pp. 3–14. Springer, Cham (2016). https://doi.org/10.1007/978-3-319-40409-7_1
28. Schmitt, B.: Experiential marketing. J. Mark. Manage. 15(1–3), 53–67 (1999). https://doi. org/10.1362/026725799784870496
29. Hwang, J., Seo, S.: A critical review of research on customer experience management. Int. J. Contemp. Hosp. Manage. 28(10), 2218–2246 (2016). https://doi.org/10.1108/IJCHM-04-2015-0192
30. Schmitt, B.: Concepts and frameworks for experience management. a framework for managing customer experiences. In: Schmitt, B.H., Rogers, D.L. (eds.) Handbook on Brand and Experience Management, pp. 113–132. Edward Elgar, Cheltenham (2008)
31. Verhoef, P.C., Lemon, K.N., Parasuraman, A., Roggeveen, A., Tsiros, M., Schlesinger, L.A.: Customer experience creation: determinants, dynamics and management strategies. J. Retail. 85(1), 31–41 (2009). https://doi.org/10.1016/j.jretai.2008.11.001
32. Bussolon, S.: The X factor: defining the concept of experience. In: Marcus, A. (ed.) Design, User Experience, and Usability, pp. 15–24. Springer International, Cham (2016). https://doi. org/10.1007/978-3-319-40409-7_2
33. Robier, J.: UX Redefined. Winning and Keeping Customers with Enhanced Usability and User Experience. Springer, Cham (2016). https://doi.org/10.1007/978-3-319-21062-9
34. Meyer, C., Schwager, A.: Customer experience. Harv. Bus. Rev. 85(2), 116–126 (2007)
35. Schmitt, B.: Experience marketing: concepts, frameworks and consumer insights. FNT in Mark. 5(2), 55–112 (2010). https://doi.org/10.1561/1700000027
36. Baker, M.J.: The Marketing Book, 5th edn. Butterworth-Heinemann, Routledge (2008)
37. Hassenzahl, M., Tractinsky, N.: User experience - a research agenda. Behav. Inf. Technol. 25(2), 91–97 (2006). https://doi.org/10.1080/01449290500330331
38. Yan, Y., Tang, C., Zhang, L.: Personalized design of food packaging driven by user preferences. In: Ahram, T., Falcão, C. (eds.) AHFE 2019. AISC, vol. 972, pp. 514–523. Springer, Cham (2020). https://doi.org/10.1007/978-3-030-19135-1_50
39. Richter, M., Flückiger, M.D.: Usability und UX kompakt. Produkte für Menschen, 4th edn. Springer Vieweg (IT kompakt), Heidelberg (2016). https://doi.org/10.1007/978-3-662-498 28-6
40. Colin, L.M., Chavez, A.R.: Evaluating interfaces and user's profiles. In: Rebelo, F., Soares, M. (eds.) Advances in Ergonomics in Design, pp. 437–446. Springer, Cham (2016). https:// doi.org/10.1007/978-3-319-41983-1_39

41. Hassenzahl, M.: User experience (UX): towards an experiential perspective on product quality. Session: Conférenciers invités. In: Association for Computing Machinery, Proceedings of the 20th Conference on l'Interaction Homme-Machine. IHM 2008, pp. 11–15. ACM Press, New York (2008)

42. Fortezza, F., Dusi, A., Pencarelli, T.: How marketing works in the experience economy: the case of the experience gift box providers. In: Pencarelli, T., Forlani, F. (eds.) The Experience Logic as a New Perspective for Marketing Management. ISAMS, pp. 111–123. Springer, Cham (2018). https://doi.org/10.1007/978-3-319-77550-0_6

43. Law, E.L.-C., van Schaik, P., Roto, V.: Attitudes towards user experience (UX) measurement. Int. J. Hum Comput Stud. **72**(6), 526–541 (2014). https://doi.org/10.1016/j.ijhcs.2013.09.006

44. Driggs, J., Diggs, A., Steinberg, D.: Building a house with a limited tool set: overcoming the challenge of incorporating usability in the acquisition Process. In: Ahram, T., Falcão, C. (eds.) AHFE 2019. AISC, vol. 972, pp. 24–31. Springer, Cham (2020). https://doi.org/10.1007/978-3-030-19135-1_3

45. Konradt, U., Wandke, H., Balazs, B., Christophersen, T.: Usability in online shops: scale construction, validation and the influence on the buyers' intention and decision. Behav. Inf. Technol. **22**(3), 165–174 (2003)

46. Barkhuus, L., Rode, J.A.: From mice to men-24 years of evaluation in CHI. In: Proceedings of the SIGCHI Conference on Human Factors in Computing Systems, CHI 2007, vol. 10, pp. 1–16. ACM Press, New York (2007)

47. Onal, E., McDonald, S., Morgan, C., Onal, O.: Enabling better user experiences across domains: challenges and opportunities facing a human factors professional. In: Marcus, A. (ed.) DUXU 2014. LNCS, vol. 8520, pp. 81–89. Springer, Cham (2014). https://doi.org/10.1007/978-3-319-07638-6_9

48. Stull, E.: UX Fundamentals for Non-UX Professionals. User Experience Principles for Managers, Writers, Designers, and Developers. Apress, Upper Arlington (2018)

49. Abelein, U., Sharp, H., Paech, B.: Does involving users in software development really influence system success? IEEE Softw. **30**(6), 17–23 (2013)

50. Nisar, T.M., Prabhakar, G.: What factors determine e-satisfaction and consumer spending in e-commerce retailing? J. Retail. Consum. Serv. **39**, 135–144 (2017)

51. Keil, M., Carmel, E.: Customer-developer links in software development. Commun. ACM **38**(5), 33–44 (1995)

52. Martin, A., Biddle, R., Noble, J.: The XP customer role in practice: three studies. In: Agile Development Conference, pp. 42–54. IEEE (2004)

53. Chamberlain, S., Sharp, H., Maiden, N.: Towards a framework for integrating agile development and user-centred design. In: Abrahamsson, P., Marchesi, M., Succi, G. (eds.) Extreme Programming and Agile Processes in Software Engineering. 7th International Conference, pp. 143–153. Springer, Heidelberg (2006). https://doi.org/10.1007/11774129_15

54. Hamachi, R., Tsukida, I., Noda, H.: Activities to improve system integration and service quality and add additional values - reducing the cost in applying human-centered-design process. In: Marcus, A. (ed.) DUXU 2014. LNCS, vol. 8520, pp. 32–38. Springer, Cham (2014). https://doi.org/10.1007/978-3-319-07638-6_4

55. Abrahamsson, P., Warsta, J., Siponen, M.T., Ronkainen, J.: New directions on agile methods: a comparative analysis. In: Proceedings of the 25th International Conference on Software Engineering. ICSE03, pp. 244–254. IEEE, Washington DC (2003)

56. Gurusamy, K., Srinivasaraghavan, N., Adikari, S.: An integrated framework for design thinking and agile methods for digital transformation. In: Marcus, A. (ed.) DUXU 2016. LNCS, vol. 9746, pp. 34–42. Springer, Cham (2016). https://doi.org/10.1007/978-3-319-40409-7_4

57. Beck, K., Beedle, M., van Bennekum, A., Cockburn, A., Cunningham, W., Fowler, M., et al.: Manifesto for agile software development. Utah (2001). http://agilemanifesto.org/

58. Pellegrini, F., Anjos, M., Florentin, F., Ribeiro, B., Correia, W., Quintino, J.: How to prioritize accessibility in agile projects. In: Ahram, T., Falcão, C. (eds.) AHFE 2019. AISC, vol. 972, pp. 271–280. Springer, Cham (2020). https://doi.org/10.1007/978-3-030-19135-1_27

59. Steffen, A.: Menschen und Organisationen im Wandel. Ein interdisziplinärer Werkzeugkasten für Veränderungsprozesse. Springer Gabler, Berlin, Heidelberg (2019). https://doi.org/10.1007/978-3-662-58851-2

60. Plonka, L., Sharp, H., Gregory, P., Taylor, K.: UX design in agile: a DSDM case study. In: Cantone, G., Marchesi, M. (eds.) Agile Processes in Software Engineering and Extreme Programming. 15th International Conference, XP, pp. 1–15. Springer Verlag (2014). https://doi.org/10.1007/978-3-319-06862-6_1

61. O'Cathain, A., Murphy, E., Nicholl, J.: Multidisciplinary, interdisciplinary, or dysfunctional? team working in mixed-methods research. Qual. Health Res. **18**(11), 1574–1585 (2008)

62. Pennington, D.: A conceptual model for knowledge integration in interdisciplinary teams: orchestrating individual learning and group processes. J. Environ. Stud. Sci. **6**(2), 300–312 (2015). https://doi.org/10.1007/s13412-015-0354-5

63. Lund, A.M.: Creating a user-centered development culture. Innov. Bus. Interact. **17**(3), 34–38 (2010)

64. Thompson, C.F., Anderson, R.I., Au, I., Ratzlaff, C., Zada, N.: Managing user experience: managing change. In: Extended Abstracts on Human Factors in Computing Systems, CHI 2010, pp. 3143–3146. ACM Press, New York (2010)

65. Szóstek, A.: A look into some practices behind Microsoft UX management. In: Extended Abstracts on Human Factors in Computing Systems, CHI 2012, pp. 605–618. ACM Press, New York (2012)

66. Bogner, A., Littig, B., Menz, W. (eds.) Das Experteninterview. VS Verlag für Sozialwissenschaften, Wiesbaden (2002)

67. Mieg, H.A., Näf, M.: Experteninterviews in den Umwelt- und Planungswissenschaften: eine Einführung und Anleitung. 2nd edn. ETH, Zürich (2005)

68. Mayring, P.: Qualitative content analysis. In: Forum Qualitative Sozialforschung/Forum: Qualitative Social Research, vol. 1, no. 2 (2000)

69. Schreier, M.: Varianten qualitativer Inhaltsanalyse: ein wegweiser im dickicht der Begrifflichkeiten. In: Forum: Qualitative Social Research, vol. 1, no. 15 (2014)

70. Müller, A., Gast, O.: Customer Experience Tracking – Online-Kunden. conversion-wirksame Erlebnisse bieten durch gezieltes Emotionsmanagement. Hochschule Offenburg. Fakultät für Betriebswirtschaft und Wirtschftsingenieuerwesen (2014)

71. Berg, B.L., Lune, H.: Qualitative Research Methods for the Social Sciences, 8th edn. Pearson, Boston (2012)

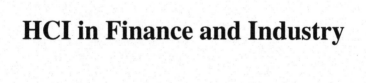

# HCI in Finance and Industry

# How Blockchain Innovations Emerge: From the Perspective of Knowledge Search

Jingxuan Huang, Lele Kang$^{(\boxtimes)}$, and Yiyang Bian

School of Information Management, Institute of Data Research in Humanities and Social Sciences, Nanjing University, Nanjing 210093, People's Republic of China
{lelekang,bianyiyang}@nju.edu.cn

**Abstract.** Emerging technologies like Blockchain are firms' important resources, rendering it significant to clarify their generation mechanisms. One potential way is knowledge search, which is an essential source of firms' lacking knowledge. There are two types of search: local search and boundary-spanning search. They have a different impact on innovative outcomes. Besides, the innovations of emerging technologies have two aspects: R&D aspect and application aspect, depending on the domain to which the target of an innovation belongs. Because of the distinct features of these two aspects, knowledge search may influence R&D innovations and application innovations differently. We empirically test our hypotheses on Blockchain patent data retrieved from PATSTAT. The results show that there exist different effects that knowledge search has on R&D innovations and application innovations. While searching across the boundary may benefit patent novelty in application innovations, it will improve patent quality in R&D innovations. Our study has many academic contributions and practical implications, and its limitations leave room for further research on the topic.

**Keywords:** Emerging technology · Knowledge search · Blockchain

## 1 Introduction

Emerging technologies are firms' important assets [1]. Therefore, the way their innovations are generated deserves further exploration. The literature distinguishes two aspects of the innovations of emerging technologies: the R&D innovation and the application innovation [2]. The former aims at addressing technical issues and advancing the performance of technology portfolio, whereas the latter tries to adapt the technology to other domains and obtain innovative outcomes. Due to the distinct features of R&D and application technologies, their generation mechanisms might be different as well.

Blockchain, a new method for recording transactional information, is a typical case of emerging technology [3, 4]. On one hand, Blockchain as a new technology has room for technical improvement, thereby attracting R&D innovations of many developers [2]. On the other hand, its fundamental technologies are mature to some extent for commercial use, so people are applying it to solve problems in other domains [5]. Since Blockchain is thriving on both aspects at the moment, it is possible for us to observe the generation

© Springer Nature Switzerland AG 2021
F. F.-H. Nah and K. Siau (Eds.): HCII 2021, LNCS 12783, pp. 181–196, 2021.
https://doi.org/10.1007/978-3-030-77750-0_12

of R&D and application of Blockchain technology, which will help us understand the underlying mechanisms. In such case, Blockchain is a good exemplar for the study of generation mechanisms of emerging technologies.

One potential road of inventing emerging technology is knowledge search that is confirmed as an important source of innovations in the literature [6, 7]. From the learning perspective [8], knowledge search refers to a strategic behavior that firms seek knowledge they lack, which is significant for finding new ideas through combining new knowledge with an existing knowledge base [7, 9]. Knowledge search is essentially important in the context of emerging technology since new knowledge is emerging in the field extremely rapidly [10], which requires firms to keep doing knowledge search to keep up with the pace. According to the boundary it takes place, knowledge search can be classified into local search and boundary-spanning search [11–13]. Local search happens within the focal technological domain, therefore the retrieved knowledge can be more similar and easier to absorb. In contrast, boundary-spanning search reaches out for wider fields, increasing the possibility of encountering novel knowledge. By studying how different types of search affect the innovations of emerging technologies, we can advance the theoretical insights of their generation mechanisms. Specifically, as R&D innovations and application innovations of emerging technologies have distinct features [2], how search boundary affects the innovative outcomes can be different between them.

The positive effect of boundary-spanning search and local search has attracted much attention in innovation research. The literature achieves the agreement that the boundary-spanning search is more likely to generate innovations of satisfactory quality as it overcomes path dependency in innovation [14] and facilitates the combination of various knowledge [15]. However, some scholars begin to recognize the unique merits of local search. Jung and Lee [13] found that when targeted at original knowledge, local search can produce more high-impact innovations than the boundary-spanning one does due to the originality firms revitalize. This finding indicates that the relationship between knowledge search types and innovative outcomes depends on the contextual factors. In the context of emerging technology, the relationship may be different in R&D innovations and application innovations. To better understand how search boundary influences the innovations of emerging technologies, it is important to take these two aspects into account.

In the context of Blockchain innovation, we mainly address two questions: (1) how does the search boundary affect quality and novelty of innovations of emerging technologies separately; (2) how does this effect differentiate when the innovation targeted at R&D innovations or application innovations. We use Blockchain patent data retrieved from PATSTAT database to empirically provide the answers to these questions. When constructing measures, we use several advanced methods. For measuring the search types, we adopt Latent Dirichlet allocation (LDA) and a Deep Learning language model RoBERTa to represent each patent abstract, which better preserves the semantic information. Besides, to measure the R&D and application innovations in patents, we combine the keyword method and the Support Vector Machine (SVM) classifier to obtain satisfying results.

This study makes several contributions. First, the findings enrich the literature on innovation theory by examining how search boundary affects innovations of emerging technologies and how the effects will be different in R&D innovations and application innovations. Second, it is also found that searching across the boundary can be useful, but the type of innovations (R&D or application) and the expected attribute of outcomes (quality or novelty) should be taken into consideration. Third, this study adopts text mining approaches and some machine learning algorithms to construct measures, which can be used in future studies in related fields.

The paper is arranged as follows: the second part reviews the literature related to this study; the third part carries out theoretical analysis and proposes the hypotheses; the fourth part describes the methodology including data, the construction of measures and regression models; the fifth part is the results of empirical research; the sixth part discusses the findings of the study and summarizes its contributions and limitations, then provides future research directions.

## 2 Literature Review

### 2.1 Search Boundary

A large body of literature distinguishes various types of search based on the boundary it takes place. Scholars differentiate boundaries that search may cross, like technological boundary [13, 16], geographical boundary [17] and organizational boundary [11]. The most concerned is the technological boundary that is regarded as the boundary of technological domains. 'Local search' refers to the one that happens within the technological domain that the focal innovation belongs to, while 'boundary-spanning search' may cover several technological domains besides the focal one. While the search itself satisfies the definition of exploration [18], local search is thought to be less explorative as it mainly focuses on knowledge within its local technological domain [19, 20]. There also exists a mapping relation between the search boundary and the nature of search: local search corresponds to exploitation and boundary-spanning search corresponds to exploration [13].

Based on the ambidexterity theory [21], Rosenkopf and Nerkar [11] proposed that these two types of search will give rise to different kinds of competence. The "first-order competence", which refers to the incremental expertise in current domain and the generation of incremental innovations, can be enhanced by local search [11]. On the other hand, searching across the boundary will promote the "second-order competence", which encourages the recombination of knowledge of different domains and also fosters the creation of new knowledge, since recombinant knowledge is the major source of novel knowledge [13, 22]. The "second-order competence" is more highlighted in innovation literature since it can create new knowledge through the reconfiguration of knowledge [11]. Therefore, boundary-spanning search attracts more attention than the local one as it can overcome path dependency to facilitate knowledge recombination [11, 14], thereby improving "second-order competence".

Recently, scholars began to reconsider the influence of local search and found the necessity to further exploring the relationship between search boundary and the outcomes of search. Jung and Lee [13] distinguished "search target" as a brand-new dimension of search and thus refining the existing boundary-based typology. They found that when firms search targeting at original knowledge, local search will lead to more high-impact breakthroughs than the boundary-spanning one. The finding indicates that search boundary may have more complicated effects on innovative outcomes and also demonstrates the capacity of local search to generate innovations of satisfactory quality. However, they only studied the effect when the search target is original knowledge and did not consider the specific innovation context. Therefore, further examination is required to fill the gap.

## 2.2 Innovation Novelty and Quality

Jung and Lee [13] distinguished path-breaking novelties and high-impact breakthroughs as two aspects of innovative outcomes. The first aspect emphasizes the discontinuous nature of an innovation, which renders the existing technologies obsolete [23]. Meanwhile, it also leaves room for further improvement [24]. The second aspect represents the usefulness of an innovation. Those highly impactful innovations resolve some of the existing uncertainty and thus being recognized and built on by abundant following innovations [25, 26]. It is worth noticing that a patent with path-breaking novelty is not bound to be a high-impact breakthrough, as a novel idea is not necessarily a successful one. While different inherently, the two aspects can be combined to give a comprehensive evaluation of an innovative outcome.

We follow this framework but substitute quality for the high-impact breakthroughs, which implies that we do not consider whether the community has recognized the innovation until now. This is in accordance with the features of Blockchain as an emerging technology whose impact is still too weak to be recognized due to the relatively early stage in technological development [2]. Therefore, we only focus on the potential usefulness of innovations and regard it as one important indicator for evaluation.

There has long been a consensus on the capability of boundary-spanning search to produce satisfactory innovative outcomes with no clear distinction between quality and novelty [11, 27]. However, Jung and Lee [13] presented us with the possibility that local search can also generate high-impact breakthroughs in a certain condition. To fully understand the impact of different search on innovation novelty and quality, we will further study the underlying mechanisms.

## 2.3 R&D and Application Innovations

Blockchain possesses all of the five features of an emerging technology [1], namely radical novelty, relatively fast growth, coherence, prominent impact, and uncertainty and ambiguity. Therefore, the framework of analysis used in assessing emerging technologies can be applied to Blockchain technology appropriately. Srinivasan [10] pointed out two dimensions of the development of emerging technologies: the relay race evolution and the revolution by application. He also mentioned that as the commercial potential of an innovation grows, the company's focus tends to shift from technology's science to its applications. Pillai and Biswas [2] also distinguished the R&D aspect and the application aspect in the technological development of emerging innovations. R&D innovations aim at conquering technical challenges of the technology itself, while application innovations reflect the adaptation of the emerging technology in other domains, which is consistent with the evolutionary theory of technological change [1].

The two aspects are different but correlated. An obvious difference is the target of innovation. The R&D innovations try to overcome technical challenges and thus improving the emerging technology itself, while the application innovations apply the technology to resolve problems in other domains. Srinivasan [10] also found that innovations aimed at tackling technical problems of the technology itself tend to have an incremental effect on its original domain, but those that are applied to a new domain are more likely to produce discontinuous "creative destruction", which have been observed in several industries [28]. Besides the different effects on technological development, these two aspects also produce different economic outcomes. The application innovations have markets and benefits that are more conceivable as they are relatively easier to be transformed into particular products, therefore being more remunerative [10]. However, only when the major technical issues are addressed, can the applications of an emerging technology be possible. In that case, the two aspects are closely connected.

Blockchain technology has witnessed a spike in its application innovations in recent years, thanks to the continuously resolved technical problems [29] and its growing commercial potential [5]. On one hand, the room for its technical improvement is still considerable, intriguing more and more researchers to explore better solutions. On the other hand, the fundamental parts of the Blockchain technology are mature enough to be adapted to other domains, where people are exploring new approaches based on it to conquer persistent problems in their field. The recent trend of the development of Blockchain technology makes the framework of analysis with R&D and application aspects extremely suitable (Fig. 1).

## 3   Research Model and Hypotheses

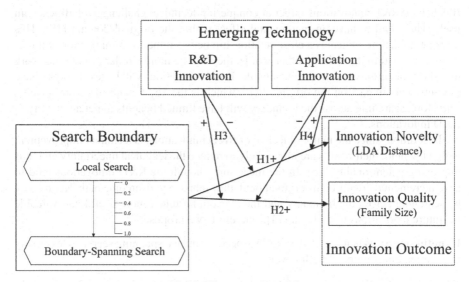

**Fig. 1.** The research model.

### 3.1 The Impact of Search Boundary

Local search focuses on knowledge within the technological domain and thus gaining incremental expertise in current domain [11]. By contrast, boundary-spanning search is more likely to generate novel knowledge by overcoming path dependency [11, 14] and promoting the recombination of knowledge of different fields [15].

The patent, an important outcome of the innovative activities, can be assessed from two perspectives. Patent novelty stresses the distinctions between the existing patents and the focal one. It highlights the discontinuous nature of an innovation [23]. Different from novelty, patent quality indicates how useful a patent is for future innovations. A patent of high quality typically resolves technological uncertainty, making it easy for other inventors to build on it.

Since boundary-spanning search is more explorative than the local one [27, 38], it is more possible to produce rather novel patents. Besides, by integrating knowledge of different fields, it is more likely to generate novel knowledge [13, 15]. Therefore, the more the search boundary is crossed, the more novel the patent will be.

In addition, as searching across the boundary exposes inventors to more unfamiliar knowledge, it can restrain the negative effect of path dependency and generate more valuable and useful innovations [15]. Besides, the novel knowledge is also of great value for future work to build on. Therefore, we propose:

**Hypothesis 1:** Search boundary is positively related to patent novelty.

**Hypothesis 2:** Search boundary is positively related to patent quality.

### 3.2 Blockchain R&D Innovation

Blockchain R&D innovations target at conquering technical challenges of Blockchain itself. They tend to have an incremental effect within the original domain [10]. This incremental nature indicates a close relationship between the focal innovation and previous work within the field. In other words, they can be more similar to previous work than the application ones. In the meanwhile, R&D innovations will be less likely to have discontinuous impact on the original field, which is the key feature of patent novelty. Therefore, searching across the boundary will have limited benefits to patent novelty in R&D innovations.

In addition, since the major objective of R&D innovations is technical improvement within the field, their results are more likely to reduce the technical uncertainty and thus improving patent quality [25]. In the meantime, though the R&D innovations tend to have incremental effects on its original field, they manage to overcome path dependency by searching across the boundary and thus becoming much more useful and valuable for future innovations to build on [14]. Therefore, we propose:

**Hypothesis 3a:** When targeted at R&D aspect, boundary-spanning search is less likely to generate innovations of high novelty.

**Hypothesis 3b:** When targeted at R&D aspect, boundary-spanning search is more likely to generate innovations of high quality.

### 3.3 Blockchain Application Innovation

On contrary to the R&D innovations, application innovations try to resolve problems in other domains by adopting Blockchain technology to those fields. The outcome is also more discontinuous than the R&D ones have, creatively destructing the existing work and even revolutionizing the industry [10]. Since the application innovations adopt the Blockchain technology to other fields, they naturally combine knowledge of different domains and create novel knowledge. As the search boundary becomes larger, the degree of recombination would only be strengthened. On the other hand, the discontinuous feature of application innovations makes it nature to lay more stress on patent novelty, which represents how much the focal one is different from the existing work.

However, the effect of the search boundary on application innovations could be much more complicated. Rosenkopf and Nerkar [11] argued that searching within technological boundary has more impact on subsequent improvement within the domain. Jung and Lee [13] found that when targeted at original knowledge (i.e. knowledge from two different fields is combined for the first time), local search will generate more high-impact patents. Capaldo et al. [16] had a similar finding, but they further clarified the underlying mechanisms. They claimed that the more distant two domains are, the more difficult to generate valuable innovations. This is because the inventor is not familiar with the distant knowledge, which increases difficulties in searching and absorbing knowledge, thus limiting the possibility of successful knowledge recombination and reducing the value of innovations. Besides, from the perspective of technological uncertainty, the introduction of distant knowledge that the inventor cannot fully understand may increase the uncertainty instead of resolving it. Therefore, we hypothesize that in application aspect, the positive effect of searching across the boundary on patent quality is weakened.

**Hypothesis 4a:** When targeted at application aspect, boundary-spanning search is more likely to generate innovations of high novelty.

**Hypothesis 4b:** When targeted at application aspect, boundary-spanning search is less likely to generate innovations of high quality.

## 4 Research Methodology

### 4.1 Data

To examine the theoretical hypotheses, we analyzes the Blockchain patents. This follows the previous work which regards patents as a measure of knowledge within firms [16, 39]. We retrieve patent data from PATSTAT (Spring 2020 Edition), a patent database containing raw patent data from more than 80 patent offices across the world [40]. It is widely used in recent innovation literature [2, 38, 41, 42]. Each patent in PATSTAT contains extensive information like forward citation, international patent classification (IPC) codes and abstract.

We initiated our data collection by identifying Blockchain-related patents. Due to its early stage of development, there is no unique IPC codes assigned to Blockchain technology [2], which makes it hard to acquire related patents. An intuitive way is to search the keyword 'Blockchain' and its modifications (e.g. 'Block-chain') in the patent title and abstract. However, it cannot wipe out unrelated patents containing the keyword referring to other concepts, such as copolymer block chain in chemistry. Pillai and Biswas [2] incorporated 21 IPC codes related to Blockchain, verified by domain experts from the European Patent Office (EPO), to improve the results from keyword search. We adopted their method and retrieved 15,100 Blockchain patents based on both keywords and IPC codes. Considering the growing trend of Blockchain patents applications [3, 43], we precluded data before 2014 due to the small total number, which is consistent with recent research on Blockchain technology [4, 31]. Because we need to know the patentee's previous patents to develop knowledge search measurements, patents with patentee that has no previous application records are excluded, trimming our dataset to 3,614. The Blockchain patents within our final dataset were applied between 2014 and 2019. These patent applications belong to 1,476 different companies. In this paper, the unit of analysis is at patent level.

## 4.2  Measures

**Dependent Variables**
*Innovation Novelty*
Patent novelty is measured with the similarity between patents [42], and the more similar two patents are, the less novel the focal patent is [3]. One approach to measuring patent similarity is text matching, which reliability has been validated by experts [42]. However, traditional keyword-based text matching suffers from several shortcomings like difficulties to select meaningful keywords, multicollinearity between keywords (e.g. "happy" and "delight" may be accounted as two features though they are synonyms) and limitation in representing semantic information. To avoid these disadvantages, new methods of measuring text similarity are in demand.

Latent Dirichlet allocation (LDA) method is a helpful approach to represent text and then to better measure novelty. LDA is an unsupervised learning model proposed by Blei et al. [44] and is widely used in nature language processing tasks nowadays. A fitted LDA model can extract topics from the corpus automatically as well as the distribution of each word in each topic. With that information, the probability that one text belongs to different topics can be generated. LDA requires no keyword list as input, wiping out the arbitrariness that comes from manual-selected features. Moreover, its superiority in capturing true innovation has been demonstrated in recent literature [45, 46]. Therefore, it is an appropriate method to present text in our research.

We use the abstract to represent each patent. We first preprocess abstracts by lowercasing the text, removing punctuation and stop words, stemming all words and then eliminating those with document frequency less than 0.02 as well as words shorter than 3 characters. Then we implement LDA in the preprocessed data and extract 20 topics from the corpus by trial. Each patent is transformed into a 20-dimension vector ($v_i$), each unit $(topic_i)$ standing for the probability of its degree of belonging to one topic. For each patent ($v_i$), we compute the cosine similarity between it and the others in the rest of the corpus $(v_j)$, then use 1 to minus this value to get a collection of distance. The average of it serves as our measurement of innovation novelty.

$$v = [\text{topic}_1, \text{topic}_2, \ldots, \text{topic}_{20}]$$

$$\text{Patent Novelty} = \frac{\sum_{j \in N, \, j \neq i} \left( 1 - \frac{v_i v_j}{\sqrt{v_i^2 v_j^2}} \right)}{N - 1}$$

*Innovation Quality*

The literature mostly uses forward citation as the measure of patent quality [46, 47]. However, due to the relatively short time the Blockchain technology has developed, it is worth noticing that Blockchain patents do not have many forward citations in general, and most of them have not been cited at all. Therefore, a new measurement that can represent the potential high quality of patents is necessary in this study.

A patent can only protect the innovation within the country that the patent is granted. Therefore, a patentee is inclined to apply patents of the same innovation in different countries respectively. This group of patents is called patent family. Since applying for patents in each country could be costly, the size of the patent family implicitly indicates how much value the patentee expects from it [47]. We search for family members of each patent by matching patent titles, and those patents are granted by patent offices from 11 countries. The family size of a patent is used to measure innovation quality of patents.

**Independent Variables**

*Search Boundary*

To measure the search boundary, we follow Jung and Lee [1] to use the technological proximity between the focal patent and the patents it cites. To calculate the proximity, we construct two vectors for each patent: the focal patent vector $(F_i)$ and cited patent vector $(F_j)$. Each dimension of the vector represents an IPC code. In order to constrain the dimension of the vector, we truncate the IPC code and keep 3 digits of each technological class. Since there are 131 unique 3-digit IPC codes among the Blockchain patents, these vectors are all 131 dimensions. For vector representing the focal patent $(F_i)$, we retrieve all patent applications that the applicant applied before the filling date of the focal patent. Then we calculate the average time that each 3-digit IPC code appears $(\text{ipc}_k)$. For the vector representing the cited patent $(F_j)$, the frequency of occurrences of IPC codes in cited patents is used to form the vector. With these two vectors, we can calculate the Jaffe's patent class-based proximity measure of two vectors [2] to get the search proximity ranging from 0 to 1. The search boundary is one minus search proximity as the wider the boundary is, the less proximate two patents would be.

$$F = [ipc_1, \, ipc_2, \, \ldots, \, ipc_{131}]$$

$$\text{Search Boundary} = 1 - \frac{F_i F_j}{\sqrt{F_i^2 F_j^2}}$$

*R&D Innovation and Application Innovation*
Another difficulty in the research is to measure the R&D innovation and application innovation of patents. Pillai and Biswas [2] implemented a rule-based text classification based on patent title and abstract to classify them. This method, however, suffers from the arbitrariness in manual screening as well as the inability to classify patents without those identified keywords. To make up for these deficiencies, we propose a hybrid approach that combines the rule-based method and machine learning classification models to get satisfactory results.

To be specific, we search for keywords of R&D and application innovations in preprocessed patent abstract according to the keyword list that Pillai and Biswas provided [2]. 579 patents can be classified in this way, while the others remain unknown. To conduct the classification task, we adopt the Support Vector Machine (SVM) classifier and input these 579 labeled patents as the training set, then apply the trained model to classify the rest of the patents.

In order to transform patent abstract into numeric features so that they can serve as model input, we apply a pre-trained language model to obtain word embedding for each patent. The pre-trained language model is a cutting-edge methodology in Natural Language Processing with deep learning. It is capable of generating word embedding of satisfactory quality, capturing semantic and syntactic similarity in natural language. It is increasingly used in recent literature to examine patents [49, 50]. Specifically, we employ RoBERTa, a robustly optimized BERT pre-trained model [51], to obtain word embedding for each patent.

Since sometimes the keywords of R&D and application innovations can be found in the same patent abstract, we train two SVM classifiers separately and use two dummy variables to indicate the type of patent. This demonstrates that the classification of R&D innovations and application innovations is not a strict one. The accuracy of the R&D SVM classifier is 77.7%, while the application SVM classifier is 77.2%. After implementing models in unlabeled patents, we obtain 1,562 R&D innovations and 2,287 application innovations as some patents could be regarded as both R&D and application.

**Controls**
Table 1 summarizes all control variables and their explanation.

**Table 1.** Control variables and corresponding explanation.

| Control | Explanation |
|---|---|
| Authority (dummy) | The country of the patent office that grants the focal patent |
| Year (dummy) | The filing year of the focal patent |
| Citing total | The backward citations of the focal paten |
| Science knowledge | The number of nonpatent citations of the focal patent |
| Knowledge maturity | The average number of years passed when a patent is cited by the focal patent |
| Knowledge maturity diversity | The standard deviation of intervals between filing years of the focal patent and the patents it cites |
| Team size | The number of inventors related to the focal patent |
| Team diversity | The number of occurrences of each 3-digit IPC codes in patents that inventors applied prior to the focal one. Calculate the entropy to represent a team as a whole |
| Team experience | The average number of patents that inventors applied in the past 5 years before filing the focal one |
| Team experience diversity | The standard deviation of Team Experience |
| Team success | The average number of patents that inventors of the focal patent applied in the past 5 years are granted |
| Team Success diversity | The standard deviation of Team Success |

## 4.3 Analyses

### Regressions

Since we have innovation novelty and innovation quality with a different distribution, we choose the estimation models accordingly. As innovation novelty distributes evenly between 0 and 1, we use an ordinal least square (OLS) regression in estimation. Innovation quality is patent family size counting how many countries the same patent applies in, so we use the Poisson regression, which is recommended in such situation [55].

### Estimation Models

We construct 6 models for each dependent variable. Model 1 serves as a baseline model, which includes only control variables. Then we incorporate three independent variables (search boundary, R&D innovation and application innovation) separately in Model 2, 3 and 4. We put an interaction term of search boundary and R&D innovation in Model 5 to study their interaction effect. Model 6 is designed for similar reasons, but it examines the interaction effect between search boundary and application innovation.

## 5 Results

For innovation novelty, in both Model 2 and 5, the coefficients of search boundary are significantly positive ($\beta = 0.019$, $p < 0.1$; $\beta = 0.025$, $p < 0.05$). This indicates that searching across the boundary will produce innovations of higher novelty, which supports Hypothesis 1. In Model 5, the interaction term between search boundary and R&D innovation does not have a significant coefficient, which rejects Hypothesis 3a. However, in Model 6, the interaction term between search boundary and application innovation has a positive coefficient ($\beta = 0.009$, $p < 0.01$), strongly supporting Hypothesis 4a.

For innovation quality, in Model 2 and Model 5, the significant positive coefficient ($\beta = 1.323$, $p < 0.01$; $\beta = 0.757$, $p < 0.01$) between search boundary and innovation quality demonstrates that boundary-spanning search is more likely to generate innovations of high quality, which supports Hypothesis 2. In Model 5, the interaction term between search boundary and R&D innovation has a positive coefficient ($\beta = 0.103$, $p < 0.01$), strongly supporting Hypothesis 3b. However, the interaction term in Model 6 shows that application innovation does not enhance or weaken the impact of search boundary on innovation quality, which is against Hypothesis 4b that boundary-crossing search is not so helpful in improving the quality of application innovation.

# 6   Discussion and Conclusion

Blockchain technology, an emerging technology, is changing the world. It not only reshapes the transaction system as the fundamental technology of Bitcoin, but also catches the attention of people from different fields to resolve problems in those domains. Considering the great potential of Blockchain, scholars become interested in how its innovations are generated within companies. If we are clear about their generation mechanism, it would be much easier to promote the effectiveness and efficiency of innovative activities. This study explores how search boundary influences the innovation quality and novelty of Blockchain patents. Specifically, we study the impact of search boundary on Blockchain patents, then investigate the patents from two aspects, namely R&D aspect and application aspect. We find the effects of search boundary will be different in different kinds of Blockchain innovations.

## 6.1   Theoretical Contributions

This study has several contributions to theory. First, our findings enrich knowledge search theory. There exists a trade-off when searching across the technological boundary [11], so the degree of crossing boundary is worth in-depth study. By testing empirically in Blockchain patents retrieved from PATSTAT, we reveal the effects of search boundary on patent quality and novelty in the context of emerging technologies. Specifically, it is found that boundary-spanning search benefits both innovation novelty and quality.

Second, we further measure Blockchain patents according to two aspects of emerging technologies, namely R&D innovation and application innovation. We explore how the effects of search boundary will be different in specified kinds of innovations. Our empirical results support our hypotheses that its positive effect on patent novelty will be enhanced in application innovation but not in R&D innovation. On the other hand, searching across the boundary will be more helpful to improve innovation quality when it focuses on R&D aspect, but application innovation have no such strengthening effect.

Another theoretical contribution of this study is the innovations we make when constructing measures. To preserve the semantic information in numeric representation of patent abstract, we deploy Latent Dirichlet allocation (LDA) and a deep learning language model RoBERTa. In addition, we combine the keyword method and the Support Vector Machine (SVM) to measure R&D and application innovation. The introduction of state-of-the-art machine learning models can improve the results of empirical analysis [56].

## 6.2 Practical Contributions

This study also has some practical implications. The results of empirical estimation show that the degree of search boundary depends on the type of focal patent and the feature of the outcome that the firm cares about. For R&D innovations, it would be useful to search across the boundary if the objective is to produce patents of high quality. However, patent novelty does not benefit so much from the boundary-spanning search as the patent quality does. On the contrary, for application innovations, searching across the boundary can remarkably promote patent novelty, but it will not be so helpful for improvement in patent quality. It is important for firms to design proper strategies accordingly.

## 6.3 Limitations and Future Research Directions

This study has some limitations, leaving room for future work to make improvements. First, the unit of analysis of most literature about knowledge search theory is firm [23, 57]. We adopt patent unit as we believe the knowledge of a group of inventors will be more stable and measurable than a firm, making it much easier to recognize whether the boundary-spanning search happens or not. However, it would be meaningful to test our hypotheses in firm unit. Second, when it comes to boundary-spanning search, we only consider the technological boundary. There also exist other boundaries like organizational [11] and geographical boundary [17], which require further examination. Besides, several measures of this study have the room for improvement. For patent novelty, we use the LDA method to represent each patent, but the number of topic we choose is somewhat arbitrary. For patent quality, we use the size of the patent family to indicate the potential quality, but it may not be representative and comprehensive enough. Future research in better measures of patent novelty and quality will be fruitful. Furthermore, the results of some control variables exhibit interesting points that deserve further exploration. We find that a patent will have lower novelty and quality if it has more backward citations in total, but it would be helpful to cite more literature that is nonpatent. It seems that different kinds of citations will have a different impact on patents. Besides, even though diverse knowledge in a group of inventors will make the patent quality decrease, searching for different knowledge is helpful for patent quality. Future work can delve into the differences in these two phenomena. Finally, we only consider Blockchain to investigate the emerging technologies, which may not be fully generalizable. Future work can explore different emerging technologies to test the hypotheses in this study.

**Acknowledgement.** The work was partially supported by the National Natural Science Foundation of China (#72072087), Natural Science Foundation of Jiangsu Province (No.

BK20200339), Shenzhen Special Fund for the Development of Strategic Emerging Industries (No. JCYJ20170818100156260), research fund of Science and Technology Department of Sichuan Province (2020YFSY0061), and Institute of Data Research in Humanities and Social Sciences at Nanjing University.

# References

1.  Rotolo, D., Hicks, D., Martin, B.R.: What is an emerging technology? Res. Pol. **44**(10), 1827–1843 (2015)
2.  Filippova, E., Scharl, A., Filippov, P.: Blockchain: an empirical investigation of its scope for improvement. In: International Conference on Blockchain (2019)
3.  Bruens, B., Moehrle, M.G.: Understanding the diffusion of the blockchain technology: a patent-based analysis using the tf-lag-idf for term novelty evaluation. In: PICMET 2018 Portland International Conference on Management of Engineering and Technology (2018)
4.  Kim, H., Kim, J., Jang, K., Han, J.: Are the blockchain-based patents sustainable for increasing firm value? Sustainability **12**(5), 1–17 (2020)
5.  Salviotti, G., De Rossi, L.M., Abbatemarco, N.: A structured framework to assess the business application landscape of blockchain technologies. In: Proceedings of the 51st Hawaii International Conference on System Sciences (2018)
6.  Lin, R., Xie, Z., Hao, Y., Wang, J.: Improving high-tech enterprise innovation in big data environment: a combinative view of internal and external governance. Int. J. Inf. Manage. **50**, 575–585 (2020)
7.  Ferreras-Méndez, J.L., Newell, S., Fernández-Mesa, A., Alegre, J.: Depth and breadth of external knowledge search and performance: the mediating role of absorptive capacity. Ind. Mark. Manage. **47**, 86–97 (2015)
8.  Teece, D.J.: Profiting from technological innovation: Implications for integration, collaboration, licensing and public policy. Res. Pol. **15**(6), 285–305 (1986)
9.  Shenkar, O., Li, J.: Knowledge search in international cooperative ventures. Organ. Sci. **10**(2), 134–143 (1999)
10. Srinivasan, R.: Sources, characteristics and effects of emerging technologies: research opportunities in innovation. Ind. Mark. Manage. **37**(6), 633–640 (2008)
11. Rosenkopf, L., Nerkar, A.: Beyond local search: Boundary-spanning, exploration, and impact in the optical disk industry. Strateg. Manage. J. **22**(4), 287–306 (2001)
12. Sidhu, J.S., Commandeur, H.R., Volberda, H.W.: The multifaceted nature of exploration and exploitation: value of supply, demand, and spatial search for innovation. Organ. Sci. **18**(1), 20–38 (2007)
13. Jung, H.J., Lee, J.J.: The quest for originality: a new typology of knowledge search and breakthrough inventions. Acad. Manage. J. **59**(5), 1725–1753 (2016)
14. Ahuja, G., Lampert, C.M.: Entrepreneurship in the large corporation: A longitudinal study of how established firms create breakthrough inventions. Strateg. Manage. J. **22**(6–7), 521–543 (2001)
15. Fleming, L.: Recombinant uncertainty in technological search. Manage. Sci. **47**(1), 117–132 (2001)
16. Capaldo, A., Lavie, D., Messeni Petruzzelli, A.: Knowledge maturity and the scientific value of innovations: the roles of knowledge distance and adoption. J. Manage. **43**(2), 503–533 (2017)
17. Rosenkopf, L., Almeida, P.: Overcoming local search through alliances and mobility. Manage. Sci. **49**(6), 751–766 (2003)

18. March, J.G.: Exploration and exploitation in organizational learning. Organ. Sci. **2**(1), 71–87 (1991)
19. Katila, R., Ahuja, G.: Something old, something new: a longitudinal study of search behavior and new product introduction. Acad. Manage. J. **45**(6), 1183–1194 (2002)
20. Stuart, T.E., Podolny, J.M.: Local search and the evolution of technological capabilities. Strateg. Manage. J. **17**(S1), 21–38 (1996)
21. Tushman, M.L., O'Reilly, C.A.: Ambidextrous organizations: managing evolutionary and revolutionary change. Calif. Manage. Rev. **38**(4), 8–29 (1996)
22. Weitzman, M.L.: Recombinant growth. Q. J. Econ. **113**(2), 331–360 (1998)
23. Lavie, D., Stettner, U., Tushman, M.L.: Exploration and exploitation within and across organizations. Acad. Manage. Ann. **4**(1), 109–155 (2010)
24. Trajtenberg, M., Henderson, R., Jaffe, A.: University versus corporate patents: a window on the basicness of invention. Econ. Innov. New Technol. **5**(1), 19–50 (1997)
25. Singh, J., Fleming, L.: Lone inventors as sources of breakthroughs: myth or reality? Manage. Sci. **56**(1), 41–56 (2010)
26. Fleming, L., Mingo, S., Chen, D.: Collaborative brokerage, generative creativity, and creative success. Adm. Sci. Q. **52**(3), 443–475 (2007)
27. Ahuja, G., Katila, R.: Where do resources come from? The role of idiosyncratic situations. Strateg. Manag. J. **25**(8–9), 887–907 (2004)
28. Birnbaum, R., Christensen, C., Raynor, M.: The innovator's dilemma: when new technologies cause great firms to fail. Academe (2005)
29. Swan, M.: Blockchain: Blueprint for a New Economy. O'Reilly Media, Inc. (2015)
30. Nomura Research Institute: Survey on blockchain technologies and related services. In: Japan's Ministry of Economy, Trade and Industry, no. March, pp. 1–78 (2016)
31. Frizzo-Barker, J., Chow-White, P.A., Adams, P.R., Mentanko, J., Ha, D., Green, S.: Blockchain as a disruptive technology for business: a systematic review. Int. J. Inf. Manage. **51**, 102029 (2020)
32. Hughes, L., Dwivedi, Y.K., Misra, S.K., Rana, N.P., Raghavan, V., Akella, V.: Blockchain research, practice and policy: applications, benefits, limitations, emerging research themes and research agenda. Int. J. Inf. Manage. **49**(April), 114–129 (2019)
33. Kshetri, N.: 1 Blockchain's roles in meeting key supply chain management objectives. Int. J. Inf. Manage. **39**, 80–89 (2018)
34. Leng, J., et al.: Blockchain-empowered sustainable manufacturing and product lifecycle management in industry 4.0: a survey. Renew. Sustain. Energy Rev. **132**, 110112 (2020)
35. Bumblauskas, D., Mann, A., Dugan, B., Rittmer, J.: A blockchain use case in food distribution: do you know where your food has been? Int. J. Inf. Manage. **52**, 102008 (2020)
36. Yli-Huumo, J., Ko, D., Choi, S., Park, S., Smolander, K.: Where is current research on Blockchain technology? - a systematic review. PLoS One **11**(10), e0163477 (2016)
37. Frizzo-Barker, J., Chow-White, P.A., Mozafari, M., Ha, D.: An empirical study of the rise of big data in business scholarship. Int. J. Inf. Manage. **36**(3), 403–413 (2016)
38. Arts, S., Veugelers, R.: Technology familiarity, recombinant novelty, and breakthrough invention. Ind. Corp. Chang. **24**(6), 1215–1246 (2015)
39. Wu, L., Hitt, L., Lou, B.: Data analytics, innovation, and firm productivity. Manage. Sci. **66**(5), 2017–2039 (2020)
40. de Rassenfosse, G., Dernis, H., Boedt, G.: An introduction to the patstat database with example queries. Aust. Econ. Rev. **47**(3), 395–408 (2014)
41. Zhou, X., Zhang, Y., Porter, A.L., Guo, Y., Zhu, D.: A patent analysis method to trace technology evolutionary pathways. Scientometrics **100**(3), 705–721 (2014). https://doi.org/10.1007/s11192-014-1317-4
42. Arts, S., Cassiman, B., Gomez, J.C.: Text matching to measure patent similarity. Strateg. Manage. J. **39**(1), 62–84 (2018)

43. Drobyazko, S., Makedon, V., Zhuravlov, D., Buglak, Y., Stetsenko, V.: Ethical, technological and patent aspects of technology blockchain distribution. J. Leg. Ethical Regul. Issues **22**(Special Issue 2), 1–6 (2019)
44. Blei, D.M., Ng, A.Y., Jordan, M.I.: Latent Dirichlet allocation. J. Mach. Learn. Res. **3**, 993–1022 (2003)
45. Bellstam, G., Bhagat, S., Cookson, J.A.: A text-based analysis of corporate innovation. SSRN Electron. J. (2016)
46. Trevor Rogers, F.: Patent text similarity and cross-cultural venture-backed innovation. J. Behav. Exp. Financ. **26**, 100319 (2020)
47. Lanjouw, J.O., Schankerman, M.: Patent quality and research productivity: measuring innovation with multiple indicators. Econ. J. **114**(495), 441–465 (2004)
48. Jaffe, A.B.: Technological opportunity and spillovers of R&D: evidence from firms' patents, profits, and market value. Am. Econ. Rev. **76**, 984–999 (1986)
49. Chen, L., Xu, S., Zhu, L., Zhang, J., Lei, X., Yang, G.: A deep learning based method for extracting semantic information from patent documents. Scientometrics **125**(1), 289–312 (2020). https://doi.org/10.1007/s11192-020-03634-y
50. Lee, J.S., Hsiang, J.: Measuring patent claim generation by span relevancy arXiv. 2019
51. Liu, Y., et al.: RoBERTa: a robustly optimized BERT pretraining approach, arXiv. 2019
52. Nerkar, A.: Old is gold? The value of temporal exploration in the creation of new knowledge. Manage. Sci. **49**(2), 211–229 (2003)
53. Singh, J.: Distributed R&D, cross-regional knowledge integration and quality of innovative output. Res. Pol. **37**(1), 77–96 (2008)
54. Islam, E., Zein, J.: Inventor CEOs. J. Financ. Econ. **135**(2), 505–527 (2020)
55. Valtakoski, A.: The evolution and impact of qualitative research. J. Serv. Mark. **34**(1), 8–23 (2019)
56. Zheng, E., et al.: When econometrics meets machine learning. Data Inf. Manag. **1**(2), 75–83 (2018)
57. Wang, C., Chin, T., Lin, J.H.: Openness and firm innovation performance: the moderating effect of ambidextrous knowledge search strategy. J. Knowl. Manage. **24**(2), 301–323 (2020)

# The Impact of Integrated Market Power on Trade Credit and Cash Holding in US Retail Sector

Shih-Sian Jhang[1], Chih-Yang Cheng[1(✉)], and Winston T. Lin[2]

[1] Department of Finance, College of Management, National Sun Yat-sen University, NO. 70, Lian Hai Rd., Gushan Dist., Kaohsiung City 80424, Taiwan
shihsian@mail.nsysu.edu.tw, chihyang@g-mail.nsysu.edu.tw
[2] Department of Operations Management and Strategy, School of Management, University at Buffalo-SUNY, 325A Jacobs Hall, Buffalo, NY 14260-4000, USA
mgtfewtl@buffalo.edu

**Abstract.** This paper explores how integrated market power (Fscore) affects upstream trade credit and cash holding in the US retail sector. We investigate the above relationship via the COMPUSTAT database and focus on publicly traded firms in the US from 1984 to 2014. Applying factor analysis, we first retrieve a common factor (i.e., Fscore) in the retail sector based on three dimensions, including industry completion, finance, and operations management. Then, we run the regression analysis by ordinary least squares, Fama-Macbeth regression, and year fixed effects models. Overall, we also find that Fscore performs a negative influence on demand uncertainty and upstream trade credit. Instead, the Fscore is positively associated with the retailer's internal cash holdings. Lastly, we reexamine the above relationships across industries within the retail sector and provide several managerial implications for this study.

**Keywords:** Integrated market power · Retail sector · Trade credit · Cash holding

## 1 Introduction

Owning market power in a competitive environment is vital for a firm's operations since it will lead to the redistribution of resources and affect a company's survival. Extant studies have shown that a firm's market power may drive its operations or financial decisions in the manufacturing sector [1–3]. However, retailers and manufacturers may have different business models. First, the bullwhip effect exhibits that demand uncertainty in manufacturers should be more considerable than that in retailers since the manufacturers (retailers) are located at the upstream (downstream) of the supply chain [4]. Second, there exists more information asymmetry problems and moral hazard for manufacturers than retailers to use upstream trade credit [5, 6]. Third, the utilization of market power may be different. For example, [7] show suppliers with more concentrated customers can mitigate inventory problems via supply chain practices, such as, Collaborative Planning,

© Springer Nature Switzerland AG 2021
F. F.-H. Nah and K. Siau (Eds.): HCII 2021, LNCS 12783, pp. 197–212, 2021.
https://doi.org/10.1007/978-3-030-77750-0_13

Forecasting, and Replenishment (CPFR), Vendor-Managed-Inventory (VMI), and Just-In-Time (JIT) (See also [7–9]). This finding support firms with high bargaining power tend to cooperate with their supplier to increase inventory efficiency. In contrast, taking Amazon, a leading e-commerce giant and accounts for more than 50% of US retail sales, for example. News from Bloomberg.com (2018.3) exhibits that "*Amazon.com Inc., locked in a margin-crushing price war, is offloading costs onto suppliers and limiting the number of single, low-priced items shoppers can purchase in an effort to offset rising shipping costs…*". Recognizing the difference and restrictions in the existing literature and real world, we investigate the market power in the retail sector and shed light on the relationship between a companies' market power and upstream trade credit as well as cash holdings.

Accurately measuring market power from different dimensions may not be easy. Most existing literature attempts to gauge the proxy of market power from various aspects, including sales, market concentration, market shares, firm size, etc. [10–13]. However, these measures are limited since an integrated market power should involve several dimensions. As such, we follow extant researchc approach [3] and try to construct a new market power proxy suitable for the retail sector. Specifically, we try to gauge a new market power based on three aspects, industry competition (gross profit margin and asset turnover), corporate operations (inventory), and finance (growth opportunities). We then use this proxy to verify two hypotheses.

Our data is from the COMPUSTAT database. We focus on publicly traded retail firms in the US from 1984 to 2014 with 5,628 firm-year observations. We first use factor analysis to retrieve a common factor of integrated market power and then perform various regression analyses, including ordinary least squares (OLS), Fama-Macbeth regression, and fixed-effects model [14, 15]. The empirical results show that retailers with high (low) integrated market power are associated with low (high) demand uncertainty. Also, high (low) market power retailers tend to have relatively high (low) cash holding and could utilize relatively low (high) upstream trade credit balances. Even though most industries in the retail sector embrace the above relationships, the industry of automotive dealers and gasoline service stations may be an exception. The post hoc analysis also shows that high market power retailers' profit margins are more than five times that of low market power retailers. High market power retailers also get more than twice the growth opportunity and market evaluations than low market power retailers. Furthermore, we show that high market power retailers keep a 75% lower inventory than low market power retailers.

The results of this study will contribute to the field in the following ways. First of all, this interdisciplinary research provides integration from various interfaces, including managerial economics, supply chain management, operations management, accounting, and finance. Second, we provide evidence to support that market power may drive short-term financing from upstream supliers and cash holdings of companies, broadening the literature of working capital management. Third, we extend the market power from the manufacturing sector to the retail sector, which compensates for extant literature. Lastly, we have developed a multi-faceted market power proxy covering gross margins, assets turnover, inventory, and growth opportunities. This proxy can help managers verify the current status of their firms' market power and offer an early warning signal in case their market power statuses change. This proxy can also help managers find potential approaches to enhance companies' market power and improve operational and financial performance.

The structure of this article is as follows. We review the relevant literature and construct two hypotheses in Sect. 2. We introduce the data and variables in Sect. 3. The main empirical results are exhibited in Sect. 4. The conclusions will be shown in Sect. 5.

## 2 Literature Review and Hypotheses Development

### 2.1 Market Power

The Lerner Index (Lerner, 1934), a traditional measure of the extent of market power, is widely used in economics, corporate finance, and operations management [1, 16, 17]. However, most of the proxies of market power that we know about are concentrated in the manufacturing industry, and the selected factors are biased towards finance and accounting [3, 18–21]. Therefore, how to construct a unique market power in the retail sector has been overlooked. Here, we try to propose a new proxy to integrate the industry competition in managerial economics, inventory status in operations management, and growth opportunity in finance. Following that, we use this proxy to examine the general decisions, such as cash holding and trade credit in the retail sector.

### 2.2 Cash Holding

Firms may keep cash for the transaction, precautionary, and operational motive [22, 23]. Specifically, keeping cash on hand can minimize transaction costs of raising additional funds. Also, firms can use cash to finance operational activities or prey on competitors, which may increase industry competitiveness. Extant studies already examine cash holding may be driven by a couple of firm-specific variables. For example, [24] finds that the cash-to-assets ratios vary across industries. Firms with high profitability tend to have higher cash. [25] proves that companies will hold more cash when they bear higher financial distress costs, supporting precautionary motive. [26] show that cash can be driven by firm size, growth opportunity, and risk characteristics. [27] find that the increase of cash holding can be explained by (1) the fewer accounts receivables, inventory, and capital expenditure, (2) the increase of R&D expenses and cash flow volatility. [28] found that diversified companies have higher cash holdings. In sum, existing research focuses mostly on how firm-specific variables drive the cash holding. Very little literature considers three dimensions simultaneously to examine their relationship in holding cash. We argue that integrated market power can affect a firm's cash holding decision.

### 2.3 Upstream Trade Credit

Extant empirical studies that examine upstream trade credit are usually survey-based or do not consider the retail sector. For example, [29] argue that firms with growth opportunities and lower internal resources tend to use more upstream trade credit. Using data from China, [30] find that non-state-owned firms tend to utilize trade credit than state-owned firms based on financial motive. [31] claim that large firms can get more purchase discounts from suppliers. [32] find a substitution effect between bank loans and trade credit. [33] find that firms may use trade credit to replace alternative sources when they are in financial distress. Based on the transaction motive, [3] show that firms with high market power tend to use less trade credit. [34] find that suppliers' industry competition may influence their trade credit decision. [35] document that suppliers' market share also plays an important role on trade credit. However, few literatures mention the impact of integrated market power on upstream trade credit, especially for retailing companies. Our study tends to fill the gap in the literature.

### 2.4   Integrated Market Power and Demand Uncertainty

In operation management, how to build up inventory to reduce demand uncertainty and improve company performance is a common topic [36]. The competitive environment forces companies to transfer shocks to suppliers and customers so as to protect their production and profits [3, 37]. In other words, we assume that companies with high integrated market power have higher competitive advantages or produce unique products, so they can reduce demand uncertainty by setting price flexibility.

### 2.5   Market Power and Cash

We infer that the integrated market may have a positive correlation with the cash holding for various reasons. To begin with, companies with a highly integrated market power may take VMI and CPFR practices. In terms of VMI, retailers can lower administrative costs and ordering costs, minimize the double buffering of inventory, and cut purchase lead time for order fulfillment. In the same vein, retailers taking CPFR could cooperate with supply chain partners to create a joint business plan and sales forecast. They can share information and cooperate with the management process to cope with exceptions. These practices allow retailers to communicate and collaborate efficiently with supply chain partners and effectively reduce the negative impact of supply chain [38–40]. Due to effective integration within the supply chain, retailers may not only save unnecessary expenses or waste but also create efficient sales plans. This kind of operations model could attract customers' attention and purchases, which allows a retailer to accumulate sufficient cash flow and cash holdings.

Besides, a company with higher integrated market power may hold a large amount of cash as a strategic tool to enhance competitiveness. Retailers can utilize abundant cash to engage in mergers and acquisitions activities to maintain or increase market share in the long run [41]. Based on the previous arguments, we construct the following hypothesis.

*Hypothesis 1: Retailers with high (low) Integrated Market power tend to keep high (low) cash holding.*

### 2.6   Integrated Market Power and Upstream Trade Credit

We argue that retailers' market power is negatively related to the upstream trade credit based on the following transactional and financial motives. First of all, retailers with low market power tend to have high delivery and demand uncertainty [42]. These kinds of uncertainty exist not only at retailers' customers but also at retailers' suppliers. To mitigate the fluctuations in operations, low power retailers may adjust trade credit terms rather than set the prices. Furthermore, due to the bullwhip effect, these firms tend to utilize relatively high upstream trade credit to mitigate the negative impact of operations disruptions.

Different from the operational motives above, our second argument is related to financial motives. Specifically, firms with high market power can easily integrate resources within the supply chain and access the capital market for external financing. Also, these firms with inventory leanness have relatively high credit ratings and reputation [43, 44]. As such, companies facing stable cash flow in revenue or having creditworthiness (i.e., high market power firms) will rely less on alternative financing resources (i.e., AP) provided by upstream suppliers. Based on the above arguments, our second hypothesis is as follows:

*Hypothesis 2: Retailers with high (low) Integrated Market power tend to utilize low (high) upstream trade credit (AP).*

## 3  Data, Variables, Research Methods, and Preliminary Evidence

### 3.1  Data

We use data of publicly retailing firms in the US (SIC code from 5200 to 5999) from the COMPUSTAT database. Our data covers the period from 1984 to 2014. We require that the selected sample must be publicly traded for at least five years, and the stock price of the fiscal year should be greater than 1 USD. Also, we eliminate inefficient firms that assets turnover is below 25%. The final sample included 5,638 firm-year observations.

### 3.2  Model Variables

**Integrated Market power Proxy**
We follow the method discussed in [3] to construct our integrated market power. However, we do some minor revision to better fit the condition in the retail sector. We replace Tobin's Q with cash activity since investment or growth opportunities are better to capture the retail sector's financial activities. Retailers with substantial market power should have high-quality management performance and investment opportunities [45, 46]. Furthermore, Tobin's Q can measure the return on investment, goodwill, or the value of intangible assets such as information technology, which is also essential in retail sector [47, 48]. Overall, our integrated market power proxy in this study considers three perspectives, including (1) industry competition, related to profit margin (PM) and asset turnover (ATO), (2) operations management, related to inventory (INV), and (3) growth or investment opportunity (Tobin's Q) in finance.

**Model Variables Measures**

Table 9 records the definitions and references of the nine model variables discussed in this paper, including seven independent variables and two control variables. We scaled most variables by total assets so that it is easy for us to compare financial information across firms and mitigate the impact of firm size. To mitigate the impact of outliers on the regression coefficients, we winsorize the data at 5% and 95% level [3, 49–51].

**Research Methods**

This study follows extant literature and used a two-step process to capture the market power proxy [3, 52]. First of all, using factor analysis, we use four variables, including PM, ATO, INV, and Tobin's Q, to obtain a common factor, defined as integrated market power (Fscore). Next, we use the integrated market power to identify its relationship with demand uncertainty, upstream trade credit, and cash holding. Following that, we perform various regression analyses, including ordinary least squares (OLS), Fama-Macbeth regression, and fixed-effects model [14, 15].

## 4    Main Empirical Analysis

### 4.1    Summary Statistics and Correlation Tables

Table 1 lists the descriptive statistics of the full sample. Comparing with related studies proposed by [3], we find that the PM of retailers (0.08) is slightly lower than that in the manufacturer (0.116). However, the ATO in retailers (2.226) is higher than that in the manufacturer (1.278). This finding imply that US retailers face more intensive completion than US manufacturers. Furthermore, the inventory level in retail (0.275) is also higher than that in the manufacturing sector (0.182), implying that the US retail

**Table 1.** Summary statistics

| Variable | N | Mean | Std Dev | Minimum | Q1 | Median | Q3 | Maximum |
|---|---|---|---|---|---|---|---|---|
| *Model variables* | | | | | | | | |
| PM | 5,638 | 0.080 | 0.048 | −0.031 | 0.044 | 0.074 | 0.111 | 0.213 |
| ATO | 5,638 | 2.260 | 0.914 | 0.749 | 1.595 | 2.060 | 2.775 | 6.164 |
| INV | 5,638 | 0.275 | 0.188 | 0.008 | 0.115 | 0.256 | 0.414 | 0.685 |
| Tobin's Q | 5,638 | 1.602 | 0.807 | 0.621 | 1.032 | 1.331 | 1.923 | 4.871 |
| CASH | 5,638 | 0.092 | 0.098 | 0.002 | 0.019 | 0.052 | 0.137 | 0.447 |
| AP | 5,638 | 0.128 | 0.077 | 0.020 | 0.064 | 0.114 | 0.179 | 0.339 |
| σ(ATO) | 5,638 | 0.249 | 0.196 | 0.012 | 0.116 | 0.194 | 0.321 | 1.841 |
| *Control variables* | | | | | | | | |
| SIZE | 5,638 | 5.687 | 1.622 | 2.322 | 4.557 | 5.488 | 6.704 | 11.354 |
| TANG | 5,638 | 0.397 | 0.206 | 0.050 | 0.237 | 0.361 | 0.538 | 0.853 |

N = 5,638

sector encounters some inventory problems. We also exhibit the correlations among variables in Table 2. We find that clearly shows that PM[1] has a significant negative relationship with ATO and INV and a positive relationship with Tobins'Q. All of which is consistent with our expectations of market power. The results also exhibit that PM is positively related to CASH but negatively associated with AP. These findings provide strong preliminary support for two hypotheses.

**Table 2.** Pearson correlations among model variables

|  | PM | ATO | INV | Tobin's Q | CASH | AP | σ(ATO) | SIZE | TANG |
|---|---|---|---|---|---|---|---|---|---|
| **PM** | 1.000 | -0.372 *** | -0.370 *** | 0.526 *** | 0.134 *** | -0.438 *** | -0.193 *** | 0.219 *** | 0.248 *** |
| (p value) |  | (<.0001) | (<.0001) | (<.0001) | (<.0001) | (<.0001) | (<.0001) | (<.0001) | (<.0001) |
| **ATO** |  | 1.000 | 0.280 *** | 0.139 *** | 0.000 | 0.530 *** | 0.214 *** | -0.043 *** | -0.077 *** |
| (p value) |  |  | (<.0001) | (<.0001) | (0.982) | (<.0001) | (<.0001) | (0.001) | (<.0001) |
| **INV** |  |  | 1.000 | -0.110 *** | -0.135 *** | 0.555 *** | 0.043 *** | -0.014 | -0.566 *** |
| (p value) |  |  |  | (<.0001) | (<.0001) | (<.0001) | (0.001) | (0.291) | (<.0001) |
| **Tobin's Q** |  |  |  | 1.000 | 0.279 *** | -0.042 *** | 0.009 | 0.226 *** | 0.042 *** |
| (p value) |  |  |  |  | (<.0001) | (0.002) | (0.488) | (<.0001) | (0.002) |
| **CASH** |  |  |  |  | 1.000 | -0.016 | 0.069 *** | -0.093 *** | -0.247 *** |
| (p value) |  |  |  |  |  | (0.229) | (<.0001) | (<.0001) | (<.0001) |
| **AP** |  |  |  |  |  | 1.000 | 0.073 *** | 0.032 ** | -0.322 *** |
| (p value) |  |  |  |  |  |  | (<.0001) | (0.015) | (<.0001) |
| **σ(ATO)** |  |  |  |  |  |  | 1.000 | -0.122 *** | -0.116 *** |
| (p value) |  |  |  |  |  |  |  | (<.0001) | (<.0001) |
| **SIZE** |  |  |  |  |  |  |  | 1.000 | 0.015 |
| (p value) |  |  |  |  |  |  |  |  | (0.269) |
| **TANG** |  |  |  |  |  |  |  |  | 1.000 |

N=5,638.***, **, and * indicate significance at the 0.01, 0.05, and 0.1 level, resp.

### 4.2  Factor Analysis Results

According to the principal component method, a primary factor is extracted from the data of PM, ATO, INV, and Tobin's Q. We exhibit the results in Table 3. We denote the score of the main factor as Fscore, our proxy of market power. Based on the factor analysis, the eigenvalue is 1.826, which implies that this factor could explain 45.7% of the common variance of four variables (PM, ATO, INV, and Tobin's Q). We also find that Fscore has a significant positive correlation with PM (0.893) and Tobin's Q (0.567), but negatively related to ATO (−0.529) and INV (−0.655). Since Fscore follows a normal distribution with mean equaling zero and standard deviation equaling 1, we generate an equation (See Eq. (1) for Fscore. The cutoff point for Eq. (1) is zero. If a firm's Fscore is above zero, it will be classified as a high market power firm. In contrast, a firm can be considered as low market power once its Fscore is below zero.

---

[1] PM (i.e., Lerner Index) is used as an indicator of market power (Lerner, 1934).

**Table 3.** Results of factor analysis.

| | |
|---|---|
| *Eigenvalue of major factor:* | 1.826 |
| *Percent of common variance explained:* | 45.7% |

*Correlations of major factor scores, Fscore, with input variables (Factor pattern):*

| Input variable | Corr. | p value |
|---|---|---|
| PM | 0.893 | (<0.0001) *** |
| ATO | -0.529 | (<0.0001) *** |
| INV | -0.655 | (<0.0001) *** |
| Tobin's Q | 0.567 | (<0.0001) *** |

*Generating equation for Fscore:*

Fscore = -0.18705 +10.18089(PM) -0.31688 (ATO) -1.90268 (INV)+ 0.38457 (Tobin's Q)     (1)

Factor analysis method is principal components with varimax rotation, and is applied to the full-sample panel data (N=5,638). ***, **, and * indicate significance at the 0.01, 0.05, and 0.1 level, resp.

## 4.3   The Relationship Between Market Power and Demand Uncertainty

**Table 4.** Regressions of Fscore.

| | VIF | OLS^ | Fixed effects | OLS^ | Fama-Macbeth | Fixed effects |
|---|---|---|---|---|---|---|
| Intercept | | 0.215 *** | | -1.144 *** | -1.123 *** | |
| | | (9.56) | | (-21.53) | (-16.01) | |
| □(ATO) | 1.03 | -0.862 *** | -0.770 *** | -0.549 *** | -0.471 *** | -0.440 *** |
| | | (-13.39) | (-11.49) | (-8.74) | (-9.47) | (-7.09) |
| SIZE | 1.02 | | | 0.109 *** | 0.090 *** | 0.090 *** |
| | | | | (16.22) | (23.14) | (12.04) |
| TANG | 1.01 | | | 1.669 *** | 1.790 *** | 1.790 *** |
| | | | | (29.67) | (23.30) | (30.75) |
| Industry fixed effects | | | | | | |
| Year fixed effects | | No | Yes | No | No | Yes |
| Adj. R², Avg. R², or R² | | 0.03 | 0.06 | 0.18 | 0.19 | 0.22 |

N=5,638. ***, **, and * indicate significance at the 0.01, 0.05, and 0.1 level, resp.

We first examine the relationship between Fscore and demand uncertainty and exhibit the results in Table 4. In the first column, the variance inflation factor (VIF) shows no multicollinearity among the regression variables since the values of VIF are far less than 10 [53][2]. The next two columns show the results of the ordinary least squares (OLS) method and the year fixed effect regression. We do find that the Fscore is negatively associated with QUOTE , suggesting that there exists a negative correlation between integrated market power and demand uncertainty. The negative relationship is also confirmed by the Fama-Macbeth approach and the inclusion of the control variables. In terms of control variables, the coefficients of SIZE and TANG are significantly positive in all regressions. The findings are consistent with integrated market power usually increases with the company's scale.

---

[2] The VIF values do not exceed this threshold at the following tables. Therefore, we will not further present the VIF values.

## 4.4 Regressions of Cash

We examine the regression of cash on market power and show the results in Table 5. The first column shows the OLS regression of Cash on Fscore alone. The coefficient of Fscore is significantly positive, indicating a positive relationship between cash and the integrated market power without considering other control variables.

**Table 5.** Regressions of cash.

|  | OLS^ | OLS^ | OLS^ | Fama-Macbeth | Fixed effects |
|---|---|---|---|---|---|
| Intercept | 0.092 *** | 0.169 *** | 0.218 *** | 0.215 *** |  |
|  | (68.41) | (29.57) | (34.43) | (24.99) |  |
| Fscore | 0.020 *** |  | 0.036 *** | 0.032 *** | 0.033 *** |
|  | (15.17) |  | (23.61) | (16.95) | (25.51) |
| SIZE |  | -0.005 *** | -0.010 *** | -0.011 *** | -0.011 *** |
|  |  | (-7.61) | (-13.33) | (-14.09) | (-14.53) |
| TANG |  | -0.116 *** | -0.178 *** | -0.158 *** | -0.167 *** |
|  |  | (-20.89) | (-26.31) | (-16.53) | (-27.08) |
| Year fixed effects | No | No | No | No | Yes |
| Adj. R², Avg. R², or R² | 0.04 | 0.07 | 0.18 | 0.15 | 0.21 |

N=5,638. t-statistics are shown in parentheses, and for OLS^ results are Newey-West adjusted.
***, **, and * indicate significance at the 0.01, 0.05, and 0.1 level, resp.

We also include Fscore and all control variables and test it by different econometric methods. The results of the last three regressions all produced similar results, and the coefficients of market power were significantly positive. It means that the higher the integrated market power, the higher the cash holding, which supports *Hypothesis 1*. The coefficients of SIZE and TANG are significantly negative. Take SIZE for an example; the reason might come from that company with small size hold more cash based on precautionary motive [54, 55].

## 4.5 Regressions of Trade Credit (AP)

Lastly, we discuss results for regressions of AP in Table 6. The first column of OLS regression shows that the coefficient of Fscore for AR is −0.045, which is significantly negative. In addition, the adjusted QUOTE is substantially 0.34. Next, we perform OLS regression of AP on QUOTE, and the results are displayed in the second column. Evidence supports that AP increases with demand uncertainty because the coefficient of QUOTE is significantly positive. In the third OLS regression, only control variables are included as regressors, and the coefficients of SIZE and TANG are reliably positive and negative, respectively. The results of the next three regressions all create similar results. In sum, the coefficients of Fscore remain negatively significant and is robust to the inclusion of control variables and alternative econometric methods. These findings also provide strong support for our *Hypothesis 2*, indicating that companies with high (low) market power will utilize relatively low (high) upstream trade credit.

**Table 6.** Regressions of accounts payable (AP).

|  | OLS | OLS | OLS | OLS | Fama-Macbeth | Fixed effects |
|---|---|---|---|---|---|---|
| Intercept | 0.128 *** | 0.121 *** | 0.166 *** | 0.107 *** | 0.101 *** |  |
|  | (154.45) | (74.12) | (39.46) | (29.39) | (29.02) |  |
| Fscore | -0.045 *** |  |  | -0.043 *** | -0.044 *** | -0.043 *** |
|  | (-53.17) |  |  | (-49.14) | (-27.27) | (-46.93) |
| □(ATO) |  | 0.029 *** |  |  |  |  |
|  |  | (5.68) |  |  |  |  |
| SIZE |  |  | 0.002 *** | 0.007 *** | 0.007 *** | 0.007 *** |
|  |  |  | (3.05) | (13.56) | (15.80) | (14.37) |
| TANG |  |  | -0.120 *** | -0.045 *** | -0.042 *** | -0.048 *** |
|  |  |  | (-26.38) | (-11.60) | (-7.44) | (-11.20) |
| Year fixed effects | No | No | No | No | No | Yes |
| Adj. $R^2$, Avg. $R^2$, or $R^2$ | 0.34 | 0.01 | 0.10 | 0.37 | 0.38 | 0.38 |

N=5,638. t-statistics are shown in parentheses, and for OLS results are Newey-West adjusted.

***, **, and * indicate significance at the 0.01, 0.05, and 0.1 level, resp.

## 4.6  Post-hoc Analysis

In Table 7, we sort the company's annual observations into quintiles by Fscore and calculate all model variables' average values. The value of Diff represents the difference between quintile 1 and quintile 5. As to the four variables of market power, we observe that PM and Tobin's Q monotonically increase with the Fscore quintiles; however, ATO and INV decrease with the Fscore quintiles. For example, PM's Diff value is −0.118, which indicates that companies with high integrated market power (Q5) generally have profit margins around 11.8% higher than companies with low integrated market power (Q1). Furthermore, the ratio of Q5/Q1 for PM equals 5.12, suggesting the profit margins are more than five times higher for high market power firms versus low market power firms. In the same vein, the ratio of Q5/Q1 for INV equals 0.25, suggesting high market

**Table 7.** Mean values of variables by quintiles of Fscore

| Variable | Q1 (MP low) | Q2 | Q3 | Q4 | Q5 (MP high) | Q1-Q5: Diff | t-statistic |
|---|---|---|---|---|---|---|---|
| Fscore | -1.289 | -0.638 | -0.069 | 0.548 | 1.439 | -2.728 | n/a |
| *Model variables used as factor analysis inputs:* | | | | | | | |
| PM | 0.029 | 0.050 | 0.072 | 0.100 | 0.147 | -0.118 | n/a |
| ATO | 2.979 | 2.545 | 2.233 | 1.884 | 1.667 | 1.312 | n/a |
| INV | 0.459 | 0.350 | 0.271 | 0.185 | 0.114 | 0.345 | n/a |
| Tobin's Q | 1.100 | 1.324 | 1.584 | 1.727 | 2.274 | -1.174 | n/a |
| *Remaining model variables:* | | | | | | | |
| CASH | 0.060 | 0.088 | 0.106 | 0.098 | 0.109 | -0.049 *** | -12.51 |
| σ(ATO) | 0.282 | 0.280 | 0.262 | 0.218 | 0.206 | 0.076 *** | 10.13 |
| AP | 0.188 | 0.159 | 0.131 | 0.096 | 0.067 | 0.120 *** | 43.69 |
| *Control variables:* | | | | | | | |
| SIZE | 5.076 | 5.666 | 5.822 | 5.963 | 5.901 | -0.824 *** | -13.97 |
| TANG | 0.289 | 0.344 | 0.386 | 0.453 | 0.514 | -0.226 *** | -27.4 |
| N (Firm-years) | 1114 | 1,135 | 1,131 | 1,135 | 1,123 | | |

N=5,638. t-statistics are shown in parentheses, and for OLS results are Newey-West adjusted.

***, **, and * indicate significance at the 0.01, 0.05, and 0.1 level, resp.

power retailers have 75% lower inventory than low market power firms. Besides, high market power retailers get more than twice market evaluation or investment opportunity than that of low market power retailers.

**Table 8.** Regressions across retail industries

Panel A: Regressions of Cash on Fscore across Retail Industries

|  | SIC-52 | SIC-53 | SIC-54 | SIC-55 | SIC-56 | SIC-57 | SIC-58 | SIC-59 |
|---|---|---|---|---|---|---|---|---|
| Fscore | 0.024 *** | 0.027 *** | 0.043 *** | 0.000 | 0.076 *** | 0.021 *** | 0.035 *** | 0.024 *** |
|  | (3.91) | (7.88) | (9.76) | (-0.07) | (21.05) | (3.98) | (10.60) | (8.18) |
| SIZE | 0.004 | -0.007 *** | -0.023 *** | -0.012 *** | -0.026 *** | 0.011 *** | -0.013 *** | -0.012 *** |
|  | (0.80) | (-5.01) | (-12.06) | (-3.64) | (-10.39) | (3.08) | (-7.76) | (-6.36) |
| TANG | -0.145 *** | -0.122 *** | -0.313 *** | 0.007 *** | -0.261 *** | -0.290 *** | -0.283 *** | -0.030 *** |
|  | (-2.98) | (-5.90) | (-14.63) | (0.41) | (-8.81) | (-7.65) | (-21.14) | (-1.34) |
| Year fixed effects | Yes | Yes | Yes | Yes | Yes | Yes | Yes | Yes |
| Adj. R², Avg. R², or R² | 0.26 | 0.21 | 0.46 | 0.19 | 0.43 | 0.31 | 0.40 | 0.15 |

Panel B: Regressions of upstream trade credit on Fscore across Retail Industries

|  | SIC-52 | SIC-53 | SIC-54 | SIC-55 | SIC-56 | SIC-57 | SIC-58 | SIC-59 |
|---|---|---|---|---|---|---|---|---|
| Fscore | -0.049 *** | -0.048 *** | -0.058 *** | 0.030 *** | -0.035 *** | -0.061 *** | -0.017 *** | -0.063 *** |
|  | (-11.59) | (-15.23) | (-21.13) | (5.06) | (-15.95) | (-14.62) | (-12.78) | (-29.20) |
| SIZE | 0.013 *** | 0.007 *** | 0.000 | 0.007 ** | 0.008 *** | 0.028 *** | -0.001 * | 0.006 *** |
|  | (3.88) | (5.27) | (0.21) | (1.77) | (5.09) | (10.37) | (-1.91) | (4.42) |
| TANG | -0.070 ** | 0.031 | -0.014 | 0.023 | 0.009 | -0.083 *** | -0.017 *** | -0.054 *** |
|  | (-2.07) | (1.60) | (-1.03) | (1.01) | (0.52) | (-2.79) | (-3.08) | (-3.37) |
| Year fixed effects | Yes | Yes | Yes | Yes | Yes | Yes | Yes | Yes |
| Adj. R², Avg. R², or R² | 0.46 | 0.28 | 0.53 | 0.30 | 0.27 | 0.42 | 0.31 | 0.44 |

N=5,638. t-statistics are shown in parentheses, ***, **, and * indicate significance at the 0.01, 0.05, and 0.1 level, resp.

We further examine the market power on cash and upstream trade credit across different retail industries, including SIC-52 (*Building Materials, Hardware, Garden Supply, and Mobile Home Dealers*), SIC-53 (*General Merchandise Stores*), 54 (*Food Stores*), 55 (*Automotive Dealers and Gasoline Service Stations*), 56 (*Apparel and Accessory Stores*), 57 (*Home Furniture, Furnishings, and Equipment Stores*), 58 (*Eating and Drinking Places*), and 59 (*Miscellaneous Retail*). Table 8 Panel A and Panel B show the results of cash and upstream trade credit across retail industries, respectively. Interestingly, we find that market power has various impacts on different retail industries. For example, firms' market power essentially drives the cash utilization in the apparel and accessory industry, but not in the automotive dealers and gasoline service stations industry. In a similar vein, the impact of market power on upstream trade credit varies within the retail sector. Even though firms with high market power utilize less upstream trade credit based on our previous results, firms in automotive dealers and gasoline service stations act differently. Future research could reexamine the characteristics of this industry.

### 4.7 Discussions and Implications

Our research evaluates market power through three dimensions of industry competition (gross profit margin and asset turnover), company operations (inventory), and finance (growth opportunities), replacing the previous literature that defines market power from a single perspective. We prove that market forces may impact the management decisions of retailers. The empirical results show that market power negatively relates to upstream

**Table 9.** Model variables measures

| | Variables | Measurement | Reference |
|---|---|---|---|
| Main variables | Profit Margin (*PM*) | $PM_{i,t} =$ <br> $(SALES_{i,t} - COGS_{i,t} - SGA_{i,t})/SALES_{i,t}$ <br> $SALES_{i,t}$, $COGS_{i,t}$, and $SGA_{i,t}$ are firm i's total sales, cost of goods sold, and selling, general and administrative expense at year-end t, respectively | [58, 59] |
| | Asset Turnover (*ATO*) | $ATO_{i,t} = SALES_{i,t}/AT_{i,t-1}$ <br> $AT_{i,t-1}$ is firm i's total assets at year-end t − 1 | [59] |
| | Inventory (*INV*) | $INV_{i,t} = INVENTORY_{i,t}/AT_{i,t}$ <br> $INVENTORY_{i,t}$ is firm i's balances of total inventory at year-end t | [60] |
| | Tobin's Q (*Tobin's Q*) | *Tobin's* <br> $Q_{i,t} = (AT_{i,t} - BEV_{i,t} + MEV_{i,t})/AT_{i,t}$ <br> $BEV_{i,t}$ and $MEV_{i,t}$ are firm i's book and market equity values at year-end t, respectively | [55, 61] |
| | Cash (*CASH*) | $CASH_{i,t} = CASHBAL_{i,t}/AT_{i,t}$ <br> $CASHBAL_{i,t}$ is firm i's balance of cash and equivalents at year-end t | [27] |
| | Accounts Payable (*AP*) | $AP_{i,t} = ACCTPAY_{i,t}/AT_{i,t}$ <br> $ACCTPAY_{i,t}$ are firm i 's balances of accounts payable at the end of year t | [3] |
| | Demand Uncertainty ($\sigma(ATO)$) | $\sigma(ATO)_{i,t} =$ <br> $\left\{ \sum_{t-4}^{t} [ATO_{i,t} - E(ATO_{i,t})]^2 \right\}^{1/2}$ <br> demand uncertainty is the standard deviation of asset turnover over the past five years | [7, 62] |
| Control Variables | Size (*SIZE*) | $SIZE_{i,t} = \ln(AT_{i,t}/GDPdeflator_t)$ <br> $GDPdeflator_t$ is GDP deflator at year-end t | [31, 63] |
| | Tangibility (*TANG*) | $TANG_{i,t} = PP\&E_{i,t}/AT_{i,t}$ <br> $PP\&E_{i,t}$ is firm i's net property, plant and equipment at year-end t | [7, 64, 65] |

trade credit and demand uncertainty. In other words, retail companies with high market power have more stable operations and less seasonality, leading that firms have less motivation to utilize upstream trade credit. However, the finding between market power and cash holding may suggest that firms should keep high market power to enrich the cash holdings. As such, to increase the company's market power, managers may design business models based on the factors developed from this paper. These actions include the increase of gross profit margin, the enhancement of investment opportunity, and reduction of inventory level as well as asset turnover.

First of all, retailers may introduce high-profit products, rather than the creation of new sales, to hance market power. Besides, to increase gross profit margin, managers can lower the cost of goods sold and sales/administrative expenses related to operations. For example, Wal-Mart requires poultry suppliers to provide standard weights on the packaging of chicken pallets. This action can lower administrative costs and improve pricing efficiency or profit margins [56]. Also, Tesco, a major retailer in the UK, is good at building connections with consumers through loyalty programs. This action may attract potential investors or financial analysts and increase the investment opportunity of firms. Third, since retailers need to cope with various products, firms may adopt effective supply chain practices, such as JIT, CPFR, or VMI, to maintain low inventories and enhance the market power. Furthermore, retailers may increase the operational efficiency by reducing the inventory ordering costs, tracking costs, and allocation costs. Like Costco, a US wholesaler, this company controls the number of its stock keeping unit (SKU) at a relatively low level, approximately 3,800 pieces [57]. Overall, the above actions may help retailers for operational decisions and enhance their market power status.

## 5  Conclusions

This paper explores how integrated market power affects trade credit and cash holding in retailing firms. We apply the COMPUSTAT database and focus on publicly traded retailing firms in the US (SIC code from 5200 to 5999) from 1984 to 2014. Using factor analysis and regression analysis, including ordinary least squares, Fama-Macbeth regression, and fixed effects model, we generalize the empirical results: First, we find that a decisive integration factor (Fscore) exists from three dimensions, including industry competition, operations management, and finance. Second, US retailers' market power negatively influences demand uncertainty and trade credit. It suggests that retailers with low market power tend to utilize relatively high upstream trade credit to mitigate the negative impact of operations disruptions or have more needs on financing resources from suppliers. Lastly, US retailers' market power has a positive impact on cash holdings. In addition to the strategic purpose for holding cash, we can find that high market power firms taking effectively supply chain practices, such as CPFR or VMI, could attract customers' attention and create sufficient cash flow.

## References

1. Datta, S., Iskandar-Datta, M., Singh, V.: Product market power, industry structure, and corporate earnings management. J. Bank. Financ. **37**(8), 3273–3285 (2013)

2. Grullon, G., Michaely, R.: Corporate payout policy and product market competition. In: AFA 2008 New Orleans meetings paper (2007)
3. Jhang, S.-S.S., Ogden, J.P., Suresh, N.C.: Operational and financial configurations contingent on market power status. Omega **88**, 91–109 (2019)
4. Lee, H.L., Padmanabhan, V., Whang, S.: The bullwhip effect in supply chains. Sloan Manag. Rev. **38**, 93–102 (1997)
5. Kim, S.-J., Shin, H.S.: Sustaining production chains through financial linkages. Am. Econ. Rev. **102**(3), 402–406 (2012)
6. Long, M.S., Malitz, I.B., Ravid, S.A.: Trade credit, quality guarantees, and product marketability. Financ. Manage. **22**(4), 117–127 (1993)
7. Ak, B.K., Patatoukas, P.N.: Customer-base concentration and inventory efficiencies: evidence from the manufacturing sector. Prod. Oper. Manag. **25**(2), 258–272 (2016)
8. Ren, Z.J., Cohen, M.A., Ho, T.H., Terwiesch, C.: Information sharing in a long-term supply chain relationship: the role of customer review strategy. Oper. Res. **58**(1), 81–93 (2010)
9. Terwiesch, C., Ren, Z.J., Ho, T.H., Cohen, M.A.: An empirical analysis of forecast sharing in the semiconductor equipment supply chain. Manage. Sci. **51**(2), 208–220 (2005)
10. Elzinga, K.G., Mills, D.E.: The Lerner index of monopoly power: origins and uses. Am. Econ. Rev. **101**(3), 558–564 (2011)
11. Fu, X.M., Lin, Y.R., Molyneux, P.: Bank competition and financial stability in Asia pacific. J. Bank. Finance **38**, 64–77 (2014)
12. Hannan, T., Berger, A.: The rigidity of prices: evidence form the banking sector. Am. Econ. Rev. **81**, 938–945 (1991)
13. Pavic, I., Galetic, F., Piplica, D.: Similarities and differences between the CR and HHI as an indicator of market concentration and market power. J. Econ. Manag. Trade. **13**(1), 1–8 (2016)
14. Fama, E.F., MacBeth, J.D.: Risk, return, and equilibrium: empirical tests. J. Polit. Econ. **81**(3), 607–636 (1973)
15. Greene, W.H.: Econometric Analysis. Pearson Education India (2003)
16. Akdoğu, E., MacKay, P.: Product markets and corporate investment: theory and evidence. J. Bank. Finance **36**(2), 439–453 (2012)
17. Datta, S., Iskandar-Datta, M., Sharma, V.: Product market pricing power, industry concentration and analysts' earnings forecasts. J. Bank. Financ. **35**(6), 1352–1366 (2011)
18. Beccarello, M.: Time series analysis of market power: evidence from G-7 manufacturing. Int. J. Ind. Organ. **15**(1), 123–136 (1997)
19. Katics, M.M., Petersen, B.C.: The effect of rising import competition on market power: a panel data study of US manufacturing. J. Ind. Econ. **42**(3), 277–286 (1994)
20. Lee, M.: Environmental regulations and market power: the case of the Korean manufacturing industries. Ecol. Econ. **68**(1–2), 205–209 (2008)
21. Rezitis, A.N., Kalantzi, M.A.: Measuring the degree of market power in the Greek manufacturing industry. Int. Rev. Appl. Econ. **27**(3), 339–359 (2013)
22. Jensen, M.C.: Agency costs of free cash flow, corporate finance, and takeovers. Am. Econ. Rev. **76**(2), 323–329 (1986)
23. Keynes, J.M.: La auto-suficiencia nacional. El Trimestre Econ. **1**(2), 174–189 (1934)
24. Chudson, W.A.: The pattern of corporate financial structure: a cross-section view of manufacturing, mining, trade, and construction, 1937 (1945)
25. John, T.A.: Accounting measures of corporate liquidity, leverage, and costs of financial distress. Financ. Manag. **22**, 91–100 (1993)
26. Opler, T., Pinkowitz, L., Stulz, R., Williamson, R.: The determinants and implications of corporate cash holdings. J. Financ. Econ. **52**(1), 3–46 (1999)
27. Bates, T.W., Kahle, K.M., Stulz, R.M.: Why do US firms hold so much more cash than they used to? J. Financ. **64**(5), 1985–2021 (2009)

28. Subramaniam, V., Tang, T.T., Yue, H., Zhou, X.: Firm structure and corporate cash holdings. J. Corp. Finan. **17**(3), 759–773 (2011)
29. Petersen, M.A., Rajan, R.G.: Trade credit: theories and evidence. Rev. Financ. Stud. **10**(3), 661–691 (1997)
30. Ge, Y., Qiu, J.: Financial development, bank discrimination and trade credit. J. Bank. Financ. **31**(2), 513–530 (2007)
31. Giannetti, M., Burkart, M., Ellingsen, T.: What you sell is what you lend? Explaining trade credit contracts. Rev. Financ. Stud. **24**(4), 1261–1298 (2011)
32. Huang, H., Shi, X., Zhang, S.: Counter-cyclical substitution between trade credit and bank credit. J. Bank. Financ. **35**(8), 1859–1878 (2011)
33. Molina, C.A., Preve, L.A.: An empirical analysis of the effect of financial distress on trade credit. Financ. Manage. **41**(1), 187–205 (2012)
34. Chod, J., Lyandres, E., Yang, S.A.: Trade credit and supplier competition. J. Financ. Econ. **131**(2), 484–505 (2019)
35. Lee, H.-H., Zhou, J., Wang, J.: Trade credit financing under competition and its impact on firm performance in supply chains. Manuf. Serv. Oper. Manag. **20**(1), 36–52 (2018)
36. Isaksson, O.H., Seifert, R.W.: Inventory leanness and the financial performance of firms. Prod. Plan. Control **25**(12), 999–1014 (2014)
37. Peress, J.: Product market competition, insider trading, and stock market efficiency. J. Financ. **65**(1), 1–43 (2010)
38. Flynn, B.B., Huo, B., Zhao, X.: The impact of supply chain integration on performance: a contingency and configuration approach. J. Oper. Manag. **28**(1), 58–71 (2010)
39. Prajogo, D., Olhager, J.: Supply chain integration and performance: the effects of long-term relationships, information technology and sharing, and logistics integration. Int. J. Prod. Econ. **135**(1), 514–522 (2012)
40. Yin, Y., Cheng, S.-R., Cheng, T., Wang, D.-J., Wu, C.-C.: Just-in-time scheduling with two competing agents on unrelated parallel machines. Omega **63**, 41–47 (2016)
41. Fresard, L.: Financial strength and product market behavior: the real effects of corporate cash holdings. J. Financ. **65**(3), 1097–1122 (2010)
42. Ferris, J.S.: A transactions theory of trade credit use. Q. J. Econ. **96**(2), 243–270 (1981)
43. Bendig, D., Strese, S., Brettel, M.: The link between operational leanness and credit ratings. J. Oper. Manag. **52**, 46–55 (2017)
44. Ng, C.K., Smith, J.K., Smith, R.L.: Evidence on the determinants of credit terms used in interfirm trade. J. Financ. **54**(3), 1109–1129 (1999)
45. Lang, L.H., Stulz, R., Walkling, R.A.: Managerial performance, Tobin's Q, and the gains from successful tender offers. J. Financ. Econ. **24**(1), 137–154 (1989)
46. Tobin, J.: A general equilibrium approach to monetary theory. J. Money Credit Bank. **1**(1), 15–29 (1969)
47. Arcelus, F.J., Mitra, D., Srinivasan, G.: On the incidence of deferred taxes, intangibles and non-linearities in the relationship between Tobin's Q and ROI. J. Econ. Bus. **57**(2), 165–185 (2005)
48. Bharadwaj, A.S., Bharadwaj, S.G., Konsynski, B.R.: Information technology effects on firm performance as measured by Tobin's q. Manage. Sci. **45**(7), 1008–1024 (1999)
49. Doidge, C., Karolyi, G.A., Stulz, R.M.: The US left behind? Financial globalization and the rise of IPOs outside the US. J. Financ. Econ. **110**(3), 546–573 (2013)
50. Fahlenbrach, R., Stulz, R.M.: Bank CEO incentives and the credit crisis. J. Financ. Econ. **99**(1), 11–26 (2011)
51. Jhang, S.-S.S., Lin, W.T., Fang, I.-H.: How does firms' integrated market power affect upstream trade credit and institutional ownership? Evidence from Taiwan. Asia Pac. Manag. Rev. **25**(2), 75–86 (2020)

52. Shervani, T.A., Frazier, G., Challagalla, G.: The moderating influence of firm market power on the transaction cost economics model: an empirical test in a forward channel integration context. Strateg. Manag. J. **28**(6), 635–652 (2007)
53. Kutner, M., Nachtsheim, C., Neter, J.: Simultaneous inferences and other topics in regression analysis. In: Applied Linear Regression Models. 4th edn., pp. 168–170. McGraw-Hill Irwin, New York (2004)
54. Fazzari, S.M., Petersen, B.C.: Working capital and fixed investment: new evidence on financing constraints. RAND J. Econ. **24**, 328–342 (1993)
55. Whited, T.M.: Debt, liquidity constraints, and corporate investment: evidence from panel data. J. Financ. **47**(4), 1425–1460 (1992)
56. Callahan, P., Zimmerman, A.: Price war in Aisle 3—Wal-Mart tops grocery list with supercenter format; but fewer choices, amenities. Wall Street J. May 27, B1 (2003)
57. Berman, B.R.: Competing in Tough Times: Business Lessons from LL Bean, Trader Joe's, Costco, and Other World-Class Retailers (Paperback). FT Press (2010)
58. Lerner, A.: VThe concept of monopoly and the measurement of monopoly power. V Rev. Econ. Stud. **1**(157), 75 (1934)
59. Mottner, S., Smith, S.: Wal-mart: supplier performance and market power. J. Bus. Res. **62**(5), 535–541 (2009)
60. Chen, H., Frank, M.Z., Wu, O.Q.: US retail and wholesale inventory performance from 1981 to 2004. Manuf. Serv. Oper. Manag. **9**(4), 430–456 (2007)
61. Myers, J.N., Myers, L.A., Omer, T.C.: Exploring the term of the auditor-client relationship and the quality of earnings: a case for mandatory auditor rotation? Acc. Rev. **78**(3), 779–799 (2003)
62. Rumyantsev, S., Netessine, S.: What can be learned from classical inventory models? A cross-industry exploratory investigation. Manuf. Serv. Oper. Manag. **9**(4), 409–429 (2007)
63. Cao, M., Zhang, Q.: Supply chain collaboration: impact on collaborative advantage and firm performance. J. Oper. Manag. **29**(3), 163–180 (2011)
64. Ogden, J.P., Jen, F.C., O'Connor, P.F.: Advanced Corporate Finance: Policies and Strategies. Pearson College Division (2003)
65. Williams, J.T.: Financial and industrial structure with agency. Rev. Financ. Stud. **8**(2), 431–474 (1995)

# Disentangling Technostress and Financial Stress Impacts on Users' Psychophysiological Responses and Coping Behaviors in the Context of Mobile Banking

Marion Korosec-Serfaty[(✉)], Aurélie Vasseur[(✉)], Pierre-Majorique Léger[(✉)], and Sylvain Sénécal[(✉)]

Tech3Lab, HEC Montreal, Montreal, QC, Canada
{marion.korosec-serfaty,aurelie.vasseur,pierre-majorique.leger,
syvlain.senecal}@hec.ca

**Abstract.** In the mobile banking context, the decision to discontinue using a certain service has received sparse attention. Previous research has identified this behavior as one potential coping strategy to avoid stressful situations related to the use of technology. Considering that forms of stress are multidimensional, complex, and situational, this research proposal investigates the determining factors influencing users' responses and coping behaviors through the perspective of a potential interaction between technostress and financial stress in the mobile banking context. Our literature review on mobile banking, technostress, and financial stress research, shows that prior research on technostress 1) has not explored the context of mobile banking; 2) does not investigate simultaneously users' psychophysiological and behavioral responses and; 3) that the interaction between technostress and non-technological stress has not been explored. It also shows that 4) even though factors of technostress and financial stress differ, their outcomes seem generally similar. Based on these findings and in order to disentangle financial stress and technostress impacts on users' responses and behaviors, an experimental design based on an adapted version of the Trust Game is proposed.

**Keywords:** Technostress · Financial stress · Mobile banking · Discontinuance behavior

## 1 Introduction

Mobile-banking transactions increase banks' overall efficiency by offering transactions that are up to ten times cheaper than Automated Teller Machine (ATM) transactions, not only increasing efficiency but also lowering operating costs. In fact, the cost of mobile banking transactions is, on average, 50 times lower than branch transactions, 10 times lower than transactions via ATMs and 5 times lower than transactions via online platforms [1]. Moreover, by increasing mobile banking adoption rates, average banking institutions can generate millions in additional revenue and reduce attrition

© Springer Nature Switzerland AG 2021
F. F.-H. Nah and K. Siau (Eds.): HCII 2021, LNCS 12783, pp. 213–227, 2021.
https://doi.org/10.1007/978-3-030-77750-0_14

by up to 15% [2]. As such, compared to branch-only customers, mobile banking users hold more products from their financial institutions, stay longer with them and complete transactions more frequently. Thus, to maintain profitability, banking institutions must retain existing mobile banking users and facilitate their continuance usage.

However, despite increased adoption rates, mobile banking continuance usage rates are still low [3]. Studies report individuals' intention to stop using and eventually deleting their mobile banking applications when facing privacy concerns and account management issues [4]. Whereas information system (IS) research covers extensively mobile banking adoption and usage phases [5], only one study explores its termination phase [6], where users develop discontinuance usage behaviors and potentially switch to alternatives.

General IS research identified these discontinuance behaviors as one of the coping strategies to avoid IS-caused threatening situations [7]. In the context of technology voluntary usage, technostress was established as one the factors of IS discontinuance [8]. For instance, studies showed that discontinuance usage behaviors were prevalent among Social Network Services users who felt that their personal information might be threatened (techno-privacy) or forced to meet technological expectations (techno-overload) as an effort to cope with these technostressors [9]. However, these dimensions have not been explored in regard to mobile banking.

Technostress has been approached as a phenomenon dissociated from other forms of stress [10], while it is indeed part of a spectrum of interactions with other types of stress [11]. It is thus crucial to explore the nature and extent of the relationship between technostress and non-technological forms of stress. One form of the latter is financial stress that is due, among others, to perceived potential financial loss [12]. As no study has focused on the relationship between financial stress and mobile banking usage discontinuance, this research aims to *disentangle financial stress and technostress impacts on users' responses and coping behaviors in that context.*

To reach this objective and to reproduce a mobile banking usage context, we will develop an adapted version of the Trust Game (TG) [13]. This paradigm, widely used in neuroeconomics to study cognitive mechanisms underlying decision-making in economic situations [14], will allow us to assess users' responses and behaviors in situations of exposition vs. non-exposition to financial stress and technostress. As studies found that technostressors and sources of financial stress produce significant physiological changes, we will record electrodermal activity [15] and heart rate [16] measures to assess stress levels. Perceptual stress will be assessed through questionnaires and interviews and discontinuance behaviors as the decision not to invest. This experiment will provide preliminary results on how users perceive, react to and cope with potential non-technological stress and technostress-related situations in the mobile-banking usage context, thus suggesting design guidelines to prevent discontinuance and switching behaviors.

This research proposal is organized as follows. First, mobile banking, general stress, technostress, and financial stress research are presented. Subsequently, the proposed methodology, including the experimental design and measurements, is introduced.

At this stage of the research, the contribution of this article is twofold. First, it characterizes mobile banking, general stress, technostress, and financial stress research, highlighting the elements that still need to be addressed to understand users' discontinuance behaviors. Second, it provides a proposed experimental design to investigate the nature and outcomes of potential interactions between specific factors of technostress and financial stress on users' psychophysiological responses and coping behaviors in the context of mobile banking.

## 2 Literature Review

### 2.1 Mobile Banking

Mobile banking is generally defined as mobile commerce application, supported by mobile technology and products that allow users to make financial transactions using portable technologies, such as mobile phones and tablets [5]. While individuals tend to use their mobile devices for everyday financial account management, simple banking transactions or transferring funds [5], the services offered by mobile banking vary from simple financial services such as balance inquiries, fund transfers, bill payment to more complex services such as stock exchange transactions.

At the introduction of mobile web services, mobile banking was mainly done via text or Short Message Service (SMS) and was known as SMS banking. In 1999, after the introduction of smartphones with Wireless application protocol support, which allowed the use of the mobile web, the first banks began offering mobile banking via this platform [17]. Until 2010, SMS banking and internet banking were the most popular mobile banking services offered [17]. However, the development of smartphones operating with iOS and Android systems contributed to the evolution of mobile banking applications. Users were now able to download mobile banking applications on their smartphones with more sophisticated interfaces and improved transactional abilities.

This transition to mobile banking services was not without impediments. Whereas banking institutions adopted mobile services at a fairly rapid pace, users were skeptical and hesitant to adopt them despite their potential benefits [18]. Banking institutions had thus to evaluate their readiness to adopt and their willingness to use these services to offer suitable experiences for users. Since the early 2000s [18], the focus of scholars has therefore primarily been on understanding the adoption, intention to use and usage continuance of these systems.

An abundance of IS studies, mainly relying on the Technology Acceptance Model [19, 20] and the Continuance Model [21, 22], have investigated users' mobile banking adoption and continuous usage intention. For example, numerous studies have shown that users may adopt mobile banking because of its perceived usefulness, credibility [e.g., 23] and compatibility [e.g., 24]. Users may also decide not to adopt mobile banking because of specific sociodemographic and cultural factors [e.g., 25] greater uncertainty or risk perception [e.g., 26]. Users may also use mobile banking because of their perceived ease of use [e.g., 27] or task self-efficiency [e.g., 28].

Nevertheless, mobile banking continuance usage rates are still low [3]. Studies report that, when confronted with privacy concerns and account management issues, people express their intention to cease using these applications, and potentially delete them [4]. Indeed, mobile banking evolves in an impersonal environment that enables increased opportunities for fraud, and privacy risks are multiplying exponentially as users' lives are increasingly digitized. Over the past several years, instances of identity theft and application fraud combined with high-profile data breaches have placed privacy concerns at the top of the mind of users [29]. Moreover, [30] reports that users feel that account management issues, such as having to delve several layers beyond the home screen to be able to deal or to comply with an excessive number of features to perform basic tasks, such as viewing balances and recent transactions, are common concerns when making regular mobile banking usage.

Despite these growing concerns, reports on mobile banking users' discontinuance usage intentions and low continuance rates, the termination phase and the corresponding discontinuance and switching usage behaviors have been largely overlooked by IS research. To the best of our knowledge, only one study has addressed discontinuance usage intention in the mobile banking context in relation to users' personality traits [6].

Nevertheless, general IS research indicates that continuance and discontinuance usage are not opposite extremities of the same continuum. As such, [31] showed that continuous and discontinuance usage intentions are motivated by different factors and [32] that individuals' perceptions differ while continuing to use IS or when discontinuing its usage. Users may decide to discard using IS because of low perceived usefulness [32], reliability or compatibility [33]. On the other hand, they may choose to continue using IS because of habit [31] or social support [32]. Finally, users may also adopt discontinuance behaviors as one potential coping strategy to avoid IS-caused threatening situations, such as technology-related stress [7].

To better understand technology-related stress and the extent of its potential influence on users' responses and coping strategies, the next section will underline the basic foundations of human stress.

## 2.2 What is Stress?

Stress is a familiar and omnipresent part of life and can be a motivator or a burden. It is generally understood as a combination of events, or demands, consisting of a stimulus (stressor), that activates fight-or-flight physiological systems, and triggers psychological and behavioral responses [34].

As such, the experience of a stressful event will first prompt a distress signal from the amygdala, an area of the brain that contributes to emotions processing, to the hypothalamus. The latter will then trigger the sympathetic division of the autonomic nervous system by sending signals to the adrenal glands which will respond by sending adrenaline hormones into the bloodstream. As adrenaline circulates through the body, it will bring several physiological changes including pupil dilation, electrodermal conductance elevation, airway relaxation, heart rate acceleration, strong glucose release, muscle tension to blood pressure elevation [35]. The hypothalamus will also release the corticotropin-releasing hormone, which will trigger the pituitary gland to release the adrenocorticotropic hormone, which will travel to the adrenal glands, prompting them to release cortisol, noradrenaline, and dopamine hormones [35]. Once the levels of cortisol fall, the parasympathetic division of the autonomic nervous system will dampen the stress response, and the physiological system will return to its normal state. These physiological responses are often unconscious. In fact, they often happen so fast that individuals are not always aware of them.

Psychological and behavioral responses to stress will usually appear quickly after the stressful event. Even though feelings such as anger, irritability and aggressive or reckless behaviors [36] normally settle rapidly, they can sometimes last several days. In the long run, when the sources of stress persist, it may also create a long-term stimulation of the fight-or-flight response which can have a profound effect on one's ability to function. Feelings of increased mental load, overwhelm or depression may lead to socially unacceptable behaviors, such as absenteeism and tardiness, or that interfere with one's ability to function such as addiction, eating and sleeping disorders, social withdrawing, or procrastination. Nevertheless, stress can also generate positive reactions such as enhancing memory [36] or increasing motivation to reach specific goals and enhance performance to reach specific goals requiring a high level of arousal [37].

In fact, one's ability to cope with stress will have an impact on their success or failure in controlling potential stressful situations. These psychophysiological reactions to sources of stress differ, in part, on one's cognitive appraisal: a stressor may have a stronger negative impact when perceived as a threat versus as a challenge [37]. As such, some may try to mitigate stressful situations by adopting problem-focused coping strategies aiming to alter or eliminate the source of stress by directly focusing on the problem. Others will cope by adopting emotion-focused strategies as, for instance, avoiding or distracting themselves from the source of stress, venting to others about it, seeking social support, or denying it [38, 39].

Sources of stress can also take many forms. They can be situational, environmental, personal, professional, financial, or technology-related, to name a few. As a matter of fact, each form of stress occurrence is part of a full range of complex interactions with other forms of stress that one might feel at a given time and in a specific context [11]. An individual may very well be confronted with work, financial or personal-related stress at the same time, but to varying degrees, and with different outcomes.

To summarize, stress is a multidimensional situation, complex and situational, hence requiring investigating, and understanding factors influencing the intensity of the stressful event, their psychophysiological and behavioral outcomes, and coping strategies.

In light of the general stress process and the importance of its outcomes, it is necessary to understand the extent to which research has addressed technostress as a specific form of stress, within which usage context. To this end, we will provide in the following a conceptualization of technostress as well as an overview of technostress research, before introducing different technology-related stressors relevant to mobile banking.

## 2.3 Technostress

Technostress research investigates how and why the use of IS causes various demands on individuals. The concept was first introduced by psychologist Craig Brod [40], in the early 80s, at a time when the technological revolution was starting to change work environments. He described technostress as a modern adaptation disease caused by the inability to deal healthily with new computer technology [40]. In the late 90s, [41] extended this definition to any negative effect caused directly or indirectly by technology on beliefs, emotions, behaviors, or body psychology. In the early 2000s, [42] defined technostress as stress created by usage, explaining that it is one of the consequences of the attempts and difficulties of users to cope with continuously evolving IS and the changing cognitive and social demands associated with their use. The latest definition generally accepted by scholars is that technostress is a form of stress that individuals experience due to their use of information systems [43].

Technostress is understood as the result of an interaction between individuals and their environment [44] and is conceptualized as a process activated by the use of is where the latter acts as an interfering variable [45]. As such, this process includes the presence of individual, task, technology and/or organizational environmental characteristics. These characteristics, referred to as antecedents are appraised by users as demands, namely technostressors, that are taxing and require a change [43]. These technostressors, then activate coping strategies that lead to psychophysiological and behavioral outcomes [46], referred to as strains. The users' evaluation of the extent of this demand, namely primary appraisal, influences the intensity of the relationship between the antecedents and technostressors. The users' assessment of their available alternatives and resources [43] referred to as secondary appraisal, impacts the relationship between technostressors and coping responses.

As shown in a recent systematic review of the literature [10], technostress research has mainly focused on work-related technostress in mandatory technology usage context. An extensive body of research has explored the relation between organizational characteristics, technostressors and its psychological consequences [10] wherein a few have investigated its coping strategies and physiological and behavioral outcomes or addressed psychological outcomes in relation to task characteristics and context stressors [10]. More recently, research has started to take interest in Social Network Services (SNS) related context usage, making it the most non-mandatory-work-related technology context [e.g., 9]. These studies considered individual and situational factors, coping strategies and psychobehavioral outcomes related to SNS technostress. While SNS-related technostress is an emerging trend in non-work-related technostress studies, other non-work-related usage contexts are still under-explored by IS research. To date, the latter contexts investigated include (a) individual factors and technology characteristics as antecedents of online-shopping-related technostress and their neuropsychological consequences [15, 47, 48]; (b) individual and technology characteristics in the intensity of the technostress effect, coping strategies and behavioral consequences of mobile-application usage context and (c) the effect of technostress among users over 60 years old in the daily usage context [49].

Overall, only three studies [50–52] have simultaneously investigated psychophysiological and behavioral outcomes of technostress. However, as mentioned, physiological responses to general stress are often unconscious. Research has shown that users do not necessarily perceive stress consciously while interacting with an IS [53]. Understanding physiological outcomes are an essential complement to the comprehension of psychological and behavioral responses [54]. These results add to the fact that technostress impacts beliefs, emotions, behaviors, or physiology [55], leading us to emphasize on the importance of exploring simultaneously all three consequential outcomes of technostress.

This systematic overview of the technostress literature not only shows that, aforesaid, technostress has not yet been explored in the context of mobile banking, but also demonstrates that prior research has mostly focused on investigating separately physio-logical, psychological, and behavioral outcomes of technostress as well as users coping strategies.

It now allows us to look at specific sources of technostress, namely techostressors, their consequences and introduce the ones relevant to the context of mobile banking.

Under the technostress framework, technostressors are technology-related stimuli assessed by users as harmful and-or threatening [56]. Several technostressors have been identified by IS research, among which techno-overload [e.g., 57, 58], techno-invasion [e.g., 59, 60], techno-insecurity [e.g., 61, 62], techno-unreliability [e.g., 44, 56], techno-uncertainty [e.g., 59, 63], techno-complexity [e.g., 42, 64] and techno-privacy [49]. Techno-overload and techno-privacy correspond to a serious reality of mobile banking. The present research proposal focuses on these two specific technostressors which are presented in the following.

*Techno-Overload.* Techno-overload refers to the general perception of overload felt by users from the use of IS [42]. In mandatory technology work-related usage contexts, techno-overload is understood as users' perception of being forced to do more to use the technology [42], resulting in lower job satisfaction [e.g., 61], organizational commit-ment [e.g., 65] and productivity [42]. Furthermore, in non-mandatory technology-usage contexts, techno-overload embodies SNS users' feeling of being obliged to meet expec-tations of others [9], deal with redundant and excessive features [66], manage mobile shopping applications' push notifications [8] and, in the daily usage context, cope with more problems than necessary, hence executing tasks slower [49]. In the SNS-related usage context, techno-overload has been shown to lower users' satisfaction, increase exhaustion leading to discontinuance usage intention [58] and avoidance coping strate-gies [67]. SNS-related techno-overload has also been linked to distraction coping strate-gies [68] where users either engage in another activity within the same application or in another activity outside the application. In the mobile shopping application context, techno-overload from push notifications have proven to exert a significant influence on users' coping strategies [8]. Users will in fact develop negative emotions such as avoid-ance intention or self-deception towards the usefulness of these notifications which will consequently develop into discontinued usage. Considering the particular context of mobile banking, we, therefore identify techno-overload as having to deal or to comply with an excessive number of technological features to perform basic tasks, as a critical technostressor for mobile banking users.

*Techno-Privacy.* Another significant technostressor is techno-privacy which represents the perception of disclosure that users experience when using IS [43]. It embodies users' feelings that too much personal information is disclosed on an SNS by them or by their friends [9]. In the daily usage context, techno-privacy refers to users' perception of having their personal information threatened because their use of technology can be tracked, recorded, and exploited by third parties [49], resulting in a decrease in subjective well-being and a compulsion to undergo a cognitive and social adaptation process to technology as a coping strategy. In the specific context of mobile banking, we identify techno-privacy, as users' perception of having their personal information threatened, as a significant technostressor for mobile banking users.

In sum, previous research has shown that the perception of techno-overload and techno-privacy lead to psychobehavioral strains, as well as to avoidance or adaptive coping strategies. Given the human specific experience of stress, besides these technology-related factors which trigger these responses, other non-technological sources of stress might also have an impact on users' responses in general technological-related context and in the specific case of mobile banking. However, our systematic research [10] revealed only one article aiming to identify the effect of the interaction between technostress and non-technological stress. As such, [69], in a tentative model development, demonstrated the importance of examining the interaction between technostress and work-related stress such as management expectations for productivity, as both forms of stress may impact satisfaction and organizational commitment. This model does not seem to have been pursued in an experimental study as no published article from the same author on this subject has been found. The potential effect of an eventual interaction between technostress and non-technological stress is thus still currently unknown. We choose to contribute to the filling of this gap by exploring one form of non-technological stress underlying the economic decision-making context of mobile banking, i.e., financial stress, which we present next.

## 2.4  Financial Stress

Financial stress is defined as the psychophysiological and behavioral responses resulting from financial and or/economic events in the sphere of financial resource management and decision making [70]. It is conceptualized and operationalized through financial strain, the perception of an economic pressure which creates a possibly harmful, threatening, or challenging situation [71] and aligns with the definition of a stressor to individuals. The psychophysiological and behavioral responses to financial strain are defined as financial stress [72].

Studied by scholars since the 19th century, financial stress has covered a wide range of heterogeneous contexts from financial stress experienced by university students [73], U.S. farmers [74], public sector employees [75], families and societies [76] to cancer patients [77]. As already underlined here, no study on financial stress has focused on the mobile banking context.

Financial stress has been identified as coming from three distinct sources: (1) personal stressors such as investment losses, accidents, wage reductions and perceived potential financial loss; (2) family stressors such as major life-cycle events requiring substantial amounts of money to resolve and; (3) financial stressors including personal consumer choice situations [12]. In the specific context of mobile banking, we therefore identify perceived potential financial loss due to online daily banking or investment transactions as the financial stressor.

Consistent findings on financial stress have shown a significant positive relationship between financial stress, psychological outcomes such as lowered self-esteem and an increase in depression [76], behavioral consequences such as lower work productivity [77] academic performance [73] increase in absenteeism [78], physiological outcomes such as higher blood pressure and heart rate [75] and a general declining of physical and mental health [76].

# 3  Proposed Experiment

In this part, we outline our proposed experimental design to disentangle technostress and financial stress on users' responses and coping behaviors, as well as the measurements used.

## 3.1  Experimental Design

We propose to use a 3-factor within-subject experimental design and manipulate financial stress, techno-overload, and techno-privacy. The experiment will have two subsequent stages: earning and investing.

**Earning Stage.**  To increase user behaviors' ecology [79], the earning stage will legitimize "wealth with effort" [80] by having subjects take a 10 simple questions quiz, earning $10 when answering correctly to 5 of them.

**Investing State.**  In the investing stage, and to reproduce a mobile banking usage context, participants will play 20 rounds of an adapted version of the TG, divided into four randomized blocks (5 rounds each), a widely used paradigm in neuroeconomics to study cognitive mechanisms underlying economic decision-making [14].

In the classic version of the TG, a player (the trustor) chooses whether to trust a second player (the trustee) by deciding to send or not, and how much, money from an initial endowment to this anonymous second player. This amount is then tripled by the experimenter and passed to the trustee who can then decide whether to return or defect the trust. In some cases, the roles of trustor and trustee are taken in alternation by each of the players until one of them refuses to return the money. Furthermore, the number of stages is either limited or not [81].

In our case, the experimental task will see participants acting as trustors and decide how much previously won money ($0 to $10) to invest into a fictional bank's financial product (the trustee) [13] given the actual return rate on a mobile-banking platform. Participants will be informed that the accrued total amount of the obtained returns determines a bonus at the end of the experiment based on a conversion chart [82]. Across blocks, the central independent variable will be the amount invested [83] under each condition.

Return on investment will constitute the financial stressor. Techno-overload will be induced as a text-based CAPTCHA before completing the investment transaction, and techno-privacy as a phishing attack message simulating an information breach [84], momentarily preventing participants from carrying on their investment decision.

Block A will be conducted on a non-technological platform to eliminate possible stress sources from using the TG software and induces financial stress over two conditions: High (potential gain/loss of 50% of the investment) vs. low (potential gain/loss of 5%) (Fig. 1).

Blocks B, C and D will use a TG software. Block B will randomly expose participants to financial stress and techno-overload, over four conditions: (high vs. low) and (captcha vs. no captcha). Block C will randomly expose participants to financial stress and techno-privacy, over four conditions: (high vs. low) and (message vs. no message). Block D will

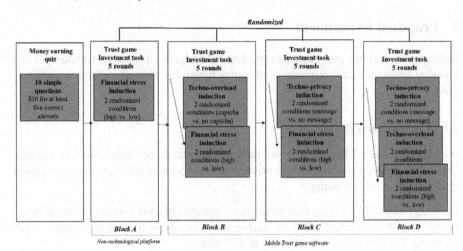

**Fig. 1.** Proposed experimental design.

manipulate all inductions and randomly assesses participants' reactions in a 2 (financial stress: high vs. low) × 2 (techno-overload: captcha vs. no captcha) × 2 (techno-privacy: message vs. no message) design.

### 3.2 Measurements

Psychophysiological and behavioral data will be captured pre- and post- and during the experiment.

**Physiological Responses Measurements.** Throughout the experiment, physiological responses to financial stress and technostress will be measured by recording electrodermal activity and heart rate as evidence of physiological arousal. After each round, a fixation cross will be displayed to allow recovery of physiological responses [82].

**Psychometric Responses Measurements.** Psychobehavioral responses will be measured using pre- and post-experiment questionnaires. The first questionnaire, which will be conducted in the pre-experiment stage, will collect sociodemographic data, including age, gender, and education status. The second questionnaire, which will be conducted in the post-experiment stage, will assess perceptions of techno-overload [65], techno-privacy [49], financial stress [70], discontinuance behaviors [8, 9], switching behaviors [85] and privacy security-efficiency [86]. All constructs will be measured on a 5-point Likert scale.

## 4    Conclusion and Next Phase

In conclusion, while the factors of technostress and financial stress differ, their outcomes seem generally similar. The question now is, on one hand, to determine the extent to which the effects of technostress and financial stress, and more specifically techno-overload, techno-privacy, and potential financial loss, affect users' reactions and perceptions and, on the other hand, whether they have different impacts in the specific context of mobile banking. To address this gap in the literature, we propose to conduct a pilot study to help disentangle these constructs and to ascertain the experiment's feasibility and ecological validity. The experimental design is presented to obtain feedback and help prepare the experiment.

# References

1. Johnstone, B.: Mobile banking: a catalyst for improving bank performance. Deloitte Consulting (2010)
2. Anastasia D.: Why banks need mobile apps: 7 significant benefits. RubyGarage. https://rub ygarage.org/blog/mobile-banking-benefits#:~:text=Full%20control%20over%20customer% 20finances,deposits%2C%20and%20do%20much%20more. Accessed 09 Sept 2020
3. Letić, J., Mobile banking statistics: the future of money is in the palm of your hand. Data Prot. https://dataprot.net/statistics/mobile-banking-statistics/. Accessed 09 Sept 2020
4. Heo, W., Lee, J.M., Rabbani, A.G.: Mediation effect of financial education between financial stress and use of financial technology. J. Fam. Econ. Issues 1–16 (2020). https://doi.org/10. 1007/s10834-020-09720-w
5. Tam, C., Oliveira, T.: Literature review of mobile banking and individual performance. Int. J. Bank Mark. 35(7), 1044–1067 (2017)
6. Avornyo, P., Fang, J., Antwi, C.O., Aboagye, M.O., Boadi, E.A.: Are customers still with us? The influence of optimum stimulation level and IT-specific traits on mobile banking discontinuous usage intentions. J. Retail. Consum. Serv. 47, 348–360 (2019)
7. Beaudry, A., Pinsonneault, A.: Understanding user responses to information technology: A coping model of user adaptation. MIS Q. 29(3), 493–524 (2005)
8. Chen, J.V., Tran, A., Nguyen, T.: Understanding the discontinuance behavior of mobile shoppers as a consequence of technostress: an application of the stress-coping theory. Comput. Hum. Behav. 95, 83–93 (2019)
9. Maier, C., Laumer, S., Weinert, C., Weitzel, T.: The effects of technostress and switching stress on discontinued use of social networking services: a study of Facebook use. Inf. Syst. J. 25(3), 275–308 (2015)
10. Korosec-Serfaty, M., Léger., P-M., Sénécal., S.: Technostress in work-related and non-work-related usage contexts: a systematic literature review. In: SIGHCI 2020 Proceedings, p. 11 (2020)
11. Godbold, N.: Researching emotions in interactions: seeing and analysing live processes. Emot. Rev. 7(2), 163–168 (2015)
12. Joo, S.H., Grable, J.E.: An exploratory framework of the determinants of financial satisfaction. J. Fam. Econ. Issues 25(1), 25–50 (2004)
13. Nofer, M., Hinz, O., Muntermann, J., Roßnagel, H.: The economic impact of privacy violations and security breaches. Bus. Inf. Syst. Eng. 6(6), 339–348 (2014)
14. Fehr, E., Fischbacher, U., Kosfeld, M.: Neuroeconomic foundations of trust and social preferences: initial evidence. Am. Econ. Rev. 95(2), 346–351 (2005)
15. Riedl, R., Kindermann, H., Auinger, A., Javor, A.: Computer breakdown as a stress factor during task completion under time pressure: identifying gender differences based on skin conductance. Adv. Hum. Comput. Interact. 2013, 1–8 (2013)
16. Emurian, H.H.: Cardiovascular and electromyograph effects of low and high density work on an interactive information system. Comput. Hum. Behav. 9(4), 353–370 (1993)

17. Corporate Finance Institute: What is Mobile Banking. https://corporatefinanceinstitute.com/resources/knowledge/finance/mobile-banking/. Accessed 02 Apr 2021
18. Souiden, N., Ladhari, R., Chaouali, W.: Mobile banking adoption: a systematic review. Int. J. Bank Mark. 39(2), 214–2441 (2021)
19. Davis, F.D.: User acceptance of information technology: system characteristics, user perceptions and behavior impacts. Int. J. Man Mach. Stud. 38, 475–487 (1993)
20. Davis, F.D.: Perceived usefulness, perceived ease of use, and user acceptance of information technology. MIS Q. 13, 31–340 (1989)
21. Bhattacherjee, A., Lin, C.P.: A unified model of IT continuance: three complementary perspectives and crossover effects. Eur. J. Inf. Syst. 24(4), 364–373 (2015)
22. Bhattacherjee, A.: Understanding information systems continuance: an expectation-confirmation model. MIS Q. 25(3), 351–370 (2001). (Sep. 2001)
23. Koenig-Lewis, N., Palmer, A., Moll, A.: Predicting young consumers' take up of mobile banking services. Int. J. Bank Mark. 28(5), 410–432 (2010)
24. Püschel, J., Mazzon, J.A., Hernandez, J.M.C.: Mobile banking: proposition of an integrated adoption intention framework. Int. J. Bank Mark. 28(5), 389–409 (2010)
25. Alafeef, M., Singh, D., Ahmad, K.: Influence of demographic factors on the adoption level of mobile banking applications in Jordan. Res. J. Appl. Sci. 6(6), 373–377 (2011)
26. Alalwan, A.A., Dwivedi, Y.K., Rana, N.P.P., Williams, M.D.: Consumer adoption of mobile banking in Jordan: examining the role of usefulness, ease of use, perceived risk and self-efficacy. J. Enterp. Inf. Manag. 29(1), 118–139 (2016)
27. Saleem, Z., Rashid, K.: Relationship between customer satisfaction and mobile banking adoption in Pakistan. Int. J. Trade Econ. Financ. 2(6), 537 (2011)
28. Zhou, T.: Understanding users' initial trust in mobile banking: an elaboration likelihood perspective. Comput. Hum. Behav. 28(4), 1518–1525 (2012)
29. Elm, A., Van Dyke, D.: The banking digital trust report 2020: how consumers rank the top 10 US banks on security, privacy, reputation, reliability, feature breadth, and ease of use. eMarketer. https://www.emarketer.com/content/the-banking-digital-trust-report-2020-how-consumers-rank-the-top-10-us-banks-on-security-privacy-reputation-reliability-feature-bre adth-and-ease-of-use-2020-2. Accessed 02 Jan 2021
30. Financial Brand Newsletter: Mobile Banking: Financial Institutions Must Clean Up Their Apps. https://thefinancialbrand.com/96850/covid-19-coronavirus-mobile-banking-app-digital-channel-website/. Accessed 02 Jan 2021
31. Turel, O.: Quitting the use of a habituated hedonic information system: a theoretical model and empirical examination of Facebook users. Eur. J. Inf. Syst. 24(4), 431–446 (2015)
32. Parthasarathy, M., Bhattacherjee, A.: Understanding post-adoption behavior in the context of online services. Inf. Syst. Res. 9(4), 362–379 (1998)
33. Pollard, C.: Exploring continued and discontinued use of IT: a case study of OptionFinder, a group support system. Group Decis. Negot. 12(3), 171–193 (2003)
34. Dhabhar, F.S.: Effects of stress on immune function: the good, the bad, and the beautiful. Immunol. Res. 58(2–3), 193–210 (2014). https://doi.org/10.1007/s12026-014-8517-0
35. Riedl, R.: On the biology of technostress: literature review and research agenda. ACM SIGMIS Database: DATABASE for Adv. Inf. Syst. 44(1), 18–55 (2013)
36. Ulifeline: Good Stress. Bad stress. http://www.ulifeline.org/articles/450-good-stress-bad-str ess#:~:text=In%20fact%2C%20stress%20can%20help,like%20epinephrine%2C%20nore pinephrine%20and%20cortisol. Accessed 09 Sept 2020
37. Course Hero: Stress, Coping, and Health Psychology. https://www.coursehero.com/sg/introd uction-to-psychology/emotional-and-behavioral-responses-to-stress/. Accessed 09 Sept 2020
38. Folkman, S., Lazarus, R.S., Dunkel-Schetter, C., DeLongis, A., Gruen, R.J.: Dynamics of a stressful encounter: cognitive appraisal, coping, and encounter outcomes. J. Pers. Soc. Psychol. 50(5), 992 (1986)

39. Lazarus, R.S., Folkman, S.: Stress, Appraisal, and Coping. Springer, Heidelberg (1984)
40. Brod, C.: Technostress: The Human Cost of the Computer Revolution. Addison Wesley, Reading (1984)
41. Rosen, L., Weil, M.: Technostress: Coping with Technology@ Work@ Home@ Play. Wiley, Etobicoke (1997)
42. Tarafdar, M., Tu, Q., Ragu-Nathan, B.S., Ragu-Nathan, T.S.: The impact of technostress on role stress and productivity. J. Manag. Inf. Syst. 24(1), 301–328 (2007)
43. Tarafdar, M., Cooper, C.L., Stich, J.F.: The technostress trifecta-techno eustress, techno distress and design: theoretical directions and an agenda for research. Inf. Syst. J. 29(1), 6–42 (2019)
44. Fischer, T., Riedl, R.: Theorizing technostress in organizations: a cybernetic approach. In 12th International Conference on Wirtschaftsinformatik Proceedings, pp. 1453–1467 (2015)
45. Ayyagari, R.: What and why of technostress: technology antecedents and implications. All Dissertations. 133 (2007)
46. Pirkkalainen, H., Salo, M., Makkonen, M., Tarafdar, M: Coping with technostress: when emotional responses fail. In: Proceedings the 38th International Conference on Information Systems, pp. 1–17 (2017)
47. Riedl, R., Kindermann, H., Auinger, A., Javor, A.: Technostress from a neurobiological perspective. Bus. Inf. Syst. Eng. 4(2), 61–69 (2012)
48. Trimmel, M., Meixner-Pendleton, M., Haring, S.: Stress response caused by system response time when searching for information on the Internet. Hum. Factors 45(4), 615–622 (2003)
49. Nimrod, G.: Technostress: measuring a new threat to well-being in later life. Aging Ment. Health 22(8), 1086–1093 (2018)
50. Galluch, P.S., Grover, V., Thatcher, J.B.: Interrupting the workplace: examining stressors in an information technology context. J. Assoc. Inf. Syst. 16(1), 2 (2015)
51. Galluch, P.: Interrupting the workplace: examining stressors in an information technology context. All Dissertations. 448 (2009)
52. Tams, S.: The Role of Age in Technology-induced Workplace Stress. All Dissertations. 779 (2011)
53. Korunka, C., Huemer, K.H., Litschauer, B., Karetta, B., Kafka-Lützow, A.: Working with new technologies: hormone excretion as an indicator for sustained arousal. A pilot study. Biol. Psychol. 42(3), 439–452 (1996)
54. De Guinea, A.O., Titah, R., Léger, P.M.: Explicit and implicit antecedents of users' behavioral beliefs in information systems: a neuropsychological investigation. J. Manag. Inf. Syst. 30(4), 179–210 (2014)
55. Riedl, R., Léger, P.M.: Fundamentals of NeuroIS. Studies in Neuroscience, Psychology and Behavioral Economics. Springer, Heidelberg (2016). https://doi.org/10.1007/978-3-662-450 91-8
56. Weinert, C., Christian, M., Laumer, S., Weitzel, T.: Technostress mitigation: an experimental study of social support during a computer freeze. J. Bus. Econ. 90, 1199–1249 (2020). https://doi.org/10.1007/s11573-020-00986-y
57. Califf, C., Brooks, S.L.: An empirical study of techno-stressors, literacy facilitation, burnout, and turnover intention as experienced by K-12 teachers. Computers and Education 157, 103971 (2020)
58. Maier, C., Laumer, S., Wirth, J., Weitzel, T.: Technostress and the hierarchical levels of personality: a two-wave study with multiple data samples. Eur. J. Inf. Syst. 28(5), 496–522 (2019)
59. Tarafdar, M., Pullins, E.B., Ragu-Nathan, T.S.: Technostress: negative effect on performance and possible mitigations. Inf. Syst. J. 25, 103–132 (2015)

60. Fieseler, C., Grubenmann, S., Meckel, M., Müller, S.: The leadership dimension of coping with technostress. In: 47th Hawaii International Conference on System Sciences, pp. 530–539 (2014)
61. Khan, A., Rehman, H., Rehman, D.S.U.: An empirical analysis of correlation between technostress and job satisfaction: a case of KPK, Pakistan. Pak. J. Inf. Manage. Libr. **14**, 9–15 (2016)
62. Tu, Q., Wang, K., Shu, Q.: Computer-related technostress in China. Commun. ACM **48**(4), 77–81 (2005)
63. Oh, S.T., Park, S.: A study of the connected smart workers Techno-Stress. Proc. Comput. Sci. **91**, 725–733 (2016)
64. Tarafdar, M., Tu, Q., Ragu-Nathan, T.S.: Impact of technostress on end-user satisfaction and performance. J. Manag. Inf. Syst. **27**(3), 303–334 (2010)
65. Ragu-Nathan, T.S., Tarafdar, M., Ragu-Nathan, B.S., Tu, Q.: The consequences of technostress for end users in organizations: conceptual development and empirical validation. Inf. Syst. Res. **19**(4), 417–433 (2008)
66. Zhang, S., Zhao, L., Lu, Y., Yang, J.: Do you get tired of socializing? An empirical explanation of discontinuous usage behaviour in social network services. Inf. Manage. **53**(7), 904–914 (2016)
67. Wang, W., Daneshvar Kakhki, M., Uppala, V.: The interaction effect of technostress and non-technological stress on employees' performance. In: Proceedings of the Twenty-third Americas Conference on Information Systems (2017)
68. Luqman, A., Cao, X., Ali, A.: Empirical investigation of Facebook discontinues usage intentions based on SOR paradigm. Comput. Hum. Behav. **70**, 544–555 (2017)
69. Tarafdar, M., Maier, C., Laumer, S., Weitzel, T.: Explaining the link between technostress and technology addiction for social networking sites: a study of distraction as a coping behavior. Inf. Syst. J. **30**(1), 96–124 (2020)
70. Heo, W., Cho, S.H., Lee, P.: APR Financial Stress Scale: Development and validation of a multidimensional measurement. J. Financ. Ther. **11**(1), 2 (2020)
71. Asebedo, S.D., Wilmarth, M.J.: Does how we feel about financial strain matter for mental health? J. Financ. Ther. **8**(1), Article 5 (2017)
72. Martin, J., Boyer, M., Léger, P.-M., Dumont, L.: Cognitive fit and visual pattern recognition in financial information system: an experimental study. In: Davis, F.D., Riedl, R., vom Brocke, J., Léger, P.-M., Randolph, A.B. (eds.) Information Systems and Neuroscience. LNISO, vol. 29, pp. 147–153. Springer, Cham (2019). https://doi.org/10.1007/978-3-030-01087-4_18
73. Britt, S.L., Mendiola, M.R., Schink, G.H., Tibbetts, R.H., Jones, S.H.: Financial stress, coping strategy, and academic achievement of college students. J. Financ. Couns. Plan. **27**(2), 172–183 (2016)
74. Heo, W., Lee, J.M., Park, N.: Financial-related psychological factors affect life satisfaction of farmers. J. Rural. Stud. **80**, 185–194 (2020)
75. Nag, D., Smith, C., Morgan, W.B., Walker, S.S.: Effects of financial stress on employees' physiological health, financial hassle, and performance. In: Proceedings of the Graduate Student Research Conference in Business and Economics: Volume 1 (2017)
76. Davis, C.G., Mantler, J.: The consequences of financial stress for individuals, families, and society. Centre for Research on Stress, Coping and Well-being. Carleton University, Ottawa: Department of Psychology (2004)
77. Hanratty, B., Holland, P., Jacoby, A., Whitehead, M.: Financial stress and strain associated with terminal cancer—a review of the evidence. Palliat. Med. **21**(7), 595–607 (2007)
78. Kim, J., Sorhaindo, B., Garman, E.T.: Relationship between financial stress and workplace absenteeism of credit counseling clients. J. Family Econ. Issues **27**(3), 458–478 (2006)
79. Tzieropoulos, H.: The trust Game in neuroscience: a short review. Soc. Neurosci. **8**(5), 407–416 (2013)

80. Cherry, T.L., Frykblom, P., Shogren, J.F.: Hardnose the dictator. Am. Econ. Rev. **92**(4), 1218–1221 (2002)
81. Roszczynska-Kurasinska, M., Kacprzyk, M.: The dynamics of trust from the perspective of a trust game. In: Nowak, A., Winkowska-Nowak, K., Brée, D. (eds.) Complex Human Dynamics. Understanding Complex Systems, pp. 191–207. Springer, Heidelberg (2013). https://doi.org/10.1007/978-3-642-31436-0_11
82. Studer, B., Scheibehenne, B., Clark, L.: Psychophysiological arousal and inter-and intraindividual differences in risk-sensitive decision making. Psychophysiology **53**(6), 940–950 (2016)
83. Zürn, M., Topolinski, S.: When trust comes easy: articulatory fluency increases transfers in the trust game. J. Econ. Psychol. **61**, 74–86 (2017)
84. Terlizzi, M. A.: Privacy concerns and protection motivation theory in the context of mobile banking. [doctoral dissertation], Sao Paulo, School of Business Administration (2019)
85. Wang, L., Luo, X.R., Yang, X., Qiao, Z.: Easy come or easy go? Empirical evidence on switching behaviors in mobile payment applications. Information & Management **56**(7), 103150 (2019)
86. Mamonov, S., Benbunan-Fich, R.: The impact of information security threat awareness on privacy-protective behaviors. Comput. Hum. Behav. **83**, 32–44 (2018)

# Structure-Behavior Coalescence Method for Mobile Payment FinTech Service Systems Design

Wei-Ming Ma[1], Yu-Chen Yang[2(✉)], and William S. Chao[3]

[1] Cheng Shiu University, Kaohsiung, Taiwan
k3666@gcloud.csu.edu.tw
[2] National Sun Yat-Sen University, Kaohsiung, Taiwan
ycyang@mis.nsysu.edu.tw
[3] Association of Systems Architects, Taipei, Taiwan

**Abstract.** The core theme of systems engineering is a modeling language with model consistency of static systems structure and dynamic systems behavior. In this research, we developed Channel-Based Multi-Queue Structure-Behavior Coalescence Process Algebra (C-M-SBC-PA) as the formal language for the model singularity of the mobile payment FinTech service systems design. In C-M-SBC-PA, a sole diagram is adopted to describe the syntax and semantics of the design of the service system. Overall, the model consistency will be fully guaranteed in the mobile payment FinTech service systems design when the C-M-SBC-PA method is used.

**Keywords:** Mobile payment FinTech service systems design ·
Structure-behavior coalescence · Formal language · Model singularity · Model consistency

## 1 Introduction

As a general application of modeling to support systems planning, specification, design, verification, and testing tasks beginning in the conceptual planning phase and continuing throughout development and later life cycle phases, systems engineering aims to promote systems engineering activities that have traditionally been performed using the document-based approach and result in the enhanced specification and design quality, reuse of system specification and design artifacts, as well as communication between development teams [1–5].

The kernel theme of systems engineering is a consistent model, i.e., systems modeling language (SysML), of the static systems structure and dynamic systems behavior, with an emphasis on using model-based methods and tools to enhance and ameliorate the model. However, because SysML is a multiple diagram method based on UML 2.0, there are always remarkable inconsistencies between varied diagrams in the SysML design of a system [6–10].

© Springer Nature Switzerland AG 2021
F. F.-H. Nah and K. Siau (Eds.): HCII 2021, LNCS 12783, pp. 228–241, 2021.
https://doi.org/10.1007/978-3-030-77750-0_15

In this research, we developed channel-based multi-queue structure-behavior coalescence process algebra (C-M-SBC-PA) [11, 12] as the modeling language for the model singularity of the mobile payment FinTech service systems design. Using C-M-SBC-PA, only a single diagram is used to specify the semantics of the system. Therefore, the model consistency will be completely ensured in the mobile payment FinTech service systems design.

The rest of this paper is organized as follows. Section 2 deals with the related systems engineering modeling studies. C-M-SBC-PA, as a single diagram for service systems design, is detailed in Sect. 3. After describing the structure-behavior coalescence method adopted in this paper, we will apply it to the mobile payment FinTech service systems design in Sect. 4. The conclusions of this paper are in Sect. 5.

## 2  Background

In the systems engineering user group, people often use the Systems Modeling Language (SysML) to specify the static systems structure and dynamic systems behavior of the system. The SysML concepts include (1) an abstract syntax that defines the language concepts and is described by a meta-model, and (2) a concrete syntax, or notation, that defines how the language concepts are represented and are described by a user model [4, 5]. Because SysML is a multiple diagram method based on UML 2.0, there are always some inconsistencies between various diagrams in the user model [6–10].

There are two ways to resolve inconsistencies in the SysML design of a system. The first method is to use a meta model. To ensure and check consistency, the meta-model defining the abstract syntax of the modeling language needs to provide a unified semantic framework for specifying consistency rules to press constraints on the structure or behavior constructs of the SysML systems specification. The Object Management Group (OMG) specifies a language that represents meta-models, called Meta Object Facility (MOF) that is used to define UML, SysML, and other meta-models. Various mechanisms are used in MOF, such as Object Constraint Language (OCL) [13], Foundational UML (fUML) [14], The Action Language for Foundational UML (Alf) [15], Process Specification Language (PSL) [16], and so on. However, all the mechanisms used in MOF do not provide a unified semantic framework from which each diagram in the user model will be projected as a view of the SysML meta-model.

The second method to ensure and check model consistency is to provide a single diagram for the SysML user model specification. The Object Process Methodology (OPM) [17] which is able to consider processes that are parallel to the object, depicting an excellent single diagram framework that avoids model inconsistencies by unifying all the information into the unified model and limiting the complexity through a scaling mechanism.

In this paper, we developed channel-based multi-queue structure-behavior coalescence process algebra (C-M-SBC-PA) as the modeling language for mobile payment FinTech service systems design. In C-M-SBC-PA, only a single diagram is used to design the syntax and semantics of the system. Therefore, by using the C-M-SBC-PA method, the model consistency can be completely guaranteed in the mobile payment FinTech service systems design.

# 3  Method of Structure-behavior Coalescence

## 3.1  Channel-Based Mechanism

The block is the fundamental modular unit for specifying the systems structure in SysML [4, 5]. It can define a type of virtual or real entity; a software, hardware, or object; a person; a facility. A channel is a mechanism for agent communication via message passing [11, 12]. A message may send over a channel, and another agent can receive messages sent by a channel it has a reference. Each channel defines a set of parameters that describes the arguments passed in with the request or passed back out once a $K \subseteq \Lambda \times \Theta$ request has been handled. The signature for a channel is a combination of its name along with parameters as follows:

&lt;channel name&gt;(&lt;parameter list&gt;)

The parameters in the parameter list represent the inputs or outputs of the channel. Each parameter in the list displayed with the following format:

&lt;direction&gt; &lt;parameter name&gt; : &lt;parameter type&gt;

Parameter direction may be in, out, or inout. We formally describe the "channel signature" as a relation where $\Lambda$ is a set of "channel names", and $\Theta$ is a set of "parameter lists".

An interaction [11, 12] describes an integrated communication between the caller agent (actor or block) and the callee block. In the channel-based value-passing approach, as shown in Fig. 1, the caller agent interacts with the callee block through the "calculateSum(in a: Real; in b: Real; out c: Real)" channel signature.

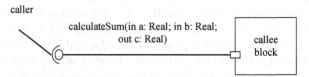

Fig. 1.  Channel-based value-passing interaction

The outside environment uses a "type 1 interaction" to interact with a block. We specify the channel-based value-passing "type 1 interaction" as a relation $G \subseteq B \times K \times \Gamma$ where $B$ is a set of "external environment's actors", and $K$ is a set of "channel signatures", and $\Gamma$ is a set of "blocks".

Two blocks use a "type 2 interaction" to interact with each other. We specify the channel-based value-passing "type 2 interaction" as a relation $V \subseteq \Gamma \times K \times \Gamma$ where $\Gamma$ is a set of "blocks" and $K$ is a set of "channel signatures".

We can also specify the channel-based value-passing "type 1 or 2 interaction" as a relation $\Delta \subseteq \Xi \times K \times \Gamma$ where $\Xi$ is a set of "external environment's actors or blocks" and $K$ is a set of "channel signatures", and $\Gamma$ is a set of "blocks".

## 3.2   Entities of C-M-SBC-PA

As shown in Table 1, we define $K$ be the relation of channel signatures then utilize $k1$, $k2$... to scope over $K$. We further define $\Lambda$ be the set of channel names then utilize $ch1$, $ch2$... to scope over $\Lambda$. Further, we define $\Theta$ be the finite set of parameters then utilize $p1$, $p2$... to scope over $\Theta$. We define $G$ be the relation of interactions of type 1 then utilize $g1$, $g2$... to scope over $G$. We define $V$ be the relation of interactions of type 2 then utilize $v1$, $v2$... to scope over $V$. Further, we define $\Delta$ be the relation of interactions of type 1 or 2 then utilize $a1$, $a2$... to scope over $\Delta$. We define $\Psi$ be the finite set of state expressions then utilize $s1$, $s2$... to scope over $\Psi$. Further, we define $X$ be the finite set of state variables then utilize $X1$, $X2$...to scope over $X$. We define $B$ be the finite set of actors then utilize $\beta1$, $\beta2$... to scope over $B$. We further define $\Gamma$ be the finite set of blocks then utilize $b1$, $b2$... to scope over $\Gamma$. Finally, we define $\Xi$ be the finite set of actors or blocks then utilize $\rho1$, $\rho2$... to scope over $\Xi$.

**Table 1.**   Entities of C-M-SBC-PA

| Entity Set | Entity name | Type of entity |
|---|---|---|
| $K$ | $k_1, k_2$... | Channel signatures |
| $\Lambda$ | $ch_1, ch_2$ | Channel names |
| $\Theta$ | $p_1, p_2$... | Parameter lists |
| $G$ | $g_1, g_2$... | Interaction of type 1 |
| $V$ | $v_1, v_2$... | Interaction of type 2 |
| $\Delta$ | $a_1, a_2$...to scope over $\Delta$ | Interaction of type 1 or 2 |
|  | I, J,... | Indexing sets |
| $\Psi$ | $s_1, s_2$... | State expressions |
| $X$ | $X_1, X_2$... | State variables |
| $B$ | $\beta_1, \beta_2$... | Actors |
| $\Gamma$ | $b_1, b_2$... | Blocks |
| $\Xi$ | $\rho_1, \rho_2$... | Actors or blocks |

## 3.3   Syntax of C-M-SBC-PA

Figure 2 shows the syntax of C-M-SBC-PA, which is specified by the grammar of Backus-Naur Form.

(1) <System> ::=   <FixIFD> {" $\coprod$ " <FixIFD>}

(2) <FixIFD> ::=" **fix**(" <State_Variable>"="<IFD>
    " $\bullet$ " <State_Variable> ")"

(3) <IFD> ::= <Type_1_Interaction> {" $\bullet$ " Type_1_Or_2_Interaction>}

(4) <Type_1_Or_2_Interaction> ::= <Type_1_Interaction>

                                  | <Type_2_Interaction>

**Fig. 2.** Syntax of C-M-SBC-PA

## 3.4 State Expression of the System in C-M-SBC-PA

In C-M-SBC-PA, the state expression of a mobile payment FinTech service systems design is defined as $\coprod_{i=1,m} FixIFD_i$ and the expression of FixIFD$_i$ is defined as **fix**$(X_i = \bigoplus_{j=1,n} a_{ij} \bullet X_i)$ where $a_{i1} = g_{i1}$ for all $i \in 1, m$.

To combine them together, we summarize that in C-M-SBC-PA, the mobile payment FinTech service systems design is then formally defined as

" **fix**$(X_1 = g_{11} \bullet a_{12} \bullet a_{13} \bullet \ldots \bullet a_{1n} \bullet X_1)$ $\coprod$ **fix**$(X_2 = g_{21} \bullet a_{22} \bullet a_{23} \bullet \ldots \bullet a_{2n} \bullet X_2)$ $\coprod$ ...$\coprod$,"
**fix**$(X_m = g_{m1} \bullet a_{m2} \bullet a_{m3} \bullet \ldots \bullet a_{mn} \bullet X_m)$

## 3.5 Transitional Semantics of C-M-SBC-PA

In giving meaning to C-M-SBC-PA, we use the transition graph (TG) as a single diagram to specify the semantics of a system. The C-M-SBC-PA transition graph is a labeled transition system (LTS) [18].

**DEFINITION** (TRANSITION GRAPH) A C-M-SBC-PA transition graph $TG = (\Psi, s_0, \Delta, TGR)$ consists of

- *a finite set $\Psi$ of states,*
- *an initial state $s_0 \in \Psi$,*
- *a finite set $\Delta$ of "type 1 or 2 interactions",*
- *a transition relation $TGR \subseteq \Psi_1 X \Delta X \Psi_2$, where $(s_j, a, s_k) \in TGR$ is denoted by $s_j \xrightarrow{a} s_k$.*

We can draw a diagram to represent the transition graph. Figure 3 shows the diagram of the transition graph $TG_{01}$. In the diagrammed transition graph, the state is represented by a circle containing its name; the transition from the source state to the target state is denoted by an arrow and labelled with an interaction; the initial state (e.g., "$s_1$") is the target state of the arrow which has no source state.

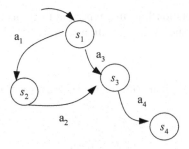

**Fig. 3.** Diagram of the transition graph $TG_{01}$

We can also list the relationships that represent the transition graph. Table 2 shows the transition relation "$TGR_{01}$" of the transition graph "$TG_{01}$".

**Table 2.** Relation $TGR_{01}$ of the transition graph $TG_{01}$.

| $\Psi_1$ | $\Delta$ | $\Psi_2$ |
|---|---|---|
| $s_1$ | $a_1$ | $s_2$ |
| $s_2$ | $a_2$ | $s_3$ |
| $s_1$ | $a_3$ | $s_3$ |
| $s_3$ | $a_4$ | $s_4$ |

## 3.6 Transition Graph of FixIFD in C-M-SBC-PA

In C-M-SBC-PA, the state expression of $FixIFD_i$ is formally specified as "$\mathbf{fix}(X_i = g_{i1} \bullet a_{i2} \bullet a_{i3} \bullet \ldots \bullet a_{in} \bullet X_i)$". As shown in Fig. 4, we use the C-M-SBC-PA transition graph $TG_i$ to specify the execution of the "$FixIFD_i$" state expression.

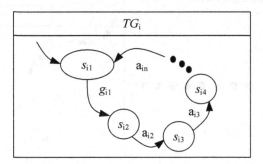

**Fig. 4.** Transition graph for $FixIFD_i$.

We can also list the relationships that represent the transition graph of the FixIFD$_i$ state expression. Table 3 shows the transition relation "$TGR_i$" of the transition graph "$TG_i$".

**Table 3.** Relation $TGR_i$ for the state expression "FixIFD$_i$".

| $\Psi_1$ | $\Delta$ | $\Psi_2$ |
|---|---|---|
| $s_{i1}$ | $g_{i1}$ | $s_{i2}$ |
| $s_{i2}$ | $a_{i2}$ | $s_{i3}$ |
| $s_{i3}$ | $a_{i3}$ | $s_{i4}$ |
| • | • | • |
| $s_{in}$ | $a_{in}$ | $s_{i1}$ |

In C-M-SBC-PA, the state expression of the mobile payment FinTech service systems design is formally defined as "$\mathbf{fix}(X_1 = g_{11} \bullet a_{12} \bullet a_{13} \bullet \ldots \bullet a_{1n} \bullet X_1)$ $\square$ $\mathbf{fix}(X_2 = g_{21} \bullet a_{22} \bullet a_{23} \bullet \ldots \bullet a_{2n} \bullet X_2)$ $\square$ $\ldots \square$ $\mathbf{fix}(X_m = g_{m1} \bullet a_{m2} \bullet a_{m3} \bullet \ldots \bullet a_{mn} \bullet X_m)$".

We use the C-M-SBC-PA transition graph $TG_{system}$ to specify the execution of the mobile payment FinTech service systems design, as shown in Fig. 5.

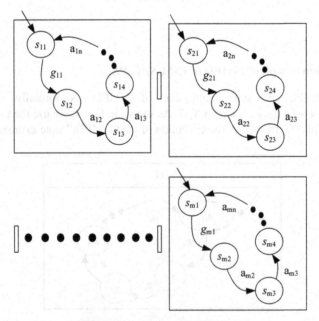

**Fig. 5.** Transition graph $TG_{system}$.

We can also list the relationships that represent the transition graph of a system. Table 4 shows the transition relation $TGR_{system}$ of the transition graph $TG_{system}$.

**Table 4.** Relation $TGR_{system}$.

| $\Psi_1$ | $\Delta$ | $\Psi_2$ |
|---|---|---|
| $s_{11}$ | $g_{11}$ | $s_{12}$ |
| $s_{12}$ | $a_{12}$ | $s_{13}$ |
| $s_{13}$ | $a_{13}$ | $s_{14}$ |
| • | • | • |
| $s_{1n}$ | $a_{1n}$ | $s_{11}$ |

| $\Psi_1$ | $\Delta$ | $\Psi_2$ |
|---|---|---|
| $s_{21}$ | $g_{21}$ | $s_{22}$ |
| $s_{22}$ | $a_{22}$ | $s_{23}$ |
| $s_{23}$ | $a_{23}$ | $s_{24}$ |
| • | • | • |
| $s_{2n}$ | $a_{2n}$ | $s_{21}$ |

| $\Psi_1$ | $\Delta$ | $\Psi_2$ |
|---|---|---|
| $s_{m1}$ | $g_{m1}$ | $s_{m2}$ |
| $s_{m2}$ | $a_{m2}$ | $s_{m3}$ |
| $s_{m3}$ | $a_{m3}$ | $s_{m4}$ |
| • | • | • |
| $s_{mn}$ | $a_{mn}$ | $s_{m1}$ |

# 4 Application of Mobile Payment Fintech Service System

## 4.1 Mobile Payment FinTech Service System

Financial technology, also named FinTech, is the new mechanization that aims to compete with traditional financial approaches in the delivery of financial solutions [19]. The use of smart phones for mobile banking, financial services, and cryptocurrency are examples of mechanizations aiming to make financial solutions more accessible to the public. Financial technology companies consist of both startups and established financial companies trying to improve or ameliorate the usage of financial solutions provided by existing financial companies.

Mobile Payment FinTech service system (MPFSS), shown in Fig. 6, links customers to stores that offer cell phone QR code scanning payments. Mobile payment is a significant financial technology application.

Behaviors of MPFSS consist of a) behavior of *Registering_Member_Account*, b) behavior of *Depositing_Money_into_the_Account*, c) behavior of *Setting_QR_Code_to_Collect_Money*, d) behavior of *Scanning_QR_Code_to_Pay*, and e) behavior of W*ithdrawing_Money_from_the_Account*.

In the behavior of *Registering_Member_Account*, a future member shall use the *Register_Member_Account_UI* component to input the corresponding data for this account registration. After that, the account registration data will be saved to the *MPFSS_Database* block. In the behavior of *Depositing_Money_into_the_Account*, each member can use MPFSS to transfer money from his bank to his mobile payment account. After confirming the transfer, all relevant data will be saved to the *MPFSS_Database* block. In the behavior of *Setting_QR_Code_to_Collect_Money*, a store can use MPFSS

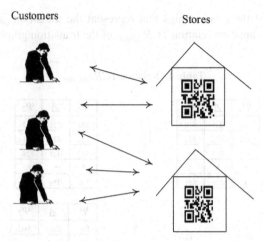

Customers                    Stores

**Fig. 6.** MPFSS operates autonomously within networks.

to set the QR code for payment. After confirming the settings, all relevant data will be saved to the *MPFSS_Database* block. In the behavior of *Scanning_QR_Code_to_Pay*, customers can use MPFSS for scanning and payment. After confirming the payment, all relevant data will be saved to the *MPFSS_Database* block. In the behavior of *Withdrawing_Money_from_the_Account*, each member can use MPFSS to transfer money from his mobile payment account to his bank. After confirming the transfer, all relevant data will be saved to the *MPFSS_Database* block.

### 4.2   C-M-SBC-PA State Expression of the Mobile Payment FinTech Service System

We first use the C-M-SBC-PA to design the Mobile Payment FinTech service system. The C-M-SBC-PA state expression of the Mobile Payment FinTech service system, $s_{MPFSS}$, is defined as "$\mathbf{fix}(X_1 = g_{11} \bullet v_{12} \bullet X_1) \bigsqcup \mathbf{fix}(X_2 = g_{21} \bullet v_{22} \bullet v_{23} \bullet g_{24} \bullet X_2) \bigsqcup$
$\mathbf{fix}(X_3 = g_{31} \bullet v_{32} \bullet g_{33} \bullet X_3) \bigsqcup \mathbf{fix}(X_4 = g_{41} \bullet v_{42} \bullet g_{43} \bullet v_{44} \bullet g_{45} \bullet X_4) \bigsqcup$
$\mathbf{fix}(X_5 = g_{51} \bullet v_{52} \bullet v_{53} \bullet g_{54} \bullet X_5)$".

We use the C-M-SBC-PA transition graph $TG_{MPFSS}$ defined as "$TG_1 \bigsqcup TG_2 \bigsqcup TG_3 \bigsqcup TG_4 \bigsqcup TG_5$" to represent the state expression of the Mobile Payment FinTech service systems design, as shown in Fig. 7.

We use a TG relation $TGR_{MPFSS} \subseteq \Psi_1 X X \Lambda X \Theta X \Gamma X \Psi_2$ defined as "$TGR_1 \bigsqcup TGR_2 \bigsqcup TGR_3 \bigsqcup TGR_4 \bigsqcup TGR_5$" to represent the C-M-SBC-PA transition graph $TG_{MPFSS}$ of the state expression of the Mobile Payment FinTech service systems design, as shown in Table 5.

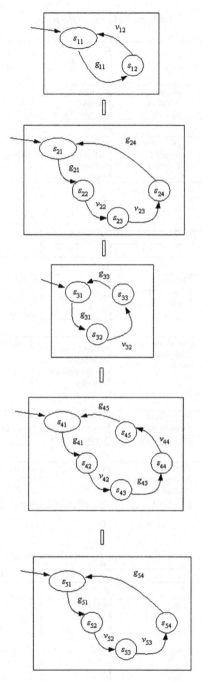

**Fig. 7.** Transition graph $TG_{\text{MPFSS}}$

**Table 5.** Relation $TGR_{MPFSS}$.

| $\Psi_1$ | $\Delta$ | | | | $\Psi_2$ |
|---|---|---|---|---|---|
| | $\Xi$ | $\Lambda$ | $\Theta$ | $\Gamma$ | |
| | $g_{11}$ | | | | |
| $s_{11}$ | Member | Register_Member_Account | in Register_Member_Account_Form | Register_Member_Account_UI | $s_{12}$ |
| | $v_{12}$ | | | | |
| $s_{12}$ | Register_Member_Account_UI | SQL_Insert_Register_Member_Account | in Register_Member_Account_Query | MPFSS_Database | $s_{11}$ |

| $\Psi_1$ | $\Delta$ | | | | $\Psi_2$ |
|---|---|---|---|---|---|
| | $\Xi$ | $\Lambda$ | $\Theta$ | $\Gamma$ | |
| | $g_{21}$ | | | | |
| $s_{21}$ | Member | Deposit_Money_into_the_Account_CALL | in Bank_Account; in Amount | Deposit_Money_into_the_Account_UI | $s_{22}$ |
| | $v_{22}$ | | | | |
| $s_{22}$ | Deposit_Money_into_the_Account_UI | Withdraw_Money_from_the_Bank | in Bank_Account; in Amount; out Authorization_Response | Bank_Service | $s_{23}$ |
| | $v_{23}$ | | | | |
| $s_{23}$ | Bank_Service | SQL_Insert_Deposit_Money_into_the_Account | in Deposit_Money_into_the_Account_Query | MPFSS_Database | $s_{24}$ |
| | $g_{24}$ | | | | |
| $s_{24}$ | Member | Deposit_Money_into_the_Account_RETURN | out Deposit_Money_into_the_Account_Report | Deposit_Money_into_the_Account_UI | $s_{25}$ |

| $\Psi_1$ | $\Delta$ | | | | $\Psi_2$ |
|---|---|---|---|---|---|
| | $\Xi$ | $\Lambda$ | $\Theta$ | $\Gamma$ | |
| | $g_{31}$ | | | | |
| $s_{31}$ | Store | Set_QR_Code_CALL | in Set_QR_Code_Form | Set_QR_Code_UI | $s_{32}$ |
| | $v_{32}$ | | | | |
| $s_{32}$ | Set_QR_Code_UI | SQL_Insert_Set_QR_Code | in Set_QR_Code_Query | MPFSS_Database | $s_{33}$ |
| | $g_{33}$ | | | | |
| $s_{33}$ | Store | Set_QR_Code_RETURN | out QR_Code | Set_QR_Code_UI | $s_{31}$ |

(*continued*)

**Table 5.** (*continued*)

| $\Psi_1$ | $\Delta$ | | | | $\Psi_2$ |
|---|---|---|---|---|---|
| | $B$ | $\Lambda$ | $\Theta$ | $\Gamma$ | |
| $s_{41}$ | Customer | Scan_to_Pay | *g41* | Scan_QR_Code_to_Pay_UI | $s_{42}$ |
| $s_{42}$ | Scan_QR_Code_to_Pay_UI | Scan_QR_Code | *v42* out QR_Code_Content | Store's_QR_Code | $s_{43}$ |
| $s_{43}$ | Customer | Agree_to_Pay_CALL | *g43* in Agree_to_Pay_Form | Scan_QR_Code_to_Pay_UI | $s_{44}$ |
| $s_{44}$ | Scan_QR_Code_to_Pay_UI | SQL_Insert_Agree_to_Pay | *g44* in Agree_to_Pay_Query | MPFSS_Database | $s_{45}$ |
| $s_{45}$ | Customer | Agree_to_Pay_RETURN | *g45* out Agree_to_Pay_Report | Scan_QR_Code_to_Pay_UI | $s_{41}$ |

| $\Psi_1$ | $\Delta$ | | | | $\Psi_2$ |
|---|---|---|---|---|---|
| | $B$ | $\Lambda$ | $\Theta$ | $\Gamma$ | |
| $s_{51}$ | Member | Withdraw_Money_from_the_Account CALL | *g51* in Bank_Account; in Amount; | Withdraw_Money_from_the_Account_UI | $s_{52}$ |
| $s_{52}$ | Withdraw_Money_from_the_Account_UI | Deposit_Money_into_the_Bank | *v52* in Bank_Account; in Amount; out Authorization_Response | Bank_Service | $s_{53}$ |
| $s_{53}$ | Withdraw_Money_from_the_Account_UI | SQL_Insert_Withdraw_Money_from_the_Account | *v53* in Bank_Account; in Amount; out Authorization_Response | MPFSS_Database | $s_{54}$ |
| $s_{54}$ | Member | Withdraw_Money_from_the_Account RETURN | *g54* out Withdraw_Money_from_the_Account_Report | Withdraw_Money_from_the_Account_UI | $s_{51}$ |

## 5 Conclusion

This paper proposed C-M-SBC-PA as the modeling language for the model singularity of the mobile payment FinTech service systems design. In C-M-SBC-PA, only a single diagram is used to specify the semantics of the design of the mobile payment FinTech service system. In general, when the C-M-SBC-PA method is adopted, the model consistency in the mobile payment FinTech service system design will be fully guaranteed.

**Acknowledgment.** The authors wish to express thanks to the anonymous references for their valuable comments, which help clarify subtle points and triggered new ideas.

## References

1. Blaha, M.R., Rumbaugh, J.R.: Object-Oriented Modeling and Design with UML, 2nd edn. Pearson, Upper Saddle River (2004)
2. Arlow, J., Neustadt, I.: UML 2, and the Unified Process: Practical Object-Oriented Analysis and Design. Addison-Wesley, Boston (2005)
3. Dori, D.: Model-Based Systems Engineering with OPM and SysML. Springer, New York (2016). https://doi.org/10.1007/978-1-4939-3295-5
4. Friedenthal, S., Moore, A., Steiner, R.: A Practical Guide to SysML The Systems Modeling Language, 3rd edn. Morgan Kaufmann, Burlington (2014)
5. Weilkiens, T.: Systems Engineering with SysML/UML: Modeling, Analysis, Design. Morgan Kaufmann, Burlington (2008)
6. Allaki, D., Dahchour, M., Ennouaary, A.: A new taxonomy of inconsistencies in UML models with their detection methods for better MDE. Int. J. Comput. Sci. Appl. **12**(1), 48–65 (2015)
7. Bashir, R.S., Lee, S.P., Khan, S.U.R.: UML models consistency management: guidelines for software quality manager. Int. J. Inf. Manage. **36**, 883–899 (2016)
8. Malgouyres, H., Motet, G.: A UML model consistency verification approach based on meta-modeling formalization. In: Proceedings of the 2006 ACM Symposium on Applied Computing, pp. 1804–1809 (2006)
9. Apvrille, L., Courtiat, J., Lohr, C., de Saqui-Sannes, P.: TURTLE: a real-time UML profile supported by a formal validation toolkit. IEEE Trans. Softw. Eng. **30**(7), 473–487 (2004)
10. Paige, R.F., Brooke, P.J., Ostroff, J.S.: Metamodel-based model conformance and multiview consistency checking. ACM Trans. Softw. Eng. Methodol. **16**(3), B1–B49 (2007). Article 11
11. Yang, Y.-C., Tsai, C.-T., Chao, W.S.: A structure-behavior coalescence systems modeling approach for service systems design. In: Nah, F.F.-H., Xiao, B.S. (eds.) HCIBGO 2018. LNCS, vol. 10923, pp. 236–249. Springer, Cham (2018). https://doi.org/10.1007/978-3-319-91716-0_18
12. Qin, G.-P., Sun, S.-P., Lee, Z.-J., Chao, W.S.: A Structure-behavior coalescence approach for model singularity. In: Bhatia, S., Tiwari, S., Mishra, K., Trivedi, M. (eds.) Advances in Computer Communication and Computational Sciences, vol. 759, pp. 343–350. Springer, Singapore (2018). https://doi.org/10.1007/978-981-13-0341-8_31
13. Przigoda, N., Wille, R., Drechsler, R.: Analyzing inconsistencies in UML/OCL models. J. Circ. Syst. Comput. **25**(3), 1640021:1-1640021:21 (2016)
14. OMG: Semantics of a Foundational Subset for Executable UML Models (fUML). Object Management Group, Needham, MA (2013)

15. OMG: Action Language for Foundational UML (Alf). Object Management Group, Needham, MA (2013)
16. ISO TC-184 (Technical Committee on Industrial Automation Systems and Integration), ISO 18629 Process Specification Languages (PSL) (2006)
17. Dori, D.: Object-Process Methodology: A Holistic Systems Paradigm. Springer, New York (2002)
18. Chao, W.S.: System: Contemporary Concept, Definition, and Language. CreateSpace Independent Publishing (2016)
19. Wilson, J.: Creating Strategic Value through Financial Technology. Wiley, Hoboken (2017)

# Human Factors in Industry 4.0 and Lean Information Management: Remodeling the Instructions in a Shop Floor

Juliana Salvadorinho[1] ⓘ, Leonor Teixeira[2](✉) ⓘ, Beatriz Sousa Santos[3] ⓘ, and Carlos Ferreira[2] ⓘ

[1] Department of Economics, Management, Industrial Engineering and Tourism, University of Aveiro, 3010-193 Aveiro, Portugal
juliana.salvadorinho@ua.pt
[2] Institute of Electronics and Informatics Engineering of Aveiro, Department of Economics, Management, Industrial Engineering and Tourism, University of Aveiro, 3010-193 Aveiro, Portugal
{lteixeira,carlosf}@ua.pt
[3] Institute of Electronics and Informatics Engineering of Aveiro, Department of Electronics, Telecommunications and Informatics, University of Aveiro, 3010-193 Aveiro, Portugal
bss@ua.pt

**Abstract.** Industry 4.0 or also called the digital paradigm brings with it an environment where information sharing, and agile flows can improve the results of organizations but also create great challenges for operators. The digital paradigm promotes the globalization of human capital, with an impact on worker turnover, as well as on the potential increase in the loss of organizational knowledge, as workers leave companies. Thus, this work, through the combination of the concepts of digital transformation and information management, joint with the techniques of BPM and Lean, clarifies a methodology (using BPMN) for the creation of a repository of organizational knowledge (enhancing instruction modelling work routines), while promoting the introduction of digital tools in daily tasks, placing the operator in the foreground. This digital introduction promotes the elimination of waste connected with Lean Information Management, creating more fluid information flows in the company. The human factor is then valued and new points of connection between the human workforce and digital tools are established, while organizational knowledge is updated, created, and retained.

**Keywords:** Human factors · Digitalization · Industry 4.0 · Organizational knowledge · BPMN · Shop floor

## 1 Introduction

The Fourth Industrial Revolution ($4^{th}$IR) adds a new state (digital) in the organizations, by moving them into a new work cycle that combines the digital with the physical world. Particularly in the digital world, new challenges arise due to the power of technologies

© Springer Nature Switzerland AG 2021
F. F.-H. Nah and K. Siau (Eds.): HCII 2021, LNCS 12783, pp. 242–255, 2021.
https://doi.org/10.1007/978-3-030-77750-0_16

such as internet of things (IoT) devices, big data and analytics systems, additive manufacturing, advanced and autonomous robotics tools, augmented and virtual reality, cloud computing, artificial intelligence and cognitive systems. All these technological drivers are related to the most sophisticated and innovative developments where the internet serve as a pillar to integrate computer agents, humans, processes, materials and products, and the information serves as a binding element to create a new kind of intelligence within an organization [1]. In fact, the emerging technologies behind Industry 4.0 can change the organizational value chain, creating new ways of working and of looking at business. However, despite the benefits arising from digitalization, this phenomenon leads to drastic changes in organizations with impacts on physical processes, information flows and on the way people work (human capital).

Another phenomenon that is strongly rooted in organizations today, and that should not be ignored in this new industrial revolution context, is Lean Thinking (LT). Although this concept has emerged in the manufacturing industry, it is already spreading to other areas, namely services, including data and information flows [2]. Considering some studies in the literature, LT can contribute to information management by eliminating waste, i.e., activities that do not add value on the information processes [3, 4]. These authors believe that wastes associated with information management, besides not adding value to the information chain, contribute negatively to the decision-making process. Among the various waste types [5] identify excess information, information over-processing and poor data quality, as the main wastes that occur in most organizations. Lean Information Management is defined by [6] as an approach for improving organizational systems, to reduce waste and to increase the value of information, eliminating activities without added value. It focuses on exposing and solving problems of information waste, variability and inflexibility.

To introduce changes concerning I4.0 and implement Lean Thinking among shop floor resources, companies must attend to their processes (core in any organization) and manage them it is vital to know how they are used at the organization and how they are linked to each other. Thus the modelling and documentation of processes are a matter of concern related to their maturity within the organization [7]. In fact, some researchers [8–10] have been already emphasizing that there is a need to extend the concepts of Business Process Management (BPM) to support knowledge flow in organizations. In the context of an organization operative business processes and even from a knowledge management perspective, process orientation is critical to providing task relevant knowledge In line with this thought, Business Process Management can be seen not only as important for process engineering, but also as a methodology that allows the transformation of informal into formal knowledge.

According to [11], lean manufacturing integrated with I4.0 represents an important research field that should be extensively explored. The human element should be in the centre of the shift, and companies are challenged to develop a group of competencies (a whole new curricula), in an effort to handle the increasing technological and organizational complexity of operations [12, 13]. Skills gain will not only be achieved through said "normal" education, but also through lifelong learning [14]. In this way and since the knowledge flow will be preponderant in the I4.0 paradigm, it is essential that companies are able to retain all the skills of their employees (tacit knowledge), in order to make the workforce rotation easier, so that the process on-site learning be also easier and more effective. In this sense, the purpose of this paper is to examine the relationship between I4.0, lean and information management on the perspective of the human factors and organizational knowledge. For this, a case study was carried out in a chemical industry company, where the collaborators' work instructions were modeled on the shop floor and activities of added value, non-added value, and inappropriate information flows were detected. This analysis allowed to specify an application to support decision making in a group of manufacturing cells. A remodeling of the instructions previously executed was conceived in order to consider the software functionalities and with the purpose of establishing a new role for collaborators (with the team leader example). The result is a starting point for an Organizational Knowledge Lean Repository (establishing new connection points between information and communication technologies and human resources on the shop floor) and a Lean Information System (only retaining information relevant to the company core processes).

## 2  Theoretical Background

### 2.1  Human Factor in Industry 4.0 and Operator 4.0

Cyberphysical systems will transform functions into manufacturing systems, which despite the increase the role of the computerization and automation, reveal that human work will be very important for the future [15]. Thus, in the Industry 4.0 environments, work is expected to be less repetitive and more challenging, but more qualified with a view to the use of cyberphysical systems [15], with the new concept of Operator 4.0 emerging. Operator 4.0 is understood as an intelligent and skillful operator who performs cooperative work with robots, presents assistance by machines, being used for that very reason, human cyberphysical systems, advanced technologies of human-machine interaction and adaptive automation to reach automation symbiosis work systems human [16]. It is expected that following Operator 4.0 principles, the factories of the future will be suitable for workers with different preferences, capacities and skills and driven by solutions that empower employees and involve the work community. There is, however, the argument that operators of the future will transition from operators to manufacturers, taking advantage of collaboration with digitized and automated production systems and using creativity to solve unexpected and unforeseen challenges [17].

Operator 4.0 converges on the intelligent and skilled operators of the future who will be assisted by automated systems (which will relieve physical and mental stress), fostering the growth of creative, innovative and improvisational skills, without compromising production objectives [18].

Companies now realize that new people being recruited are ill-equipped in terms of skills to face the reality of modern engineering. Technical knowledge is not enough and the strong and rapid advances in technology are showing that, increasingly, engineers face challenges that involve large-scale complex systems, requiring interdisciplinary interaction. Competencies for commerciality, customer management skills, relationship and communication skills, collaboration, systemic thinking and a stronger external market focus will be fundamental in the new paradigm [19].

Flores et al. [20] classify human capital 4.0 as having five major dimensions of competencies, categorizing them as soft, hard, cognitive, emotional and digital workforce. The soft workforce is considered flexible and social and includes communication, teamwork and cooperation, leadership, willingness to learn, self-development, negotiating power, flexibility and/or adaptability. The hard workforce, which is professional and skillful, encompasses technical knowledge that, in the paradigm of the future, is based on competencies at the level of industrial organization, industrial processes, understanding of patterns, problem solving techniques, software design, man interactions -machine, digital network settings, digital security and coding or programming. The cognitive workforce converges into intelligence and analytical skills, which in turn are divided into verbal aptitude, numerical aptitude and spatial aptitude (coordination, memory, decision making, abstract and analytical thinking). The emotional competence of the workforce is revealed in the breadth of self-awareness and empathy. Characteristics of this dimension are revealed as being self-control, empathy, orientation towards achievement and motivation. The competence of the digital workforce encompasses digitally literate and digital interactive. And it incorporates in itself programming skills, cybersecurity, digital networks, cloud computing, database architecture and web development.

As mentioned in [18] and [21], Operator 4.0 can be differentiated in Super-strength Operator (due to the use of exoskeletons), in Augmented Operator (due to the application of the augmented reality tool), in Virtual Operator (from the use of a virtual factory), the Healthy Operator (using wearable devices to track employee well-being), the Smarter Operator (applying agents or artificial intelligence to planning activities), the Collaborative Operator (through interaction with CoBots), the Social Operator (due to knowledge sharing using a social network) and the Analytical Operator (through the application of Big Data analysis).

Li et al. [21], in their research, despite mentioning the previous Operator 4.0 models, they funnel their characteristics in four dimensions, being the Augmented Operator (able to enjoy remote orientation and specialized capture, where they register their work and place it in a place where other operators can search), the Virtual Operator (creating ease of learning and training, such as showing availability for meetings to plan new factory layouts), the Smart Operator (supported by artificial intelligence systems, where it is possible to create shop-floor memory, digital checklists and digital immediate transfer of information for follow-up of operators) and, finally, the Social Operator (where social networks operate that provide knowledge sharing, advice and function as knowledge repositories).

Human resources are considered essential in smart manufacturing. In the past, it was the operator who had to adapt to processes and systems, with efficiency, productivity and cost savings being the main drivers of adaptation. With the emergence of technologies, machines and processes are so automated that these performance measures are already guaranteed. However, exploiting the flexibility and creativity of human workers is becoming more important to gain a competitive advantage in today's business. Thereafter, the paradigm is changing, as systems must be adapted to the human operator and satisfaction in the workplace will be a key issue. The adaptation according to the human operator was developed under four dimensions, adaptation to human physics with ergonomics at work, adaptation to human skills, adaptation to interaction and adaptation to the Level of Automation (LoA) [18].

## 2.2 Lean Information Management

Information management (IM) consists of sharing information to support the decision-making process, learning and coordination of activities, thus being transversal to any organization [1, 22]. Here, the information (product) follows a flow in order to satisfy a specific user (customer), ensuring that valuable and quality information is available at the right time to the right people, in order to help people, access and use the information. information efficiently and effectively [1].

Lean thinking is a philosophy that has the potential to be applied to any system or process, to identify critical areas of improvement. The principles of lean involve the elimination of waste and the guarantee of value flows, therefore it is necessary to ensure the identification of value, understanding of the flow and characterization of waste [23].

In the context of philosophy, all activities can be classified into three categories: activities with added value, activities with no added value, mandatory / necessary and activities with no added value. Activities with no added value are those for which customers are not willing to pay, and it is in this type of task that Lean principles must be applied (as they are activities that are understood as waste). However, there are the necessary activities without added value, which should not be eliminated blindly, because although they do not add value from the customer's perspective, they are necessary for production, however, there is a need to explore another way of reduce or eliminate them in the long run [24].

Lean Information Management is a theory that combines two well-established concepts in the literature: lean and information management [1]. It is therefore an approach that tries to improve the flow of information, applying its focus on reducing waste (arising from activities with no added value), thus incorporating more value in the information [1, 24]. It concentrates, as a whole, practices, functions and responsibilities that aim to manage the public value of information and knowledge [25].

When thinking about manufacturing and production, the underlying cause of waste is generally well understood and visible. However, in the context of information management, visualizing waste is less clear, so, before applying the Lean philosophy at the level of processes associated with information management, it is necessary to develop an understanding of waste within the context itself and characterize the types of waste present in the system and infrastructure [23].

According to [1, 26] and [25], seven wastes (inspiring in the Lean Manufacturing' seven wastes) of lean from the perspective of information management were established and are summarized at Table 1.

The principles inherent in the theme of Lean Information Management, can be summarized as follows [1, 24]: (i) the information should only be created if it is valuable for decision makers, being therefore useful to simplify each process to minimize the need for information management; (ii) the information must be directed only to those who need it, programming each flow of value from just one point; (iii) the information must be handled quickly (preferably in real time), avoiding waiting by users, being crucial that all stages of the processes are capable and available; and (iv) the information must be delivered by sources deprived of replication of data, which must be sent in small batches.

**Table 1.** The seven lean wastes on information processes [1, 25, 26]

| Waste category | Implications |
|---|---|
| Overproduction | Too many systems and multiple data sources with no added value information that the process client will not use immediately |
| Waiting | Time and resources used to identify information that is not readily available (which usually results in people waiting for the right information or in collaborators waiting for a program to run) |
| Extra Work | Activities that are carried out to overcome the lack of information (delays in changing information, for example), which may consist of creating new information or even taking corrective actions |
| Defects | Errors in data entry, reprocessing of electronic transactions, information systems with problems in converting information, information formats with incompatible standards, inappropriate actions based on inaccurate information (can result in poor decision making) |
| Conveyance | It consists of moving information that does not add value to the user (an example of this is the approval of documents that require more than one signature - which means that the documents have to be moved between folders) |
| Inventory | Excessive information (with consequent loss of essential information, due to unnecessary details) from legacy databases and files |
| Motion | Unnecessary movement to acquire information due to the organization and inadequate representation of it that was previously performed. Manual intervention due to the lack of integration between systems and information transferred to the wrong destination are considered unnecessary movements (and therefore waste) |

## 3 Remodeling the Routine Work Instruction in a Shop Floor: A Practical Case

### 3.1 Context Goals and Methods

This article focuses on a practical problem related to a company whose production is concentrated in flush toilets, which belongs to the chemical industry. The production area is the main task, with around 80% of the employees working (a total of around 400 employees) in two different areas: injection and assembly. In the assembly area, there are numerous manufacturing cells where automation can effectively make a difference and the currently most automated, with data capture through IoT mechanisms, is the tap cell. The data acquired in this cell is meaningless to the decision maker; still, they can produce potentially relevant information.

The proposed objective for this practical case is the analysis and reformulation, through Business Process Model and Notation (BPMN 2.0) and the concept of Lean Information Management, of the assembly operator's work instruction, due to the introduction of a digital tool to support management and cell decision making. In [27] the authors established the BPMN tool as a facilitator to create and increase the organizational knowledge, transmuting the tacit knowledge to explicit one, producing working instructions in the company's shop floor. This work focuses on placing the human factor among the new digital paradigm, demonstrating the impact on working instructions, considering new digital tools to support production management.

The modeling of the initial work instruction was achieved through informal interviews and direct observation at the workstation. When the analysis related to the current function of the assembly operator was carried out, it was realized that the incorporation of a digital tool would facilitate the flow of information at the task level, as well as the greater visualization of the processes themselves. In addition, and as of now, the modeling of work instructions is deterministic in establishing a repository of organizational knowledge, with a view to facilitating turnover (since new employees are more easily able to adapt to work) and, still, with a view to maintaining competitive advantage (in which the tacit knowledge of operators is retained). A technological tool was idealized and designed using UML notation on parity with the new work instruction, in order to establish the human factor at the center of the process.

## 3.2 Results and Discussion

**AS-IS Map of Work Instruction Before the Digital Tool Implementation.** As already discussed, in the scope of industry 4.0, where we easily reach the globalization of the human workforce, it is essential to retain the tacit knowledge of employees, constituting repositories of organizational knowledge. In this matter, the mapping of work instructions (which represent the employees' work routine) is essential. Thus, the assembly operator's work instruction was mapped, with a view to understanding the routine associated, as well as a source of analysis for potential waste in the tasks performed.

Figure 1 show the AS-IS map of routine work instruction (which includes the assembly operator daily tasks), before the introduction of the digital tool. Very briefly, here, the operator must, on arrival at the workstation (immediately after the Kaizen Daily meeting) perform autonomous maintenance, as well as checking the conditions of the workstation. Then, the operator must start the assembly of the products, and there may be the occurrence of several events, they are: stops (in this case it is necessary to fill in the OEE paper sheet); breakdowns (the operator must contact the team leader to report the problem); production order finalization (the number of non-conformities must be recorded on the OEE sheet). In case the finished production is pallet, the issuing of the label for tracking is necessary. Hence, the operator, either continues production, or in the event of the end of the shift, he must record on the production sheet (if he was in the middle of a manufacturing order) the quantity produced of parts. To be able to leave the site, new autonomous maintenance must be performed.

To assist in the performance of the tasks of the operators of the future (Operator 4.0), it is essential that the dissemination of information and knowledge becomes the focus of the action, which must be verified between operators and managers [28, 29].

Ensuring that this information reaches its destination in a way that is perceived by the end user, assisting him in the execution of his operations and in making decisions is extremely important [29, 30]. Information and communication technologies accelerate the collection, storage and retrieval of knowledge, but the retention of tacit knowledge for them still goes a long way. The application of the Business Process Management subject to the elaboration of work instructions, which was executed with this diagram, allows the beginning to the creation of a knowledge repository, essential to standardize the flow of information in the company and thus respond to the challenges of the digital paradigm. It should also be noted that this I4.0 paradigm brings with it the promotion of the globalization of human resources, which emphasizes the need to retain tacit knowledge, knowledge that is allocated to the minds of employees. It is therefore necessary to retain as much organizational knowledge as possible, highlighting the competitive advantage of organizations.

**Digital Tool Creation for the Tap Cell Station.** The Taps Cell Station display sensors, PLC's and other equipment with IoT capability (recording machines and testers) that can record the following data: Stops/micro stops; Number of non-compliant parts; Number of conforming parts; Manufacturing orders to be produced; Binaries. These data were already stored in a database; however, they presented no context. Thus, with a view to enhancing information regarding the performance of the workstation, the conceptualization of a digital tool that was capable of processing and presenting indicators that enabled the demonstration of the station's level of efficiency was carried out. Figure 3 shows the class diagram, representing the database scheme.

The specified software of the tap cell presents itself as a homemade solution created for the automatic counting of parts, also following the cadence of the stations. The presented classes aggregate the data presented and calculate the production rate, while calculating the number of parts, as well as signaling equipment stops.

The report table was created as being the fact table, where some calculations were done in order to have numbers related to efficiency level, such as the global overall equipment effectiveness (OEE), that results from the multiplication of the availability OEE, the performance OEE and the quality OEE.

**TO-BE Map of Work Instruction and Main Improvements.** The modeling of the work instruction (as-is diagram) allowed the perception of some problems with a focus on: (i) performance of redundant tasks; (ii) manual records (high paper traffic); (iv) outdated information in the computer system and (v) low level of real-time machine state interpretation. The introduction of the digital tool makes possible a new way of working, which potentially will reduce the waste listed. Considering this thought and after the design of the digital tool, a new work instruction was mapped, aiming to recreate the operator's workplace, so that it was placed as a central part of the process.

With the introduction of the digital tool, the operator, when starting a new manufacturing order, must enter the production order number (using a bar code device) and, immediately afterwards, the program will ask for your operator number. While the products are being assembled, the system saves the data (referring to the number of parts assembled and stops), it should be noted that when a stop is made, the system issues a warning for the operator to justify the stop. The performance level (OEE) is automatically calculated, and, in this case, there is no need to fill in tracing paper sheets.

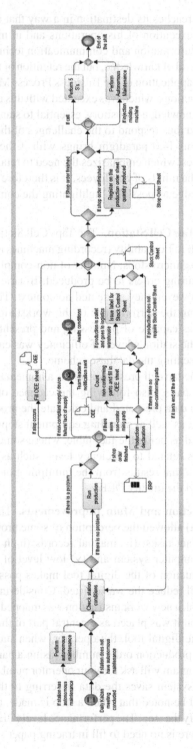

**Fig. 1.** Working instruction before the digital tool application

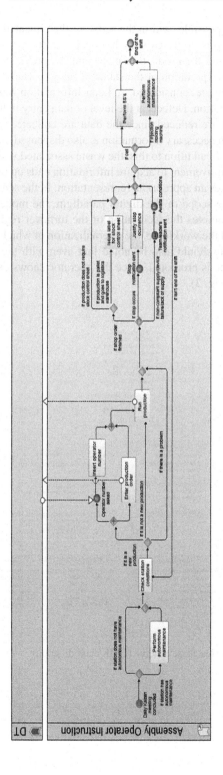

**Fig. 2.** Working instruction after the digital tool application

The digital tool made it possible, within the scope of the allocated tasks, to reduce the existing manual records (due to the existing high paper traffic, specifically in terms of filling out the OEE file and the production plan) and the provision of information in real time with superior interpretation of the status of the job. The changes indicated make it possible to reduce waste, considered by Lean Information Management to be friction in the flow of information. Defects at the level of data entry in the system (later, for the calculation of OEE) are reduced since the data are collected automatically by sensors. Extra work to obtain necessary information is also dispensed, making operators more focused on their tasks. In addition to this, the waste associated with Motion is also reduced, since unnecessary movement to acquire information ends up being eliminated, and even the information takes an appropriate representation. In the sense of knowledge management, and within the scope of the digital paradigm, the modeling of the new routine work instruction promotes the facilitation of the turnover regime, since when introducing new elements of the workforce, the internalization of which tasks that make up the job is made easier. It should also be noted that even with the introduction of digital tools, their acceptance is promoted, since the operator knows exactly where his interaction is taking place (Fig. 2).

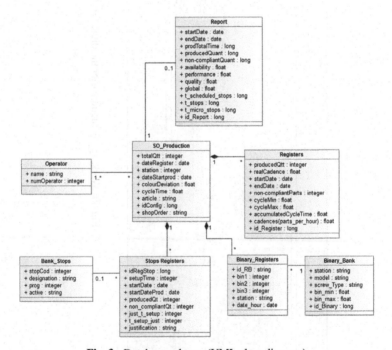

**Fig. 3.** Database scheme (UML class diagram)

## 4   Final Remarks and Future Work

This practical work promotes the view that articulating the digital transformation concepts of Business Process Management and Lean Manufacturing is essential in the constitution of work instructions that will facilitate the turnover regime in the new digital and competitive environment that organizations face.

This union of efforts makes it possible not only to enable new employees to learn faster (due to the phenomenon of globalization of human resources), but also to create uniform flows by the organization (with the capture of tacit organizational knowledge), which will be essential in determining the success of the digital paradigm.

The modelling of work instructions and their subsequent analysis within the scope of the digital paradigm, promotes the full perspective of the existing waste associated with Lean Information Management, as well as the re-adaptation of the workstation to receive digital tools (as presented in this case), placing the operator as a central part of the process.

The integration of the digital tool in the daily tasks of the assembly operator presented in this practical case, promoted the reduction of waste with a focus on defects, motion and extra work. In fact, it is known from the literature that ICTs are a key element of information management, as they can integrate fragmented information, eliminating communication barriers in organizations. Thus, the tool applied within this organization allowed the creation of more fluid flows, where the employee is the focus of the process and, therefore, is integrated into the flow. But even if the integration of digitalization in a paradigm of rapid change in knowledge, such as that which characterizes Industry 4.0, it is essential to ensure the mapping of work instructions, as well as the management of these processes. This is because, new connection points between human operators and digital systems must be created, as well as learning by new operators must be facilitated as much as possible. The application of BPM, with the notation on which it is based, BPMN, was the focus of study of this work, where it was possible to originate organizational knowledge.

Hence, the approach presented in this paper promotes a new methodology to create a culture where a repository of knowledge is endorsed in organization's environment and also reveals to be a means to backing the establishment of digitization in organizations.

It is believed that the operator's productivity will be stimulated by the increased flexibility of the work environment and the ability to learn more easily, points in which this work was applied.

As a future work, the integration of the digital tool in a more collaborative management system oriented towards decision making close to the manufacturing floor will be a hypothesis, with subsequent validation by users.

**Acknowledgement.** This work was supported by Portuguese funds through the Institute of Electronics and Informatics Engineering of Aveiro (IEETA) and Foundation for Science and Technology, in the context of the project UIDB/00127/2020.

# References

1. Teixeira, L., Ferreira, C., Santos, B.S.: An information management framework to industry 4.0: a lean thinking approach. In: Ahram, T., Karwowski, W., Taiar, R. (eds.) IHSED 2018. AISC, vol. 876, pp. 1063–1069. Springer, Cham (2019). https://doi.org/10.1007/978-3-030-02053-8_162
2. Lopes, R., Teixeira, L., Ferrira, C.: Lean thinking across the company: successful cases in the manufacturing industry. In: Silva, F., Ferreira, L. (eds.) Lean Manufacturing: Implementation, Opportunities and Challenges, pp. 1–31. Nova Science Publishers (2019)
3. Meissner, A., Müller, M., Hermann, A., Metternich, J.: Digitalization as a catalyst for lean production: a learning factory approach for digital shop floor management. Proc. Manuf. **23**, 81–86 (2018). https://doi.org/10.1016/j.promfg.2018.03.165
4. Arromba, A.R., Teixeira, L., Xambre, A.R.: Information flows improvement in production planning using lean concepts and BPMN an exploratory study in industrial context. In: 2019 14th Iberian Conference on Information Systems and Technologies (CISTI), pp. 206–211, June 2019. https://doi.org/10.23919/CISTI.2019.8760699
5. Bell, S., Orzen, M.: What Is Information Waste? Lean Enterprise Institute, Inc., Lean Enterprise Institute, Inc. (2011)
6. Ibbitson, A., Smith, R.: The Lean Information Management. Toolkit. Ark Group (2011)
7. Ongena, G., Ravesteyn, P.: Business process management maturity and performance a multi group analysis of sectors and organization sizes. Bus. Process Manag. J. **26**(1), 132–149 (2020). https://doi.org/10.1108/BPMJ-08-2018-0224
8. Sarnikar, S., Deokar, A.: Knowledge management systems for knowledge-intensive processes: design approach and an illustrative example. In: Proceedings of the 36th Annual Hawaii International Conference on System Sciences, pp. 1–10 (2010). https://doi.org/10.1109/HICSS.2010.248
9. Bosilj-Vukšić, V.: Business process modelling: a foundation for knowledge management. J. Inf. Organ. Sci. **30**(2), 185–198 (2006)
10. Kalpič, B., Bernus, P.: Business process modeling through the knowledge management perspective. J. Knowl. Manag. **10**(3), 40–56 (2006). https://doi.org/10.1108/13673270610670849
11. Sanders, A., Elangeswaran, C., Wulfsberg, J.: Industry 4.0 implies lean manufacturing: research activities in industry 4.0 function as enablers for lean manufacturing. J. Ind. Eng. Manag. **9**(3), 811–833 (2016). https://doi.org/10.3926/jiem.1940
12. Zangiacomi, A., et al.: The management of operations moving towards digitalization: a multiple case study in manufacturing. Prod. Plan. Control **31**(2–3), 143–157 (2020). https://doi.org/10.1080/09537287.2019.1631468
13. Caldarola, E.G., Modoni, G.E., Sacco, M.: A knowledge-based approach to enhance the workforce skills and competences within the industry 4.0. In: Tenth International Conference on Information, Process, and Knowledge Management, Rome, April 2018
14. Jerman, A., Aleksi, A.: Transformation towards smart factory system: examining new job profiles and competencies. Syst. Res. Behav. Sci. **2020**, 388–402 (2020). https://doi.org/10.1002/sres.2657
15. Stern, H., Becker, T.: Concept and evaluation of a method for the integration of human factors into human-oriented work design in cyber-physical production systems. Sustainability **11**(16), 1–33 (2019). https://doi.org/10.3390/su11164508
16. Romero, D., Stahre, J., Taisch, M.: The Operator 4.0: towards socially sustainable factories of the future. Comput. Ind. Eng. **139**(November 2019) (2020). https://doi.org/10.1016/j.cie.2019.106128

17. Kadir, B.A., Broberg, O.: Human-centered design of work systems in the transition to industry 4.0. Appl. Ergon. **92**(November 2020), 103334 (2021). https://doi.org/10.1016/j.apergo.2020. 103334
18. Kaasinen, E., et al.: Empowering and engaging industrial workers with Operator 4.0 solutions. Comput. Ind. Eng. **139**(January 2019), 105678 (2020). https://doi.org/10.1016/j.cie.2019. 01.052
19. Whysall, Z., Owtram, M., Brittain, S.: The new talent management challenges of Industry 4.0. J. Manag. Dev. **38**(2), 118–129 (2019). https://doi.org/10.1108/JMD-06-2018-0181
20. Flores, E., Xu, X., Lu, Y.: Human capital 4.0: a workforce competence typology for Industry 4.0. J. Manuf. Technol. Manag. **31**(4), 687–703 (2020). https://doi.org/10.1108/JMTM-08-2019-0309
21. Li, D., Fast-Berglund, A., Paulin, D.: Production innovation and effective dissemination of information for operator 4.0. Adv. Transdiscipl. Eng. **13**, 229–238 (2020). https://doi.org/10. 3233/ATDE200160
22. Hammer, D.K.: Lean information management. J. Comput. Inf. Technol. **5**(3), 145–157 (1997)
23. Hicks, B.J.: Lean information management: understanding and eliminating waste. Int. J. Inf. Manag. **27**(4), 233–249 (2007). https://doi.org/10.1016/j.ijinfomgt.2006.12.001
24. Bevilacqua, M., Ciarapica, F.E., Paciarotti, C.: Implementing lean information management: The case study of an automotive company. Prod. Plan. Control **26**(10), 753–768 (2015). https://doi.org/10.1080/09537287.2014.975167
25. Soares, S., Teixeira, L.: Lean information management in industrial context: An experience based on a practical case. Int. J. Ind. Eng. Manag. **5**(2), 107–114 (2014)
26. Redeker, G.A., Kessler, G.Z., Kipper, L.M.: Lean information for lean communication: Analysis of concepts, tools, references, and terms. Int. J. Inf. Manag. **47**(January), 31–43 (2019). https://doi.org/10.1016/j.ijinfomgt.2018.12.018
27. Salvadorinho, J., Teixeira, L.: Organizational knowledge in the I4.0 using BPMN: a case study. Proc. Comput. Sci. **181**, 981–988 (2020). https://doi.org/10.1016/j.procs.2021.01.266
28. Li, D., Fast-Berglund, Å., Paulin, D.: Current and future Industry 4.0 capabilities for information and knowledge sharing. Int. J. Adv. Manuf. Technol. **105**(9), 3951–3963 (2019). https:// doi.org/10.1007/s00170-019-03942-5
29. Sandbergs, V., Stief, P., Dantan, J., Etienne, A., Siadat, A.: Human-centred dissemination of data, information and knowledge in industry 4.0. Pro. CIRP **84**, 380–386 (2019). https://doi. org/10.1016/j.procir.2019.04.261
30. Mourtzis, D., Zogopoulos, V., Xanthi, F.: Augmented reality application to support the assembly of highly customized products and to adapt to production re-scheduling. Int. J. Adv. Manuf. Technol. **105**(9), 3899–3910 (2019). https://doi.org/10.1007/s00170-019-03941-6

# Customer Solution Design – A New Agile Role Needed in the Automotive Industry to Support Digital Transformation?

Aline Schnurr[1], Pamela Renz[2], and Andrea Müller[1（✉）]

[1] Hochschule Offenburg – University of Applied Sciences, Badstrasse 24,
77652 Offenburg, Germany
andrea.mueller@hs-offenburg.de
[2] Robert Bosch GmbH, Hoferstrasse 30, 71636 Ludwigsburg, Germany

**Abstract.** As one result of the digital transformation in the automotive industry, new digital business models comprising software-based solutions are demanded by OEMs. To adequately meet these new requirements, automotive suppliers implement interdisciplinary roles – called Customer Solution Designers. However, due to the novelty, the Customer Solution Design research field is not yet well developed, neither in theory nor in practice. Besides giving an overview of the current state of the Customer Solution Design research field, the core of this paper is two-fold: Based on the conduction of 14 guided expert interviews with selected experts of a large German automotive supplier, we establish a uniform understanding of the Customer Solution Design role by using the Role Model Canvas (I). In addition, a case study strategy comprising two software-based projects, which are executed by a large German automotive supplier, is used to derive a common approach for Customer Solution Design in the context of an agile business framework (II).

**Keywords:** Customer solution design · Digital transformation · Automotive industry · Automotive supplier industry · Agile business · Agile role · Digital business models · Software-based solutions · Role Model Canvas

## 1  Introduction

It is undeniable that the digitalization has already fundamentally transformed various industry sectors around the globe in recent years and will continue to change them further in the future. Even established branches such as the automotive industry could thus not escape this far-reaching process of change and became aware of the disruptive and dynamic character of the digital transformation. These fundamental changes of the automotive industry were clearly visible with the emergence of new customer needs and competitors from completely different industries, accompanied by new technologies that came onto the market in ever shorter intervals. However, the digital transformation brought also enormous business opportunities for the automotive industry, as there is potential for many new digital business models around the physical product of the car.

© Springer Nature Switzerland AG 2021
F. F.-H. Nah and K. Siau (Eds.): HCII 2021, LNCS 12783, pp. 256–276, 2021.
https://doi.org/10.1007/978-3-030-77750-0_17

Against the background of the changing end customer needs for digital solutions, the requirements of the original equipment manufacturers (OEMs) on the automotive suppliers have also evolved. In order to protect their market position, automotive suppliers are therefore challenged to complement their existing physical product range with digital products. This product expansion requires the creation of new structures within the company that are designed to generate digital solutions. In this context, special attention is paid to the establishment of an agile business framework that is able to react flexibly and target-oriented to the continuously changing customer requirements and needs and the emergence of new technologies. Linked to that, automotive suppliers have to identify and implement new suitable digital business models. Faced with these major challenges, companies in the automotive supplier industry must therefore reinvent themselves.

Building on the requirements already mentioned, it is thus necessary for automotive suppliers to integrate new roles and approaches within the company to deal with the complexity, uncertainty and dynamics that come with the generation of new digital solutions. To counter these specifics of digital solutions, interdisciplinary teams and roles are of central importance.

One of these new roles and approaches, which comprises various disciplines, is Customer Solution Design. This approach and the associated role are designed to cope with the increased complexity of new digital customer solutions and ensure the successful implementation of complex customer requirements for a digital solution within an interdisciplinary project team.

A key challenge that goes hand in hand with the creation and effective implementation of such a new type of role is that it requires a clear understanding of the role itself as well as the associated scope of tasks, in order to avoid parallels with existing roles and equally to create transparency and a general understanding of Customer Solution Design within the company and for the customer.

To evaluate the Customer Solution Design research field, it is important to first consider both the digital transforming automotive industry as well as fundamental changes that go along with it and the current state of this research field by analyzing related work. Against the background of the novelty of this research field, the focus of the paper at hand is on the analyzation of the Customer Solution Design role (I) and on the derivation of a common approach for this role in an agile business framework (II). For establishing a uniform understanding of the Customer Solution Design role, guided expert interviews with in total 14 selected experts of a large German automotive supplier were conducted. The interviews were evaluated based on the qualitative content analysis method and the results were additionally visualized via the Role Model Canvas. With regard to the derivation of a common approach for Customer Solution Design, the case study method comprising two software-based projects executed by a large German automotive supplier was chosen as the research method. One project was evaluated retrospectively by a Lessons Learned Workshop, whereas the second project was analyzed based on an active project participation.

## 2  Current State of Customer Solution Design

### 2.1  Background

The automotive industry has established itself as one of the world's most important industry sectors [1]. With regard to the entrepreneurial actors within the automotive branch, these are generally differentiated into the actual automakers – the Original Equipment Manufacturers (OEMs) – and the upstream automotive suppliers [2]. It is of vital importance that the largest share of automotive value added – with on average 70% – is generated by the automotive supplier industry, whereby the automotive suppliers make a decisive contribution to the success of the OEMs [3]. Against the background of this economic dependence between the central automotive players – the OEMs and the suppliers – the automotive industry is currently facing several challenges: Ranging from a fast-changing environment characterized as volatile, uncertain, complex and ambiguous – short defined as VUCA – to global megatrends such as digitalization [4].

The resulting digital transformation in the automotive supplier industry entails various impacts that change this branch fundamentally. In the context of the rapidly changing automotive environment, the automotive suppliers have to operate agile as well as flexible and their innovation cycles regarding developing and running the business have to be speeded up [1]. Both the organizational and operational structure of the automotive supplier companies is thus transformed by the digitalization. In addition, new players push into the automotive market including start-ups as well as companies from completely different industries like Apple and Google as IT enterprises [5]. These new competitors enter the automotive ecosystem by providing innovative digital concepts [6]. The focus of creating automotive value is thus shifted from physical aspects to IT, which means that digitalization generally opens up innovative, technical-based business opportunities based on digital data for the automotive suppliers [7]. In the course of the ever-changing digital-based customer needs, highly flexible, scalable as well as customized software-based solutions are demanded from automotive suppliers [8]. Traditional, linear business models of the automotive industry are therefore disrupted due to the digitalization [8].

As a result, automotive suppliers have to generate new digital offerings focusing on connectivity functionalities as well as on information technologies for the automotive sector in order to survive in the digital automotive era and thus to turn the disruptive forces of the digital transformation into business benefits [9]. So-called new digital business models are the nowadays basis for creating automotive value [9]. To remain competitive and successful, automotive suppliers therefore generate digitally focused business concepts mainly based on customer-centric needs [5]. These innovative business models are based on various digital offerings [5]. In this context, mobility services and connected services represent two central pillars for the automotive business of the future: Mobility services aim at enabling mobility users to switch between different means of transport by generating intermodal and flexible solutions [10]. The importance of such mobility business models is based on environmental issues, increasing traffic density and customer trends regarding sustainability and mentality of sharing [6]. In order to generate new mobility usership concepts, the automotive industry thus focuses on the provision of sharing services such as car sharing, e-scooter sharing and ride sharing, carpooling as well as mobility platforms [11]. In the context of connected services as new digital business models of the automotive supplier industry, automobiles are equipped with connectivity functionalities based on automotive and IT know-how [9]. Connected vehicles act both as transmitters and as receivers of data. Data exchange with the automotive ecosystem is thus enabled via defined application programming interfaces (APIs). There are various vehicle management services resulting from the integration of connectivity functionalities into automobiles: Over-the-air firmware and software updates – called FOTA and SOTA – providing updates for vehicle control units, predictive diagnostics functions offering information regarding the status of maintenance-relevant vehicle components and systems, and road condition services delivering real-time information regarding traffic, weather or topography are among such connected concepts [10]. Based on these exemplary digital business models, added values such as safety, navigation, information and convenience are generated for customers.

The basis for successfully addressing the digital transformation in the automotive supplier industry is thus created by both digital concepts – mobility services as well as connected services. Nevertheless, the prerequisite to generate such digital business models is specific expertise comprising automotive, business and mainly IT knowledge. For this reason, automotive suppliers are implementing interdisciplinary teams including roles – called Customer Solution Designers – which are aimed at designing software-based solutions.

## 3 Related Work

For giving an overview of the current state of the Customer Solution Design research field, related work comprising a literature review as well as a related design methodology was analyzed.

The approach established by the scientists *Webster and Watson* was chosen as the methodology for the literature review. According to these guidelines, an exhaustive review of literature related to the research field of Customer Solution Design was performed. The focus was on research results related to the search term *"Customer Solution Design"*; this ensures that a structured overview of the current research status with regard to the defined research field – the Customer Solution Design field – is given. Based on this, the aim of the literature review was on the one hand, to examine whether the term Customer Solution Design is already anchored within the literature and on the other hand, to check which related terms and concepts have already been established in relation to the Customer Solution Design research field.

Against the backdrop of the novelty of the Customer Solution Design research field and thus for ensuring the relevance and the quality of the reviewed publications, there was no focus on a specific number of articles. Therefore, all articles found were initially considered. For identifying relevant literature, a modified approach based on Webster and Watson, which is illustrated in Fig. 1, was used.

Scientific databases were initially selected. In this regard, the focus was on the literature database *Google Scholar* as well as on the database of the *Association for Information System* (AIS) the so-called *AIS Electronic Library* (AISeL), which is a specific database for information system literature. With regard to the selected databases – Google Scholar and AISeL – the author searched for titles, keywords, abstracts and full texts by using the search term *"Customer Solution Design"*. September and October 2019 were set as the period for the database queries. For considering the interdisciplinary of the information system field, an extension of the search process to adjacent research fields such as economics, especially marketing and finance as well as computer science was done. Publications that were not labelled as research papers, for example news, research commentaries, keynotes or book reviews, were not considered.

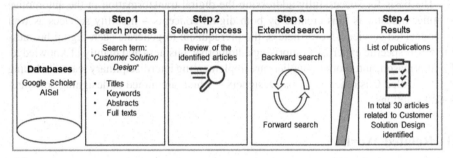

**Fig. 1.** Steps of the literature review.

Second, based on the database queries, a primary set of relevant articles was selected. For identifying a primary set of relevant research literature, each article was reviewed in detail. As a result, studies that neither contain the specific keyword *"Customer Solution Design"* nor have a focus on respectively a relation to the research field of Customer Solution Design or an adjacent research field, were not considered within the further research process.

In the third step, a backward search as well as a forward search were done for the remaining literature. The backward search was conducted in the following way: Articles, which were listed within the lists of references of the remaining literature resulting out of the second step, were considered for further evaluation if their titles were related to the research field of Customer Solution Design. In addition, articles cited within the relevant Customer Solution Design-related text passages of the remaining literature were reviewed in detail. Articles, which were related to the Customer Solution Design research field, were through this also included within the further process. Regarding the forward search, this was performed by using the function *cited by* offered by the database Google Scholar. Articles found via this function were taken into account if there was a relation to the Customer Solution Design field. In short, publications that were identified either by the backward search or by the forward search were added to the selection of relevant literature. The procedure out of step 3 was repeated until the literature search did not yield any new results.

As a result, a list of publications with a relation to the research field of Customer Solution Design was created as a foundation for the further evaluation; this list contains all publications, which were identified as relevant within the structured literature review but does not claim to be a complete overview of existing Customer Solution Design-related research.

With regard to the database Google Scholar in total 18 publications for the search term "Customer Solution Design" were listed. Based on the database AISeL just one article referring to the Customer Solution Design field was found. This means that the search process yielded initially 19 publications. The analysis showed that just one article was relevant for the further evaluation. Based on the defined selection criteria, the other publications either had no relation to the Customer Solution Design field or were not scientific in nature. Due to the backward and forward searches, which were performed on the basis of the one remaining article, in total 30 relevant publications referring to the defined research field were finally identified for the further evaluation. In the course of the further classification process, the key aspects were extracted out of the relevant articles. Based on the key aspects, central terminologies were identified and thus the following concepts regarding the Customer Solution Design research field were derived: *Customer solution, customer solution provider, customer solution process, design of the solution* and *customer solution performance*. Through these concepts a theoretical foundation was created as well as the importance of Customer Solution Design was demonstrated.

In order to create a theoretical understanding regarding Customer Solution Design for this paper, the establishment of a literature-based definition for this concept is needed. Based on the combination of the two identified Customer Solution Design-related terminologies – *customer solution* and *solution design* – a common literature-based understanding for Customer Solution Design is derived by using extant views of different authors in the following. In the tables below (Table 1 and Table 2), the selected views for both terms are listed.

**Table 1.** Extant view of the understand of a customer solution

| Customer Solution | |
|---|---|
| Reference | Concepts |
| Johansson, J. E./Krishnamurthy, C./Schlissberg, H. E. (2003) | o is a **combination of services** that creates value beyond the sum of its parts (p. 118) |
| Davies, A./Brady, T./Hobday, M. (2006) | o involves the provision of **tailored innovative combinations of services** as high-value 'integrated solutions' that **address the specific needs of large business** (pp. 39-40) |
| Sawhney, M. (2006) | o an **integrated combination of services** customized for a set of customers that allows customers to achieve better outcomes than the sum of the individual components of the solution (p. 372) |
| Tuli, K./Kohli, A. K./Bharadwaj, S. G. (2007) | o a **customized and integrated combination of services** for **meeting the needs of the customers** (p. 1) |
| Evanschitzky, H./von Wangenheim, F./Woisetschläger, D. M. (2011) | o **individualized offers for complex customer problems** that are **interactively designed** and whose components offer an integrative **added value by combining services** (p. 647) |

**Table 2.** Extant views of the understand of solution design

| Solution Design | |
|---|---|
| Reference | Concepts |
| Mohammad, A. F. (2009) | o a process in which a **conversion of requirements documentation into a conceptual model** is done and then used to get the **required solution designed and developed** (w.p.) |
| Offermann, P./Levina, O./Schönherr, M./Bub, U. (2009) | o comprises develop **system architecture, analyze** and **design the system, observe** and **evaluate the system** (p. 4) |
| Wieringa, R. (2009) | o viewing design as a **plan** which is used to **reach one of more stakeholder goals** by using e.g. a **new or improved technique, notation, instrument, device, algorithm, process, business structure**, etc. (p. 4) |
| Bertram/Schaarschmidt/von Korflesch, H. (2016) | o **capability to design a future-proof software solution** based on existing product functionalities and **specific customer's needs** (p. 11) |
| Hevner/vom Brocke/Maedche (2019) | o solution design entities **collect the prescriptive knowledge** as represented in the **tangible artifacts, systems**, and **processes** designed and applied in the **problem solution space** (p. 4) |

Due to the shown extant views, for both concepts – customer solution and solution design – certain characteristics could be identified. In the context of the previous literature review and based on the identified characteristics, the following common literature-based understanding for Customer Solution Design was derived: *Customer Solution Design comprises an interdisciplinary information system concept, which is used to solve a complex customer problem by designing suitable software-based services and thus is aimed at remaining competitive in an agile business environment by meeting the ever-changing needs of the customer.*

Due to the grounding of Customer Solution Design in an agile ecosystem, in addition to the literature review, the so-called Scaled Agile Framework, which was first introduced by Dean Leffingwell and his collaborators in 2011, was considered [17]. This framework designed to deliver software-based services and solutions in the shortest sustainable lead-time consists of four different levels: Starting from *Team Level* to *Program Level, Large Solution Level* to *Portfolio Level* [18]. Due to the relation to the Customer Solution Design research field, the Large Solution Level was considered. The focus of the *Large Solution Level* is on the development of large-scale, multidisciplinary software systems [19]. Against this background, this level comprises specific components including roles, artifacts and processes, which are needed for developing such large and complex solutions [19]. In this regard, the Large Solution Level consists of a trio of roles: *Solution Management, Solution Train Engineer* (STE) and *Solution Architect* resp. *Solution Engineering*; this trio is required for coordinating the Large Solution Level and thus for advancing the development as well as the delivering of complex software and IT systems [19]. The detailed analyzation of these roles is waived in this paper. By the consideration should only show that solution-oriented concepts are needed to design customer-oriented digital business models and to successfully competing in the digitally transforming industries. A relation to focus on the design of software-based solutions and the Customer Solution Design research field was additionally stated.

Based on the related work comprising a literature review and a related design methodology a theoretical foundation for the Customer Solution Design research field was created.

## 4 Research Approach

In cooperation with the Offenburg University and the Robert Bosch GmbH as a leading global supplier of technology and services, the study at hand has been initiated. There are two central research aims: The evaluation of the role understanding of Customer Solution Design as well as the derivation of a common approach for this new agile role. In addition, the results have been prepared accordingly in order to make a decisive contribution to the Customer Solution Design research field.

### 4.1 Investigation of the Customer Solution Design Role

For evaluating the Customer Solution Design role, guided expert interviews are selected as research method. This research method focuses on entering special knowledge regarding a specific object of investigation by interviewing selected experts [12]. By using this variant, the expert interview is additionally controlled and structured by the guide, which ensures that all relevant aspects regarding the object of investigation are covered. The guide consists of a list of questions to be asked: Neither the order nor the formulation of the questions are binding, whereby further inquiries as well as additions are also possible [13].

The guide, on which the expert interviews are conducted, was created based on a comprehensive analysis of the Customer Solution Design research field. To achieve the establishment of a uniform role understanding, the focus of the questions formulated in the guide is on various characteristics needed for defining a role: Ranging from tasks, aims, stakeholders to temporal and process-related aspects. The selection of the interview partners was intended to ensure that the Customer Solution Design role is covered from different perspectives. Besides Customer Solution Designers themselves, central stakeholders of this role were thus selected as experts for the interviews. In this context, an expert is someone having extensive Customer Solution Design-related experience through intensive cooperation with Customer Solution Design based on software-based customer projects. Derived from this, in total fourteen interview partners comprising both technical and commercial disciplines were identified.

The guided expert interviews lasted between 20 and 60 min. The results gathered out of the interviews have been evaluated by using the qualitative content analysis method of Mayring and additionally visualized via the Role Model Canvas – a template, which aims at the definition of both project and organizational roles. Based on this research approach, a common understanding of the Customer Solution Design role is generated.

## 4.2  Derivation of a Customer Solution Design Approach

In order to derive a common approach for the Customer Solution Design role, the case study method is chosen. The exploration and understanding of emerging, complex research fields is allowed by this qualitative research method [14]. Probably the best-known definition originates from Yin: "A case study is an empirical inquiry that investigates a contemporary phenomenon in depth and within its real-life context, especially when the boundaries between phenomenon and context are not clearly evident." [15] Within this definition, the concept of a case is broad: Case in this context refers to the exploration of a current phenomenon [15] The case study method is thus an open research approach with regard to the use of different methods and the evaluation of data from different sources [14].

With regard to the case selection, two software-based projects referring to two international truck manufacturers as customers are defined as cases and thus a multiple-case design is chosen for this study. For collecting data out of the projects, one project was evaluated retrospectively by conducting a Lessons Learned Workshop and the second project was analyzed based on an active project participation. Based on these two defined data collection methods – the Lessons Learned Workshop and the active project participation, the case study method offers the possibility of combining different data sources to evaluate a case comprehensively [16].

There is no general approach for the case study analysis, whereby the analysis is conducted individually on the basis of the specific case. Starting point of the analysis phase is nonetheless the structuring and sorting of the gathered data material. For the case study design of this study – the multiple-case design – a cross-case analysis is intended. This means that each individual case of the study is first evaluated separately and then, the key results of all case studies are compared and discussed.

## 5  Analysis and Findings

### 5.1  Role of Customer Solution Design

Against the background of the literature-based foundation regarding the Customer Solution Design research field and based on the results of the guided expert interviews, the analysis of the role of Customer Solution Design is done in the following based on established questions.

*Why is the role of Customer Solution Design in an agile business framework of an automotive supplier needed?*

The need of the Customer Solution Design role in the agile context of an automotive supplier is based on various reasons. These reasons illustrating the existence of Customer Solution Design are thus varied in nature. Customer Solution Design is needed to generate software-based customer solutions, which are required by the OEMs in the context of the digitally transformed automotive industry. These solutions are characterized as extremely complex. In order to adequately address this complexity and thus to design the most suitable solution for the OEMs, appropriate competencies are essential. Customer Solution Design ties in with this: The Customer Solution Design role comprises technical, commercial, automotive as well as customer-oriented disciplines. Derived from this, Customer Solution Design combines the competencies, which are necessary for generating the required digital solutions within an agile business framework. Based on the various fields of competence, the Customer Solution Designer holistically understands the complex acquisition process, which results out of the required digital services. Customer Solution Design is therefore essential to manage the acquisition phase in a target-oriented manner by consolidating various information and thus to successfully complete the acquisition project, which refers to the creation of a software-based customer solution. In this context, the Customer Solution Design role is furthermore needed to advise the OEM as the customer comprehensively regarding digital business models in the course of the acquisition phase. This advice process is necessary to capture all customer requirements and thus to provide a solution, which fulfills specific customer needs. Based on this solution created by the Customer Solution Design role, a high customer satisfaction is realized and thus a corresponding future-oriented establishment with the customer is reached. This also clearly shows the need of Customer Solution Design. In addition, Customer Solution Design deals intensively with the latest requirements of the digitally transformed automotive market. For this reason, the Customer Solution Design role is essential to realize software-based innovations that both address future customer problems and meet the ever-changing needs of the customer. To sum up, the Customer Solution Design role is a central foundation for creating digital automotive value by designing the most appropriate software-based solutions in an agile business framework. Customer Solution Design is therefore crucial for remaining competitive in an agile business framework. The next question refers to the procedure of Customer Solution Design:

*How does Customer Solution Design proceed in an agile business framework of an automotive supplier?*

In order to realize the various added values of Customer Solution Design and thus in particular to create the most appropriate software-based customer solution, a certain working procedure is needed. For successfully managing the acquisition project in an agile business framework, the Customer Solution Design role refers to the establishment of a cross-functional project team. This means that the project team consists of stakeholders, which cover various disciplines, mainly technical, commercial and legal aspects. Derived from this, the intense cooperation with the project-relevant stakeholders is essential. In this context, Customer Solution Designers define an individual cooperation model with each stakeholder in order to gather the relevant information, which is needed for designing software-based solutions. This required information thus comprises commercial, technical, legal, project-related or costumer-oriented project data depending on the respective stakeholder. Moreover, the Customer Solution Design role implements setting up and leading workshops and, regular as well as ad hoc meetings in the course of the acquisition project. Based on these project events, Customer Solution Designers ensure that the requirements of the project are holistically covered by considering each project-related perspective. In this context, the regular organization of customer workshops is essential to actively involve the customer in the acquisition project. This customer involvement is needed to cover all customer requirements and therefore to successfully design the required digital service. The Customer Solution Design role thus refers to the connection between internal project stakeholders and the customer as the central external interface of such projects. With regard to the realization of software-based innovations, the Customer Solution Design role additionally focuses on expert conferences, trade fairs and future-oriented research on automotive connectivity issues. In brief, the Customer Solution Design role consolidates project-relevant information provided by both the interdisciplinary project team and the customer in order to design the required innovative software-based customer solutions and thus to proceed in an agile business framework. A further question analyzed regarding the Customer Solution Design role is refers to their value proposition:

*What does Customer Solution Design deliver in an agile business framework of an automotive supplier?*

The overall result of the Customer Solution Design role is the generation of the most appropriate software-based customer solution that comprehensively fulfills the specific customer requirements in the context of an agile business framework. These delivered solutions, which are based on solutions out of the existing portfolio and customer-specific adaptions, are characterized as flexible, scalable and customized. Based on the detailed solution concept created for the OEM as the customer, the Customer Solution Design role delivers further valuable results arising out of the acquisition project. With regard to the customer, the Customer Solution Designer provides – in addition to the requested software-based solution – comprehensive advisory services, particularly with regard to innovative digital business models in the connected automotive context. As a result out of the successful management of software-based acquisition projects, the Customer Solution Design role additionally delivers a detailed project preparation including comprehensive project documentations to the official project manager. Regarding the innovation process, which is another central component of Customer Solution Design, innovative software-based solution concepts are provided by the Customer Solution Design role. Derived from this, the delivered results of the Customer Solution Design role are both stakeholder- and project-dependent. As an overall result, the focus is – besides the design of digital offerings addressing customer needs – on the provision of customer and market requirements, specific expertise and further relevant information for the project-related stakeholders.

Based on the evaluation of the guided expert interviews, a comprehensive foundation for the understanding of the Customer Solution Design role was established. Building on this, a common understanding is established in the following based on this question: *What is the understanding of the Customer Solution Design role in an agile business framework of an automotive supplier?*

In the context of the digital transformation of the automotive industry, new digital business models comprising software-based solutions are required by the OEMs. To provide such solutions, which are characterized as extremely complex, automotive suppliers implement interdisciplinary roles – called Customer Solution Designers – in the course of the acquisition phase.

Customer Solution Design is thus an interdisciplinary role covering various competencies. These competencies, mainly referring to technical, commercial and automotive disciplines, are essential in order to generate the required software-based customer solution in an agile business framework. Derived from this, the overall aim of the Customer Solution Design role is the design of the most appropriate software-based solution, which fulfills specific customer needs. Within the acquisition phase, the Customer Solution Design role additionally advises the OEMs regarding new digital business models and thus manages the acquisition project, which refers to the creation of the required solution based on existing solutions out of the portfolio and customer-specific adaptions. In this context, Customer Solution Design establishes a cross-functional project team consisting of both internal and external stakeholders from various disciplines. Based on such cross-functional project teams, the Customer Solution Design role consolidates project-relevant information to successfully manage the acquisition project, which represents the overall task of this role. Besides the acquisition phase, the innovation process is another central component of the Customer Solution Design role in an agile business framework. In this context, the Customer Solution Design role creates innovative software-based solutions referring to the latest market and customer requirements as a basis for remaining competitive in the digitally transformed automotive ecosystem.

In summary, Customer Solution Design is the central interface between the company and the OEM as the customer in the context of the generation of innovative, software-based solutions. In order to create the required solution, the Customer Solution Design role successfully manages the acquisition project by coordinating the cross-functional project team and consolidating project-related information. With regard to the innovation process and acquisition phase, Customer Solution Design as interdisciplinary role is thus a central foundation for generating software-based, future-oriented automotive value added for the customer in an agile business framework. To provide an overview of the Customer Solution Design role, the central results were additionally visualized by using a role model canvas (Fig. 2).

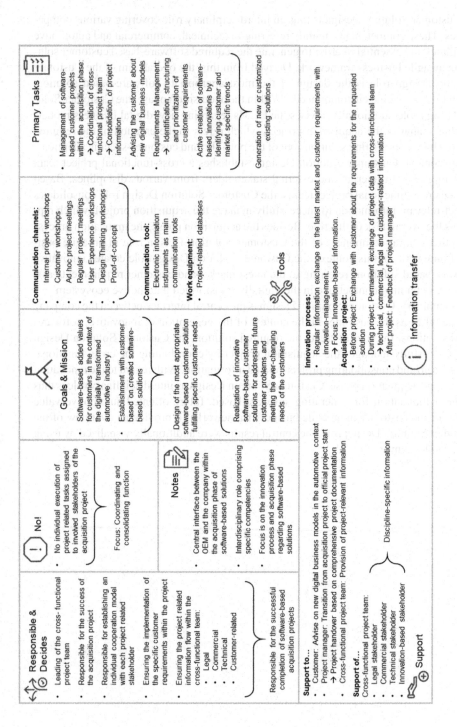

**Fig. 2.** Role Model Canvas of Customer Solution Design.

## 5.2   Approach for Customer Solution Design

The derivation of a common Customer Solution Design approach focusing on work packages is done in the following. The Customer Solution Design-related work packages, which were identified based on the conducted case study comprising two software-based projects, were categorized and thus systematically classified into customer-related, project-related, technical, commercial, legal and innovation-based categories. For each category, a table was created as seen below (Tables 3, 4, 5, 6, 7 and 8).

**Table 3.** Customer-related work package of Customer Solution Design

| Customer-related work packages of Customer Solution Design | | |
|---|---|---|
| Work package | Specification of the work package | Chronology |
| Creation of software-based customer solutions | - Analyzation of customer problems and needs<br>- Definition of customer requirements<br>- Prioritization of customer requirements<br>- Design the required software-based customer solution | - Acquisition kick off<br>- Project execution |
| Cooperation with the customer | - Advise the customer regarding new digital business models<br>- Support the customer in finding the appropriate solution<br>- Active integration of the customer into the project | - Acquisition kick off<br>- Project execution |

**Table 4.** Project-related work package of Customer Solution Design

| Project-related work packages of Customer Solution Design | | |
|---|---|---|
| Work package | Specification of the work package | Chronology |
| Management of software-based projects | - Stakeholder management:<br>  • Identification of internal and external project stakeholders<br>- Project organization:<br>  • Set-up of an agile, cross-functional project team<br>  • Establishment of an internal project cooperation model<br>  • Creation of a project schedule<br>  • Organization of project meetings and workshops<br>- Project coordination:<br>  • Coordination of the cross-functional project team<br>  • Coordination of the project work packages<br>  • Coordination of meetings and workshops<br>- Project documentation:<br>  • Consolidation of project information<br>  • Documentation of the respective project status | - Acquisition kick off<br>- Project execution<br>- Quotation phase<br>- Project completion |
| Risk management | - Identification of project-related risks<br>- Evaluation of project-related risks<br>- Definition of countermeasures<br>- Tracking of project-related risks | - Acquisition kick off<br>- Project execution |
| Project reporting | - Reporting of project status to project stakeholders<br>- Preparation of decision-relevant information<br>- Presentation to the management committee | - Project execution<br>- Quotation phase |
| Preparation of binding proposal | - Consolidation of the project information<br>- Preparation of the quotation document<br>- Review of the final quotation document | - Quotation phase |
| Project handover | - Preparation of handover documents<br>- Handover of the project to the official project manager<br>- Support of the official project manager during transition phase | - Transition phase |

**Table 5.** Technical work package of Customer Solution Design

| Technical work packages of Customer Solution Design | | |
|---|---|---|
| Work package | Specification of the work package | Chronology |
| Requirements management | - Identification of customer requirements<br>- Creation of a requirements list:<br>  • Description of the requirements<br>  • Categorization of the requirements<br>  • Classification into functional/non-functional requirements<br>  • Prioritization of customer requirements<br>- Discussion of requirements with project stakeholders | - Acquisition kick off<br>- Project execution<br>- Quotation phase |
| Definition of the software architecture | - Determination of technical solution components<br>- Determination of the required APIs<br>- Technical description of the software architecture<br>- Cost calculation of the software architecture | - Project execution<br>- Quotation phase |
| Service descriptions | - Gather requirements of the offered services<br>- Definition of the requirements regarding the offered services<br>- Preparation of technical descriptions of the offered services | - Project execution |

**Table 6.** Commercial work package of Customer Solution Design

| Commercial work packages of Customer Solution Design | | |
|---|---|---|
| Work package | Specification of the work package | Chronology |
| Definition of the business model | - Cost structure:<br>  • Definition of the cost components<br>  • Cost calculation of the project<br>  • Discussion of the costs with project stakeholders<br>- Pricing models:<br>  • Definition of the pricing of the offered services<br>  • Preparation of pricing models | - Project execution<br>- Quotation phase |
| Operations concept | - Operational scope:<br>  • Determination of service level objectives and agreements<br>  • Definition of support layer: First-, second-, third-level support<br>  • Planning of incident and problem management | - Quotation phase |

**Table 7.** Legal work package of Customer Solution Design

| Legal work package of Customer Solution Design | | |
|---|---|---|
| Work package | Specification of the work package | Chronology |
| Legal requirements | - Ensuring the compliance of legal standards and regulations<br>- Preparation of terms and conditions<br>- Security concept:<br>  • Ensure data privacy<br>  • Preparation of the data privacy concept<br>  • Ensure information security<br>  • Preparation of the security concept | - Project execution<br>- Quotation phase |

**Table 8.** Customer-related work package of Customer Solution Design

| Innovation-based work package of Customer Solution Design | | |
|---|---|---|
| Work package | Specification of the work package | Chronology |
| Innovation management | - Trend identification:<br>  • Identification of the latest market trends<br>  • Identification of the latest customer trends<br>- Trend evaluation:<br>  • Evaluation of the latest market trends<br>  • Evaluation of the latest customer trends<br>- Creation of innovative software-based solution concepts | - Entire process |

As shown in the tables, the work packages of Customer Solution Design in an agile business framework within the automotive branch are varied in nature. The derived common Customer Solution Design approach consisting of five specific steps and the identified work packages including related subtasks is visualized in the figure below (Fig. 3).

As depicted in the figure (Fig. 3), each step of the derived common Customer Solution Design approach consists of specific work packages including various subtasks. The implementation of these work packages is essential in order to fulfill the central aim of each phase and, consequently, to reach the overall aim of Customer Solution Design – the creation of the most appropriate software-based customer solution.

The derived common Customer Solution Design approach starts with the approval of the acquisition project, which refers to the creation of a specific software-based customer solution. Based on this, the central aim of the first step – the acquisition kick off – is to establish a comprehensive basis to ensure a successful execution of the respective acquisition project. Besides the identification of the customer requirements and the advice of the customer based on the analyzed customer problems and needs, project organizational work packages are thus also essential for this step. These project organizational work packages mainly refer to the set-up of an agile, cross-functional project-team, the establishment of an internal cooperation model with the identified project stakeholders and the organization of project-related meetings and workshops throughout the entire common Customer Solution Design approach. Building on this, the central aim of the second step – the project execution – refers to the creation of the required software-based solution concept. The work packages within this step are therefore interdisciplinary comprising customer-related, project-related, technical, commercial and legal tasks. Nevertheless, the focus of Customer Solution Design is on the target-oriented coordination of the acquisition project in this regard. As in the execution step, the quotation phase also comprises interdisciplinary work packages. These tasks are needed in order to create the final quotation document, which is the central aim of this third step. In this context, the overall work package of the quotation phase thus refers to the preparation of the binding proposal by consolidating project-related information. As the name of the next step – the project completion – implies, the focus within this phase is on the final, successful completion of the respective acquisition project. This successful completion includes the final project documentation on the related data base as well as project organizational work packages. In this context, a concluding Lessons Learned Workshop forms the central project organizational task within this step of the common Customer Solution Design approach. Based on this workshop, project-related experiences are identified and documented for future acquisition projects. With regard to the last step – the transition phase – the aim is on the successful handover of the project. The main focus thereby is on the preparation of the handover documents and the execution of the final project handover to the official project manager. In addition, the official project manager is supported by Customer Solution Design within the transition phase to ensure the successful continuation of the respective acquisition project. It should also be emphasized that the innovation management – as the central innovation-based work package of Customer Solution Design – is an essential component throughout the entire common Customer

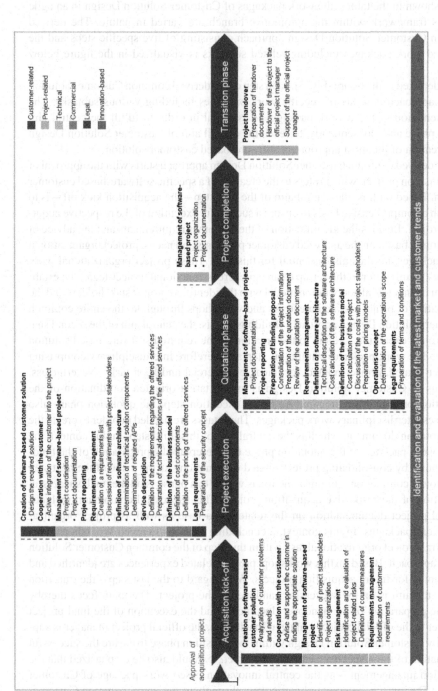

**Fig. 3.** Common Customer Solution Design approach.

Solution Design approach. In this context, the focus is on the identification and evaluation of the latest market and customer trends in order to ensure the continuous creation of innovative software-based customer solutions.

In summary, the derived common Customer Solution Design approach comprising specific work packages is a possible basis to successfully manage software-based customer projects within the digitally transformed automotive industry. In order to establish a common approach within this paper, both the approach as well as the included Customer Solution Design-related work packages were generalized. For this reason, the derived common Customer Solution Design approach has to be adapted to the respective acquisition project. Particularly against the background of the agile business framework, a constant adaption of the derived approach will additionally be needed so that a successful Customer Solution Design can also be ensured in the future.

## 6 Final Evaluation and Recommendations

The paper makes two central theoretical contributions for the Customer Solution Design research field. By the establishment of a detailed role description of Customer Solution Design, on the one hand, the paper at hand supports the addressing of the research gap that exists with regard to the lack of understanding of the Customer Solution Design role. On the other hand, a generalized common Customer Solution Design approach was developed in the course of this paper. This approach comprises specific Customer Solution Design-related steps and related work packages. Based on the established approach, a theoretical framework for the research field of Customer Solution Design was created. The results obtained in this paper extend the Customer Solution Design research field mentioned in previous related literature and thus generated a theoretical foundation, which is essential for further constructive research regarding the Customer Solution Design role and approach.

The tasks and competencies of Customer Solution Design are an essential basis for successfully managing customer-oriented software-based projects within the automotive supplier industry. For this reason, it is recommended to implement the role of Customer Solution Design as a uniform standard for such projects. Against this background of the importance of Customer Solution Design for customer projects, the role should not only be introduced within the acquisition phase, but over the entire life cycle. In order to exploit the full potential of the Customer Solution Design role, it is recommended to define an internal cooperation model with both each project stakeholder and the entire project team based on an internal project contract at the beginning of future projects. This internal cooperation model clearly determines the responsibilities of each project-related role and is thus especially needed when the Customer Solution Design role is newly introduced. It is furthermore recommended: To successfully execute the Customer Solution Design role in an agile business framework, the Customer Solution Design approach derived within this paper represents an important foundation. This approach focusing on work packages is therefore an essential component for Customer Solution Design. Nevertheless, the recommendation is that each Customer Solution Designer has to adapt this derived approach individually according to the project and its characteristics.

There are limitations to mention for the paper at hand. These limitations simultaneously imply valuable starting points for future Customer Solution Design-related research, as shown below. The theoretical background was focused on the Scaled Agile Framework to identify similar solution-oriented roles within a related field. This implies that further design methods – such as Design Thinking or User Experience – should be evaluated to extend the theoretical consideration of Customer Solution Design. With regard to the evaluation of the Customer Solution Design role, one limitation is that this was just analyzed based on guided expert interviews with internal stakeholders. For further evaluating the role of Customer Solution Design, it is thus essential to extend the questions as well as to recruit more interview partners including external stakeholders such as customers. A further limitation is that the derivation of the common Customer Solution Design approach was based on two selected projects only. In order to elaborate and extend this approach more detailed, on the one hand additional projects have to be considered and on the other hand, projects have to be evaluated for a longer period. Furthermore, the use of qualitative methods for the evaluation left a large scope for interpretation, which is why the results are to be checked in follow-up studies. Derived from this, the use of further research methods – both qualitative and quantitative – is additionally required to gain additional findings regarding the role and the approach of Customer Solution Design. Similarly, a further limitation can be seen in the focus on the automotive supplier industry as well as on a single company, in this case the Robert Bosch GmbH. This implies for future research to analyze if Customer Solution Design or similar concepts are already established in other digitally transformed branches, whereby cross-industry research is needed. Based on the emphasis of this paper – the evaluation of the Customer Solution Design role and the derivation of a common approach – it should be noted that further aspects of Customer Solution Design such as success criteria have also to be analyzed in future research to expand the understanding of this research field in general.

# 7   Conclusion

To sum up, the paper emphasizes that Customer Solution Design is a central interface between the company and the OEM in the context of acquisition projects comprising the generation of new digital business models. In this context the Customer Solution Design as interdisciplinary roles refers to a cross-functional team. Regarding the common approach, the management of software-based acquisition projects and thus the successful creation of software-based customer solutions are seen as the overall work packages.

For providing an outlook, it should be stated that – according to the authors– the need for Customer Solution Design will continue to grow in the future. This is especially due to the increasing importance of new digital business models in the digitally transformed automotive supplier industry. In this context, Customer Solution Design will thus become an integral part for the generation of software-based solutions within automotive supplier companies. Against the background of continuous generating digital-based automotive added value for the customer, the demand for Customer Solution Design will in future additionally go beyond the acquisition process and establish itself throughout the entire project life cycle.

Finally, it should be noted that Customer Solution Design is important for generating the most appropriate software-based customer solutions required by the OEMs in the context of an agile business framework and thus makes an essential contribution to the successful addressing of the digital transformation in the automotive supplier industry. Referring to the overall question of this paper – Customer Solution Design - A new agile role needed in the automotive industry to support digital transformation? – it can definitely be stated: The Customer Solution Design role is an important basis for supporting the digital transformation within the automotive industry.

# References

1. Möller, D.P.F., Haas, R.E.: Guide to Automotive Connectivity and Cybersecurity: Trends, Technologies, Innovations and Applications. Springer, Cham (2019). https://doi.org/10.1007/978-3-319-73512-2
2. Wallentowitz, H., Freialdenhoven, A., Olschewski, I.: Strategien in der Automobilindustrie: Technologietrends und Marktentwicklungen. Springer, Wiesbaden (2009). https://doi.org/10.1007/978-3-8348-9311-6
3. Gropp, M.: Verbunden auf Gedeih und Verderb (2016). https://www.faz.net/aktuell/wirtschaft/unternehmen/autohersteller-und-zulieferer-verbunden-auf-gedeih-und-verderb-14402472.html
4. Dannenberg, J., Reichhardt, M.: Automobilzulieferer: Acht neue Herausforderungen für CEOs von Zulieferern (2019). https://www.automobil-industrie.vogel.de/acht-neue-herausforderungen-fuer-ceos-von-zulieferern-a-838511/
5. Kessler, T., Buck, C.: How digitization affects mobility and the business models of automotive OEMs. In: Khare, A., Stewart, B., Schatz, R. (eds.) Phantom Ex Machina, pp. 107–118. Springer, Cham (2017). https://doi.org/10.1007/978-3-319-44468-0_7
6. Winkelhake, U.: The Digital Transformation of the Automotive Industry: Catalysts, Roadmap, Practice. Springer, Cham (2018). https://doi.org/10.1007/978-3-319-71610-7
7. Büttner, R., Müller, E.: Changeability of manufacturing companies in the context of digitalization. In: 28th International Conference on Flexible Automation and Intelligent Manufacturing, pp. 539–546 (2018)
8. Piccinini, E., Hanelt, A., Gregory, R.W., Kolbe, L.M.: Transforming industrial business: the impact of digital transformation on automotive organizations. In: 36th International Conference on Information Systems, pp. 1–20 (2015)
9. Bosler, M., Burr, W., Ihring, L.: HMD Praxis der Wirtschaftsinformatik **55**(2), 329–348 (2018). https://doi.org/10.1365/s40702-018-0396-8
10. Kallenbach, R., Reichert, C., Hieronymi, F., Nicodemus, R.: Mobility 4.0 – on the road toward mobility services. ATZ Worldwide **121**, 64–69 (2019)
11. Wittmann, J.: Electrification and digitalization as disruptive trends: new perspectives for the automotive industry? In: Khare, A., Stewart, B., Schatz, R. (eds.) Phantom Ex Machina, pp. 137–159. Springer, Cham (2017). https://doi.org/10.1007/978-3-319-44468-0_9
12. Gläser, J., Laudel, G.: Experteninterviews und qualitative Inhaltsanalyse: als Instrumente rekonstruierender Untersuchungen, 4th edn. VS Verlag für Sozialwissenschaften, Wiesbaden (2010)
13. Misoch, S.: Qualitative Interviews. Berlin/München/Boston: Walter de Gruyter GmbH (2015)
14. Borchardt, A., Göthlich, S.E.: Erkenntnisgewinnung durch Fallstudien. In: Albers, S., Klapper, D., Konradt, U., Walter, A., Wolf, J. (eds.) Methodik der empirischen Forschung, pp. 33–48. Gabler Verlag, Wiesbaden (2009). https://doi.org/10.1007/978-3-322-96406-9_3
15. Yin, R.K.: Case Study Research: Design and Methods, 4th edn. SAGE Publications, Thousand Oaks (2009)

16. Göthlich, S.E.: Fallstudien als Forschungsmethode: Plädoyer für einen Methodenpluralismus in der deutschen betriebswirtschaftlichen Forschung. In: Manuskripte aus den Instituten für Betriebswirtschaftslehre an der Universität Kiel, No. 578 (2003)
17. Leffingwell, D.: Scaling software agility: advanced practices for large enterprises (2011). https://www.agilealliance.org/agile2011/
18. Scaled Agile, Inc.: What Is SAFe? (2017). https://v45.scaledagileframework.com/what-is-safe/
19. Scaled Agile, Inc.: Large Solution Level (2017). https://v45.scaledagileframework.com/large-solution-level/

# Mobile Wallet Adoption: Does Ubiquity Make a Difference?

Norman Shaw[1]([⊠]) and Brenda Eschenbrenner[2]

[1] Ryerson University, Toronto, Canada
norman.shaw@ryerson.ca
[2] University of Nebraska at Kearney, Kearney, NE, USA
eschenbrenbl@unk.edu

**Abstract.** Smartphones have become versatile in their functionality, including providing an alternate method of contactless payment. Mobile wallets have become popular, and this popularity is expected to continue to grow. Enticements such as convenience and efficiency have led some to adopt mobile wallets. However, challenges and apprehensions of adoption still exist. Our research investigates potential factors influencing adoption of mobile wallets in USA and Canada and explores the differences between the two countries. We utilize Diffusion of Innovation Theory and extend it to include ubiquity to understand important factors of mobile wallet adoption. Our survey findings suggest that relative advantage, results demonstrability, and ubiquity are influential factors for mobile wallet adoption, except for females in the USA. Complexity, however, was not significant. Trialability was only marginally significant for the USA and compatibility had mixed effects. Our results provide guidance to practitioners regarding factors to consider in their endeavors to understand and expand mobile wallet adoption, as well as suggesting avenues for future research.

**Keywords:** Mobile wallet · Diffusion of innovations · Ubiquity · PLS-SEM

## 1 Introduction

In today's mobile world, smartphones have become an essential part of daily life, playing a crucial role in the way various services have become accessible [1]. When connected to the Internet, consumers can pay for merchandise by waving their smartphone over the payment terminal [2]. The origin of this contactless means of payment can be attributed to the steps taken by credit card companies to make transactions less prone to fraud.

Payment via credit has been used widely in physical stores since the introduction of the Diners Club card in 1950 [3]. A payment card is presented, the credit worthiness is checked, the customer signs to authenticate identity and, if all criteria have been met, the payee's account is debited and the merchant's account credited. Unfortunately, fraudulent activities can and have occurred with this process. Guarding against fraud is a continuous endeavor of credit card companies. In 1998, the three major credit card companies (i.e., Europay, Mastercard, and Visa) introduced the EMV standard which required a chip to

© Springer Nature Switzerland AG 2021
F. F.-H. Nah and K. Siau (Eds.): HCII 2021, LNCS 12783, pp. 277–292, 2021.
https://doi.org/10.1007/978-3-030-77750-0_18

be inserted into the credit card [4]. With an encrypted personal identification number (PIN) stored in the chip, this added an extra level of security, making the transaction more secure than one with just a signature. The adoption of EMV standards required that consumers receive a new credit card with an embedded chip, and that retailers upgraded their payment terminal to accept this 'chip and pin' card.

Consumers were issued these chip and pin cards at no cost to them [4]. However, to be effective, retailers needed to upgrade their terminal for a fee in order for the embedded chips to be usable. Retailers who did not upgrade would be liable for fraudulent transactions if a chip and pin card was not used. To give retailers time to upgrade their payment terminals, the EMV consortium gave deadlines by geographical region, after which the liability moved from the credit card company to the retailer [5]. For Europe, where the EMV standard was first introduced, the deadline was 1 January 2005. For Canada, the date was 11 March 2011 and for the USA, the date was 1 October 2015. The later date for the USA market was due to the US payment market having multiple, smaller card issuers in comparison to the other geographic regions [6].

In addition to storing encrypted payment data, the chip can communicate with Near Field Communication (NFC) [7] when close to an NFC-enabled payment terminal. If the transaction is less than a specified amount, tap and pay transactions are accepted by these NFC-enabled payment terminals. In addition, a smartphone with NFC capability can, in effect, mimic the cards. In 2010, Android phones were NFC enabled thereby allowing mobile wallet apps to perform contactless payments. When Apple added NFC to their iPhones in late 2014, NFC became the de facto standard for mobile wallets [8, 9].

Mobile payment solutions have been growing in many countries [10]. It is estimated that there will be approximately 1.3 billion mobile payment transactions worldwide by 2023 [11]. In 2020, there has been a further increase in adoption due to the COVID-19 pandemic. When consumers shop in physical stores, they may prefer not to use cash or touch a payment terminal [12]. Major credit card companies have recognized and responded to this demand by increasing their tap limit for smaller transactions. COVID-19 has accelerated the adoption of contactless payments with an 'expected stickiness factor' for the long term [13].

Although mobile wallet usage has been increasing, there are still barriers to adoption. For instance, individuals may be hesitant on using an alternate form of payment if an existing form has been reliable. Also, individuals may have concerns regarding experiencing more technical issues if using their smartphones to pay. In addition, the availability of merchants capable of processing contactless payments will be influential in mobile wallet adoption – tap and pay cards and mobile wallets cannot be used if the payment terminal is not NFC enabled. If not fully understood, these barriers could limit future adoption and usage.

Therefore, the research questions posed in this study are: What factors influence the adoption of mobile wallets? Do these factors differ between countries (i.e., Canada and the USA)? Rogers studied the adoption of agricultural innovations and found that there were five factors that impacted adoption [14]. He proposed the Diffusion of Innovation (DOI) Theory which posits that relative advantage, complexity, compatibility, observability and trialability influence adoption. In the context of mobile wallet adoption, another potential factor could be ubiquity considering the inability to utilize mobile wallets if payment terminals are not properly enabled. To answer our research question, we explore the factors proposed in the DOI model extended with the construct of ubiquity. Contributions from this study will include a deeper understanding of the relevant factors influencing mobile wallet adoption and potential differences between the US and Canadian markets. The findings can provide valuable insights to those in industry, such as credit card companies, as well as researchers interested in mobile wallet adoption.

The paper is structured as follows. We begin with the theoretical foundation, discussions of the constructs of the research model, and our proposed hypotheses. The research model, methodology, and data analysis follow. Results, discussions, contributions, implications and the scope of future research are addressed in the latter sections.

## 2  Theoretical Foundation and Hypotheses

### 2.1  Technology Adoption

Innovation is the creation and application of new ideas, which in turn may lead to new services and products [15, 16]. Some innovations are more widely adopted than others and various theories of adoption have sought to understand individuals' motivations to start using a new technology. One well-researched theory is the Technology Acceptance Model (TAM) [17], which posits that an innovation is adopted when it is useful and easy to use. However, this model has been criticized as being too parsimonious [18] and consequently it has been extended with other constructs [19]. Another well-researched theory is the Diffusion of Innovations (DOI) [14]. Rogers studied the diffusion of agricultural innovations and concluded that five conditions had to be satisfied for an innovation to be successfully adopted. These conditions or factors for adoption include users perceiving a relative advantage, the innovation is not too complex and is perceived as being compatible, the results of usage are observable, and users are able to try it before full scale use.

Because relative advantage is similar to perceived usefulness and simplicity (the opposite of complexity) is similar to perceived ease of use, TAM has been expanded with the constructs of DOI [20, 21]. For instance, Lee et al. [22] integrated TAM with DOI in a study of employees' adoption of an e-learning system. In a study of the adoption of the Uber app, Min et al. [23] combined TAM with DOI. This combination increased the explanatory power of TAM alone.

The Diffusion of Innovations Theory has been used by researchers to understand the consumer adoption behavior in various fields like mobile banking [24], Uber mobile application adoption [23], and innovative technological solutions in the field of medicine [25]. A few recent studies that have tested DOI in the context of mobile wallets include Johnson et al. [26] and Sivathanu [27]. Information Systems (IS) scholars have argued that DOI is a suitable framework for understanding innovation diffusion across different types of users irrespective of their background [26, 28]. DOI has been cited as a well-known theoretical framework to gain an in depth understanding of technology adoption in social settings [29].

However, external conditions must also be considered [30]. When a technology, such as the mobile wallet, depends upon the network of payment providers, terminals, and connectivity, adoption will also depend upon the availability and reliability of these necessary components [31]. Extending DOI-TAM further with the construct of ubiquity will provide insights into the significant factors that are influencing the adoption of the mobile wallet across two distinct countries, USA and Canada.

Hence, in this study, we utilized the Diffusion of Innovations Theory and extended it with ubiquity. The hypotheses are proposed below.

## 2.2 Relative Advantage

Relative advantage 'is the degree to which an innovation is perceived as better than the idea it supersedes' [32]. Similarly, perceived usefulness from TAM is defined as 'the degree to which a person believes that using a particular system would enhance his or her job performance' [17]. Various studies of TAM have found that relative advantage is the most consistent variable that significantly influences adoption [33]. For instance, in Singapore, the post office implemented a self-collection service to improve the delivery of home packages that could not be delivered if the recipient was not home [34]. With the lens of DOI, the relative advantage of self-managing the collection lead to the adoption of the service.

Paying with a mobile wallet has advantages over the alternatives. For example, cash can be more unhygienic, which has become an even greater concern during the COVID-19 pandemic. It can also be more efficient and convenient than having to obtain and/or calculate the correct currency or retrieve a payment card. The mobile wallet also has additional functions readily available, such as transferring money to a friend. We therefore hypothesize:

- H1: Relative advantage positively influences the intention to use a mobile wallet.

## 2.3 Complexity or Perceived Ease of Use

Rogers [32] defined complexity as the 'degree to which an innovation is perceived as difficult to understand and use'. TAM's construct, perceived ease of use (PEOU), is the opposite and defined as 'the degree to which a person believes that using a particular system would be free of effort' [17]. In this study, we use PEOU as the opposite of complexity. In a meta-analysis of extant studies of TAM, PEOU was found to be significant but less influential than relative advantage [33].

Waving a mobile wallet over a payment terminal is similar to waving a payment card. It is simple to learn and doesn't require significant amounts of training or additional knowledge to operate. Studies of mobile wallet acceptance have shown that PEOU is significant [10, 35]. We therefore hypothesize:

- H2: Perceived ease of use positively influences the intention to use a mobile wallet.

### 2.4  Compatibility

Compatibility is defined as 'the degree to which a service is perceived as consistent with the consumer's existing values and experiences' [32]. Zhang et al. [36] found that managers were more likely to adopt an email system if its use was compatible with their prior experience. When implementing a new hospital information system, users looked for compatibility [25]. Customers who use mobile banking are more likely to adopt it if they perceive that it is compatible with their needs [37].

Mobile wallets and payment terminals with tap and pay capabilities provide similar experiences and the same value to consumers who have previously used payment cards. Also, when paying with the mobile wallet, the transaction needs to be approved in the same manner as if it originated from a payment card. This compatibility will encourage consumers to have their mobile wallets enabled and ready to pay considering the consistency with their existing values and experiences with payment cards. Hence:

- H3: Compatibility positively influences the intention to use a mobile wallet.

### 2.5  Observability or Results Demonstrability

Observability is 'the extent to which an innovation is visible to the members of a social system and the benefits can be easily observed' [32]. In a study of mobile banking in Saudi Arabia, observability was significant [38]. When employees were being introduced to an e-learning system, they were encouraged when they saw others using the system successfully [22]. On reviewing the literature, Moore and Benbasat [20] were not satisfied with the measures of observability. Therefore, they revised the construct as "results demonstrability" and developed a new instrument for it. We adopt this as the construct in our model.

Smartphone owners may become aware that a mobile wallet app exists when they see someone paying with their smartphone. When they observe the results that the merchant receives credit and the payment is successfully completed, they may be persuaded to start using their smartphone to pay. We therefore add our fourth hypothesis:

- H4: Results demonstrability positively influences the intention to use a mobile wallet.

### 2.6  Trialability

From Rogers' research [39], individuals were more likely to adopt an innovation if they were able to try it before making a full commitment. This 'risk free exploration' encourages experimentation, builds confidence, and allows the user to gauge the relative advantage [34]. On-line gaming players were significantly influenced by the trialability of a game: they were more likely to adopt the game if they were able to play it first [40]. Tan & Teo [41] found that trialability was a necessary pre-cursor prior to the full adoption of Internet banking. This was explained by the associated risks where a mistake could be costly. Similarly, users of the mobile wallet may be concerned about loss of funds and they would therefore wish to try the innovation first. Therefore, we hypothesize:

- H5: Trialability positively influences the intention to use a mobile wallet.

### 2.7 Ubiquity

Smartphones connected to the Internet permit access to the worldwide web via the Internet. The small size of the phone makes it portable with connectivity to high Internet availability. Also, communication via a network is feasible anytime and anyplace [31]. Access to information is unconstrained by time and place [42]. Mobile commerce benefits from uninterrupted connectivity [43]. From a meta-analysis of the literature, the dimensions of ubiquity included portability, immediacy, and continuity [44]. Users of the mobile wallet want to be able to pay with their smartphone wherever they shop. Their device is portable and always connected, which allows payments to occur wherever an NFC-enabled payment terminal is available. Therefore, we hypothesize:

- H6: Ubiquity positively influences the intention to use a mobile wallet.

### 2.8 Intention to Use

Intention to use is a measure of the likelihood that a person would adopt an innovation [45]. In comparison to actual usage, it has the advantage that it includes those individuals that have heard of the innovation but have not yet adopted it. Although no actual usage is currently occurring, they may be very likely to use the innovation in the future [46]. Because actual use is strongly correlated with intention [47] and we are most interested in individuals intending to use mobile wallet, intention to use is the dependent variable in our research model.

### 2.9 Research Model

The research model is illustrated in Fig. 1.

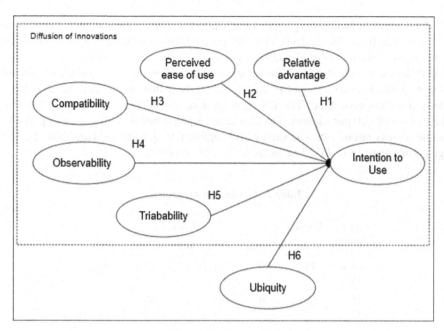

**Fig. 1.** Research model

## 3 Methodology

The proposed research model was assessed using a survey research method. The constructs were measured with items adapted from existing literature (see Table 1) and measured using a 5-point Likert scale with 1 being strongly disagree and 5 being strongly agree.

**Table 1.** Source of indicators

| Construct | Indicators adapted from |
| --- | --- |
| Relative advantage | Chandra, Srivastava & Theng, 2010 [48] |
| | Jaradat, Moustafa & Al-Mashaqba 2018 [49] |
| Perceived ease of use (opposite of Complexity) | Venkatesh, Morris, Davis & Davis, 2003 [50] |
| Compatibility | Jaradat, Moustafa & Al-Mashaqba 2018 [49] |
| Observability OR Results demonstrability | Kapoor, Dwivedi & Williams, 2014 [51] |
| | Moore & Benbasat, 1991 [20] |
| | Venkatesh & Bala, 2009 [52] |
| Trialability | Kapoor, Dwivedi & Williams, 2014 [51] |
| | Moore & Benbasat, 1991 [20] |
| Ubiquity | Kranz, 2012 [53] |
| | Okazaki & Mendez,2013 [44] |
| | D-H Shin, 2007 [54] |
| Intention to use | Chandra, Srivastava & Theng, 2010 [48] |

A pilot questionnaire was prepared and trialed to refine the measurement items. Data was collected from US residents using MTurk and from Canadian residents through a panel sourced from Qualtrics, a US company specializing in quantitative surveys. The data collected was cleansed by eliminating those responses that had significant amounts of same-value answers (straight-lining) as well as those that significantly deviated from the average response time. The US response rate was 87%, resulting in 398 usable surveys out of 460 participants. The Canadian response rate was 90%, resulting in 447 usable surveys out of 498. The survey also captured gender and age (see Table 2). The age groups were 18 to 24, 25 to 38, as well as 39 and over.

**Table 2.** Gender and age groups

| Age group | Canada | | | USA | | |
|---|---|---|---|---|---|---|
| | Male | Female | Total | Male | Female | Total |
| 18 to 24 | 74 | 70 | 144 | 42 | 52 | 94 |
| 25 to 38 | 69 | 74 | 143 | 123 | 60 | 183 |
| 39 plus | 80 | 80 | 160 | 62 | 59 | 121 |
| **Totals** | **223** | **224** | **447** | **227** | **171** | **398** |

Using SmartPLS software, PLS-SEM was used for the data analysis [55]. PLS-SEM is an accepted exploratory statistical tool [56, 57]. It does not require a normal distribution and is also robust to smaller sample sizes. In this study, the number of responses is considered relatively large, but the data by country-gender-age group is smaller. PLS-SEM allows comparisons between these smaller groups.

We followed a two-step analysis, starting with the measurement model followed by the structural model. The measurement model tests for reliability as well as discriminant validity. For the structural model assessment, the path analysis calculates the path coefficients and with a bootstrap procedure with 5,000 subsamples, the significance of each path is estimated. Also, data can be assigned to groups within SmartPLS software enabling multigroup analysis.

## 4　Results

### 4.1　The Measurement Model

The PLS-SEM algorithm calculates the loadings for each of the indicators. To assess the reliability of the indicators, the loadings must be greater than 0.7 [58]. In the first round, some of the indicators were less than 0.7 and were dropped. Subsequently, all indicators loaded on their respective construct and with loadings above 0.7.

In order to assess discriminant validity, the Fornell-Larcker criterion was used [59] in which the square root of the average variance extracted (AVE) for each latent variable should be more than the other correlation values among the latent variables. Table 3 shows that the criterion has been satisfied.

**Table 3.** Fornell-Larcker criterion

|      | COMP | ITU | PEOU | RA | RD | TRI | UB |
|------|------|-----|------|-----|-----|-----|-----|
| COMP | **0.878** | | | | | | |
| ITU  | 0.601 | **0.894** | | | | | |
| PEOU | 0.681 | 0.525 | **0.778** | | | | |
| RA   | 0.718 | 0.615 | 0.745 | **0.72** | | | |
| RD   | 0.638 | 0.69 | 0.644 | 0.634 | **0.76** | | |
| TRI  | 0.583 | 0.398 | 0.72 | 0.672 | 0.53 | **0.804** | |
| UB   | 0.456 | 0.591 | 0.375 | 0.428 | 0.592 | 0.278 | **0.784** |

A second discriminant test is the heterotrait-monotrait ratio (HTMT), which is a measure of similarity between variables, and has been found to be more sensitive than Fornell-Larcker [55]. All ratios were less than 0.85, confirming the discriminant validity of the variables [60] (see Table 4 for results).

**Table 4.** HTMT ratio

|      | COMP | ITU | PEOU | RA | RD |
|------|------|-----|------|-----|-----|
| COMP | | | | | |
| ITU  | 0.823 | | | | |
| PEOU | 0.849 | 0.684 | | | |
| RA   | 0.846 | 0.808 | 0.848 | | |
| RD   | 0.84 | 0.847 | 0.795 | 0.817 | |
| TRI  | 0.792 | 0.639 | 0.848 | 0.822 | 0.79 |

### 4.2 The Structural Model

The PLS-SEM algorithm calculated the path coefficients, followed by bootstrapping to find the significance of the paths. The coefficient of determination ($R^2$) represents the percent of variance explained from the independent variables [61]. The populations of the two countries were analyzed separately, with Canada $R^2 = 0.609$ and USA $R^2 = 0.587$. The results (see Table 5) suggest that all factors are significant except perceived ease of use (i.e., complexity), compatibility being marginally significant for the USA, and trialability being marginally significant for the USA and not significant for Canada.

**Table 5.** Path coefficients for USA and Canada

|  | Canada | | | USA | | |
|---|---|---|---|---|---|---|
|  | Path coeff | T statistic | P Values | Path coeff | T statistic | P Values |
| RA -> ITU | 0.243 | 5.353 | 0*** | 0.265 | 4.011 | 0*** |
| PEOU -> ITU | −0.062 | 1.315 | 0.189 | −0.012 | 0.153 | 0.878 |
| COMP -> ITU | 0.251 | 5.124 | 0*** | 0.154 | 2.329 | 0.02** |
| RD -> ITU | 0.252 | 5.581 | 0*** | 0.349 | 6.4 | 0*** |
| TRI -> ITU | −0.006 | 0.117 | 0.907 | −0.113 | 2.188 | 0.029** |
| UB -> ITU | 0.237 | 5.129 | 0*** | 0.242 | 4.983 | 0*** |
| R squared | 0.609 | | | 0.587 | | |
| Sample size | 447 | | | 398 | | |

*** $p < 0.001$, ** $p < 0.05$

## 4.3 Analysis by Data Group

Data groups were further defined by gender/country. The samples sizes for each group are shown in Table 2 above and for each group, the sample size was sufficient for statistical significance, i.e., the sample size was greater than ten times the maximum number of paths [62]. Table 6 shows the path coefficients for each group: Canada/male, Canada/female, USA/male, USA/female.

**Table 6.** Path coefficients for gender/country

| Row labels | Canada | | | | USA | | | |
|---|---|---|---|---|---|---|---|---|
|  | Male | | Female | | Male | | Female | |
|  | Path coeff | T | Path coeff | T | Path coeff | T | Path coeff | T |
| RA -> ITU | 0.22 | 3.238*** | 0.303 | 4.58*** | 0.304 | 3.561*** | 0.181 | 1.65 |
| PEOU -> ITU | −0.034 | 0.426 | −0.078 | 1.239 | 0.069 | 0.753 | −0.075 | 0.869 |
| COMP -> ITU | 0.246 | 3.488 | 0.235 | 3.637*** | 0.058 | 0.725 | 0.29 | 3.358*** |
| RD -> ITU | 0.214 | 3.193*** | 0.255 | 4.815*** | 0.387 | 5.201*** | 0.308 | 3.744*** |
| TRI -> ITU | −0.006 | 0.145 | −0.014 | 0.288 | −0.155 | 1.952 | −0.082 | 1.154 |
| UB -> ITU | 0.237 | 2.988** | 0.256 | 4.297*** | 0.201 | 3.065** | 0.287 | 4.072*** |
| R squared | 0.532 | | 0.682 | | 0.564 | | 0.644 | |
| Sample size | 223 | | 224 | | 227 | | 171 | |

*** $p < 0.001$; ** $p < 0.01$

The findings suggest that there are differences between the path coefficients when comparing males and females for each country. There are also differences between the path coefficients when comparing Canadian males to USA males and Canadian females to USA females. We ran multigroup analysis for each of these comparisons. There were no significant differences. We also evaluated age groups and found no significant differences.

### 4.4 Summary of Results

To summarize our findings (see Table 7), results demonstrability and ubiquity are significant factors influencing the adoption of mobile wallets. Relative advantage is as well except for females in the USA. Perceived ease of use (i.e., complexity) is not a significant factor and trialability is only significant for the USA. Compatibility is significant for Canada and females, and marginally significant for the USA.

**Table 7.** Summary of results

| H | Path | Canada | USA | Can-M | Can-F | USA-M | USA-F |
|---|------|--------|-----|-------|-------|-------|-------|
| H1 | RA → ITU | ✓ | ✓ | ✓ | ✓ | ✓ | |
| H2 | PEOU → ITU | | | | | | |
| H3 | Comp → ITU | ✓ | ✓* | | ✓ | | ✓ |
| H4 | RD → ITU | ✓ | ✓ | ✓ | ✓ | ✓ | ✓ |
| H5 | TRI → ITU | | ✓* | | | | |
| H6 | UB → ITU | ✓ | ✓ | ✓ | ✓ | ✓ | ✓ |

*Marginally significant

## 5   Discussion

Consistent with extant research [42], relative advantage is significant for both populations. This further confirms the importance of this construct, which is equivalent to perceived usefulness [50, 63]. Not surprisingly, individuals would not adopt the mobile wallet if they did not perceive an advantage over current means of paying with cash or a payment card and they considered this to be useful [64]. For all subgroups, except USA females, relative advantage was significant. This is surprising and could be the subject of future research to determine if another study would produce the same results. Alternatively, other constructs could be added to enrich the model and determine if USA females are influenced by, for example, social factors.

Results demonstrability (or observability) was significant for all groups. In a study of Brazilian Internet banking, Hernandez and Mazzon [65] found that users were influenced by results demonstrability. As much as perceived usefulness is significant, consumers need to be convinced that the benefits are realizable and this can occur when they observe the results from others. For example, shoppers in physical stores may be waiting in line to check out and can easily observe other customers waving their smartphone over the payment terminal. They can observe the speed of the transaction and its convenience as there is no need to search in their pocket or handbag to find their physical wallet and produce a payment card or cash.

Ubiquity was significant for all groups. Johnson et al. [26] found that ubiquity was an important factor for the adoption of m-payment services. To use the mobile wallet, retailers must provide an up-to-date payment terminal capable of accepting NFC. If these terminals have not achieved a critical penetration of the market, users of the mobile wallet will be forced to have another payment option available when tap and pay is not. This study expected a significant difference between Canada and the USA as NFC-enabled payment terminals are more widely installed in Canada, which can be partially attributed to Canada's earlier adoption of EMV standards and the more fragmented card issuer market in the USA [6]. However, a multigroup analysis found no difference.

Compatibility was significant for females from both countries, compared to non-significant for males. Compatibility means that it is consistent with existing values and experiences: consumers can pay with the smartphone using a similar process to when they pay with cash or payment card. This can be congruent to existing values of making the payment decision at the last moment. From our results, males attach less importance to compatibility than females. Future research could investigate this further, adding additional constructs to the model or specifying dimensions of compatibility.

## 5.1 Theoretical Contribution

Diffusion of Innovation Theory has been applied to understand users of smartphones [66] and extended with variables such as perceived risk [38]. Studies have also recognized that smartphones operate best in a ubiquitous environment [67]. We offer a novel contribution by adding the construct of ubiquity to DOI in the domain of mobile wallet adoption. In our study, this model has been applied to mobile wallets and can be equally applied in any ubiquitous environment. For example, the model may be applied in the context of mobile device adoption to monitor health or motivate exercising. Also, the model may be applied to the adoption of event ticketing applications.

## 5.2 Implication for Practitioners

Practitioners will want to ensure that factors that influence mobile wallet adoption are taken into consideration in their endeavors. For instance, users need to understand the advantage of the mobile wallet. Also, users want to see results and be convinced that adoption is worthwhile. Practitioners should concentrate on early adopters, who will be influencers, demonstrating results as others observe the advantages. Ubiquity must be addressed by investment in infrastructure, to ensure that payment terminals are installed and ready to use, thereby demonstrating to adopters that the mobile wallet is advantageous and can be used anytime and anyplace.

## 5.3 Limitations and Future Research

Canadian data was collected from panels that have been recruited by Qualtrics [68]. These individuals receive a reward for participation which may have influenced their responses (i.e., being more focused on completing the survey to receive a reward). Similarly, USA participants were recruited via MTurk, which also offers a reward for participation. The survey was limited to owners of smartphones who are assumed to have a knowledge of mobile payments, but some of these owners may have limited understanding of the functionality which would impact their answers. Sampling took place in Canada and USA only, and the results may not be generalizable to other countries.

Future research could extend the model further. For example, privacy and security are potential concerns and these constructs could be added. As mentioned, Canadian and US culture and attitudes are potentially different from other countries so collecting data from other areas would highlight differences between regions.

## 6 Conclusion

Smartphones are in the hands of most of the population [69] and, with the help of the Internet, consumers have the choice of thousands of apps [70]. Some apps, such as Facebook, are adopted by millions of people, whilst others have only a few adopters, ending their digital life soon after launch. Practitioners are interested in what motivates individuals to adopt technology so that their app becomes widely adopted. Hence, it will be important to identify factors influential in adoption. Leveraging and extended the Diffusion of Innovation Theory, our research identifies factors that are important for mobile wallet adoption. These factors can provide guidance to practitioners looking to expand the usage of this alternate payment method and provides the potential for future research.

## References

1. Baah, B., Naghavi, N.: Beyond the basics: how smartphones will drive future opportunities for the mobile money industry (2018). https://www.gsma.com/mobilefordevelopment/wp-content/uploads/2018/09/2017-SOTIR-deep-dive-How-smartphones-will-drive-future-opportunities.pdf
2. Mordor Intelligence. Retail industry - growth, trends (2019). https://www.mordorintelligence.com/industry-reports/retail-industry.
3. Davenport, W.B.: Bank credit cards and the uniform commercial code. Val. UL Rev. 1, 218 (1966)
4. King, D.: Chip-and-PIN: success and challenges in reducing fraud. In: Retail Payments Risk Forum, January 2012
5. Krickett, J.D.: The high cost of missing the EMV chip card switch. Podiatry Manag. 34(7), 59–64 (2015)
6. IBISWorld. Credit Card issuing in the US (2020). https://www.ibisworld.com/industry-statistics/market-size/credit-card-issuing-united-states/
7. Amoroso, D.L., Magnier-Watanabe, R.: Building a research model for mobile wallet consumer adoption: the case of mobile Suica in Japan. J. Theor. Appl. Electron. Commer. Res. 7(1), 94–110 (2012)
8. PYMNTS.com: Mobile Wallet Adoption 2020. PYMNTS.com (2020)
9. Smith, S.M., et al.: System and method of conducting transactions using a mobile wallet system. Google Patents (2010)
10. Shin, D.: Towards an understanding of the consumer acceptance of mobile wallet. Comput. Hum. Behav. 25(6), 1343–1354 (2009)

11. Clement, J.: Global proximity mobile payment usage penetration 2019. eMarketer (2019)
12. Beatty, A.: COVID-19 Proves Digital Banking Is No Longer Optional. Finextra, Toronto (2020)
13. InteracCorp. COVID-19 accelerating the move to digital payments across Canada (2020). https://www.newswire.ca/news-releases/covid-19-accelerating-the-move-to-digital-payments-across-canada-810549777.html
14. Rogers, E.M.: Diffusion of Innovations. 3rd edn. Free Press; Collier Macmillan, New York, London (1983). xix, 453 p.
15. Hlavacek, J.D., Thompson, V.A.: Bureaucracy and new product innovation. Acad. Manag. J. **16**(3), 361–372 (1973)
16. Thompson, V.A.: Bureaucracy and innovation. Adm. Sci. Q. 1–20 (1965)
17. Davis, F.D.: Perceived usefulness, perceived ease of use, and user acceptance of information technology. MIS Q. **13**(3), 319–340 (1989)
18. Benbasat, I., Barki, H.: Quo vadis, TAM? J. Assoc. Inf. Syst. **8**(4), 211–218 (2007)
19. King, W.R., He, J.: A meta-analysis of the technology acceptance model. Inf. Manag. **43**(6), 740–755 (2006)
20. Moore, G.C., Benbasat, I.: Development of an instrument to measure the perceptions of adopting an information technology innovation. Inf. Syst. Res. **2**(3), 192–222 (1991)
21. Plouffe, C.R., Hulland, J.S., Vandenbosch, M.: Research report: richness versus parsimony in modeling technology adoption decisions - Understanding merchant adoption of a smart card-based payment system. Inf. Syst. Res. **12**(2), 208 (2001)
22. Lee, Y.-H., Hsieh, Y.-C., Hsu, C.-N.: Adding innovation diffusion theory to the technology acceptance model: Supporting employees' intentions to use e-learning systems. J. Educ. Technol. Soc. **14**(4), 124–137 (2011)
23. Min, S., So, K.K.F., Jeong, M.: Consumer adoption of the Uber mobile application: Insights from diffusion of innovation theory and technology acceptance model. J. Travel Tour. Mark. **36**(7), 770–783 (2019)
24. van der Boor, P., Oliveira, P., Veloso, F.: Users as innovators in developing countries: the global sources of innovation and diffusion in mobile banking services. Res. Policy **43**, 1594–1607 (2014)
25. Tung, F.-C., Chang, S.-C., Chou, C.-M.: An extension of trust and TAM model with IDT in the adoption of the electronic logistics information system in HIS in the medical industry. Int. J. Med. Inform. **77**(5), 324–335 (2008)
26. Johnson, V.L., et al.: Limitations to the rapid adoption of M-payment services: understanding the impact of privacy risk on M-Payment services. Comput. Hum. Behav. **79**, 111–122 (2018)
27. Sivathanu, B.: Adoption of digital payment systems in the era of demonetization in India. J. Sci. Technol. Policy Manag. **10**, 143–171 (2019)
28. Kaur, P., et al.: Why do people use and recommend m-wallets? J. Retail. Consum. Serv. **56**, 102091 (2020)
29. Yates, B.L.: Applying diffusion theory: adoption of media literacy programs in schools. In: International Communication Association Conference, Washington, DC, USA (2001)
30. Taylor, S., Todd, P.A.: Understanding information technology usage: a test of competing models. Inf. Syst. Res. **6**(2), 144–176 (1995)
31. Junglas, I., Watson, R.T.: The u-constructs: four information drives. Commun. Assoc. Inf. Syst. **17**(1), 26 (2006)
32. Rogers, E.M.: Diffusion of preventive innovations. Addict. Behav. **27**(6), 989–993 (2002)
33. Legris, P., Ingham, J., Collerette, P.: Why do people use information technology? A critical review of the technology acceptance model. Inf. Manag. **40**(3), 191–204 (2003)
34. Wang, X., et al.: An innovation diffusion perspective of e-consumers' initial adoption of self-collection service via automated parcel station. Int. J. Logist. Manag. **29**(1), 237–260 (2018)

35. Shaw, N.: The mediating influence of trust in the adoption of the mobile wallet. J. Retail. Consum. Serv. **21**(4), 449–459 (2014)
36. Zhang, N., Guo, X., Chen, G.: IDT-TAM integrated model for IT adoption. Tsinghua Sci. Technol. **13**(3), 306–311 (2008)
37. Sitorus, H.M., et al.: Examining the Role of Usability, Compatibility and Social Influence in Mobile Banking Adoption in Indonesia
38. Al-Jabri, I.M., Sohail, M.S.: Mobile banking adoption: application of diffusion of innovation theory. J. Electron. Commer. Res. **13**(4), 379–391 (2012)
39. Rogers, E.M.: Diffusion of Innovations. London Free Press, New York (1995)
40. Wang, E.S.-T.: Perceived control and gender difference on the relationship between trialability and intent to play new online games. Comput. Hum. Behav. **30**, 315–320 (2014)
41. Tan, M., Teo, T.S.: Factors influencing the adoption of Internet banking. J. Assoc. Inf. Syst. **1**(1), 5 (2000)
42. Weigel, F.K., et al.: Diffusion of innovations and the theory of planned behavior in information systems research: a metaanalysis. Commun. Assoc. Inf. Syst. **34**(1), 31 (2014)
43. Roy, S., Moorthi, Y.: Technology readiness, perceived ubiquity and M-commerce adoption: the moderating role of privacy. J. Res. Interact. Mark. **11**(3), 268–295 (2017)
44. Okazaki, S., Mendez, F.: Exploring convenience in mobile commerce: moderating effects of gender. Comput. Hum. Behav. **29**(3), 1234–1242 (2013)
45. Ajzen, I.: The theory of planned behavior. Organ. Behav. Hum. Decis. Process. **50**(2), 179 (1991)
46. Schepers, J., Wetzels, M.: A meta-analysis of the technology acceptance model: investigating subjective norm and moderation effects. Inf. Manag. **44**(1), 90–103 (2007)
47. Slade, E.L., et al.: Modeling consumers' adoption intentions of remote mobile payments in the United Kingdom: extending UTAUT with innovativeness, risk, and trust. Psychol. Mark. **32**(8), 860–873 (2015)
48. Chandra, S., Srivastava, S.C., Theng, Y.-L.: Evaluating the role of trust in consumer adoption of mobile payment systems: an empirical analysis. Commun. Assoc. Inf. Syst. **27**(1), 561–588 (2010)
49. Jaradat, M.-I.R.M., Moustafa, A.A., Al-Mashaqba, A.M.: Exploring perceived risk, perceived trust, perceived quality and the innovative characteristics in the adoption of smart government services in Jordan. Int. J. Mobile Commun. **16**(4), 399–439 (2018)
50. Venkatesh, V., et al.: User acceptance of information technology: toward a unified view. MIS Q. **27**(3), 425–478 (2003)
51. Kapoor, K.K., Dwivedi, Y.K., Williams, M.D.: Rogers' innovation adoption attributes: a systematic review and synthesis of existing research. Inf. Syst. Manag. **31**(1), 74–91 (2014)
52. Venkatesh, V., Bala, H.: Technology acceptance model 3 and a research agenda on interventions. Decis. Sci. **39**(2), 273–315 (2008)
53. Kranz, J.J.: The difference of determinants of mobile data services' adoption and continuance – a longitudinal study (2012)
54. Shin, D.-H.: User acceptance of mobile Internet: implication for convergence technologies. Interact. Comput. **19**(4), 472–483 (2007)
55. Henseler, J., Ringle, C.M., Sarstedt, M.: A new criterion for assessing discriminant validity in variance-based structural equation modeling. J. Acad. Mark. Sci. **43**(1), 115–135 (2014). https://doi.org/10.1007/s11747-014-0403-8
56. Hair, J.F., Ringle, C.M., Sarstedt, M.: PLS-SEM: indeed a silver bullet. J. Mark. Theory Pract. **19**(2), 139–152 (2011)
57. Wold, H.: Partial least squares. In: Encyclopedia of Statistical Sciences (1985)
58. Henseler, J., Ringle, C.M., Sinkovics, R.R.: The use of partial least squares path modeling in international marketing. Adv. Int. Mark. **20**, 277–319 (2009)

59. Fornell, C., Larcker, D.F.: Evaluating structural equation models with unobservable variables and measurement error. J. Mark. Res. **18**, 39–50 (1981)
60. Voorhees, C.M., Brady, M.K., Calantone, R., Ramirez, E.: Discriminant validity testing in marketing: an analysis, causes for concern, and proposed remedies. J. Acad. Mark. Sci. **44**(1), 119–134 (2015). https://doi.org/10.1007/s11747-015-0455-4
61. Hair, J.F.: Multivariate Data Analysis, 6th edn. Pearson Prentice Hall, Upper Saddle River (2006). xxiv, 899 p.
62. Hair, J.F., et al.: A Primer on Partial Least Squares Structural Equations Modeling (PLS-SEM). SAGE Publications (2014)
63. Venkatesh, V., Thong, J., Xu, X.: Consumer acceptance and use of information technology: extending the unified theory of acceptance and use of technology. MIS Q. **36**(1), 157–178 (2012)
64. Tamilmani, K., Rana, N.P., Dwivedi, Y.K.: Consumer acceptance and use of information technology: a meta-analytic evaluation of UTAUT2. Inf. Syst. Front. **2020**, 1–19 (2020). https://doi.org/10.1007/s10796-020-10007-6
65. Hernandez, J.M.C., Mazzon, J.A.: Adoption of internet banking: proposition and implementation of an integrated methodology approach. Int. J. Bank Mark. **25**, 72–88 (2007)
66. Nickerson, R., Austreich, M., Eng, J.: Mobile technology and smartphone apps: a diffusion of innovations analysis (2014)
67. Kim, Y., et al.: Analyzing user's intention and innovation diffusion of smartphones. In: 2010 Proceedings of the 5th International Conference on Ubiquitous Information Technologies and Applications. IEEE (2010)
68. Qualtrics. Qualtrics: What is Qualtrics? (2020). Accessed 20 Mar 2020. https://csulb.libgui des.com/qualtrics
69. Statista: Smartphone ownership (2020)
70. Statista. Number of apps available in leading app stores as of 1st quarter 2018 (2018). https:// www.statista.com/statistics/276623/number-of-apps-available-in-leading-app-stores/

# Transferring Customers Trust and Loyalty on Offline Banks Towards Online Payment Platforms in Integrated Ecosystem

Bo-chiuan Su[1], Li-Wei Wu[2(✉)], and Ying-Chi Yen[3]

[1] Department of Information Management, National Dong Hwa University, Hualien, Taiwan
bsu@gms.ndhu.edu.tw
[2] Department of International Business, Tunghai University, Taichung City, Taiwan
lwwu@thu.edu.tw
[3] Citibank, Taipei, Taiwan

**Abstract.** Cashless society is becoming popular due to the advanced development of technology. The ubiquity of mobile payment is astounding. Consumers have shifting from physical to mobile payment, making payment process more convenient and seamlessness. This paper is exploring the possibility of transferring customers trust and loyalty on offline banks to online payment platforms. Customers can extend their positive evaluations of the online channel to the offline channel by the halo effect. Particularly, based on the synergistic combination, the offline bank and the online payment platforms may collaborate to enhance customer's payment stickiness and create a more integrated ecosystem. To address these research questions, we analyze 353 users. A LISERSL for Structural Equation Modeling was used to test the research hypotheses, indicating a good fit of measurement model. Eight of the ten research hypotheses are supported. The results show significant transferring customers trust on offline banks to online payment platforms, but perceived quality has no significant effect on transferring customers trust on offline banks to online payment platforms. Offline bank loyalty has significantly positively affected online payment platforms loyalty, proving the halo effect. Theoretical and practical implications are provided.

**Keywords:** Mobile payment · Trust · Corporate reputation · Perceived risk · Perceived quality · Structural assurance

## 1 Introduction

Mobile payment is defined as a combination between mobile device and payment system that enables users making payment process through mobile devices [1]. Despite the concept of non-monetary system has a long history, it is only the advancement of technology and support such system that make mobile payments prevalent.

Although mobile payment is still way behind traditional payment methods in terms of usage frequency on the basis of PricewaterhouseCoopers market survey. From the global perspective, the mobile payment market had grown from $450 billion to $1800

© Springer Nature Switzerland AG 2021
F. F.-H. Nah and K. Siau (Eds.): HCII 2021, LNCS 12783, pp. 293–306, 2021.
https://doi.org/10.1007/978-3-030-77750-0_19

billion in 2015 to 2019. Based on the report by Mordor Intelligence has predicted that mobile payments are becoming the second most common payment method after debit cards by 2022.

From the domestic perspective, the cognition of the mobile payment has reached up to 96.6% in Taiwan. The government has declared that the penetration rate of mobile payment will reach up to 60% by 2020 and 90% by 2025. To strengthen industrial cooperation and integration, different industry including payment operators, financial operators and so on have dedicated to participate the development of such technologies.

The popularity of mobile devices has spawned the development of the fintech industry and industry cross-border integration have let customer behaviors turn into a virtual way on payments. The popularity of mobile devices has gradually become a development trend. In order to keep up with the trend, many traditional bankers are also proactively giving consumers more convenient services, and allied with mobile payment platforms in order to attract more users and provide users with better services to enhance customer stickiness so as to gain more customer size to react to a volatile market.

For the research purpose, as we have mentioned that there are rarely studies about the relationship between partners who collaborate in the mobile payment industry, therefore, we want to explore the correlations between issuing banks and payment platforms to see whether there are any psychological impact while using physical and virtual credit cards as the medium. As for the contribution of this study, the issuing bank and the payment platform provider could have a concept for what they should focus on to enhance consumers' or users' confidence toward the offline side and the online side. Not merely does the payment providers should focus on consumers experience, but likewise the internal improvement of itself is also a significant part.

## 2   Literature Review and Hypotheses

### 2.1   Trust

Trust is defined as the willingness of a party to be susceptible to the actions of another party based on the expectation that the other will perform a particular action important to the trustor (Hong and Cho, 2011). From a psychological perspective, some scholars believe that trust is a state comprising the intention to accept vulnerability based upon positive expectations of the intentions or behavior of another (Rousseau, Sitkin, Burt and Camerer, 1998). In addition, trust can be build-up by one party's positive response and generate the other's expectation.

This study distinguishes trust into offline and online trust. Offline trust represents the attitude toward the issuing bank services of the physical credit card while the online trust represents the attitude toward the payment platform system of the virtual credit card. Trust in issuing banks and other financial institutions is crucial for the functioning of the banking system and for society as a whole [2]. Offline trust can build by customers' perception of a belief to the physical card that could provide reliable services to meet their needs based on the financial procedures and its issuing bank's reputation and so on.

On the other hand, in a mobile commerce environment, prior studies have also identified trust as of most important antecedents that facilitate customers' acceptance and succeeding usage of m-payment in various situations [2]. Online trust involves user's perception of the faith to the virtual card on the platform that could provide a stable and secure transaction for users.

## 2.2 Trust Transfer

Contemporary Internet-oriented world has made trust transfer further significant for marketers to study the interaction between offline and online channels when analyzing customer behavior [3]. Trust transfer is a process that a cognitive one in which the trust in one domain has an influence on attitudes and perceptions in another domain [4]. The trust transfer process is related to how one's trust in a familiar target can be transferred to another target because there exist certain associations [5]. Apply to this study, we will explore the trust transfer due to the different context of the physical card of the issuing bank and the virtual credit card on the platform. However, there is little research on trust transfer from the offline to the online mobile domain as the latter is relatively new. So far, this study has focused on the transfer between offline and online mobile domain. Thus, we consider that credit cards are an intermediary between the offline and the online. Therefore, the trust in the entity services of the card will affect positive perception of the virtual services of the card. Therefore, we have:

H1: Trust towards the issuing bank will positively affect trust towards the payment platform.

## 2.3 Loyalty

It is defined that customer loyalty as a mentality of having a good attitude towards the company, promising to repurchase the company's products or services and recommending to others (Pearson, 1996). Loyalty is also defined as the repeated purchase behavior presented over a period of time due to a favorable attitude toward the subject from both attitude and behavioral aspects [6].

In this study, we distinguished loyalty into offline loyalty toward the bank which provides physical credit card and online loyalty toward the platform which provide virtual credit card. The offline loyalty is the service or the product loyalty [7], thus, we accounted offline loyalty indicates the customer will tend to use the service of the bank they are assured. With respect to the service loyalty, it is considered to repurchase or reuse only this provider when the certain services or products are needed [8]. In the offline environment, high level of trust allows parties to focus on the long-term benefits of the relationship [9]. Customers may feel the reliance of the services which issuing bank provides and tend to use it in the long-term. Therefore, we have:

H2-1: Trust towards the bank will positively affect loyalty towards the bank.

Online loyalty is regarded as the users will prefer using virtual credit card that the payment platform they are assured and further provides multi-services for the users. Loyalty towards online side is defined as a user's intention to do more transaction and recommend it to other people [10]. Thus, their intention may drive them to use the virtual credit card on the platform in the long-term. Numerous studies found that trust has positive effect on customer loyalty and also emphasized it is fundamental determinant of customer loyalty in online environment [11]. On the online platform, customer may prefer to transact on the online environment which they are accustomed to and trustworthy for them due to the high level of risk perception. Therefore, we have:

H2-2: Trust towards the payment platform will positively affect loyalty towards the payment platform.

## 2.4 Loyalty Transfer

Many transactions that start in the online environment are performed in the offline environment [12] and the results obtained in the offline environment have an impact on the online environment [13]. According to halo effect proposed by Thorndike [14] the entire assessment affects one's response to other attributes, or the impression of one attribute affects the impression of other independent attributes [15]. In other words, customers can extend their positive evaluations of the online channel to the offline channel by the halo effect. By means of offering a multi-channel of services to meet customer needs will leads to increased customer loyalty [16]. Based on the synergistic combination, the issuing bank and the payment platform may collaborate on launching programs to enhance customers stickiness on both sides of the system. As a result, customers transfer existing attitudes and beliefs built from offline side to online side. Therefore, we have:

H3: Loyalty towards the bank will positively affect loyalty towards the payment platform.

## 2.5 Corporate Reputation

Reputation is considered to be one of the main standards to assess the trustworthiness of a potential trustee. The company's reputation is considered as a means to win the trust of stakeholders, and therefore to obtain their continuous support and commitment to help ensure the long-term sustainability of the organization [17]. Furthermore, the second-hand information or word of mouth can influence a person's perception of service when they do not have first-hand knowledge of the company. As confidence is a crucial factor in the creation of relational trust [18], while the company possess a favorable reputation, it can strengthen customers' confidence and lower risk perceptions when they make judgment on organizational performance and quality of products or services [19], and even result in a munificent revenue and greater value in the market [20]. Good corporate reputation can bring advantages for the issuing bank. In order to establish good reputation, therefore, we considered that customers will contact physically and processed banking directly to the issuing bank which is well-known or with high reputation in the market, and at the psychological level customers trust will increase when the bank has a high reputable impression toward customers. Therefore, we have:

H4: Corporate reputation will positively affect trust on the bank.

## 2.6 Perceived Risk

The concept of perceived risk is defined as an attribute of a decision alternative that reflects the variance of its possible outcomes. An attribute of the conceptualization of perceived risk within consumer psychology is mainly from the potentially negative outcomes [21].

The level of perceived risk is mainly supported by the purchase situation [22] when the transaction process is related to finance problems, therefore, good caring of the physical credit card service improves the usage situation of customers toward the issuing bank. Brand trust can reduce risk perception in an offline context, and the cognitive dimension plays a vital role in this environment [14]. As discussed above, perceived risk is concerned with the unfavorable result on physical card services, the reason is likely caused by the experience and might affect the customer's impression of the issuing bank. They might feel anxious if they have a hardly ideal experience, thus, customers will diminish their trust on the issuing bank. Therefore, we have:

H5-1: Perceived risk will negatively affect trust on the bank.

Risk about the technology being used becomes integral to customer decisions while engaged in mobile payments. Concerns over privacy risks have negative influence on perceptions of security [23]. Customers may pay more attention to their rights and interests; therefore, they form a higher risk perception of internet commerce [24]. While they are not familiar with the mobile payment, customers might have a resistive mentality on psychological aspect if virtual credit card embed on the platform have no stable and secure protection. They might diminish their trust on the payment platform. In addition, the financial loss is also one of the major concerns on an impediment to the adoption of mobile payment [2]. Overall, hesitation on using virtual credit card on the payment platform might have a negative impact on customers' degree of trust. Therefore, we have:

H5-2: Perceived risk will negatively affect trust on the payment platform.

## 2.7 Perceived Quality

Perceived quality is determined as the customer's perception of the overall quality or superiority of a product or service relative to alternatives regarding its intended purpose (Zeithaml, 1988). Perceived quality is also defined as the consumers' judgments about physical services including integrated excellence or superiority [25]. Different from the objective quality, which used to describe technical advantages of a product, perceived quality may not exist and invaluable because all qualities are comprehend in distinct perception by someone [26].

In this research, we distinguished the perceived quality between the service quality of the issuing bank and the system quality of the payment platform. Service quality is derived from the comparison between what is provided and what the customer feels should be offered [27]. And the perception of service quality is derived by comparing expectations with perceptions of performance [28]. In the research, we will apply to the performance of physical card services of the issuing bank. Those invisible soft power may affect customers' trustworthiness and enhance their willingness of usage of the services. Therefore, we have:

H6-1: Perceived quality will positively affect trust on the bank services.

So as to increase the perceived quality level of a website requires convincing users that the website is promptly and precise, and will provide helpful information [29]. While people using the virtual credit card on the payment platform, they not merely attracted by the convenience but likewise the system's feature will also affect their attitude to the usage of the mobile payment. The convenience of using the platform interface is also an important factor which affects customers' perception of the system quality. System quality including navigational structure and visual appeal on the platform will affects users' trust in mobile commerce technologies. With a stable and reliable system of the transaction and the friendly layout of the payment platform comes the reduction of users' potential risk and strengthen their sense of trust. Therefore, we have:

H6-2: Perceived quality will positively affect trust on the payment platform system.

### 2.8 Structure Assurance

Structural assurance means the belief in the web having a protective legal or technical structure [30] to ensure that web business can be carried out safely and reliably. In terms of security and privacy, the online environment exist high risk and additional uncertainties compared to an offline environment; therefore, consumers would respond well to such structural assurances [31]. Due to the lack of direct experience and knowledge about online system of mobile payments, users may depend much on the structural assurance to build their trust from mobile payments. Previous studies also demonstrate that structure assurance of the online environment positively affects users' trust. For the Internet has a high standard of structural assurance, it will produce a sense of structurally guaranteed security, so people are more likely to rely upon specific Internet providers [32]. It could be demonstrated that structural assurance of the virtual card on the payment platform should affect willingness to depend on the platform provider since high structural assurance indicates consumers have been capable of prevailing over fears of the online side such that they are comfortable dealing with it. Therefore, we have:

H7: Structure assurance will positively affect trust on the payment platform.

## 3   Research Methodology

### 3.1   Conceptual Framework

These relationships can be summarized in the conceptual framework as the following Fig. 1:

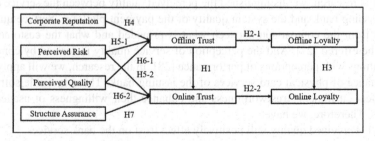

**Fig. 1.** Conceptual framework

## 3.2 Sample and Data Collection

This research collected data throughout paper-based questionnaires and web-based questionnaires through Google. The questionnaires were survey for those people who have experience in using the banking services and in using mobile payment platform when processing payment for goods or services. The duration of data collection lasted from February 4, 2020 to April 10, 2020. In total, 445 were delivered as the online questionnaire and 74 were delivered as the paper questionnaire, all entries were returned by both ways, with a returning rate of 100%. 353 out of 519 questionnaires were valid (68% valid rate).

The respondent demographic characteristics show as follows: gender (male, 44%; female, 56%), age (less than or equal to 20 years of age, 7.4%; 21–30 years of age, 37%; 31–40 years of age, 15%; 41–50 years of age, 16%; greater than or equal to 51 years of age, 25%), education (high school graduate, 3.4%; high school diploma or equivalent, 4.2%; bachelor degree, 34.8%; master degree or above, 57.5%).

## 3.3 Analysis Method

**Validation of Measures.** The Cronbach's alphas of all constructs were all greater than 0.70, supporting the reliability of the measurement. In addition, all composite reliabilities were greater than 0.60 and most of the average variance extracted (AVE) estimates were greater than 0.50 [33] except for perceived risk, which means the perceived risk has no convergence validity. Discriminant validity was tested between all constructs according to Fornell and Larcker [34] recommendations and confirmed for all pairs of constructs. Specifically, AVE estimate for each construct was greater than the squared correlation of all construct pairs. Table 1 shows the means, standard deviations, and correlations matrix for the constructs.

**Table 1.** Means, standard deviations, and correlation matrix

|      | Mean  | S. D  | CR      | PR      | PQ      | SA      | OFFT    | ONT     | OFFL    | ONL   |
|------|-------|-------|---------|---------|---------|---------|---------|---------|---------|-------|
| CR   | 4.259 | 0.594 | 0.814   |         |         |         |         |         |         |       |
| PR   | 2.513 | 0.896 | − .124** | 0.675   |         |         |         |         |         |       |
| PQ   | 4.131 | 0.577 | .503**  | − .273** | 0.736   |         |         |         |         |       |
| SA   | 4.077 | 0.678 | .452**  | − .241** | .763**  | 0.863   |         |         |         |       |
| OFFT | 4.136 | 0.616 | .587**  | − .225** | .716**  | .648**  | 0.785   |         |         |       |
| ONT  | 4.113 | 0.642 | .494**  | − .283** | .744**  | .760**  | .726**  | 0.835   |         |       |
| OFFL | 4.132 | 0.737 | .523**  | − .184** | .602**  | .506**  | .707**  | .578**  | 0.847   |       |
| ONL  | 4.044 | 0.805 | .385**  | − .249** | .670**  | .628**  | .558**  | .703**  | .570**  | 0.894 |

# 4 Data Analysis and Empirical Results

## 4.1 Structural Equation Modeling

The hypothesized relationships in the model were tested simultaneously through SEM. The standardized path coefficients of the structural model as estimated by LISREL are given in Table 2. The fit of the model was as following (NFI = 0.952, RFI = 0.948, IFI = 0.965, CFI = 0.965, PNFI = 0.883, PGFI = 0.625, RMR = 0.051, RMSEA = 0.093). In the above model, NFI, RFI, CFI were greater than the suggested 0.9. These three fit indices indicate a good fit of measurement model.

## 4.2 Hypotheses Test

According to the results, H1 is supported as offline trust will have a positive effect on online trust ($\beta = 0.355$, t = 4.838). Furthermore, in terms of variables of trust toward loyalty, H2-1 and H2-2 which affirmed that offline trust is positively related to offline loyalty and online trust is positively related to online loyalty ($\beta = 0.885$, t = 15.003) ($\beta = 0.763$, t = 10.731), thus H2-1 and H2-2 are supported. Additionally, H3 is supported since offline loyalty will have positive effect on online loyalty ($\beta = 0.290$, t = 4.102). The positive relationship between corporate reputation and offline trust in H4 is also supported ($\gamma = 0.289$, t = 6.818). H5-1 and H5-2 are indicate the same direction, which means that perceived risk will have negative effect on offline trust and online trust, however, the result has shown that H5-1 is not supported ($\gamma = 0.019$, t = 0.550), on the other hand, H5-2 is supported as the path is significant ($\gamma = 0.289$, t = 6.818). Subsequently, H6-1 and H6-2 are affirmed perceived quality have positive effect on both offline trust and online trust, yet the evidences have the opposite result since H6–1 is supported ($\gamma = 0.662$, t = 10.929) but H6-2 is not supported ($\gamma = 0.166$, t = 1.526). Structure assurance have a positive influence on online trust ($\gamma = 0.459$, t = 6.637), therefore, H7 is supported.

**Table 2.** Path analysis

| Path | | $\beta/\gamma$ | t-value | P-value | Results |
|---|---|---|---|---|---|
| H1 | Offline Trust Online Trust | $\beta = 0.355$ | 4.838 | *** | Supported |
| H2-1 | Offline Trust Offline Loyalty | $\beta = 0.885$ | 15.003 | *** | Supported |
| H2-2 | Online Trust Online Loyalty | $\beta = 0.763$ | 10.731 | *** | Supported |
| H3 | Offline Loyalty Online Loyalty | $\beta = 0.290$ | 4.102 | *** | Supported |
| H4 | Corporate Reputation Offline Trust | $\gamma = 0.289$ | 6.818 | *** | Supported |
| H5-1 | Perceived Risk Offline Trust | $\gamma = 0.019$ | 0.550 | P > .05 | Not Supported |
| H5-2 | Perceived Risk Online Trust | $\gamma = 0.289$ | −2.626 | *** | Supported |
| H6-1 | Perceived Quality Offline Trust | $\gamma = 0.662$ | 10.929 | *** | Supported |
| H6–2 | Perceived Quality Online Trust | $\gamma = 0.166$ | 1.526 | P > .05 | Not Supported |
| H7 | Structural Assurance Online Trust | $\gamma = 0.459$ | 6.637 | *** | Supported |

# 5 Discussion and Suggestions

## 5.1 Discussion and Conclusions

**Offline Trust, Online Trust, Offline Loyalty and Online Loyalty.** According to the statistical analysis results, offline trust has a significant effect on online trust in terms of the different environment of the physical card issued by the bank and the virtual card embed in the payment platform. Such outcome is slightly similar to the previous researches whereas the trust is mostly based on the same brand in an offline firm to an online business [3]. In this study, users have faith toward the issuing bank which will do the right and moral things, thus, regarding the credit card as an intermediary of the offline and online side, customers reliance will also transfer to the online environment and believing the trading contract process on the payment platform.

In addition, trust has positively influence loyalty from both offline and online context. As numerous preceding studies had affirmatory results of effects on trust toward loyalty in the certain services or products [7], customers are tending to have a positive attitude toward the service or the product, further, recommend their own positive views to others. From the offline bank, since customers have confidence attitude toward the services, including services of employees or accounting services of the issuing bank which will be the profound expression of the bank. Therefore, perfect and sound accounting services will also attract users and further recommend to people around them through word of mouth and turn their faithful into loyal attitude.

From the online mobile payment platform, due to the complete and immediate service of the virtual credit card, further trust the system provides by the payment platform, it will enhance reliance toward the payment platform. The online trust for the system refers to this study indicates such as its stability and immediacy regarding to the transaction process. With respect to the user, while possessing truthfulness toward the virtual card which will provide immediate transaction on the payment platform, they will have tendency on using the payment system repeatedly and it is not easy for them to switch to another payment platform. Therefore, when users are accustomed using the mobile payment platform, the online trust will influence positively on the online loyalty of payment system. Furthermore, also increases users' stickiness on the platform.

Based on the analysis outcomes, offline loyalty has positively affected online loyalty. It had mentioned that the halo effect will play a part in two different attributes and enhance customers' loyalty. In this study, while customers have held the loyalty from the offline issuing bank of its services, they will prone to use the physical credit card which bank provides. Simultaneously, owing to the virtual credit cards embed in the payment platform, the effect will thence transfer to the online payment platform. Furthermore, as the description we have addressed in the previous section as regards the offline trust will have a significant and a positively influence toward the offline loyalty and the online trust, therefore, it has a forceful evidence to prove that there is a transformation from offline loyalty to online loyalty.

**Corporate Reputation, Perceived Risk, Perceived Quality, Structure Assurance, Offline Trust and Online Trust.** Corporate reputation is a criterion that evaluate the level of trustworthiness of a potential trustee, since customers will tend to use the issuing bank of the physical credit card, which has a high recognition from them due to the status in the market, and the corporate reputation will deeply rooted in their heart. Believing the bank which they have used will be responsible on the financial services and establish the moral standard, customers will trust the value of the bank. As the high attention or influence of the bank among the financial market, it will affect the economic pulse of the entire financial industry, further customers will prone to entrust their confidence on the offline bank as a result of status and further believe services of the physical credit card.

The experimental evidence on effect on perceived risk toward offline trust. It shows that perceived risk does not have significant influence on offline trust. Since physical credit cards of issuing banks have been in the market for a long history, customers have ingrained knowledge of physical credit cards and do not have concerns about its services or even mode of operation. Customers feel more relieved by means of using the actual cards while its services are more familiar with to them. On the other hand, the consequence of the analysis examination of perceived risk to the online trust is similar to the earlier paragraph, which had mentioned that customers will have concerns about the reliability or the resistance mentality toward unfamiliar objects. Since perceived risk affect the level of online trust, users are not willing to use the virtual credit card on the mobile payment due to certain apprehensions. Consequently, anxiety caused by perceived risk will lead to diminished customers truthfulness and reliance on the online payment platform.

It is demonstrated by survey results that the perceived quality providing positive outcomes toward the offline trust is in accordance with the previous study which had elaborated the service quality is derived from customers expectation of certain performances [28]. Consumers will take notice of its completeness and immediacy on the service system construction. Further, their perception on the service quality will have an impact on the reliance of the physical credit card and further toward the issuing bank. Moreover, the result of the analysis of perceived quality has no positive effect on the online trust. The insignificant result may cause from the following two reasons. From platform providers' view, they prone to offer comprehensive services to gain stickiness from users and lead to messy platform interfaces, yet consumers are easily accepted streamlined information, therefore, they may be confused when browsing the platform interface. The other is that the users may not familiar with the mobile payment system may lead to some doubts about its professional ability of system on mobile payment. Therefore, perceived quality did not positively affect online trust on payment platforms.

At last, the factor of structure assurance has a directly effect on online trust in the line with the extent literature which had discovered the structural assurances have a significant influence when parties involved in the financial transactions via online channels [35]. Employing the theories to examine the influence of the structural assurance on the online trust, it can show that the mobile payment platform users will perceive security and privacy when the virtual card provides sound protection mechanism to users. Thus, it will further cause them to build their confidence upon the payment platform. While they are accustomed to deal with the financial transaction with the virtual card on the payment platform, it will enhance their online trust toward system of the virtual card and the platform.

## 5.2  Managerial Implications

We have several practical suggestions to both offline and online side of the payment providers. To start with, offline issuing banks should put more effort on enhancing customers trust of its credit cards services, involving benefits from purchasing, experience using counter services by the staff or even the problem of credit card fraud could cause their reliance of the issuing bank. Once customers have the confidence of bank services, it is important for retaining the customer by aiming their target customers and providing suitable services for the purpose of strengthening their loyalty. Likewise, from the online perspective, payment platform should pay more attention on customer trust of its payment system service, including secured transactions, virtualization of various services and feedbacks. For the purpose of attracting more users, it should collaborate with more issuing banks and service providers in order to create a more integrated ecosystem.

In addition, favorable reputation of the issuing bank will induce customers to take further steps to banking services and increase the customers trust of the issuing bank. For instance, it should protect the rights and interests of consumers, which is indispensable duty and an objective requirement for improving its business development level. In terms of the perceived quality, the bank could strengthen service awareness by cultivating good service attitude and improve customers experience by providing multiple service contents. In this case, due to good reputation and perfect perceived quality, the issuing bank will gain more users and increase reliance from them rapidly.

For online payment platform providers, it should take an eye on customers perception of platform risk and the structure assurance of the transaction system. While the virtual credit card embeds on the platform, users will be affected by the risk of the platform system. When consumers have lack knowledge of online system, they will refuse to accept the new payment method. Thus, the platform provider could put more effort on simplifying payment operation mode further reduce users' doubts and make ease of use about the payment platform. Our finding revealed that the structure assurance plays an essential role on payment platform. Users may have certain concerns including the procedure of transaction and their personal information. Platform provides should establish a secure and private environment for users. For instance, they could establish a more complete security verification mechanism on the platform and update it regularly. Wherefore, as a result of the protecting users' transaction, they can lower their anxiety on the online environment.

For the purpose of achieving the goal of cashless society, the issue of people's trust has received considerable critical attention to be discussed. Entity and virtual payment providers could figure out what factors are relatively considerable in their service procedures and come up with suitable solutions for their target customers and further increase their trust and loyalty. Moreover, payment providers could collaborate with multi merchants launching more convenient and preferential services to draw consumers and assimilate mobile payment into their daily lives for increasing trust and decrease risk from using the payment service.

## 5.3  Limitations and Future Research

The empirical results reported herein should be considered in the light of several limitations. The first is the collected questionnaires are non-randomly on account of the respondents are mostly students and young people, therefore, there may be differences with regard to the pre-factors that they valued. The second limitation concerns the questionnaire was delivered to participants mainly throughout the Internet. It may neglect the results of those respondents who might not accustomed to use the mobile payment and resulting in the response of trust and loyalty, and it may let slip the potential customers who are not willing to fill in the survey. Third, regional restrictions should also be pondered due to customers who have used the mobile payment are mostly in urban areas, thus, it may lead to incomplete consequences. The fourth limitation factor is considered that there are little researches about transfer between the offline and online mobile side in the past, For the reason that there may not be adequate literatures on the research structure. The last is that the promotion may be essential to customers attitude and behavior on mobile payment. When there are new preferential schemes, some customers may shift to other payment platform, there may be no loyalty to them at all as a consequence.

For future research, Internet-only banking have launched out in the recent year. Although it still provides physical credit cards and other services for users, however, the business model is different from physical banks. Therefore, researchers may figure out some not similar influences on the issues. Furthermore, different cultures of people may have different level of trust toward the payment platform based on the habits of usage. For instance, the penetration rate of mobile payment of Britain and China is much greater than that of Taiwan, thence, people may have less risk or other attitude on payment platforms. Last, subsequent researchers may add different variables on the relationship for the level of customers trust for more outcome of the research.

# References

1. Srivastava, S.C., Chandra, S., Theng, Y.L.: Evaluating the role of trust in consumer adoption of mobile payment systems: an empirical analysis. Commun. Assoc. Inf. Syst. 27(1), 561–588 (2010)
2. Liébana-Cabanillas, F., Sánchez-Fernández, J., Muñoz-Leiva, F.: Antecedents of the adoption of the new mobile payment systems: the moderating effect of age. Comput. Hum. Behav. 35, 464–478 (2014)
3. Lee, K.C., Kang, I., McKnight, D.H.: Transfer from offline trust to key online perceptions: an empirical study. IEEE Trans. Eng. Manag. 54(4), 729–741 (2007)
4. Lu, Y., Yang, S., Chau, P.Y., Cao, Y.: Dynamics between the trust transfer process and intention to use mobile payment services: a cross-environment perspective. Inf. Manag. 48(8), 393–403 (2001)
5. Kim, D.J.: Self-perception-based versus transference-based trust determinants in computer mediated transactions: a cross-cultural comparison study. J. Manag. Inf. Syst. 24(4), 13–45 (2008)
6. Keller, K.L.: Conceptualizing, measuring, and managing customer-based brand equity. J. Mark. 57(1), 1–22 (1993)
7. Lim, K.S., Razzaque, M.A.: Brand loyalty and situational effects: an interactionist perspective. J. Int. Consum. Mark. 9(4), 95–115 (1997)
8. Gremler, D.D., Brown, S.W.: Service loyalty: its nature, importance, and implications. Adv. Serv. Qual.: Global Perspect. 5(1), 171–181 (1996)
9. Ganesan, S.: Determinants of long-term orientation in buyer-seller relationships. J. Mark. 58(2), 1–19 (1994)

10. Chen, J., Zhang, C., Xu, Y.: The role of mutual trust in building members' loyalty to a C2C platform provider. Int. J. Electron. Commer. **14**(1), 147–171 (2009)
11. Doney, P.M., Cannon, J.P.: An examination of the nature of trust in buyer-seller relationships. J. Mark. **61**(2), 35–51 (1997)
12. Kim, J., Jin, B., Swinney, J.L.: The role of retail quality, e-satisfaction and e-trust in online loyalty development process. J. Retail. Consum. Serv. **16**(4), 239–247 (2009)
13. Forgas, S., Palau, R., Sánchez, J., Huertas-García, R.: Online drivers and offline influences related to loyalty to airline websites. J. Air Transp. Manag. **18**(1), 43–46 (2012)
14. Tedeschi, M., Galli, G., Martini, M.C.: On and off-line purchase intention: the role of brand trust as moderator of risk perception. J. Emerg. Trends Mark. Manag. **1**(1), 194–203 (2017)
15. Nisbett, R.E., Wilson, T.D.: The Halo effect: evidence for unconscious alteration of judgments. J. Pers. Soc. Psychol. **35**(4), 250 (1977)
16. Shankar, V., Smith, A.K., Rangaswamy, A.: Customer satisfaction and loyalty in online and offline environments. Int. J. Res. Mark. **20**(2), 153–175 (2003)
17. Van Der Merwe, A.W., Puth, G.: Towards a conceptual model of the relationship between corporate trust and corporate reputation. Corp. Reput. Rev. **17**(2), 138–156 (2014)
18. Morgan, R.M., Hunt, S.D.: The commitment-trust theory of relationship marketing. J. Mark. **58**(3), 20–38 (1994)
19. Keh, H.T., Xie, Y.: Corporate reputation and customer behavioral intentions: the roles of trust, identification and commitment. Ind. Mark. Manag. **38**(7), 732–742 (2009)
20. Smith, K.T., Smith, M., Wang, K.: Does brand management of corporate reputation translate into higher market value? J. Strateg. Mark. **18**(3), 201–221 (2010)
21. Dholakia, U.M.: A motivational process model of product involvement and consumer risk perception. Eur. J. Mark. **35**(11/12), 1340–1362 (2001)
22. Dowling, G.R., Staelin, R.: A model of perceived risk and intended risk-handling activity. J. Consum. Res. **21**(1), 119–134 (1994)
23. Johnson, V.L., Kiser, A., Washington, R., Torres, R.: Limitations to the rapid adoption of M-payment services: understanding the impact of privacy risk on M-Payment services. Comput. Hum. Behav. **79**, 111–122 (2018)
24. Corbitt, B.J., Thanasankit, T., Yi, H.: Trust and e-commerce: a study of consumer perceptions. Electron. Commer. Res. Appl. **2**(3), 203–215 (2003)
25. Snoj, B., Pisnik Korda, A., Mumel, D.: The relationships among perceived quality, perceived risk and perceived product value. J. Product Brand Manag. **13**(3), 156–167 (2004)
26. Zeithaml, V.A.: Consumer perceptions of price, quality, and value: a means-end model and synthesis of evidence. J. Mark. **52**(3), 2–22 (1988)
27. Parasuraman, A., Zeithaml, V.A., Berry, L.L.: A conceptual model of service quality and its implications for future research. J. Mark. **49**(4), 41–50 (1985)
28. Rowley, J.: Quality measurement in the public sector: some perspectives from the service quality literature. Total Qual. Manag. **9**(2/3), 321–333 (1998)
29. Everard, A., Galletta, D.F.: How presentation flaws affect perceived site quality, trust, and intention to purchase from an online store. J. Manag. Inf. Syst. **22**(3), 56–95 (2005)
30. Borenstein, N.S.: Perils and pitfalls of practical cybercommerce. Commun. ACM **39**(6), 36–44 (1996)
31. Wu, G., Hu, X., Wu, Y.: Effects of perceived interactivity, perceived web assurance and disposition to trust on initial online trust. J. Comput.-Mediat. Commun. **16**(1), 1–26 (2010)
32. Van Esterik-Plasmeijer, P., Van Raaij, W.F.: Banking system trust, bank trust, and bank loyalty. Int. J. Bank Mark. **35**(1), 97–111 (2017)
33. McKnight, D.H., Chervany, N.L.: Conceptualizing trust: a typology and E-commerce customer relationships model. In: Proceedings of the 34th Annual Hawaii International Conference on System Sciences, vol. 7, p. 7022 (2001)

34. Fornell, C., Larcker, D.F.: Evaluating structural equation models with unobservable variables and measurement error. J. Mark. Res. **18**(1), 39–50 (1981)

35. Kim, K.K., Prabhakar, B.: Initial trust and the adoption of B2C e-commerce: the case of internet banking. ACM SIGMIS Database: DATABASE Adv. Inf. Syst. **35**(2), 50–64 (2004)

# Information Technology as Enabler of Transparency in Food Supply Chains - An Empirical Study

Robert Zimmermann[1]([✉]), Werner Wetzlinger[1], Magdalena Mayer[2],
Gabriele Obermeier[1], and Andreas Auinger[1]

[1] University of Applied Sciences Upper Austria, Steyr, Austria
robert.zimmermann@fh-steyr.at
[2] HOFER KG, Hofer Straße 1, 4642 Sattledt, Austria

**Abstract.** Due to globalization, food supply chains are scattered around the globe. As a result, they become more complex and anonymous, potentially confusing customers of the food's origin and production conditions. In addition, due to higher living standards, consumers are demanding greater transparency in the food production process in terms of safety, quality, and sustainability. Simultaneously, technological developments have made various technologies available to track and provide information about food production to consumers at the physical Point of Sale (POS). However, current literature does not provide a comprehensive overview of technologies presenting transparent product information and guidelines about additional information consumers want to know. Therefore, the authors present a literature review of transparent product information and an outline of technologies to provide such information at the POS. Additionally, the authors present the results of an online survey highlighting the importance of individual transparent product information from a consumer point of view. Combining this information, the authors deduct guidelines on how to use technology to present transparent information to the consumer at the POS.

**Keywords:** Food supply chain · Transparency · Transparent product information

## 1 Introduction

Globalization permanently changed our economy, our lives, and consumer needs. Food travel distances have increased significantly while delivery times have shortened, resulting in a year-round season-independent food supply [1]. Meanwhile, consumers benefit from lower prices, higher quality, and a greater variety of food [2]. However, globalization has also increased the complexity and anonymity of food supply and value chains [3]. This unsettles consumers as it becomes difficult to understand the complex dynamics of today's food supply chains [1]. In addition, past food and livestock production related affairs, such as mad cow disease (BSE), swine fever, avian flu, and influenza, or the horsemeat scandal, have raised consumer awareness of food safety and drawn more

© Springer Nature Switzerland AG 2021
F. F.-H. Nah and K. Siau (Eds.): HCII 2021, LNCS 12783, pp. 307–323, 2021.
https://doi.org/10.1007/978-3-030-77750-0_20

attention to the production, processing, and distribution of our nutrition [4, 5]. Communicating the advantages of ecologically better food choices can positively influence consumers' purchase decisions [6]. Hence, global food supply chains are under increased pressure due to growing consumer demands [7] as their superior living standards imply that consumers are not only concerned about the taste but also about quality and authenticity [8]. Consumers have become more critical in recent years, demanding greater transparency in the food production process, wanting to be informed about the origins, processes of food procurement, the safety level, production methods, the use of pesticides, and the effects on environmental aspects [9]. Therefore, the traceability of food in global supply chains is of great importance [10]. However, current food supply chains show an information asymmetry towards the consumers, as the aspects of food safety and food quality are insufficiently transparent [11]. Though, for producers, traceability is also essential as it guarantees the quality of raw materials in the food chain, enables certification and approval of their products, and allows monitoring systems to be introduced [12]. Furthermore, with regard to corporate social responsibility, it is crucial to implement transparency in order to differentiate producers from other competitors [13]. Additionally, the sustainability of food supply chains is linked to social, ecological, and economic factors, which implies that increasing transparency and traceability of food supply chains has the potential to improve the social and environmental sustainability of food supplying companies' business practices [14].

Agrawal & Pal [15] emphasize that little is known about consumers' preferences regarding the provision of traceability information. New traceability technologies are available, and organizations are driven to use these technologies in order to offer additional information to their customers. However, the provision of large amounts of information is controversially discussed in literature as it can lead to information overload. Thus, Agrawal & Pal point out the necessity to separate between essential and non-essential information in order to enable an optimal exchange of information. In addition, the complexity of modern retail stores and personal time constraints force consumers to act economically and selective in their information intake [16]. However, this is countered by the fact that technological developments have made various technologies available that allow consumers to trace the path of food along the supply chain. Thus, making it easier for them to access product information providing transparency along the food supply chain (in the following: "transparent product information") and therefore supporting their decision-making process at the POS.

Previously published literature on transparent product information mainly focuses on the region of Asia (e.g. [16–19]). Additionally, a literature review done by Siddh et al. [20] illustrates that the majority of existing literature on food supply chain quality (from 1994–2016) concerns information, sustainability, and logistics management. However, only a minority of literature covers the management of food quality and safety [20]. With reference to this research gap, this study aims to find out more about consumers' preferences in German-speaking countries with regard to the use of technology at the POS and the most desired transparent product information.

Resulting from these problem fields, the authors derived the following research questions on food supply chain-related transparent product information.

RQ1: Which transparent product information can be provided according to previous research?

RQ2: Which transparent product information is most valuable for consumers?

RQ3: Which technology presenting transparent product information do consumers prefer?

The paper is structured in the following way: Following this introduction, the method section summarizes our literature review as well as the conducted survey. Subsequently, the results of the literature reviews and the survey are presented and discussed. The paper concludes with a summary of the results and provides implications for the field of HCI and opportunities for future work.

## 2   Method

This paper consists of a theoretical and an empirical part. The first research question is answered with a systematic literature review. Following the review, the paper presents an empirical investigation conducted in the form of an online survey. The results of the empirical part answer the second and third research questions. Combining the answers of all research questions, the authors deduct implications for companies and academics.

### 2.1   Literature Review

Various types of enabling technologies are available for the transparent presentation of supply chain information. For example, technologies for recording, storing, and transferring information (e.g., blockchains [21, 22]), linking between products and information (e.g., barcodes [23]), and enabling transparent product information to be displayed at the POS (e.g., smartphones [24]). However, due to the emerging trend of smart retail [25], a retail scenario that uses innovative technologies to enhance the shopping experience, we consider the POS a key element when providing transparent product information. This is because consumers often make unplanned purchases at the POS and thus can be influenced directly when making their purchase decision [25]. Therefore, this study focuses on technologies, which enable consumers to display information about the supply chain and the product directly in the store. From a typology of digital technology in stores, we considered the categories (i) *information/ product display technologies* and (ii) *information search technologies* and only included technologies that are used already to a certain extend (excluding technologies like *augmented reality* that few consumers have experience with) [26]:

- **Smartphones**: Smartphones are the most widely used personal mobile devices [27]. They are characterized by the fact that they are always at hand so that information can be received, recorded, or sent at any time. In retail stores, smartphones can be used to scan products and display associated information [24].
- **Smart Displays**: Smart displays are digital screens that display various content types among animated or interactive elements. In retail stores, smart displays can be placed above shelves to display additional information about products on the shelf [28].

- **Interactive In-Store Kiosks/Terminals**: In-store kiosk systems, also known as terminals, are free-standing, physical information and service units with touch-screen monitors. In-store kiosks provide an interface that allows users to interactively call up specific information, such as in-store navigation, purchase suggestions, or additional product characteristics [26].
- **Smart Shopping Carts**: Intelligent shopping carts, also known as smart trolleys or smart shopping carts, are equipped with scanners (e.g., hand scanners) and a screen (e.g., tablet). This provides additional services like scanning products to access further information or self-service payment [29].

The literature review to identify transparent product information elements, to be displayed via the above-listed technologies, was carried out from March to April 2020 in various online databases. It comprised the four steps shown in Fig. 1.

**Step 1:** In the first step, we used a predefined set of keywords on a predefined set of databases to identify relevant scientific papers and industry case studies. The following keywords were used to identify relevant papers and industry case studies: transparency OR traceability AND food AND "supply chain" AND "consumer preferences" AND sustainability OR quality. These keywords were used as search strings in the following databases: AIS, EBSCO Business Source Premier, Emerald Insight, Google Scholar, IEEE Xplore, Science Direct, Taylor and Francis, Web of Science, Wiley, WISO. This led to 15 articles and 7 industry case studies.

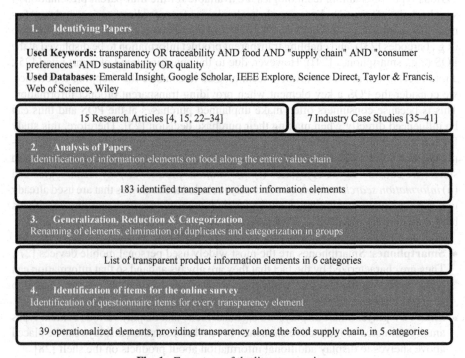

**Fig. 1.** Four steps of the literature review

**Step 2:** In the second step, we deducted relevant transparent product information elements from the papers and industry case studies. The identified papers also included studies that conducted literature reviews to identify characteristics that customers consider essential for assessing products and their supply chain (e.g. [15, 30, 31]). Thus, by analyzing these papers, 183 transparent product information elements could be identified. This included duplicate entries because numerous elements have been mentioned in multiple papers.

**Step 3:** Since transparent product information elements are named differently in the identified scientific papers and industry case studies, in a third step, we conducted a summarizing qualitative content analysis to consolidate them [32]. The elements were consolidated by renaming elements that were named differently but had the same meaning (generalization) and eliminating duplicate elements that resulted from this generalization process (reduction). This procedure resulted in a list of transparent product information elements that were further categorized (categorization) into the following groups (i) origin, (ii) freshness, (iii) cultivation & production methods, (iv) transport, (v) sustainability, and (vi) product properties. These categories facilitated the survey and analysis.

**Step 4:** In a final step, the identified transparent product information elements were operationalized for the online survey by generating items based on other questionnaires in the literature. Since the elements in the category (vi) product properties (e.g., price, packaging, brand, etc.) did not describe the characteristics of the food supply chain, this category was omitted. Consequently, this process led to 39 transparent product information items in five categories that were operationalized via survey items.

## 2.2 Online Survey

An empirical investigation was conducted using an online survey in Germany, Austria, and Switzerland between June 2, 2020, and June 20, 2020. To ensure comprehensiveness and understandability of the survey, and that no misunderstandings arise, a pretest with 15 persons was conducted. The survey aims to determine which transparent product information elements are most valuable for consumers and which technology presenting transparent product information consumers prefer. The elements identified in the literature review were used in the questionnaire to determine the elements of interest regarding product information transparency.

As a result of the survey, the elements are ranked based on the respondents' ranking, which elements they perceive as most valuable when shopping for groceries at the POS. Further, the survey provides results on the preference among four different technologies presenting transparent product information. The survey consists of 37 questions and is divided into six sections containing 32 closed or hybrid questions and 5 open questions. The outline of the survey is displayed in Table 1.

As suggested by Rugel et al. [18], nominally scaled questions, where there is concern that the order in which the answers are given will influence voting behavior, answer options were randomized. For questions with ordinally scaled answer options, the natural

**Table 1.** Survey outline

| Question | Source |
|---|---|
| **Shopping Behavior** | |
| Who is the person responsible for grocery shopping in your household? | [36] |
| For how many persons do you go grocery shopping? | |
| How would you describe your household? | |
| How often do you go grocery shopping? | [37] |
| In which shopping location do you do grocery shopping? | [38] |
| **Product Information** | |
| How important are these product characteristics for you when shopping for groceries? | SD |
| How important are these criteria when shopping for groceries? | |
| Please rank the importance of these product information when doing grocery shopping | |
| Are you satisfied with the product information currently available on the packaging/shelf? | [37] |
| Which product information are missing regarding origin, ingredients, production, transport, or sustainability? | |
| **Food Security** | |
| Which topics concern you the most when thinking about groceries? | [39] |
| What is your opinion regarding food safety? | |
| **Interest in transparency information** | |
| Which of the following information regarding the origin of food is interesting for you? | SDI [37] |
| Which of the following information regarding the freshness of food is interesting for you? | |
| Which of the following information regarding cultivation and production methods of food is interesting for you? | |
| Which of the following information regarding the transport of food is interesting for you? | |
| Which of the following information regarding sustainability when buying food is interesting for you? | |
| **Transparency Usage** | |
| Have you used the following transparency applications? | SD |
| How satisfied are you with used transparency applications? | |
| Why are you dissatisfied with the used transparency application? | |

*(continued)*

**Table 1.** (*continued*)

| Question | Source |
|---|---|
| Where would you like to see these information regarding food to be displayed? | |
| How would you prefer food information to be displayed on a smartphone? | |
| What would be the preferred design of a smartphone food transparency application for you? | |
| In which buying phase would you like to receive transparent product information? | |
| For which food product groups would you like to receive transparent product information? | SDI [40] |
| In general, I am interested in the transparent product information for food | SD |
| In general, I interest in a technological application providing traceability information | |
| Why are you not interested in a technological application providing traceability information | |
| I would use a technological application providing traceability information | |
| Why would you not use a technological application providing traceability information? | |
| Would you prefer buying a product that could be traced back to where it was produced? | |
| **Demographics** | |
| Gender | SDI [41] |
| Age | |
| In which country do you live? | SD |
| Choose the answer which describes your occupation situation best | SDI [41] |
| Please choose your highest educational level | |
| What is your net household income? | [38] |
| SD (Self-developed, based on the literature review), SDI (Self-developed but inspired by [Source]) <br> All questions were translated from German | |

ordering of the response options remained. However, for ordinally scaled questions, the individual items' order was sorted randomly to avoid adverse effects on voting behavior [33]. The online survey was distributed by the platform Surveycircle, which currently represents the largest community for online research on whose website one's own survey can be published in order to attract survey participants [34]. Pictures accompanied questions on technology preference to give respondents a visual impression of the four selected technologies, as depicted in Fig. 2.

314     R. Zimmermann et al.

The complete survey can be accessed at https://doi.org/10.5281/zenodo.4438820 [35]. The survey data are analyzed with the help of MS Excel and the statistical program SPSS.

**Fig. 2.** Visualization of technologies in the online questionnaire

## 2.3 Survey Sample

After the survey collection phase was completed, 578 entries could be recorded. Before the results were evaluated, data cleaning and error checking was carried out. In total, 174 entries were not completed in full or were aborted, and three entries were excluded because of their participation from countries not being Germany, Austria, or Switzerland, resulting in 401 complete data records used for the evaluation.

Looking at the descriptive statistics, Table 2 shows the demographics of the sample, and Table 3 provides insights into the sample's shopping behavior. On average, the respondents prefer to go to 2.8 shopping places to do their grocery shopping. As the separate analysis of Austria, Germany, and Switzerland only yielded minimal deviations, a separate evaluation for each country was not carried out, and all countries were included in a single analysis.

**Table 2.** Demographics

| | N | % | | N | % |
|---|---|---|---|---|---|
| **Age** ($M_{age}$ = 31.93 years, $\sigma$ = 12.927) | | | **Education** | | |
| Less than 25 years | 172 | 42.9% | University Degree | 163 | 40.6% |
| 25–35 years | 131 | 32.7% | Baccalaureate | 144 | 35.9% |
| 36–50 years | 39 | 9.7% | High School | 46 | 11.5% |
| Above 50 | 59 | 14.7% | Apprenticeship | 36 | 9.0% |
| | | | Other | 7 | 1.7% |
| **Gender** | | | | | |
| Male | 141 | 35.2% | **Occupation** | | |
| Female | 260 | 64.8% | Employed | 204 | 50.9% |
| | | | Student | 154 | 38.4% |
| **Nationality** | | | Unemployed | 18 | 4.5% |
| Austria | 297 | 74.1% | In retirement | 12 | 3.0% |
| Germany | 97 | 24.2% | "Other" | 6 | 1.5% |
| Switzerland | 7 | 1.7% | Pupils | 5 | 1.2% |
| | | | In apprenticeship | 2 | 0.5% |
| **Household** | | | | | |
| Couple without children | 134 | 33.4% | **Net household income (per month in EUR)** | | |
| Single living with parents | 77 | 19.2% | <2,400 | 176 | 43.9% |
| Single household | 67 | 16.7% | > 2,400 and <3,799 | 135 | 33.7% |
| Couple with children | 62 | 15.5% | >4,800 | 49 | 12.2% |
| Other | 47 | 11.7% | No Answer | 41 | 10.2% |
| Single with children | 14 | 3.5% | | | |
| **Total** | 401 | 100% | | 401 | 100% |

**Table 3.** Shopping behavior

| | N | % | | N | % |
|---|---|---|---|---|---|
| **Grocery shopping for** | | | **Grocery Shopping Responsibility** | | |
| 1 person | 75 | 18.7% | With household members | 230 | 57.4% |
| 2 persons | 171 | 42.6% | Alone | 119 | 29.7% |
| 3–4 persons | 126 | 31.4% | Household members | 49 | 12.2% |
| 5 persons | 25 | 6.2% | Other person | 3 | 0.7% |
| >5 persons | 4 | 1.0% | | | |
| | | | **Preferred Location to shop groceries** | | |
| **Frequency of grocery shopping per week** | | | Supermarket | 134 | 33.5% |
| 1 | 128 | 31.9% | Discount Store | 86 | 21.5% |
| 2–3 | 238 | 59.4% | Specialty Store | 52 | 13.1% |
| 4–5 | 26 | 6.5% | Drugstore | 46 | 11.5% |
| 6–7 | 9 | 2.2% | Farmer / Producer | 34 | 8.5% |
| | | | Farmers Market | 26 | 6.5% |
| | | | Organic Food Store | 22 | 5.7% |
| | | | Other | 1 | 0.3% |
| **Total** | 401 | 100% | | 401 | 100% |

# 3   Results

The following section presents the results of the conducted survey and its underlying literature review.

## 3.1   Literature Review

The result of the literature analysis process is shown in Table 4. It provides a list of transparent product information items that can be used for decision-making when selecting

**Table 4.**  Ranking of transparency elements by importance

| Category | Transparency element | L | Mean | Median | ER |
|---|---|---|---|---|---|
| Sustainability (M = 5.34) | **Species appropriate animal husbandry** | | **6,10** | 7 | 3 |
| | Recycling (recyclability of the packaging) | x | 5,57 | 6 | 8 |
| | **Workers' rights & working conditions, child labor, etc** | | **5,55** | 6 | 9 |
| | **Environmentally-friendly production impact** | | **5,41** | 6 | 10 |
| | Labels (e.g. fair trade, organic) | x | 5,27 | 6 | 12 |
| | Amount of packaging, generated waste | | 4,97 | 5 | 16 |
| | CO2 footprint of the food (production + transport) | | 4,97 | 5 | 17 |
| | Resources used (e.g., water consumption) | | 4,85 | 5 | 23 |
| Cultivation and Production methods (M = 5.26) | Type of animal husbandry (free-range/stable/etc.) | x | 6,17 | 7 | 2 |
| | **Pesticide use (sprayed) on fruits and vegetables** | | **5,82** | 6 | 6 |
| | Organic/conventional farming | x | 5,65 | 6 | 7 |
| | Type of farming method for fish | x | 5,20 | 6 | 13 |
| | Farming method (greenhouse/field/etc.) | | 4,86 | 5 | 22 |
| | Type of fishing method (trawl/fishing/etc.) | x | 4,63 | 5 | 29 |
| | Processing steps of the food | | 4,52 | 5 | 31 |
| Freshness (M = 5.06) | Best before date | x | 5,91 | 7 | 5 |

*(continued)*

**Table 4.** (*continued*)

| Category | Transparency element | L | Mean | Median | ER |
|---|---|---|---|---|---|
| | Slaughter date for meat | | 4,98 | 5 | 15 |
| | Packing date of food | | 4,95 | 5 | 18 |
| | Harvest/picking date for fruit & vegetables | | 4,89 | 5 | 19 |
| | Catch date for fish | | 4,87 | 5 | 21 |
| | Laying date for eggs | | 4,76 | 5 | 26 |
| Transport (M = 4.54) | Distance from farm field to the shelf in km | | 4,79 | 5 | 25 |
| | Duration from farm field to shelf | | 4,68 | 5 | 27 |
| | Tracking of compliance with the cold chain | | 4,65 | 5 | 28 |
| | CO2 consumption due to transport | | 4,56 | 5 | 30 |
| | All means of transport used (plane/ship, truck/rail/etc.) | | 4,29 | 4 | 32 |
| | Primary means of transport used | | 4,25 | 4 | 33 |
| Origin (M = 4.40) | Country of origin for fruit & vegetables | x | 6,24 | 7 | 1 |
| | Country of origin for meat | x | 6,06 | 7 | 4 |
| | Country of aquaculture/fishing area for fish | x | 5,33 | 6 | 11 |
| | **Food inspection protocol** | | **5,01** | **5** | **14** |
| | Exact place of origin for fruits & vegetables | | 4,87 | 5 | 20 |
| | Exact place of origin for fish | x | 4,79 | 5 | 24 |
| | Additional information on species/fish | | 3,97 | 4 | 34 |
| | Name of the producer(s) | x | 3,84 | 4 | 35 |
| | Address of the producer(s) | x | 3,54 | 4 | 36 |
| | Name of the supplier(s) | | 3,24 | 3 | 37 |
| | Address of the supplier(s) | | 3,01 | 3 | 38 |
| | Additional information about the company | | 2,94 | 3 | 39 |

**\*ER = Element Rank**
**\*L = Mostly labelled on Packaging**

food (used research articles: [4, 15, 17, 30, 31, 37, 39, 42–49]; used industry case studies: [50–56]).

## 3.2 Transparent Product Information Survey

Resulting from the survey responses, Table 4 also provides the ranking of the importance of the individual transparent product information items and their corresponding categories (sorted by the mean ranking per category).

It becomes apparent that the five most important transparency elements (see Element Rank (ER) 1–5 in Table 4) are "Country of origin for fruit and vegetables" followed by the "Type of animal husbandry", the "Species-appropriate animal husbandry", and "Country of origin for meat". In addition, essential for respondents is the "Best-before date" and the "Pesticide use in fruits and vegetables". It has to be noted that grocery products in the European Union already require several of these transparency elements to be displayed on the product packaging (e.g., free-range husbandry of eggs) or signs at the product shelf (e.g., Bananas from Brasil) [57].

When focusing on additional product information that is typically not (yet) available at the POS but could be provided by an additional information source, such as technology, the five most important transparency elements are the following (highlighted with bold letters in Table 4):

1. Species appropriate animal husbandry
2. Pesticide use (sprayed) on fruits and vegetables
3. Workers' rights & working conditions, child labor, etc.
4. Environmentally-friendly production impact
5. Food inspection protocol

Additionally, we surveyed the participants to determine which technological application is preferred for providing transparent product information. The "Smart Display" was selected by 32% of respondents, followed by the "Smart Shopping Cart" (30.6%), the user's self-owned smartphone (29.3%), and the Terminal (8%). Multiple answers were possible for this question. On average, one person selected 1.6 answer options for this question.

## 4 Discussion

The online ranking results on the participants' preferred technology choice show that customers may value smartphones, smart displays, and smart shopping carts higher to retrieve the product information of interest than a stationary terminal. One possible reason for this low ranking might be that specific product information should be available at the moment of decision-making. Therefore, it might be advisable for retailers to consider that grocery shoppers prefer technology, which allows retrieving additional product information and does not force a specific movement through the store. The difference between the three most preferred technology options is less than 3%. Therefore, it could be beneficial for retailers to design a type of cross-device application providing additional transparent product information to consumers, which is not yet provided on product labels or signs at the POS. Among the three preferred options, smartphones represent the most cost-efficient and scalable option. As of its customer-owned nature, retailers would not need to invest in additional technological infrastructure among the entire store landscape.

Based on the conducted literature review, we identified 38 transparency elements that potentially lead to improved transparency of the food supply chain, of which 13 are already commonly available on the products packaging, labels, or signs at the POS. From the quantitative survey results, four of the five most essential transparency elements are already provided at the POS in German-speaking countries, which refer to the country of origin of fruits, vegetables, and meat, as well as the type of animal husbandry, and the expiration date. Looking at the most important transparency elements which are not (yet) available at the POS, consumers request more information on the appropriateness of animal husbandry (ER 3), if pesticides have been used on organic food (ER 6), the workers' rights and working conditions (ER 9), whether the production had an environmentally-friendly production impact (ER 10), and would like to see a proof in the form of a food inspection protocol (ER 14). These five highly preferred transparency elements mainly refer to the category of sustainability (ER 3, 9, 10), as well as to cultivation and production methods (ER 6) and origin (ER 14). These results support current research on consumers' increasing awareness of sustainable and "green" consumption choices [58]. In contrast to the ongoing discussion in research and industry [e.g., 59], the ranking of product information preferences in this study revealed that information transparency of the category "Transport", for example, the distance and the related cause of $CO_2$ emissions, are less important to consumers.

The study has some research limitations that can be venues for future research. The sample consists of young adults perceiving higher education and includes more female participants than the average population, limiting this study's generalizability. Moreover, a person's fundamental principles and values are strongly related to product information seeking, which were not enquired in the present work. For instance, customers who value tradition, security, and conformity are less susceptible to consider sustainability aspects in their purchase decision [58]. Moreover, the study was carried out in German-speaking countries only. Future research could investigate product transparency in other countries, where more/less additional product information is available at the POS and where value orientations differ on a societal level [58]. An additional approach is to investigate the differences in product information of low and high involvement products and the customer's trust in the displayed information [6].

Building on this study results, researchers could focus on one specific information type (e.g., environmentally-friendly production impact) and investigate the consumer's technology preference. Therefore, researchers could address how certain product information is linked to technology preferences and vice versa. Moreover, the study design could be enriched by presenting the respective technology with various media types (e.g., a video of various technologies in use). Finally, the study could also be conducted in a lab environment or in the field where users can directly interact with the technology.

As the presented results focus on comparing general preferences for different customer-facing in-store technologies, it calls for a more in-depth view of User Experience (UX) abilities and the technologies' actual usage. Forthcoming studies could investigate the influence of an application providing transparent product information on consumer adoption and behavior. Additionally, various design and UX factors of a cross-device application might play a crucial role in the fast-paced food shopping environment to ensure a strong and positive impact on consumer behavior. New and innovative in-store technologies could also play a crucial role at the POS. For instance, a head-mounted mixed-reality shopping device (e.g., Microsoft HoloLens) that can merge pervasive, computer-generated transparency product information (virtual objects) into the real world could play a crucial role in future shopping scenarios [60].

## 5  Conclusion

Customers demand greater transparency and traceability about the food products they are purchasing and consuming [4, 5]. Industry follows this upward trend by increasingly providing more transparent information on product packing, labels, and signs at the physical POS.

In this paper, we examined this topic by (RQ1) identifying transparent product information from the literature and conducting a survey to investigate (RQ2) which transparent product information are most valuable for consumers and (RQ3) which technology to present this information consumers prefer. In the systematic literature review we found 15 scientific papers and seven industry case studies and identified 39 transparent product information elements in the categories (i) origin, (ii) freshness, (iii) cultivation & production methods, (iv) transport, and (v) sustainability. We used these 39 transparent product information elements to design a survey to answer research questions RQ2 and RQ3.

Results show that the most important transparent product information are already present on the packaging of most products or shelves in the region of the survey (Germany, Austria, Switzerland). Further important but currently not available transparent product information should be provided via additional technology: (i) species-appropriate animal husbandry, (ii) pesticide use (sprayed) on fruits and vegetables, (iii) workers' rights & working conditions, child labor, etc., (iv) environmentally-friendly production impact, and (v) food inspection protocol.

The survey also revealed that consumers do not have a preferred technology to display this information. Smart displays (32.0%), smart shopping carts (30.6%), and smartphones (29.3%) had similar results. Only terminals (8%) can be considered as an inept technology.

**Acknowledgment.** This study has been conducted within the training network project PERFORM funded by the European Union's Horizon 2020 research and innovation program under the Marie Skłodowska-Curie grant agreement No. 765395. Note: This research reflects only the authors' view. The Agency is not responsible for any use that may be made of the information it contains.

# References

1. Aung, M.M., Chang, Y.S.: Traceability in a food supply chain: safety and quality perspectives. Food Control **39**, 172–184 (2014)
2. Buzby, J.C.: International Trade and Food Safety. Economic Theory and Case Studies. Bibliogov (2012)
3. Cannella, S., Dominguez, R., Framinan, J.M., Ponte, B.: Evolving trends in supply chain management: complexity, new technologies, and innovative methodological approaches. Complexity **2018**, 1–3 (2018)
4. Hooker, N.H., Caswell, J.A.: Trends in food quality regulation: implications for processed food trade and foreign direct investment. Agribusiness **12**, 411–419 (1996)
5. van Plaggenhoef, W.: Integration and self regulation of quality management in Dutch agri-food supply chains. A cross-chain analysis of the poultry meat, the fruit and vegetable and the flower and potted plant chains. [S.l.s.n.] (2007)
6. Frank, P., Brock, C.: Bridging the intention-behavior gap among organic grocery customers: the crucial role of point-of-sale information. Psychol. Mark. **35**, 586–602 (2018)
7. Qian, J., et al.: Food traceability system from governmental, corporate, and consumer perspectives in the European Union and China: a comparative review. Trends Food Sci. Technol. **99**, 402–412 (2020)
8. George, R.V., Harsh, H.O., Ray, P., Babu, A.K.: Food quality traceability prototype for restaurants using blockchain and food quality data index. J. Clean. Prod. **240**, 118021 (2019)
9. Trienekens, J.H. (ed.): European Pork Chains. Diversity and Quality Challenges in Consumer-Oriented Production and Distribution. Wageningen Academic Publishers, Wageningen (2009)
10. Behnke, K., Janssen, M.F.W.H.A.: Boundary conditions for traceability in food supply chains using blockchain technology. Int. J. Inf. Manag. **52**, 101969 (2020)
11. Hobbs, J.E.: Information asymmetry and the role of traceability systems. Agribusiness **20**, 397–415 (2004)
12. Espiñeira, M., Santaclara, F.J.: Advances in Food Traceability Techniques and Technologies. Elsevier Science (2016)
13. Nilsson, F., Göransson, M., Båth, K.: Models and technologies for the enhancement of transparency and visibility in food supply chains. In: Sustainable Food Supply Chains, pp. 219–236. Elsevier (2019)
14. Astill, J., et al.: Transparency in food supply chains: a review of enabling technology solutions. Trends Food Sci. Technol. **91**, 240–247 (2019)
15. Agrawal, T., Pal, R.: Traceability in textile and clothing supply chains: classifying implementation factors and information sets via Delphi study. Sustainability **11**, 8–9 (2019)
16. Hou, B., Hou, J., Wu, L.: Consumer preferences for traceable food with different functions of safety information attributes: evidence from a menu-based choice experiment in China. Int. J. Environ. Res. Public Health **17**, 146 (2019)
17. Jin, S., Zhang, Y., Xu, Y.: Amount of information and the willingness of consumers to pay for food traceability in China. Food Control **77**, 163–170 (2017)
18. Liu, R., Gao, Z., Snell, H.A., Ma, H.: Food safety concerns and consumer preferences for food safety attributes: evidence from China. Food Control **112**, 107157 (2020)
19. Zhang, B., Fu, Z., Huang, J., Wang, J., Xu, S., Zhang, L.: Consumers' perceptions, purchase intention, and willingness to pay a premium price for safe vegetables: a case study of Beijing, China. J. Clean. Prod. **197**, 1498–1507 (2018)
20. Siddh, M.M., Soni, G., Jain, R., Sharma, M.K., Yadav, V.: Agri-fresh food supply chain quality (AFSCQ): a literature review. IMDS **117**, 2015–2044 (2017)
21. Manski, S.: Building the blockchain world: technological commonwealth or just more of the same? Strateg. Chang. **26**, 511–522 (2017)

22. Kamilaris, A., Fonts, A., Prenafeta-Boldú, F.X.: The rise of blockchain technology in agriculture and food supply chains. Trends Food Sci. Technol. **91**, 640–652 (2019)
23. Opara, L.U., Mazaud, F.: Food traceability from field to plate. Outlook Agric. **30**, 239–247 (2001)
24. Dacko, S.G.: Enabling smart retail settings via mobile augmented reality shopping apps. Technol. Forecast. Soc. Change **124**, 243–256 (2017)
25. Pantano, E., Priporas, C.V., Dennis, C.: A new approach to retailing for successful competition in the new smart scenario. IJRDM **46**, 264–282 (2018)
26. Pantano, E., Vannucci, V.: Who is innovating? An exploratory research of digital technologies diffusion in retail industry. J. Retail. Consum. Serv. **49**, 297–304 (2019)
27. EUROSTAT: Almost 8 out of 10 internet users in the EU surfed via a mobile or smart phone in 2016. https://ec.europa.eu/eurostat/documents/2995521/7771139/9-20122016-BP-EN.pdf. Accessed 14 Jan 2021
28. Microsoft News Centre Europe: Is this the supermarket of the future? Coop's digital transformation. https://news.microsoft.com/europe/features/supermarket-of-the-future/. Accessed 10 Feb 2021
29. Vojvodić, K.: Brick-and-mortar retailers: Becoming smarter with innovative technologies. Strat. Manag. **24**, 3–11 (2019)
30. Román, S., Sánchez-Siles, L.M., Siegrist, M.: The importance of food naturalness for consumers: Results of a systematic review. Trends Food Sci. Technol. **67**, 44–57 (2017)
31. Petrescu, D.C., Vermeir, I., Petrescu-Mag, R.M.: Consumer understanding of food quality, healthiness, and environmental impact: a cross-national perspective. Int. J. Environ. Res. Public Health **17**, 169 (2019)
32. Mayring, P.: Qualitative content analysis: theoretical foundation, basic procedures and software solution. Klagenfurt
33. Rugel, M., Jaskolla, L., Skulschus, M.: System und Systematik von Fragebögen. Innovativer ontologiebasierter Ansatz. Comelio-Medien, Berlin (2010)
34. SurveyCircle.com: Das ist SurveyCircle. https://www.surveycircle.com/de/. Accessed 22 Dec 2020
35. Zimmermann, R., Wetzlinger, W., Mayer, M., Obermeier, G., Auinger, A.: Annex - Information Technology as Enabler of Transparency in Food Supply Chains. Zenodo (2021)
36. Beer-Borst, S.: Fragebogen eingesetzt im Projekt „Gesund & Gut: Na Klar!" NFP69 Salzkonsum. Institut für Sozial- und Präventivmedizin der Universität Bern (2017)
37. Meise, J.N.: Communicating Supply Chain Transparency to Consumers. The Impact of Supply Chain Information Provision on Consumers' Preference and Willingness to Pay. Shaker, Aachen (2010)
38. Gremmer, P., Hempel, C., Hamm, U., Busch, C.: Zielkonflikt beim Lebensmitteleinkauf: Konventionell regional, ökologisch regional oder ökologisch aus entfernteren Regionen? (2016)
39. EFSA: Food safety in the EU. [Publications Office of the European Union], [Luxembourg] (2019)
40. ECR: SERVICEPLATTFORM WARENGRUPPENKLASSIFIKATION. https://ecr-austria.at/arbeitsgruppen/serviceplattform-warengruppenklassifikation/. Accessed 13 Jan 2021
41. Universität Innsbruck: Liebe in Zeiten des Corona-Virus. https://ec.europa.eu/eurostat/documents/2995521/7771139/9-20122016-BP-EN.pdf. Accessed 13 Jan 2021
42. Denver, S., Jensen, J.D., Olsen, S.B., Christensen, T.: Consumer preferences for 'Localness' and organic food production. J. Food Prod. Mark. **25**, 668–689 (2019)
43. Louise, E., Datta, K.: From beef to bananas. Consumer preferences and local food flows in Honolulu, Hawai. In: Sahakian, M., Saloma, C.A., Erkman, S. (eds.) Food Consumption in the City. Practices and Patterns in Urban Asia and the Pacific. Routledge, London, New York (2016)

44. Martínez-Ruiz, M.P., Gómez-Cantó, C.M.: Key external influences affecting consumers' decisions regarding food. Front. Psychol. **7**, 1618 (2016)
45. Meyerding, S.G.H., Trajer, N., Lehberger, M.: What is local food? The case of consumer preferences for local food labeling of tomatoes in Germany. J. Clean. Prod. **207**, 30–43 (2019)
46. Sanchez-Siles, L.M., et al.: The Food Naturalness Index (FNI): an integrative tool to measure the degree of food naturalness. Trends Food Sci. Technol. **91**, 681–690 (2019)
47. Sigurdsson, V., Larsen, N.M., Alemu, M.H., Gallogly, J.K., Menon, R.G.V., Fagerstrøm, A.: Assisting sustainable food consumption: the effects of quality signals stemming from consumers and stores in online and physical grocery retailing. J. Bus. Res. **112**, 458–471 (2020)
48. Trienekens, J.H., Wognum, P.M., Beulens, A.J.M., van der Vorst, J.G.A.J.: Transparency in complex dynamic food supply chains. Adv. Eng. Inform. **26**, 55–65 (2012)
49. Zander, K., Risius, A., Feucht, Y., Janssen, M., Hamm, U.: Sustainable aquaculture products: implications of consumer awareness and of consumer preferences for promising market communication in Germany. J. Aquat. Food Prod. Technol. **27**, 5–20 (2018)
50. Prüf nach!: Rückverfolgung Ihres Produktes—Zurück zum Ursprung. https://www.zuruec kzumursprung.at/grundwerte/qualitaetssicherung-und-rueckverfolgung/rueckverfolgung-ihres-produktes/. Accessed 14 Jan 2021
51. Metro Pro Trace: PRO TRACE Fisch—METRO. https://www.metro.de/unternehmen/nachha ltigkeit/pro-trace/fisch. Accessed 14 Jan 2021
52. Check Your Product: Check Your Product. https://www.check-your-product.com. Accessed 14 Jan 2021
53. Ocean Disclosure Project: Ocean Disclosure Project. https://oceandisclosureproject.org/. Accessed 14 Jan 2021
54. Codecheck: Codecheck.info - Produkte checken und gesund einkaufen. https://eur-lex.europa. eu/legal-content/EN/TXT/PDF/?uri=CELEX:02011R1169-20140219&from=DE. Accessed 14 Jan 2021
55. Verein Österreichische Eierdatenbank: Verein Österreichische Eierdatenbank. https://www. eierdatenbank.at/#was-steht-auf-dem-ei. Accessed 14 Jan 2021
56. REWE Rückverfolgbarkeit bis zum Erzeugerbetrieb: REWE führt Rückverfolgbarkeit bis zum Erzeugerbetrieb per QR-Code ein. https://www.rewe-group.com/de/newsroom/presse mitteilungen/1710-rueckverfolgbarkeit-bis-zum-erzeugerbetrieb. Accessed 14 Jan 2021
57. European Parliament: Regulation (EU) No 1169/2011 of the European Parliament and of the Council of 25 October 2011 on the provision of food information to consumers. https://eur-lex.europa.eu/eli/reg/2011/1169/oj/eng. Accessed 10 Feb 2021
58. Pekkanen, T.-L., Pätäri, S., Albadera, L., Jantunen, A.: Who cares about product sustainability information at the moment of purchase? Consumer evidence from three countries. Sust. Dev. **26**, 229–242 (2018)
59. Caputo, V., Nayga, R.M., Scarpa, R.: Food miles or carbon emissions? Exploring labelling preference for food transport footprint with a stated choice study. Aust. J. Agric. Resour. Econ. **57**, 465–482 (2013)
60. Mora, D., Jain, S., Nalbach, O., Werth, D.: Holographic recommendations in brick-and-mortar stores. In: AMCIS 2020 Proceedings, vol. 12 (2020)

# Work and Business Operations

# The New Normal? Motivators
# for and Hindrances to Telework

Thomas Fischer(iD), Stefan Küll, Ursula Niederländer,
and Martin Stabauer(✉)(iD)

Johannes Kepler University, Linz, Austria
{thomas.fischer,stefan.kuell,ursula.niederlaender,
martin.stabauer}@jku.at

**Abstract.** Telework or telecommuting – a concept of flexible work
arrangements predominantly driven by the Human-Computer Interaction (HCI) community – has vastly increased in recent months due to
lockdowns and other measures in response to the COVID-19 pandemic.
In this paper, we explicitly exclude outside forces (such as a pandemic)
as grounds for adopting telework, but rather ask: What are the reasons for organizations and/or individuals to voluntarily decide for or
against telework? In this effort to identify the most relevant antecedents
of the adoption of telework at both the organizational and the individual level, we present the results of a comprehensive literature review of
72 papers conducted in Q4/2020. The discovered characteristics influencing the decision for or against telework were then structured in a 6
(rationales) by 2 (organization vs individual) matrix, each of which was
further analyzed in detail. The multifaceted results fall into three broad
categories that impact telework adoption: (i) the type of work, (ii) the
way this work is organized and (iii) its organizational environment.

**Keywords:** Telework · Telecommuting · Literature review

## 1  Introduction

The COVID-19 pandemic has created an unparalleled demand for more flexible work arrangements that allow employees to work outside of their typical
work environment (e.g., from home). For example, at the time of writing, in
the European Union (EU) almost half of the employed population has worked
from home for at least some time in the course of the COVID-19 pandemic [3].
Such arrangements are commonly referred to as "telework", a concept formulated as early as in the 1970s, but which has spread only slowly since then [15]. In
recent years, however, information and communication technologies (ICT) have
increased the potential for work outside the normal office environment, which
was then exploited in response to the pandemic. Numerous studies (not only)
in the field of Human-Computer Interaction (HCI) have been conducted and
examined various facets of telework (e.g., [33,90]).

© Springer Nature Switzerland AG 2021
F. F.-H. Nah and K. Siau (Eds.): HCII 2021, LNCS 12783, pp. 327–346, 2021.
https://doi.org/10.1007/978-3-030-77750-0_21

However, telework should not be viewed just as part of a contingency plan (e.g., during a health crisis), but its benefit as a complement to existing work arrangements that place the employee mostly within an office environment provided by the employer should also be considered. It is important that the blend be decided on a case-by-case basis [16], though it is not clear what should be considered when reaching this conclusion in an organizational context.

To support this decision-making process, we reviewed the literature to identify aspects that are considered (i) by employers when they decide to provide telework arrangements, and (ii) by employees when they decide to make use of such arrangements. In particular, we focused on the factors that drive or hinder organizations when they consider offering telework arrangements and what motivations and deterrents then influence an employee's decision to work away from the employer's premises.

We present the methodology of our systematic literature review (SLR) in the next section, which includes the literature search, the selection process and the categories used for classification. In Sect. 3, we then summarize our findings regarding factors that influence employer and employee decisions, before we discuss results and conclude the paper in Sect. 4.

## 2   Methodology

We conducted an SLR based on the recommendations by Webster and Watson [89]. This involved an initial phase of a keyword-based search of a publication database followed by backward and forward searches. Peer-reviewed articles (journal articles or conference proceedings) were selected based on a set of inclusion and exclusion criteria, and the remaining articles were then analyzed based on an existing set of categories developed by Belzunegui-Eraso and Erro-Garcés [12].

### 2.1   Literature Search and Selection

For the initial literature search, we used the Web of Science (WoS) database and a set of keywords drawn from landmark publications on telework (e.g., [15, 24, 26, 52]). The keywords for this search were supposed to reflect two types of concept: (i) forms of telework and related terms (e.g., telecommuting or home office) and (ii) the adoption or acceptance of such arrangements (e.g., adoption or use). We used the advanced search in the WoS and combined both types of terms in the following string: *TS=(Telework OR telecommuting OR "home office" OR "mobile office" OR "virtual office") AND TS=(acceptance OR adoption OR application OR agreement OR use OR implementation).*

We also limited our results to articles published in 2006 or later, for two main reasons: First, since then policies have been implemented to support and telework in major economies such as the EU (e.g., the "Framework agreement on telework"[1]) or the USA (e.g., the "Telework Enhancement Act of 2010"[2]). Second, while working outside a normal office environment is not new, developments in ICT have certainly made it more common [26].

This initial database search yielded 953 hits on November 26, 2020. Based on title and abstract, 79 of these articles were selected for further investigation. The following inclusion and exclusion criteria were then applied to select papers for further analyses:

*Inclusion*: Papers had to focus on telework, which we specified based on the description by Taskin [81] as "work at a distance" (i.e., work outside the main office) enabled through the use of ICT. We did not exclude papers based on type of research (e.g., empirical papers, conceptual papers, or reviews), data collection method (e.g., surveys or interviews), or context of investigation (e.g., private or public companies).

*Exclusion 1*: We excluded papers if they focused on telework arrangements that were implemented in response to outside forces (e.g., a pandemic) and not based on the employer's or employee's own volition (examples of papers excluded based on this criterion: [12,39]).

*Exclusion 2*: We also excluded papers if they did not focus on the antecedents of the decision to adopt telework, but rather on the variables that influence the negotation process or the success of telework (examples of papers excluded based on this criterion: [33,72,82]).

*Exclusion 3*: Further, we excluded papers which focused on a set of flexible work practices (e.g., flexible work hours, or social benefits such as parental leave) that included work away from the office, but did not provide analyses that were specific to telework (examples of papers excluded based on this criterion: [77,78]).

After the application of these inclusion and exclusion criteria, 40 papers remained for further analysis. These papers were also used as input for a round of backward search, which yielded 15 additional papers. The resulting 55 papers were then used as input for forward search using Google Scholar from December 4 to 13, 2020. This led to a total of 2,670 hits, from which 22 additional papers were selected, yielding a total of 77 papers for our review.

## 2.2 Literature Classification

Of the 77 papers in our review, 72 were used for further analysis. Five review papers (i.e., [21,37,63,67,74]) were excluded, as their classification according to our criteria would have led to conceptual overlap, which we sought to avoid. We used the categories presented by Belzunegui-Eraso and Erro-Garcés [12] as a basis for classifying the antecedents investigated by the papers in our review. Their classification scheme includes five categories that could affect telework: Individual, Home and Family, Organization, Job, and Environment. Due to our

---

[1] https://www.etuc.org/en/framework-agreement-telework.

[2] https://www.congress.gov/bill/111th-congress/house-bill/1722/text.

specific focus on ICT-enabled work, we decided to treat Technology as a separate category and not as part of the Job category.

In the category *Individual*, we included variables that relate to personal characteristics (e.g., skills and abilities) and circumstances (e.g., family situation). In the category *Home and Family*, we included variables that relate to boundaries between work and personal life, such as considerations related to work-life balance. In the category *Organization*, we included variables that relate to the characteristics of the employer (e.g., supervisor's attitude towards telework or organizational culture) and the circumstances at work (e.g., social environment or level of disruptions). In the category *Job*, we included variables that relate to the nature of work (e.g., knowledge-based tasks, need for communication) and how it is managed and organized (e.g., interdependence with the work of others, output-based performance assessment). In the category *Technology*, we included variables that relate to the technological resources of an organization (e.g., existing ICT infrastructure) and the technological consequences of telework (e.g., potential for malfunction). Finally, in the category *Miscellaneous*, we included variables that have so far received little attention (e.g., related to environmental considerations of telework, its technical safety implications, legal influences, and external influences such as industry standards or national culture), which is also in line with Belzunegui-Eraso and Erro-Garcés [12] as most of these variables have only been considered in more recent research into telework.

**Table 1.** Findings

|  | Organizational adoption | Individual adoption |
|---|---|---|
| Individual | [2,11,20,25,32,35,40,41,53, 59–61,68,76,86,88] | [1,2,6–9,13,14,17,19,20,22,23,27– 32,34,40,42,43,48,56– 58,65,66,69– 71,79,80,83,85,87,88,91,92] |
| Home & Family | [32,49,60,61,68,73,76] | [1,2,5,6,8,9,13,14,18–20,27– 29,31,32,34,43,48,57,58,66,70,79, 80,83,92] |
| Organization | [2,6,11,17,20,25,32,35,36,38, 40,41,46,47,49,51,53–55,59– 61,68,73,75,76,86,88] | [2,5,6,8–10,13,16,20,23,25,27– 29,31,32,34,40,43,48,50,57,62,64, 66,70,71,79,83,86,87,91] |
| Job | [2,6,11,20,32,35,36,40,41,44– 47,53,60,61,68,73,76,86,88] | [2,5,6,8,9,13,14,16,18– 20,22,23,25,27,29–32,34,43– 45,48,50,58,66,80,83–88,92] |
| Technology | [2,6,17,25,32,40,41,51,54,55, 60,61,68,76,86,88] | [2,5,6,9,13,16,18,22,25,29,31,32, 40,57,66,79,85,92] |
| Miscellaneous | [20,38,46,47,54,55,60,61,68, 75,76,86] | [4,6,9,31,42,57,58,62,65,70] |

For the classification process it has to be noted though that these categories are not fully disjunctive, as the included variables are often closely related to each other (e.g., *Individual* and *Home and Family* or *Organization, Job,* and *Technology*). Nevertheless, we assigned the investigated variables to only one category, which was done by authors 1, 2, and 4 independently. The independent classifications were then reviewed by authors 1 and 4 to create a more coherent classification of all papers. The result of this classification into the six categories listed is shown in Table 1. A more detailed discussion of the main findings for organizational and individual adoption of telework within each of these categories is presented in the next section.

# 3 Results

In this section, we highlight the main findings for each of our six categories both at the employer and the employee level. As summarized in Table 1, 30 and 53 studies focused on criteria that influence organizational and individual telework adoption respectively. Only 11 studies in our sample concentrated on both sides (i.e., [2, 6, 17, 20, 25, 32, 40, 44, 45, 86, 88]).

## 3.1 Organizational Adoption

On the organizational side, the main categories investigated included characteristics of the organization (28 studies), the job (21 studies) and the individual (16 studies), and the technology employed (16 studies), while individual home and family characteristics (7 studies) received only minor attention. Variables outside of these categories (i.e., "Miscellaneous"), were investigated in 12 studies.

**Individual.** Several studies investigated whether managers offer the opportunity to telework based on *individual demography*. These characteristics include: gender of the individual asking for telework, although there were no conclusive results in this regard [11,53,61]; age [53,76]; and their organizational tenure [20,53,88], where Vogel et al. [88] pointed out that managers tended to worry that colleagues with shorter tenure in the university context would not get socialized sufficiently if they stayed at home, while Donnelly [20] pointed out that managers expressed the view that senior members had earned the right to be able to work outside the main office. Certain attitudes and personality characteristics (e.g., independence, team player, skepticism and resistance towards telework) were also highlighted as potential influencing factors in several studies [32,53,68,88], although managers (deans and administrators) interviewed by Vogel et al. [88] expressed the fear that some of these characteristics could be used as an excuse to push unpopular colleagues out of sight.

Having relevant *skills and abilities* was also considered an important employee characteristic that motivated managers to allow telework arrangements. General self-management skills (e.g., time management, independent decision-making, technological skills, communication skills) were frequently shown to positively influence this decision [2,11,25,35,40,53,68,76]. Aside from these more general skills, Peters et al. [61] found that individuals with knowledge and skills that were particularly valuable to their employers were also more often allowed to telework, and according to the findings by Lembrechts et al. [41], this even holds true when individuals are part of a heterogeneous team (i.e., several specialized individuals working collaboratively). Another major driver for offering telework that was confirmed in several studies was a *high level of trust* between the individual and their supervisor [11,32,35,53,60,61,86], with only one study in our sample not showing support for this relationship [40].

**Home and Family.** Several studies showed that companies with managers that valued *work-life balance* were more likely to allow telework [49,60,68], particularly within an environment (e.g., a particular municipality) or culture that also valued work-life balance [60,76]. However, this relationship can be weak [49] and can be accompanied by the rarely expressed fear that employees might be more distracted when working from home [68]. Rather, in some studies managers highlighted that it depends on the personality and working style of an individual whether they can effectively cope with such distractions [32], and some managers even allowed telework for the expressed reason that individuals may experience fewer work interruptions at home than in the office [61]. In a few studies, it was also found that *home-related reasons* for not coming to the office (e.g., childcare responsibilities) were also considered as relevant to a manager's decision to grant telework [73], although this consideration was also culture/country-dependent (e.g., accepted by managers in the UK and in Sweden, but not in the Netherlands, [61]).

**Organization.** Characteristics of the organization, its members and its processes and practices that influence the decision to adopt teleworking were highly diverse, and we therefore highlight the main variables investigated that relate to (i) the type of organization (e.g., industry), (ii) its culture, (iii) practices and support mechanisms, (iv) management style and forms of control, and (v) work processes.

Regarding the *type of an organization*, there were mixed results for the positive influence of company size on telework adoption [11,51,54,55,75]. Some studies also found that public sector and more knowledge-oriented companies (e.g., corporate service or information technology) were more likely to adopt teleworking than capital-intensive companies in manufacturing-related domains [47,49,54,61,75], although this relationship was not always confirmed [11]. Further, studies that investigated the positive influence a company's international scope (e.g., multinationals or companies with international clients) on teleworking adoption confirmed this relationship [49,54,55,60], with one exception [75].

An *organizational culture* that is supportive of family life did not seem to significantly influence the adoption of telework [11,59], while a culture that supports individual responsibility or innovativeness (e.g., related to technology) [40,55,86] and a more bureaucratic culture (e.g., in the university or governmental context) [76,88] had a positive and negative impact, respectively.

For implemented *policies and support mechanisms*, a number of studies found that companies that provide supportive human resource development practices (e.g., telework training, additional administrative resources, pilot projects to try telework) were also more likely to provide the opportunity to telework [25,35, 46,47,54,73,75,76]. Further, while Beham et al. [11] reported that companies with a formal telework policy were more likely to offer telework arrangements, this finding was not supported by Peters et al. [61]. In addition, while Peters and Batenburg [59] found that companies that offer other forms of flexible work arrangements (e.g., flexible working hours and mobile work) were also more likely to offer telework, this finding was not confirmed by Martínez-Sánchez et al. [46].

For *characteristics of management*, Beham et al. [11] and Silva-C et al. [73] found that managers who had previous experience with telework were more likely to encourage it, and a number of studies highlighted that top management support is crucial for telework to be adopted in an organization [17,40,60,76,86]. While there is some evidence that concerns related to control over employee work might contribute to a manager's decision against telework [2,6], this was not supported by all studies [40,68]. Managers who tended to evaluate employee performance based mainly on their output and the results of their work were more likely to allow telework [53,59,86].

In the context of *organizational processes*, it was found that managers preferred not to allow telework because they feared that both the necessary interaction between employees [2,17,68,88] and more spontaneous allocation of work that becomes critical [32] would become more difficult. This problem can, at least to some extent, be overcome by using electronic communication [86].

**Job.** Characteristics of an employee's work that influence organizational adoption of telework for a particular occupation mostly relate to the overall type of job, the type of tasks involved and the ability to independently organize these tasks. For the *type of occupation*, we found that the results of several studies concurred in describing knowledge-based work (e.g., research) particularly suited to telework [46,47,73,88], while production work was in most cases considered unsuitable [36]. In addition, individuals in a managerial position were also more likely to be allowed to telework [53,60], although this observation did not apply to the public sector (e.g., universities) in which higher-ranking individuals are often expected to be present in the office for face-to-face interaction [32,88]. This finding also recurred in several studies that reported that jobs which are composed mainly of *tasks* that require physical presence in the office for communication or quality assurance purposes were less likely to be regarded as suitable for telework [2,20,44,53]. Work that does not require much communication, is highly standardized and has clear goals and outputs is more often regarded as suitable for telework [32,53,61,68]. Another important aspect was whether certain jobs and tasks can be done autonomously by an individual or whether they are highly interdependent on the work of others, with tasks being regarded as less suitable for telework in the latter case [6,11,20,35,41,76,86].

**Technology.** The presence or absence of *technology* that managers perceive to be necessary for telework in a company was found, respectively, to be an enabler or barrier to telework in several studies [25,40,41,54,55,61,86]. Neirotti et al. [54] reported that enterprise information systems (e.g., ERP) and e-learning tools had a positive effect on telework adoption, while Neirotti et al. [55] found the same to be true for Enterprise 2.0 tools (e.g., social media), as they facilitate communication. According to Brodt and Verburg [17], technology that supports telework, and in particular mobile work, needs to be optimized especially in terms of its human interface design (e.g., low weight, voice recognition, simplified user identification and personalisation).

In several studies [2,51,68,88], managers mentioned the *investment* involved in setting up the necessary technological infrastructure and the potential indirect costs of using telework (e.g., due to having to deal with technological malfunctions) as deterrents to telework. In addition, extensive investments in workstations at the office (e.g., for increased ergonomics or specialized equipment for workers with poor vision) were also cited as reasons for managers not to support telework, as this would incurr aditional costs and result in underuse of equipment already acquired [6,32].

Finally, in the studies by Peters et al. [60] and van der Merwe and Smith [86], it was also discussed whether technological developments are a driver or just an enabler of telework adoption. While Peters et al. [60] argued that technological developments are a driver because they force organizations to adapt, which also entails new types of work arrangements, such as telework, van der Merwe and Smith [86] argued that implementation of new technology alone will not drive diffusion of telework, but can be a barrier if the implementation is not managed well.

**Miscellaneous.** Some studies showed that companies with an *environmental orientation* support telework as a means of promoting environmental awareness and corporate social responsibility [20,68], which seems to be particularly important in the public sector [38,76]. The potential of telework-related *data security* issues related to telework to hamper telework adoption was reported in only one study [59]. Further, *legal concerns* were focused on to a negligible extent, with Svidronova et al. [76] reporting that legal restrictions (e.g., related to data privacy) may be a hindrance to telework adoption in public organizations, and Stavrou et al. [75] finding no support for the idea that stricter employment laws may be beneficial to the adoption of telework. Some factors that are mostly outside an organization's sphere of influence also have an impact, for instance, a tight labor market, which pressures companies to adopt telework in order to be more attractive employers or to retain staff when turnover is generally high [20,46,47,61,68]. Finally, aspects of national culture also seem to influence telework adoption, although evidence remains inconclusive, as it is not clear which specific aspects are helpful or a hindrance in this context [60,75,86].

## 3.2 Individual Adoption

On the individual side, the main categories investigated included characteristics of the individual (40 studies), characteristics of the job (35 studies), characteristics of the organization (32 studies) and home and family issues (27 studies), while technological characteristics (18 studies) received only minor attention. Variables outside these categories (i.e., "Miscellaneous"), were investigated in 10 studies.

**Individual.** The most frequent motivator in this category is the opportunity to avoid or at least reduce *commuting* time [1,8,14,19,28,31,32,43,79,80]. Some studies also highlighted the costs of commuting and/or business trips [9,23,28, 31,32,66], others identified a positive correlation with the commute distance [29,34,43,57], and Loo and Wang [42] argued that employees commuting by car preferred part-day telework. For a telework frequency of 2–4 days/month, Tang et al. [80] showed that employees who enjoyed riding their bikes were more inclined to telework. Moreover, engaging in shopping, maintenance and discretionary activities was shown to positively influence the decision to telework [7].

The *worker most likely to adopt telework* is male and has a college degree [14,27,56,85,87]. The more valuable in terms of qualifications an employee is to a firm, the higher the rate of home-based telework [57]. The "evening type" of worker is also found most likely to adopt telework [30]; the same is true for employees described as workaholics [42] and those with a high income [43,70]. Understandably, a similar effect holds for employees with a positive attitude towards telework and for those with high needs for autonomy, competence and relatedness [91]. The most important characteristics of potential teleworkers include self-discipline, the ability to work alone, technological literacy, good communication skills [13], and self-efficacy [71].

The fear of isolation [6,20,23,29,31,66] and perceived limitations to decision-making capabilities (lack of employee autonomy) [17] were both shown to cause reluctance to telecommute. Maruyama and Tietze [48] and Robert and Börjesson [66] argued that teleworkers can be motivated by an increase in work efficiency. However, performance risk and psychological risk reduced the desire to telework [71]. Robelski et al. [65] elaborated on an individual's choice between co-working spaces and home office, which is mainly dependent on perceived productivity, self-organization and social aspects.

Improved health and well-being is a motivator highlighted by Houghton et al. [32]. Reduced stress is another one found by Robert and Börjesson [66] and Wilton et al. [92], while Tahavori [79] pointed out an increase in workload and consequently an increase in work stress as potential hindrances. The teleworking status of one's social network positively influences the decision for telework [69]. Preferred communication type [40] and higher productivity due to fewer interruptions [92] were also found to affect an individual's inclination for telework.

**Home and Family.** The most widely discussed theme in this category is successfully reconciling one's professional life with family life and leisure time (*work-life balance*), which is frequently found to motivate employees to adopt home-based telework [1,13,14,19,32,43,57,88,92]. However, downsides are also evident, some studies question the strong positive correlation and see a desire to separate home and work [2,20,83]. Asatiani and Penttinen [6] reported problems with integrating employees' private lives with work practices and rhythms. Savings in commute time leading to more time for the family, was another factor discussed in this context, for example, in [9,43,48,79,83]; Hopkins and McKay also mentioned improved support for family management [31].

Another aspect is the number of *children* in the household. A higher number of children tends to increase the probability of telework [8,34,70], at least for women [66] and for children aged 6 to 10 [58]. However, Beno's study in Austria [14] and Ellder's study in Sweden [22] reported differently and found that telework is favored more by childless employees.

*Distraction by family members* is another common theme [6,66]. The availability of an adequate environment for telework can be a motivator [18,28], and its absence [6,66] or its costs [31,83] can be hindrances. Asgari et al. [8] and Hamsa et al. [29] found negative correlations of both household size and the number of cars owned with the willingness to telecommute; the latter was confirmed by Paleti and Vukovic [58]. Hazak [30], in contrast, found that household size positively influenced telework adoption. Goñi-Legaz and Ollo-López [27] stated that having either no partner or a working partner positively affected the decision for telework.

Furthermore, other household members' telecommuting [58] and the overall household income [80] were both shown to have strong effects on an individual's choice. A supportive family was also seen as a motivator for telework [5].

**Organization.** Telework requires the employer's permission, as Hopkins and McKay [31] pointed out. *Organizational support* is among the most important factors that positively influence the inclination for telework [23,28,40,86,91], while the employer's opposition [2,48,66] or perception of an organizational norm to fall behind or losing a chance for promotion when working from home [6,25, 29,79,83] were frequently mentioned hindrances. Sener and Bhat [70] argued that full-time employment has a positive influence on telework adoption, but a negative one on telework frequency. *A good relationship with one's supervisor* [13], their support for telework [5,50], and telework as a sign of trust [5,32,86] were motivators; a lack of support [9] or a lack of trust [25] had the opposite effect. Peters et al. [62] found that a supervisor's hard indirect controls positively influenced the adoption of telework, while Vilhelmson and Thulin [87] argued for a shift from direct supervision to result-based control. Female supervisors were found to more likely offer telework arrangements to their subordinates [10].

The form of *supervision* needed to encourage employees to adopt telework was shown to differ between cultures [25]: Individualistic cultures in Western countries prefer individual decisions, and a participative culture fosters telework

[57], while in Confucian cultures with high power distance (mainly in Asia) functioning within norms of hierarchy is of greater importance to the employee than the convenience of telework, but telecommuting supervisors can encourage their subordinates to follow suit [64]. *Colleague opinion* has a substantial influence on an individual's choice to telework [25,91]. This was confirmed by Seol et al. [71], who additionally found a similar effect of one's perceived social image. However, being less visible to colleagues, and a social norm of doing more work from home [20] and a lack of immediate peer feedback [16] can be hindering factors.

Malik et al. [43] pointed out a significant negative influence of *firm size*, while Goñi-Legaz and Ollo-López [27] saw little adoption with very small and very large firms, and a peak of adoption for companies with 50 to 99 employees. Employees in the public sector showed a higher willingness to telecommute than those in the private sector [8,27]. Existence of an organizational policy for telework [31,43] and informal telecommuting arrangements [34] were both shown to foster support telework adoption.

**Job.** The most researched factor in this category is the *nature of an employee's work* [2,5,8,23,29,31,44,45,66,86]. This includes levels of autonomy [18,27,86] and feedback [86]. Employees at the management level appear diverse: Tremblay and Thomsin [85] found a positive effect, and Goñi-Legaz and Ollo-López [27] and McNamara et al. [50] a negative one. Other studies [58,80] discussed a correlation between work status (full-time vs part-time) and the frequency of telework. IT and product development jobs [30], computational and mathematical jobs [50], knowledge-intensive jobs [22,87], and analytical jobs [84] were all shown to be conducive to an individual's choice for telework, while jobs in health care [50] and in the fields of manufacturing, administration or professional business [58] were not. Telework adoption was higher when employee work included creative, contemplative or intellectual activities [16,30]; studies conducted at universities revealed that a motivator for academic staff was the potential for relatively undisturbed research activities [34,88]. Ismail et al. [34] showed a negative influence of employees' accustomed frequency of face-to-face communication and a positive one of ICT-based communication on their inclination for telework.

Weekly work hours were another factor affecting telework adoption [43], Asgari et al. [8] found a positive correlation; work time variability and flexible working hours [8,19] were determinants as well. The expectations of higher productivity [2,6,9,13,23,32,48,92], flexible work schedule, better organization of one's work time [9,83,92], and better concentration [13] were major drivers for telework adoption. Concerns expressed by clients [20,25], however, can discourage employees from choosing telework.

**Technology.** At the individual level, technology is often seen as a *hygiene factor*. Clearly, technological issues hinder the introduction of telework [32]. Not having the right technology package [25] (e.g., a setup of multiple screens [6], or an adequate home office setup in general [92]) can be such an issue; low speed of hardware, software or internet connection are further obstacles [5,31,66,79].

Ellder [22] stressed the importance of access to essential material such as emails and one's work computer. The costs of hard- and software [9] and a lack of communication tools [2] can also have impairing effects.

However, adequate technological equipment can foster telework. This includes factors such as ICT infrastructure at the country level [57] and the availability of PCs and tablets [13] and supporting devices [5] at home. Low perceived IT complexity [18], technical possibilities [85], and smartphone usage [29] were all found to have a positive correlation with the willingness to telecommute. According to Boell et al. [16], electronic communication may be preferred to face-to-face situations to avoid interruptions and to maintain records of exchanges. This was also supported by Lebopo et al. [40], who showed that use of suitable communication tools positively influences the willingness to adopt telework.

**Miscellaneous.** Contrary to our expectations, *environmental factors* played a subordinate role in the literature analyzed; only Sener and Bhat [70] saw telecommuting as a means of reducing auto travel for environmentally conscious individuals. Similarly, *safety concerns* as motivators for telework were underrepresented. Paleti and Vukovic [58] stated that workers with significant concerns regarding safety were more likely to telecommute. Other papers demonstrated information security threats [6,31] as potential hindrances; Robelski et al. [65] also saw privacy concerns in co-working settings. Regarding *legal issues*, it was shown that higher levels of national telework regulation have a positive influence on telework adoption [57], while a lack of policies and regulations had the opposite effect [9]. Alizadeh and Sipe [4] pointed out the motivational effect of tax incentives.

Other relevant antecedents for telework included a country's culture. Ollo-López et al. [57] showed that, in countries with high levels of individualism and femininity and low power distance, telework adoption is high. According to Peters et al. [62], this also applies to nations characterized by strong national values, i.e. individualism and collectivism. Another aspect is the location of an employee's home: A greater distance to the workplace leads to more home-based telework, while a greater distance to the nearest shopping center reduces it [42]; Tang et al. [80] also showed effects of the regional accessibility for a household's neighborhood and the number of restaurants, and institutional establishments within 400 m.

## 4  Discussion and Conclusion

Based on our review of 72 articles, we find that, for both employers and employees, adoption of telework depends mainly upon a *set of factors* related to (i) the type of work done outside of the main office, (ii) the way that this work is organized and (iii) the organizational environment within which it is conducted. Considerations related to the type of work included whether an individual is already working on tasks that are done mainly with the help of ICT (i.e., more knowledge-based work) and is therefore not spatially tied (e.g., when shared workspaces are used within an office environment and the individual can switch workstations throughout the workweek). In relation to job organization, considerations included, for instance, the level of autonomy granted to employees (e.g., individuals being able to structure their workday independent of the work of others) and, in particular, how performance of the individual is assessed (e.g., with output-based management being more conducive to telework). A particular factor that was investigated extensively in this context is the level of trust between supervisor and employee, which was repeatedly found to be crucial to the adoption of telework. Regarding the organizational environment, considerations included the organizational culture and in particular the need for social interaction as an element that is difficult to fully replace in telework arrangements. In addition, support for telework at the top level of the organization, often indicated by elements such as a formal telework policy or human development practices (e.g., training on technology needed for telework) have a positive influence.

We can also see clear *differences between employers and employees*. For organizations, the reasoning to adopt telework was often centered around the potential advantages of telework in terms of individual work performance (e.g., fewer disruptions and therefore higher productivity at home) and it is also often used as an incentive mechanism (e.g., for senior employees). For individual employees, in contrast, telework is often seen as a means to improve work-life balance (e.g., by saving commute time, which can then be spent with family members) and to improve individual well-being (e.g., by creating a work environment and a job structure that fits better to the own work needs and work style).

The review also yielded some insights that might be *counter-intuitive and therefore surprising*. First, neither employers nor employees regard technological developments as drivers for telework; rather, both sides seem to agree that technology serves as an enabling factor. Hence, while ICT may have led to other types of human behavior being changed drastically (e.g., communication using social media), it is more of a complement in the work context (e.g., enabling formal communication, but unable to fully replace face-to-face conversations). This also applies to HCI-related concepts. Second, some considerations that are closely related to remote work (e.g., legal implications of working from home, such as documentation of hours worked or the insurance consequences of accidents at home) and its technological implementation (e.g., safety threats related to data transfers and data storage on devices used within the network at home) were covered in very few studies.

Our review, like every piece of research, has *limitations* that may have influenced these findings. In particular, a lack of publications focusing on legal or data privacy issues could be the result of a publication bias in our review. As our approach to searching and selecting the articles was rigorous, we expect this not to be the case - with one exception: We did not consider some of the more recent research published in the wake of the COVID-19 pandemic (Exclusion Criterion 1). Hence, an update to this review that focuses specifically on research published from 2020 onwards is called for.

There are further areas for *future research*. First, the type of an organization (in addition to the type of industry it operates in) should be considered when arguing for the generalization of study findings. Some studies, for example, focused on small and medium-sized companies (SME) [2,51], family-run businesses [51], and public-sector organizations such as universities and government agencies [32,76]. In the context of public-sector organizations, for instance, we saw a more frequent focus on factors related to the environment or the social context within the organization as potential influencers of telework adoption. Therefore, established relationships should also be tested with a more varied sample of organizations to ensure the validity of findings. Second, the samples used in the studies reviewed have a wide geographical distribution (e.g., with samples from Europe [47,48,54], the Americas [19,69,70], Africa [1,5,86], Asia [23,29,42], and Australia and Oceania [31,68]), although the majority focused on one specific country only. Of those few studies that focused on more than one country (i.e., [4,16,17,25,57,60–62,75], some found country-level differences, such as the influence of national culture on telework adoption [25,60]. Further studies are needed to assess what and how country-level differences affect telework adoption. In this context, there is an opportunity to combine country-level comparisons with research into aspects that have thus far been widely omitted such as the impact of legislation on telework adoption. For example, Belzunegui-Eraso and Erro-Garcés [12] recently highlighted that many countries lack telework-specific regulations, which hinders uptake of this practice. This lack could be due to state and local government rules that impede nation-wide teleworking regulations, such as zoning laws forbidding any kind of business including teleworking in certain areas, or labor law, which, for example, often demands safety precautions regarding the place of employment. Besides, a legal framework for working from home is not easily applicable to all different kinds of working situations and conditions, which could be why in so many countries teleworking arrangements are often agreed on individually based on employment contract clauses or company agreements. At the moment, there is also a discussion about "the right to disconnect" with regard to telework, which could also promote further legal regulations.

# References

1. Abdel-Wahab, A.G.: Employees' attitudes towards telecommuting. An empirical investigation in the egyptian governorate of dakahlia. Behav. Inf. Technol. **26**(5), 367–375 (2007). https://doi.org/10.1080/01449290500535426
2. Aguilera, A., Lethiais, V., Rallet, A., Proulhac, L.: Home-based telework in France: characteristics, barriers and perspectives. Transp. Rese. Part A: Policy Pract. **92**, 1–11 (2016). https://doi.org/10.1016/j.tra.2016.06.021
3. Ahrendt, D., et al.: Living, working and COVID-19. Eurofound, Publications Office of the European Union, Luxembourg (2020). https://doi.org/10.2806/467608
4. Alizadeh, T., Sipe, N.: Impediments to teleworking in live/work communities: local planning regulations and tax policies. Urban Policy Res. **31**(2), 208–224 (2013). https://doi.org/10.1080/08111146.2013.779919

5. Ansong, E., Boateng, R.: Organisational adoption of telecommuting: evidence from a developing country. Electron. J. Inf. Syst. Dev. Countr. **84**(1), e12008 (2018). https://doi.org/10.1002/isd2.12008

6. Asatiani, A., Penttinen, E.: Constructing continuities in virtual work environments: a multiple case study of two firms with differing degrees of virtuality. Inf. Syst. J. **29**(2), 484–513 (2019). https://doi.org/10.1111/isj.12217

7. Asgari, H., Jin, X.: Impacts of telecommuting on nonmandatory activity participation: role of endogeneity. Transp. Res. Rec. **2666**(1), 47–57 (2017). https://doi.org/10.3141/2666-06

8. Asgari, H., Jin, X., Mohseni, A.: Choice, frequency, and engagement: framework for telecommuting behavior analysis and modeling. Transp. Res. Rec. **2413**(1), 101–109 (2014). https://doi.org/10.3141/2413-11

9. Azami, M., Okhovati, M., Mokhtari, H., Khodabakhs, S.: Teleworking in health libraries: a survey of academic librarians' viewpoints. J. Biochem. Technol. **9**(2), 78–83 (2018)

10. Bae, K.B., Lee, D., Sohn, H.: How to increase participation in telework programs in U.S. federal agencies: examining the effects of being a female supervisor, supportive leadership, and diversity management. Public Pers. Manage. **48**(4), 565–583 (2019). https://doi.org/10.1177/0091026019832920

11. Beham, B., Baierl, A., Poelmans, S.: Managerial telework allowance decisions - a vignette study among German managers. Int. J. Hum. Resour. Manage. **26**(11), 1385–1406 (2015). https://doi.org/10.1080/09585192.2014.934894

12. Belzunegui-Eraso, A., Erro-Garcés, A.: Teleworking in the context of the covid-19 crisis. Sustainability **12**(9), Article 3662 (2020). https://doi.org/10.3390/su12093662

13. Beno, M.: An empirical study on teleworking among slovakia's office-based academics. In: Proceedings of the International Conference on Computational Science and Engineering (CSE), pp. 164–170. IEEE (2018). https://doi.org/10.1109/CSE.2018.00030

14. Beno, M.: Home-based telework and the role of gender - results of a study in Austria. In: AIS (ed.) Proceedings of the International Conference on Information Resources Management (Conf-IRM) (2019)

15. Blount, Y.: Pondering the fault lines of anywhere working (telework, telecommuting): a literature review. Found. Trends Inf. Syst. **1**(3), 163–276 (2015). https://doi.org/10.1561/2900000001

16. Boell, S.K., Cecez-Kecmanovic, D., Campbell, J.: Telework paradoxes and practices: the importance of the nature of work. New Technol. Work. Employ. **31**(2), 114–131 (2016). https://doi.org/10.1111/ntwe.12063

17. Brodt, T.L., Verburg, R.M.: Managing mobile work? Insights from European practice. New Technol. Work. Employ. **22**(1), 52–65 (2007). https://doi.org/10.1111/j.1468-005X.2007.00183.x

18. Carillo, K., Cachat-Rosset, G., Marsan, J., Saba, T., Klarsfeld, A.: Adjusting to epidemic-induced telework: empirical insights from teleworkers in France. Eur. J. Inf. Syst. **27**(4), 1–20 (2020). https://doi.org/10.1080/0960085X.2020.1829512

19. Coelho, F.A., Faiad, C., Rêgo, M.C.B., Ramos, W.: What Brazilian workers think about flexible work and telework? Int. J. Bus. Excell. **20**(1), 16–31 (2020). https://doi.org/10.1504/IJBEX.2019.10017773

20. Donnelly, R.: How "free" is the free worker? An investigation into the working arrangements available to knowledge workers. Pers. Rev. **35**(1), 78–97 (2006). https://doi.org/10.1108/00483480610636803

21. Dropkin, J., Moline, J., Kim, H., Gold, J.E.: Blended work as a bridge between traditional workplace employment and retirement: a conceptual review. Work Aging Retire. **2**(4), 373–383 (2016). https://doi.org/10.1093/workar/waw017
22. Elldér, E.: Who is eligible for telework? Exploring the fast-growing acceptance of and ability to telework in Sweden, 2005–2006 to 2011–2014. Soc. Sci. **8**(7), Article 200 (2019). https://doi.org/10.3390/socsci8070200
23. Eom, S.J., Choi, N., Sung, W.: The use of smart work in government: empirical analysis of Korean experiences. Gov. Inf. Q. **33**(3), 562–571 (2016). https://doi.org/10.1016/j.giq.2016.01.005
24. Gajendran, R.S., Harrison, D.A.: The good, the bad, and the unknown about telecommuting: meta-analysis of psychological mediators and individual consequences. J. Appl. Psychol. **92**(6), 1524–1541 (2007). https://doi.org/10.1037/0021-9010.92.6.1524
25. Gani, Z., Toleman, M.: Success factors and barriers to telework adoption in e-business in Australia and Singapore: the influence of culture and organizational culture. J. Theor. Appl. Electron. Commer. Res. **1**(3), 81–92 (2006)
26. Garrett, R.K., Danziger, J.N.: Which telework? Defining and testing a taxonomy of technology-mediated work at a distance. Soc. Sci. Comput. Rev. **25**(1), 27–47 (2007). https://doi.org/10.1177/0894439306293819
27. Goñi-Legaz, S., Ollo-López, A.: Factors that determine the use of flexible work arrangement practices in Spain. J. Fam. Econ. Issues **36**(3), 463–476 (2015). https://doi.org/10.1007/s10834-014-9408-1
28. Haddad, H., Lyons, G., Chatterjee, K.: An examination of determinants influencing the desire for and frequency of part-day and whole-day homeworking. J. Transp. Geogr. **17**(2), 124–133 (2009). https://doi.org/10.1016/j.jtrangeo.2008.11.008
29. Hamsa, A.A.K., Jaff, M.M., Ibrahim, M., Mohamed, M.Z., Zahari, R.K.: Exploring the effects of factors on the willingness of female employees to telecommute in Kuala Lumpur, Malaysia. Transp. Res. Proc. **17**, 408–417 (2016). https://doi.org/10.1016/j.trpro.2016.11.082
30. Hazak, A.: Perceived usability of teleworking options in creative knowledge work. In: Proceedings of the 10th International Conference on Knowledge and Smart Technology (KST), pp. 112–116. IEEE (2018). https://doi.org/10.1109/KST.2018.8426117
31. Hopkins, J.L., McKay, J.: Investigating 'anywhere working' as a mechanism for alleviating traffic congestion in smart cities. Technol. Forecast. Soc. Chang. **142**, 258–272 (2019). https://doi.org/10.1016/j.techfore.2018.07.032
32. Houghton, K.R., Foth, M., Hearn, G.: Working from the other office: trialling co-working spaces for public servants. Aust. J. Public Adm. **77**(4), 757–778 (2018). https://doi.org/10.1111/1467-8500.12317
33. Igeltjørn, A., Habib, L.: Homebased telework as a tool for inclusion? A literature review of telework, disabilities and work-life balance. In: Antona, M., Stephanidis, C. (eds.) HCII 2020. LNCS, vol. 12189, pp. 420–436. Springer, Cham (2020). https://doi.org/10.1007/978-3-030-49108-6_30
34. Ismail, F.D., Kadar Hamsa, A.A., Mohamed, M.Z.: Modelling the effects of factors on the stated preference towards telecommuting in IIUM campus, Gombak. Int. J. Urban Sci. **23**(1), 122–147 (2019). https://doi.org/10.1080/12265934.2018.1446352
35. Kaplan, S., Engelsted, L., Lei, X., Lockwood, K.: Unpackaging manager mistrust in allowing telework: comparing and integrating theoretical perspectives. J. Bus. Psychol. **33**(3), 365–382 (2018). https://doi.org/10.1007/s10869-017-9498-5

36. Kelly, E.L., Kalev, A.: Managing flexible work arrangements in us organizations: formalized discretion or 'a right to ask'. Soc. Econ. Rev. **4**(3), 379–416 (2006). https://doi.org/10.1093/ser/mwl001

37. Kossek, E.E., Thompson, R.J., Lautsch, B.A.: Balanced workplace flexibility: avoiding the traps. Calif. Manage. Rev. **57**(4), 5–25 (2015). https://doi.org/10.1525/cmr.2015.57.4.5

38. Kwon, M., Jeon, S.H.: Why permit telework? Exploring the determinants of California city governments' decisions to permit telework. Public Pers. Manage. **46**(3), 239–262 (2017). https://doi.org/10.1177/0091026017717240

39. Lapierre, L.M., van Steenbergen, E.F., Peeters, M.C.W., Kluwer, E.S.: Juggling work and family responsibilities when involuntarily working more from home: a multiwave study of financial sales professionals. J. Organ. Behav. **37**(6), 804–822 (2015). https://doi.org/10.1002/job.2075

40. Lebopo, C.M., Seymour, L.F., Knoesen, H.: Explaining factors affecting telework adoption in south african organisations pre-covid-19. In: ACM (ed.) Proceedings of the Conference of the South African Institute of Computer Scientists and Information Technologists. Association for Computing Machinery (2020)

41. Lembrechts, L., Zanoni, P., Verbruggen, M.: The impact of team characteristics on the supervisor's attitude towards telework: a mixed-method study. Int. J. Hum. Resour. Manage. **29**(21), 3118–3146 (2018). https://doi.org/10.1080/09585192.2016.1255984

42. Loo, B.P.Y., Wang, B.: Factors associated with home-based e-working and e-shopping in Nanjing, China. Transportation **45**(2), 365–384 (2018). https://doi.org/10.1007/s11116-017-9792-0

43. Malik, A., Rosenberger, P.J., Fitzgerald, M., Houlcroft, L.: Factors affecting smart working: evidence from Australia. Int. J. Manpow. **37**(6), 1042–1066 (2016). https://doi.org/10.1108/IJM-12-2015-0225

44. Mamdoohi, A.R., Kermanshah, M., Poorzahedy, H.: Telecommuting suitability modeling: an approach based on the concept of abstract job. Transportation **33**(4), 329–346 (2006). https://doi.org/10.1007/s11116-005-2308-3

45. Mamdoohi, A.R., Kermanshah, M., Poorzahedy, H.: Fuzzy random utility choice models: the case of telecommuting suitability. Int. J. Transp. Eng. **1**(4), 255–270 (2014)

46. Martínez-Sánchez, A., Pérez-Pérez, M., José Vela-Jiménez, M., de Luis-Carnicer, P.: Telework adoption, change management, and firm performance. J. Organ. Chang. Manag. **21**(1), 7–31 (2008). https://doi.org/10.1108/09534810810847011

47. Martínez-Sánchez, A., Pérez-Pérez, M., de Luis-Carnicer, P., Vela-Jiménez, M.J.: Telework, human resource flexibility and firm performance. New Technol. Work. Employ. **22**(3), 208–223 (2007). https://doi.org/10.1111/j.1468-005X.2007.00195.x

48. Maruyama, T., Tietze, S.: From anxiety to assurance: concerns and outcomes of telework. Pers. Rev. **41**(4), 450–469 (2012). https://doi.org/10.1108/00483481211229375

49. Mayo, M., Gomez-Mejia, L., Firfiray, S., Berrone, P., Villena, V.H.: Leader beliefs and CSR for employees: the case of telework provision. Leadersh. Organ. Dev. J. **37**(5), 609–634 (2016). https://doi.org/10.1108/LODJ-09-2014-0177

50. McNamara, T.K., Pitt-Catsouphes, M., Brown, M., Matz-Costa, C.: Access to and utilization of flexible work options. Ind. Relat.: J. Econ. Soc. **51**(4), 936–965 (2012). https://doi.org/10.1111/j.1468-232X.2012.00703.x

51. Meroño-Cerdán, A.L.: Perceived benefits of and barriers to the adoption of tele-working: peculiarities of Spanish family firms. Behav. Inf. Technol. **36**(1), 63–74 (2017). https://doi.org/10.1080/0144929X.2016.1192684

52. Messenger, J.C., Gschwind, L.: Three generations of telework: new ICTs and the (r)evolution from home office to virtual office. New Technol. Work. Employ. **31**(3), 195–208 (2016). https://doi.org/10.1111/ntwe.12073

53. Mihhailova, G., Õun, K., Türk, K.: Virtual work usage and challenges in different service sector branches. Balt. J. Manag. **6**(3), 342–356 (2011). https://doi.org/10.1108/17465261111167984

54. Neirotti, P., Paolucci, E., Raguseo, E.: Mapping the antecedents of telework diffusion: firm-level evidence from Italy. New Technol. Work. Employ. **28**(1), 16–36 (2013). https://doi.org/10.1111/ntwe.12001

55. Neirotti, P., Raguseo, E., Paolucci, E.: Flexible work practices and the firm's need for external orientation. J. Enterp. Inf. Manag. **30**(6), 922–943 (2017). https://doi.org/10.1108/JEIM-04-2016-0090

56. Nicholas, A.J., Guzman, I.R.: Is teleworking for the millennials? In: Power, N., Kaiser, K., Downey, J., Joseph, D. (eds.) Proceedings of the Special Interest Group on Management Information System's 47th Annual Conference on Computer Personnel Research, pp. 197–208. ACM Press, New York (2009). https://doi.org/10.1145/1542130.1542168

57. Ollo-López, A., Goñi-Legaz, S., Erro-Garcés, A.: Home-based telework: usefulness and facilitators. Int. J. Manpower **ahead-of-print**(ahead-of-print), 1 (2020). https://doi.org/10.1108/IJM-02-2020-0062

58. Paleti, R., Vukovic, I.: Telecommuting and its impact on activity-time use patterns of dual-earner households. Transp. Res. Rec. **2658**(1), 17–25 (2017). https://doi.org/10.3141/2658-03

59. Peters, P., Batenburg, R.: Telework adoption and formalisation in organisations from a knowlegde transfer perspective. Int. J. Work Innov. **1**(3), 251–270 (2015). https://doi.org/10.1504/IJWI.2015.074169

60. Peters, P., Bleijenbergh, I., Oldenkamp, E.: Cultural sources of variance in telework adoption in two subsidiaries of an ICT-multinational. Int. J. Employ. Stud. **17**(2), 66–101 (2009)

61. Peters, P., Heusinkveld, S.: Institutional explanations for managers' attitudes towards telehomeworking. Hum. Relat. **63**(1), 107–135 (2010). https://doi.org/10.1177/0018726709336025

62. Peters, P., Ligthart, P.E., Bardoel, A., Poutsma, E.: 'Fit' for telework? Cross-cultural variance and task-control explanations in organizations' formal telework practices. Int. J. Hum. Resour. Manage. **27**(21), 2582–2603 (2016). https://doi.org/10.1080/09585192.2016.1232294

63. Quttainah, M.A., Paczkowski, W.: Telework regulatory and legal contingencies for employers and consultants. Donn. J. Bus. Financ. Manage. Res. **1**(4), 30–39 (2015)

64. Raghuram, S., Fang, D.: Telecommuting and the role of supervisory power in China. Asia Pac. J. Manage. **31**(2), 523–547 (2014). https://doi.org/10.1007/s10490-013-9360-x

65. Robelski, S., Keller, H., Harth, V., Mache, S.: Coworking spaces: the better home office? A psychosocial and health-related perspective on an emerging work environment. Int. J. Environ. Res. Public Health **16**(13), 1–22 (2019). https://doi.org/10.3390/ijerph16132379

66. Robèrt, M., Börjesson, M.: Company incentives and tools for promoting telecommuting. Environ. Behav. **38**(4), 521–549 (2006). https://doi.org/10.1177/0013916505283422

67. Saludin, N.A., Hassan, H.: A conceptual study on working from home in Malaysian construction industry. Int. Proc. Econ. Dev. Res. **56**, 67–72 (2012)

68. Scholefield, G., Peel, S.: Managers' attitudes to teleworking. New Zealand J. Employ. Relat. **34**(3), 1–13 (2009)

69. Scott, D.M., Dam, I., Páez, A., Wilton, R.D.: Investigating the effects of social influence on the choice to telework. Environ. Plan. A: Econ. Space **44**(5), 1016–1031 (2012). https://doi.org/10.1068/a43223

70. Sener, I.N., Bhat, C.R.: A copula-based sample selection model of telecommuting choice and frequency. Environ. Plan. A: Econ. Space **43**(1), 126–145 (2011). https://doi.org/10.1068/a43133

71. Seol, S., Lee, H., Zo, H.: Exploring factors affecting the adoption of mobile office in business: an integration of TPB with perceived value. Int. J. Mobile Commun. **14**(1), 1–25 (2016). https://doi.org/10.1504/IJMC.2016.073341

72. Sewell, G., Taskin, L.: Out of sight, out of mind in a new world of work? Autonomy, control, and spatiotemporal scaling in telework. Organ. Stud. **36**(11), 1507–1529 (2015). https://doi.org/10.1177/0170840615593587

73. Silva-C, A., Montoya R, I.A., Valencia A, J.A.: The attitude of managers toward telework, why is it so difficult to adopt it in organizations? Technol. Soc. **59**, 101133 (2019). https://doi.org/10.1016/j.techsoc.2019.04.009

74. Singh, P., Paleti, R., Jenkins, S., Bhat, C.R.: On modeling telecommuting behavior: option, choice, and frequency. Transportation **40**(2), 373–396 (2013). https://doi.org/10.1007/s11116-012-9429-2

75. Stavrou, E.T., Parry, E., Anderson, D.: Nonstandard work arrangements and configurations of firm and societal systems. Int. J. Hum. Resour. Manage. **26**(19), 2412–2433 (2015). https://doi.org/10.1080/09585192.2014.992456

76. Svidronova, M.M., Merickova, B.M., Stejskal, J.: Social innovations in work organizing: telework in slovakia. In: XIX. mezinárodní kolokvium o regionálních vědách. Sborník příspěvků, pp. 431–438. Masaryk university, Brno (2016). https://doi.org/10.5817/CZ.MUNI.P210-8273-2016-55

77. Sweet, S., Pitt-Catsouphes, M., Besen, E., Golden, L.: Explaining organizational variation in flexible work arrangements: why the pattern and scale of availability matter. Commun. Work Family **17**(2), 115–141 (2014). https://doi.org/10.1080/13668803.2014.887553

78. Sweet, S., Pitt-Catsouphes, M., James, J.B.: Manager attitudes concerning flexible work arrangements: fixed or changeable? Commun. Work Family **20**(1), 50–71 (2017). https://doi.org/10.1080/13668803.2016.1271311

79. Tahavori, Z.: Teleworking in the national library and archives of Iran: teleworkers' attitudes. J. Librariansh. Inf. Sci. **47**(4), 341–355 (2015). https://doi.org/10.1177/0961000614532676

80. Tang, W., Mokhtarian, P.L., Handy, S.L.: The impact of the residential built environment on work at home adoption frequency: an example from northern California. J. Transp. Land Use **4**(3), 3–22 (2011). https://doi.org/10.5198/jtlu.v4i3.76

81. Taskin, L.: Introducing telework in a public and bureaucratic environment: a re-regulationist perspective on a non-conventional change. Int. J. Manag. Concepts Philos. **4**(3/4), 294–310 (2010). https://doi.org/10.1504/IJMCP.2010.037814

82. Taskin, L., Edwards, P.: The possibilities and limits of telework in a bureaucratic environment: lessons from the public sector. N. Technol. Work. Employ. **22**(3), 195–207 (2007). https://doi.org/10.1111/j.1468-005X.2007.00194.x
83. Thomsin, L., Tremblay, D.G.: Exploring the diversity of mobile working: a detailed examination on the sequences of workplaces and job satisfaction. J. e-Work. **2**, 47–66 (2008)
84. Thulin, E., Vilhelmson, B., Johansson, M.: New telework, time pressure, and time use control in everyday life. Sustainability **11**(11), 3067 (2019). https://doi.org/10.3390/su11113067
85. Tremblay, D.G., Thomsin, L.: Telework and mobile working: analysis of its benefits and drawbacks. Int. J. Work Innov. **1**(1), 100–113 (2012). https://doi.org/10.1504/IJWI.2012.047995
86. van der Merwe, F.I., Smith, D.C.: Telework: enablers and moderators when assessing organisational fit. In: de Villiers, C., van der Merwe, A.J., van Deventer, J.P., Matthee, M.C., Gelderblom, H., Gerber, A. (eds.) Proceedings of the Southern African Institute for Computer Scientist and Information Technologists Annual Conference, pp. 323–333. ACM Press, New York (2014). https://doi.org/10.1145/2664591.2664599
87. Vilhelmson, B., Thulin, E.: Who and where are the flexible workers? Exploring the current diffusion of telework in Sweden. New Technol. Work. Employ. **31**(1), 77–96 (2016). https://doi.org/10.1111/ntwe.12060
88. Vogel, E., Percival, J., Muirhead, B.: Can telecommuting work in a traditional university environment? Exploring perspectives of deans and senior academic administrators. In: Gómez Chova, L., Candel Torres, I., López Martínez, A. (eds.) Proceedings of the International Technology, Education and Development Conference, pp. 1–11. International Association of Technology, Education and Development (IATED) (2011)
89. Webster, J., Watson, R.T.: Analyzing the past to prepare for the future: writing a literature review. MIS Q. **26**(2), xiii–xxiii (2002)
90. Weiss, D., Damianos, L.E., Drozdetski, S.: Teleworkers and their use of an enterprise social networking platform. In: Nah, F.F.-H., Tan, C.-H. (eds.) HCIB 2015. LNCS, vol. 9191, pp. 532–541. Springer, Cham (2015). https://doi.org/10.1007/978-3-319-20895-4_49
91. Wessels, C., Schippers, M.C., Stegmann, S., Bakker, A.B., van Baalen, P.J., Proper, K.I.: Fostering flexibility in the new world of work: a model of time-spatial job crafting. Front. Psychol. **10**, Article 505 (2019). https://doi.org/10.3389/fpsyg.2019.00505
92. Wilton, R.D., Páez, A., Scott, D.M.: Why do you care what other people think? A qualitative investigation of social influence and telecommuting. Transp. Res. Part A: Policy Pract. **45**(4), 269–282 (2011). https://doi.org/10.1016/j.tra.2011.01.002

# Addressing the "Unseens": Digital Wellbeing in the Remote Workplace

Holtjona Galanxhi[1]([⊠]) and Fiona Fui-Hoon Nah[2]

[1] University of Nebraska-Lincoln, Lincoln, NE 68588, USA
[2] Missouri University of Science and Technology, Rolla, MO 65409, USA
nahf@mst.edu

**Abstract.** The ubiquity of sophisticated devices, along with uninterrupted access to the Internet and organizational computerized systems, allows for the "anyplace" workplace to be established. Technology has the potential to deliberately or inadvertently impact psychological wellbeing. Specific psychological demands are inadvertently imposed on remote employees whose permanent online presence is required. Hence, it is important to understand factors affecting digital wellbeing and steps that can be taken to maximize the wellbeing of remote employees. This paper provides suggestions for future research on studying the digital wellbeing of (fully or partially) remote employees. A research framework is proposed to demonstrate the different levels of analysis at which digital wellbeing could be explored and studied.

**Keywords:** Remote work · Digital wellbeing · Digital wellness · Technostress

## 1 Remote Work

Due to the increased pervasiveness of new communication technologies, new ways of working (that resulted in a mobile, multi-locational, remote, flexible, distributed, or virtual workplace) have become increasingly feasible. A new digital workplace has emerged from breaking down information silos and channels once available only on desktop computers in the physical workplace (Byström 2016). As discussed later, the literature has documented both positive and negative effects of remote work on wellbeing. The coronavirus crisis has demonstrated that remote work may become commonplace even for professions that are deemed more inclined toward in-person interactions such as teachers, lawyers, and priests. Therefore, new questions arise from remote work becoming increasingly ubiquitous: Does it matter where you work? How does remote work impact our lifestyle and wellbeing? How do employees negotiate their work-life boundaries under these circumstances?

Many companies intend to maintain remote work even after the pandemic is over because both employees and organizations see benefits in terms of cost-saving, lowering costs of commuting, saving time and organizational resources, and higher employee satisfaction (Barbuto et al. 2020; Thulin et al. 2019). However, certain negative effects in terms of employees' wellbeing might also occur (De Menezes and Kelliher 2011;

© Springer Nature Switzerland AG 2021
F. F.-H. Nah and K. Siau (Eds.): HCII 2021, LNCS 12783, pp. 347–364, 2021.
https://doi.org/10.1007/978-3-030-77750-0_22

Grant et al. 2007; Michel 2011; Moen et al. 2013; Parker 2014). Therefore, further research is necessary to study these unintended consequences of remote work on digital wellbeing, which refers to the impact of digital technologies on what it means to live a life that is good for a human being (Burr et al. 2020; Floridi 2014; Nah and Siau 2020).

Working from home is not a new phenomenon, but the coronavirus crisis intensified and accelerated workplace changes that normally would have taken far longer to materialize. Instead of a hybrid digital-physical workplace that is already customary for many organizations, a fully virtual and digital workplace has become the norm in a very short time. These changes have affected how information is created and consumed in organizations. It is expected that 'when' and 'where' people work may not only affect their productivity and innovativeness but can also affect employees' digital wellbeing.

Several studies have shown that the use of information and communication technologies (ICTs) during the coronavirus crisis has made a positive impact on digital wellbeing (e.g. García del Castillo-Rodríguez et al. 2020). But for others, working from home is associated with a negative impact on digital wellbeing (Song and Gao 2020). It does "Matter Where You Work".

## 1.1 It Does Matter Where You Work

Remote work, also known as telecommuting or telework, is an arrangement between an employee and the employer where the employee's work is performed remotely outside the employer's physical premises (Messenger et al. 2017). People who work away from a "formal" desk show a remarkable diversity in their work patterns (Bjerrum and Bødker 2003). Burmeister et al. (2018) found that the environment affects concentration, accuracy, and decision-making; more specifically, participants in the 'formal' work environment showed higher accuracy compared to participants in the non-work environment. Further, remote workers demonstrate significantly lower satisfaction with work-life balance and higher negative work-home interaction (Jacukowicz and Merecz-Kot 2020).

Several studies conducted during the coronavirus pandemic found that remote employees emphasize the importance of and difficulty in maintaining work contacts and intense use of communication systems. Most remote employees found themselves working longer hours than normal, and some even indicated that they accomplished less. However, it is possible for remote employees to efficiently and effectively perform their tasks and maintain good relations with colleagues, but with the downside that it may require working longer than normal (Bolisani et al. 2020).

## 1.2 Work-Life Boundaries

The distinction between work-related and non-work-related activities is becoming less and less meaningful, as the spheres of work and life blur into each other (Bødker 2016). The "always-on" mode has extended work beyond the walls of physical buildings, creating an intrusion into people's personal life (Bjerrum and Bødker 2003; Bødker and Christiansen 2006). Because home is normally a place of restoration, the blurring of work-home boundaries may reduce opportunities to disconnect from work for restoration, and hence, it can negatively impact wellbeing.

Bødker (2016) advocates rethinking technology and how it contributes to the boundaries of work and life. She argues that work-life boundaries are not fixed, and technology should not, and is not meant to, remove the boundaries. She calls for controllable/negotiable dynamic boundaries made possible through flexibility in technological settings. In this regard, seams and boundaries are not static, and they are considered resources for: 1) reducing the complexity of information and activity; 2) standardizing shared objects across activities, communities, and groups; 3) making boundaries visible so groups can define and distinguish themselves from others; 4) supporting individual/group privacy and legitimacy.

## 2  Digital Wellbeing in the Remote Workplace

Digital wellbeing has been defined as "A state where subjective wellbeing is maintained in an environment characterized by digital communication overabundance. Research has shown that it does "matter where you work" (Hill et al. 2003; Moskaliuk et al. 2017) as the physical environment can influence cognition and work performance (e.g., Kay et al. 2004).

### 2.1  Digital Wellbeing and HCI Research

There seems to be a need for a new cross-cutting research field that focuses on the identification, analysis, and management of vulnerabilities and the unintended side effects emerging as a result of the sociotechnical digital transition (Scholz et al. 2018).

According to Schalock et al. (Schalock et al. 2002), there are more than 200 definitions of wellbeing across different contexts and there are three factors in the wellbeing construct: *1) independence* (personal development and self-determination); 2) *social participation* (relationships, social acceptance, and rights); 3) *wellbeing* (psychological, physical and material). Burr et al. (2020) identified three themes in wellbeing research: *1) positive computing; 2) personalized human-computer interaction; 3) autonomy and self-determination.* They believe these themes are central to ongoing discussions and research on digital wellbeing.

**Positive Computing.**  This theme builds on positive psychology research and adopts an interdisciplinary perspective to study the individual and social factors that foster wellbeing (human flourishing) to understand how to promote digital wellbeing by embedding ethics more closely within the design process (Calvo and Peters 2017; Desmet and Pohlmeyer 2013).

**Personalized Human-Computer Interaction.**  Personalization has been defined as "the ability to provide contents and services tailored to individuals based on knowledge about their needs, expectations, preferences, constraints, and behaviours" (Vallée et al. 2016, p. 186). The ubiquity of complex digital technologies and advances in data management and analytics has increased the viability of personalized human-computer interaction (Burr et al. 2020).

**Autonomy and Self-determination.** Five dimensions of autonomy may clarify the mediating role of health and wellbeing applications on the communication of information: *1) degree of control and involvement* that the user has within the app; 2) *degree of personalization* over the app's functionality; 3) *degree of truthfulness and reliability* related to the information presented to the user, and how it affects the user's decisions; 4) *user's self-understanding* regarding the goal-pursuit, and whether the app promotes or hinders a user's awareness of their agency; 5) *whether the app promotes some form of moral deliberation or moral values* in the actions it recommends (Rughiniş et al. 2015).

## 2.2 Designing for Wellbeing

Peters et al. (Peters et al. 2020) suggest that designing for wellbeing must be distinguished from designing for positive emotions. In this view, wellbeing involves more than positive emotions. Tools should be built in a way to help safeguard against psychological harm and support sustainable wellbeing. While recognizing its importance, design for positive emotion, will not necessarily result in wellbeing, as feeling good is different from functioning well (Ryan and Deci 2017; Keyes and Annas 2009).

Specker Sullivan and Reiner (2019) describe several ethical frameworks to assess the justification of the influence of digital wellness technologies on users. They argue that "while some technologies help users to complete tasks and satisfy immediate preferences, other technologies encourage users to reflect on the values underlying their habits and teach them to evaluate their lives' competing demands" (p. 1). They conclude that applications take a more *maternalistic* approach to wellbeing and focus on both immediate wellness and long-term reflection on wellbeing are preferable.

## 2.3 Levels of Analyzing Digital Wellbeing

The "Digital Revolution" is a double-edged sword with benefits and challenges such that special attention should be given to what Scholz et al. (2018) call the "unseens". They suggest that these unseen effects should be studied at multiple levels: *1) the Human Individual; 2) Human Groups; 3) Organizations (Companies); 4) Institutions (Governmental Organizations); 5) Societies (Nation States); 6) Human Species*. The authors argue that human-machine interaction must be seen as a form of social interaction and self-reflection.

**Individual.** Countless studies have shown that communication medium affects communication itself, and thereof expected to play a significant role in wellbeing (Taylor et al. 2008; Caplan 2007).

*Theories of Computer-Mediated Communication (CMC).* CMC theories can be useful in wellbeing research within HCI. One of the most influential CMC theories is the media richness theory (MRT) (Daft and Lengel 1986; Dennis and Kinney 1998). According to MRT, which is also known as information richness theory, different media vary in their capacity for *1) immediate feedback; 2) multiple cues; 3) language variety; 4) personal focus*. Leaner media might be best used to reduce uncertainty, while richer media are best used to reduce equivocality. Media synchronicity theory (MST) (Dennis et al. 2008) is another prominent theory. MST focuses on the ability of media to support synchronous communication. According to MST, when the main objective is to convey information, low synchronicity media are more suitable, but when the main objective is convergence on shared meanings, high synchronicity media are more suitable. Both MRT and MST are focused on which media should be chosen in different contexts. The Uses and Gratification (U&G) theory explores which channels are chosen and the reasons for them. According to U&G, users are looking to satisfy certain needs when using media. Recently, U&G has focused more on connecting the needs, goals, benefits, and consequences of media consumption and uses, along with individual factors, making U&G more predictive and explanatory (West and Turner 2010).

Gui et al. (2017) define digital wellbeing skills as "a set of skills needed to manage the side effects of digital communication overabundance" (p. 163). These skills are necessary to achieve strategic attention focus, avoid the stress caused by an overwhelming flow of information, minimize time wasted, and reduce attention on irrelevant activities. Digital stimuli should be managed so that they can be efficiently filtered and finalized toward personal goals and wellbeing. Two types of digital wellbeing skills are: 1) *attentional skills* (cognitive skills required for maintaining focus on specific issues for sufficient lapses of time, without getting interrupted); 2) *strategic or meta-cognitive skills* (cognitive strategies that envisage "constraints that an agent imposes on himself for the sake of some expected benefit to himself" (Elster and Jon 2000, p. 4).

**Group.** Communication (formal and informal) and awareness are key to working in teams/groups. The social dimension of remote work and digital wellbeing also needs a conscious reflection on digital etiquette (Montag and Diefenbach 2018) and consists of examining how technology is integrated within the existing culture of a group/team, the organization, or society as a whole. It includes determining what is considered an appropriate or adequate use of technology in social settings and areas intentionally made technologically-free (e.g., for certain hours of the day). This aspect is of importance especially in the context of the fully or partially remote workplace.

Wang et al. (2014) for example, used the feedback process model and the dissonance reduction theory to examine the effects of two types of emoticons (i.e., liking and disliking emoticons) on negative feedback acceptance. Their results showed that liking and disliking emoticons have different effects on the acceptance of negative feedback. They found that the perceived good intention of the provider and the perceived feedback negativity are contingent upon feedback specificity.

**Organizational.** Kulkarni et al. (2017) have used the structurational model of technology (Orlikowski 1992), which is based on structuration theory (Giddens 1979; Giddens 1984), to reconstruct the relationship between organizations and technology. In the context of remote work and when communication channels are porous (e.g., constant switching between email vs. chat), the question becomes how business intelligence (BI) capability is affected, and how can an organization improve its BI capability. Additionally, user participation is found to affect general information capability and BI capability. Hence, remote work outcomes at the individual and group levels have an impact at higher levels of analysis.

**Government and Society.** The fulfillment of psychological needs at the societal level contributes to long-term wellbeing (Sheldon et al. 2001). Evidence shows that the extent to which the needs of other people and society are fulfilled is also a determinant factor of individual subjective wellbeing (Tay and Diener 2011).

Because human relationships with one another and their environment has been changed by the rapid deployment and ubiquity of digital technologies, the wellbeing of individuals is now intimately connected to the information environment and the digital technologies that mediate human interactions with that environment (Burr et al. 2020). Therefore, ethical questions concerning the impact of digital technologies need to be considered at the societal level.

Capability Approach. Taddeo (2015) has proposed using a capability approach (Sen 1980) in analyzing the online persona in the context of individual wellbeing. He states that there is a "struggle between liberties and authorities" which will then be reconsidered based on an analysis of the wellbeing of the online persona, and the individual rights that come with it. Society today faces a compelling need to strive for a harmonious combination of liberties and authorities to ensure the wellbeing of individuals and society.

**Human Species.** In the longer term, different modalities of communication and working environments will cause changes in our brains by changing the nature of work itself, our expectations, and our employers' expectations. With continuous and repeated feedback loops between us and these systems, our psyches will change and adapt (Bednar and Welch 2019).

### 2.4 The Net Effect on Wellbeing

The lack of theoretical and empirical understanding of the goals of digital wellbeing could be due, partially or fully. to disagreements regarding the optimal way to measure the wellbeing construct, and/or from the uncertainty about the causal relationship between the use of digital technology (e.g., a smartphone) and the psychological effects (e.g., increased anxiety or depression) (Peters et al. 2018).

**Advantages.** Research shows that the use of ICTs can improve life satisfaction in the elderly population by, for example, increasing feelings of self-sufficiency (Klein 2017); ICTs can also provide young people and adults with more social and emotional support, which improves their psychological wellbeing (e.g., Meng et al. 2017; Pérez 2018; Verduyn et al. 2017).

Peters et al. (2020) contend that there is a gap in commercial digital wellbeing initiatives because the focus is mostly on changing human behavior rather than changing technologies. From a design perspective, Desmet and Fokkinga (2020) contend that need profiles can support a systematic approach to design for positive experiences and subjective wellbeing (Hassenzahl et al. 2010; Desmet et al. 2001; Desmet and Hekkert 2007). Wellbeing-supportive design tools should satisfy the need for proof, buy-in, tangibility, and the need for clear instruction (Peters et al. 2020).

Garcia del Castillo-Rodriguez et al. (2020) examined the use of the Quality of Life scale (acronym in Spanish is TICO) and ICTs in the context of coronavirus. They found that the factors examined in the instrument account for the following dimensions: *1) satisfaction with life; 2) emotional support;* 3) *"social support"*. The conclusion is that these factors present an adequate correlation to assess personal perceptions of quality of life associated with the use of ICTs in the context examined. Evidence also suggests that positive work factors (*collegial support, rewards,* meaning, *and cohesion*) promote wellbeing (Rogerson et al. 2016). Therefore, when technology supports these needs, it promotes their wellbeing.

*Digital Wellness.* Digital wellness technologies are tools that are designed to address immediate needs in digital wellbeing. Some technologies are geared toward helping users to complete tasks and satisfy immediate preferences, while others focus on encouraging users to reflect on the values underlying their habits and teaching them to evaluate and prioritize their lives' competing demands. Specker Sullivan and Reiner (2019) proposed that a maternalistic approach that incorporates these wellness technologies is more effective than a paternalistic approach as the former is more likely to lead to more skillful user engagement with technology. The main difference between the two approaches is that paternalism involves a local constraint of an individual's liberty for the sake of their immediate benefit (but not necessarily their global autonomy competencies), while maternalism involves a local intervention on an agent that benefits their overall autonomy competencies in conjunction with their wellbeing.

**Disadvantages.** Recent research during the coronavirus pandemic has shown contrary evidence to what was generally assumed in the pre-COVID literature. It was found that working from home is not always a positive factor for employees as it depends on their specific home conditions (Bolisani et al. 2020). A large portion of employees can keep sufficiently good and fruitful interactions, although it depends on the type of job they perform and the availability of appropriate communication technologies. There are still many employees who struggle with using different communication systems, and this struggle can be a stress factor for them.

*Fragmentation of Everyday Life.* Duke and Montag (2017) have provided evidence that smartphone addiction is inversely related to self-reported productivity. In terms of fragmentation of daily life, they suggest that it can be partly explained by the high number of daily interruptions. When working from home, the number of non-related interruptions is expected to be higher.

Interruptions caused by ICTs can potentially reduce business productivity and increase employee stress. In this context, Galluch, Grover, and Thatcher (2015) examined the quantity and content of ICT-enabled interruptions. They found that ICT-enabled interruptions may negatively affect individual productivity and therefore decrease organizational productivity. Additionally, interruptions may lead to technostress which can, initially, be in the form of short-term episodes of technostress, but cumulatively, can cause harm to sustainable wellbeing.

*Technostress.* The term technostress was originally coined by Craig Brod (1984), and more recently has been defined as "the stress that users experience as a result of application multitasking, constant connectivity, information overload, frequent system upgrades and consequent uncertainty, continual relearning and consequent job-related insecurities, and technical problems associated with the organizational use of ICT" (Tarafdar et al. 2010, pp. 304–305). Kushlev and Dunn (2015) demonstrated that there is a positive correlation between the number of times a day a person checks emails and his or her stress level, while other studies show that the mere presence of a mobile phone diminishes the quality of face-to-face interaction (Przybylski and Weinstein 2013). Molino et al. (2020) examined technostress in the context of coronavirus pandemic and found that it negatively affects work-family conflict and behavioral stress.

*Fatigue, Isolation, and Digital Depression.* Research has shown that social factors (social comparison, social interaction overload, social surveillance, and social information overload) and the technical factors of system complexity can all be contributing factors to fatigue.

Isolation increases with remote work (Mann and Holdsworth 2003). Moreover, there is a perceived obligation to maintain connections and stay updated, which can negatively affect wellbeing (Brooks 2015; Fox and Moreland 2015). Toscano and Zappalà (2020) investigated the experience of isolation in terms of stress, perceived productivity, and work satisfaction in the context of the coronavirus crisis. They found that social isolation is negatively related to remote work satisfaction, confirming previous studies (Orhan et al. 2016; Lee and Brand 2005). Social isolation and stress were also found to be linked to each other which is consistent with previous studies (Stephenson and Bauer 2010; Weinert et al. 2015). The findings also indicate a negative influence of social isolation on perceived productivity. Their study emphasized the importance of social relationships and found that feelings of loneliness are related to perceived productivity and work satisfaction.

Brown and Kuss (2020) looked at the *fear-of-missing-out* (FOMO) phenomenon, mental wellbeing, and social connectedness, and how they were influenced by a social media abstinence trial. FOMO is a strong motivator for social media use and may impact individual wellbeing. A significant positive relationship between mental wellbeing and social connectedness was found. The authors also provide additional insights regarding distracting nature of notifications from many platforms (such as email, chat, etc.). They found that the removal of notifications was associated with a more positive experience, suggesting that notifications trigger FOMO.

Although long-term effects of technology use on the human brain have not been sufficiently conclusive, they can change the human brain because technology pervades all aspects of our lives and exerts an impact on thinking, feeling, and social interaction (e.g., Small et al. 2020; Sparrow et al. 2011). The term "Digital Depression" underlines threats to wellbeing and happiness (Diefenbach and Ullrich 2016). Evidence has shown that overuse of digital channels is strongly linked to depression (e.g., Montag et al. 2017).

# 3  Research Models and Measures

We review related research in digital wellbeing and discuss the research models and their measurement in this section.

Bednar and Welch (2019) argue that human action, along with changes in personal and organizational life, is driven by desire. They proposed using a socio-technical approach that reflects *multiple boundaries* drawn from the perspectives of different human actors within the space. This approach recognizes the fact that individuals interact within an organized working system, *continually creating and recreating it*. Multiple roles with unique perspectives join, interact in, and leave the system making it open and dynamic.

Vanden Abeele (2020) proposed a theoretical model of digital wellbeing that accounts for the dynamic and complex nature of peoples' relationships to continuous connectivity. The model considers the balance *between connectivity and disconnectivity* that results in digital wellbeing, contingent upon a constellation of *person-, device- and context-specific factors*. Different combinations of these factors represent pathways to digital wellbeing, and with continuous repetitions, affect long-term digital wellbeing.

### 3.1 Design to Support Wellbeing

Two of the methods proposed for investigating wellbeing-supportive design are: 1) *a six-step process of Positive-Practice Canvas (PPC)* (Klapperich et al. 2019), and 2) METUX - a model for *Motivation, Engagement, and Thriving in User Experience* (Peters et al. 2018).

**Positive-Practice Canvas.** The PPC is based on a model of social practices (Shove et al. 2012) combined with the notion of psychological needs (Hassenzahl et al. 2013). It takes a *multi-level model*, which connects wellbeing, positive experiences, and psychological needs (*the 'Why'*) through activities (*the 'What'*) with concrete technologies, their form, and interaction possibilities (*the 'How'*). This methodology allows for positive practices to be accumulated and serve as a starting point for further design activities.

**METUX.** This model draws on SDT to understand the impact of digital technology on motivation, engagement, and wellbeing. SDT identifies three basic needs which must be satisfied for an individual to experience digital wellbeing: *1) autonomy; 2) competence; 3) relatedness*. They propose that to address wellbeing, psychological needs must be considered within the following *five spheres of analysis*, which sit within a *sixth sphere* that addresses the direct and collateral effects of technology use and non-user experiences: 1) at the point of technology adoption; 2) during interaction with the interface; 3) as a result of engagement with technology-specific tasks; 4) as part of the technology-supported behavior; 5) as part of an individual's life overall.

### 3.2 Measurement

**Screen Use/Screen Time.** People find it difficult to identify a healthy routine of technology use (e.g., Blabst and Diefenbach 2017). A debate about the psychological impacts of screen time is ongoing. Some evidence routinely shows negative correlations between screen time and wellbeing (e.g., Twenge and Campbell 2018). However, recent meta-analyses (Odgers and Jensen 2020; Orben 2020) have found that research in this area is difficult to interpret and there are mixed findings. Overall, there are criticisms concerning poor conceptualizations, the use of non-standardized measures that are predominantly based on self-report, and issues with measuring screen time as a ratio over time and context (Kaye et al. 2020).

Kaye et al. (2020) suggest replacing "screen time" with "screen use" which varies across time and context. In this way, the measurements are more centrally developed around behaviors rather than what "functions and features" people are using. The authors view "screen use" to be irrespective of platforms or features; it is based on the behavior(s) facilitated by the screens: entertainment, social, education/work, and informational. Therefore, this view suggests that the needs of users should be the main concern, and users themselves should be co-creators. Once again, a more user-participative and context-relevant approach is advocated in addressing relevant aspects of digital wellbeing.

# 4   Future Research

Particularly during the coronavirus pandemic, many practitioners have looked for best practices to address the digital wellbeing of remote employees. For example, Greenwood and Krol (2020) offer eight concrete actions managers and leaders can take:

- Be vulnerable
- Model healthy behaviors
- Build a culture of connection through check-ins
- Offer flexibility and be inclusive
- Communicate more than you think you need to
- Invest in training - prioritize proactive and preventive workplace mental health training
- Modify policies and practices - to reduce stress for everyone
- Measure – to ensure accountability.

While the above suggestions are all useful tips, the new realities of remote work require a better understanding of digital wellbeing. As Tarafdar, Gupta, and Turel (2013) have stated, "the very qualities that make IT useful - reliability, portability, user friendliness and fast processing - may also be undermining employee productivity, innovation and wellbeing". In the rest of this section, we present future research areas/themes for exploring, understanding, and enhancing digital wellbeing, in the context of fully or partially remote work.

We expand on research avenues proposed by Montag and Diefenbach (2018) below. The literature review provided strong support for cross-cutting research on digital wellbeing, which should take place at different levels of analysis (as first presented by Scholz et al. 2018). Additionally, it has become evident that context and repeated experiences (loops) play a significant role and should be factored in when examining digital wellbeing. Several authors also distinguish between near-term and long-term digital wellbeing.

Further research is needed to look at the different levels of analysis – from individuals, groups of individuals, organizations, etc. – in *a work setting that can take place anywhere* (see Fig. 1). More specifically, areas for future digital wellbeing research include (starting at the lowest level of analysis):

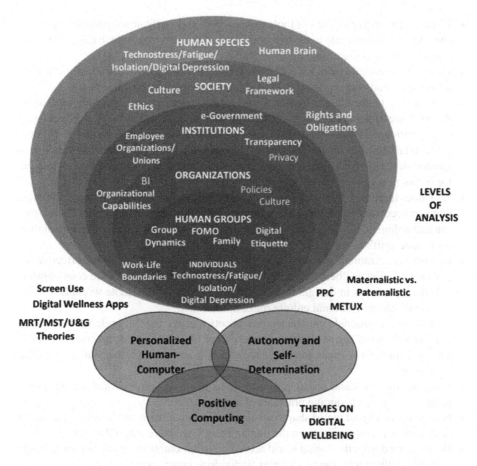

**Fig. 1.** A multi-level approach to research on digital wellbeing

- How do new forms of self-perception, self-reflection, and self–presentation affect the social communication of remote employees?
- What kinds of self-control mechanisms and other digital skills are employed by the individual employee when it comes to his/her online work persona? How are these digital skills used to maximize the net short-term and long-term (sustainable) wellbeing?
- What ICT support is needed for the individual employees to remain effective and efficient in meeting their performance goals of remote work while preserving their wellbeing?
- How do pragmatic and symbolic reasons for media choice operate in the context of remote work?
- What are strategies to promote flow experiences in times of fragmented lifestyle of individuals and the groups/teams they belong to?
- What is the impact of group/team features, such as social inclusion, group identity, norm-building (e.g., digital etiquette), and group dynamics, on digital wellbeing?

- What are the characteristics of tools that can help and facilitate individual employees and teams in managing work-life boundaries? What is the right balance between seamlessness and seamfulness?
- What are meaningful rules for social communication in times of abundantly available access to digital distractions (for individual, group, and organization)?
- How can one better adapt to hybrid or fully virtual meetings, and "decision-making by Zoom"? Are decision-makers going to adapt their styles considering digital wellbeing considerations? What tools do they need to be able to remain efficient and efficient while maintaining everyone's digital wellbeing? At what level should feature-control be exercised (e.g., individual, group, meeting level, etc.)? What are employees looking for in this new context for decision-making?
- How does increased autonomy impact digital wellbeing? What are the technological features necessary to preserve trust and minimize stress from autonomy? What role can technological tools/features play in performance feedback and conflict resolution for remote staff?
- In what organizational contexts are maternalistic approaches the most effective for designing digital wellbeing organizational tools? What are the pros and cons of paternalistic approaches in designing technologies to be used in remote workplaces? Do organizational and national culture make a difference?
- How do organizations/companies/governments manage the "struggle between liberties and authorities" in the context of remote work? In what ways do practices, policies, and legal frameworks need to change to reflect the new realities to ensure sustainable wellbeing?
- What are the roles and social responsibilities of digital professionals in designing online settings to encourage practices of wellbeing?
- How does the digital world shape or change the human brain and how can we hinder or minimize harmful effects on the human brain? Are there cultural differences?
- How can we design the digital world according to our emotional evolutionary heritage to foster wellbeing in digital societies (individual, group, society)?
- Do we need a better measure for the digital wellbeing construct and its antecedents (e.g., technostress creators)? How can we better understand the relationships between remote work and digital wellbeing?

## 5   Conclusion

Creating a better understanding of the direct and indirect effects of the "unseens" on digital wellbeing requires experience and expertise from different fields of science. The proliferation of technology supporting a culture that is "always-on" and its impact on wellbeing warrants further research in order to propose solutions to maximize individual digital wellbeing. In this paper, we propose a multi-level framework that demonstrates the effects of different technological affordances on the digital wellbeing of users. We also provide suggestions for future research at each level of analysis.

In this paper, we highlight the importance of recognizing the dynamic and complex nature of the relationships between people and the continuous connectivity that they experience to more fully understand their impact on wellbeing. Remote employees operate in a system where boundaries open and close at different times, and there are continuous information and feedback not only at the individual level but also at the higher levels. Therefore, cross-cutting research that utilizes mixed methodologies would be the most promising. The questions identified in this paper are not meant to be comprehensive, but they serve as an initial blueprint in advancing digital wellbeing research.

# References

Barbuto, A., Gilliland, A., Peebles, R., Rossi, N., Shrout, T.: Telecommuting: smarter workplaces. Retrieved from The Ohio State University. Campus as a living laboratory. Environment, Economy, Development and Sustainability (EEDS) Capstone (2020). http://hdl.handle.net/1811/91648

Bednar, P.M., Welch, C.: Socio-technical perspectives on smart working: creating meaningful and sustainable systems. Inf. Syst. Front. **22**(2), 281–298 (2019). https://doi.org/10.1007/s10796-019-09921-1

Bjerrum, E., Bødker, S.: Knowledge sharing in the 'new office'. In: Eighth European Conference on Computer Supported Cooperative Work, pp. 199–219. Kluwer Academic Publishers, Netherlands (2003)

Blabst, N., Diefenbach, S.: WhatsApp and well-being: a study on WhatsApp usage, communication quality and stress. In: Proceedings of the 31st International BCS Human Computer Interaction Conference (HCI 2017), Sunderland, UK (2017)

Bolisani, E., Scarso, E., Ipsen, C., Kirchner, K., Hansen, J.P.: Working from home during COVID-19 pandemic: lessons learned and issues. Manage. Mark. Challenges Knowl. Soc. **15**(s1), 458–476 (2020). https://doi.org/10.2478/mmcks-2020-0027

Brod, C.: Technostress: The Human Cost of the Computer Revolution. Addison-Wesley, Reading (1984)

Brooks, S.: Does personal social media usage affect efficiency and well-being. Comput. Hum. Behav. **46**, 26–37 (2015)

Brown, L., Kuss, D.J.: Fear of missing out, mental wellbeing, and social connectedness: a seven-day social media abstinence trial. Int. J. Environ. Res. Public Health **17**(12), 4566 (2020). https://doi.org/10.3390/ijerph17124566

Burmeister, C.P., Moskaliuk, J., Cress, U.: Ubiquitous working: do work versus non-work environments affect decision-making and concentration? Front. Psychol. **9** (2018). https://doi.org/10.3389/fpsyg.2018.00310

Burr, C., Taddeo, M., Floridi, L.: The ethics of digital well-being: a thematic review. Sci. Eng. Ethics **26**(4), 2313–2343 (2020). https://doi.org/10.1007/s11948-020-00175-8

Byström, K.: Information challenges, challenging information in digital workplaces: report from the European network for workplace information symposium 2015. J. Libr. Inf. Sci. **42**(1) (2016). https://search.proquest.com/scholarly-journals/information-challenges-challenging-digital/docview/1999243693/se-2?accountid=37193

Bødker, S.: Rethinking technology on the boundaries of life and work. Pers. Ubiquit. Comput. **20**(4), 533–544 (2016). https://doi.org/10.1007/s00779-016-0933-9

Bødker, S., Christiansen, E.: Computer support for social awareness in flexible work. Comput. Support. Cooper. Work **15**(1), 1–28 (2006). https://doi.org/10.1007/s10606-005-9011-y

Calvo, R.A., Peters, D.: Positive Computing: Technology for Wellbeing and Human Potential. The MIT Press, Cambridge (2017)

Caplan, S.: Relations among loneliness, social anxiety, and problematic internet use. Cycberpsychol. Behav. **10**(2), 234–242 (2007)

Daft, R.L., Lengel, R.H.: Organizational information requirements, media richness and structural design. Manage. Sci. **32**(5), 554–571 (1986). https://doi.org/10.1287/mnsc.32.5.554

De Menezes, L.M., Kelliher, C.: Flexible working and performance: a systematic review of the evidence for a business case. Int. J. Manag. Rev. **13**(4), 452–474 (2011). https://doi.org/10.1111/j.1468-2370.2011.00301.x

Dennis, A.R., Kinney, S.T.: Testing media richness theory in the new media: the effects of cues, feedback, and task equivocality. Inf. Syst. Res. **9**(3), 256–274 (1998). https://doi.org/10.1287/isre.9.3.256

Dennis, A.R., Fuller, R.M., Valacich, J.S.: Media, tasks, and communication processes: a theory of media synchronicity. MIS Q. **32**(3), 575 (2008). https://doi.org/10.2307/25148857

Desmet, P., Fokkinga, S.: Beyond Maslow's pyramid: introducing a typology of thirteen fundamental needs for human-centered design. Multimodal Technol. Interact. **4**(3), 38 (2020). https://doi.org/10.3390/mti4030038

Desmet, P., Hekkert, P.: Framework of product experience. Int. J. Design **1**(1), 57–66 (2007). https://search.proquest.com/scholarly-journals/framework-product-experience/docview/921466399/se-2?accountid=37193

Desmet, P., Overbeeke, K., Tax, S.: Designing products with added emotional value: development and application of an approach for research through design. Des. J. **4**(1), 32–47 (2001). https://doi.org/10.2752/146069201789378496

Desmet, P., Pohlmeyer, A.: Positive design: an introduction to design for subjective well-being. Int. J. Design **7**(3), 5–19 (2013). https://search.proquest.com/scholarly-journals/positive-design-introduction-subjective-well/docview/1468157524/se-2?accountid=37193

Diefenbach, S., Ullrich, D.: Digitale depression: wie neue Medien unser Glücksempfinden verändern. MVG Verlag, München (2016)

Duke, É., Montag, C.: Smartphone addiction, daily interruptions and self-reported productivity. Addict. Behav. Rep. **6**, 90–95 (2017). https://doi.org/10.1016/j.abrep.2017.07.002

Duxbury, L., Smart, R.: The "myth of separate worlds": an exploration of how mobile technology has redefined work-life balance. In: Creating Balance (2011). https://doi.org/10.1007/978-3-642-16199-5_15

Elster, J., Jon, E.: Ulysses Unbound: Studies in Rationality, Precommitment, and Constraints. Cambridge University Press, Cambridge (2000)

Floridi, L.: The Fourth Revolution: How the Infosphere is Reshaping Human Reality. Oxford University Press, New York (2014)

Fox, J., Moreland, J.J.: The dark side of social networking sites: an exploration of the relational and psychological stressors associated with Facebook use and affordances. Comput. Hum. Behav. **45**, 168–176 (2015). https://doi.org/10.1016/j.chb.2014.11.083

Galluch, P., Grover, V., Thatcher, J.: Interrupting the workplace: examining stressors in an information technology context. J. Assoc. Inf. Syst. **16**(1), 1–47 (2015). https://doi.org/10.17705/1jais.00387

García del Castillo-Rodríguez, J.A., Ramos-Soler, I., López-Sánchez, C., Quiles-Soler, C.: Information and communication technologies and quality of life in home confinement: development and validation of the TICO scale. PLoS One **15**(11), e0241948 (2020). https://doi.org/10.1371/journal.pone.0241948

Giddens, A.: Central Problems in Social Theory: Action, Structure, and Contradiction in Social Analysis. University of California Press, Oakland (1979)

Giddens, A.: The Constitution of Society: Outline of the Theory of Structuration. University of California Press, Oakland (1984)

Grant, A.M., Christianson, M.K., Price, R.H.: Happiness, health, or relationships? Managerial practices and employee well-being tradeoffs. Acad. Manag. Perspect. **21**(3), 51–63 (2007). https://doi.org/10.5465/amp.2007.26421238

Greenwood, K., Krol, N.: 8 ways managers can support employees' mental health [Harvard Business Review online] (2020). https://hbr.org/2020/08/8-ways-managers-can-support-emp loyees-mental-health

Gui, M., Fasoli, M., Carradore, R.: "Digital wellbeing": developing a new theoretical tool for media literacy research. Ital. J. Sociol. Educ. **9**, 155–173 (2017). https://doi.org/10.14658/pupj-ijse-2017-1-8

Hancock, P.A., Pepe, A.A., Murphy, L.L.: Hedonomics: the power of positive and pleasurable ergonomics. Ergon. Design: Quart. Hum. Factors Appl. **13**(1), 8–14 (2005). https://doi.org/10.1177/106480460501300104

Hassenzahl, M., Diefenbach, S., Göritz, A.: Needs, affect, and interactive products – Facets of user experience. Interact. Comput. **22**(5), 353–362 (2010). https://doi.org/10.1016/j.intcom.2010.04.002

Hassenzahl, M., Eckoldt, K., Diefenbach, S., Laschke, M., Len, E., Kim, J.: Designing moments of meaning and pleasure. Experience design and happiness. Int. J. Design **7**(3), 21–31 (2013). https://search.proquest.com/scholarly-journals/designing-moments-mea ning-pleasure-experience/docview/1468157555/se-2?accountid=37193h

Hill, E., Ferris, M., Märtinson, V.: Does it matter where you work? A comparison of how three work venues (traditional office, virtual office, and home office) influence aspects of work and personal/family life. J. Vocat. Behav. **63**(2), 220–241 (2003). https://doi.org/10.1016/s0001-8791(03)00042-3

Jacukowicz, A., Merecz-Kot, D.: Work-related Internet use as a threat to work-life balance – a comparison between the emerging on-line professions and traditional office work. Int. J. Occup. Med. Environ. Health **33**(1), 21–33 (2020). https://doi.org/10.13075/ijomeh.1896.01494

Kay, A.C., Wheeler, S., Bargh, J.A., Ross, L.: Material priming: the influence of mundane physical objects on situational construal and competitive behavioral choice. Organ. Behav. Hum. Decis. Process. **95**(1), 83–96 (2004). https://doi.org/10.1016/j.obhdp.2004.06.003

Kaye, L.K., Orben, A., Ellis, D.A., Hunter, S.C., Houghton, S.: The conceptual and methodological mayhem of "screen-time." Int. J. Environ. Res. Public Health **17**(10), 3661 (2020). https://doi.org/10.31219/osf.io/u4hqn

Keyes, C.L., Annas, J.: Feeling good and functioning well: distinctive concepts in ancient philosophy and contemporary science. J. Posit. Psychol. **4**(3), 197–201 (2009). https://doi.org/10.1080/17439760902844228

Klapperich, H., et al.: Mind the gap; a social practice approach to wellbeing-driven design. In: Petermans, A., Cain, R. (eds.) Design for Wellbeing: An Applied Approach. Routledge, London (2019)

Klein, A.: El creciente uso de las nuevas technologias en adultos mayores. Estud. Interdisc. sobre Envelhecimento **22**(2), 95–111 (2017). https://doi.org/10.22456/2316-2171.61313

Kulkarni, U., Robles-Flores, J., Popovič, A.: Business intelligence capability: the effect of top management and the mediating roles of user participation and analytical decision making orientation. J. Assoc. Inf. Syst. **18**(7), 516–541 (2017). https://doi.org/10.17705/1jais.00462

Kushlev, K., Dunn, E.W.: Checking email less frequently reduces stress. Comput. Hum. Behav. **43**, 220–228 (2015). https://doi.org/10.1016/j.chb.2014.11.005

Lee, S.Y., Brand, J.L.: Effects of control over office workspace on perceptions of the work environment and work outcomes. J. Environ. Psychol. **25**(3), 323–333 (2005). https://doi.org/10.1016/j.jenvp.2005.08.001

Mann, S., Holdsworth, L.: The psychological impact of teleworking: stress, emotions and health. New Technol. Work Employ. **18**(3), 196–211 (2003). https://doi.org/10.1111/1468-005x.00121

Meng, J., Martinez, L., Holmstrom, A., Chung, M., Cox, J.: Research on social networking sites and social support from 2004 to 2015: a narrative review and directions for future research. Cyberpsychol. Behav. Soc. Netw. **20**(1), 44–51 (2017). https://doi.org/10.1089/cyber.2016.0325

Messenger, M., Vargas Llave, O., Gschwind, L., Boehmer, S., Vermeylen, G., Wilkens, M.: Working anytime, anywhere: the effects on the world of work. Publications Office of the European Union (2017)

Michel, A.: Transcending socialization. Adm. Sci. Q. **56**(3), 325–368 (2011). https://doi.org/10.1177/0001839212437519

Moen, P., Kelly, E.L., Lam, J.: Healthy work revisited: do changes in time strain predict well-being? J. Occup. Health Psychol. **18**(2), 157–172 (2013). https://doi.org/10.1037/a0031804

Molino, M., et al.: Wellbeing costs of technology use during Covid-19 remote working: an investigation using the Italian translation of the technostress creators scale. Sustainability **12**(15), 5911 (2020). https://doi.org/10.3390/su12155911

Montag, C., Diefenbach, S.: Towards homo digitalis: important research issues for psychology and the neurosciences at the dawn of the internet of things and the digital society. Sustainability **10**(2), 415 (2018). https://doi.org/10.3390/su10020415

Montag, C., Widenhorn-Müller, K., Panksepp, J., Kiefer, M.: Individual differences in Affective Neuroscience Personality Scale (ANPS) primary emotional traits and depressive tendencies. Compr. Psychiatry **73**, 136–142 (2017). https://doi.org/10.1016/j.comppsych.2016.11.007

Moskaliuk, J., Burmeister, C.P., Landkammer, F., Renner, B., Cress, U.: Environmental effects on cognition and decision making of knowledge workers. J. Environ. Psychol. **49**, 43–54 (2017). https://doi.org/10.1016/j.jenvp.2016.12.001

Nah, F.-H., Siau, K.: COVID-19 Pandemic – role of technology in transforming business to the new normal. In: Stephanidis, C., et al. (eds.) HCII 2020. LNCS, vol. 12427, pp. 585–600. Springer, Cham (2020). https://doi.org/10.1007/978-3-030-60152-2_43

Odgers, C.L., Jensen, M.R.: Annual research review: adolescent mental health in the digital age: facts, fears, and future directions. J. Child Psychol. Psychiatry **61**(3), 336–348 (2020). https://doi.org/10.1111/jcpp.13190

Orben, A.: Teenagers, screens and social media: a narrative review of reviews and key studies. Soc. Psychiatry Psychiatr. Epidemiol. **55**(4), 407–414 (2020). https://doi.org/10.1007/s00127-019-01825-4

Orhan, M.A., Rijsman, J.B., Van Dijk, G.M.: Invisible, therefore isolated: comparative effects of team virtuality with task virtuality on workplace isolation and work outcomes. Rev. Psicol. Trabajo las Organ. **32**(2), 109–122 (2016). https://doi.org/10.1016/j.rpto.2016.02.002

Orlikowski, W.J.: The duality of technology: rethinking the concept of technology in organizations. Organ. Sci. **3**(3), 398–427 (1992). https://doi.org/10.1287/orsc.3.3.398

Parker, S.K.: Beyond motivation: job and work design for development, health, ambidexterity, and more. Ann. Rev. Psychol. **65**(1), 661–691 (2014). https://doi.org/10.1146/annurev-psych-010213-115208

Peters, D., Ahmadpour, N., Calvo, R.A.: Tools for wellbeing-supportive design: features, characteristics, and prototypes. Multimodal Technol. Interact. **4**(3), 40 (2020). https://doi.org/10.3390/mti4030040

Peters, D., Calvo, R.A., Ryan, R.M.: Designing for motivation, engagement and wellbeing in digital experience. Front. Psychol. **9**, 797 (2018). https://doi.org/10.3389/fpsyg.2018.00797

Przybylski, A.K., Weinstein, N.: Can you connect with me now? How the presence of mobile communication technology influences face-to-face conversation quality. J. Soc. Pers. Relat. **30**(3), 237–246 (2013). https://doi.org/10.1177/0265407512453827

Pérez, V.: Aproximación a la investigación psicológica en Internet y redes sociales. Summa Psicol. **15**(1), 98–105 (2018). https://doi.org/10.18774/448x.2018.15.vp

Rogerson, S., Meir, R., Crowley-McHattan, Z., McEwen, K., Pastoors, R.: A randomized controlled pilot trial investigating the impact of a workplace resilience program during a time of significant organizational change. J. Occup. Environ. Med. **58**(4), 329–334 (2016). https://doi.org/10.1097/jom.0000000000000677

Rughiniş, C., Rughiniş, R., Matei, Ş: A touching app voice thinking about ethics of persuasive technology through an analysis of mobile smoking-cessation apps. Ethics Inf. Technol. **17**(4), 295–309 (2016). https://doi.org/10.1007/s10676-016-9385-1

Ryan, R.M., Deci, E.L.: Self-determination Theory: Basic Psychological Needs in Motivation, Development, and Wellness. Guilford Publications, New York (2017)

Schalock, R.L., Verdugo, M.A., Alonso, M.A., Braddock, D.L.: Handbook on Quality of Life for Human Service Practitioners. Amer Assn on Intellectual & Devel, Washington, DC (2002)

Scholz, R., et al.: Unintended side-effects of the digital transition: European scientists' messages from a proposition-based expert round table. Sustainability **10**(6), 2001 (2018). https://doi.org/10.3390/su10062001

Sen, A.: Equality of what? The Tanner Lecture on Human Values, I, pp. 197–220, 22 May 1979. https://www.ophi.org.uk/wp-content/uploads/Sen-1979_Equality-of-What.pdf

Sheldon, K.M., Elliot, A.J., Kim, Y., Kasser, T.: What is satisfying about satisfying events? Testing 10 candidate psychological needs. J. Pers. Soc. Psychol. **80**(2), 325–339 (2001). https://doi.org/10.1037/0022-3514.80.2.325

Shove, E., Pantzar, M., Watson, M.: The Dynamics of Social Practice: Everyday Life and How it Changes. Sage Publications, London (2012)

Small, G., et al.: Brain health consequences of digital technology use. Dialogues Clin. Neurosci. **22**(2), 179–187 (2020). https://doi.org/10.31887/dcns.2020.22.2/gsmall

Song, Y., Gao, J.: Does telework stress employees out? A study on working at home and subjective well-being for wage/salary workers. J. Happiness Stud. **21**(7), 2649–2668 (2019). https://doi.org/10.1007/s10902-019-00196-6

Sparrow, B., Liu, J., Wegner, D.M.: Google effects on memory: cognitive consequences of having information at our fingertips. Science **333**(6043), 776–778 (2011). https://doi.org/10.1126/science.1207745

Specker Sullivan, L., Reiner, P.B.: Digital wellness and persuasive technologies. SSRN Electron. J. (2019). https://doi.org/10.2139/ssrn.3394952

Stephenson, L.E., Bauer, S.C.: The role of isolation in predicting new principals' burnout. Int. J. Educ. Policy Leadersh. **5**(9), 1–17 (2010). https://doi.org/10.22230/ijepl.2010v5n9a275

Taddeo, M.: The struggle between liberties and authorities in the information age. Sci. Eng. Ethics **21**(5), 1125–1138 (2014). https://doi.org/10.1007/s11948-014-9586-0

Tarafdar, M., Gupta, A., Turel, O.: The dark side of information technology use. Inf. Syst. J. **23**(3), 269–275 (2013). https://doi.org/10.1111/isj.12015

Tarafdar, M., Tu, Q., Ragu-Nathan, T.S.: Impact of technostress on end-user satisfaction and performance. J. Manag. Inf. Syst. **27**(3), 303–334 (2010). https://doi.org/10.2753/mis0742-1222270311

Tay, L., Diener, E.: Needs and subjective well-being around the world. J. Pers. Soc. Psychol. **101**(2), 354–365 (2011). https://doi.org/10.1037/a0023779

Taylor, H., Fieldman, G., Altman, Y.: E-mail at work: a cause for concern? The implications of the new communication technologies for health, wellbeing and productivity at work. J. Organ. Transf. Soc. Change **5**(2), 159–173 (2008). https://doi.org/10.1386/jots.5.2.159_1

Thulin, E., Vilhelmson, B., Johansson, M.: New telework, time pressure, and time use control in everyday life. Sustainability **11**(11), 3067 (2019). https://doi.org/10.3390/su11113067

Toscano, F., Zappalà, S.: Social isolation and stress as predictors of productivity perception and remote work satisfaction during the COVID-19 pandemic: the role of concern about the virus in a moderated double mediation. Sustainability **12**(23), 9804 (2020). https://doi.org/10.3390/su12239804

Twenge, J.M., Campbell, W.K.: Associations between screen time and lower psychological well-being among children and adolescents: evidence from a population-based study. Prevent. Med. Rep. **12**, 271–283 (2018). https://doi.org/10.1016/j.pmedr.2018.10.003

Vallée, T., Sedki, K., Despres, S., Jaulant, M., Tabia, K., Ugon, A.: On personalization in IoT. In: International Conference on Computational Science and Computational Intelligence. 2016 Presented at CSCI 2016, Las Vegas, USA (2016)

Vanden Abeele, M.M.: Digital wellbeing as a dynamic construct. Commun. Theory (2020). https:// academic.oup.com/ct/advance-article-abstract/doi/10.1093/ct/qtaa024/5927565

Verduyn, P., Ybarra, O., Résibois, M., Jonides, J., Kross, E.: Do social network sites enhance or undermine subjective well-being? A critical review. Soc. Issues Policy Rev. 11(1), 274–302 (2017). https://doi.org/10.1111/sipr.12033

Wang, W., Zhao, Y., Qiu, L., Zhu, Y.: Effects of emoticons on the acceptance of negative feedback in computer-mediated communication. J. Assoc. Inf. Syst. 15(8), 454–483 (2014). https://doi. org/10.17705/1jais.00370

Weinert, C., Maier, C., Laumer, S., Weitzel, T.: Does teleworking negatively influence IT professionals? In: Proceedings of the 52nd ACM Conference on Computers and People Research - SIGSIM-CPR 2014 (2015). https://doi.org/10.1145/2599990.2600011

West, R.L., Turner, L.H.: Introducing Communication Theory: Analysis and Application. McGraw-Hill, Boston (2010)

# An Analysis and Evaluation of the Design Space for Online Job Hunting and Recruitment Software

Bowen Hui[1]([✉]), Eileen Wood[2], and Carlos Khalil[2]

[1] University of British Columbia, Kelowna, BC, Canada
`bowen.hui@ubc.ca`
[2] Wilfrid Laurier University, Waterloo, ON, Canada
`ewood@wlu.ca, khal4170@mylaurier.ca`

**Abstract.** Despite heavy usage of social networking sites during the job hunting and recruitment process, little academic research has examined how these sites are used, the value they provide to the end-users, or how they should ideally be designed. The present study describes the use of a participatory design methodology to actively include end-users as part of the design process in creating an online job website. Participants who acted as job seekers and job providers both identified unique and overlapping requirements for an ideal prototype. The results enabled the production of a minimal viable product called EdgeMap. This prototype was evaluated in a usability study where participants endorsed EdgeMap as one they would use for recruitment and job hunting. The process and outcomes are discussed in terms of implementing participatory design methodology, design implications, and future directions for software design and adoption.

**Keywords:** Participatory design · Design requirements · Recruitment software · Social networking sites · Employment selection

## 1 Introduction

Online job boards, such as monster.com and Workopolis.com, are common tools used by recruiters and job seekers. While online job boards are useful, their functionality is limited and the usability is often poor. Job boards usually feature search functions that let job seekers find and browse postings and let job providers find and browse résumés. The typical structure of a job posting includes the job title, location, salary, general description about the position, more specific responsibilities, required/preferred qualifications, and how to apply. Typical job boards provide no opportunity for applicants to interact with potential employers beyond submitting a résumé. This online experience is thus restricted to

This work was in part supported by the Social Sciences and Humanities Research Council (SSHRC) in Canada.

F. F.-H. Nah and K. Siau (Eds.): HCII 2021, LNCS 12783, pp. 365–383, 2021.
https://doi.org/10.1007/978-3-030-77750-0_23

the process of viewing content-heavy job postings. Moreover, there is not much opportunity for individual companies to personalize their job ads. In some cases, a hyperlink to a company website may be provided, however, corporate websites can be perceived as overly complicated for job hunting purposes [1]. Ease of use is an important design requirement as 25% of job seekers reject potential work opportunities simply due to poor website usability [13]. Initial website impressions, therefore, are important during the recruitment process [2,3,16].

Meanwhile, many large organizations have adopted the use of social networking sites (SNSs) for recruitment. Existing SNSs are populated with a multitude of features to support many user groups, including job seekers, recruiters, and community learners across different expertise levels. While SNSs have been widely used for recruitment purposes since the mid 2000's, there is a lack of design and empirical research on how these sites should ideally be designed and used in the job search process. The goal of this research is to explore the design space of software that is used for online recruitment and job hunting purposes.

In this work, we adopt a participatory design methodology by involving the end-users in co-design sessions to gather design requirements of an online system that would be used in today's job hunting and recruitment process. Section 3 describes a participatory design study involving 9 youth job seekers and 5 business owners as job providers. This study involved activities for brainstorming, card sorting, and paper prototyping. Based on the session outcomes, Sect. 4 identifies five categories of software requirements to illustrate what the software should ideally do for the two user groups. Among these, our participants highlighted novel software features that would improve the user experience and confidence in the job search and hiring process. These elicited results led to our working prototype called EdgeMap, which is also presented in Sect. 4.

To evaluate our prototype, we conducted a preliminary usability study summarized in Sect. 5 involving 45 youths and 7 business representatives. The results indicated that most users found EdgeMap easy to use and liked the value that it provided. Moreover, the business participants identified specific criteria for software adoption, which we discuss in the context of future work in Sect. 6. Ultimately, our research goal is to deepen our understanding about the role of new technologies in the pre-employment process.

## 2    Literature Review

Although networking through social networking sites (SNS) has become one of the most widely used job search methods [15], there is limited research on how SNSs impact the job hunting and recruitment process [12]. Research examining how SNSs are used by potential employers indicates that recruiters regularly use these sites to make person-organization fit judgments [14]. Davidson et al. [4] report that recruiters used SNSs to identify counter productive work behaviors such as negative expressions of one's job, co-workers, or employer. Another study compared the degree of deception between paper résumés and LinkedIn profiles [6]. The researchers found that public LinkedIn profiles were less deceptive with an individual's work experience, but more deceptive regarding interests and hobbies. The authors hypothesized that the observed level of deception was due to the public nature of online profiles that allows others, including past employers and co-workers, to view and (in)validate another individual's listed expertise. Research has also identified the types of information recruiters look for when viewing LinkedIn profiles [17]. Through interviews with recruiters for positions in sales/marketing, human resources, and finance, this work indicated that recruiters unanimously look for presence of spelling or grammar mistakes, hobbies or interests similar to the recruiter, a college degree, number of years of work experience, sufficient content provided, the professionalism of email used, and the presence of a professional photograph in the profile. To summarize, previous research provides some guidelines on how user profiles should be designed in order to facilitate access to the desired content that recruiters want to see.

From the job seeker's perspective, Gerard [5] reported SNS usage data from business students in an undergraduate capstone strategy course. Survey data collected after the participants had completed assignments that involved in-depth usage of LinkedIn indicated that participants were very engaged when using features that related to the maintenance of their own profile and connections. However, they spent very little time on professional development activities such as asking for career or résumé advice, identifying themselves as a job-seeker, joining groups, looking up companies of interest, conducting advanced job searches, or promoting themselves. The authors suspected that the participants did not engage in professional development activities was due to a lack of incentive in the research study and a greater demand on the participants' effort and time. Other research on job seeker attitudes show that the ease, simplicity, and perceived usefulness of an online job site affect the job seeker's attitudes and the site features are used [8, 9]. This body of research suggest the need to train job seekers to engage in professional development activities online.

We are unaware of any published design research on SNSs or empirical analyses of these sites to assess whether they meet user needs. However, from a general design perspective, Maurer and Liu [10] proposed that an online recruiting site should tailor its design to emphasize either "central processing" or "peripheral processing" of information depending on the software's target user. The authors define *central cues* as information pertaining to relevant content and *peripheral cues* as information that reflect relatively cursory content or reference to the medium used to present content. They suggest using central cues to target job seekers who are serious or have more work experience, while using peripheral cues to target new graduates or those who are just browsing for jobs. The authors also draw on marketing literature that suggests two key software features which are consistent with the findings of our studies below: a user's active control of a site (e.g., the ability to personalize and save search results) and the support for a two-way communication between a potential employer and candidate (e.g., online messaging). Site vividness, in terms of providing rich sensory information that evokes multiple perceptual channels, was also identified as a means for improving site receptiveness and usability when used appropriately. This model offers important design suggestions for two types of end-users. Unfortunately, the authors did not provide an application of the model to evaluate existing software or a design of the software that is prescribed by the model. Such an extension is necessary to fully understand the relative contributions of their proposed research.

In order for designers to develop software that better fits the target user's conception of the process, Muller and Kuhn [11] propose employing participatory design methodology to bring the user and designer together through "co-design sessions". These types of sessions would enable potential users to act as designers, and work together to complete design tasks that lead to concrete artifacts used in building software prototypes. Example artifacts may include an organization of information into categories, sketches of screen mock-ups, preference evaluations of sample screenshots, and paper prototypes built using craft materials. This process allows designers to better understand the user's way of thinking and users can better appreciate the designer's constraints. For this reason, we adopt a participatory design approach to conduct our design study.

## 3  Design Research

Our first study uses a participatory design methodology by bringing the end-users into the design loop. Participatory design research is a well-established area within the field of human-computer interaction (HCI) in computer science. Traditionally, software design is mainly driven by business needs. In cases where gaps exist, design decisions are often made by programmers developing the software. Consequently, such software often ends up being unintuitive and fails to gain broad user acceptance. To solve this problem, the main premise of participatory design is to involve potential users throughout the design process to ensure that software is designed to meet real user needs and is implemented in a way that reflects how real users would actually want to use the software. This section describes the participatory design activities used to elicit user needs and preferences for an online job hunting and recruitment software.

### 3.1  Participatory Design with Job Seekers and Job Providers

The goal of this study was to explore the design space of job hunting and recruiting software. We elicited user needs from two groups of potential users – youth as job seekers and business owners as job providers. The results provided insights into the software needs of the two user populations and their general technology usage and preferences. This research was reviewed and approved by a university research ethics board and all participants were treated in accordance with APA ethical standards.

### 3.2  Participants

In total, we had 14 participants from community organizations and schools from two small Canadian communities. There were 9 youth participants for our first target user group: 3 male students in grades 10 to 12 from one community and 4 females and 2 males in grades 9 and 10 in the other community. All the youth participants were comfortable with basic computer technologies, common social media applications, and mobile applications. In addition, none of them had knowledge of LinkedIn prior to this study.

For our second target user group, there were 5 business owners or organization leaders: 2 female and 1 male from the first community and 2 females from the second. Our business participants' ages spanned from mid-thirties to mid-fifties, and all of them were familiar with basic computer technology and recognized the need for a job hunting software in today's market.

### 3.3   Materials and Procedure

There were three design activities in this study: brainstorming, card sorting, and paper prototyping. Both participant groups conducted the brainstorming and card sorting activities. Due to limited time available, only the youth participants completed the paper prototyping activity.

In each community, we conducted two 90-min sessions for each participant group. Sessions were held in a community high school. Each session was facilitated by one research assistant. For materials, the facilitator brought in sticky notes, blank paper, and colorful writing implements to each session. In order to keep the structure of these sessions consistent, the facilitator followed a process script and had a list of goals and questions to use in probing the participants during the sessions to encourage participation. At the beginning of the first session, participants were introduced to each other and the research facilitator who led the session. The remainder of the time was devoted to the design activities.

**Brainstorming.** Participants were asked to generate as many ideas as possible to express how job hunting software could ideally help them search for jobs. (Alternatively, the context for business participants was recruitment software looking for qualified candidates.) At times when participants were stuck, the facilitator prompted them with questions related to functionality and usability (e.g., "How do you search for jobs?", "What would you like to do differently", "Which features do you like from other apps that you enjoy?"). Each idea was written on a sticky note. These ideas reflect user needs as either functional requirements that define what the software is supposed to do or non-functional requirements that specify how the software does it.

Once everyone was finished, participants were asked to post their sticky notes onto the wall for sharing. They reviewed each other's ideas, made clarifications in the wording, and identified additional features to add to the wall. The activity ended when everyone was comfortable with the posted information.

**Card Sorting.** The card sorting exercise is a well-established usability technique used in HCI research that helps designers identify how information is organized from the user's perspective [7]. With all the ideas generated from the brainstorming activity, participants were asked to sort all the labeled sticky notes into meaningful categories with approximately the same number of items. After establishing all the groups, they were asked to provide an umbrella label that represents the ideas in each category with a word or a short phrase. The goal here was to understand the organization of the desired software features in terms of what was intuitive and natural from the user's perspective.

**Paper Prototyping.** Focusing on the categories identified from the card sorting activity, participants were asked to pick a category and sketch an interface that works best that would incorporate all the features in it. For example, a participant who chose the category "User Profile" with three items (e.g., personal information, upload résumé, and calendar reminder) would need to sketch out various user information while considering where upload résumé and the calendar reminders would be located and how they would be visualized on that page. This activity is helpful for eliciting interface layout requirements because users typically do not have the design vocabulary to articulate how they want the interface to look and feel.

### 3.4    Results

**Brainstorming.** Overall, the youth participants were highly engaged during the co-design sessions. The first group of youths generated 50 notes and the second group generated 76 notes. Considerable time was spent together clarifying the wording used, as the youths often found it hard to articulate their ideas. Redundant notes were removed. For example, "easy to use" and "app has to be basic" were considered as one requirement.

The business participants were also productive, where one group generated 36 notes while the other generated 45 notes. There were many instances where participants said, "If the app could have [such and such] feature, it would be very effective for me". At times, the business participants also considered functionality that would be useful for youth job seekers. Overall, the participants were very thoughtful and thorough in this activity.

**Card Sorting.** The results of the card sorting activity from both participant groups produced the following categories of functional requirements: usability, user profile, job search, social media and networking, resources, and job consideration (alternatively, candidate evaluation for business participants).

In addition, usability was of high importance to all the youth participants, indicating that they did not want ads or making sure the app was simple and easy to use. Surprisingly, business participants were less concerned about usability although they do expect the software to be easy to use.

Notably, it was important to the youth participants to be able to directly communicate with potential employers or employees who had previously worked in a company of interest. On the other hand, business participants did not express in engaging with potential candidates until they reached an interview stage. One possible reason, as explained by one of the business participants, is that living in a small community makes them know many people informally already so they did not feel the need for this feature. However, business participants indicated that they wanted the ability to maintain a network with other businesses and stay connected with the community.

Ideas generated by the business participants emphasized the importance of having a wide variety of functionality available in the software and access to external resources (e.g., government funding opportunities for hiring students, incentive programs, sample interview questions).

**Paper Prototyping.** The youth participants were excited to develop sketches in this activity. We found that some participants struggled with developing the details for a mockup, as they did not reference external sources. Interestingly, we noted that all of the resulting mockups were designed for a mobile device rather than a desktop computer (although they were not instructed to do so one way or another). This suggests the importance of mobile friendly applications for our youth population.

Figure 1 presents three mockups that show how two participants visualized search results. On the left, the sketch shows a search about a business in a certain geography. Once the user selects a business, the details are displayed. In the middle and on the right in Fig. 1, another participant illustrated the search results of potential jobs and the details of a job posting. In these cases, the mockups illustrated very well-organized content, arranged using images and whitespace appropriately so that the content is easy to process.

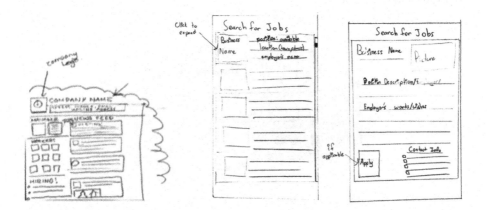

**Fig. 1.** Youth mockups showing the importance of content structure.

Other sketches included a mockup of two people messaging with each other, a mockup of two people engaged in a video or audio chat, a homepage with vivid imagery to attract the user's attention, a layout with search and filter options. These mockups resemble the interfaces of well-known mobile applications (e.g., iMessage layout for text messaging on an iPhone). In one mockup, the search bar was placed at the top of the screen, suggesting the importance of the search functionality for the participant. One of the mockups showed a page of news feeds, which suggests the importance of staying up-to-date on various events relevant to the app.

### 3.5   Discussion

The software envisioned by both participant groups resembles an SNS with job hunting and recruitment features. In contrast to a professional SNS such as LinkedIn, the focus of our software design is not networking, but rather job placement success. As such, requirements that participants identified that were not central to LinkedIn include: job management capabilities (e.g., résumé tool and calendar), job review operations (e.g., comments on job experience), online communication features (e.g., online messaging or calls with potential employers), relevant resources for funding and advancement (e.g., training, career planning, business incentive programs), and mass résumé application.

## 4   EdgeMap: A Minimal Viable Prototype

Based on the design outcomes from Sect. 3, we identified features for a minimal viable prototype of a software that supports youth and business users in their job search and recruitment process. This section presents our prototype called EdgeMap, which was developed using Ruby on Rails and is made available at http://edgemap.ok.ubc.ca/.

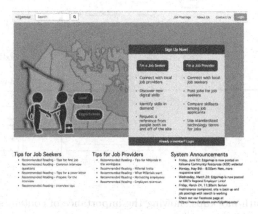

**Fig. 2.** Homepage of the EdgeMap system showing various functionalities at the top menu bar, the sign-up options, and tips and announcements at the bottom.

## 4.1   System Overview

EdgeMap is an online platform designed with two target user groups in mind: job seekers—youth looking for employment, and job providers—companies posting vacancies and recruiting qualified candidates. The site combines features from traditional online job boards, e-portfolio, social networking sites, and additional requirements identified from our design research study. Figure 2 shows the landing page for this site.

## 4.2   Job Seeker Features

As a job seeker, the user can create a profile with an online portfolio to showcase projects, browse the online community, and apply for jobs. Modeled after the testimonial feature in LinkedIn, EdgeMap also enables users to electronically reach out to referees and obtain a reference to include in their own profiles. The profile enables users to highlight their skills in an e-portfolio format. The profile allows users to record personal information and select whether to keep that information private or to display it to the public (e.g., name).

One novel feature that differentiates EdgeMap from other job hunting and recruitment tools is the skills survey. The skills survey is an online survey that lets the user self-report their expertise levels across many predefined categories. We devised this skills survey as a way to standardize the types of skills that the software recognizes, as well as to facilitate the search and comparison of skills.

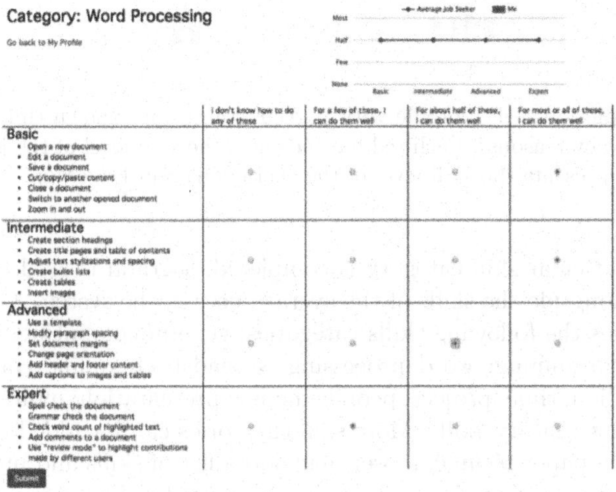

**Fig. 3.** The mini-questionnaire for the word processing category. The line graph at the top shows the average user in the system can do half of the functions in each of the basic, immediate, advanced, and expert levels. Once the user submits a completed mini-questionnaire, the system will automatically overlay the user's skills in the graph.

Each skill category operates as a mini-questionnaire which can be completed independently. Currently, each skill category has 3 or 4 related questions. For example, in the word processing category, we elicit the expertise level of the user in those related tasks, including: opening a new document, creating a new section heading, setting document margins, and checking the word count in a document. In our design, we enumerated a long list of tasks for each skill category, and grouped them into one of four levels: basic, intermediate, advanced, and expert. Thus, each level would have 5–10 associated tasks. The user completes the mini-questionnaire by indicating how well s/he can accomplish the tasks in each level (ranging from "I don't know how to do any of these tasks" to "I can do all the tasks well"). Figure 3 shows the mini-questionnaire for word processing.

A user completing the survey can choose the relevant skill categories to complete and view survey results immediately without having to wait until the other skill categories are finished. A sample screenshot of a user profile and her partial skill surveys is shown in Fig. 4.

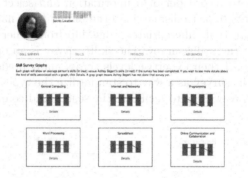

**Fig. 4.** A sample job seeker profile with partial skill graphs shown (image and name blurred for privacy reasons). Each red bar indicates the skill level of the job seeker and the blue line represents the skill level of the average user in EdgeMap.

Once a particular skill category is completed, a graph is used to visualize a user's skills alongside the skills of the average user in the system. Currently, the system includes the following skills categories: general computing; Internet and networks; programming; word processing; spreadsheet; online communication and collaboration; time, project, people; money; presentation; multimedia; social media; and 21st century skills. More skill categories can be added in the future.

Similar to a paper résumé, a user may add a list of skills and project accomplishments. Since our mini-questionnaires are worded in generic terms, users may want to add more detailed skills which can also be associated to the predefined skill categories. For example, a user can add "MS Word" and "Vim" as skills under "word processing". Furthermore, these skills can be linked to specific projects where they were applied. An example screenshot showcasing a user's projects is shown in Fig. 5.

**Fig. 5.** Sample projects page in a job seeker's profile. Each project has a month/year, representative image, title, description, and associated skills.

EdgeMap is designed to combine features of a job hunting app with online social networking abilities. As such, our system serves as a virtual community platform with several key search functionalities. A job seeker can search for companies and read their profiles to learn about a company's culture and job postings. In addition, a job seeker can search for people in the online community to learn about their work and the kind of skills and expertise they have. This is especially useful for students who are thinking about their future careers and want to explore specific options in depth. If a user has certain skills in mind (e.g., python programming), the user can search directly for the skills to see who has those skills or search for projects involving those skills how those skills were applied. To take advantage of the skills survey in EdgeMap, users can compare their skills to another user to get a sense of the areas of improvement needed. This is helpful for young job seekers who are less familiar with the job market and wish to learn more about the skills they need to obtain their ideal job.

Lastly, a user can browse job postings, filter them by various criteria such as location and company, and apply to jobs. In the case where a job seeker is unsure whether she has the qualifications for a particular job of interest, she can compare her own skills to those of an "ideal candidate" as defined by the job posting. The result is a graph similar to that shown in Fig. 7 below that compares the two skill sets. This feature helps job seekers conduct an initial self-assessment of qualifications which can help them build confidence and decide whether to take the time to apply to the interested job.

### 4.3   Job Provider Features

Job providers can create a company profile and manage job postings. To create a new job posting, the user enters information about the job, such as title, location, start and end date, salary, job description, required skills, and preferred skills. Optionally, the user can complete a skills survey (same format as the one for a job seeker) to express what skills an "ideal candidate" for the job should have. Once a job posting has been created, other users on EdgeMap can apply to it. Employers can view submitted applications on demand. Clicking an applicant's name directs the user to the applicant's profile, and a visual summary of which required and preferred skills are met. The user can decide to consider (i.e., shortlist), reject, or accept the applicant (see Fig. 6). These decisions will propagate to the applicant's account and appear as a notification.

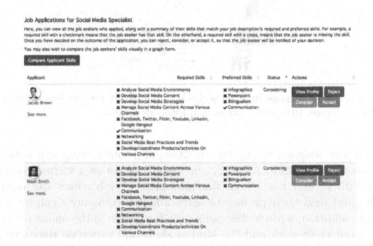

**Fig. 6.** A partial list of applicants for a particular job posting (profile images are blurred and fake names are used for privacy reasons).

Figure 6 also shows the option to compare applicant skills. This feature makes use of the skills surveys in EdgeMap to help job providers in evaluating the candidates. More often than not, a job provider has several seemingly good candidates who applied for a particular job and is unsure how to rank them. By clicking on this compare button, the system will aggregate the data in the skills survey and present them in a single graph with each candidate's skills stacked side-by-side. A sample comparison graph is shown in Fig. 7 for the programming and social media categories. The line in the graph represents the skill levels of an average user on EdgeMap while the coloured bars in the graph represent the skill levels of the ideal candidate (if available) and all the applicants of this position. Figure 7 shows that the ideal candidate (red) has few basic programming skills but many social media skills across all expertise levels. The graphs show that all the candidates have more than what is needed for programming skills, but only a few have the ideal set of social media skills. This visualization helps the decision maker tease out which applicants have the required skills quickly and provide a comparison of all the applicants in one place.

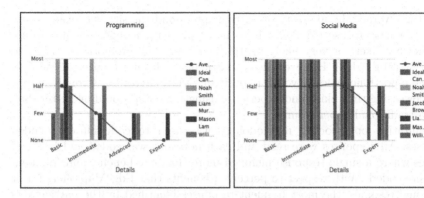

**Fig. 7.** Comparison graphs to support candidate evaluation for the Programming and Social Media skill categories. (Color figure online)

# 5  Usability Study

The purpose of this study was to assess the utility of EdgeMap. We conducted a usability study with a new group of youth and business participants. The overall methodology in the two experiments were the same, although the detailed tasks and questionnaires differed due to the two user groups. This research was reviewed and approved by a university research ethics board and all participants were treated in accordance with APA ethical standards.

## 5.1  Study with Youth Participants

We first report our usability results with youth participants as job seekers.

**Participants.** A total of 45 university students (21 females, 24 males) acted as youth job seekers in this study. Over 75% of the participants were born in 1996–1998, with the others born between 1987–1995. The majority of the participants were in their early years of a university program.

**Materials and Procedure.** We used the current prototype of EdgeMap as described in Sect. 4 above. Participants were asked to use the software to complete a list of tasks we provided, and then complete a short post-questionnaire.

In particular, participants were tasked with creating an account on EdgeMap, completing the user profile with at least 5 projects to showcase. They also needed to upload a résumé to the account, browse for jobs, and determine if they are qualified for those jobs. Then, they were asked to search other people's profiles and compare their own skills against those in the profiles.

At the end of their session, participants were asked to summarize the tasks they completed and to complete the post-questionnaire. The questionnaire had four 5-point Likert scale questions and three open-ended questions assessing perceptions about the software.

**Results.** Overall, the majority of participants found the site very easy to use (26.7%) or easy to use (51.1%). More than half of them reported they would be somewhat likely or very likely to use the site for self-promotion (53%) and for job hunting (51%). However, many participants did not realize the value of using an e-portfolio as fewer youth participants (42%) agreed or strongly agreed that showcasing their skills and experience using EdgeMap would be better than using a traditional paper résumé.

Qualitative open-coding methodology was used to code all open-ended responses. All responses were read and each new idea was coded and labelled. In cases where a single response included more than one benefit, multiple benefits were coded. With respect to perceived benefits that EdgeMap offered over traditional résumés, the most frequent responses identified by the participants include: the ability to showcase projects, display more content, emphasize skills, view information visually, and compare themselves with others. Figure 8 provides a histogram of all the elicited benefits.

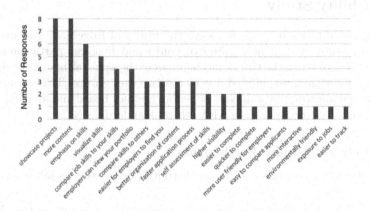

**Fig. 8.** Coded responses indicating benefits EdgeMap has over traditional résumés.

Participants were also asked to identify any other sites they felt were similar to Edgemap. Only 3 software were identified: LinkedIn (16 responses), Indeed.ca (15 responses), and social networking sites not designed for professional use such as Facebook (4 responses). Thirteen participants indicated that there was no other comparative site that they knew of.

The last question asked if participants had any other comments. Only two participants indicated concerns with EdgeMap. In particular, one participant did not know how to edit skills in the profile. Remaining comments identified strengths with the prototype with feedback such as: "This is a very useful site that I will strongly consider in the future. I loved the fact the user profile can be so informative and tell so much about an individual" and "This site has the profile and the bio as well as specific skills which is unlike any other site that I have come across. Very interesting".

## 5.2   Study with Business Participants

Here, we report our usability results with business participants as job providers. We note that it has been significantly more difficult in recruiting business participants due to their demanding workload as leaders of small businesses.

**Participants.** We had a total of 7 business participants (2 females, 5 males). Following the North American industry classification system, the primary sector of business that these participants represent are: professional, scientific, and technical services (3), health care and social assistance (2), educational services (1), and information (1). The participants reported the average employee age at their company to be mostly between 26 and 35 years old (3), with some cases of 25 years and under (2), and between 36 and 49 years old (2).

**Materials and Procedure.** Business participants were asked to complete an initial survey about their personal information, business, and attitude towards technology. They used the same EdgeMap prototype described in Sect. 4 to complete a list of tasks we provided.

The tasks that the business participants were asked to complete include creating an account on EdgeMap and posting two job advertisements that involve the use of technology (given printed content). In order to assess the utility of our system in the hiring decision process, we provided a generic business account with two technology job ads (social media specialist and web specialist). The idea is that the participant would log into this generic account as his/her own, then evaluate the applicants for the two positions. For one of the job postings, we created five fictitious applicants for it (all white males). The business participants were asked to familiarize themselves with the job ads, study and compare the applicants, and provide a final ranking of the applicants.

Lastly, we asked participants to complete a small usability questionnaire based on their experience using EdgeMap. The questionnaire had eighteen usability questions that used a combination of 5-point Likert scale questions, open-ended questions on strengths and weaknesses of the software, and open-ended questions that probed them to compare Edgemap with other systems.

**Results.** From the initial technology survey, about 95% of the participants' responses indicated positive agreement (somewhat agree or strongly agree) towards technology's role in their businesses. Specifically, participants identified a range of technologies that their businesses use. These include: email, Word processing software, video conferencing software (e.g., Skype), presentation software, spreadsheets, accounting software, search engines, and social networks.

The main part of the study took participants on average approximately 50 min to complete. The accounts and content created showed care and thought, reflecting that the participants tried to use the system genuinely. When evaluating the fictitious job applicants, all the participants reviewed traditional résumés that were uploaded along with each applicant as well as the skills comparison graphs in EdgeMap. All but one participant ranked what we expected to be the top two candidates within their top three rankings. This suggests that the participants were able to use the information available in the system to help them make effective hiring decisions.

With respect to usability, the majority of participants found the system easy to use and would be inclined to use it in their company's recruitment process. In comparison to standard online job boards, the majority of participants found the added features of candidate portfolios and the visual skills graphs to be informative and helpful (see Fig. 9). Importantly, participants found the traditional résumés less informative. This suggests that participants see value in the information provided by the portfolios and skills graphs that are not available in the résumés.

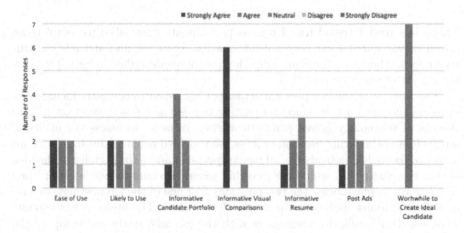

**Fig. 9.** Post-questionnaire responses on several usability aspects of EdgeMap.

Given that creating job ads on EdgeMap was an important feature for job providers, we asked the participants whether the ad creation process was easy to complete. Four felt it was easy, two were neutral, and one thought that it was slightly difficult to use. We also asked the participants to consider the time needed to prepare and post job ads in EdgeMap in comparison to other systems. When asked about the time needed to review job applicants for a given posting, six of the seven participants felt that EdgeMap was less time consuming than other systems, while one felt it was about the same. Recall that an optional feature in creating a job ad is to complete the skills survey of an ideal candidate for that position. Since this feature is unique to EdgeMap, it implies that carrying out this feature would require additional time and effort on the part of the job provider. However, all the participants indicated it was worthwhile to create an ideal candidate for a job posting, despite the added time needed.

In the open-ended section of the post-questionnaire, participants were first asked to indicate strengths and weaknesses of the system. Most participants identified the skills comparison of EdgeMap as the key strength, while others mentioned that the interface is easy to use, the content is well-organized, and the added value of the social networking aspect of the system. Some minor navigation issues were mentioned as weaknesses, with one participant indicating that they wanted a customizable skills survey and another requiring this feature to be available for future software adoption.

In another open-ended question, the participants mentioned the other sites they use for recruitment purposes include LinkedIn, indeed.ca, monster.com, Workopolis.com, university career sites, and some industry-specific systems.

Lastly, we were interested in knowing what would make businesses use a new recruitment software, despite the added overhead. Six of the participants indicated that if EdgeMap had a significant user base of job seekers, they would use it for recruitment.

# 6   Discussion and Future Work

The goal of this research was to explore the design space of software used for online recruitment and job hunting purposes. Understanding the design space of such systems enables us to analyze the value that existing software offers to the end-users and to improve upon the state-of-the-art business technology.

As SNSs become more prevalent in today's society, we also discovered that both our target user groups identified basic SNS features (such as connecting with others and online chat) as core functionality of job hunting and recruitment software. This finding suggests that traditional online job boards that only support job postings and résumé submissions will need to incorporate social media features in order to remain competitive.

Our participatory design studies identified several categories of features that job hunting and recruitment software should ideally have. For youths, they include: user profile, job search, social media and networking, training resources, and job consideration. For businesses, they include: user profile, job posting, social media and networking, funding resources, and candidate consideration. While the categories are strikingly similar for the two user groups, the detailed features within each category need to be tailored to each user group.

Given that LinkedIn is the most popular SNS designed for professional networking, we compared LinkedIn's design to this ideal conception of the software. In particular, we see that LinkedIn supports features for user profile, job search, job posting, and social media and networking. Also, there is some overlap in the set of job consideration features, such as the ability to view featured jobs and contact current or previous employees of a company of interest. However, our participants suggested the desire for the features in the resources category, which are largely absent from LinkedIn's design. Job providers, identified the need for resources that identified financial aid opportunities, business development links, connections to local entrepreneurial opportunities, and sample interview questions to support the hiring process. Although these resources could appear in the form of advertisements and discussion group posts in LinkedIn, the design of the software would be more coherent if it had a section dedicated to these resources which could then be personalized.

One of the resources that youth participants suggested they wanted in EdgeMap is resources to learn about possible career paths. At minimum, this information can be presented as articles on career development and links to educational programs. However, there is a very interesting opportunity to connect the skills graphs in EdgeMap with training resources and career paths suggested here. In EdgeMap, users can identify their skills and see how they fare in comparison to other users or an ideal candidate of a job posting. If these skills graphs were integrated within existing training programs and career options, then users could use EdgeMap to assist them in mapping out their learning goals. For example, given a user's profile, one could easily identify which training program to pursue in order to enhance a category of skills. Similarly, one could explore different career options, then backtrack to identify the necessary training programs and skills sets needed in order to pursue a career path. These are exciting ideas and they offer a very innovative design opportunity to explore in future work.

In the usability study, we saw that our business participants valued time savings offered by the skills graphs comparison feature during the candidate evaluation process. Since this feature is unique to EdgeMap, the business participants unanimously acknowledged the strength of this feature in comparison to other major competitors, such as LinkedIn and various online job boards.

Our usability results also indicated that having a rich community of job seekers is a key criterion to software adoption for businesses. Unfortunately, this is a circular dependency because job seekers will tend to use sites that have many job postings. Therefore, some mechanism needs to be in place to enter job postings onto EdgeMap to increase job seekers, which will hopefully in turn attract more job providers onto the site. In addition, the skills survey feature needs to be extended so that it can be customizable and job providers can select the categories of skills deemed most useful for their needs.

Design is an iterative process. As technology evolves, so do user expectations. Therefore, in order to ensure that software is relevant for the target users, regular technology reassessment is necessary. Our study indicates that participatory research between software designers and end-users is a particularly informative mechanism for identifying key aspects of design needed. Given that design preferences differ from one user to another, it is theoretically impossible to arrive at a single optimal design that works equally well for everyone. However, design researchers need to sample representative users, and gather both qualitative and quantitative feedback. In some cases, these evaluations may involve a comparison of multiple software so that benchmark results can be obtained. Other methods such as longitudinal studies and field studies may also be employed, depending on the researcher's evaluation goals.

# References

1. Braddy, P.W., Meade, A., Kroustalis, C.: Unwanted online job seekers swamp HR staff. Can. HR Rep. **17**(7), 1–2 (2004)
2. Braddy, P.W., Meade, A., Kroustalis, C.: Online recruiting: the effects of organizational familiarity, website usability, and website attractiveness on viewers' impressions of organizations. Comput. Hum. Behav. **24**, 2992–3001 (2008)
3. Braddy, P.W., Thompson, L., Wuensch, K., Grossnickle, W.: Internet recruiting: the effects of web page design features. Soc. Sci. Comput. Rev. **21**, 374–385 (2003)
4. Davidson, H.K., Maraist, C., Bing, M.N.: Friend of foe? The promise and pitfalls of using social networking sites for HR decisions. J. Bus. Psychol. **26**(2), 153–159 (2011)
5. Gerard, J.G.: Linking in with LinkedIn: three exercises that enhance professional social networking and career building. J. Manage. Educ. **36**(6), 866–897 (2012)
6. Guillory, J., Hancock, J.: The effect of LinkedIn on deception in résumés. Cyberpsychol. Behav. Soc. Netw. **15**(3), 135–140 (2012)
7. Hudson, W.: Card Sorting. The Interaction Design Foundation, 2 edn. (2013)
8. Lin, H.: Applicability of the extended theory of planned behavior in predicting job seeker intentions to use job-search websites. Int. J. Sel. Assess. **18**, 64–74 (2010)
9. Lin, K., Lu, H.: Why people use social networking sites: an empirical study integrating network externalities and motivation theory. Comput. Hum. Behav. **27**, 1152–1161 (2011)
10. Maurer, S., Liu, Y.: Developing effective e-recruiting websites: insights for managers from marketers. Bus. Horizons **50**, 305–314 (2007)
11. Muller, M., Kuhn, S.: Participatory design. Commun. ACM **36**(6), 24–28 (1993)
12. Nikolaou, I.: Social networking web sites in job search and employee recruitment. Int. J. Sel. Assess. **22**(2), 179–189 (2014)
13. Pastore, M.: Web expands role in corporate recruiting (2000). https://www.clickz.com/web-expands-role-in-corporate-recruiting/65037/. Accessed 4 Jan 2021
14. Roulin, N., Bangerter, A.: Social networking websites in personnel selection. J. Manage. **20**(10), 1–30 (2013)
15. Stopfer, J., Gosling, S.: Online Social Networks in the Work Context, pp. 39–59. Psychology Press, London (2013)
16. Thompson, L.F., Braddy, P.W., Wuensch, K.L.: E-recruitment and the benefits of organizational web appeal. Comput. Hum. Behav. **24**, 2384–2398 (2008)
17. Zide, J., Elman, B., Shahani-Denning, C.: LinkedIn and recruitment: how profiles differ across occupations. Empl. Relat. **36**(5), 583–604 (2014)

# Perceptions of Using Tracking and Tracing Systems in Work Environments

Christian Jandl[1]([✉]), Florian Taurer[1], Martina Hartner-Tiefenthaler[2], Markus Wagner[1], Thomas Moser[1], and Sebastian Schlund[2]

[1] UAS St. Pölten, 3100 St. Pölten, Austria
cjandl@fhstp.ac.at
[2] Vienna University of Technology, 1140 Vienna, Austria

**Abstract.** Tracking and tracing of objects have found widespread application in industry and logistics for the last decade. Profound information about the position and the status of an object allows better planning and scheduling, thus leads to more flexible processes, stock reductions and even new business models become possible. The implementation of tracking and tracing systems (TATS) precisely enables also electronic monitoring of employee performance and behavior. Therefore, this study analyzes perceptions of TATS in working environments and differentiates between the tracking of objects (AT) and the tracking of employees (EM). Our findings based on 19 qualitative interviews reveals that privacy issues predominantly emerge in the context of EM, but not so much with regard to AT. In the context of EM, we identify an imonitoring-privacy dilemma which can be solved when taking in account the acceptance factors (i.e., transparency, trust, communication, data storage, health aspect, and safety perception). Furthermore, experience seems to attenuate the perceived risks when implementing TATS.

**Keywords:** Tracking & tracing · Asset tracking · Employee behavior · Employee monitoring · Employee location monitoring

## 1 Introduction

Tracking and tracing systems (TATS) have found widespread application in industry and logistics for the last decade. Profound information about the position and the status of an object allows better planning and scheduling and might also enable various new services and business models. In addition to information about object, location-based-services also provide user-specific information of the position, orientation or logged movement or use data of individuals or groups. Within work enviroments TATS enable applications to track and trace materials and goods over entire supply networks, allow improved planning and scheduling of logistics and manufacturing processes via geofencing services and provide supply chain transparency to improve security in case of sensible or expensive goods.

Despite the similarity of use cases in consumer and business TATS, both application areas comprise very different boundary conditions with respect to privacy and the use

© Springer Nature Switzerland AG 2021
F. F.-H. Nah and K. Siau (Eds.): HCII 2021, LNCS 12783, pp. 384–398, 2021.
https://doi.org/10.1007/978-3-030-77750-0_24

of personal related data. Whereas the private use of consumer regulations bases on individual decisions to use tracking and tracing services, these conditions only account to a limited extent in business environments. Thus, we need to distinguish insights about privacy from consumer research as it does not apply for the work environment and therefore generate further knowledge about perceptions on TATS in the work environment.

The decision to implement systems that explicitly or implicitly use personal data of employees (e.g., digital assistance systems) does not only depend on the benefit gained for the respective organization, but usually requires acceptance by the users (i.e., employees) and their representative body such as the workers' council. Therefore, depending on a country's legislation, different obligational processes are in place to ensure the use of digital systems in line with individual privacy protection. In most European countries, privacy issues are very strict and usually handled in favour of the employee. We assume that the perceived values for the organization or the employees might influence the perceptions about TATS and also increase the intention to allow and use these systems. This assumption is considered as of particular interest for two further reasons: First, the boundaries between tracking and tracing an object to tracking and tracing a person remain thin and is very ambiguous within various applications. The tracking of a parcel on a truck or the tracking of a person that is hand guiding a cobot within an assembly area straightforwardly allow the tracking of both the truck driver and the cobot programmer. Secondly, when employees are aware of the benefit of TATS-based applications, their acceptance for Privacy-by-Design approaches is higher and their intended use (without unintended manipulations) of such TATS is more likely. A profound understanding of employees' perceptions about the use of TATS enables the deduction of recommendations and measures to design, implement and use privacy-related assistance systems.

In order to gain insights into this topic, 19 semi-structured interviews were conducted. Interviewees representing various stakeholders were chosen in order to get a broad spectrum of different views on TATS. The remainder of this paper is structured as follows: After providing the theoretical background of TATS in Sect. 2, the research aim is stated in Sect. 3. In Sect. 4 the research method and our strategy of analysing the interview transcripts is described. Based on a content-analytic approach according to Mayring [1], four categories emerged (i.e., experience, benefits, challenge and acceptance factors) which are presented in Sect. 5. In Sect. 6 our model about influence factors when using TATS is presented and discussed. In Sect. 7 conclusion and further research possibilities are given.

## 2   Theoretical Background

To open up this interdisciplinary field of research, it is important to gain knowledge of the entire range of TATS and influence factor on employee behavior. On the one hand, it's necessary to have a good understanding of influence factors for employee behavior in organizations, explained in Sect. 2.2. On the other hand, it is important to recognize the problems of used technologies in TATS with respect to privacy, since these often lead to unexpected privacy issues. Therefore Sect. 2.1 explains wireless sensor networks and technologies used for TATS.

## 2.1 Tracking and Tracing Systems (TATS)

Due to the constantly increasing automation in industry, the need for information on the allocation of assets in the value chain at the plant site is growing. Real-time information on the current location of a specific asset is just as important here as data from the whole production flow in the shop floor [2]. The former enables the value-added process to be accelerated, as asset search times are reduced, and the exact process progress of an asset is always recorded in the organization's information system. In this way, for example, bottlenecks in production facilities can be identified at an early stage and even bypassed [3]. On the other hand, the collection and evaluation of data across the entire value chain enables precise evaluations of a wide range of Key Performance Indicators, such as throughput time, storage time and analysis of internal transport logistics. Tracking and tracing of physical objects is called Asset Tracking (AT) and summarizes all activities and methods to collect and the use of real-time positions and status data of goods, tools and load carriers and is already standard in entire industries.

Current AT systems use so-called Wireless Sensor Networks (WSN) to estimate the position of an asset. These systems are based on standardized radio technologies such as Wifi [4], Bluetooth [5], RFID [6, 7] or ZigBee [8, 9]. Each asset needs to be equipped with a tag for this purpose. These tags are active or passive radio transmitters that send their identification number in intervals. In the area where the tracking is carried out, so-called readers are static positioned to ensure optimal detection of the radio signals from these tags. The readers collect the Received Signal Strength Indicator (RSSI), which represents an indicator for the reception field strength, and a unique identification number of the tag. Using various algorithms such as trilateration or triangulation, the RSSI values of several readers can be used to calculate the physical position of a tag [10]. In addition to asset tracking, these technologies also offer new possibilities for collecting information and analyzing the location of individual employees in the organization including the exact time and duration of location [11]. Employee (Location) Monitoring (EM) plays a growing role in many jobs. In delivery jobs, for example, it is now common practice for these employees to constantly transmit their position to headquarters in order to be able to take on orders in the vicinity. Furthermore, trucks are equipped with GPS-transmitters so that dispatchers know where their vehicles are in real time [12].

## 2.2 Consequences of TATS on Employees

Improvements in technology have significantly changed the workplace environment. TATS have enabled employers to monitor employees in the workplace. This monitoring could help reduce employee misconduct, increase productivity, and prevent the leakage of confidential information. It may also lead to loss of employees' morale and the invasion of their privacy [13]. In the organizational context, it is particularly important to consider how electronic monitoring is introduced as literature reveals that negative reactions to monitoring might arise: A) Feelings of privacy invasion [14, 15], B) Perceptions of unfairness [16, 17], C) Decreased job satisfaction and organizational commitment [18], D) Lower task performance and productivity [19], E) Greater perceptions of stress on work-related tasks [19]. However, despite of EM's potentially negative consequences on employees' wellbeing in the organization, EM is well-accepted by employees for using it for the following purposes: to improve safety at work, improve productivity and work process instruction [11].

To get added value in the organization with EM, it is necessary to also take the concerns of employees very seriously. Employee monitoring offers a multitude of helpful services for organizations. However, there are several factors to take into consideration when implementing an EPM system. Tomczak et al. recommends the following recommendations for using electronic monitoring systems: A) Be transparent with employees about employee monitoring use; B) Be aware of all potential employee reactions to being monitored; C) Use employee for learning and development rather than deterrence; D) Restrict employee monitoring to only work-related behaviors; E) Consider organizational makeup when implementing an employee monitoring system [20].

## 3 Research Aim

The usage of TATS in working environments is increasing, but little is known about which factors influence employees' perceptions about TATS in the industrial environment. For example, 10% of German industrial organizations already use indoor positioning systems, and it is expected that these systems will soon become standard in the industry [21]. Therefore, it is necessary to establish new guidelines in order to support the positive possibilities of this technology on the one hand, but also to consciously limit the possibilities for unwanted monitoring. Especially, the knowledge about the impact on the behavior of the employees is often forgotten. Implementing TATS in the work environment without taking care of the employee's needs could bring unexpected effects with it, such as decreasing employee acceptance or diminishing productivity, or even lower quality of work. To prevent negative effects, it is necessary to become aware of possible factors influencing the perceptions prior to the implementation of these systems. Thus, the question remains, which factors influence employee perceptions when using TATS in work environments?

Full transparency in the collection and evaluation of data obtained from TATS would mean that every employee would have access to the evaluations of all other employees. This in turn contradicts the required data protection and would promote social blaming within the organization. If the goal is to maximize employee privacy, the use of TATS would need to be completely avoided. This creates a *monitoring-privacy dilemma* for organizations: on the one hand, they are required to use new technologies to increase their competitiveness and to foster employee safety, and on the other hand, they must ensure that existing laws on data protection are complied with and that employees are not harmed. Therefore, organizations are required to carefully weigh the costs and benefits of TATS.

## 4 Method

In order to elaborate the perception of the use of TATS on employees, we carried out a qualitative interview study with different stakeholders such as executives from several industries, employee representatives and the Austrian Chamber of Commerce. This led to various, detailed opinions on the topic, to cover most aspects about TATS. Interviews seem to be ideal to capture rich information about individual perceptions of TATS as well as receive knowledge about the prevalent discourse in the community which is communicated and understood through narratives. Narratives provide a means through which perceptions about TATS are enacted and perpetuated among peers [22].

## 4.1 Data Collection and Interviewees

Our primary source of data consisted of 19 audio-recorded interviews conducted by the first author between 4th December 2019 and 29th June 2020. Eight interviews were held face-to-face at the interviewees' organization site and eleven interviews took place via online video conferencing. The interviews were semi-structured and asked questions about asset tracking and employee (location) tracking. In addition to that, the interviewees were asked about their opinion about two possible tracking scenarios. The first scenario described the use of TATS for emergency evacuation purposes only whereas the second scenario described continuous tracking in the work environment. All interviews had narrative elements and the interviewees were encouraged to elaborate on their answers. They received the opportunity to disclose their opinions without much interruption from the interviewers. The interviews were conducted in German and lasted between

Table 1. Interviewees and interview profile

| Nr. | Pseudonym | Position in the organization | Gender | Length (min) |
|-----|-----------|------------------------------|--------|--------------|
| 1 | Sandra | Compliance in the legal department | Woman | 46,0 |
| 2 | Michael | Head of lean management | Man | 40,0 |
| 3 | Peter | Development manager IoT | Man | 30,7 |
| 4 | Stefan | Hardware | Man | 29,6 |
| 5 | Matthias | Head of lean management | Man | 25,4 |
| 6 | Daniel | Programmer software | Man | 21,0 |
| 7 | Markus | Head of accident prevention division | Man | 68,2 |
| 8 | Florian | Head of department | Man | 68,2 |
| 9 | Andre | Head of department | Man | 68,2 |
| 10 | Alexander | Order management | Man | 17,6 |
| 11 | Patrick | Production manager | Man | 41,0 |
| 12 | Robert | Innovation service employee | Man | 36,2 |
| 13 | Manfred | Trade union | Man | 38,2 |
| 14 | Thomas | Sales management | Man | 36,6 |
| 15 | Philipp | Safety specialist | Man | 28,5 |
| 16 | Andreas | IT area manager | Man | 38,3 |
| 17 | Christian | Digital transformation manager | Man | 15,8 |
| 18 | Manuela | Senior HR specialist | Woman | 15,8 |
| 19 | Christoph | Technician | Man | 34,2 |

15,8 and 68,2 min (36,82 min on average). All interviewees participated voluntarily in the study and were not compensated for their time. However, they were able to decline at any point in time and anonymity was assured in treatment of the data. In this paper, the interviewees are identified only using pseudonyms in order to ensure anonymity (see Table 1 for an overview of interviewees).

### 4.2  Data Analysis

The interview protocols encompassed a total of 114 DIN A4 pages of 12-point Arial font, single-spaced. We opted for a content-analytic approach following Mayring [1] as it is a typical approach for qualitative research and aims at the development of hypotheses and building of theories. As a basic form of interpretation, structuring was chosen to extract the information. In more detail, we carried out the following steps to analyze the material: In a first phase, three researchers openly coded the interview material. First, we identified the chunks of content and copied them into Excel (in addition with interview number, position, assessment of experience in TATS, scenario answers). resulting in 392 quotes. Second, based on these quotes, 25 categories emerged (description of categories available upon request) due to semantic similarity. Third, we grouped the categories to nine super-categories on a more abstract level. Based on these categories, we generated a category scheme which is displayed in the appendix.

## 5  Findings

Four topics emerged as being most relevant with regard to our research question: benefits, challenges, acceptance factors and experiences with TATS. Thus, in this section we present how these aspects relate to each other. With regard to EM, one of the most important challenges was privacy. We argue that organization also have to tackle privacy issues when implementing AT as technically, AT provides the possibility to implicitly track employees.

Figure 1 illustrates how organizations have to weigh benefits and challenges when deciding whether they should implement TATS. First of all, they experience an imonitoring-privacydilemma as although they can use TATS to gain valuable informa- tion, the privacy of the user might be violated. Our research highlights several factors that help to manage this challenge and reveals that users' experience in TATS further influence the evaluation of these acceptance factors. In the following these topics will be further elaborated on.

### 5.1  Benefits of Using TATS

When asking the interviewees for which purpose they use or would use TATS, the most frequently cited reasons were that it enables organizations to gain information for pro- cess optimization and traceability. AT has high potential when it comes to understanding production processes in their entirety. On the one hand, real-time monitoring enables the early detection of possible bottlenecks, but also the analysis of throughput periods in production helps to reduce downtimes and to optimize the inhouse transport. The

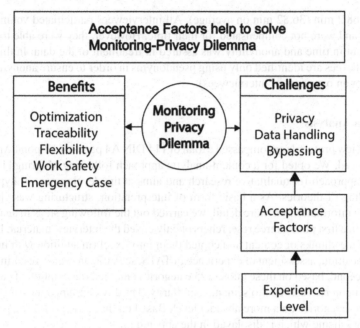

**Fig. 1.** Model for influence factors for acceptance of TATS

essential thing here is that employees are also offered the data that is being determined. This information gives them transparent insights into current processes. Accurate information quality can give real-time insights in the processes and are helpful in daily work. For example Thomas, a Sales Manager commented:

*If process data are collected and visualized on info terminals, where the employees also recognize it, then they get certainly a much better understanding of the value chain.*
(Thomas, Sales Management)

In the area of industrial production, process data is usually more relevant than the position data of employees. The interviewees report that EM is mostly in use for work in hazardous environments, for emergencies or optimizing workplaces. When used in harsh or dangerous working conditions, the interviewees find the use of EM as justifiable. Examples for that are dangerous environmental influences such as radioactive radiation or oxygen-deficient atmospheres. One important aspect here is that the technology improves the speed of reaction, which can be crucial for life savings: EM can ensure that maximum contamination limits are not exceeded and no long-term damage to the health of employees may occur.

Furthermore, it was raised that biofeedback on possibility of monitoring of health data by the employer was also mentioned. For example, the continuous recording and evaluation of the heartbeat per minute with wearables could indicate to the employee whether he or she is working too hard or whether he or she is currently very stressed. This corporate health care could help to reduce the sick leave rate in organizations. For example WHO from a TYPE OF ORGANIZATION gave an example about an internal fitness competition in his or her organization. Employees, who wanted to join that competition were equipped with smart watches and shared their activities with the organization. That competition was so well attended, that the group management decided to do another competition the following year. Despite its obvious benefit, there are also challenges connected to TATS.

### 5.2 Challenges in the Operation of TATS

Challenges can vary depending on the use case they were developed for. In the case of AT, technical constraints and economic reasons were mentioned in the interviews as the main factors why it is not applied for large scale. For example, WHO from TYPE OF ORGANIZATION reported that their organization has about 3000 containers in circulation, in which their products are transported between the processing steps. To equip all containers with tags and the whole shop floor with readers, a large investment would be required. A further constraint is the maintenance of the system, which also needs resources. Another challenge with regard to AT is how the organization should provide the information to the employees. It is important to consider that not all employees have the same level of understanding of such visualizations. Employees may feel overwhelmed by too much information, which might lead to stress. Patrick from an industrial company proposes an iterative data provision process:

*[…] it makes sense to provide the given information in steps. If employees ask for more information, then more data should be made available. If you make all the data directly available right at the beginning, you overburden the employees.*

(Patrick, Production Manager)

When using EM systems, the most important concern raised was with regard to privacy issues., EM implies that sensitive data about employees are being collected. This data could be used to evaluate performance of employees. It also allows detailed surveillance, e.g. the employer could monitor how long an employee is at the workplace, the break room or in the restrooms. Our interviewees reported that most organizations take data protection and employee privacy into account. They are aware of the potential threat and Daniel from the production industry brings it to the point:

*Until asset tracking works properly in our organization, EM is not an option anyway. It makes no sense to start here with the most sensitive topic.*

(Peter, Development Manager IoT)

Due to country differences in the legislation, this issue is particularly relevant in international corporations. The problem is significantly intensified if the organization's headquarters has less stringent data protection regulations than the national division. The local organizations are now challenged to comply to applicable data protection regulations in order to ensure employee privacy locally. Florian highlights this issue in the following quote:

*The challenge for large corporations is that their headquarters may be in countries where the use of EM is not regulated as precisely. The headquarter then demands that these measures should be implemented everywhere. The task of the national group then must be to reject these measures because they are not permitted by law.*

(Florian, Head of Department)

### 5.3 Acceptance Factors for Operation

The reported challenges can only be overcome when several factors have to be taken into account. Factors that were found to influence the acceptance of TATS are: transparency, trust, communication, data storage, health aspect, and safety perception.

Many of the interviewees stated that these acceptance factors are particularly important when the information can be tied to individual employees. These acceptance factors are particularly important in the following situations:

**Transparency** - It is important to address employees' concerns at an early stage. Most interviewees stated that transparency is essential in the introduction and operation of TATS. It is important that the expected benefits and the impact on the process are communicated in advance. In most situations, employees are initially opposed to the change or conversion of processes. However, if it is clearly communicated which data is collected and for which purpose, the acceptance is higher.

**Trust** - Several aspects were mentioned with regard to trust and the use of TATS. According to the interviewees, it is fundamentally important that the organization is known as reliable and trustworthy. Another factor is how strong the influence of works councils is on organization management, whether they are merely tolerated or whether there is a good relationship.

**Communication** - One of the most frequently cited factor influencing acceptance of TATS was the organizational communication. Interviewees stated that it is important to speak with all affected employees and not just with certain supervisors. In addition, all concerns must be taken seriously and only then, the next steps of the project can be implemented. It is also important that the organization's management stands behind the project; it must support the project managers in their communication.

**Data Storage** - Especially with EM, privacy of the employee is a very crucial issue that must be considered from the very beginning of the implementation. Only data that has been defined for the fulfillment of the intended task should be logged. In addition, EM should not be used to determine the performance of one specific employee, data should be anonymized and evaluated over a whole department. The duration of the monitoring is also essential. If EM is used for a limited period of time to optimize workplaces, acceptance is stronger than with permanent monitoring.

**Safety Perception** - EM was usually rejected by the interviewees unless it can significantly increase work safety e.g., in dangerous working environments. In this special situation, employees then normally feel more guarded than monitored. On the other hand, some interviewees mentioned, that they would only feel protected if the area is really harmful.

**Health Aspect** - Personal health data is a very sensitive area. If an organization offers to support employees in this area, this can also trigger greater health awareness among the employees themselves.

## 5.4  Influence of Experience

The interviewees were basically asked about their experience with TATS in their area of operation in the organization. It turned out that the organizations have experience in very different use cases and solutions. Since TATS are used in a very process-oriented approach, they are thus individually adapted and are strongly dependent on the value chain of the respective organization. However, from all these statements, a certain basic mood could be determined as to how the attitude to TATS is in the organizations. Nearly every interviewee had some experience with AT. Systems, based on simple barcode scanners or WSNs, have been used in a variety of use cases in the enterprises. Most respondents felt that the advantages of these systems outweighed the risks and that employees would not be negatively affected by them.

Two scenarios were presented and the interviews were asked if they rather agree or would reject the usage of TATS for the specifc scenario. Scenario 1 described a TATS that would only be activated in an emergency case to simplify evacuation of the persons who are present. This scenario had a generally high level of agreement. However, it appeared that those with more experience with TATS in particular were more likely to agree that this use of TATS was justifies, as shown in Table 2.

Scenario 2 described a TATS that should be used permanently in production to increase efficiency. Thus, assets and employees should be localizable with the system. As expected, agreement was naturally lower in this scenario, but again interviewees with less experience were fundamentally more skeptical. The results on approval and disapproval of both scenarios can be found in Table 2.

In principle, the interviews had the result that the risks of monitoring were rated lower for AT systems than for EM systems. When prior experience with TATS was reported, the risks of monitoring are also rated lower.

**Table 2.**  Consent or rejection to the scenarios in the interviews

| Experience of interviewee | Scenario 1 | | Scenario 2 | |
|---|---|---|---|---|
| | Consent | Rejection | Consent | Rejection |
| No experience | 2 | 2 | 0 | 4 |
| Medium experience | 5 | 1 | 2 | 5 |
| High experience | 8 | 1 | 4 | 4 |
| Total | **15** | **4** | **6** | **13** |

# 6 Discussion

We conducted a qualitative interview study with various stakeholders to derive knowledge about perceptions of TATS in work environments. Our analysis reveals that the type of tracking (AT vs. EM) matters, organizations have to deal with an imonitoring-privacydilemma in particularly with regard to EM and different acceptance factors such as transparent communication help to solve this dilemma in organizations.

## 6.1 Relevance of Type of Tracking

During the analysis of the interviews, it became clear that fundamental differences between the two types of tracking (AT, EM) are made. While AT is already widely used in industrial applications [21], EM normally is used explicitly in extra-ordinary work environments. Usually, use cases focused on workplace safety elicited the high acceptance under employees [11]. In the case of AT, technical constraints and economic reasons were mentioned in the interviews as the main factors why it is not applied for large scale. Although in most cases no personal data is collected, the privacy of the users should still be taken into consideration [10]. In the production industry, EM is mostly used to increase occupational safety, emergency scenarios for evacuation or for optimizing workplaces. Compared to AT, EM is more challenging since it involves organizational, privacy and social issues [23]. Data regulations and standards that are designed to ensure privacy and data protection, such as the GDPR[1] or Standard ISO/IEC 29100:2011[2] are rather strict in Europe compared to other areas in the world. In principle, these standards are also valid for employment relationships, but with the restriction that employees not always have the free decision which data they share with the employer. On the other hand, employers argue that they have the right to improve employee productivity and location monitoring is just another means of improving employee performance [24]. However, when using EM sensitive data about employees are collected which intrudes privacy rights [24].

Previous studies have shown that technology experience can moderate the relationship between attitudes and intentions to resist employee monitoring systems, such that the relationship is stronger for individuals with strong technology experience [25]. This relationship was supported in our interviews. Furthermore, the higher was the level of experience with tracking systems in the working environment, the lower were the perceived risks of monitoring. It is probable that the higher level of experience also includes the underlying knowledge about required data protection, evaluation of data and influence on employee privacy. Since the interviewees were mainly from the management level of the organizations, they already had experience with the extensive activities that are necessary to implement TATS and comply with the law.

## 6.2 Monitoring-Privacy Dilemma

Organizations are challenged to gather all relevant information on production and business processes, but they need to take the privacy of their employees into account. This creates an *monitoring-privacy dilemma* for organizations:

---

[1] https://gdpr.euT.

Therefore, they are required to carefully weigh the costs and benefits of TATS when introducing it into the organization. This dilemma cannot be completely solved because one would have to completely abandon the logging of all data in the production process that have a personal reference. However, it is a possibility to take the acceptance factors from Sect. 1.3 into consideration at the beginning of the implementation of TATS. These points can help to ensure that employees' concerns are addressed, and that employees' perceptions of these systems are more positive.

### 6.3 How to Create Acceptance for Employee Monitoring

Organizations are challenged to create acceptance when introducing TATS. Derived from our interviews, the following five guidelines might help with this endeavor:

1. **Differentiate between the use cases:** It always depends on what you need to achieve and then to decide which tracking fits best. For AT use cases it is always good practice to be as transparent as possible with information sharing. In the case of EM systems, careful decisions must be made as to who has access to the data.
2. **Privacy is an imperative need, not an option:** Not everything one agrees in his or her private life is acceptable in work environments. It is particularly important to note that decisions can be made freely and that there is the option for not using these systems.
3. **Show that you care:** Almost every employee expects a healthy workplace with a high level of work safety. Show the employees that you can meet this desire with the help of monitoring systems.
4. **Discuss also uncomfortable topics:** It is easy to talk about the benefits of TATS. For an open corporate communication, it is also necessary to address unpleasant topics such as influence on employee privacy and to act authentically.
5. **Be aware of employee perceptions:** By taking into account the acceptance factors described above, more support can be created as experience with TATS help to raise its acceptance.

## 7  Conclusion

Framing technology's end-goals as serving intrinsic goals yields higher employee acceptability than when serving extrinsic goals within a controlling work context [26]. Our interview study explored perceptions of TATS in work environments and provides a guideline for the implementation of TATS in work environments. We particularly emphasize that there are several factors influencing acceptance of TATS in organizations that have to be taken into account right at the start (or prior) the implementation. By designing the implementation consciously, the ımonitoring-privacydilemma can be defused and problems in the implementation can be solved at an early stage.

# Appendix

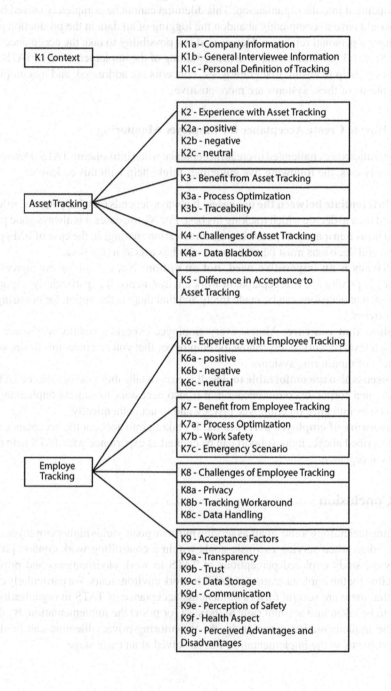

K1 Context
- K1a - Company Information
- K1b - General Interviewee Information
- K1c - Personal Definition of Tracking

Asset Tracking

K2 - Experience with Asset Tracking
- K2a - positive
- K2b - negative
- K2c - neutral

K3 - Benefit from Asset Tracking
- K3a - Process Optimization
- K3b - Traceability

K4 - Challenges of Asset Tracking
- K4a - Data Blackbox

K5 - Difference in Acceptance to Asset Tracking

Employe Tracking

K6 - Experience with Employee Tracking
- K6a - positive
- K6b - negative
- K6c - neutral

K7 - Benefit from Employee Tracking
- K7a - Process Optimization
- K7b - Work Safety
- K7c - Emergency Scenario

K8 - Challenges of Employee Tracking
- K8a - Privacy
- K8b - Tracking Workaround
- K8c - Data Handling

K9 - Acceptance Factors
- K9a - Transparency
- K9b - Trust
- K9c - Data Storage
- K9d - Communication
- K9e - Perception of Safety
- K9f - Health Aspect
- K9g - Perceived Advantages and Disadvantages

# References

1. Mayring, P.: Qualitative Inhaltsanalyse. Grundlagen und Techniken. Weinheim, vol. 3, p. 58 (2010)
2. Kousay, S., Maffei, A., Onori, M.: Real-time asset tracking; a starting point for digital twin implementation in manufacturing. Ljubljana Slovenia **81**, 719–723 (2019)
3. Frankó, A., Vida, G., Varga, P.: Reliable identification schemes for asset and production tracking in industry 4.0. Sensors **20**(13), 3709 (2020). https://doi.org/10.3390/s20133709
4. Salman, A., El-Tawab, S., Yorio, Z., Hilal, A.: Indoor localization using 802.11 WiFi and IoT edge nodes. In: 2018 IEEE Global Conference on Internet of Things (GCIoT), pp. 1–5, December 2018. https://doi.org/10.1109/GCIoT.2018.8620162
5. Jandl, C., Nurgazina, J., Schöffer, L., Reichl, C., Wagner, M., Moser, T.: SensiTrack - a privacy by design concept for industrial IoT applications. In: International Conference on Emerging Technologies and Factory Automation (ETFA 2019), Zaragossa, Spain, September 2019.
6. Moniem, S.A., Taha, S., Hamza, H.S.: An anonymous mutual authentication scheme for healthcare RFID systems. In: 2017 IEEE SmartWorld, Ubiquitous Intelligence Computing, Advanced Trusted Computed, Scalable Computing Communications, Cloud Big Data Computing, Internet of People and Smart City Innovation, pp. 1–6, August 2017. https://doi.org/10.1109/UIC-ATC.2017.8397622
7. Fan, K., Jiang, W., Li, H., Yang, Y.: Lightweight RFID protocol for medical privacy protection in IoT. IEEE Trans. Ind. Inform. **14**(4), 1656–1665 (2018). https://doi.org/10.1109/TII.2018.2794996
8. Chan, H.K.: Wireless industrial tracking system for factory automation. In: 2008 Second International Symposium on Intelligent Information Technology Application, vol. 3, pp. 862–866, December 2008. https://doi.org/10.1109/IITA.2008.548
9. Kim, S.-J., Seo, J. H., Krishna, J., Kim, S.-J.: Wireless sensor network based asset tracking service. In: PICMET 2008 - 2008 Portland International Conference on Management of Engineering Technology, pp. 2643–2647, July 2008. https://doi.org/10.1109/PICMET.2008.4599893
10. Zafari, F., Gkelias, A., Leung, K.: A survey of indoor localization systems and technologies. ArXiv170901015 Cs, September 2017
11. Jacobs, J.V., et al.: Employee acceptance of wearable technology in the workplace. Appl. Ergon. **78**, 148–156 (2019). https://doi.org/10.1016/j.apergo.2019.03.003
12. Michael, K., McNamee, A., Michael, M.G.: The emerging ethics of humancentric GPS tracking and monitoring, p. 12 (2006)
13. Lee, S., Kleiner, B.H.: Electronic surveillance in the workplace. Manag. Res. News **26**(2/3/4), 72–81 (2003). https://doi.org/10.1108/01409170310784014
14. Mcnall, L., Stanton, J.: Private eyes are watching you: reactions to location sensing technologies. J. Bus. Psychol. **26**(3), 299–309 (2010)
15. Stanton, J.M.: Reactions to employee performance monitoring: framework, review, and research directions. Hum. Perform. **13**(1), 85–113 (2000). https://doi.org/10.1207/S15327043HUP1301_4
16. Moorman, R.H., Wells, D.L.: Can electronic performance monitoring be fair? Exploring relationships among monitoring characteristics, perceived fairness, and job performance. J. Leadersh. Organ. Stud. **10**(2), 2–16 (2003). https://doi.org/10.1177/107179190301000202
17. McNall, L.A., Roch, S.G.: Effects of electronic monitoring types on perceptions of procedural justice, interpersonal justice, and privacy. J. Appl. Soc. Psychol. **37**(3), 658–682 (2007). https://doi.org/10.1111/j.1559-1816.2007.00179.x
18. Wells, D.L., Moorman, R.H., Werner, J.M.: The impact of the perceived purpose of electronic performance monitoring on an array of attitudinal variables. Hum. Resour. Dev. Q. **18**(1), 121–138 (2007). https://doi.org/10.1002/hrdq.1194

19. Aiello, J.R., Kolb, K.J.: Electronic performance monitoring and social context: impact on productivity and stress. J. Appl. Psychol. **80**, 339–353 (1995). https://doi.org/10.1037/0021-9010.80.3.339
20. Tomczak, D.L., Lanzo, L.A., Aguinis, H.: Evidence-based recommendations for employee performance monitoring
21. Schlund, S., Pokorni, B.: Industrie 4.0 – Wo steht die Revolution der Arbeitsgestaltung? Ingenics AG, Stuttgart/Ulm (2016)
22. Dunbar, R.L.M., Statler, M.: A historical perspective on organizational control. In: Sitkin, S.B., Cardinal, L.B., Bijlsma-Frankema, K.M. (eds.) Organizational Control, pp. 16–48. Cambridge University Press, Cambridge (2010)
23. Yao, W., Chu, C., Li, Z.: The use of RFID in healthcare: Benefits and barriers. In: 2010 IEEE International Conference on RFID-Technology and Applications, Guangzhou, China, pp. 128–134, June 2010. https://doi.org/10.1109/RFID-TA.2010.5529874
24. Minch, R.: Legal and ethical implications of employee location monitoring. In: gehalten auf der Hawaii International Conference on System Sciences (2005)
25. Spitzmüller, C., Stanton, J.M.: Examining employee compliance with organizational surveillance and monitoring. J. Occup. Organ. Psychol. **79**(2), 245–272 (2006). https://doi.org/10.1348/096317905X52607
26. Acker, B.B.V., Conradie, P., Vlerick, P., Saldien, J.: Employee acceptability of wearable mental workload monitoring in industry 4.0: a pilot study on motivational and contextual framing, vol. 1, no. 1, pp. 2101–2110 (2019)

# A User Interface for Personalising WS-BPEL Scenarios

Dionisis Margaris[1] ⓘ, Dimitris Spiliotopoulos[2]([✉]) ⓘ, Dionysios Vasilopoulos[3] ⓘ,
and Costas Vassilakis[3] ⓘ

[1] Department of Digital Systems, University of the Peloponnese, Sparta, Greece
margaris@uop.gr
[2] Department of Management Science and Technology, University of the Peloponnese,
Tripoli, Greece
dspiliot@uop.gr
[3] Department of Informatics and Telecommunications, University of the Peloponnese,
Tripoli, Greece
{dvasilop,costas}@uop.gr

**Abstract.** Due to the huge volume of web services available, both locally and in the cloud, the performance of users and systems need significant research attention. Since WS-BPEL is the dominant language for orchestrating individual web services into business processes, by composing WS-BPEL scripts/scenarios, graphical notations facilitating WS-BPEL design can be extremely useful. Current user interfaces allow WS-BPEL designers not only to invoke selected web services, but also to explicitly ask for recommendations. Then, the user interface appends the services achieving the highest score, according to the attributes' importance, set by the designer, to their WS-BPEL scenario. However, since the final selection is produced automatically, rather than relying on the designers' choices, many times, from a personalisation point of view, the adaptation fails. This work reports on the design, development and user evaluation of a user interface that incorporates functionalities that support the designers' selection performance, thereby upgrading the personalisation level of the WS-BPEL scenarios, as well as the success of the adaptation.

**Keywords:** User interface · Personalisation · Recommender systems · WS-BPEL scenarios · Web services · User evaluation · Usability

## 1 Introduction

WS-BPEL (Web Services Business Process Execution Language) is the typical language that orchestrates individual web services (WSs) in order to build high level business processes [1, 2]. A WS-BPEL scenario requires multiple invocations to WSs. Those invocations may be either user-specified, i.e., the user selects the services to invoke and the exact parameters, or system-adapted, i.e. a query is made to a recommender engine to retrieve the WSs that realize the desired functionality and select the one best suited

© Springer Nature Switzerland AG 2021
F. F.-H. Nah and K. Siau (Eds.): HCII 2021, LNCS 12783, pp. 399–416, 2021.
https://doi.org/10.1007/978-3-030-77750-0_25

to the user's needs. The desired functionality may be specified in terms of categories of interest [3, 4], such as Hotel, Sea Travel, and Car Rental services.

The recommender engine queries may impose restrictions on quality of service (QoS) attribute values, according to the user's choices, such as cost, availability, reliability, and others [5, 6]. Existing research has reported algorithms that perform adaptation of WS-BPEL scenario execution based on user specifications of limits and importance of QoS parameters, however, these proposals involve automatic computation and execution of the optimal query plan, without allowing the user to intervene and customize the execution according to his preferences [7, 8]. As a result, in many cases, the invoked service is not the one that a user would select and, as a result, from a personalisation point of view, the WS-BPEL scenario execution adaptation yields suboptimal results. Recent HCI research addresses the problem by offering a user interface (UI) that enables the users to both preview the recommended WSs and make the final selection based on their own preferences [9]. Although that is a major step towards the personalisation of the WS-BPEL scenario execution adaptation, experienced WS-BPEL designers/developers that are the end-users of this approach reported the need for functionalities such as user-directed exclusions and automatic assignment of the top candidate WSs in the scenario code, which no WS-BPEL IDE provides.

This work presents three WS-BPEL scenario adaptation functionalities, which assist the WS-BPEL designers to upgrade the personalisation level of their scenarios and are not supported by any other IDE, as well as the design, implementation and user evaluation of the corresponding UI that supports them.

The rest of the paper is structured as follows: Sect. 2 overviews related work, while Sect. 3 presents the necessary foundations for our work, for self-containment purposes. Sect. 4 presents and analyses the proposed functionalities and the overall UI design, while Sect. 5 presents the results of the user evaluation. Finally, Sect. 6 concludes the paper and outlines the future work.

## 2   Related Work

Over the last years the research field of WS-BPEL scenarios' adaptation process has attracted significant research efforts [10–13]. Moser et al. [14] propose an aspect-oriented approach by intercepting SOAP messages and allowing service exchange during run-time with minimum performance penalty costs in high-availability BPEL environments. Margaris et al. [15] introduce a framework that incorporates runtime quality of BPEL scenarios WS-based adaptation, allowing for tailoring their execution to the needs of each user. Furthermore, their framework supports automatic resolution of system-level exceptions, while both exception resolution and scenario execution adaptation manage to maintain the transactional semantics that may bear invocations to multiple WSs offered by the same provider.

Kareliotis et al. [16] present a framework that includes mechanisms for considering the qualitative parameters of the invoked WSs, so that the WS-BPEL scenarios tailor their execution to each designer's needs or adapt to the WWW dynamic environment, where old WSs may be withdrawn or change their qualitative parameters, or new ones may be deployed. Furthermore, the proposed framework includes mechanisms that are able to handle infrastructure failures in the distributed WWW environment, as well as allows the designers to specify the qualitative parameters that they require and locate and invoke suitable WSs. Charfi et al. [17] present a plug-in architecture for self-adaptive WS composition with well-modularized self-adaptation features in aspect-based plug-ins. Their approach is easily extensible, supports application-specific adaptation WS-BPEL scenarios and finally allows self-adaptation logic to be deployed on running business process instances. Agarwal and Jalote [18] propose an approach for dynamically adapting WS compositions based on non-functional requirements. Their approach selects the suitable WSs at runtime, while the selected WSs need only be semantically equivalent since their system is able to automatically take care of the syntactical differences between the WSs' interfaces. Margaris et al. [19] introduce a framework which extends the qualitative adaptation mechanisms with collaborative filtering techniques, allowing the WS-BPEL designers to further refine the adaptation process by considering WS selections made by other designers in the past. Wu and Doshi [20] incorporate constraint enforcement models and generalized adaptation in order to transform the traditional WS-BPEL process into an adaptive one, producing a WS-BPEL process able to execute on standard BPEL implementations and to respect coordination constraints.

Liu et al. [21] present a middleware-based approach which deploys mobility, tasks and user interactions into WS-BPEL engines. Their approach provides a Domain-Specific Language which includes facilities which support the declarative development of mobile-oriented adaptive and Web-based UIs in WS-BPEL. Hermosillo et al. [22] introduce a framework which combines the strengths of dynamic business process adaptation and complex event processing that is able to maintain the qualitative characteristics of the business processes by dynamically adapting them according to each case. Hielscher et al. [23] present a framework that aims to enable proactive self-adaptation, by exploiting online testing techniques to detect deviations and process them accordingly before they lead to undesired consequences. Furthermore, they present online testing activities required to trigger proactive adaptation, as well as discuss how these testing activities can be implemented by existing adaptation and testing techniques.

Erradi et al. [24] present a policy-based middleware for dynamic self-adaptation of WS compositions to various changes. Their middleware manages to improve reliability by addressing business exceptions and supporting fault management of WS compositions. Mei et al. [25] exploit the XML-based artifacts' structural similarity between test cases and propose a set of test case prioritisation techniques that selects test case pairs without replacement, in an iteratively way, which proved to be cost-effective in exposing faults. Kareliotis et al. [26] introduce a middleware-based framework for system exception resolution that undertakes the tasks of failure interception and discovery and invocation of alternative services, driven by consumer-specified process qualitative policy. Furthermore, the proposed middleware employs XSLT-based transformations [27–29] to solve syntactic differences between the functionally equivalent WS and the originally invoked one.

However, none of the above-mentioned works addressed the personalisation processes from the user interaction perspective by offering useful functionalities to the WS-BPEL designer, while at the same time upgrading the personalisation level of the WS-BPEL scenario adaptation process.

Recently, Margaris et al. [9] presented a UI for WS-BPEL designers, which produced personalised recommendations, based on user generated criteria, enabling the designers to have the final selection choice. In this work a specialized UI for WS-BPEL designers, that allows personalised recommendation and selection of business process functionalities based on user generated criteria is introduced. Compared to previous works, the proposed UI embeds additional functionalities, such as default values and selections for multiple recommendation candidates and user-directed relational bounds based on non-qualitative criteria, aiming to enhance both the personalisation level of the WS-BPEL scenarios, as well as the adaptation success.

# 3  Prerequisites

For conciseness purposes, the following subsections summarize the major concepts and underpinnings from the areas of WS substitution relationships and WS QoS attributes domains, which are used in our work.

## 3.1  Web Services QoS Attributes

The overall performance of WSs is typically described using non-functional parameters expressed as WS QoS attributes, such as reliability, availability, cost, etc. [30–33]. In our work, for conciseness purposes and without loss of generality, we consider the attributes of *reliability* (rel), *cost* (c), and *response time* (rt). For information considering their typical definitions, the interested reader is referred to [34–37].

In a WS-BPEL scenario execution, constraints regarding the upper and lower bounds on each of the QoS attributes delivered by each WS in the context of a specific invocation may be specified using two vectors, which will be denoted as *MIN* and *MAX*, correspondingly. Additionally, a weight vector, which will be denoted as *W*, can be used to indicate the importance of each attribute in the context of the particular invocation of the WS-BPEL scenario [38]:

- $MIN_x(min_{rt,x}, min_{c,x}, min_{rel,x})$,
- $MAX_x(max_{rt,x}, max_{c,x}, max_{rel,x})$ and
- $W(rt_w, c_w, rel_w)$.

The weight vector is used to calculate an overall score for the whole composition, through the application of a weight sum approach. Effectively, after the value each QoS attribute of the whole composition is determined, each QoS attribute value is multiplied by the respective weight, and the partial sums are added to produce the overall score for the particular WS-BPEL scenario adaptation. Notably, while the MIN and MAX vectors, are applied to each WS selection (regulating thus each individual invocation), while the W vector is applied to the whole WS-BPEL scenario (the whole composition).

Furthermore, in this work:

- All attributes are normalized in the range [0, 10], using a standard normalization (min-max) formula.

- We consider that larger attribute values correspond to higher QoS levels and, hence, an inversion transformation is needed for the attributes where smaller attribute values correspond to higher QoS levels (such as latency and price).

The aforementioned approach is typically followed for QoS attribute values handling in the context of WS selection and composition [2, 39, 40].

Table 1 depicts an example of the repository form that contains four indicative WSs.

**Table 1.** Example of repository contents.

| Service | Response time | Cost | Reliability |
|---------|---------------|------|-------------|
| $S_1$ | 6 | 6 | 6 |
| $S_2$ | 8 | 8 | 4 |
| $S_3$ | 2 | 2 | 2 |
| $S_4$ | 3 | 10 | 4 |

It has to be noted that our framework is also able to handle (a) service selection affinity (i.e. interdependencies between service selections, in the sense that the selection that some functionality $F_j$ is realized through service implementation $SI_{j,k}$ binds the selection of the service to realize some functionality $F_m \neq F_j$ to some specific implementation $SI_{m,n}$; the affinity concept preserves the transactional semantics of WS-BPEL scenarios [15]), (b) parallel (concurrent invocations) and sequential structures and (c) exception resolution in WS-BPEL scenarios [15, 26].

## 3.2 Substitution Relationship Representation

In order for a WS implementation A to realize a particular requested functionality B, in the context of a WS-BPEL scenario, the WS matchmaking relationships [36, 41, 42] are used, where the selected WS must either provide:

- the exact same functionality as B, or
- more specific functionality than B.

In order for an adaptation software to compute the matchmaking relationships between an implementation and a functionality, a WS taxonomy must be used. An example taxonomy is depicted in Fig. 1, concerning an airline ticket booking WS, where the white shaded rectangles (lower levels) represent WS implementations, while the orange shaded rectangles (upper level) represent (sub-)categories [43, 44]. The line between two orange shaded rectangles denotes that the higher-level node includes the lower-level one in a superclass-subclass relation.

The WS repository stores the QoS attributes values for each node corresponding to a WS implementation (white shaded rectangles), as depicted in Fig. 2.

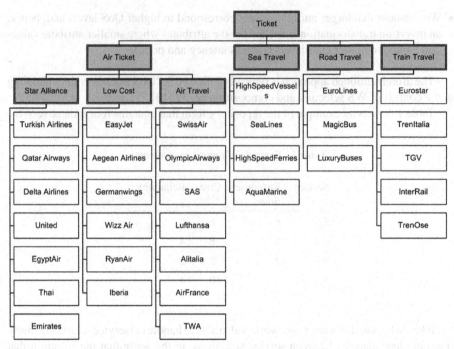

**Fig. 1.** Hierarchy of WSs (sub-)categories and implementations for the airline ticket booking service.

```
Category: Ticket
  Category: Air Ticket
    Category: Star Alliance
      Implementation: Turkish Airlines (rt=6, cost=2, rel=9)
      Implementation: Qatar Airways (rt=5, cost=8, rel=3)
      Implementation: Delta Airlines (rt=2, cost=6, rel=6)
```

**Fig. 2.** Excerpt of the WS taxonomy repository.

### 3.3 WS-BPEL Scenario and Dataset Example

Our WS-BPEL scenario example contains one sequential structure, concerning the process of booking a summer holiday vacation package that includes the following three functionalities:

1. *asking for a recommendation* considering an airline ticket,
2. booking a *specific* (direct invocation to a WS by the user) luxury hotel room, and
3. renting a car from a *specific* (direct invocation to a WS by the user) car rental WS.

The aforementioned scenario's pseudocode is depicted in Fig. 3.

```
SHVP
WEIGHTS(respTime=0.2, cost=0.3, reliability=0.5)
  SEQ
    (name=bookAirTravel, REC, Ticket / Air Ticket / Low Cost , min=(-,3,5), max=(-,9,-) )
    (name=bookHotel, INV, "Hilton")
    (name=bookCarRental, INV, "Rent a Car")
  END_SEQ
```

**Fig. 3.** Pseudocode of the summer holiday vacation package business process execution request example.

Each functionality, in Fig. 3, either:

- asks for a WS recommendation (term *REC*): in this case, the user enters the full path to the WS (sub-)category in the repository, as well as the upper and lower QoS attributes' bounds (or enters the "-" symbol, denoting that no specific binding is requested), or
- indicates an invocation to a specific WS (term *INV*).

## 4 Interface Design and Functionalities

The proposed UI was designed and implemented in order to cover the following three functionalities:

- Preselection of the top candidate service, to allow automatic preloading for all *REC* recommendations, reducing the user effort required to perform manual selection.
- User-directed relational bounds based on non-qualitative criteria, such as "exclude *CountryOrigin* airline" or "exclude *airline_name = RyanAir*", thereby satisfying the personalisation user criteria.
- N-result visualization based on user personalisation parameters, such as combination of score/bound metrics and user-specified preference criteria.

In the following subsections the above functionalities will be analysed.

### 4.1 Preselection of the Top Candidate Service

The UI allows the user to enter the BPEL scenario specification using pseudocode, utilising the *REC* and *INV* commands as illustrated in Fig. 3. For every *REC* placeholder, the services that satisfy the criteria are retrieved and presented to the user as a list ranked by the highest criteria values (Fig. 4). The right-hand side shows the retrieved services for line 4 of the user code that used *REC* for the WS recommendation for specific criteria. It shows the line it refers to, the criteria values for easy user lookup and the retrieved services ordered by highest-to-lowest criteria satisfaction.

The user may adjust the criteria at any time. When so, the list is repopulated with the items and ranking that satisfies the new criteria.

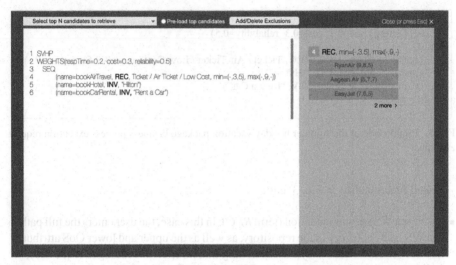

**Fig. 4.** The UI showing the user code and the WS recommendation request list if retrieved services.

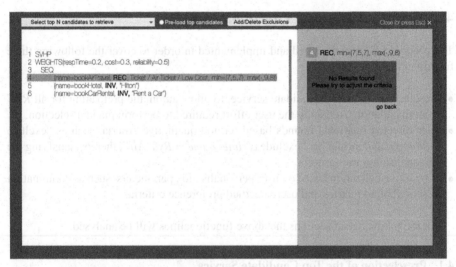

**Fig. 5.** The UI showing the user adjusted criteria and the case where no services that satisfy the criteria can be retrieved.

When no services can be retrieved, the REC line is highlighted in red allowing the user to go back to their previous criteria values or further adjust the criteria that were too strict. The realisation of this functionality is depicted in Fig. 5.

Many BPEL scenarios are characterized by several requests for WSs' recommendations (e.g., over 20). In this case, the BPEL designer has to devote considerable amount of time in order to manually select each specific WSs, so that the BPEL scenario can be executed. To tackle this issue, the proposed system may automatically make selections for the WS implementations that will be used for each *REC* placeholder, selecting for each placeholder the WS implementation that has the highest score, considering the QoS attribute weight vector and the overall composition. Automatic choices are clearly highlighted on the user interface, and the user has the ability to modify the selections.

The user may request the system to pre-load the top candidate services for all *REC* lines using the "Pre-load top candidates" button. When this action is performed, the *REC* code is replaced by specifications of the concrete service invocations of the top candidate preselected by the system, i.e. the top service from the retrieved list. The system preselection is highlighted, both for the lines of code and their selections, as depicted in Fig. 6 (elements coloured in light orange).

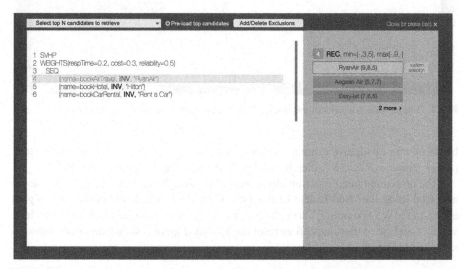

**Fig. 6.** The system preselection of the top candidate service is pre-loaded and inserted into the user code.

The user may also make a manual selection after the most prominent selections are automatically filled in by the system. In that case, the user's selection replaces the system automatic selection in the code and the highlighting properties are changed to make the fact that a manual selection is applied clear on the UI. The user selection is also shown in blue on the list of the retrieved services (Fig. 7). That is also the case for every user manual selection thereafter.

This functionality allows the user to directly use the system's automatic selections or apply manual selection as many times as necessary, highlighting the current selection and the system preselection. Currently, light orange and blue colours are used for highlighting automatic and manual selections, respectively, making the different cases clearly discernible at a visual level within the UI.

## 4.2 User-Specified Exclusions

A functionality that would be very useful for WS-BPEL designers, would be the ability to exclude specific or full categories of WSs (e.g., for personal reasons), from being considered in the recommendation process, despite the values in their qualitative attributes,

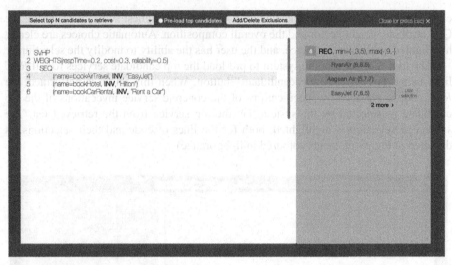

**Fig. 7.** The manual user selection is inserted into the code, overriding the system pre-loaded code.

based on non-qualitative criteria, such as "exclude *CountryOrigin* airline" or "exclude *airline_name* = *RyanAir*", thereby satisfying the personalisation user criteria.

The aforementioned functionality is available through the user interface and can be accessed using the "Add/Delete Exclusions" UI control, which allows the user to gain access to the WS taxonomy. Through this taxonomy, the user may exclude and re-include services and categories, as well as reset the actions. Figure 8 shows the user exclusion management page.

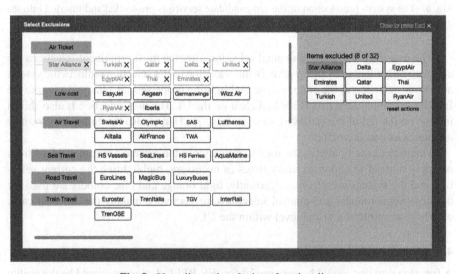

**Fig. 8.** User-directed exclusions functionality.

The user-specified exclusions lead to the retrieval of filtered results that encompasses only the non-excluded services, as shown in Fig. 9. In this example, the retrieved results exclude all the services under the *Category: "Star Alliance"*, as well as the *airline_name = "RyanAir"*. The "pre-load top candidate" function will populate the code using the filtered list items. However, the user may choose to view the excluded items and manually select services that were initially excluded based on the user exclusion actions.

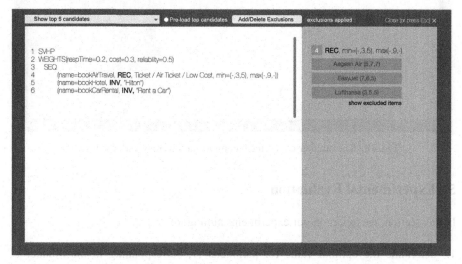

**Fig. 9.** The WS recommendation results filtered by the user-set exclusions.

### 4.3   Number of Retrieved Candidates

A very useful feature that WS-BPEL designers have requested is to be able to choose the top-N candidate WSs, based on their feature values and designer parameters (weights and limits), which should appear when requesting for a recommendation, by the same token that some users who perform Google search, stay at the first 4–5 results, while others do a more thorough work, reaching up to the 4th–5th page [45].

This functionality is illustrated in Fig. 10. The optimal value for the top-N parameter, will be experimentally determined in the next section.

The next section presents the evaluation of the UI by WS-BPEL designers, after determining the optimal value for the top-N parameter, concerning the number of candidate WSs that should appear in the right-hand-side list when requesting for a recommendation.

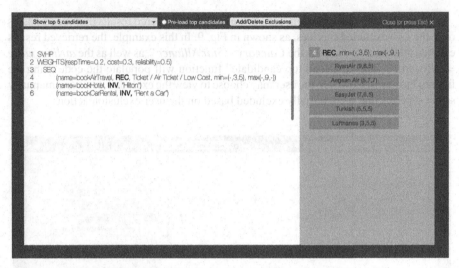

**Fig. 10.** The number of service recommendations may vary by design.

## 5    Experimental Evaluation

In this section, we report on our experiments aiming to:

1. determine the optimal value for parameter $N$, corresponding to the number of candidate WSs that should become available to the user when requesting for a recommendation, and
2. evaluate the usability of the proposed UI, in terms of user satisfaction regarding the offered functionalities [46–50].

### 5.1    Determining the Number of the Candidates Displayed Per Recommendation

The first experiment is aimed at determining the number of alternative WSs, $N$, that should be initially shown to the user on the UI when a WS-BPEL designer requests for a recommendation, so that, on the one hand designers may have enough options to be displayed to them, while on the other hand this list of WSs is appropriately presented in a manageable, low-cognitive-load fashion. Therefore, in this experiment we vary the number of the candidate WSs considered, seeking the optimal point between "enough alternatives" and "too many alternatives" for a WS-BPEL designer. In this experiment 8 WS-BPEL designers (6 male and 2 female) were used, each with more than 2 years of experience in BPEL design using various commercial or in-house software development platforms [51–53].

In Fig. 11, we can observe that the optimal number of alternative WSs, the designers opted, is 4, marginally outperforming the case of 5 alternatives (9.4/10 versus 9.3/10) and hence, in the subsequent experiments we set parameter $N$ to 4. It has to be mentioned that the results shown in Fig. 11 have been found to be fairly independent of the service category within which each designer requested for a recommendation.

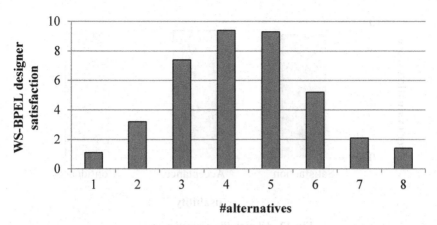

**Fig. 11.** User feedback on the preference for the number of top N WS recommendations.

### 5.2 Evaluation

After having determined the optimal number of candidate WSs, $N$, per recommendation to the user, the next experiment is aimed at quantifying the participant satisfaction from the proposed UI, including the three functionalities analysed in the previous section.

In the UI evaluation process, 10 WS-BPEL designers (3 female and 7 male) took part, each with more than 2 years of experience in BPEL design.

The 10 designers were asked to create simple BPEL code (consisting only of WS invocations) using the pseudocode supported by the proposed UI (see Fig. 3) which included at least two recommendation cases. After completing the BPEL design, the participants were asked to report on their user experience, by filling a usability questionnaire, through which satisfaction from the tool, acceptance (i.e. willingness to use the tool) and confidence in tool usage (i.e. self-assessed level of proficiency with the usage of the tool). For each dimension, a score was given in a Likert scale from 0 to10. Figure 12 depicts the user-reported acceptance, confidence and satisfaction. The user evaluation results show that the BPEL designers appreciated the UI features (access to recommendation computation engine, assignment of defaults, customization, exclusion of services or service branches in the taxonomy), commenting that these features provide a good mixture of automation and tailorability.

The main outcome of the follow up discussion was that the vast majority of the designers mentioned they would happily use this IDE in its current state. Two main points for further improvement were reported. Regarding the weights, it was suggested that the $W$ values can be adjusted globally as well as individually for specific *RECs*. A similar suggestion was reported for the exclusion functionality, that is to allow for global and individual adjustment. Both suggestions will be considered in the context of our future work.

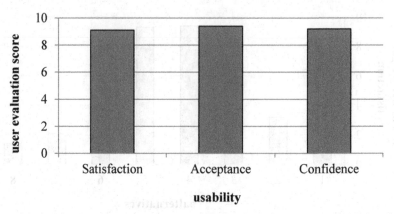

**Fig. 12.** UI usability evaluation results.

## 6  Conclusion and Future Work

In this work, a specialised UI for WS-BPEL designers, which allows personalised recommendation and selection of business process functionalities based on user generated criteria, was introduced. Compared to previous work, the proposed UI incorporates three extra functionalities: (a) preselection of the WS with the highest score for all *REC* requests of the BPEL scenario, (b) user-specified restrictions based on non-qualitative criteria, thereby satisfying the personalisation user criteria, and (c) tuning of the number of retrieved candidate service implementations shown to the user, to achieve a balance between (a) increased tailorability through a high number of choices and (b) tackling information overload. Experienced WS-BPEL designers participated in an experiment through which the UI and the recommendation-selection process were evaluated. The evaluation process showed very high levels acceptance, confidence and satisfaction, while the majority of them mentioned that they would happily use this IDE in its current state.

Our future work will focus on considering social media data for search enrichment and personalised ranking of the results by recommending information retrieved from the users' social networks [54–59], as well as collaborative filtering techniques between users sharing similar/identical functionalities [60–63].

## References

1. Moser, O., Rosenberg, F., Dustdar, S.: VieDAME - flexible and robust BPEL processes through monitoring and adaptation. In: Companion of the 13th International Conference on Software Engineering - ICSE Companion 2008, p. 917. ACM Press, New York (2008). https://doi.org/10.1145/1370175.1370186
2. Margaris, D., Vassilakis, C., Georgiadis, P.: A hybrid framework for WS-BPEL scenario execution adaptation, using monitoring and feedback data. In: Proceedings of the 30th Annual ACM Symposium on Applied Computing - SAC 2015, pp. 1672–1679. ACM Press, New York (2015). https://doi.org/10.1145/2695664.2695687

3. Zhang, H., Gao, Y., Chen, H., Li, Y.: TravelHub: a semantics-based mobile recommender for composite services. In: Proceedings of the 2012 IEEE 16th International Conference on Computer Supported Cooperative Work in Design (CSCWD), pp. 476–482. IEEE (2012). https://doi.org/10.1109/CSCWD.2012.6221861

4. Chen, X., Liu, X., Huang, Z., Sun, H.: RegionKNN: a scalable hybrid collaborative filtering algorithm for personalized web service recommendation. In: 2010 IEEE International Conference on Web Services, pp. 9–16. IEEE (2010). https://doi.org/10.1109/ICWS.2010.27

5. Mukherjee, D., Jalote, P., Gowri Nanda, M.: Determining QoS of WS-BPEL compositions. In: Bouguettaya, A., Krueger, I., Margaria, T. (eds.) ICSOC 2008. LNCS, vol. 5364, pp. 378–393. Springer, Heidelberg (2008). https://doi.org/10.1007/978-3-540-89652-4_29

6. Margaris, D., Vassilakis, C., Georgiadis, P.: Improving QoS delivered by WS-BPEL scenario adaptation through service execution parallelization. In: Proceedings of the 31st Annual ACM Symposium on Applied Computing, pp. 1590–1596. Association for Computing Machinery, New York (2016). https://doi.org/10.1145/2851613.2851805

7. Rosenberg, F., Enzi, C., Michlmayr, A., Platzer, C., Dustdar, S.: Integrating quality of service aspects in top-down business process development using WS-CDL and WS-BPEL. In: 11th IEEE International Enterprise Distributed Object Computing Conference (EDOC 2007), p. 15. IEEE (2007). https://doi.org/10.1109/EDOC.2007.23

8. Sakka Rouis, T., Bhiri, M.T., Kmimech, M., Sliman, L.: A generic approach for the verification of static and dynamic behavioral properties of SCDL/WS-BPEL service-component architectures. In: Park, J.H., Shen, H., Sung, Y., Tian, H. (eds.) PDCAT 2018. CCIS, vol. 931, pp. 381–389. Springer, Singapore (2019). https://doi.org/10.1007/978-981-13-5907-1_41

9. Margaris, D., Spiliotopoulos, D., Vassilakis, C., Karagiorgos, G.: A user interface for personalized web service selection in business processes. In: Stephanidis, C., et al. (eds.) HCII 2020. LNCS, vol. 12427, pp. 560–573. Springer, Cham (2020). https://doi.org/10.1007/978-3-030-60152-2_41

10. Maâlej, A.J., Krichen, M., Jmaïel, M.: WSCLim: a tool for model-based testing of WS-BPEL compositions under load conditions. In: Gabmeyer, S., Johnsen, E.B. (eds.) TAP 2017. LNCS, vol. 10375, pp. 139–151. Springer, Cham (2017). https://doi.org/10.1007/978-3-319-61467-0_9

11. Wang, X., Feng, Z., Huang, K., Tan, W.: An automatic self-adaptation framework for service-based process based on exception handling. Concurr. Comput. Pract. Exp. 29, e3984 (2017). https://doi.org/10.1002/cpe.3984

12. Margaris, D., Vassilakis, C.: Improving collaborative filtering's rating prediction quality in dense datasets, by pruning old ratings. In: 2017 IEEE Symposium on Computers and Communication, pp. 1168–1174 (2017). https://doi.org/10.1109/ISCC.2017.8024683

13. Ding, Z., Zhou, Z.: RaceTest: harmful data race detection based on testing technology in WS-BPEL. SOCA 13(2), 141–154 (2019). https://doi.org/10.1007/s11761-019-00261-1

14. Moser, O., Rosenberg, F., Dustdar, S.: Non-intrusive monitoring and service adaptation for WS-BPEL. In: Proceeding of the 17th international conference on World Wide Web - WWW 2008, p. 815. ACM Press, New York (2008). https://doi.org/10.1145/1367497.1367607

15. Margaris, D., Vassilakis, C., Georgiadis, P.: An integrated framework for QoS-based adaptation and exception resolution in WS-BPEL scenarios. In: Proceedings of the 28th Annual ACM Symposium on Applied Computing - SAC 2013, p. 1900. ACM Press, New York (2013). https://doi.org/10.1145/2480362.2480714

16. Kareliotis, C., Vassilakis, C., Rouvas, E., Georgiadis, P.: QoS-driven adaptation of BPEL scenario execution. In: 2009 IEEE International Conference on Web Services, pp. 271–278. IEEE (2009). https://doi.org/10.1109/ICWS.2009.80

17. Charfi, A., Dinkelaker, T., Mezini, M.: A plug-in architecture for self-adaptive web service compositions. In: 2009 IEEE International Conference on Web Services, pp. 35–42. IEEE (2009). https://doi.org/10.1109/ICWS.2009.125

18. Agarwal, V., Jalote, P.: From specification to adaptation: an integrated QoS-driven approach for dynamic adaptation of web service compositions. In: 2010 IEEE International Conference on Web Services, pp. 275–282. IEEE (2010). https://doi.org/10.1109/ICWS.2010.39

19. Margaris, D., Georgiadis, P., Vassilakis, C.: Adapting WS-BPEL scenario execution using collaborative filtering techniques. In: Proceedings - International Conference on Research Challenges in Information Science, pp. 174–184 (2013). https://doi.org/10.1109/RCIS.2013. 6577691

20. Wu, Y., Doshi, P.: Making BPEL flexible &#150; Adapting in the context of coordination constraints using WS-BPEL. In: 2008 IEEE International Conference on Services Computing, pp. 423–430. IEEE (2008). https://doi.org/10.1109/SCC.2008.71

21. Liu, X., Xu, M., Teng, T., Huang, G., Mei, H.: MUIT: a domain-specific language and its middleware for adaptive mobile web-based user interfaces in WS-BPEL. IEEE Trans. Serv. Comput. 12, 955–969 (2019). https://doi.org/10.1109/TSC.2016.2633535

22. Hermosillo, G., Seinturier, L., Duchien, L.: Using complex event processing for dynamic business process adaptation. In: 2010 IEEE International Conference on Services Computing, pp. 466–473. IEEE (2010). https://doi.org/10.1109/SCC.2010.48

23. Hielscher, J., Kazhamiakin, R., Metzger, A., Pistore, M.: A Framework for proactive self-adaptation of service-based applications based on online testing. In: Mähönen, P., Pohl, K., Priol, T. (eds.) ServiceWave 2008. LNCS, vol. 5377, pp. 122–133. Springer, Heidelberg (2008). https://doi.org/10.1007/978-3-540-89897-9_11

24. Erradi, A., Maheshwari, P., Tosic, V.: Policy-driven middleware for self-adaptation of web services compositions. In: van Steen, M., Henning, M. (eds.) Middleware 2006. LNCS, vol. 4290, pp. 62–80. Springer, Heidelberg (2006). https://doi.org/10.1007/11925071_4

25. Mei, L., Cai, Y., Jia, C., Jiang, B., Chan, W.K.: Prioritizing structurally complex test pairs for validating WS-BPEL evolutions. In: 2013 IEEE 20th International Conference on Web Services, pp. 147–154. IEEE (2013). https://doi.org/10.1109/ICWS.2013.29

26. Kareliotis, C., Vassilakis, C., Rouvas, E., Georgiadis, P.: IQoS-aware exception resolution for BPEL processes: a middleware-based framework and performance evaluation. Int. J. Web Grid Serv. 5, 284 (2009). https://doi.org/10.1504/IJWGS.2009.028346

27. Gu, G.P., Petriu, D.C.: XSLT transformation from UML models to LQN performance models. In: Proceedings of the Third International Workshop on Software and Performance - WOSP 2002, p. 227. ACM Press, New York (2002). https://doi.org/10.1145/584369.584402

28. Janssen, W., Korlyukov, A., Van den Bussche, J.: On the tree-transformation power of XSLT. Acta Inform. 43, 371–393 (2007). https://doi.org/10.1007/s00236-006-0026-8

29. Spiliotopoulos, D., Xydas, G., Kouroupetroglou, G.: Diction based prosody modeling in table-to-speech synthesis. In: Matoušek, V., Mautner, P., Pavelka, T. (eds.) TSD 2005. LNCS (LNAI), vol. 3658, pp. 294–301. Springer, Heidelberg (2005). https://doi.org/10.1007/115 51874_38

30. Kalepu, S., Krishnaswamy, S., Loke, S.W.: Verity: a QoS metric for selecting web services and providers. In:2003 Proceedings of Fourth International Conference on Web Information Systems Engineering Workshops, pp. 131–139. IEEE. https://doi.org/10.1109/WISEW.2003. 1286795

31. Margaris, D., Georgiadis, P., Vassilakis, C.: A collaborative filtering algorithm with clustering for personalized web service selection in business processes. In: 2015 IEEE 9th International Conference on Research Challenges in Information Science (RCIS), pp. 169–180 (2015). https://doi.org/10.1109/RCIS.2015.7128877

32. Alrifai, M., Skoutas, D., Risse, T.: Selecting skyline services for QoS-based web service composition. In: Proceedings of the 19th International Conference on World Wide Web - WWW 2010, p. 11. ACM Press, New York (2010). https://doi.org/10.1145/1772690.1772693

33. Kobusinska, A., Boron, M., Kerebinska, A., Margaris, D.: Exploiting recommender service to enhance efficiency of replication. In: 2019 IEEE 12th Conference on Service-Oriented Computing and Applications (SOCA), pp. 64–72. IEEE (2019). https://doi.org/10.1109/SOCA.2019.00017

34. Comerio, M., De Paoli, F., Grega, S., Maurino, A., Batini, C.: WSMoD. Int. J. Web Serv. Res. **4**, 33–60 (2007). https://doi.org/10.4018/jwsr.2007040102

35. Tran, V.X., Tsuji, H.: QoS based ranking for web services: fuzzy approaches. In: 2008 4th International Conference on Next Generation Web Services Practices, pp. 77–82. IEEE (2008). https://doi.org/10.1109/NWeSP.2008.41

36. Margaris, D., Georgiadis, P., Vassilakis, C.: On replacement service selection in WS-BPEL scenario adaptation. In: Proceedings - 2015 IEEE 8th International Conference on Service-Oriented Computing and Applications, SOCA 2015, pp. 10–17 (2015). https://doi.org/10.1109/SOCA.2015.11

37. Varitimiadis, S., Kotis, K., Spiliotopoulos, D., Vassilakis, C., Margaris, D.: "Talking" triples to museum chatbots. In: Rauterberg, M. (ed.) HCII 2020. LNCS, vol. 12215, pp. 281–299. Springer, Cham (2020). https://doi.org/10.1007/978-3-030-50267-6_22

38. Margaris, D., Vassilakis, C., Georgiadis, P.: An integrated framework for adapting WS-BPEL scenario execution using QoS and collaborative filtering techniques. Sci. Comput. Program. **98**, 707–734 (2015). https://doi.org/10.1016/j.scico.2014.10.007

39. Yu, T., Zhang, Y., Lin, K.-J.: Efficient algorithms for Web services selection with end-to-end QoS constraints. ACM Trans. Web. **1**, 6 (2007). https://doi.org/10.1145/1232722.1232728

40. Zeng, L., Benatallah, B., Ngu, A.H.H., Dumas, M., Kalagnanam, J., Chang, H.: QoS-aware middleware for web services composition. IEEE Trans. Softw. Eng. **30**, 311–327 (2004). https://doi.org/10.1109/TSE.2004.11

41. Bellur, U., Kulkarni, R.: Improved matchmaking algorithm for semantic web services based on bipartite graph matching. In: IEEE International Conference on Web Services (ICWS 2007), pp. 86–93. IEEE (2007). https://doi.org/10.1109/ICWS.2007.105

42. Pal, K.: A semantic web service architecture for supply chain management. Proc. Comput. Sci. **109**, 999–1004 (2017). https://doi.org/10.1016/j.procs.2017.05.442

43. Qu, C., Calheiros, R.N., Buyya, R.: Auto-scaling web applications in clouds. ACM Comput. Surv. **51**, 1–33 (2018). https://doi.org/10.1145/3148149

44. Mezni, H., Fayala, M.: Time-aware service recommendation: taxonomy, review, and challenges. Softw. Pract. Exp. (2018). https://doi.org/10.1002/spe.2605

45. Beel, J., Gipp, B.: Google Scholar's ranking algorithm: the impact of citation counts (an empirical study). In: Third International Conference on Research Challenges in Information Science. IEEE, Fez (2009). https://doi.org/10.1109/RCIS.2009.5089308

46. Kouroupetroglou, G., Spiliotopoulos, D.: Usability methodologies for real-life voice user interfaces. Int. J. Inf. Technol. Web Eng. **4**, 78–94 (2009). https://doi.org/10.4018/jitwe.2009100105

47. Spiliotopoulos, D., Stavropoulou, P., Kouroupetroglou, G.: Spoken dialogue interfaces: integrating usability. In: Holzinger, A., Miesenberger, K. (eds.) USAB 2009. LNCS, vol. 5889, pp. 484–499. Springer, Heidelberg (2009). https://doi.org/10.1007/978-3-642-10308-7_36

48. Spiliotopoulos, D., Tzoannos, E., Stavropoulou, P., Kouroupetroglou, G., Pino, A.: Designing user interfaces for social media driven digital preservation and information retrieval. In: Miesenberger, K., Karshmer, A., Penaz, P., Zagler, W. (eds.) ICCHP 2012. LNCS, vol. 7382, pp. 581–584. Springer, Heidelberg (2012). https://doi.org/10.1007/978-3-642-31522-0_87

49. Korableva, O., Durand, T., Kalimullina, O., Stepanova, I.: Studying user satisfaction with the MOOC platform interfaces using the example of coursera and open education platforms. In: Proceedings of the 2019 International Conference on Big Data and Education – ICBDE 2019, pp. 26–30. ACM Press, New York (2019). https://doi.org/10.1145/3322134.3322139

50. Spiliotopoulos, D., Xydas, G., Kouroupetroglou, G., Argyropoulos, V., Ikospentaki, K.: Auditory universal accessibility of data tables using naturally derived prosody specification. Univers. Access Inf. Soc. **9**, 169–183 (2010). https://doi.org/10.1007/s10209-009-0165-0

51. Adadi, N., Berrada, M., Chenouni, D., Halim, M.: AWSCPM: a framework for automation of web services composition processes. In: 2019 7th Mediterranean Congress of Telecommunications (CMT), pp. 1–4. IEEE (2019). https://doi.org/10.1109/CMT.2019.893 1389

52. Anvari, M., Takht, M.D., Sefid-Dashti, B.: Thrift service composition. In: Proceedings of the International Conference on Smart Cities and Internet of Things - SCIOT 2018, pp. 1–5. ACM Press, New York (2018). https://doi.org/10.1145/3269961.3269973.

53. Demidova, E., et al.: Analysing and enriching focused semantic web archives for parliament applications. Futur. Internet. **6**, 433–456 (2014). https://doi.org/10.3390/fi6030433

54. Margaris, D., Vassilakis, C., Spiliotopoulos, D.: Handling uncertainty in social media textual information for improving venue recommendation formulation quality in social networks. Soc. Netw. Anal. Min. **9**(1), 1–19 (2019). https://doi.org/10.1007/s13278-019-0610-x

55. Margaris, D., Vassilakis, C., Spiliotopoulos, D.: What makes a review a reliable rating in recommender systems? Inf. Process. Manag. **57**, 102304 (2020). https://doi.org/10.1016/j.ipm.2020.102304

56. Aivazoglou, M., et al.: A fine-grained social network recommender system. Soc. Netw. Anal. Min. **10**(1), 1–18 (2019). https://doi.org/10.1007/s13278-019-0621-7

57. Risse, T., et al.: The ARCOMEM architecture for social- and semantic-driven web archiving. Future Internet **6**, 688–716 (2014). https://doi.org/10.3390/fi6040688

58. Petasis, G., Spiliotopoulos, D., Tsirakis, N., Tsantilas, P.: Sentiment analysis for reputation management: mining the Greek web. In: Likas, A., Blekas, K., Kalles, D. (eds.) SETN 2014. LNCS (LNAI), vol. 8445, pp. 327–340. Springer, Cham (2014). https://doi.org/10.1007/978-3-319-07064-3_26

59. Campana, M.G., Delmastro, F.: Recommender systems for online and mobile social networks: a survey. Online Soc. Netw. Media **3–4**, 75–97 (2017). https://doi.org/10.1016/j.osnem.2017.10.005

60. Margaris, D., Spiliotopoulos, D., Vassilakis, C.: Social relations versus near neighbours: reliable recommenders in limited information social network collaborative filtering for online advertising. In: Proceedings of the 2019 IEEE/ACM International Conference on Advances in Social Networks Analysis and Mining (ASONAM 2019), pp. 1160–1167. ACM, Vancouver (2019). https://doi.org/10.1145/3341161.3345620

61. Margaris, D., Kobusinska, A., Spiliotopoulos, D., Vassilakis, C.: An adaptive social network-aware collaborative filtering algorithm for improved rating prediction accuracy. IEEE Access **8**, 68301–68310 (2020). https://doi.org/10.1109/ACCESS.2020.2981567

62. Nilashi, M., Ibrahim, O., Bagherifard, K.: A recommender system based on collaborative filtering using ontology and dimensionality reduction techniques. Expert Syst. Appl. **92**, 507–520 (2018). https://doi.org/10.1016/j.eswa.2017.09.058

63. Raghuwanshi, S.K., Pateriya, R.K.: Collaborative filtering techniques in recommendation systems. In: Shukla, R.K., Agrawal, J., Sharma, S., Singh Tomer, G. (eds.) Data, Engineering and Applications, pp. 11–21. Springer, Singapore (2019). https://doi.org/10.1007/978-981-13-6347-4_2

# Blockchain-Based Load Carrier Management in the Physical Internet

Wolfgang Narzt[1(✉)], Philipp Schützeneder[1], Petko Dragoev[1],
Bartosz Schatzlmayr-Piekarz[2], and Martin Schwaiger[3]

[1] Johannes Kepler University, Altenbergerstr. 69, 4040 Linz, Austria
{wolfgang.narzt,philipp.schuetzeneder,petko.dragoev}@jku.at
[2] Österreichische Donaulager GmbH, Regensburgerstr. 3, 4020 Linz, Austria
b.schatzlmayr-piekarz@linzag.at
[3] Satiamo GmbH, Bahnhofstr. 16, 4600 Wels, Austria
msc@satiamo.com

**Abstract.** Although recent studies have shown that the concepts of the Physical Internet (PI) can sustainably improve logistics processes, this new paradigm has not yet become established in practice. Companies fear losing control over their business and resist disclosing internal data. Even if some see a long-term improvement in the PI, current practical tests fail because the potential benefits can only be leveraged with a sufficiently large number of participants. We are therefore convinced that the introduction of the PI can only take place in small steps, in which companies retain control over their business. The technical platform required to operate the PI must be set up in a kind of parallel operation and disseminated via incentives without interfering with critical process flows. Such an incentive could be provided, e.g., by a shareable accounting platform that documents the exchange of pallets, boxes, etc. and keeps balance lists in sync with any trading partner. Companies continue to control their processes themselves, but at the same time they enable the construction of a backbone for distributed data exchange with arbitrary partners – a first step towards the establishment of a PI platform. In this paper we show how such a load carrier management platform can look like, how manipulation can be prevented with the use of Blockchain and how human handling can be improved.

**Keywords:** Physical internet · Load carrier management · Blockchain

## 1 Introduction

The way goods are currently transported, handled, stored and delivered around the world is economically, environmentally and socially unsustainable. There are too many empty runs or transports that could be bundled if the players involved were mutually aware of the transport orders. The currently much-discussed approach to this problem is called Physical Internet (PI) [1], a model analogy to the digital Internet, in which data packets are routed through a network in a standardized manner in compliance with the TCP/IP

© Springer Nature Switzerland AG 2021
F. F.-H. Nah and K. Siau (Eds.): HCII 2021, LNCS 12783, pp. 417–432, 2021.
https://doi.org/10.1007/978-3-030-77750-0_26

protocol, with no central control or global optimization, but with packets being forwarded on the basis of locally available data between neighboring network nodes.

In the same way, the Physical Internet, in which concrete objects are transported, should take communication and collaboration mechanisms from the digital Internet and adapt them for the transport domain [2]. Although there are fundamental differences between the physical and the digital world [5] (especially with regard to the duration of transport and associated costs), the vision of a Physical Internet is generally considered to be both a solution and a major challenge to global logistical sustainability.

The basic prerequisite for the realization of a Physical Internet is a network structure modeled on the digital Internet, which is not centrally controlled and is unrestricted in terms of its global scalability [4]. Such a system consists of a large number of network nodes in the same way as the digital Internet (equivalent to routers), which on the one hand share the network load among themselves and on the other hand ensure the optimal onward transport of packets without controlling instance or optimization procedures, only by means of restricted, neighboring communication [6].

While in conventional transport processes the involved stakeholders usually cooperate with each other via contracts regulating the transfer of goods and liability by bilateral agreements, the transport process in the PI that is open per se is unclear, i.e. the transport companies cooperating for a transmission order are not yet known at the time the order is placed. It therefore makes sense to integrate Blockchain technology [7, 10] into such an open, cooperative logistics network in which the parties involved do not always know each other directly. In this way, manipulation security is ensured and there is no need for an intermediary settlement point between the actors [8].

Transport orders in a Physical Internet are placed in a virtual "black box", and anyone who has available transport resources in the vicinity and at the same time meets the transport requirements set by the customer can accept the transport order. In a first step, this can be controlled by the companies themselves within an open information network; in the final expansion step, an automatic service is to ensure optimal use of resources and synergies and thus an economic improvement.

And this is the crux of why the Physical Internet has not yet become established in practice [3]. Companies would have to disclose their transport orders and would thus allow conclusions to be drawn about their business activities, which hardly any company wants to do. Transport companies would lose control in an automatically controlled allocation process, and on top, there's a chicken-and-egg problem, because participating in a Physical Internet only pays off when there are enough players on board. Suitable concepts are therefore needed to introduce the Physical Internet step by step.

We believe that the widespread adoption of a Physical Internet can only succeed if we manage to build an unrestricted collaboration platform that gives companies certain advantages (possibly in other thematic areas than directly in transport operations) without losing control over their process flows. This platform already allows interactions and business processes between unknown participants, while at the same time offering all security standards in terms of data integrity and tamper-proofing (Blockchain) and, in the first instance, dispensing with general disclosure of company data. In this way, the technological basis for a collaboration network of a Physical Internet can be created and the necessary number of system participants can be acquired, with which economic synergies can be created in a later step in the synopsis of overlapping business processes in the sense of the Physical Internet.

Such a platform could deal with the accounting for the exchange of load carriers and their quality during the transfer of goods – a sideshow, so to speak, which has so far only been recorded with paper or Excel spreadsheets, in the best case via digital internal company balance lists, which, however, are not reconciled with any trading partner. In the event of a dispute, there are thus always two figures, the accuracy of which is almost impossible to verify. Providing a distributed system in which the balances are recorded in a way that cannot be manipulated and is transparent for both sides would deliver corresponding added value for the companies, while neither interfering with critical process flows nor having to publish company data.

In this paper, we therefore address the development of an open collaboration platform for load carrier management as a precursor to a platform for the PI, including global scaling concepts via a distributed network architecture. We show which Blockchain model is necessary or suitable for ensuring data integrity [9] and explain the concept and realization of multi-signature transactions [12, 16] (requiring the consent of two or more parties), which are needed for the two-sided confirmation of an entry in the Blockchain. We show how Blockchain can be used as a byproduct for recovery as well, and deal with use cases from load carrier management, showing how the interaction mechanisms for the operational staff look like, what kind of interface for humans is provided by the collaboration platform and how information exchange is handled by the interference of humans in the transportation process.

## 2 State of the Art

### 2.1 Blockchain in Logistics and SCM

The property that the stored data cannot be manipulated in a distributed system without the attempted manipulation being immediately detected has established the Blockchain as a trading platform for a large number of cryptocurrencies [17]. However, the Blockchain can be used not only for financial transactions, but in general for applications in open systems where security is required over processes between participating parties [18]. These are speculative transactions, decentralized storage, voting systems, notary services, energy markets, crowdfunding and prediction markets, etc. [19]. A comprehensive overview is provided by Nussbaum [20].

In the same line, the Blockchain is interesting for the logistics industry and especially for supply chain management (SCM) [22]. Keywords such as digital identity, traceability of products, authenticity, settlements, provenance, property and ownership are intended to show the potentials of Blockchain technology in these areas [23].

International and complex supply chains of products and services from production to the customer including storage, logistics and transport require modern IT support and IT integration across organizations, which can be mapped via Blockchain [22]. They offer the advantage that all participants in the supply chain have the ability to view the status of the transaction or delivery at any time [24]. As a result, the efficiency of the supply chain can be increased and logistics processes from storage to delivery and billing can be made more efficient. Blockchain can also increase transparency and security, and the flow of physical goods can be accelerated [28]. Monitoring goods in the logistics process can also improve the decision-making process in terms of higher customer satisfaction. Smart contracts create new opportunities to design and implement new business models and services in logistics. For example, at each step along the supply chain, data can be captured and documented as transactions to prove the product history, e.g., tracking orders, receipts, invoices, payments, official documents, warranties, certifications, copyrights, licenses, serial numbers, and bar codes [22].

There are already initial joint projects of international logistics groups that are testing the use of Blockchain technology to reduce administrative effort and paperwork. For example, Maersk and IBM are testing Blockchain (Hyperledger) to manage their transactions between freight forwarders, ocean carriers, ports, and customs authorities [21]. Kamath [29] conducted a case study in 2018 that showed how the supply chain of food (pork in china and mangos in America) from production on the farm to the consumer can be mapped and tracked on a Blockchain. Other examples of Blockchain supporting supply chain management include Skuchain [25], Provenance [26], or Everledger [27].

In 2018, a research group from GS1-Germany conducted a pilot project together with around 35 companies from trade, industry, logistics, the start-up scene, science and associations on a specific logistics use case: the pallet exchange process. The aim was to gain reliable insights into the strengths, weaknesses and potentials of Blockchain on a topic with great potential for optimization [30]. While the GS1 development group focused primarily on using Blockchain (Hyperledger) in general to support the exchange process, we see this use case as an opportunity to introduce a distributed, technical system base for a Physical Internet, in which Blockchain must of course be an essential component in the backend to ensure data integrity. Our focus is on providing an incentive system to encourage logistics companies to participate without exposing critical company data. As part of this incentive system, we are also extending the functionality of GS1's prototype, additionally documenting pallet quality and value, thus creating an open, distributed collaboration network through which consistent balance data is stored. The companies benefit not only from data integrity, but also from the possibility to record exchange processes with load carriers of different quality in a structured way and to settle them with the trading counterparts. Abuse with regard to exchange transactions with different pallet quality is to be reduced in this way.

## 2.2   Complex and Collaborative System Networks

Creating a technical basis for open, distributed networks is by no means trivial. There are a number of viable approaches to distributed network architectures, but the requirements for a globally scaling, decentralized, and extensible network are high, and additional concepts are needed to make the complexity of the applications manageable.

Let us start with architectures for IoT platforms: The challenge with IoT systems is the unified networking of a heterogeneous landscape of (technical) units equipped with computing power, wireless data transmission, sensors or actuators. Established standards and IoT protocols now enable the uniform integration of these entities into the Internet, mostly using cloud-based and centrally controlled architectures, regardless of whether they are academic prototypes or industrial or commercial products. Examples from the literature are (and the following lists are only exemplary due to the abundance of already existing platforms) collaborative working architectures for IoT-based applications [31], or cloud-based information- and collaboration platforms for supply chain networks [32]. There are also a number of commercial cloud-based IoT platforms, e.g. Cisco IoT Edge Intelligence [33], SolutionDot IoT Platform [34] and various (European) initiatives for the further development of IoT collaboration networks [35].

We observe the use of distributed network architectures in newer and more concrete use case scenarios. Here again, the following list can only be exemplary: Awais et al. [36] deal with the acceleration of High-Performance Computing (HPC) networks by setting up regional HPC data centers, managing them locally and achieving a performance gain through a decentralized interaction of these distributed data units. Especially in the business area, we are observing an increase in the importance of distributed network architectures in order to be able to handle business processes fast, securely and quickly, taking regional conditions (e.g. the location of a company or the origin of a measured signal) into account for integrated calculations and optimizations. We are registering the development of distributed security middleware architectures [37] as well as distributed platforms in supply chain management (SCM) scenarios to prepare for transport processing along the lines of the Physical Internet [38].

## 3 Approach

### 3.1 Challenges

While the importance of distributed network architectures is clearly increasing alongside new, complex and global challenges, we still observe that there are many isolated developments tailor-made for specific applications, although in the area of open, collaborative networks there is a common base that can be used for a variety of applications. In particular, we refer here to the data exchange/process handling of geographically relevant system parts (e.g. companies and their data, products and resources) within a system of systems, meaning that the ownership and location of resources used is transparent. Considering a PI context, we can identify the following challenges to the design of a generic system base for a distributed collaboration network:

- The platform must link business processes by connecting unknown stakeholders [1] and ensure manipulation safety. It must be capable of handling a flood of data generated by each logistics transaction and provide mechanisms for data recreation if parts of the network fail. We refer to challenges that have already been addressed in fog/edge computing, where locally generated data can be processed in peripheral nodes [6], such that large-scale, regionally unrestricted, networked applications can be created.
- In addition to these basic technical and functional requirements, such collaborative platforms must also meet non-functional quality criteria. They must be extensible, fail-safe and performant and require secure and manipulation-free transaction concepts for data exchange between potentially unknown stakeholders [4].
- There is a number of further challenges regarding the construction of collaboration networks: The distributed approach must ensure that the addition of new nodes complies with specified standards and does not endanger the stability of the system. Similarly,

it must also be possible to remove nodes without endangering the integrity of the network, or, in the event of an unintentional failure, to create suitable recovery methods that allow the content, state and resources of a node to be fully restored.

## 3.2  Architecture

In the following, we want to give an insight into the network architecture and system behavior in order to be able to grasp the complexity of the system. It should be noted, however, that all subsequent presentations and figures are abstract views of the overall system and do not claim to be technically complete.

Our proposed platform is constructed in the form of distributed networks in order to be able to scale globally. Each individual node is self-sufficient, works with regionally limited resources and data and, when combined with other nodes, forms a global system of systems. Processes are handled by the interaction of individual nodes, and optimization is achieved by self-organizing and/or learning mechanisms within the overall network. In principle, the system works along the lines of the Internet, where TCP packets are sent to their destination via routers that only have a local view of the network.

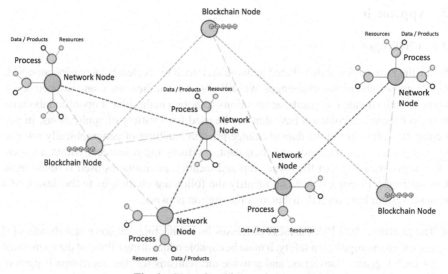

**Fig. 1.**  General architectural structure.

Figure 1 shows the backbone of our system architecture – a network node that handles all activities in spatial proximity. It can be considered a local information hub that enables interaction of processes by transmitting data or products using available resources beyond the scope of single applications [39]. Each network node is connected to a limited number of other nodes referring to the real spatial collaboration structure.

With this basic structure, it should be possible to spatially assign information without having to perform time-consuming geo searches in spatial databases. The question of who offers certain information or products or has resources in a certain region can be answered easily and efficiently with this structure. New nodes can be added arbitrarily, and it is also possible to assign existing processes to another, newly added node if they are spatially closer. If a node is removed from the network, the processes (and also the associated data, products and resources) that were assigned to this node must be distributed to other suitable nodes. This is to ensure unlimited scalability within the network. The overall system can grow and change without affecting the integrity of the network.

The innovation here is probably not the design of a distributed network approach, for which there are numerous variants in a multitude of application domains in the literature [35, 36, 37, 38]. It is rather about the generic nature of this approach, which is intended to create a systemic basis for modern collaboration networks beyond the Physical Internet (e.g., in the areas of IoT, CPS, AI, etc.). This systemic basis also includes the integration of the Blockchain in order to be able to handle secure and manipulation-free transactions within a huge, open network. Such transactions involve processes or parties that usually have no mutual contact points, so that trust and security play an important role in process handling.

The Blockchain exists parallel to the described network structure and itself represents a distributed system of (redundant) Blockchain nodes (see Fig. 1) and further increases the complexity of the general system architecture. Each network node of the collaboration network is connected to one of these Blockchain nodes, so that transactions that are executed within the network can be stored directly in the Blockchain, already as a function of the network base. This means that the Blockchain is not only integrated into the system at application level.

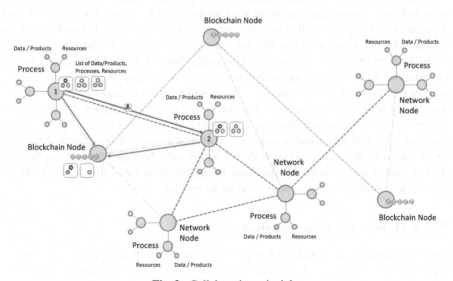

**Fig. 2.** Collaboration principle.

Data exchange between two network nodes (which is equivalent to inter-process communication or a business transaction, depending on the level of abstraction or application domain in which a collaborative act is to be seen) functions in principle as follows: All processes, data, products and resources involved are stored on both the sending and the receiving network node (see Fig. 2, symbolic list of red, green and yellow bubbles). The redundant data storage enables both nodes to query locally where their data, products and resources are located or who owns them without having to perform a complex network search. Information is available in constant runtime complexity O(1). Even if redundant storage means synchronization effort, the processing only takes place in a few selected network nodes and does not affect the rest of the network.

The redundant data storage is maintained until the affected processes are completed and the associated data and products have been completely transferred. As far as (physical) resources are concerned, information about their location is stored redundantly until they are returned to the network node with which the owner process is associated.

If one of these network nodes fails, it can restore its content due to redundancies with its neighboring nodes. However, if several network nodes fail, information from the entire network is irretrievably lost. To prevent this, we use the Blockchain as a recovery backbone. Every data exchange between two network nodes (and of course also within a network node) is stored as a transaction in the Blockchain.

We differentiate between simple transactions, in which (as in the conventional sense of crypto-currencies) information is transferred from a sender to a receiver, and multi-signature transactions, which require the confirmation of both parties/processes in order for information to be exchanged (e.g. confirmation of a delivery). This means that, from case to case, the information transferred is stored differently in the Blockchain compared to its redundant counterparts at the network nodes (see Fig. 2, schematically indicated differentiated storage in the Blockchain). However, seen as a whole they yield the same information, and it is exactly this fact that we use for a recovery mechanism.

In the event of a failure, each network node goes through the Blockchain and extracts the information concerning the failed node. In the worst case, the entire Blockchain must be run through in order to find those transactions that are necessary for a complete recovery. In many cases, however, it will only be necessary to go back to a certain point in time because the transactions before that point are no longer relevant for restoring a current system status (which is always a momentary image of the current situation). By the way, the Blockchain as such should be fail-safe, because due to the redundant storage of the entire content on a multitude of globally distributed Blockchain nodes, it is extremely unlikely that the entire Blockchain will fail.

### 3.3 Blockchain Technology Selection

As the Blockchain must meet two requirements in our architecture (data integrity at application level and recovery function at system level), the choice of Blockchain technology is critical: The development of an own Blockchain is usually not necessary, since the required functions are available on existing Blockchain systems (developed by experts and well tested). First, there is the question of whether to use a public or a private Blockchain.

A public Blockchain is automatically always permissionless. A private Blockchain can be permissionless or permissioned. Wüst and Gervais [10] suggest an approach for selecting a Blockchain technology for a specific use case. In our use case, the requirement is that transactions should not be public despite encryption in order to not allow any inferences about transactions between two business partners. This requirement rules out public permissionless Blockchains such as Ethereum. Scalability and low operational or transaction costs are also important, as in the final design many participants around the world would use the system and a large number of transactions would occur. The costs are high for permissionless Blockchains and the throughput is low [11].

Therefore, the choice falls on a permissioned Blockchain. The Blockchain network and the participants should also be controlled by a consortium or association of organizations, which is another reason why the Blockchain should be permissioned. Participants therefore need an invitation to become a member of the Blockchain system. In the last step of the Blockchain selection approach, we distinguish between public permissioned Blockchains and private permissioned Blockchains. In our case, participants outside the network have no interest in verification, so the Blockchain will not be freely accessible and viewable. There are now several Blockchain systems to choose from, with "Hyperledger Fabric" [11], "Quorum (JP-Morgan)" [14, 15] and "R3 Corda" [12, 13] currently being the most widely used in practice. Quorum is an extension of Ethereum and allows the use of smart contracts, which are necessary for multi-signature transactions, and the use of anonymous transactions. Quorum is also open source and due to its similarity to Ethereum and use of the Solidity programming language, there is good support and guides online. We chose Quorum for these reasons.

We implemented our test system on a server with virtual nodes using Docker containers. There are nodes that represent the general network structure as well as blockchain nodes (created with Quorum Maker) with internal IP addresses and corresponding routings for external access.

## 4   Use Case

Using and testing this platform for exactly the purpose for which it is designed (namely, for the open transport of goods in the sense of PI) is difficult because it requires the disclosure of company data and companies would lose control over their own processes, which makes it hard to find partners willing to test such a system. We believe that the widespread adoption of a PI platform can only succeed if it is set up in a kind of parallel operation allowing uncritical interactions and business processes between unknown participants, while at the same time using the whole functionality of the platform. Such an operation could be the exchange of pallets, boxes, and other load carriers, where balance lists are kept in sync with any trading partner. Companies continue to control their processes themselves, but at the same time the necessary number of system participants can be acquired, with which economic synergies can be created later. In the frame of the following use-case scenario we show how such a load carrier management platform can look like (as a first step towards the establishment of a PI platform) and indicate how human handling can be improved.

In principle, the exchange of goods and commodities works in such a way that they are transported on load carriers whose ownership is documented individually in the current process flow via paper or proprietary storage (e.g., in Excel tables), but is not reconciled across companies. With the presented collaboration platform, the number of pallets exchanged between two system partners and their quality – based on a predefined classification scheme – should be recorded. In addition to the exchange object pallet, its nominal value is recorded, since newer / better pallets have a higher nominal value than heavily worn ones. The process is only to be clearly documented by the mutual confirmation of the exchange quality by the two partners involved in the exchange process – the "handshake procedure". In this way, it should be prevented that one partner exchanges allegedly better pallet qualities than they are actually allowed to have according to the stock account.

Thus, a very practical topic – which was formulated as a significant to critical concern by all the practical partners interviewed – was to be tested here with the Blockchain prototype in a real environment. The development of this system and the associated tests were funded by the Austrian Research Promotion Agency (FFG) as part of the project "Generic Data Platform for the Physical Internet" (GDP4PI, FFG No. 867181).

The process begins with the shipper, who picks a load for delivery to a customer and dispatches it via a transport company. Each load is initially assembled in a separate process and forwarded to warehouse employees for picking. The warehouse employees see all the loads assigned to them that are to be picked on a mobile terminal. The warehouse employees are also operationally responsible for handling the transfer of goods and thus the load carrier management vis-à-vis the transport company. The transfer must be made as simple as possible for all people operationally involved. Both the warehouse worker and the transporter should be able to implement a handshake with as little interaction as possible. One button press on each side would be the optimal situation for this. We decided on a QR code for the technical relaying, which is automatically displayed on the warehouse employee's mobile terminal according to the picked goods.

The transport company's operative (usually the truck driver) scans the QR code on the warehouse worker's device using his mobile terminal and thus receives all the information about the load and the load carriers. The takeover can then be confirmed by the truck driver simply by pressing a button via a web interface. There are no additional steps for those involved. QR code display, scan and confirmation are the only steps to be carried out electronically during a takeover (see Fig. 3).

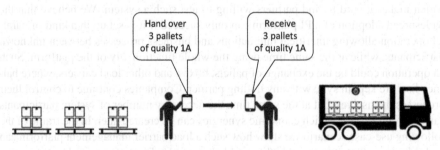

**Fig. 3.** Load carrier transfer.

All goods transfers between the various parties in the supply chain (shipper, carrier, consignee/trader) function in the same way (Fig. 4). There is a uniform electronic interface for all parties for the proper documentation of the goods transfers (and thus also for the load carrier exchange).

Shipper                    Carrier                    Trader

**Fig. 4.** Load carrier transfer in the supply chain.

Pallet transfer can take place in both directions. For each pallet received, a pallet of the same quality (empty) is exchanged so that there is a zero balance after a loading or unloading step. A zero balance is not always possible in practice, so people work with vouchers if they are unable to physically balance the pallet debit on site. With an electronic system, where each transfer is clearly documented, the physical pallet voucher is no longer necessary. Each company automatically sees the balances in terms of quantity and quality against third parties. This ensures at all times how many load carriers in which quality a company owes to whom or receives from whom.

However, the concept of the voucher will still remain (but now in an electronic and manipulation-free form), because in an open system, it may also happen that one company cooperates with another only by chance and on a single occasion. If, in this single transaction, the balance cannot be settled, there would be a perpetual debt or credit to the other. Electronic vouchers (or the balances) can accordingly be forwarded to other parties, or negative balances can be "sold" to others with them.

## 5   User Interface

The concepts described for the process flows of the use case scenarios for load carrier management were technically implemented via web application. In the following, we show some selected screenshots from the user interface, which looks the same for all stakeholders in the supply chain, but always displays only the data relevant for the respective company. The decisive factor in the design of the UI was that, on the one hand, all persons and companies involved in the process can view all transport and order data at any time (a function that currently does not exist in any open, distributed system) and, on the other hand, the work processes can be significantly accelerated with mobile terminals. In contrast to the tedious visual data reconciliation on paper (as it is currently handled), the data transfer and legal transition can be done by scanning and pressing a button. The accuracy of the data is checked electronically in the background and without further human intervention.

Figure 5 shows a captured transport order of the shipper (desktop view of the dispatcher) that can be accepted by a transport company. The screen shows the sender and

**Fig. 5.** Details of a transport order

recipient together with their Blockchain addresses, number and quality of pallets and an automatically generated QR code, which can be scanned by the truck driver of the transport service provider.

**Fig. 6.** Truck driver mobile terminal

The transfer from the shipper to the carrier is done with the QR code scan (Fig. 6). The information about the transport order (including pallet count and quality) is transmitted and visible at the receiving party. Process statuses are automatically updated with each step for all parties involved, so that everyone always has the same information status. The carrier can see the order and its details after scanning the QR code.

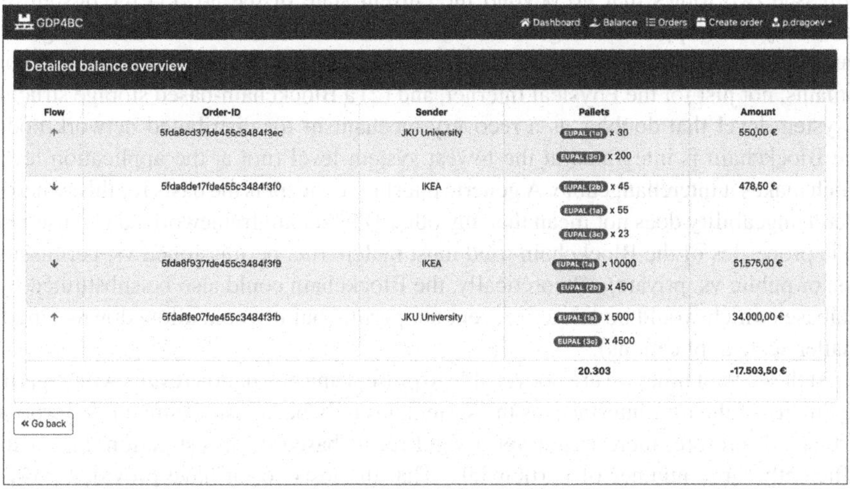

**Fig. 7.** Balance overview

With the mutual handshake after the QR-Code scan, the transaction for the load carrier exchange is stored in the Blockchain. Each company automatically receives a constantly updated and consolidated (no longer manipulable) balance overview of credit and debit vis-à-vis its trading partners (Fig. 7). The user interface not only lists the number and quality of the pallets, but also links this data directly to a current market value and expresses the balances in monetary units.

## 6  Findings and Future Work

With such a platform, we can offer participating companies added value in a variety of ways: First, the previously tedious recording work on paper or proprietary lists is eliminated (a simple QR code scan and the press of a button to confirm the transfer are sufficient), which in turn reduces errors in manual recording and consequently disputes due to differing data. On the other hand, the transport process becomes transparent for the involved companies: everyone knows the status of a delivery and the recipients even receive notification data on a coarse-grained level – information that was previously unavailable to many companies. In this way, we are introducing a technical collaboration platform in parallel with the actual goods transport process, which can be used quasi risk-free with regard to the disclosure of business data, generates added value and in this way (we hope) can be disseminated as widely as possible. As a result, at a later point in time we will be confronted with a completely new starting situation with regard to the introduction of Physical Internet concepts, in which there is already a large, registered community that is networked with each other via this platform, and with which the first synergy effects can be achieved in transport processing in the sense of the Physical Internet.

In summary, we can say that within the framework of this research project we have addressed two topics that go beyond the current state of the art: (1) the design of a scalable systems approach for generic collaboration networks, which allows the general management of location-based information and processes for a variety of application domains, not just for the Physical Internet, and (2) a Blockchain-based storage structure at system level that doubles as a recovery mechanism for distributed network nodes. The Blockchain is integrated at the lowest system level (not at the application level), which makes it interchangeable. A generic interface concept is the basis for this, whereby interchangeability does not mean that any other Blockchain framework can be used; the basic properties of the Blockchain used must match. (i.e. permissioned vs. permissionless, or public vs. private). Theoretically, the Blockchain could also be substituted by a database (which would no longer prevent tampering, but it would allow downsizing for smaller-scale applications).

At the current time, we are not yet able to present any evaluation results with regard to the quality of the user interface, as the system has only been tested with a few corporate partners. Therefore, there is not yet a valid result based on investigation data with a sufficiently large number of participants. That the tests so far have provided positive feedback in terms of shortening process flows is something we expected, because manual visual data matching on paper delivery bills is apparently more time-consuming than a simple QR code scan and confirmation of the transfer of goods at the push of a button. In this respect, based on subjective observations, we were able to determine that the user interface makes work easier for those involved. So, while the corporate partners have given the system high marks in our research project, the next step will be to get out of the prototype stage, while observing the German development around GS1 and testing the platform with a larger target group in order to get founded evaluation data on the quality of our implemented interaction paradigms. The goal here is to gain as large a number of participants as possible in order to create the best possible starting point for the next step in the development of a Physical Internet.

## References

1. Montreuil, B.: Toward a physical Internet: meeting the global logistics sustainability grand challenge. Logist. Res. 3(2–3), 71–87 (2011). https://doi.org/10.1007/s12159-011-0045-x
2. Montreuil, B.: Physical Internet Manifesto: Transforming the Way Physical Objects are Moved, Stored, Realized, Supplied and Used, Aiming Towards Greater Efficiency and Sustainability, Cirrelt, Quebec Canada (2012)
3. ALICE: WP1: Sustainable, Safe and Secure Supply Chain: Research & Innovation Framework, Alliance for Logistics Innovation through Collaboration in Europe (2015)
4. Bucherer, E., Uckelmann, D.: Business models for the internet of things. In: Uckelmann, D., Harrison, M., Michahelles, F. (eds.) Architecting the Internet of Things. Springer, Heidelberg (2011). https://doi.org/10.1007/978-3-642-19157-2_10
5. Ballot, E., Montreuil, B., Meller, R.D.: The Physical Internet - the network of logistics networks. La documemtation Francaise/Predit, Paris (2014)

6. Pach, C., Sallez, Y., Berger, T., Bonte, T., Trentesaux, D., Montreuil, B.: Routing management in physical internet crossdocking hubs: study of grouping strategies for truck loading. In: Grabot, B., Vallespir, B., Gomes, S., Bouras, A., Kiritsis, D. (eds.) APMS 2014. IAICT, vol. 438, pp. 483–490. Springer, Heidelberg (2014). https://doi.org/10.1007/978-3-662-44739-0_59

7. Nakamoto, S.: Bitcoin: A Peer-to-Peer Electronic Cash System, 31 October 2008, White Paper (2008). https://bitcoin.org/en/bitcoin-paper.

8. Antonopoulos, A.M.: Mastering Bitcoin: Unlocking Digital Crypto-Currencies, 1st edn. O'Reilly Media, Inc. (2014)

9. Yang, L.: The blockchain: state-of-the-art and research challenges. J. Ind. Inf. Integr. **15**, 80–90 (2019)

10. Wüst, K., Gervais, A.: Do you need a Blockchain?, Department of Computer Science ETH Zurich, Switzerland (2017)

11. Androulaki, E., et al.: Hyperledger fabric: a distributed operating system for permissioned blockchains. In: EuroSys 2018 Proceedings of the Thirteenth EuroSys Conference, Article No. 30, Porto, Portogal – 23–26 April 2018. ACM New York (2018)

12. Sheth, H., Dattani, J.: Overview of blockchain technology. Asian J. Convergence Technol. (AJCT) (2019). http://asianssr.org/index.php/ajct/article/view/728

13. Gmbh, M.: Difference between Ethereum, Hyperledger Fabric and R3 corda (2018). https://medium.com/@micobo/technical-difference-betweenethereum-hyperledger-fabric-and-r3-corda-5a58d0a6e347

14. Baliga, A., Subhod, I., Kamat, P., Chatterjee, S.: Performance Evaluation of the Quorum Blockchain Platform, arXiv preprint arXiv:1809.03421 (2018)

15. Quorum Maker (2019). https://github.com/synechron-finlabs/quorum-maker

16. Aitzhan, N., Svetinovic, D.L.: Security and privacy in decentralized energy trading through multi-signatures, blockchain and anonymous messaging streams. IEEE Trans. Dependable Secure Comput. 1. https://doi.org/10.1109/TDSC.2016.2616861

17. Pierro, M.D.: (2017) What is the blockchain? Comput. Sci. Eng. **19**(5), 92–95 (2017). https://doi.org/10.1109/MCSE.2017.3421554

18. Ahram, T., Sargolzaei, A., Sargolzaei, S., Daniels, J., Amaba, B.: Blockchain technology innovations. In: 2017 IEEE Technology & Engineering Management Conference (TEMSCON). Santa Clara, CA, pp. 137–141 (2017). https://doi.org/10.1109/TEMSCON.2017.7998367

19. Zeinzinger, T.: Bitcoin & Co – Das neue Gold Blockchain in Recht & Praxis, Blockchain – Anwendungen, BlockchainHub Graz (2017)

20. Nussbaum, J.: Mapping the blockchain project ecosystem (2017). https://bitnewsbot.com/mapping-the-blockchain-project-ecosystem/. entnommen am 4.1.2018

21. IBM. Maersk and IBM Unveil First Industry-Wide Cross-Border Supply Chain Solution on Blockchain (2017). http://www-03.ibm.com/press/us/en/pressrelease/51712.wss

22. Tijan, E., Aksentijević, S., Ivanić, K., Jardas, M.: Blockchain technology implementation in logistics. Sustainability **11**, 1185 (2019)

23. Treiblmaier, H.: Toward more rigorous blockchain research: recommendations for writing blockchain case studies. In: Treiblmaier, H., Clohessy, T. (eds.) Blockchain and Distributed Ledger Technology Use Cases. PI, pp. 1–31. Springer, Cham (2020). https://doi.org/10.1007/978-3-030-44337-5_1

24. Perboli, G., Musso, S., Rosano, M.: Blockchain in logistics and supply chain: a lean approach for designing real-world use cases. IEEE Access **6**, 62018–62028 (2018). https://doi.org/10.1109/ACCESS.2018.2875782

25. Skuchain (2020). https://www.skuchain.com/

26. Provenance (2020). https://www.provenance.org/

27. Everledger (2020). https://www.everledger.io/

432     W. Narzt et al.

28. Lindman, J., Rossi, M., Tuunainen, V.K.: Opportunities and risks of blockchain technologies in payment—a research agenda. In: Proceedings of the 50th Hawaii International Conference on System Sciences, HICSS/IEEE Computer Society, Waikoloa, HI, USA, 4–7 January 2017; pp. 1533–1542 (2017)
29. Kamath, R.: Food traceability on blockchain: Walmart's Pork and mango pilots with IBM. J. Br. Blockchain Assoc. **1**, 1–12 (2018). https://doi.org/10.31585/jbba-1-1-(10)2018
30. GS1 Germany. https://www.gs1-germany.de/innovation/trendforschung/blockchain/pilot/
31. Mora, H.M., Pont, M.T.S., Gil, D., Johnsson, M.: Collaborative working architecture for IoT-based applications. Sensors **18**(6), 1676 (2018). https://doi.org/10.3390/s18061676
32. David, Z., Gnimpieba, R., Nait-Sidi-Moh, A., Durand, D., Fortin, J.: Using Internet of Things technologies for a collaborative supply chain: application to tracking of pallets and containers. In: The 10th International Conference on Future Networks and Communications (FNC 2015)/The 12th International Conference on Mobile Systems and Pervasive Computing (MobiSPC 2015) (2015)
33. Cisco IoT Edge Intelligence. https://www.cisco.com/c/en/us/solutions/internet-of-things/edge-intelligence.html
34. SolutionDot. https://solutiondots.com/internet-of-things/
35. ECCP 2020, European Cluster Collaboration Platform. https://www.clustercollaboration.eu/tags/iot
36. Khan, A., Kim, T., Byun, H., Kim, Y., Park, S., Sim, H.: SCISPACE: A Scientific Collaboration Workspace for File Systems in Geo-Distributed HPC Data Centers, arXiv:1803.08228 [cs.DC] (2018)
37. Beni, E.H., Lagaisse, B., Joosen, W., Aly, A., Brackx, M.: DataBlinder: a distributed data protection middleware supporting search and computation on encrypted data. In: Middleware Conference, Middleware 2019 Proceedings of the 20th International Middleware Conference Industrial Track, pp. 50–57, Davis, CA, USA, 9–13 December 2019
38. GDP4PI 2020, Generic Data Platform for the Physical Internet, aus dem Programm der Österreichischen Forschungsförderungsgesellschaft FFG, Mobilität der Zukunft, 10. Ausschreibung, laufendes Projekt
39. Broy, M., Schmidt, A.: Challenges in engineering cyber-physical systems. Computer **47**(2), 70–72 (2014)

# A Study of Factors Influencing the Adoption of Cloud-Based ERP System: The Perspective of Transaction Cost Economics

Bo-chiuan Su[1] and Chun-Der Chen[2(✉)]

[1] Department of Information Management, National Dong Hwa University,
Hualien City, Taiwan, R.O.C.
bsu@gms.ndhu.edu.tw
[2] Department of Business Administration, Ming Chuan University,
Taoyuan City, Taiwan, R.O.C.
marschen@mail.mcu.edu.tw

**Abstract.** As the fast speed of bandwidth and rapidly growing utilization of the Internet and associated information technologies, cloud computing has become as a popular solution for organization's performance improving and competitive advantage maintenance. Cloud-based enterprise resource planning (ERP) system is an important application of cloud computing, and firms can thus receive various gains or benefit by shifting their local information systems to a cloud platform, in order to increase data accessibility, decrease the total cost of ownership and so on. Though there are many benefits provided by cloud-based ERP, the adoption seems to be difficult due to several major inhibitors, and it is called to provide a deeper understanding of cloud-based ERP system implementation intention from manager's viewpoint. However, limited studies have been conducted in investigating such phenomenon. In order to fulfill the above research gaps, the objective of this study is to explore the factors relevant to transaction attributes affecting the intention of cloud-based ERP system adoption from the perspective of transaction cost economics. We collect empirical data from Taiwan top 1000 manufacturing firms list, and we found (1) uncertainty and switching cost positively increase perceived risk, (2) perceived risk negatively and switching benefits positively affect the adoption intention of cloud-based EPR platform. We conclude our study with a discussion of the theoretical insights and practical contributions and relevant implications for managers. Suggestions for future research are also addressed in this study.

**Keywords:** Cloud computing · Enterprise resource planning · Transaction cost economics · Software as a service · Information system adoption

## 1 Introduction

As the fast speed of bandwidth and rapidly growing utilization of the Internet and associated information technologies (e.g., 5G), cloud computing has become not only as a popular answer or solution for organization's performance improving and competitive

© Springer Nature Switzerland AG 2021
F. F.-H. Nah and K. Siau (Eds.): HCII 2021, LNCS 12783, pp. 433–443, 2021.
https://doi.org/10.1007/978-3-030-77750-0_27

advantage maintenance, but it has also provided a better way for creative businesses to deliver or apply innovative services through IT (Cusumano 2019). For example, Amazon's Elastic Compute Cloud (EC2) has provided users with necessary computational resources through a pay-per-use platform since March 2006 (Ben-Yehuda et al. 2014). In August 2006, Eric Schmidt, CEO of Google, announced the concept of cloud computing at the Search Engine Strategies (SES) Seminar in San Jose. Through cloud computing, users or companies can utilize highly scalable hardware and software more efficiently, and thus they could generate individual or business agilities through rapid deployment, parallel batching processing, and mobile interactive applications that respond to user or business requirements in real time (Kathuria et al. 2018; Marston et al. 2011).

Cloud-based ERP (enterprise resource planning) system, namely software-as-a-service (SaaS), is an important application for cloud computing. Firms can thus receive various gains or benefit by shifting their local information systems to a cloud platform, in order to increase data accessibility, decrease the total cost of ownership and so on (Gupta et al. 2020; Lee et al. 2013a). Though the trend of cloud ERP system adoption continues to grow in size, and the promises from a technological perspective are relatively attractive for many firms (Castellina 2012), the shift from traditional onsite and locally installed ERP system to cloud ERP services is still in the early stage. Though there are many benefits provided by cloud-based ERP, the adoption seems to be difficult due to several major inhibitors, and it is called to provide a deeper understanding of cloud-based ERP system implementation intention from manager's viewpoint. However, limited studies have been conducted in investigating such phenomenon, for example, the perspective of transaction cost economics. In order to fulfill these research gaps, the objective of this study is to explore the factors related to transaction attributes influencing the adoption intention of cloud ERP system, from the perspective of transaction cost economics. We collect our empirical data from Taiwan top 1000 manufacturing firms list, and hope to provide deeper implications for understanding the inhibitors and facilitators of the adoption intention of cloud-based ERP platform.

## 2    Theoretical Background and Hypotheses

We develop our research model by identifying key constructs and hypotheses, as illustrated in Fig. 1. We assert several hypotheses: (1) service uncertainty, asset specificity and switching cost will affect firm's perceived risk toward cloud ERP system adoption intention and (2) firm's perceived risk and switching benefits will influence firm's cloud ERP system adoption intention. The following sections then clarify on these relationships and explains the theoretical underpinning of these hypotheses.

### 2.1    The Transaction Cost Economics (TCE) Perspective

TCE explains various problems of economic organizations, and the primary principle of it is that firms rationally conduct transactions in the most efficient way (Rindfleisch and Heide 1997). A transaction refers to a process by which a product or service is transferred through several separable interfaces (Williamson 1985). In general, it is assumed that there is a market with symmetric information, and both buyers and sellers have same

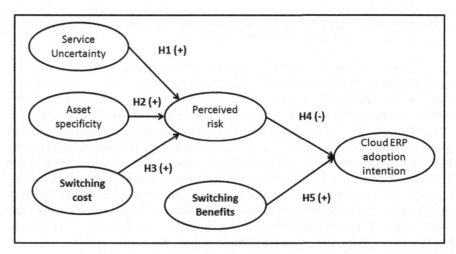

**Fig. 1.** Research model

amount of information to execute their transactions without cost (Liang and Huang 1998). However, transactions within open markets involve considerable transaction costs (e.g., information searching, contract negotiation, transaction monitoring for ensure a favorable deal). Likewise, TCE explains the underpinned reason why a transaction subject (e.g., a firm or an individual) chooses a particular and forms related transactions instead of others. Three key components from TCE, namely uncertainty, asset specificity, and transaction frequency, are used to characterize any transaction (Paswan et al. 2020). For example, transactions may have low or high uncertainty; may deal with specific or non-specific assets; or transaction may be in quite rare times or frequent ones. Since the use of ERP system is relatively frequent in most firms, transaction frequency will not be an issue for discussion in this study, and the other two factors, namely switching cost and switching benefits will be discussed for this study.

Uncertainty is defined as the unanticipated changes in circumstances surrounding a transaction. There are various forms for the formation of uncertainty. In this study, service uncertainty of cloud-based ERP system related to the theoretical framework is investigated. Service uncertainty represents to one type of behavioral uncertainty, and it refers to the difficulty in ascertaining the actual performance or service quality of vendors, or their adherence to contractual agreements (Susarla et al. 2009). In case of cloud ERP system, for example, guarantee for 100% availability, data safety and security, integration of cloud ERP and other legacy systems, technical standards for cloud platforms and so on are of great concern to most firms (Lee et al. 2013b). Firms are likely to wonder if their implemented cloud ERP system meets their expectations and whether they will perform well. Likewise, service uncertainty would affect firm's likelihood of implementing such cloud service. In such case, when firms perceive higher service uncertainty of cloud ERP system service, the concerns of performance risk will also be engendered since firms might be aware of several negative outcomes and associated transaction costs related to adoption of cloud ERP system. Hence we hypothesize that:

**Hypothesis 1 (H1):** *Perceived service uncertainty will positively increase perceived risk on cloud ERP system adoption.*

Asset specificity is the second key component for conducting. Williamson (1989) define the meaning of asset specificity as the transaction which the investments in asset would only be valuable from their use of the specific transaction. The related asset specificity within transactions is treated as an important means behind contractual arrangements (Vazquez 2004). When stakeholders (e.g., buyers or sellers) in a transaction endow specific design elements or unique resources, an asset specificity is then occurred. Therefore, such unique investment will have a lower value in alternative uses (Williamson 1996), and highly asset-specific investments will create potential costs in such transaction, since these investments might have little or no value outside the exchange relationship. If buyer or seller tries to break their contracts, the value of such specific investments would be then decreased. Such effect can also be call lock-in effect, where much can be lost to one or both parties if the relationship dissolves (Kern et al. 2002).

In case of cloud ERP system adoption, system functionalities, business processes and databases provided and stored in the cloud platform could be treated as firm's dedicated asset or specific investment. Since these specific assets can only be used in that particular relationship, and they could possibly become the hostage and lock-in effect when providers potentially increase the likelihood of their opportunistic behaviors, thereby generating adoption firm's perception of implementation risks (Wathne and Heide 2004). In sum, these conditions imply that firms need to invest great asset specificity in order to adopt cloud-based ERP system service with thereby generating great lock-in effects and the associated risk factors. Hence the following is hypothesized:

**Hypothesis 2 (H2):** *Perceived asset specificity will positively increase perceived risk on cloud ERP system adoption.*

For considering asset specificity in adopting cloud ERP system as a sunk cost with possible lock-in effect, another kind of aroused cost will be switching cost for migrating legacy system into cloud one. In order to avoid possible migration costs or uncertainty, firms assess relevant switching cost and benefits before implementing new alternative solutions (Kim and Kankanhalli 2009). In the situation of cloud ERP adoption, switching costs represent constrains for migrating legacy system into a new cloud platform, and these costs mainly include system migration, personnel training, service consulting, system maintenance expenses and so on. When perceiving higher costs for switching to cloud ERP system, it might thus lead to perceptions of higher risks and several behavioral outcomes that are performed unwillingly to avoid the relationship termination with the incumbent platform or provider (Kim and Son 2009). As such, we argue that switching cost will increase perceived risk on the adoption of cloud-based ERP system, and the following hypothesis is developed:

**Hypothesis 3 (H3):** *Perceived switching cost will positively increase perceived risk on cloud ERP system adoption.*

In general, it is said that the higher the risk, the lower is the likelihood of transaction. Firms might adopt cloud-based ERP system when their risk perceptions were low

(Ajzen 1991). From the study of Sitkin and Weingart (1995), they found that perceived risk significantly increased the higher degree of perceived loss. As such, the firm then perceived lower value can be obtained from the transaction. In the context of this study, when firms perceive higher risk degree of uncertainty, asset specificity and switching cost, these firms might thus lower their adoption intention of cloud-based ERP system. Thus the following hypothesis is developed:

> **Hypothesis 4 (H4):** *Perceived risk will positively decrease the intention of cloud ERP system adoption.*

As mentioned in the above, firms assess relevant switching cost and benefits before implementing new alternative solutions. Switching benefits refer to the perceived utility that firms would be gained or acquired in switching from the current system situation to the new information system (Kim and Kankanhalli 2009). There is no doubt that switching to a new information system such as cloud ERP system could result in several performance enhancement or productivities both in operational and strategic tasks for firms. Likewise, if firms perceived higher benefits could be gained from cloud-based ERP system implementation, firms should increase their intentions to adopt such cloud-based ERP system accordingly. Thus, we propose the following hypothesis:

> **Hypothesis 5 (H5):** *Perceived switching benefits will positively increase the intention of cloud ERP system adoption.*

## 3 Methodology and Research Design

### 3.1 Sample and Data Collection

A cross-sectional mail survey was used to collect data from randomly selected manufacturing firms in Taiwan. The sample firms were drawn from the "Taiwan Top 1000" list issued by the Common Wealth Magazine, a leading business magazine in Taiwan. In all, respondents of this study should need the relevant knowledge of ERP system utilization and implementation about their firms, and thus senior IT executives and managers are treated as our target respondents for this study. 1,000 questionnaires were sent out and 145 were returned. Since four questionnaires were invalid, a total of 141 valid and complete responses were then obtained for analysis. The samples of this study consisted of manufacturers in a variety of fields. The majority of the respondents are from Electronics (18.80%), Computers (14.53%), Metal (12,393%), Optoelectronics (11.11%), and so on. Compared to the Taiwan Top 1000 list, we argue that the distribution of our sampled firms is an appropriate representation to our sampling frame. Besides, the majority of the respondents were managers (41.91%), followed by senior managers (30.03%), and senior executives (21.45%). The average working experience of the respondents was 11.38 years, and the average number of years for which the respondents had held the current position was 6.3 years. Hence, we believed that the respondents were sufficiently knowledgeable to answer the survey.

## 3.2 Measurement Development/Operationalization of Constructs

All the constructs were measured by using multiple-item scales, and measurement items were adapted from prior literature. In additions, the questionnaire items were reviewed by several information management scholars for content description, and these items were revised following a pretest of the survey instrument with a certain number of real-case sample firms. All items were seven-point, Likert-type scales anchored at "strongly disagree" (1), "strongly agree" (7), and "neither agree nor disagree" (4).

The service uncertainty scales are adapted from Susarla et al. (2009). The asset specificity items are based on Benlian et al. (2009). As for the switching cost construct, we adopt it from Kim and Kankanhalli (2009) and Chau and Tam (1997). For the switching benefits construct, we adopt it from Kim and Kankanhalli (2009). The perceived risk scales are adapted from Falk et al. (2007). Finally, intention to adopt cloud ERP system is adapted from Teo et al. (2003).

# 4  Data Analysis and Results

## 4.1  Convergent and Discriminant Validity

Our data analysis is conducted with two sections: scale validation and hypothesis testing. First, scale validation proceeded in two steps, namely convergent and discriminant validity analyses. Convergent validity was evaluated using three criteria proposed by Fornell and Larcker (1981): (1) all item factor loadings (alpha) should be equal or greater than 0.5, (2) the value of composite reliabilities (CRs) and Cronbach's alpha for each construct, should be equal or greater than 0.8, and (3) average variance extracted (AVE) should be equal or greater than 0.5 (Nunnally, 1978). As indicated in Table 1, standardized confirmatory factor analysis (CFA) loadings for all measurement items of this study are exceed the minimum loading criterion of 0.5, and all are significant at $p < 0.001$ and. Besides, the AVE of each construct exceeds 0.5, and CRs and Cronbach's alpha for all factors exceed the required minimum of 0.8 and 0.7 respectively. Hence, all three conditions for convergent validity are met.

Next, discriminant validity refers to the degree to which measures of two constructs are empirically distinct. Discriminant validity is existed when the square root of each construct's AVE is larger than its correlations with other constructs (Chin et al. 2003). As indicated in Table 1, the highest correlation between any pair of constructs in the CFA model was 0.54, and this number is lower than the lowest square root of AVE among all of the constructs, which was 0.76. Hence, the discriminant validity criterion was also met for our data sample.

## 4.2  Hypothesis Testing

We use partial least square (PLS) to test the main effects specified in hypotheses H1 through H5, as shown in Fig. 2. With regard to the specific hypotheses, we found:

- Hypotheses 1, 2 and 3: Our results supported the hypotheses that both higher service uncertainty and higher switching cost would have significant effects on firm's

**Table 1.** Reliability, correlation coefficients and AVE results

| Variable | Mean | S.D. | Cronbach's Alpha | C.R. | AVE | (1) | (2) | (3) | (4) | (5) | (6) |
|---|---|---|---|---|---|---|---|---|---|---|---|
| 1. SVC_UNC | 5.01 | 1.36 | 0.92 | 0.94 | 0.75 | **0.87** | | | | | |
| 2. ASSET | 5.21 | 1.46 | 0.79 | 0.83 | 0.72 | 0.11 | **0.85** | | | | |
| 3. SWT_COST | 5.03 | 1.36 | 0.71 | 0.84 | 0.57 | 0.54 | 0.24 | **0.76** | | | |
| 4. RISK | 5.17 | 1.70 | 0.98 | 0.99 | 0.98 | 0.52 | 0.10 | 0.46 | **0.99** | | |
| 5. INTENTION | 2.88 | 1.59 | 0.97 | 0.98 | 0.95 | −0.24 | 0.09 | 0.13 | −0.20 | **0.97** | |
| 6. SWT_BENFIT | 3.98 | 1.37 | 0.97 | 0.98 | 0.92 | −0.10 | 0.01 | 0.20 | −0.13 | 0.34 | **0.96** |

Notes:
1. The main diagonal shows the square root of the AVE (Average Variance Extracted).
2. Significant at $p < 0.01$ level is shown in bold.
3. **C.R.** for Composite Reliability, **SVC_UNC** for Service Uncertainty, **ASSET** for Asset Specificity, **SWT_COST** for Switching Cost, **RISK** for Perceived Risk, **SWT_BENFIT** for Switching Benefits, and **INTENTION** for intention to adopt cloud ERP system.

perceived risk ($t = 4.287$ and $2.51$, $p < 0.001$ and $p < 0.05$), thereby supporting Hypotheses 1 and 3. However, asset specificity has no any significant effect on firm's perceived risk ($t = 0.045$), and Hypothesis 2 is not supported. In additions, the effect of service uncertainty on perceived risk (beta $= 0.39$) is higher than the one of switching cost on perceived risk (beta $= 0.25$).

- Hypothesis 4: As expected, higher level of firm's perceived risks had a significant but strong negative effect on the intention of cloud ERP system adoption ($t = -1.983$, $p < 0.005$).
- Hypothesis 5: As predicted, higher level of switching benefits had a significant but strong positive effect on the intention of cloud ERP system adoption ($t = 3.74$, $p < 0.001$).

## 5 Implications and Conclusions

### 5.1 Implications and Suggestions

This purpose of this research tries to explore the possible obstacles and facilitators on the adoption intention of cloud-based ERP system, from the TCE perspective. As shown in Fig. 2, the overall explanatory power of our research model was acceptable, a R-square of 31.6% for perceived risk and a R-square of 13.8% for the intention of cloud ERP system adoption were obtained.

First, service uncertainty and switching cost were found to be significant in engendering firm's perceived risk, and the effect of service uncertainty on perceived risk is higher than the one of switching cost on perceived risk. As such, service uncertainty is the most critical factor on firm's perceived risk toward cloud ERP system adoption. Firms might mostly worry about the service uncertainty of cloud ERP service in terms of security or efficiency because they might not foresee whether cloud ERP service might work smoothly as their expectation, thereby increasing their perceived risks towards cloud ERP system. The next possible inhibitor related to perceived risk is switching cost. Switching cost includes all possible expenses or efforts occurred during system

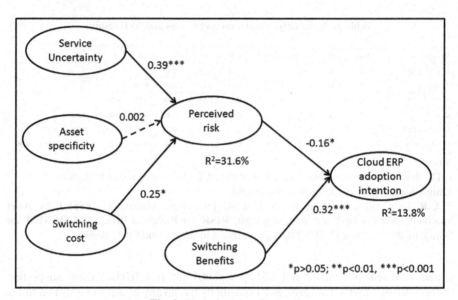

**Fig. 2.** Hypotheses testing results

migration, such as training, consulting, after service, business process change and so on. As such, if switching cost is higher and can not be affordable for firms, they could possible temporarily suspend such migration plan and remain the same in current ERP system usage. Bearing these possible inhibitors in mind, the best way to mitigate service uncertainty is to provide better governance mechanism and evidence for firms by cloud ERP system vendors. For example, service level agreement (SLA) is the best way for vendors to alleviate firm's perception of possible service uncertainty toward the usage of cloud ERP. Besides, providing persuasive evidences such as certificated service guarantee or other firms that have successfully implemented cloud EPR service could also be better ways to decrease firm's perception of service uncertainty and associated risks. For mitigating the concerns of switching cost for firms, our study suggests that cloud ERP vendors could provide seamless and valuable services with lowest expenses to harmonize it.

Second, unexpected to our prediction, asset specificity has no significant effect on perceived risk. Asset specificity refers to the degree to which an asset can be redeployed to alternative uses without sacrifice of productive value (Williamson 1989). A possible explanation for the insignificant effect on perceived risk could be as follows. Asset specificity may include tangible (e.g., facilities or dedicated personnel) and intangible specific ones (e.g., business process or domain knowledge) (Subramani and Venkatraman 2003). In the implementation of cloud ERP system, it allows firms to reduce tangible hardware infrastructure and relevant maintenance investments. Likewise, firms have no any tangible specific investment during the adoption of cloud service. Moreover, intangible specific investments in organizations as comprising two components: "know-how" and "know-what" (Kogut and Zander 1992). "Know-how" refers to the firm's understanding of task execution, in terms of operating procedures for efficient task execution. "Know-what" refers to context-sensitive or tacit understanding of subtleties that allows effective action and the resolving of ambiguities in task planning and execution. In fact, these two kinds of intangible assets are mostly related to firm's own and internalized business processes and domain knowledge, as such, firms might do not feel these investments will be relationship-specific investments to cloud ERP system vendor. Likewise, intangible asset specificity seems not a critical issue and thus is insignificant in affecting firm's perceived risk toward cloud ERP system adoption.

Lastly, we hypothesized that perceived risk is negatively and switching benefits is positively related to the intention of cloud ERP system adoption and these tow hypothesized relationships were supported by empirical data in this study. However, we also found that switching benefits have a greater influence on firm's intention of adopting cloud EPR service than firm's perceived risk. These results are expected and consistent wit TCE perspective which stated that firms will choose transaction methods that economize on transaction cost and perceived risks (Williamson 1985). When making information system implementation decision, firm tends to select a service or information system with the least costs, in terms of all needed services. In other words, when choosing a service or information system, firms always weigh all related costs and benefits. These related costs and benefits, or total ownership costs/benefits considerations, will influence firms' decisions whether to adopt cloud ERP system service or not. Likewise, if firms perceive high transaction cost or risks in cloud system, they will be less willing to adopt it. Conversely, if firms perceive high switching benefits in cloud ERP system, they will be more willing to adopt it. Since firm's perceived switching benefits have greater influences on adoption intention, this study strongly suggests that cloud ERP vendors should significantly promote what benefits firms can obtain from the implementation of cloud service, including operational, strategic or even mobile commerce ones.

## 5.2  Limitations and Suggestions for Future Researches

A few number of research limitations exist in this study, which should be considered in the future. First, the conclusions of this study are from cross-sectional data of Top 1000 manufacturing firm list in Taiwan. With such data and analysis, we only took a snapshot of this model. However, it is believed that it will be good to conduct a longitudinal study to evaluate the adoption of cloud-based ERP, since the implementation of such service is still in the beginning so far. Second, though this study could provides several meaningful insights for the explanation of the adoption intention of cloud ERP platform, some possible moderating effects between the relationship between perceived risk, switching benefits and the adoption intention of cloud ERP system is not well understood. More academic works may benefit from comprehending possible moderating factors such as industrial types (e.g., manufacturing, banking, information service and so on) that enhance or impede such cloud-based ERP adoption intention that are most compatible with such purposes. In sum, these questions open up fertile grounds for future research opportunities.

# 6  Conclusions

Based on the perspective of transaction cost economic, this study tries to contribute to the information system marketing academic fields by providing insightful support for the relationship between transaction attributes, switching costs and benefits, perceived risks and the intention of cloud-based ERP system adoption. From the practitioner's point of view, this research found that transaction attributes, especially service uncertainty and switching costs, appear to significantly influence firm's adoption intention to cloud-based ERP service. Since the adoption of cloud-based ERP platform is still new and has unique characteristics for understanding the possible inhibitors and facilitators on the system evaluation and subsequent implementation, our study hope to offer underpinnings for much further researches on this topic, and encourage scholars to investigate the relevant issues on such topic.

# References

Benlian, A., Hess, T., Buxmann, P.: Drivers of SaaS adoption: an empirical study of different application types. Bus. Inf. Syst. Eng. **1**(5), 359–369 (2009)

Ben-Yehuda, O.A., Ben-Yehuda, M., Schuster, A., Tsafrir, D.: The rise of RaaS: the resource-as-a-service cloud. Commun. ACM **57**(7), 76–84 (2014)

Castellina, N.: SaaS and cloud ERP observations: Is cloud ERP right for you? (2012). http://www.fronde.com/assets/PDF/wp-abrdn-saas-and-cloud-erp-observations-060713.pdf. Accessed 08 Oct 2013. Aberdeen Group

Chau, P.Y.K., Tam, K.Y.: Factors affecting the adoption of open systems: an exploratory study. MIS Q. **21**(1), 1–24 (1997)

Chin, W.W., Marcolin, B.L., Newsted, P.R.: A partial least squares latent variable modeling approach for measuring interaction effects: results from a Monte Carlo simulation study and an electronic-mail emotion/adoption study. Inf. Syst. Res. **14**(2), 189–217 (2003)

Cusumano, M.A.: Technology strategy and management: the cloud as an innovation platform for software development: how cloud computing became a platform. Commun. ACM **62**(10), 20–22 (2019)

Falk, T., Schepers, J., Hammerschmidt, M., Bauer, H.H.: Identifying cross-channel dissynergies for multichannel service providers. J. Serv. Res. **10**(2), 143–160 (2007)

Fornell, C., Larker, D.F.: Structural equation models with unobservable variables and measurement errors. J. Mark. Res. **18**(2), 39–50 (1981)

Gupta, S., Meissonier, R., Drave, V.A.: Examining the impact of cloud ERP on sustainable performance: a dynamic capability view. Int. J. Inf. Manage. **51**, 1–13 (2020)

Kathuria, A., Mann, A., Khuntia, J., Saldanha, T.J.V., Kauffman, R.J.: A strategic value appropriation path for cloud computing. J. Manag. Inf. Syst. **35**(3), 740–775 (2018)

Kern, T., Willcocks, L., Van Heck, E.: The winner's curse in IT outsourcing: strategies for avoiding relational Trauma. Calif. Manag. Rev. **44**(2), 47–69 (2002)

Kim, H.W., Kankanhalli, A.: Investigating user resistance to information systems implementation: a status Quo bias perspective. MIS Q. **33**(3), 567–582 (2009)

Kim, S.S., Son, J.Y.: Out of dedication or constraint? A dual model of post-adoption phenomena and its empirical test in the context of online services. MIS Q. **33**(1), 49–70 (2009)

Kogut, B., Zander, U.: Knowledge of the firm, combinative capabilities, and the replication of technology. Organ. Sci. **3**(3), 383–397 (1992)

Lee, S., Park, S.B., Lim, G.G.: Using balanced scorecards for the evaluation of software-as-a-service. Inf. Manag. **50**(7), 553–561 (2013)

Lee, S.G., Chae, S.H., Cho, K.M.: Drivers and inhibitors of SaaS adoption in Korea. Int. J. Inf. Manag. **33**(3), 429–440 (2013)

Liang, T.P., Huang, J.S.: An empirical study on consumer acceptance of products in electronic markets: a transaction cost model. Decis. Support Syst. **24**(1), 29–43 (1998)

Marston, S., Li, Z., Bandyopadhyay, S., Zhang, J., Ghalsasi, A.: Cloud computing—the business perspective. Decis. Support Syst. **51**(1), 176–189 (2011)

Paswan, A.K., Panda, S.: B-to-B relationships: a resource, knowledge, and capability (RKC) perspective. Ind. Mark. Manag. **91**, 92–99 (2020)

Rindfleisch, A., Heide, J.B.: Transaction cost analysis: past, present and future applications. J. Mark. **61**(4), 30–54 (1997)

Subramani, M.R., Venkatraman, N.: Safeguarding investments in asymmetric interorganizational relationships: theory and evidence. Acad. Manag. J. **46**(1), 46–62 (2003)

Susarla, A., Barua, A., Whinston, A.B.: A Transaction cost perspective of the software as a service business model. J. Manag. Inf. Syst. **26**(2), 205–240 (2009)

Teo, H.H., Wei, K.K., Benbasat, I.: Predicting intention to adopt interorganizational linkages: an institutional perspective. MIS Q. **27**(1), 19–49 (2003)

Vazquez, X.H.: Allocating decision rights on the shop floor: a perspective from transaction cost economics and organization Theory. Organ. Sci. **15**(4), 463–480 (2004)

Wathne, K.H., Heide, J.B.: Relationship governance in a supply chain network. J. Mark. **68**(1), 73–89 (2004)

Williamson, O.E.: The Economic Institutions of Capitalism: Firms Markets, Relational Contracting. Free Press, New York (1985)

Williamson, O.E.: Transaction cost economics. In: Schmalensee, R., Willing, R. (eds.) Handbook of Industrial Organization, pp. 136–182. Elsevier Science, Amsterdam (1989)

Williamson, O.E.: The Mechanisms of Governance. Oxford University Press, New York (1996)

# Organizational Resilience: Examining the Influence of Information Cost and Organizational Capacity on Business Continuity Management

Wei-Ning Wu[✉]

National Sun Yat-sen University, Kaohsiung, Taiwan
weiningwu@mail.nsysu.edu.tw

**Abstract.** Business continuity management is both the main indicator of organizational resilience enhancement and the primary representation of corporate social responsibility. Emphasis has been placed on business participation in the emergency management process and business continuity planning, but little is understood about the factors influencing changes in business continuity management during the development of government–business collaboration for emergency preparedness. This study examined the influence of information cost (including information use, development opportunity, and cost saving) and organization capacity on business continuity management. The results indicated that business planning information increased sales opportunities through the use of certain technologies and reduced the cost of regulation compliance. Organization size influenced firms' changing approaches to business continuity and disaster recovery planning.

**Keywords:** Disaster recovery planning · Corporate social responsibility · Business risk management · Business-government relations

## 1 Introduction

Organizational resilience is an organization's capacity to withstand hazards, continue operating under adversity, adapt to risky situations, and improve functionality after a crisis (Lengnick-Hall et al. 2011). Over the last decade, research into the role of business continuity management in organizational resilience has increased. A common argument maintains that business continuity management in the form of organizational resilience enhancement is the most pivotal management concern (Gibb and Buchanan 2006; Hatton et al. 2016). Attaining and sustaining a competitive advantage over competitors without business risk management and business continuity planning is increasingly difficult for firms (Wang et al. 2017). Evidence suggests that businesses who commit to these processes have the potential to become the champions of sustainable development in the current market place (Herbane 2010).

In many cases, individual governments seek external assistance or resources because they lack the capital to effectively respond to crises (Jung et al. 2014). Business participation in risk management and business continuity planning initiatives are vital to

© Springer Nature Switzerland AG 2021
F. F.-H. Nah and K. Siau (Eds.): HCII 2021, LNCS 12783, pp. 444–455, 2021.
https://doi.org/10.1007/978-3-030-77750-0_28

emergency management and offer the horizontal and vertical collaborative potential to work with governments on problem-solving and environmental protection. To emphasize the essential nature of business risk management and continuity planning, governments have employed various digital technologies as tools of communication with various stakeholders within a digital governance framework (Wong 2009). Although most of the literature agrees that governments play a vital role in influencing business continuity management, in reality, this is unproven (Runyan 2006; Kitching, Hart, Wilson 2015).

Whether applying governmental information and communications technology (ICT) to business planning information and development influences the business continuity management process remains unclear. In response to the increased attention to business risk management and continuity planning, this study investigated what factors change in the business continuity management process as a result of firms using governmental ICT. A review of the literature revealed descriptions of certain causal relationships but little scholarship that has deepened our understanding of the process. To answer this research question, this paper presents an overview of the literature to distinguish the key factors and to develop a hypothesis to describe their causal relationships.

## 2 Importance of Engaging Business in the Emergency Management

Participation in the emergency planning process represents a proactive role for firms; these organizations can influence decision-making by sharing their expertise and information on emergency and risk management. By involving firms in the planning process, public organizations can quickly identify the resources of a businesses, reduce any overlap in efforts and resources, and be better prepared for emergency management. In turn, firms become familiar with the relevant procedures and can share the common goals of the government and emergency stakeholders such as nonprofit organizations, community associations, and the public (Wu et al. 2015).

The role and function of firms in the emergency management process are crucial because these organizations have the expertise, connections, and resources for effective emergency management. Firms are also regarded as vital for risk management and business continuity planning. They can be a positive influence by committing to and integrating themselves into the community through the management of this valuable shared task (Hatton et al. 2016). Their willingness to participate also encourages cohesion among interest groups and risk management processes (Carpenter et al. 2003), as opposed to scattered and unprepared initiatives that prove ineffective in disaster risk reduction.

Studies have argued that firms with emergency management plans have a positive influence on emergency response (Dushie 2014). Resource-rich businesses can financially supplement public organizations' urgent emergency responses. Researchers have identified planning, resource availability, training, and education as the key components of preparedness (Pennington-Gray et al. 2011). Regarding business continuity management, these elements are essential for inclusion in written emergency management guidelines. In addition to allowing appropriate and comprehensive emergency response, education and training teach the businesses how to recognize and respond to emergency situations.

## 3 Literature Review

Many researchers have stressed the need for business continuity management to enhance organizational resilience (Akgün and Keskin 2014; Sahebjamnia et al. 2015; Torabi et al. 2016; Duchek 2020). Organizational resilience has received increasing attention in the past decade, and it refers to the continued ability of a group or system to operate during and after an adverse event (Prayag et al. 2020). Firms that exhibit greater degrees of resilience continually adapt and enhance their risk management ability. Organizational resilience can also be exhibited through changes in management functions alongside the enhancement of risk management capacity. Firm development is dynamic, constantly responding to changes in public policy, the economy, and environmental factors.

Business continuity management is a core preparedness activity; this comprehensive and fundamental framework involves the identification of various resources and processes that should be used during risk response (Castillo 2004). Studies have emphasized the key role of leadership in the adoption of business continuity management plans (Wong 2009), and others have argued that to have effective risk management and continuity planning, owners and managers must understand the mechanisms that are used to guide the activities of business continuity management (Ee 2014). Other researchers have claimed that business risk management and continuity planning efforts are only valid if business owners and employees have their priorities of risk management of and indicated their willingness to implement plans related to business continuity management (Alesi 2008). In some cases, risk management and emergency training and education also reinforce a firm's business continuity management by allowing businesses to become accustomed to their associated rules, culture, and norms. The organization can then support disaster risk reduction activities more effectively (Orlando 2007).

Research has offered numerous normative expectations and prescriptions to guide the practice of business continuity management, and yet, many businesses still struggle with this (Niemimaa et al. 2019; Soufi et al. 2019). Businesses have undertaken various methods of gathering resources and implementing processes but have reported numerous weaknesses in plans that were insufficiently comprehensive or too cost or time intensive (Jain et al. 2020). Owners institutionalize some mechanisms for risk management and business continuity planning but can seldom identify the outcomes or direct outgrowths of their efforts (Epstein and Khan 2014).

In sum, emphasis has been placed on business participation in the emergency management process and business continuity planning, but little is understood about the factors influencing changes in business continuity management during the development of government–business collaboration for emergency preparedness. Hence, to fill out the current research gap as well as to use the second-hand survey data from Queensland State Government, this study explored the influence of information cost (including information use, development opportunity, and cost saving) and organization capacity on business continuity management.

# 4  Research Model Development and Hypotheses

The topics of business continuity and disaster recovery planning have received much attention in the literature. Empirical findings and normative prescriptions have simultaneously reached both complementary and contradictory conclusions. This section outlines the four main factors commonly described as influential in firm decisions as a result of government website use.

## 4.1  Business Planning Information

Social media-based participation increases when governments begin to use multiple types of social media; greater participation then promotes the sharing and delivery of information (Wu 2020). Based on their functions, the two main types of digital technologies are expressive oriented and collaborative oriented (Lee and Kwak 2012). Expressive-oriented digital technologies focus on information delivery, allowing the social media user to share information and opinions though media such as text, images, or video. Expressive-oriented social media platforms, such as YouTube and Myspace, focus on single-way information delivery from social media users who actively share information with other social media users (Aspasia and Ourania 2014). Collaborative digital technologies offer a virtual space for social media users to communicate and provide opportunities to work together (Smith et al. 2014). Users of collaborative digital technologies tend to share common goals, and the interaction process is dynamic when these goals attract the attention of potential social media users. Hence, through the dissemination of business planning information on governmental websites, businesses can enhance their continuity management.

> H1: An increase in business planning information searching from government websites is associated with an increase in changes in business continuity management.

## 4.2  Opportunities to Use Technologies to Increase Sales

Opportunities lead to risk-taking in business planning and development, the method of which depends on internal and external factors. The primary pursuit of business is creating opportunities and maintaining sustainable development (Patzelt and Shepherd 2011). The competitive advantage view holds that a firm's potential opportunities drive value creation by increasing risk-taking activity (Fiegenbaum and Thomas 2004). A firm's development can be considered sustainable when these opportunities enhance profits, which lead to greater development (Brockman et al. 2012). If opportunities that incorporate the use of the technologies, such as the internet, the National Broadband Network, and smart phones, result in increased sales, firms may be more likely to take risks. Hence, through the use of these opportunities to use these technologies to increase sales, businesses would be more likely to enhance their business continuity management.

> H2: An increase in opportunities to use these technologies to increase sales is associated with a decrease in changes in business continuity management.

### 4.3  Reducing the Cost of Regulation Compliance

Discussions of regulation compliance often neglect the issue of cost. The transactional costs of understanding regulations and the comparative costs between regulation compliance and noncompliance have not been subject to close scrutiny (Kitching et al. 2015). A firm that is technically trained and politically astute may reach less risky decisions after considering the cost of complying with regulations (Bailey et al. 2002). When a business situation is volatile, a strategic decision-maker may conclude that the up-front cost of complying with regulations is worth the additional effort. Hence, by reducing the cost of regulation compliance, businesses would be more likely to enhance their business continuity management.

H3: A reduction in the cost of regulation compliance is associated with an increase in changes in business continuity management.

### 4.4  Organization Size

Larger, more resource-rich organizations have more organization capacity, which is a catalyst of risk planning in business continuity and disaster recovery planning processes because more available resources create more collaborative opportunities for emergency management initiatives. Plans related to business continuity or disaster recovery planning are crucially affected by organization size. Firms use their organizational advantage to build their knowledge and skills and expand their risk management capabilities (Sahebjamnia et al. 2015). In addition, more personnel can assist in the planning and implementation of emergency response, join disaster scenario exercises, and undertake preparedness training to minimize threats to people and resources (Hatton et al. 2016). Hence, large businesses are more likely to enhance their business continuity management.

H4: An increase in organization size is associated with an increase in changes in business continuity management.

## 5  Analysis and Result

For analysis of the factors influencing firm changes in business continuity management, the 2013 Customer Impact Survey of the Queensland Government was used (Queensland Government 2013). The survey data represented firms' perceptions of online services for business usage and their impact. The 2013 Customer Impact Survey was administered by the Queensland Government; 1500 small and medium businesses (with fewer than 200 employees) in Queensland were surveyed over the telephone.

Table 1 presents the summary of indicator measurements. A detailed description of the measurements of variables of the regression model are provided in the following. Table 2 details the descriptive statistics of all variables. Table 3 presents the logistic regression results for changes in business continuity and disaster recovery planning. The estimates supported the argument and hypotheses in this research.

The dependent variable in the analysis is measured by whether firms made any change in business continuity management as a result of using of Queensland State

Government websites. The variable is a dummy variable containing the question, "In the last twelve months, have you made any changes to your business as a result of your use of Queensland State Government websites? - Business continuity or disaster recovery planning" If the survey respondents indicated that they had, the variable was coded as "1". If the respondent indicated that they had not, the variable was coded as "0", which means the respondent chose not to make any change in business continuity management.

Business planning information was a dummy variable, and was measured based on whether firms use Queensland State Government websites for business planning information in the last year. Survey participants were asked the following survey question: "What did you use Queensland State Government websites for business planning information in the last year?" When the respondents answered "yes," we viewed this firms using governmental websites for business planning information in the last year.

Opportunities to use these technologies to increase sales was operationalized based on whether there are opportunities for my business to use these technologies, technologies, such as the internet, the National Broadband Network, and smart phones, to increase sales. Survey participants were asked the following: "I'd now like to talk to you about whether technologies, such as the internet, the National Broadband Network, and smart phones, provide opportunities for - There are opportunities for my business to use these technologies to increase sales." This survey question was graded on a 5-point Likert scale ranging from 5 (strongly agree), 4 (agree), 3 (Neither agree or disagree), 2 (disagree) to 1 (strongly disagree).

Reduced the cost of complying with regulations was measured based on whether Queensland State Government website(s) helped you to stay up to date with the cost reduction of complying with regulations. For this dummy variable, respondents either answered governmental help would reduce the cost of complying with regulations (coded 1), otherwise (coded 0). Also, Organization size was a dummy variable, and was measured based on whether the business employ 200 or more Full Time Equivalent (FTE). If the survey respondents chose yes, it was coded as 1, otherwise was coded as 0.

Control variables mainly include Social media channels, international business export, optimistic attitude, and online transactions. Among these control variables, social media channels, international business export, and online transactions are dummy variables. The survey questions in this study are as follows: (1) Are you aware of Queensland Government content on any of the following social media channels?; (2) Does your business export its products or services outside of Australia?; (3) I'm also interested in whether you conduct any online transactions as part of your day to day business activity. Does your business: Accept online transactions, for example taking bookings or payments? These three questions are coded as 1 if the survey respondents chose yes, otherwise was coded as 0. Finally, optimistic attitude is measured by the firms' responses to a question about their perspectives to business prospects. There were three degrees of optimistic attitude: less positive; about the same, more positive.

In Table 3, the effect of business planning information on firm changes in business continuity management was revealed to be positive (1.30, $p < 0.01$). Firms that used the Queensland State Government websites for business planning information in the last year were, on average, more likely to make changes in their business continuity management

**Table 1.** Summary of indicator measurements

| Variables | Measurement |
|---|---|
| **Dependent Variable** | |
| Change in business continuity management | In the last twelve months, have you made any changes to your business as a result of your use of Queensland State Government websites? - Business continuity or disaster recovery planning (Yes = 1) |
| **Independent Variables** | |
| Business planning information | What did you use Queensland State Government websites for business planning information in the last year? (Business planning information = 1) |
| Opportunities to use these technologies to increase sales | I'd now like to talk to you about whether technologies, such as the internet, the National Broadband Network, and smart phones, provide opportunities for - There are opportunities for my business to use these technologies to increase sales (strongly agree = 5; agree = 4; Neither agree or disagree = 3; disagree = 2; strongly disagree = 1) |
| Reduced the cost of complying with regulations | You said that Queensland State Government website(s) helped you to stay up to date with regulations/comply with regulations in the last year. Would you say it: - Reduced the cost of complying with regulations (Yes = 1) |
| Organization Size | How many staff (Full Time Equivalent, FTE) does the business employ? - 200 or more FTEs (Yes = 1) |
| Social media channels | Are you aware of Queensland Government content on any of the following social media channels? (Yes = 1) |
| International business export | Does your business export its products or services outside of Australia? (Yes = 1) |
| Optimistic attitude | And do you feel more or less optimistic about your business prospects than you did a year ago? (More positive = 3; About the same = 2; Less positive = 1) |
| Online transactions | I'm also interested in whether you conduct any online transactions as part of your day to day business activity. Does your business: Accept online transactions, for example taking bookings or payments? (Yes = 1) |

**Table 2.** Descriptive statistics

| | Freq. | Percent | | Freq. | Percent |
|---|---|---|---|---|---|
| **Change in business continuity management** | | | **Social media channels** | | |
| No = 0 | 1463 | 97.5 | No = 0 | 337 | 22.5 |
| Yes = 1 | 37 | 2.47 | Yes = 1 | 1163 | 77.5 |
| Total | 1500 | | Total | 1500 | |
| **Opportunities to use these technologies to increase sales** | | | **Optimistic attitude** | | |
| Strongly disagree = 1 | 67 | 4.47 | Less positive = 1 | 556 | 37.5 |
| Disagree = 2 | 215 | 14.3 | About the same = 2 | 344 | 23.2 |
| Neither agree or disagree = 3 | 48 | 3.2 | More positive = 3 | 581 | 39.2 |
| Agree = 4 | 686 | 45.7 | Total | 1481 | |
| Strongly agree = 5 | 484 | 32.3 | | | |
| Total | 1500 | | | | |
| **Reduced the cost of complying with regulations** | | | **International business export** | | |
| No = 0 | 1338 | 89.2 | No = 0 | 1276 | 85.1 |
| Yes = 1 | 162 | 10.8 | Yes = 1 | 224 | 14.9 |
| Total | 1500 | | Total | 1500 | |
| **Organization Size** | | | **Online transactions** | | |
| No = 0 | 1201 | 80.1 | No = 0 | 522 | 36.5 |
| Yes = 1 | 299 | 19.9 | Yes = 1 | 908 | 36.5 |
| Total | 1500 | | Total | 1430 | |
| **Business planning information** | | | | | |
| No = 0 | 1401 | 93.4 | | | |
| Yes = 1 | 99 | 6.6 | | | |
| Total | 1500 | | | | |

when all other variables were held constant. This result supports Hypothesis 1 in this study.

Firms that strongly agreed that technologies such as the internet, the National Broadband Network, and smart phones provide opportunities for increasing sales were less likely to change their business continuity management than those who strongly disagreed with the statement were ($-1.63$, $p < 0.05$, and $-1.30$, $p < 0.05$, respectively). This result supports Hypothesis 2 in this study.

Firms indicated that consultation of the Queensland State Government website(s) led to them reducing the cost of regulation compliance in the last year and were more likely to change their business continuity management ($2.14$, $p < 0.01$), holding all other

**Table 3.** Logistic regression results for changes in business continuity management

| | Coef | Std. Err | |
|---|---|---|---|
| **Business planning information** | 1.30 | 0.41 | ** |
| **Opportunities to use these technologies to increase sales** | | | |
| Disagree Vs. Strongly disagree | −1.36 | 0.80 | |
| Neither agree or disagree Vs. Strongly disagree | −1.32 | 1.20 | |
| Agree = 4 Vs. Strongly disagree | −1.30 | 0.63 | * |
| Strongly agree Vs. Strongly disagree | −1.63 | 0.67 | * |
| **Reduced the cost of complying with regulations** | 2.14 | 0.37 | ** |
| **Organization Size** | 0.72 | 0.37 | * |
| **Social media channels** | −0.14 | 0.40 | |
| **International business export** | −0.37 | 0.57 | |
| **Optimistic attitude** | | | |
| About the same Vs. Less positive | 0.43 | 0.52 | |
| More positive Vs. Less positive | 0.53 | 0.45 | |
| **Online transactions** | −0.03 | 0.36 | |
| Constant | −3.55 | 0.76 | ** |
| Number of Obs | 1,411 | | |
| Log likelihood | 137.91 | | |
| LR Chi2 | 66.64 | | |
| Pseudo R2 | 0.19 | | |

Note: Std. Err. = standard error; ** $p < 0.01$; *$p < 0.05$

variables constant. This result supports Hypothesis 3 in this study. Finally, firms with 200 or more full-time equivalent employees were more likely to change their business continuity management than those with less than 200 full-time employees were (0.72, $p < 0.05$). This result supports Hypothesis 4 in this study.

## 6  Discussion

Government websites have the vital function of educating policy stakeholders. During the policy implementation process, public officials are generally able to explain the content of public polices and the reasons for implementing selected polices that, at first glance, would be unpopular among many stakeholders. Stakeholders with a more sophisticated level of technical and social media understanding would likely provide more input in the governance process, with mutual interaction among various participants leading to positive outcomes.

Businesses can offer positive suggestions to the government on relevant public polices when they become well informed by consulting social media platforms and websites.

They can also gain an understanding of the advantages of using social media. Most businesses are unwilling to contact public officials; social media overcomes such obstacles, allowing businesses to access policy information. Because of the cost of participation, most businesses are unwilling to participate in public affairs. Hence, municipalities sometimes have a dearth of businesses involved in public affairs, creating an information divide. However, the wide use of government website channels fosters a culture of openness within public organizations, increasing opportunities to integrate, engage, and collaborate.

This study provided a prediction of business disaster risk reduction behaviors. Four variables (business planning information, opportunities to use these technologies to increase sales, reducing the cost of regulation compliance, and organization size) were demonstrated to influence firm changes in business continuity management. The results of this study strongly support the argument that has two seemingly contradictory consequences for organizational behavior, and specifically for risk plans. Reduction in the cost of regulation compliance leads to the implementation of risk plans, but in rapidly changing environments, the probability of risk plans declines along with opportunities to use these technologies to increase sales.

Because of high environmental uncertainty, a long-term state of zero risk is unlikely, and thus, firms must develop a series of business continuity and disaster recovery plans. Business continuity and disaster recovery planning must include opportunities to use the aforementioned technologies, such as the internet, the National Broadband Network, and smart phones, to increase sales and to reduce the cost of complying with regulations. From a firm's perspective, the enhancement of business risk management begins with the creation of plans relative to business continuity or disaster recovery planning. Consequently, a business with effective risk management in place can pursue profit maximization and enjoy a competitive advantage. In turn, opportunities to use the technologies to increase sales do not contribute to effective planning for disaster protective actions.

Creating sound business continuity management processes allows firms to expand capacity while maintaining all existing advantages. Thus, a tradeoff between opportunities and cost within a firm's given environmental context ultimately determines the firms' willingness to make changes in its business continuity management. The reduced cost of complying with regulations is one positive effect. Large firms formulate risk plans more often than smaller ones do. Because resources in such highly interdependent markets are often distributed on the basis of organization size, large and prestigious firms are often able to implement the most effective risk plans, especially if they are considering using these technologies to increase sales and to reduce the cost of complying with regulations.

# 7 Conclusion

Business continuity management has been practiced in governments and businesses. However, few studies have examined whether information cost—including information use, development opportunity, and cost saving—and organization capacity influence business risk management and continuity planning. Business continuity management can enhance the sustainable management of a business and increase the likelihood that its plans can be applied to disaster risk reduction processes. The present assessment demonstrated that business continuity and disaster recovery planning encourage firms to integrate risk perspectives into their managerial thinking, moving risk reduction toward sustainable management. Some long-term challenges still remain. Business interest must be sustained, and business continuity and disaster recovery planning must be fully integrated into a firms' disaster risk reduction process. Long-term observation is required to examine the factors that influence change in risk management and business continuity planning. Many firms seem satisfied that their plans have been translated into concrete steps for sustainable management and have reported positive results (Runyan 2006).

To sustain firm interest in the long term, governments must continue to emphasize the key role of business continuity management in business sustainable management. Firms must be encouraged to integrate business continuity management into risk management and program planning for more robust organizational resilience and regularly examine the reasons for adopting and changing business continuity management strategies.

# References

Akgün, A.E., Keskin, H.: Organisational resilience capacity and firm product innovativeness and performance. Int. J. Prod. Res. **52**(23), 6918–6937 (2014)

Alesi, P.: Building enterprise-wide resilience by integrating business continuity capability into day-to-day business culture and technology. J. Bus. Contin. Emer. Plan. **2**(3), 214–220 (2008)

Aspasia, V., Ourania, N.: Social media adoption and managers' perceptions. Int. J. Strategic Innovative Market. **1**(2), 61–63 (2014)

Bailey, P.D., Haq, G., Gouldson, A.: Mind the gap! comparing ex ante and ex post assessments of the costs of complying with environmental regulation. Eur. Environ. **12**(5), 245–256 (2002)

Brockman, B.K., Jones, M.A., Becherer, R.C.: Customer orientation and performance in small firms: examining the moderating influence of risk-taking, innovativeness, and opportunity focus. J. Small Bus. Manag. **50**(3), 429–446 (2012)

Carpenter, M.A., Pollock, T.G., Leary, M.M.: Testing a model of reasoned risk-taking: governance, the experience of principals and agents, and global strategy in high-technology IPO firms. Strateg. Manag. J. **24**(9), 803–820 (2003)

Castillo, C.: Disaster preparedness and business continuity planning at Boeing: an integrated model. J. Facil. Manag. **3**(1), 8–26 (2004)

Duchek, S.: Organizational resilience: a capability-based conceptualization. Bus. Res. **13**(1), 215–246 (2019). https://doi.org/10.1007/s40685-019-0085-7

Dushie, D.Y.: Business continuity planning: an empirical study of factors that hinder effective disaster preparedness of businesses. J. Econ. Sustain. Dev. **5**(27), 185–191 (2014)

Ee, H.: Business continuity 2014: from traditional to integrated business continuity management. J. Bus. Contin. Emer. Plan. **8**(2), 102–105 (2014)

Epstein, B., Khan, D.C.: Application impact analysis: a risk-based approach to business continuity and disaster recovery. J. Bus. Contin. Emer. Plan. **7**(3), 230–237 (2014)

Fiegenbaum, A., Thomas, H.: Strategie risk and competitive advantage: an integrative perspective. Eur. Manag. Rev. **1**(1), 84–95 (2004)

Gibb, F., Buchanan, S.: A framework for business continuity management. Int. J. Inf. Manag. **26**(2), 128–141 (2006)

Hatton, T., Grimshaw, E., Vargo, J., Seville, E.: Lessons from disaster: Creating a business continuity plan that really works. J. Bus. Contin. Emer. Plan. **10**(1), 84–92 (2016)

Herbane, B.: The evolution of business continuity management: a historical review of practices and drivers. Bus. Hist. **52**(6), 978–1002 (2010)

Jain, P., Pasman, H.J., Mannan, M.S.: Process system resilience: from risk management to business continuity and sustainability. Int. J. Bus. Continuity Risk Manag. **10**(1), 47–66 (2020)

Jung, K., Andrew, S.A., Wu, W.N.: Illuminating the in-house provision of emergency services: a test of organizational capacity hypotheses. Int. Rev. Public Adm. **19**(3), 238–251 (2014)

Kitching, J., Hart, M., Wilson, N.: Burden or benefit? Regulation as a dynamic influence on small business performance. Int. Small Bus. J. **33**(2), 130–147 (2015)

Lengnick-Hall, C.A., Beck, T.E., Lengnick-Hall, M.L.: Developing a capacity for organizational resilience through strategic human resource management. Human resource management review, **21**(3), 243-255 (2011)

Lee, G., Kwak, Y.H.: An open government maturity model for social media-based public engagement. Gov. Inf. Q. **29**(4), 492–503 (2012)

Niemimaa, M., Järveläinen, J., Heikkilä, M., Heikkilä, J.: Business continuity of business models: evaluating the resilience of business models for contingencies. Int. J. Inf. Manage. **49**, 208–216 (2019)

Orlando, J.: BEST PRACTICES: business continuity planning for distance education. J. Contin. High. Educ. **55**(2), 23–29 (2007)

Patzelt, H., Shepherd, D.A.: Recognizing opportunities for sustainable development. Entrep. Theory Pract. **35**(4), 631–652 (2011)

Pennington-Gray, L., Thapa, B., Kaplanidou, K., Cahyanto, I., McLaughlin, E.: Crisis planning and preparedness in the United States tourism industry. Cornell Hospitality Q. **52**(3), 312–320 (2011)

Prayag, G., Spector, S., Orchiston, C., Chowdhury, M.: Psychological resilience, organizational resilience and life satisfaction in tourism firms: insights from the Canterbury earthquakes. Curr. Issue Tour. **23**(10), 1216–1233 (2020)

Queensland Government (2013). Customer Impact Survey 2013 [Data file]. Available from Survey Data Archive, Queensland Government. https://data.qld.gov.au/dataset/2934669f-1b40-43c1-832d-3c1528ca6974

Rezaei Soufi, H., Torabi, S.A., Sahebjamnia, N.: Developing a novel quantitative framework for business continuity planning. Int. J. Prod. Res. **57**(3), 779–800 (2019)

Runyan, R.C.: Small business in the face of crisis: identifying barriers to recovery from a natural disaster 1. J. Contingencies Crisis Manag. **14**(1), 12–26 (2006)

Sahebjamnia, N., Torabi, S.A., Mansouri, S.A.: Integrated business continuity and disaster recovery planning: towards organizational resilience. Eur. J. Oper. Res. **242**(1), 261–273 (2015)

Smith, D., Shea, M., Wu, W.N.: Collaborative resource sharing between public and school libraries. Interlending Document Supply **42**(4), 159–164 (2014)

Torabi, S.A., Giahi, R., Sahebjamnia, N.: An enhanced risk assessment framework for business continuity management systems. Saf. Sci. **89**, 201–218 (2016)

Wang, C.W., Chiu, C., Wu, W.N., Lin, C.J.: Impact of rollover risk and corporate policy on extreme risk in the taiwanese manufacturing industry. Rev. Pac. Basin Financ. Mark. Policies **20**(03), 1750019 (2017)

Wong, W.N.Z.: The strategic skills of business continuity managers: putting business continuity management into corporate long-term planning. J. Bus. Contin. Emer. Plan. **4**(1), 62–68 (2009)

Wu, W.N., Chang, S.M., Collins, B.K.: Mobilizing voluntary organizations in Taiwanese emergency response: citizen engagement and local fire branch heads. J. Contemp. East. Asia **14**(2), 45–55 (2015)

Wu, W.-N.: Features of smart city services in the local government context: a case study of San Francisco 311 system. In: Nah, F.-H., Siau, K. (eds.) HCII 2020. LNCS, vol. 12204, pp. 216–227. Springer, Cham (2020). https://doi.org/10.1007/978-3-030-50341-3_17

# Innovation, Collaboration, and Knowledge Sharing

# A Study of Teamwork's Productivity and Search Behavior Using Talent Themes for Grouping

Jeng-Her Alex Chen[1]([✉]), Bo-chiuan Su[2], and Chi-Hui Chen[1]

[1] College of Management, Yuan Ze University, Taoyuan City, Taiwan
`alex@saturn.yzu.edu.tw`, `s1022358@mail.yzu.edu.tw3`
[2] Department of Information Management, National Dong Hwa University,
Hualien City, Taiwan
`bsu@gms.ndhu.edu.tw`

**Abstract.** The purpose of this research was to find a grouping method that can instantly improve team productivity so that various organizations can use this grouping method to organize the team to achieve better performance. We conducted two experiments and evaluated the teams' productivity of all groups and recorded conversation records and search behaviors of all subjects who were identified as one of the 4 categories: Execution, Influence, Relationship Building, and Strategic Thinking. For search behavior, the results show the Influence category has higher number of average different keyword searches than that of Relationship-Building category. Influence category has higher number of average different keywords than Execution category. For self-efficacy, although there is no significant difference in the confidence level between the talent categories, the Strategic Thinking category have a higher degree of confidence compared to other categories, while people belonging to the Influence category have lower confidence level than any of the other three categories. As for teamwork's productivity, the group with the highest productivity is the heterogeneous talent group with one month time of collaboration or break-in, second is the immediate homogeneous talent group, third is the immediate random group, and the group with the lowest productivity is the immediate (with no time to break-in) heterogeneous talent group.

**Keywords:** Search behavior · Self-efficacy · Clifton strengths finder · Talent themes · Teamwork's productivity

## 1 Introduction

According to Tom Rath and Barry Conchie's research [1], Strengths Based Leadership, they grouped participants based on participants' talent themes and found that in order to achieve teams' maximum productivity, it is important to let each individual perform his/her talent and within each group individual's talents should be balanced and complimentary to each other. Marcus Buckingham and Donald O Clifton [2] classified 34 characteristics human talent themes, they advanced that people should find their own advantage, and learn and practice with the advantaged talent themes to achieve success.

© Springer Nature Switzerland AG 2021
F. F.-H. Nah and K. Siau (Eds.): HCII 2021, LNCS 12783, pp. 459–470, 2021.
https://doi.org/10.1007/978-3-030-77750-0_29

Rath and Conchie [1] further categorized all 34 talents themes into 4 categories: Execution, Influence, Relationship Building, and Strategic Thinking. Execution people know how to accomplish the expected goals and can master the focus of doing things and realize it. Influence people are good at conveying his/her own ideas to others, including members within or outside the organization, Relationship Building are good at communication, and can make the relationship within team even closer and make the whole team perform better. Finally the Strategic Thinking type of people are more foresighted, and good at analyzing information to help team make better decision. Because the 4 talent categories each has different behavior, we hypothesize that during teamwork task different talent categories would behave differently.

Among other studies of differences between talent theme categories, Chuck Tomkovick and Scott Swanson [3] studied the impact of individual talent themes on career development, they used the same categorization that Rath and Conchie [1] used in 2004 and divided talents into 4 categories. Chuck et al. found Execution people will continue to accept new ideas and can carry out intentions to make ideas come true. And those in the Influence category who have the talents of Activator will turn their thoughts into actions. People who belong to the relationship establishment category will establish a good organizational relationship. Among them, those who have a talent for relator would be called relying on others and establishing close relationships with others. Those who belong to the Strategic Thinking category will help the organization make better decisions. Rath and Conchie's study [1] argued that a successful team must contain four different types of talents. Julie Connelly [4] also believed that when building teams one should pay attention to the diversity of talents of members. This makes teams with similar talents more efficient. Teams with talented and diverse members need to be belonged to small teams, only in this way can teams have a consensus and will have better productivity. Connelly's research [4] allows company employees to use the CSF (Clifton Strengths Finder) test to find out their personal talents, the company responded to the findings and then encouraged employees develop their talents, the study found those who were encouraged to developed their talents enhanced participation and get 50% increase in productivity. Therefore, he believes that the process of developing talent can be regarded as a forward-looking element of productivity, and the diversity of talents within a team can be regarded as a forward-looking element of team productivity. Shane J Lopez and Michelle C Louis [5] in the study of educational curriculum developed by talent argued that positioning individual talents can establish interpersonal relationships with others, and education developed by talents can cultivate longer-term and good interpersonal relationships. Through a team that develops a cooperative relationship with talents, it is possible to share the talents of each other among members and to fill in each other's shortcomings. Therefore, the grouping method with heterogeneous talents can form a good team. The research of Luther N Waters [6] explored the influence of talent development on self-efficacy in education. The research results showed that the development of personal talent does have a positive effect on self-efficacy, and time is an important factor affecting the development of talent. In this research the author also classified talent themes into 4 categories: Initiators, Implementers, Actuators and Motivators. Among them, those who are Inspirers have more foresight and ideas and correspond to the Strategic Thinking category in the research classification of Rath and

Conchie [1]. Those who belong to the Implementer know how to observe the ceremony and allocate resources to achieve the goal and correspond to the Execution category. The person who belongs to the Actuator knows how to arrange appropriate work for team members and corresponds to the Relationship Building category. Those who are Motivators encourage members and help the team achieve goals and echo the Influence category. The purpose of this research was to find a grouping method that can instantly improve team productivity, and to promote this grouping method, so that various organizations such as academic units can use this grouping method to organize the team to achieve better performance.

## 2  Theoretical Background and Hypotheses

### 2.1  Search Strategy

A study by Diana Tabatabai and Bruce M Shore [7] found that Internet users have different search strategies. They found that differences in proficiency and background knowledge will affect the strategy in the search process. Experts use more keywords to search, and search faster, and even use the "Ctrl + F" search function more often when searching. Beginners use "Backspace" more often and miss related websites more often. Like the work by Lazonder, Biemans et al. [8], the study found that people with higher Internet use experience require less time during the search process. And there are fewer search errors and fewer search actions in the process. In this study, we explored the differences in the search behavior of subjects, including search behaviors such as search keywords, number of words, and the number of searches using different keywords. We hypothesized that the average number of web pages visited by the talent theory group is higher than that of the random grouping team, and the average number of different keywords used by the talent theory grouping team will be more than that of the random grouping team. Tabatabai and Shore [7] found that metacognitive, cognitive and prior knowledge are important factors that affect search strategies. Sherry Y Chen and Xiaohui Liu [9] also used cognitive theory to study students' learning patterns through the Internet, and learned that different cognitive styles do affect personal search behavior. This research was based on individual talents as a distinction. We hypothesized that different talented personalities may have different search behaviors. According to the talent theory of Rath and Conchie [1], each talent category has different characteristics, there may have different performances or behaviors in the team. Therefore, the following hypotheses are listed below:

**Hypothesis 1 (H1)**: the search behavior is different between different talent categories

H1.1 Average number of different keyword searches used is different between different talent categories.

H1.2 Average number of webpages viewed is different between different talent categories.

H1.3 Average number of search words used is different between different talent categories.

H1.4 Average number of search terms used is different between different talent categories.

H1.5 Average focusing time on websites is different between different talent categories.

## 2.2 Self-efficacy

According to the research of Albert Bandura and Dale H Schunk [10], they explored the self-motivation of individuals through setting goals, and at the same time cultivate personal competence, self-efficacy and intrinsic interest. Through the experiment of the subjects in the math test, they found that there is a high consistency between self-efficacy and test scores, which means that there is a high correlation between the two. This means that under certain circumstances, self-efficacy can be regarded as an important indicator of whether you can accomplish your goals. This study also studied the self-efficacy of subjects by recording their self-assessment, and hypothesized that the self-efficacy of teams grouped by talent theory is higher than that of teams randomly grouped.

In the research that explore the influence of personal talent advantages on self-efficacy, Elston and Boniwell [11] discussed the discovery of personal strengths and their application in the work environment, they explained Buckingham and Clifton's talent theory [2] and Govindji and Linley's [12] research on Personal Strengths. Elston and Boniwell found that personal advantage can bring positive emotions to individuals at work and workers feel more valuable to work and be more willing to act. Elston and Boniwell also quoted the research results of Govindji and Linley [12] that the cognition and application of personal strengths have a significant impact on self-efficacy. Therefore, this study explored the influence of the grouping by talent theory on personal self-efficacy, and we hypothesized that grouping by talent theory will improve the self-efficacy of the subjects, which in turn affects team performance. This study explored the influence of grouping teams by talent theory on search behavior and self-efficacy, and according to the research of Hill and Hannafin [13] and the research of Tsai and Tsai (2003), self-efficacy is a factor that affects search efficiency. Therefore, we hypothesized that the self-efficacy of different talent categories is different.

**Hypothesis 2 (H2)**: the self-efficacy of different talent categories is different.

## 2.3 Participation

Qiyun Wang et al. [14] argued that the rate of students using Facebook is quite popular, the results showed that Facebook's community function does indeed has the possibility of serving as a learning management system (Learning Management System). For students, Facebook's platform can be used as a platform for students to discuss their shoul work. Madge, Meek et al. [15] also maintained that Facebook is an important social tool for college students. Although most students do not like to use Facebook as a teaching tool, some students still use Facebook for class discussions. Therefore, in this research, Facebook's community function was used as a platform for students to discuss and communicate in groups during the research process. After dividing team into four categories according to the talent theory of Rath and Conchie [1], since each talent category has different characteristics, we hypothesized that each talent category performs differently in the teamwork task.

**Hypothesis 3 (H3)**: each talent category participates differently in the teamwork task.

H3.1 Average total number of speeches is different between different talent categories.

H3.2 Average number of speeches per person related to the production of Excel files is different between different talent categories.

H3.3 Average number of speeches per person about the division of labor for making Excel is different between different talent categories.

H3.4 The number of data sources provided per person is different between different talent categories.

### 2.4  Teamwork's Productivity

According to the research of Waters [6], "time" is an important factor affecting personal development talent. King [16] also argued that the length of time team members get along also affects whether team members can establish trust relationships. This study conducted two experiments and got 4 different kinds of teams based on talent themes grouping with "time" factor. They are: heterogeneous team with real time assignment, random team, homogeneous team with real time assignment, and heterogeneous team with one month time to break in. We hypothesized that teamwork's productivity is different among the teams with homogeneous or heterogeneous talent themes, and with time to break-in or not.

**Hypothesis 4 (H4)**: teamwork's productivity is different among the teams of heterogeneous talents and real-time grouping, the same talent and real-time grouping, random grouping, and heterogeneous talents and given about one month to break-in.

## 3  Methodology and Research Design

The first experiment enlisted 44 participants in immediate (with no time to break-in) heterogeneous talent group, and 59 participants in immediate random group. The second experiment enlisted 40 participants in immediate homogeneous talent group, and 36 participants in heterogeneous talent group with one month time of collaboration or break-in. With 4 persons form 1 group making a total of 45 groups or teams (180 subjects) participated the study. All participants were volunteers of first year student in a university taking the same course of Excel, the tool used the task of the experiment.

The experiment process consisted of three stages. The first stage is for all subjects in the experimental group to take an online test of talent theory and get each participant's top 5 talent themes. In the second stage, through the research of Rath and Conchie [1], the subjects in the experimental group were divided into heterogeneous groups according to the theory of talent (first experiment), so that each group had people with different talent categories. The third stage was to let the control group randomly grouped and the experimental group grouped by talent theory to perform the same team task. We evaluated the teams' productivity of all groups and recorded conversation records and search behaviors of all subjects. The task is to "seeking the best solution" that the subjects learned in high school. Use the Excel software learned in university courses, and use the "group" as the unit to jointly design a set of tutorials on "seeking the best solution". The tutorials must include questions and answering methods. And must be designed with Microsoft Excel software, and each group must create an Excel file together. Each group had 20 min to complete the task. Once the 20-min time limit was up, regardless of the degree of completion of each group, each group must upload the created Excel file to the designated computer host. The researcher then evaluated the task performance of each group. In order to fully collect the communication process and records of all subjects in the team, all the groups were not allowed to discuss verbally in the experiment, but they were allowed to use the Facebook social networking site as the only tool for communication. Through the Facebook community, we can completely record the conversation records of all groups. In this way, we can observe whether grouping through talent theory can increase the number of speeches and participation of team members. During the task, individual subjects was asked in the Facebook community of each group how confident they were in completing the task. In the 20-min task, the researcher asked about participants' confidence level 5 times in total including the first time asking just before participant started the task. After recording the confidence level data of all subjects, we analyzed the changes in the subjects' confidence to see whether there are differences between different talent categories.

### 3.1 Data Analysis and Results

**Hypothesis Testing**
We use ANOVA and Repeated ANOVA to test hypotheses H1 through H5.

Hypothesis 1.1: our results supported the hypotheses that the average number of different keywords used between different talent categories is statistically different ($F = 4.58$, $p < 0.0071$). Thereby supporting Hypotheses 1.1. Further investigation with Tukey multiple comparison test on Table1 shows that there is a significant difference between the Influence category and the Relationship-Building category. The Influence category has higher number of average different keyword searches than that of Relationship-Building category by at least 0.56 at most 7.4 different keyword searches at 95% confidence level. And Influence category has higher number of average different keywords than Execution category by at least 1.35 at most 9.30 different keyword searches at 95% confidence level.

Hypothesis 1.2 to 1.5: our results did not support Hypothesis 1.2 to 1.5 ($F = 2.16$, 1.24, 1.24, 0.93, $p < 0.1059$, 0.3057, 0.3050, 0.4365, respectively). In other words, Average number of webpages viewed, search words used, search terms used, and focus time is not statistically different between different talent categories.

Table 2 shows that people belonging to the Execution category have a low number of different keyword searches and search words in Table 1. In the Waters study [6], it argued

**Table 1.** Hypothesis 1 Tukey multiple comparison

| | talent Comparison | Difference Between Means | Simultaneous 95% Confidence Limits | | |
|---|---|---|---|---|---|
| Influence | - Relationship Building | 3.98 | 0.56 | 7.41 | *** |
| Influence | - Strategic Thinking | 4.18 | -0.88 | 9.24 | |
| Influence | - Execution | 5.33 | 1.35 | 9.31 | *** |
| Relationship Building | - Influence | -3.98 | -7.41 | -0.56 | *** |
| Relationship Building | - Strategic Thinking | 0.19 | -4.13 | 4.52 | |
| Relationship Building | - Execution | 1.34 | -1.64 | 4.33 | |
| Strategic Thinking | - Influence | -4.18 | -9.24 | 0.88 | |
| Strategic Thinking | - Relationship Building | -0.19 | -4.52 | 4.13 | |
| Strategic Thinking | - Execution | 1.15 | -3.62 | 5.92 | |
| Execution | - Influence | -5.33 | -9.31 | -1.35 | *** |
| Execution | - Relationship Building | -1.34 | -4.33 | 1.64 | |
| Execution | - Strategic Thinking | -1.15 | -5.92 | 3.62 | |

Comparisons significant at the 0.05 level are indicated by ***.

**Table 2.** Hypothesis 1 the search behavior between different talent categories

| Talent | Mean of 'avg different keyword searches' | Mean of 'avg view webpages | Mean of 'avg search words' | Mean of 'avg search terms' | Mean of 'avg focus time' |
|---|---|---|---|---|---|
| Execution | 3.10 | 42.90 | 4.941 | 1.57 | 848.50 |
| Influence | 8.43 | 67.71 | 6.51 | 1.70 | 964 |
| Relationship Building | 4.44 | 45.59 | 5.97 | 1.34 | 811.22 |
| Strategic Thinking | 4.25 | 59.25 | 5.45 | 1.36 | 760 |

that the leadership characteristics of Implementers is similar to the Execution category which is more prone towards the idea part, so there may be less practical actions. The results show that the search behaviors of the four categories in the team task are different. The average number of different keywords used by people belonging to the Influence category is 8.43, which is significantly higher than the other three categories.

According to Waters [6], he classified the Influence category into the Motivators category in his own way, this kind of people's traits in team tasks tend to be fulfilled (Fruition), so they pay more attention to the completion of the task. Tomkovick and

Swanson [3] argued that those who belong to the Influence category who have a talent of Activator turn their thoughts into actions. Our results are consistent with previous research that the Influence category take action on the task, so they actively searched in the team task.

Table 2 shows the average number of search words and average number of search terms for people belonging to the Influence category are 6.51 and 1.7 respectively, which are also higher than those of the other three categories. It means people in this category use more keywords and words when searching. People in this category have 67.71 views of webpages, which is also significantly higher than the other three categories. The average follow time on the webpage is 964 s, which is also higher than that of the other three categories. It indicates people in the Influence category are more focused on online search behavior. As Waters [6] said, the leadership traits of this category of people tend to be fulfilled (Fruition), so they may actively seek information to complete team tasks.

Hypothesis 2: our results did not support the hypotheses that the self-efficacy of different talent categories is different. From the results of the Repeated Measurement of the Variance Analysis from Table 2, the significant p-values of Greenhouse-Geisser Epsilon and Huynh-Feldt-Lecoutre Epsilon are 0.82 and 0.90 respectively, which are both greater than the significant level of 0.05, indicating that there is no significant difference in the interaction between the change in confidence level and the talent category. The result indicates there is no significant difference in the confidence level between the talent categories (Table 3).

**Table 3.** Hypothesis 2

| | |
|---|---|
| Greenhouse-Geisser Epsilon | 0.82 |
| Huynh-Feldt-Lecoutre Epsilon | 0.90 |

From Table 4 above, we can see how confident people in the category of Strategic Thinking responded to the five times asking their confidence level during the team's task. Strategic Thinking's five-time confidence levels are always higher than any of the other three talent categories, whether it is before the mission (C1 time), during the mission, or after the mission (C5 time). From the line chart above, we can also see that the confidence level of people in the Strategic Thinking category is different from those in the other three categories. According to Waters [6], Initiators who are similar to Strategic Thinking categories are more likely to see the potential of the team. Once the goals are set, they are confident that they can accomplish the goals. Therefore, those who belong to the Strategic Thinking category have a higher degree of confidence in this team task. Table 4 indicates that for people belonging to the Influence category all the 5 times confidence levels are lower than that of the other three categories.

**Table 4.** Confidence change

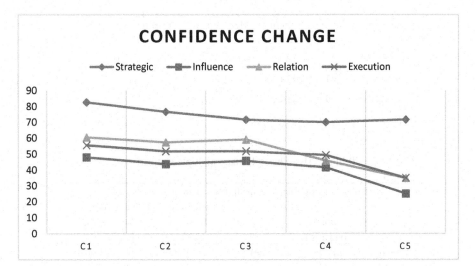

- Hypothesis 3.1 to 3.4: our results did not support the hypotheses that each talent category participates differently in the teamwork task ((F = 1.32, 1.95, 2.07, 1.95, p > 0.28, 1.14, 0.12, 0.14, respectively). That is, average total number of speeches, average number of speeches per person related to the production of Excel files, average number of speeches per person about the division of labor, and the number of data sources provided per person between different talent categories are not statistically different.
- Hypothesis 4: our results on table 5 supported the hypotheses that teamwork's productivity is different among the teams of heterogeneous talents and real-time grouping, the same talent and real-time grouping, random grouping, and heterogeneous talents and given about one month to break-in (F = 3.58, p < 0.02). Thereby supporting Hypothesis 4. Further investigation with Tukey multiple comparison test shows that there is a significant difference between heterogeneous talents group with one month to break-in and heterogeneous talents group with real-time grouping. The productivity of the heterogeneous with break-in time group is at least 0.42 at most 8.41 more than that of the real-time homogeneous group (Table 6).

Table 7 shows each of the 4 team's productivity. Teams that are grouped by heterogeneous talents and given about one month to break-in produced the greatest team productivity (productivity 11.78), followed by the same talent and real-time grouping method (productivity 10.8). The third is the method of random grouping (productivity 8.93), and the worst is the team with heterogeneous talents and real-time grouping (productivity 7.36).

**Table 5.** Hypothesis 4

| Source | DF | Sum of squares | Mean square | F value | Pr > F |
|--------|----|----|----|----|----|
| Model | 3 | 118.57 | 39.52 | 3.58 | 0.02 |
| Error | 41 | 452.63 | 11.04 | | |
| Corrected total | 44 | 571.20 | | | |

**Table 6.** Hypothesis 4 Tukey multiple comparison

| group Comparison | Difference Between Means | Simultaneous 95% Confidence Limits | | |
|----|----|----|----|----|
| Comparisons significant at the 0.05 level are indicated by ***. | | | | |
| hetero(break in) - homo(real time) | 0.98 | -3.11 | 5.067 | |
| hetero(break in) - random | 2.84 | -0.91 | 6.60 | |
| hetero(break in) - hetero(real time) | 4.41 | 0.42 | 8.41 | *** |
| homo(real time) - hetero(break in) | -0.98 | -5.07 | 3.11 | |
| homo(real time) - random | 1.87 | -1.77 | 5.50 | |
| homo(real time) - hetero(real time) | 3.44 | -0.45 | 7.32 | |
| random - hetero(break in) | -2.84 | -6.60 | 0.91 | |
| random - homo(real time) | -1.87 | -5.50 | 1.77 | |
| random - hetero(real time) | 1.57 | -1.96 | 5.10 | |
| hetero(real time) - hetero(break in) | -4.41 | -8.41 | -0.42 | *** |
| hetero(real time) - homo(real time) | -3.44 | -7.3 | 0.45 | |
| hetero(real time) - random | -1.57 | -5.10 | 1.96 | |

**Table 7.** Teamwork's productivity

| | Hetero (real time) | Random (real time) | Homo (real time) | Hetero (break in) |
|----|----|----|----|----|
| Teamwork's productivity | 7.36 | 8.93 | 10.80 | 11.78 |

# 4 Discussion

Real-time grouping with heterogeneous talents does not improve team productivity, and no previous literature has proposed the shortcomings of real-time grouping with heterogeneous talents. Therefore, this is a new finding in the related research. The Waters study [6] maintained that it is best to have 6 months to 1 year for the subjects to fully develop their personal talents. For future research, it is recommended to extend the team break-in time to at least 6 months. However, our study found that one month of breaking-in time can also increase team productivity, which is also a new finding not found in related studies.

As for the difference in confidence between the talent categories, we learned that the confidence of the people belonging to the strategic thinking category is higher than any of the other three talent categories. Moreover, the change in confidence level in the 15th and 20th min of the team task is also different from the other three talent categories. The confidence level of people who fall into the category of Strategic Thinking, on the contrary, changes from lower to higher as the task is over. Perhaps people in the Strategic Thinking category were not affected by time pressure when the team task is in progress, or they were confident that they can complete the team task.

## 5  Limitation

In the study, the control group was randomly assigned to the Random group. However, none of the subjects in the control group had ever tested the talent theory test. So we don't know the talent category of the control subjects. Perhaps, the control group has a team of the same type of talent, so it performs better in team tasks than the test team. In this study, the grouping method of talent homogeneity with break-in time is not discussed. Therefore, in future research, it is recommended to conduct further research in a homogeneous group and give time to break-in to explore the differences between homogeneous grouping and random grouping and heterogeneous grouping based on talent theory.

## 6  Conclusion

Based on the talents theory, this study tries to contribute to the academic fields by providing insightful results from two experiments to find a grouping method that can instantly improve teamwork's productivity. The results show the group with the highest productivity is the heterogeneous talent group with one month time of collaboration or break-in, second is the immediate homogeneous talent group, third is the immediate random group, and the group with the lowest productivity is the immediate (with no time to break-in) heterogeneous talent group. The results is consistent with Rath and Conchie's work (2009) which argues that the team must include members with different talents. The results are also consistent with the work of Waters (2009) which maintains that time is a very important factor for teamwork development. Therefore, we conclude when building a team, one must consider the different talents of the members, and "time" should be given to the team members to maximize the team's productivity. In other words, for enterprise organizations, if there is enough time to prepare before the task is executed, you should consider the grouping method of talent heterogeneity (with break-in time), giving at least one month or more time for breaking-in, which can achieve better results.

# References

1. Rath, T., Conchie, B.: Strengths Based Leadership. City: Gallup Pressb (2009)
2. Buckingham, M., Clifton, D.O.: Now, discover your strengths: Simon and Schuster (2001)
3. Tomkovick, C., Swanson, S.: Using strengthsfinder to identify relationships between marketing graduate strengths and career outcomes. Mark. Educ. Rev. **24**(3), 197–212 (2014)
4. Connelly, J.: All together now. Gallup Manag. J. **2**(1), 13–18 (2002)
5. Lopez, S.J., Louis, M.C.: The principles of strengths-based education. J. Coll. Character **10**(4) (2009)
6. Waters, L.N.: The effect of the knowledge and application of Signature Strengths on the perception of self-efficacy of educational administrators: Identifying hopefulness on the island of leadership. (Ed.D.). Azusa Pacific University, Ann Arbor. ProQuest Dissertations & Theses A&I database (2009)
7. Tabatabai, D., Shore, B.M.: How experts and novices search the Web. Libr. Inf. Sci. Res. **27**(2), 222–248 (2005)
8. Lazonder, A.W., Biemans, H.J., Wopereis, I.G.: Differences between novice and experienced users in searching information on the World Wide Web. J. Am. Soc. Inf. Sci. **51**(6), 576–581 (2000)
9. Chen, S.Y., Liu, X.: An integrated approach for modeling learning patterns of students in Web-based instruction: a cognitive style perspective. ACM Trans. Comput.-Hum. Interact. (TOCHI) **15**(1), 1 (2008)
10. Bandura, A., Schunk, D.H.: Cultivating competence, self-efficacy, and intrinsic interest through proximal self-motivation. J. Pers. Soc. Psychol. **41**(3), 586 (1981)
11. Elston, F., Boniwell, I.: A grounded theory study of the value derived by women in financial services through a coaching intervention to help them identify their strengths and practice using them in the workplace. Int. Coach. Psychol. Rev. **6**(1), 16–32 (2011)
12. Govindji, R., Linley, P.A.: Strengths use, self-concordance and well-being: implications for strengths coaching and coaching psychologists. Int. Coach. Psychol. Rev. **2**(2), 143–153 (2007)
13. Hill, J.R., Hannafin, M.J.: Cognitive strategies and learning from the World Wide Web. Educ. Tech. Res. Dev. **45**(4), 37–64 (1997)
14. Wang, Q., Woo, H.L., Quek, C.L., Yang, Y., Liu, M.: Using the Facebook group as a learning management system: an exploratory study. Br. J. Edu. Technol. **43**(3), 428–438 (2012)
15. Madge, C., Meek, J., Wellens, J., Hooley, T.: Facebook, social integration and informal learning at university: 'It is more for socialising and talking to friends about work than for actually doing work.' Learn. Media Technol. **34**(2), 141–155 (2009)
16. King, W.B.: Contributions made by a strengths-oriented intervention to trusting relationships within pre-existing teams. (3548187 Ed.D.). Azusa Pacific University, Ann Arbor. ProQuest Dissertations & Theses A&I database (2012)

# The Effect of Gamification on Knowledge Contribution in Online Q&A Communities: A Perspective of Social Comparison

Langtao Chen[✉] [iD]

Department of Business and Information Technology,
Missouri University of Science and Technology, Rolla, MO 65409, USA
chenla@mst.edu

**Abstract.** Online questioning and answering (Q&A) communities have become an essential social media platform for individuals to exchange specialized knowledge and collaboratively solve problems. Various gamified design elements (such as reputation scores, badges, levels, and leaderboards, etc.) have been applied in online Q&A communities to motivate users' knowledge contribution on which the sustainability of such communities depends. Current studies generally assume that motivational sources originate directly from the gamified elements. From the perspective of social comparison theory, this research proposes that the motivational affordances motivating knowledge contribution in online communities can be activated from the comparison of virtual rewards offered by gamified design features. Thus, the effect of gamified elements on a user's behavior is determined, at least partially, by the social influence of how other users in the community are rewarded by the gamification mechanism. This research contributes to theory by providing a new perspective for understanding the effect of gamification on knowledge contribution in online Q&A communities. It also provides important practical implications for the design and management of sustainable online communities.

**Keywords:** Social comparison · Gamification · Knowledge contribution · Online Q&A communities

## 1 Introduction

With the rapid spreading of information technology and the Internet, online questioning and answering (Q&A) communities have become an important source of knowledge. By participating in such communities, an individual can conveniently acquire knowledge and access a large number of experts or resources that are otherwise not available in the user's physical social network. While online communities offer significant benefits to participants, maintaining an online community relies on the voluntary contribution of a significant number of active participants. However, the reality is that most online community participants are lurkers who rarely contribute [1]. Thus, motivating user contribution is an ongoing debate in the area of online communities, given the fact that

© Springer Nature Switzerland AG 2021
F. F.-H. Nah and K. Siau (Eds.): HCII 2021, LNCS 12783, pp. 471–481, 2021.
https://doi.org/10.1007/978-3-030-77750-0_30

the service quality and sustainability of online communities are determined mainly by continuous user contribution.

Nowadays, many information systems, including online communities, have adopted the design of gamified elements to motivate user intention to use the information systems. Gamification generally refers to incorporating game elements into the design of information systems to provide motivational affordances that incentivize user behaviors in non-game contexts. Many online communities have implemented gamified elements such as usefulness votes, experience points, reputation scores, badges, levels, and leaderboards [2] to maintain existing users and attract new ones. For example, Chen et al. [3] found that usefulness voting in online knowledge communities is an important motivational affordance that incentivizes user knowledge contribution.

Although gamification has been widely regarded as a powerful means of motivating user participation in online communities, there is a lack of research in the literature that applies robust theoretical frameworks to interpret how gamification mechanisms affect user behaviors in online communities [4, 5], especially from the perspective of social comparison. To fill the research gap, this research aims to explore the effect of social comparison to understand how gamified motivational affordances drive user knowledge contribution. Given the gamified design elements implemented in online Q&A communities to evoke a relatively high level of competition among participants, the perspective of social comparison is especially important for understanding user behaviors in this competitive setting. Specifically, the following research question is asked:

*Research Question*: How does gamification affect user knowledge contribution through social comparison in online Q&A communities?

This paper is organized as follows. The next section reviews relevant theoretical background and proposes a research model with hypotheses. Then, research methods are explained in Sect. 3, followed by the discussion of implications and future research directions in Sect. 4. Section 5 concludes this research.

## 2 Theoretical Background and Hypotheses

Figure 1 presents the proposed research model with hypotheses. As illustrated clearly in the model, both upward and downward comparisons of reputation scores are suggested to be positively associated with knowledge contribution behavior. In addition, user involvement is hypothesized to moderate the main effects of upward and downward comparisons. The following subsections explain the theoretical background and rationale for the research model.

### 2.1 Gamification in Online Communities

Users participate in online communities for various reasons, such as obtaining social support, acquiring knowledge, and solving problems they encountered [3, 6, 7]. To attain

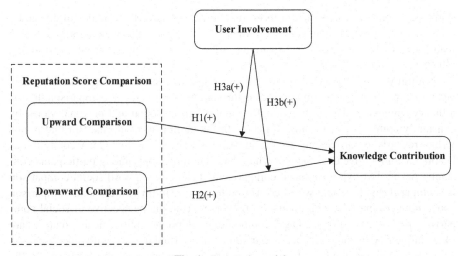

**Fig. 1.** Research model.

participants' social interaction goals, online communities need various social and technical mechanisms that facilitate social interaction and motivate user engagement. Gamification mechanisms have been applied to various non-game settings, including online communities, to engage users. Specifically, virtual rewards or statuses are granted to individuals who have achieved certain explicitly defined goals. As people have a pervasive tendency to seek self-superiority and, indeed, perceive the self as better than others [8], gamification provides a means for people to enhance their well-being. From the perspective of affordance [9], gamified design elements can offer motivational affordances to motivate preferred user behaviors. Gamification is a particularly powerful mechanism for online Q&A communities where user contributions are largely voluntary without tangible economic compensation [3].

Gamified online Q&A communities are socio-technical systems with complicated mechanisms and dynamics. Understanding user behaviors and dynamics in such systems can be from different perspectives. One way to comprehend the effect of gamification on user behaviors is to view gamified elements as a source of social influence that occurs through various processes. Previous studies have investigated a variety of factors that incentivize user contribution in online communities from various perspectives, such as self-determination theory and social learning theory. Self-determination theory is a motivation-based framework that explains how certain social-contextual factors promote the process of self-motivation and positive human potentials [10, 11]. For example, based on self-determination theory, Chen et al. [3] found that usefulness voting is an important motivational affordance that encourages knowledge contribution in online Q&A communities. On the other hand, social learning theory posits that human behavior is shaped by building a mental model of certain behavior and its consequences through observing others [12]. From the perspective of social learning theory, Cheung et al. [13] found that online social interactions, in the forms of both observational and reinforcement learning, positively affect customer information contribution behavior in online social shopping communities. Although those theoretical frameworks provide solid foundations to explain the mechanism of gamification, they generally view gamified design features as a direct source of motivational affordances, largely ignoring motivational affordances generated from social comparison.

Naturally, another perspective for understanding the impact of gamification on user behaviors in online Q&A communities is through the lens of social comparison theory, a theory suggesting that an individual evaluates her/his social and personal worth by constantly comparing with others [14]. With the gamification mechanism that grants virtual rewards to participants according to certain criteria, online Q&A communities become a competitive environment where social comparisons among participants constantly occur. Two types of social comparisons include (1) upward social comparison by comparing with people who perform better, and (2) downward social comparison concerning comparison with others doing worse. From the perspective of social comparison, participants in online Q&A communities adopting gamified design features are likely influenced by the constant comparison of their virtual rewards with other users. As a result, participants tend to adjust their knowledge contribution behavior based on the results of social comparison. Interestingly, however, research has yet to comprehensively consider the impact of social comparison in online Q&A communities.

### 2.2 Social Comparison Theory

Social comparison theory is a powerful theoretical framework for understanding human behaviors. The central tenet of social comparison theory is that humans have a natural tendency to compare themselves with others to more accurately evaluate their opinions and abilities [14]. The theoretical basis of social comparison has been applied in previous information systems studies. For example, in the context of software development, Ang and Slaughter [15] argued that contract and permanent software professionals in the same team would compare with each other and thus likely form different attitudes and behaviors. In the setting of user support forums, Jabr et al. [16] suggested that solution providers' behaviors are influenced by the number of peers as well as the performance of these peers in the community due to social comparison. In the environment of social network services, Lim and Yang [17] found that social comparison to media figures is associated with emotional responses, including envy and shame, as well as with behavioral intention and psychological consequences. In addition, Johnson and Knobloch-Westerwick [18] found that users with negative mood spend more time in social networking sites to downward comparison and less time to upward comparison. However, research has yet to examine the social comparison of gamified virtual rewards in online communities.

This research examines how participants in online Q&A communities are influenced by socially comparing each other's virtual rewards provided by gamification. Social comparison of virtual rewards becomes salient when participants are involved in social interactions in online communities. Accordingly, when participants work together to solve problems, they view or examine virtual rewards with each other. As a result, an automatic social comparison process is activated that can have a significant impact on user behaviors.

## 2.3  The Effect of Social Comparison on Knowledge Contribution

In the setting of online Q&A communities that have implemented gamification mechanisms, various virtual rewards of gamified elements are evident signals for social comparison as these rewards are often presented clearly in a variety of forms to everyone participating in the community. Thus, social comparisons are a function of experiencing these virtual rewards and an automatic comparison triggered by the experience. This research examines reputation score as a specific type of virtual rewards because it is commonly used in various online community settings and has been widely theorized or analyzed in prior studies [3, 5, 19, 20].

Social comparison literature distinguishes two main types of directional social comparisons: (1) upward comparison (i.e., comparing with people who are better off than self); and (2) downward comparison (i.e., comparing with others who are worse off). It is widely regarded that upward and downward comparisons work through different mechanisms in affecting human perceptions and behavioral consequences. Upward comparison is generally treated as a force that reduces self-esteem and mood, while downward comparison often associates with higher self-evaluation. In the organizational setting, Brown et al. [21] found that upward comparisons are negatively associated with job satisfaction and affective commitment, whereas downward comparisons positively associate with both job satisfaction and affective commitment. However, studies have suggested that upward comparison can also enhance people's self-assessments and lead to positive effects on mood and self-esteem. For example, Collins [22] suggested that people frequently seek out upward comparison as a way to achieve and maintain superiority.

Consistent with Collins [22], in the context of online Q&A communities where paths toward gaining virtual rewarding are clear and achievable, upward comparison of virtual rewards likely results in a higher level of self-esteem and commitment to the community. As Brickman and Bulman [23] argued, individuals experiencing upward comparison, though painful, may obtain more useful information by observing superior others. Upward comparison in online Q&A communities motivates the users to enhance their status by contributing more. Thus, participants experiencing upward comparison of reputation scores are likely to contribute more knowledge to the community with the hope that more knowledge contribution can help boost their reputation scores. Therefore, the following hypothesis is suggested:

*H1: Upward comparison of reputation scores is positively related to knowledge contribution.*

Likewise, downward comparison can lead to high satisfaction and commitment. According to downward comparison theory [24], people tend to choose downward comparison over upward comparison to self-enhance when they are threatened. A major benefit of downward comparison is that it can help people alleviate negative affect and thus increase their well-being [25, 26]. Accordingly, online Q&A community participants experiencing downward comparison of reputation scores are likely to achieve self-enhancement and self-satisfaction; thus their perceived competence and self-efficacy can be enhanced. As a result of the self-enhancement, participants are motivated to continue knowledge contribution in the community. Based on the above logic, the following relationship is hypothesized:

*H2: Downward comparison of reputation scores is positively related to knowledge contribution.*

### 2.4 The Moderation Effect of User Involvement

Social comparison does not occur in a vacuum. Indeed, social comparison requires individuals to actively involve in interactions with others and learn from the experience. Previous studies generally support that user involvement, operationalized as personal relevance to the social interaction or the content being exchanged, influences the cognitive processing of information [7, 27]. In online Q&A communities, users who are extensively involved in social interaction not only have more opportunity to be exposed to virtual rewards of others, but also are more likely to invest mental effort in meaningful comparison of virtual rewards. Thus, the effect of social comparison on knowledge contribution is contingent on the extent to which the users are involved in the social interaction. Accordingly, the following hypotheses are proposed:

*H3a: The positive effect of upward comparison of reputation scores on knowledge contribution is moderated by user involvement such that the effect is more positive when user involvement is greater.*

*H3b: The positive effect of downward comparison of reputation scores on knowledge contribution is moderated by user involvement such that the effect is more positive when user involvement is greater.*

## 3    Methods

### 3.1 Research Setting

A rich dataset was collected from User Experience Stack Exchange, an online Q&A community hosted on the Stack Exchange network for user experience professionals and experts. Participants can register for free to join this community for the exchange of user experience knowledge. The community provides gamification features, including reputation scores and achievement badges (gold, silver, and bronze), to encourage user participation. A typical scenario begins with a seeker posting a question relevant to user experience design or human computer interaction to the community. Then users with relevant knowledge and expertise can provide answers to this question. Users can also edit the question to refine the question description or provide comments on the question or a specific answer. An overall reputation score is calculated based on certain criteria of a user's contribution to the community. Achievement badges are also granted based on a set of conditions of user contribution. The overall reputation score and granted badges are shown in user profile as well as along with questions or answers posted by users. Figure 2 shows a sample Q&A scenario with participants' virtual rewards shown on the user interface. The whole dataset contains 29,478 questions and 76,858 answers posted by more than 23,666 participants. The raw dataset was used to extract important variables. As a result, an unbalanced monthly panel dataset ranging from January 2013 to November 2020 was constructed to explore the impact of social comparison on user knowledge contribution.

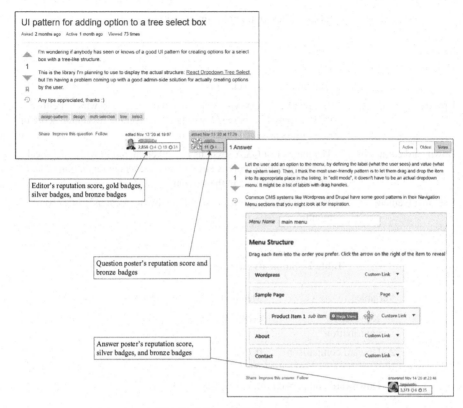

**Fig. 2.** A sample Q&A scenario.

## 3.2 Variables

Table 1 presents the description of primary variables. Summary statistics and correlations are shown in Table 2. Reputation scores and the number of badges granted (three levels including gold, silver, and bronze) are included as covariates to control for the motivational affordances directly generated from gamification. Further, other factors such as questions posted and comments posted are also included as control variables since they are associated with user knowledge contribution behavior. Additionally, yearly and monthly dummies are included to control for potential time-related effects. The unit of analysis is at individual-month level.

## 3.3 Proposed Estimation Method

The proposed method for estimating the effects of social comparison on knowledge contribution is the fixed-effects Poisson models because such models can: (1) directly model count dependent variables, and (2) control for the unobserved individual heterogeneity (time-invariant unobserved factors) that is modeled in most econometric studies of online communities [3, 6], as in this research. Other estimation methods such as fixed-effects

**Table 1.** Description of primary variables.

| Variable | Description |
|---|---|
| Knowledge contribution | The number of answers submitted by the focal user to the community in a given month |
| Upward comparison | The number of Q&A sessions in a given month in which the focal user's reputation score is lower than the average reputation score of other users involved in the session |
| Downward comparison | The number of Q&A sessions in a given month in which the focal user's reputation score is larger than the average reputation score of other users involved in the session |
| User involvement | The number of comments submitted by the focal user in a given month |

**Table 2.** Summary statistics and correlations.

| Variable | Mean | S.D | 1 | 2 | 3 | 4 |
|---|---|---|---|---|---|---|
| 1. Knowledge contribution | 0.286 | 2.012 | — | | | |
| 2. Upward comparison | 0.708 | 1.972 | 0.398 | — | | |
| 3. Downward comparison | 0.315 | 2.748 | 0.550 | 0.267 | — | |
| 4. User involvement | 0.914 | 4.131 | 0.493 | 0.569 | 0.834 | — |

negative binomial and logistic regression will also be used to test the robustness of the findings.

## 4 Discussion

This research-in-progress examines the mechanism of gamification in online Q&A communities from the theoretical lens of social comparison. Since online Q&A communities are complicated socio-technical systems designed with various functional and motivational affordances, understanding user behaviors within the communities likely requires different theoretical perspectives. Unlike other theoretical perspectives such as self-determination theory and social learning theory, the social comparison theory supports that motivational affordances of gamified design elements can be generated from the upward and downward comparisons of virtual rewards by participants. By proposing a research framework to explain the impact of upward and downward comparisons of reputation scores, this research contributes a more comprehensive understanding of the mechanism of gamification in online Q&A communities. The proposed research framework suggests that designers and managers of online communities should not only consider the motivational affordances directly generated from gamified design, but also take into account the behavioral motivations originated from the social comparison of virtual rewards offered by gamification techniques.

Future studies can investigate the similar social comparison effect by assessing other gamification factors such as badges, levels, and leaderboards, as well as non-gamified factors such as homophily [28, 29] and linguistic signals [30, 31]. Further, the same theoretical framework can be extended to understand question posting or knowledge seeking, an integrated part of user engagement in online Q&A communities. Knowledge seeking plays an important role in the success and sustainability of the communities, though its motivational sources could differ from the knowledge contribution behavior. This research can also be extended to other online settings such as customer review, social support exchange, and crowdsourcing communities where gamification mechanisms are implemented to drive user contribution and engagement.

## 5 Conclusion

Given the idiosyncratic nature of online Q&A communities that have implemented gamification mechanisms, understanding how user behaviors are motivated by gamified design elements is crucial for both research and practice. The major contribution of this research is to provide a new perspective for understanding gamification in online Q&A communities. Extending previous studies that view gamification as a direct source of motivational affordances, this research argues that motivational affordances originate, at least partially, from the comparison of virtual rewards offered by gamified design elements. Specifically, both upward and downward social comparisons are suggested to have a positive impact on user knowledge contribution. Further, user involvement is expected to moderate the effects of both upward and downward comparison on knowledge contribution. This research provides important implications for the design and management of sustainable online Q&A communities.

## References

1. Nonnecke, B., Preece, J.: Lurker demographics: counting the silent. In: Proceedings of the SIGCHI Conference on Human Factors in Computing Systems, pp. 73–80. ACM, The Hague (2000)
2. Hamari, J., Koivisto, J., Sarsa, H.: Does gamification work? - A literature review of empirical studies on gamification. In: Proceedings of the 47th Hawaii International Conference on System Sciences, pp. 3025–3034 (2014)
3. Chen, L., Baird, A., Straub, D.: Why do participants continue to contribute? Evaluation of usefulness voting and commenting motivational affordances within an online knowledge community. Decis. Support Syst. **118**, 21–32 (2019)
4. Putz, L.-M., Treiblmaier, H.: Creating a theory-based research agenda for gamification. In: 20th Americas Conference on Information Systems (2015)
5. Chen, L., Baird, A., Straub, D.: Why do users participate in online communities? The effect of motivational affordances, comments, and peer contribution on continuance. In: Proceedings of the 24th Americas Conference on Information Systems, pp. 1–5 (2018)

6. Chen, L., Baird, A., Straub, D.: Fostering participant health knowledge and attitudes: an econometric study of a chronic disease-focused online health community. J. Manag. Inf. Syst. **36**, 194–229 (2019)
7. Sussman, S.W., Siegal, W.S.: Informational influence in organizations: an integrated approach to knowledge adoption. Inf. Syst. Res. **14**, 47–65 (2003)
8. Taylor, S.E., Brown, J.D.: Illusion and well-being: a social psychological perspective on mental health. Psychol. Bull. **103**, 193–210 (1988)
9. Gibson, J.J.: The theory of affordances. In: Shaw, R.E., Bransford, J. (eds.) The People, Place, and Space Reader. Lawrence Erlbaum Associates, Hillsdale, NJ (1977)
10. Deci, E.L., Ryan, R.M.: Self-determination theory: a macrotheory of human motivation, development, and health. Can. Psychol. **49**, 182–185 (2008)
11. Ryan, R.M., Deci, E.L.: Self-determination theory and the facilitation of intrinsic motivation, social development, and well-being. Am. Psychol. **55**, 68–78 (2000)
12. Bandura, A.: Social Learning Theory. General Learning Press, New York (1977)
13. Cheung, C.M.K., Liu, I.L.B., Lee, M.K.O.: How online social interactions influence customer information contribution behavior in online social shopping communities: a social learning theory perspective. J. Am. Soc. Inf. Sci. **66**, 2511–2521 (2015)
14. Festinger, L.: A theory of social comparison processes. Hum. Relations **7**, 117–140 (1954)
15. Ang, S., Slaughter, S.A.: Work outcomes and job design for contract versus permanent information systems professionals on software development teams. MIS Q. **25**, 321–350 (2001)
16. Jabr, W., Mookerjee, R., Tan, Y., Mookerjee, V.S.: Leveraging philanthropic behavior for customer support: the case of user support forums. MIS Q. **38**, 187–208 (2014)
17. Lim, M., Yang, Y.: Effects of users' envy and shame on social comparison that occurs on social network services. Comput. Hum. Behav. **51**, 300–311 (2015)
18. Johnson, B.K., Knobloch-Westerwick, S.: Glancing up or down: mood management and selective social comparisons on social networking sites. Comput. Hum. Behav. **41**, 33–39 (2014)
19. Lou, J., Fang, Y., Lim, K.H., Peng, J.Z.: Contributing high quantity and quality knowledge to online Q&A communities. J. Am. Soc. Inform. Sci. Technol. **64**, 356–371 (2013)
20. Wasko, M.M., Faraj, S.: Why should I share? Examining social capital and knowledge contribution in electronic networks of practice. MIS Q. **29**, 35–57 (2005)
21. Brown, D.J., Ferris, D.L., Heller, D., Keeping, L.M.: Antecedents and consequences of the frequency of upward and downward social comparisons at work. Organ. Behav. Hum. Decis. Process. **102**, 59–75 (2007)
22. Collins, R.L.: For better or worse: The impact of upward social comparison on self-evaluations. Psychol. Bull. **119**, 51–69 (1996)
23. Brickman, P., Bulman, R.J.: Pleasure and pain in social comparison. Social comparison processes: Theoretical and empirical perspectives, pp. 149–186. Hemisphere, New York (1977)
24. Wills, T.A.: Downward comparison principles in social psychology. Psychol. Bull. **90**, 245–271 (1981)
25. Gibbons, F.X.: Social comparison and depression: company's effect on misery. J. Pers. Soc. Psychol. **51**, 140–148 (1986)
26. Buunk, A.P., Gibbons, F.X.: Social comparison: the end of a theory and the emergence of a field. Organ. Behav. Hum. Decis. Process. **102**, 3–21 (2007)
27. Zhang, Y., Li, X., Fan, W.: User adoption of physician's replies in an online health community: an empirical study. J. Am. Soc. Inf. Sci. **71**, 1179–1191 (2019)
28. Chen, L., Straub, D.: The impact of virtually crowdsourced social support on individual health: analyzing big datasets for underlying causalities. In: Proceedings of the 21st Americas Conference on Information Systems, pp. 1–8 (2015)

29. Wang, Z., Walther, J.B., Pingree, S., Hawkins, R.P.: Health information, credibility, homophily, and influence via the internet: Web sites versus discussion groups. Health Commun. **23**, 358–368 (2008)
30. Chen, L., Baird, A., Straub, D.: A linguistic signaling model of social support exchange in online health communities. Decis. Support Syst. **130**, 113233 (2020)
31. Chen, L.: The impact of linguistic cues on knowledge adoption in online knowledge communities: a signaling theory perspective. In: Proceedings of the 26th Americas Conference on Information Systems, pp. 1–5 (2020)

# Usability Assessment of a Jurisprudence System

Edna Dias Canedo[1]([✉]) [iD], Ana Paula Morais do Vale[2], Rafael Leite Patrão[2][iD],
Leomar Camargo de Souza[1][iD], Rogério Machado Gravina[2],
Vinicius Eloy dos Reis[3], Felipe Alberto Moreira Dias[3][iD],
Fábio Lúcio Lopes Mendonça[2][iD], and Rafael T. de Sousa Jr.[2][iD]

[1] Department of Computer Science, University of Brasília (UnB), Brasília-DF, Brazil
ednacanedo@unb.br
[2] National Science and Technology Institute on Cyber Security, Electrical
Engineering Department, University of Brasília (UnB), Brasília-DF, Brazil
{rogerio.gravina,fabio.mendonca}@redes.unb.br, desousa@unb.br
[3] General Coordination of Information Technology (CGTI), Administrative Council
for Economic Defense (CADE), Brasília-DF, Brazil
{vinicius.reis,felipe.dias}@cade.gov.br

**Abstract.** The development of a software application involves several challenges related to usability and these challenges need to be observed by the teams throughout the development process. The different forms of interaction, between users and the system, increasingly demand adaptation of human behavior. Thus, usability is an important issue, which depends on factors such as: the user, their characteristics and skills, the task that the user intends to perform, and also the context of use in which the user and the software are inserted. This paper presents a heuristic evaluation of the usability of a Jurisprudence system of the Brazilian Administrative Council for Economic Defense, using a set of 13 usability heuristics and 196 sub-heuristics. The evaluation allowed the experts to find some usability problems, mostly of small and medium severity. The evaluation results were passed on to the development team responsible for the software so that the improvements suggested by the evaluators were all implemented before the software was made available to the end-users.

**Keywords:** Heuristic evaluation · Usability heuristics · Jurisprudence system · Usability improvement

## 1  Introduction

With the progress of digital transformation carried out by the Brazilian government to offer quality public services, with less expenditure of time and money, several agencies are carrying out the automation of their provided services. In addition, the delivery of digital services makes citizens' lives easier, allowing for better monitoring of the offer of these services and their improvements. This

© Springer Nature Switzerland AG 2021
F. F.-H. Nah and K. Siau (Eds.): HCII 2021, LNCS 12783, pp. 482–499, 2021.
https://doi.org/10.1007/978-3-030-77750-0_31

makes the relationship between government agencies and the citizens who consume those services more direct and transparent. Thus, the digital transformation presents some challenges, mainly related to the usability of digital services.

Usability can be defined as how easy it is for a given user to learn a system, and how efficient this system can be, since users have already learned to use it and how pleasant its use is [21]. Usability can be described as the ability to use a product with effectiveness, efficiency, and satisfaction in a specific context of use [31].

Assessing the usability of a system is an important factor to be considered during the software development process. This assessment is performed using usability heuristics [15]. Usability heuristics assessment describes design/usability principles that serve to evaluate a given software. These assessments are largely carried out by usability experts or by ordinary users [20,23]. Usability evaluation by heuristics has been widely studied and is one of the most used methods to evaluate the quality of software, it is considered a traditional evaluation method in the literature [10,11].

In this paper, we present the results of a usability assessment of a Jurisprudence system, developed for an entity of the Federal Public Administration, called the Administrative Council for Economic Defense (CADE)[1]. The evaluation was carried out using the set of heuristics proposed by Da Costa et al. [5,6]. This set of heuristics takes the user, the context of use, the task, and the cognitive load into account as usability factors.

The results demonstrate that the system needs improvement before it is made available to end-users, containing some usability problems in the interfaces with data entry, on the visual cues and white spaces, which are not used to distinguish questions, warnings, user input instructions, and data. Regarding error prevention, the system does not inform the user in real-time, if the user is entering information in the wrong pattern.

The system also does not help the user to recognize, diagnose, and recover from errors if it is detected in a data entry field. Therefore, the system does not highlight the error or the element that needs to be changed. The system help and documentation has no relevant information and does not allow the user to resume work from where they left off. In addition, the documentation does not provide assistance for sensitive user data. The system does not allow the user to configure and customize it. Regarding Consistency and Standards, there are more than 12 to 20 different types of icons in the system.

The remaining of this work is organized as follows. Section 2 presents a contextualization of the terms usability, usability heuristics, and heuristic evaluation. In addition, the Jurisprudence system in which the heuristic evaluation was performed is presented. In Sect. 3 we present the configuration of this evaluation and the results obtained with the heuristic evaluation are presented in Sect. 4. Limitations and Threats to the result's validity are presented in Sect. 5. Finally, Sect. 6 presents conclusions and future work.

---

[1] http://www.cade.gov.br/.

## 2     Contextualization and Related Works

### 2.1     Usability

ISO/IEC 9241-11 [31] defines usability as: "to what extent can a product be used by specific users to achieve the specified goals with effectiveness (the accuracy and integrity with which the users achieve the goals they set), efficiency (the resources spent in relation to the accuracy and completeness demanded by users to reach their goals) and satisfaction (the comfort and acceptability of use) in a specified use context" [27].

ISO/IEC 9126-1 [33] describes six categories of software quality that are important in the software development process, among which is usability, being defined as the ease of use [33]. ISO/IEC 14598 [32] provides a framework for using the ISO/IEC 9126-1 model as a way to carry out the evaluation of software products [32].

ISO/IEC 25000 [34] main objective is to organize, improve and unify the concepts related to two processes of software development: quality requirements specification and quality evaluation, which are carried out together with the software quality measurement process. Shackel and Richardson [29] define usability as the human functional capacity for a system to be used easily and efficiently by a specific range of users. This is done by offering specific training and user support in order to meet the specified quantity of tasks, within the specified number of scenarios. Usability factors can impact the overall design of the product and can also affect user interaction with the application.

### 2.2     Heuristic Evaluation

In this research context, Heuristics are sentences written in a general format that represent principles or reflections that should be applied to a software system interface, and when related to usability, by evaluators who have experience in the area [1]. The heuristic evaluation can result in several improvements to the software and can show, for example, that the applications must allow the enlargement of the text size, that the colors used must be neutral to improve the contrast and that the functionalities must be clearly identified. In addition, this evaluation allows for the improvement of the consistency of navigation and the placement of icons on the screens [17].

Heuristic evaluation is one of the most widely used usability evaluation methods [27] and involves the participation of usability specialists. They analyze the interactive elements of a system using an established set of usability principles (heuristics) as a guide tool [9]. According to Matera et al. [16], the heuristic assessment [18] is one of the main methods of usability assessment.

Inostroza et al. [9] propose that each specialist, who will carry out the heuristic evaluation, inspect the user interface to identify usability problems independently. If there are several evaluators, they must be organized in such a way that each one carries out his evaluation independently of the others, and when everyone finishes, they can share their results. This restriction is necessary since in this way there is a guarantee that the evaluations are independent and impartial from each other.

Pergentino et al. [26] carried out a heuristic assessment in order to identify usability flaws in a search tool for official documents from the Brazilian Federal Court of Accounts (TCU). The work was based on Nielsen's et al. [20] heuristics and severity rates, using the heuristic evaluation method proposed by Da Costa et al. [6] and Dourado et al. [7], and associated the severity classification to the failures, in order to prioritize the correction with efficiency and agility.

### 2.3 Usability Heuristics

According to Sueyoshi [35], a system can be extraordinary in terms of development complexity, however, if the software layer that interfaces with the user are not pleasantly usable, the result of incredible technological work may end in vain, because it didn't reach those who needed it, the end-user. Through the method of heuristic evaluation, specialists can identify small and big errors related to the system's performance. The most known usability heuristics focused on widely known desktops and web systems are Nielsen's ten heuristics [22]. They consist of general principles since they are general rules and not specific usability guidelines [19], as shown in Table 1.

Although Nielsen's ten heuristics [22] are the most used in the literature, Dourado and Canedo [7] carried out a systematic literature review to find the usability heuristics focused on the mobile context. The authors found three usability heuristics in addition to Nielsen's ones in order to better align the set of heuristics for the context of mobile applications.

A heuristic assessment can contain specific or general heuristics, however, regardless of the choice between these two, the description of the heuristic must be easy to understand and apply. Very specific heuristics tend to become very difficult to apply in an assessment. On the other hand, the more general heuristics, complemented by more specific ones, tend to work better most of the time because they do not require the evaluator to have very specific knowledge of a given context. An example of this type of heuristic are those proposed by Inostroza et al. [9] which are generalists in the context of mobile device applications.

Salazar et al. [28] proposed 14 heuristics that include the usability factor 'Context of Use' to perform the heuristic assessment of a system usability. Da Costa et al. [6] proposed a set of 13 usability heuristics with 196 sub-heuristics specific to the scope of e-commerce applications. The authors concluded that the proposed set of heuristics and sub-heuristics contributed to avoid unidentified usability problems during the development of a software system, even with non-specialized developers carrying out the heuristic evaluation. In this work, we use the heuristics and sub-heuristics proposed by Da Costa et al. [6], as shown in Table 2.

Silva et al. [30] presented a list of heuristics to evaluate smartphone apps for the elderly. The heuristics were evaluated by usability experts to verify their usefulness in the heuristic evaluation of popular health applications. The methodology used comprised two main stages, the first was related to the search process

**Table 1.** Nielsen's heuristics

| Heuristics | Description |
|---|---|
| Visibility of system status | The system should always keep users informed about what is going on, through appropriate feedback within reasonable time |
| Match between system and the real world | The system should speak the users' language, with words, phrases and concepts familiar to the user, rather than system-oriented terms |
| User control and freedom | Users often choose system functions by mistake and will need a clearly marked "emergency exit" to leave the unwanted state without having to go through an extended dialogue |
| Consistency and standards | Users should not have to wonder whether different words, situations, or actions mean the same thing |
| Error prevention | Even better than good error messages is a careful design which prevents a problem from occurring in the first place |
| Recognition rather than recall | Minimize the user's memory load by making objects, actions, and options visible. The user should not have to remember information from one part of the dialogue to another |
| Flexibility and efficiency of use | Accelerators—unseen by the novice user—may often speed up the interaction for the expert user such that the system can cater to both inexperienced and experienced users |
| Aesthetic and minimalist design | Dialogues should not contain information which is irrelevant or rarely needed |
| Help users recognize, diagnose, and recover from errors | Error messages should be expressed in plain language (no codes), precisely indicate the problem, and constructively suggest a solution |
| Help and documentation | Even though it is better if the system can be used without documentation, it may be necessary to provide help and documentation. Any such information should be easy to search, focused on the user's task, list concrete steps to be carried out, and not be too large |

for a comprehensive list of heuristics to meet the needs of the research. The second stage corresponded to the application of the list found to carry out the heuristic evaluation with the group of experts to validate the heuristics. The authors identified 35 heuristics and performed 20 individual assessments and a post-assessment follow-up survey. The results of the evaluations provided an insight into the use of the heuristics list as a support tool in the evaluation of applications for the elderly.

Kumar and Goundar [12] conducted a study using heuristic evaluation to detect usability problems. The authors consider the heuristics proposed by

**Table 2.** Da Costa et al. heuristics

| ID | Heuristics | Description |
|---|---|---|
| H1 | System status visibility | The system should keep the user informed of all processes and state changes within a reasonable period of time |
| H2 | Compliance between the system and the real world | The system must speak the language of the users and not in technical system terms. The system must follow the conventions of the real world and display the information in a logical and natural order |
| H3 | User control and freedom | The system should allow the user to undo and redo their actions for clear navigation and should provide the user with an option to exit unwanted system states |
| H4 | Consistency and standards | The system must follow the established conventions, allowing the user to perform their tasks in a familiar, standardized and consistent manner |
| H5 | Error prevention | Eliminate error-prone conditions and present the user with a confirmation option with additional information before committing to the action |
| H6 | Minimization of the user's cognitive load | The system should offer visible objects, actions and options to prevent users from having to memorize information from one interface to the other |
| H7 | Customization and shortcuts | The system should provide basic and advanced settings for defining and customizing shortcuts for frequent actions |
| H8 | Efficiency of use and performance | The system must be able to load and display the information in a reasonable period of time and minimize the steps required to perform a task (number of steps to be taken by the user to achieve a goal). Animations and transitions should be displayed smoothly and fluidly |
| H9 | Aesthetic and minimalist design | The system should avoid displaying unwanted information that overloads the screen |
| H10 | User assistance to recognize, diagnose and recover from errors | The system should display error messages in a language familiar to the user, indicating the problem accurately and suggesting a constructive solution |
| H11 | Help and documentation | The system should provide easy to find documentation and help, centered on the user's current task and indicating concrete steps to be taken |
| H12 | Pleasant and respectful user interaction | The device must provide a pleasant interaction with the user, so that the user does not feel uncomfortable when using the application |
| H13 | Privacy | The system should protect the user's confidential data |

Nielsen [19] as inputs for the development of new heuristics. Since Nielsen's heuristics were judged to be too generic for the context of mobile learning applications. The heuristic evaluation used the following steps: (i) data source selection, focused on the search of relevant articles to extract usability problems; (ii) categorization of the problem, on which usability problems were extracted and mapped in traditional heuristics; (iii) development of heuristics, a phase in which new heuristics were developed through thematic analysis of usability problems; and (iv) validation of the heuristics, on which the new heuristics were submitted to validation to assess their potential benefits. As a result of the evaluation, the authors proposed three new heuristics in extension to those proposed by Nielsen [19], which were created through a structured analysis of sixteen usability studies.

## 2.4   Jurisprudence System

The development of the Jurisprudence system of the Administrative Council for Economic Defense (CADE)[2] is a project in line with the organization's Institutional Strategic Planning (PEI) and is related to the enhancement of the data generated by the agency. CADE's Master Plan for Information and Communication Technology (PDTIC) establishes the systematization of its Jurisprudence as one of the initiatives linked to the expansion of knowledge generation regarding economic competition defense.

In 2018, the Brazilian Government and the Organization for Economic Cooperation and Development (OECD) [25] published the document called Digital Government Review of Brazil [24]. The study evaluated the policies, programs, and projects of the Brazilian government, also providing recommendations for its improvement, based on OECD practices and experiences with other countries. The strengths and points of improvement of that policies and programs were identified. One of the OECD's suggestions was the development of a national strategy for digital transformation in the country.

Two years later, in April 2020, Decree 10.332/2020 was published, which instituted the Digital Government Strategy for the period from 2020 to 2022, for the Brazilian government [8]. In addition, the provision provides that each public agency draws up a Digital Transformation Plan, with actions aimed at the digital transformation of services, the unification of digital channels, and systems interoperability. Also, a Master Plan for Information and Communication Technology and an Open Data Plan should be elaborated. In CADE's Digital Transformation Plan, the project to provide a jurisprudence search solution was listed as one of the most priority.

CADE is Brazil's competition defense authority, which ultimately judges violations of the economic order. The old judgments of the CADE court must be the subject of a new decision. This brings security and prudence to the legal system.

---

[2] http://www.cade.gov.br/.

The Jurisprudence system is a solution that aims to return to its users a set of decisions by a collegiate or a court, that is, the recurring understanding within the decisions. The word jurisprudence comes from the Latin "jurisprudentia" which expresses the sense of knowledge of the law or the process of understanding the law. The jurisprudence of a given branch of law allows for a judgment consistent with other similar cases, stability, uniformity, where the interested parties have some predictability of the analysis with a specific case. Therefore, the jurisprudence search solution becomes a fundamental tool.

Among its functionalities, the system allows the search for documents related to CADE's Jurisprudence, like: technical opinions, laws, and judgments by the Brazilian Federal Court of Accounts (TCU). The consolidation of these documents searches in a system allows for quick and efficient consultation, allowing for better management of the processes and contributing to the achievement of the organization's strategic goals.

The public using this solution is made up of lawyers, businessmen, journalists, researchers, students, other antitrust authorities, etc. The usability criterion is very important for very diverse profiles of potential users.

## 3    Study Settings

We performed the heuristic assessment of the Jurisprudence system developed by the software development team, using the 13 heuristics and 196 sub-heuristics by Da Costa et al. [5,6], presented in the Table 2. Each evaluator received 13 questionnaires, developed on the Google Forms platform, containing each usability heuristic and their respective sub-heuristics to carry out the evaluation.

A document was sent to each evaluator containing instructions on the procedures to be adopted in the evaluation. In addition, we asked the evaluators to document any usability problems, identifying and classifying them into each usability heuristic. The heuristic evaluation was carried out by 4 evaluators specialized in the area. The profile of the participants in the heuristic evaluation is presented in Table 3.

**Table 3.** Heuristic evaluation evaluators' profiles

| ID | Level | Experience |
|-----|------------------|-----------|
| Ep1 | Bachelor's student | 6 months |
| Ep2 | Bachelor | 2 years |
| Ep3 | Master's student | 3 years |
| Ep4 | PhD researcher | 5 years |

All evaluators had access to all the features of the Jurisprudence system. We ask them to evaluate the maximum number of the system's functionalities, thus, increasing the chances of detecting usability problems. We also request the evaluators to use, at least twice, each system interface. The first time so they could become familiar with the user interface, and the second time to focus on evaluating each available system feature.

# 4   Results

In this section, we present the results found in the usability evaluation of the Jurisprudence system, using the 13 heuristics presented in Table 2 and their respective sub-heuristics.

## 4.1   HU1 - System Status Visibility

The evaluation for the first usability heuristic allowed us to identify that the jurisprudence system has some usability limitations, such as the lack of notifications of internal information. This leaves the user unalerted of any action that the system is taking (a search or even waiting for processing to complete). Those factors prevent the system from providing any feedback for a specific user action and, consequently, prevents the user from assimilating that there is a certain process in progress. Otherwise, the evaluation identified which objects of the interface could be selected with the provided feedback regarding which object is being selected. Also, the system has menus or pop-up notifications concerning which actions can be selected by the user. Figure 1 shows the issues found with heuristic HU1.

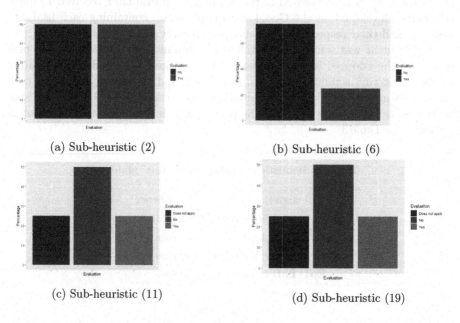

(a) Sub-heuristic (2)

(b) Sub-heuristic (6)

(c) Sub-heuristic (11)

(d) Sub-heuristic (19)

**Fig. 1.** Some evaluations for HU1.

## 4.2    HU2 - Compliance Between the System and the Real World

Unlike the heuristic HU1, in this one, the evaluation identified a small number of usability problems. Among these identified problems, the lack of interactive elements with the real world stands out, such as scrolling list physics and the absence of function keys presented in a clear and distinct way in the system. System's aspects like elements ordered in a logical way considering the user's context, familiar icons, and metaphors that correspond to the users' actions were mentioned as usability elements that are present in the application. Figure 2 shows the issues found with heuristic HU2.

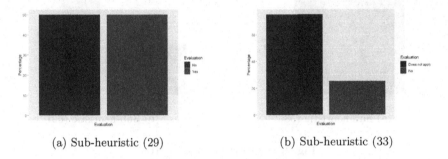

(a) Sub-heuristic (29)                (b) Sub-heuristic (33)

**Fig. 2.** Some evaluations for HU2.

## 4.3    HU3 - User Control and Freedom

Regarding the control and freedom of users, it is noteworthy that the system does not provide a fluid interaction, without constantly crashing or freezing (a factor that all the evaluators agreed on). Another aspect is the lack of possibility for the user to cancel operations in progress and the lack of screen transitions (something fundamental for the user to have the perception of where he/she is within the system). Among the positive factors, we highlight the possibility for users to move forward and backward between the forms fields, such as the search form for jurisprudence. Also, the possibility of making character changes in the input fields was considered a positive aspect. Figure 3 shows the issues found with heuristic HU3.

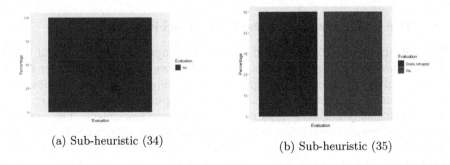

(a) Sub-heuristic (34)

(b) Sub-heuristic (35)

**Fig. 3.** Some evaluations for HU3.

## 4.4   HU4 - Consistency and Standards

The evaluations carried out for this heuristic showed that the system has few usability problems. In general, problems such as the existence of 12 to 20 different icons or the use of multiple typefaces were not identified in the evaluation carried out by the 04 evaluators. The other questions addressed by this heuristic had basically the same level of agreement among all evaluators. Figure 4 shows the issues found with heuristic HU4.

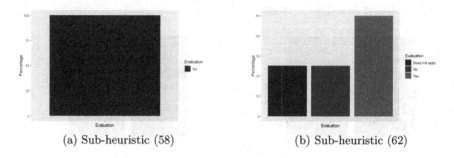

(a) Sub-heuristic (58)                    (b) Sub-heuristic (62)

**Fig. 4.** Some evaluations for HU4.

## 4.5   HU5 - Error Prevention

Regarding the prevention of errors, the evaluations pointed out this as one of the most critical usability problems in the Jurisprudence system. Some usability issues, such as preventing possible errors caused by users, lack of warnings about risks, and data insertions in the wrong format, were identified in the assessment. However, the evaluators were able to identify positive factors such as menu options that are logical and distinct, in addition to visual differences between interaction objects (fields) and information objects (messages/alerts). In addition, it is important to note that clickable objects on the screen are not very close (this is related to the fields and forms present in the system). Figure 5 shows the issues found with heuristic HU5.

## 4.6   HU6 - Minimization of the User's Cognitive Load

The evaluations identified the need for usability improvements in most of these usability heuristic metrics. Factors such as the lack of visual clues and blank spaces to allow the user to distinguish some warnings, questions, and instructions for entries. The absence of messages alerting users to fill mandatory data entries also had a negative impact on this heuristic assessment. The positive factors found were the spacing between the text areas, allowing a better visualization, and elements with a good visual distinction that facilitates users to choose between elements. Figure 6 shows the issues found with heuristic HU6.

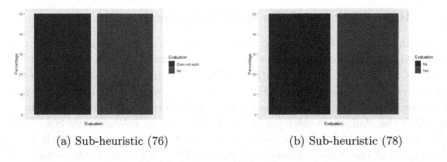

(a) Sub-heuristic (76)                    (b) Sub-heuristic (78)

**Fig. 5.** Some evaluations for HU5.

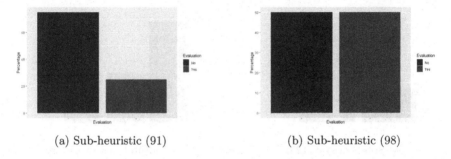

(a) Sub-heuristic (91)                    (b) Sub-heuristic (98)

**Fig. 6.** Some evaluations for HU6.

### 4.7    HU7 - Customization and Shortcuts

In general, almost all the evaluations for this heuristic and its sub-heuristics identified that the metrics present in this evaluation do not apply to the Jurisprudence system context. This is due to the absence of customization features in all pages and specific areas (an element somewhat common to many web systems). Figure 7 shows the issues found with heuristic HU7.

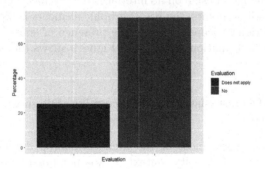

**Fig. 7.** Sub-heuristic (120)

## 4.8    HU8 - Efficiency of Use and Performance

Regarding the efficiency of use and the performance of the application, the evaluations identified more positive than negative factors. Among those, one that stands out is the accessible positions of the most often used menus, also that pages that have tasks processing in the background were avoided by the developers. One of the negative factors is related to the screen's transition, a situation in which the evaluators were unable to be unanimous in their answers. Therefore, we believe that this is a usability item that should be better work by the developers of the Jurisprudence system. Figure 8 shows the issues found with heuristic HU8.

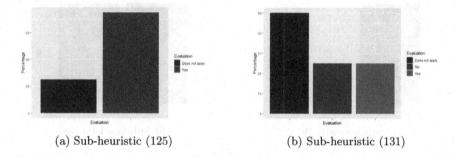

(a) Sub-heuristic (125)                    (b) Sub-heuristic (131)

**Fig. 8.** Some evaluations for HU8.

## 4.9    HU9 - Aesthetic and Minimalist Design

In this heuristic, the evaluators also pointed out some usability problems, such as the display of non-essential information for decision making, as well as the absence of images or icons on the screen. These are important factors since systems with minimalist design on its interfaces tend to have better performance. Regarding the positive points, the use of graphic elements is highlighted so that there is a distinction of icons and also the presence of short titles, presenting simple and direct information to the user. Figure 9 shows the issues found with heuristic HU9.

## 4.10    HU10 - User Assistance to Recognize, Diagnose and Recover from Errors

In this specific heuristic, most of the items evaluated did not apply to the Jurisprudence system. Given its context, it was not possible to observe points where the system emitted errors during its use, since the functionalities do not have critical levels regarding error handling and recovery.

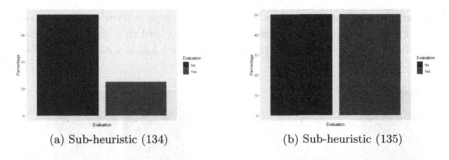

(a) Sub-heuristic (134)          (b) Sub-heuristic (135)

**Fig. 9.** Some evaluations for HU9.

### 4.11  HU11 - Help and Documentation

Regarding this heuristic, the evaluation identified that the Jurisprudence system needs information that better guides the user in the use of its functionalities. Aspects such as the user's capacity to define the desired level of detail for the information, and to recover the state of the system after accessing the assistance information were some items identified by the evaluators. In addition, an evaluator also mentioned that the system layout was not well designed and needs improvement. It is worth mentioning that not all items in this heuristic had negative evaluations, with all evaluators agreeing that the system has understandable and easy to find information. Figure 10 shows the issues found with heuristic HU11.

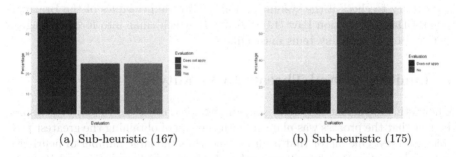

(a) Sub-heuristic (167)          (b) Sub-heuristic (175)

**Fig. 10.** Some evaluations for HU11.

### 4.12  HU12 - Pleasant and Respectful User Interaction

Among all the heuristics evaluated, this was the one with the most positive evaluations identified by the evaluators. Only two negative aspects were observed: (i) the lack of optimization of the system for the context in which the users are inserted; (ii) the lack of colors that call the user's attention regarding the change of system status. Changing colors as the system status evolves can help the end-user to identify the progress of their activities and lead to a good acceptance of the application by users. Figure 11 shows the issues found with heuristic HU12.

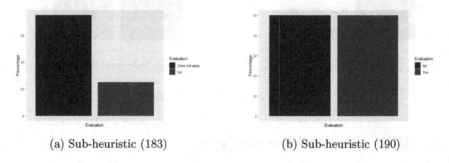

(a) Sub-heuristic (183)          (b) Sub-heuristic (190)

Fig. 11. Some evaluations for HU12.

### 4.13   HU13 - Privacy

Regarding privacy, the evaluation identified that most of the items evaluated do not fit the context of the Jurisprudence system. Aspects such as multi-user systems and protected areas do not fit the purpose of the system. Therefore, we believe that although this heuristic has not identified many problems, it is ideal to carry out an analysis in relation to the privacy of the system users' data [3,4], since the Jurisprudence system stores sensitive information. In addition, it is necessary to check if the system complies with the principles of the Brazilian General Data Protection Law (LGPD) [2,14], which came into force in August 2020 and to which all systems must adhere.

## 5   Limitations and Threats to Validity

A heuristic assessment may have some limitations or threats to validity, despite the fact that the process was planned with the aim of obtaining the greatest possible accuracy. One factor that arouses concern is the large number of heuristics and sub-heuristics that have been analyzed, a total of 13 heuristics and 196 sub-heuristics. However, for a complete analysis of the usability of the Jurisprudence system, it was necessary to analyze all the questions presented by each heuristic and their respective sub-heuristics. As the evaluation process was long and time-consuming, the evaluators may have felt tired or had been distracted during the process. This could lead to errors in the final evaluations of the sub-heuristics, such as not mentioning all identified problems.

One of the evaluators also mentioned the system's latency as a possible threat, since it may have happened due to the great geographical distance between him and the servers hosting the system. Another aspect is the application challenge and the specificity of this system since usability heuristics are general principles, not necessarily adapted to the jurisprudence context. One way to mitigate this threat is to carry out other heuristic assessments between different systems of jurisprudence and to compare the results.

## 6   Conclusions

This paper presented a usability evaluation of CADE's Jurisprudence System, using the usability heuristics and sub-heuristics by Da Costa et al. [5,13]. The evaluation was conducted by four evaluators from different academic areas for two weeks, who had access to all the functionalities of the Jurisprudence system, developed by the system's development team. The interdisciplinarity of the experts allowed a more holistic and approximate view of the system's end-user, which contributes to a more accurate feedback on possible usability problems existing in the analyzed system.

The results of the evaluation demonstrated that the Jurisprudence system needs improvements in relation to its usability. An example case is that, after the user completes an action (or group of actions), the Jurisprudence system does not indicate whether it is possible to initiate a new action (or group of actions). In addition, the data entry screens do not inform the user when the fields are optional. These usability problems, although simple at first sight, negatively impact the use of the application and the users' perception of the system. As future work, we will carry out new evaluations in the system, when new features are made available by the development team. Also, a set of different heuristics tailored to the legal and jurisprudence context could be added to the existing heuristics list in order to better analyze those kinds of systems.

**Acknowledgments.** The authors would like to thank the support of the Brazilian research, development and innovation agencies CAPES (grants 23038.007604/2014-69 FORTE and 88887.144009/2017-00 PROBRAL), CNPq (grants 312180/2019-5 PQ-2, BRICS2017-591 LargEWiN, and 465741/2014-2 INCT in Cybersecurity) and FAP-DF (grants 0193.001366/2016 UIoT and 0193.001365/2016 SSDDC), as well as the cooperation projects with the Ministry of the Economy (grants DIPLA 005/2016 and ENAP 083/2016), the Institutional Security Office of the Presidency of the Republic (grant ABIN 002/2017), the Administrative Council for Economic Defense (grant CADE 08700.000047/2019-14), and the General Attorney of the Union (grant AGU 697.935/2019).

## References

1. Botella, F., Gallud, J.A., Tesoreiro, R.: Using interaction patterns in heuristic evaluation. In: Marcus, A. (ed.) DUXU 2011. LNCS, vol. 6769, pp. 23–32. Springer, Heidelberg (2011). https://doi.org/10.1007/978-3-642-21675-6_3
2. Canedo, E.D., Calazans, A.T.S., Masson, E.T.S., Costa, P.H.T., Lima, F.: Perceptions of ICT practitioners regarding software privacy. Entropy **22**(4), 429 (2020)
3. Carvalho, A.P., Canedo, E.D., Carvalho, F.P., Carvalho, P.H.P.: Anonymisation and compliance to protection data: impacts and challenges into big data. In: ICEIS (1), pp. 31–41. SciTePress (2020)

4. Carvalho, A.P., Carvalho, F.P., Canedo, E.D., Carvalho, P.H.P.: Big data, anonymisation and governance to personal data protection. In: DG.O, pp. 185–195. ACM (2020)
5. Parente da Costa, R., Dias Canedo, E.: A set of usability heuristics for mobile applications. In: Kurosu, M. (ed.) HCII 2019. LNCS, vol. 11566, pp. 180–193. Springer, Cham (2019). https://doi.org/10.1007/978-3-030-22646-6_13
6. da Costa, R.P., Canedo, E.D., de Sousa, R.T., de Oliveira Albuquerque, R., Villalba, L.J.G.: Set of usability heuristics for quality assessment of mobile applications on smartphones. IEEE Access (2019). https://doi.org/10.1109/ACCESS.2019.2910778
7. Dourado, M.A.D., Canedo, E.D.: Usability heuristics for mobile applications - a systematic review. In: Proceedings of the 20th International Conference on Enterprise Information Systems, ICEIS 2018, Funchal, Madeira, Portugal, 21–24 March 2018, vol.2, pp. 483–494 (2018). https://doi.org/10.5220/0006781404830494
8. Governo Federal: Estratégia de governo digital, April 2020. https://www.in.gov.br/en/web/dou/-/decreto-n-10.332-de-28-de-abril-de-2020-254430358
9. Inostroza, R., Rusu, C., Roncagliolo, S., Jiménez, C., Rusu, V.: Usability heuristics validation through empirical evidences: a touchscreen-based mobile devices proposal. In: 2012 31st International Conference of the Chilean Computer Science Society (SCCC), pp. 60–68. IEEE (2012). https://doi.org/10.1109/SCCC.2012.15
10. Inostroza, R., Rusu, C., Roncagliolo, S., Rusu, V.: Usability heuristics for touchscreen-based mobile devices: update. In: First Chilean Conference on Human - Computer Interaction, ChileCHI 2013, Temuco, Chile, 11–15 November 2013, pp. 24–29 (2013). https://doi.org/10.1145/2535597.2535602. https://doi.acm.org/10.1145/2535597.2535602
11. Kjeldskov, J., Stage, J.: New techniques for usability evaluation of mobile systems. Int. J. Hum. Comput. Stud. **60**(5–6), 599–620 (2004). https://doi.org/10.1016/j.ijhcs.2003.11.001
12. Kumar, B.A., Goundar, M.S.: Usability heuristics for mobile learning applications. EAIT **24**(2), 1819–1833 (2019). https://doi.org/10.1007/s10639-019-09860-z
13. de Lima Salgado, A., Freire, A.P.: Heuristic evaluation of mobile usability: a mapping study. In: Kurosu, M. (ed.) HCI 2014. LNCS, vol. 8512, pp. 178–188. Springer, Cham (2014). https://doi.org/10.1007/978-3-319-07227-2_18
14. Macedo, P.N.: Brazilian general data protection law (LGPD). National Congress, vol. 1, pp. 1–20 (2018). https://www.pnm.adv.br/wp-content/uploads/2018/08/Brazilian-General-Data-Protection-Law.pdf. Accessed 18 Oct 2019
15. Mack, Z., Sharples, S.: The importance of usability in product choice: a mobile phone case study. Ergonomics **52**(12), 1514–1528 (2009). https://doi.org/10.1080/00140130903197446
16. Matera, M., Rizzo, F., Carughi, G.T.: Web usability: principles and evaluation methods. In: Mendes, E., Mosley, N. (eds.) Web Engineering, pp. 143–180. Springer, Heidelberg (2006). https://doi.org/10.1007/3-540-28218-1_5
17. Memedi, M., Tshering, G., Fogelberg, M., Jusufi, I., Kolkowska, E., Klein, G.: An interface for IoT: feeding back health-related data to Parkinson's disease patients. J. Sensor Actuator Netw. **7**(1), 14 (2018). https://doi.org/10.3390/jsan7010014
18. Nielsen, J.: Finding usability problems through heuristic evaluation. In: Proceedings of the Conference on Human Factors in Computing Systems, CHI 1992, Monterey, CA, USA, 3–7 May 1992, pp. 373–380 (1992). https://doi.org/10.1145/142750.142834
19. Nielsen, J.: 10 heuristics for user interface design, April 1994. https://www.nngroup.com/articles/ten-usability-heuristics/

20. Nielsen, J.: Guerrilla HCI: using discount usability engineering to penetrate the intimidation barrier. Cost-Justifying Usability, pp. 245–272 (1994). ftp://ftp.cs. umanitoba.ca/pub/cs371/Readings/Guerrilla.pdf
21. Nielsen, J.: Usability inspection methods. In: Conference on Human Factors in Computing Systems, CHI 1994, Boston, Massachusetts, USA, 24–28 April 1994, Conference Companion, pp. 413–414 (1994). https://doi.org/10.1145/259963. 260531. http://doi.acm.org/10.1145/259963.260531
22. Nielsen, J.: 10 usability heuristics for user interface design. Nielsen Norman Group (1995). http://courses.ischool.utexas.edu/rbias/2014/Spring/
23. Nielsen, J., Molich, R.: Heuristic evaluation of user interfaces. In: Proceedings of the Conference on Human Factors in Computing Systems, CHI 1990, Seattle, WA, USA, 1–5 April 1990, pp. 249–256 (1990). https://doi.org/10.1145/97243.97281. http://doi.acm.org/10.1145/97243.97281
24. OECD: Digital Government Review of Brazil: Towards the Digital Transformation of the Public Sector. OECD iLibrary (2018). https://doi.org/ 10.1787/9789264307636-en. https://www.oecd-ilibrary.org/content/publication/ 9789264307636-en
25. OCDE OECD: The OECD principles of corporate governance. Contaduría y Administración 216 (2004)
26. dos Santos Pergentino, A.C., Canedo, E.D., Lima, F., de Mendonça, F.L.L.: Usability heuristics evaluation in search engine. In: Marcus, A., Rosenzweig, E. (eds.) HCII 2020. LNCS, vol. 12200, pp. 351–369. Springer, Cham (2020). https://doi. org/10.1007/978-3-030-49713-2_25
27. Sagar, K., Saha, A.: A systematic review of software usability studies. Int. J. Inf. Technol. 1–24 (2017). https://doi.org/10.1007/s41870-017-0048-1
28. Salazar, L.H.A., Lacerda, T., Nunes, J.V., von Wangenheim, C.G.: A systematic literature review on usability heuristics for mobile phones. IJMHCI 5(2), 50–61 (2013). https://doi.org/10.4018/jmhci.2013040103
29. Shackel, B., Richardson, S.J.: Human Factors for Informatics Usability. Cambridge University Press, Cambridge (1991)
30. Silva, P.A., Holden, K., Jordan, P.: Towards a list of heuristics to evaluate smartphone apps targeted at older adults: a study with apps that aim at promoting health and well-being. In: 48th Hawaii International Conference on System Sciences, HICSS 2015, Kauai, Hawaii, USA, 5–8 January 2015, pp. 3237–3246 (2015). https://doi.org/10.1109/HICSS.2015.390
31. I.I.O. for Standardization: ISO 9241-11:1998: Ergonomic requirements for office work with visual display terminals (VDTs) - Part 11: Guidance on usability (1998)
32. I.I.O. for Standardization: ISO/IEC 14598-1: Information technology - software product evaluation - Part 1: General overview. International Organization for Standardization, Geneva, Switzerland (1999)
33. I.I.O. for Standardization: ISO/IEC 9126-1: Software engineering - product quality. International Organization for Standardization, Geneva, Switzerland (2001)
34. I.I.O. for Standardization: ISO/IEC 25000: Systems and software engineering - systems and software quality requirements and evaluation (square) - guide to square. International Organization for Standardization, Geneva, Switzerland (2005)
35. Sueyoshi, E.: Prefácio. In: Introdução e boas práticas em UX Design. Casa do Código (2014). https://books.google.com.br/books?id=vWuCCwAAQBAJ

# Inside-Out: How Internal Social Media Platforms Can Accelerate Innovation and Push External Crowdsourcing Towards New Frontiers

Maximilian Rapp[1,3]($\boxtimes$), Niclas Kröger[2], and Samira Scheerer[3]

[1] Skolkovo Institute of Science and Technology, Moscow, Russia
maximilian.rapp@de.ey.com
[2] HYVE, Munich, Germany
niclas.kroeger@hyve.net
[3] EY (Ernst & Young), Munich, Germany
samira.scheerer@de.ey.com

**Abstract.** Continuous Improvement Processes (CIP) in companies and organizations alike have been part of a widespread metamorphosis to a more strategic internal crowdsourcing process with professional campaigns as well as sophisticated ideation platforms to gather knowledge and experiences from the organizations' employees and stakeholders. While its counterpart, namely external crowdsourcing with users, customers, or external stakeholders is a matter of myriad research, the use, process, metamorphosis, and environments of internal crowds are lacking a deeper understanding through in-depth analysis. In this paper, we will answer 1) why most organizations use either internal or external crowdsourcing, and 2) what key success factors exist for effective internal campaigns. In order to answer these questions, we accompanied 10 organizations using an active research approach based on a variety of data, including interviews. We sum up by consolidating all findings in managerial implications for practical execution.

**Keywords:** Open innovation · Co-creation · Ideation · Community · Crowdsourcing · Continuous Improvement Process · Employee integration

## 1 Introduction: White Spot Internal Crowdsourcing

The strategic use of social media mechanisms through crowdsourcing platforms is not just omnipresent but seems also partly jaded through a broad variety of research and documentation which makes it hard to identify white spots for enlightening and controversial findings. Interestingly, the use of external social media platforms for creating new ideas, concepts, and designs by including external stakeholders and customers to strengthen the internal innovation pipeline has been studied extensively. However, its use for internal purposes (integration of employees and not users from outside the organization) has still much potential to offer and findings to share [1, 2]. Building crowdsourcing platforms internally to accelerate the innovation potential has been cut short in research compared to the use of external crowdsourcing platforms due to different reasons, most

© Springer Nature Switzerland AG 2021
F. F.-H. Nah and K. Siau (Eds.): HCII 2021, LNCS 12783, pp. 500–514, 2021.
https://doi.org/10.1007/978-3-030-77750-0_32

notably a lack of data and transparency, as well as a certain creeping effect which is hard to analyze:

- As internal social media platforms are producing highly confidential data, the access for research is limited, especially in comparison with external crowdsourcing platforms, where data is accessible for literally everybody (Open Innovation). For competitive reasons, organizations also seem to avoid sharing their efforts and findings on how to accelerate internal R&D and innovation processes.
- Platforms for generating ideas or solving problems within an organization have been an organic development starting through older systems, such as a Continuous Improvement Process (CIP) [3]. In many organizations, this development is creeping and very hard to analyze. On the other hand, the desire for more customer centricity and design thinking over the past 10 years has brought a spotlight to external platforms where dynamic and direct communication with customers takes place and represents a stark contrast to internal innovation.
- Internal social media platforms lack an outside-in perspective due to the exclusive engagement of the organization's employees. Shared ideas are then taken by the responsible department for execution (most likely R&D) and absorbed without highlighting the origin of the idea. Here it is hard to follow the data and see how successful those engagements (especially in addition to the creeping process) really are and hence a limitation for potential researchers.

In our research, we analyze the true potential of internal social media platforms to accelerate innovation [4]. We specifically aim to analyze the key success factors and outcomes on an organizational, strategic, and operational level. In detail we will investigate the following research questions:

- Which key factors do exist regarding successful internal crowdsourcing initiatives?
- Why do organizations mainly use either internal or external crowdsourcing platforms and rarely combine both potentials?
- How can internal crowdsourcing accelerate external initiatives?

To set the right stage and finally answer those questions for further practical use, the paper is structured as follows. First, we give an overview of related theories and current research. Second, we show an analysis of our conducted in-depth case studies, which include ten companies across different industries using either internal, external, or combined ways of crowdsourcing. Our research team actively participated in the projects from beginning to end [5]. Hereof, we conducted various interviews with the decision-makers and stakeholders of those organizations to further back-up the results. Third, we combine our findings from our action research and interviews to derive insights into our leading questions. Finally, we summarize our findings and conclude managerial implications and guidelines to help practitioners achieve the best outcome when using internal social media platforms and by providing rudiments for further research.

## 2 Theoretical Background

This paper focuses on the topic of online social media platforms that help organizations generate innovations. These platforms, often referred to as (online) innovation communities, allow organizations to innovate by developing new products and services, solving problems, improving processes, finding new applications, or even designing new strategies [6–9]. Involving large groups of people to engage in these activities is now generally referred to as crowdsourcing [10]. Crowdsourcing, most of the time, is strongly linked with the research field of Open Innovation and entails opening up with one's challenges to the public. In the scope of this paper, we refer to crowdsourcing with external stakeholders (e.g., users, customers, partners, universities) as external crowdsourcing. In contrast, we use the term internal crowdsourcing to address innovation processes that leverage very similar mechanics but only with internal stakeholders (i.e., employees).

External crowdsourcing spans a wide field of research and has been studied thoroughly since the phenomenon gained traction. Studies dive deep into a variety of factors regarding external crowdsourcing [11]. A large area of research has scoped the participants' activity in such communities, their motives for doing so, and identified both intrinsic and extrinsic factors which drive motivation [12, 13]. Furthermore, the participants have been clustered to be distinguished based on their behavior [14] and found to show different characteristics [15]. In addition to the communities, the general design elements are also well researched and understood [16]. Even though there seems to be a broad understanding of the underlying mechanics within the communities and crowdsourcing's possibilities, many organizations still struggle to institutionalize crowdsourcing as a sustainable innovation practice. Research suggests that in order for organizations to profit from Open Innovation sustainably, processes [17] or the development of capabilities [18] are required.

Internal crowdsourcing on the other hand has not received the same attention from the research community. For the purpose of this research, it is important to distinguish internal crowdsourcing from Continuous Improvement Processes (CIP) also referred to as employee suggestion schemes, employee suggestion systems (ESS), or Kaizen (continuous improvement) [19]. While CIP has successfully been transferred by many organizations from analog into digital processes, they still focus on incremental improvements with methods such as Lean, Six Sigma, or total quality management (TQM). Internal crowdsourcing as referred to in this research is more than collecting ideas for efficiency improvements (incremental innovation), but rather the empowerment of the employees to help solve challenges or share transformative and disruptive ideas. Therefore, the platforms and processes used in internal crowdsourcing are similar to those used for external crowdsourcing, making use of gamification elements like winner selection through a jury, co-creation possibilities, and social-media-like interaction of the participants. The topic has gained traction in recent years but still lacks the in-depth research conducted on external crowdsourcing [2, 20]. The technical set-up is well understood and similar to external crowdsourcing [21], other mechanics in internal crowdsourcing seem to differ in various ways. Participants seem to be motivated by managerial recognition rather than peer recognition, which points towards extrinsic motivation [22]. In general, management commitment was found to be an important success factor [23].

Only a few studies have taken a deeper look into the differences between internal and external approaches. Zhu et al. [24] have taken a first look into the differences between the two approaches and developed a framework to decide on the most suitable approach depending on the "task-crowd-interrelationship", "crowd-outcome-interrelationship", and "task-outcome-interrelationship". Both approaches offer different benefits and barriers and the use of internal or external crowdsourcing may therefore depend on the circumstances [25].

With only limited research into the adoption of internal crowdsourcing and even fewer scholars looking at the intersection and interdependencies of internal and external crowdsourcing, our research aims to initially fill this gap. Our research provides insights into why organizations may choose one approach over the other and how one can accelerate the other.

## 3 Empirical Analysis

### 3.1 Methodical Approach

To answer our research questions, we conducted a participatory action research approach (PAR). In PAR the researchers actively become part of the social object they want to study. It allows the researchers to get a thorough understanding of complex social systems [5].

Our research is also based on an in-depth case study [26] of crowdsourcing activities conducted at two leading innovation consultancies: HYVE – the innovation company, based in Munich, Germany, and Ernst & Young, headquartered in London, UK. Over the last decade, the researchers have accompanied over 70 organizations in their efforts to run both internal and external crowdsourcing challenges. The researchers can therefore draw on their accumulated observations, insights, and knowledge generated from these activities and introduce them to the action research approach.

### 3.2 Data Collection

A variety of data points form the basis of the research. They include (1) the active participation in and observation of the crowdsourcing platforms, (2) interviews and discussions with project partners, (3) insights from discussions with organizations who are interested in using social media platforms for innovation but have not yet executed initiatives, as well as (4) secondary data sources. More details about the data are provided in the following paragraphs:

(1) The researchers have actively managed part of the projects in their role as external consultants. They have conducted projects on different crowdsourcing platforms and were part of activities such as conception, topic framing, communication and recruiting of participants, community management, accompanying the selection process, and handover to implementation.

(2) During the projects, in a variety of meetings, discussions were held on strategic as well as operational topics. Most of these meetings included the project partners who

were mostly project managers or innovation managers. Furthermore, stakeholders from different backgrounds were part of the meetings. These included for example experts from the IT, legal, or marketing departments, as well as board members. In the meetings, notes were taken for further analysis. In addition, the researchers interviewed selected project managers to gain further insights into the initial findings. For reasons of confidentiality, the names of the project partners, as well as the companies they work for, are not disclosed.

(3) In the process of offering consulting services, the researchers had contact with more than 200 companies to discuss the possibilities of using crowdsourcing. From these discussions, pain points and fears of using the method could be identified. These discussions mostly took place in one-on-one conversations, but also after presentations or webinars providing insights about the perception of crowdsourcing.

(4) Secondary data was further added to the data pool. These included notes, presentations, and documents from the projects, as well as data from the platforms such as user activity, submissions, comments, contest descriptions, or participants.

While the researchers draw on their active participation in over 70 crowdsourcing projects, in-depth analysis of 10 selected companies builds the foundation of this research. Table 1 shows an overview of the companies that were part of the in-depth analysis, the industries in which they operate, their size in terms of employees, the number of contests they have run either internally, externally, or both as well as the project leaders.

**Table 1.** Overview of companies for in-depth analysis

| Industry | No. of employees/members (approx.) | Internal contests | External contests | Project driver |
|---|---|---|---|---|
| Automotive | 240,000 | 3 | 0 | Head of Incubation, Innovation Manager |
| Politics | 140,000 | 2 | 1 | General Secretary of Political Party |
| FMCG | 100,000 | 0 | 3 | Innovation Manager |
| FMCG | 50,000 | 0 | 2 | Innovation Manager, Marketing Manager |
| Bank | 50,000 | 2 | 0 | Innovation Manager |
| Aerospace | 35,000 | 2 | 0 | CTO, Head of Marketing |
| Insurance | 15,000 | 0 | 1 | Project Manager |
| Government | 6,000 | 3 | 0 | Head of Innovation, Innovation Manager |
| Government | 6,000 | 0 | 3 | Project Manager |
| Food | 3,000 | 0 | 2 | Board Member, Innovation Manager |

In the following paragraphs, we present two selected projects (one internal and one external contest) to give the reader a better understanding of a typical contest that is part of our research sample. We indicate the processes and people involved as well as the typical scope in terms of the number of participants, contributions, and discussion happening within the contest.

**Example Case - External Contest in the Steel Industry**
In this contest, the host company was looking for new use cases for two steel technologies they had developed. After already finding many use cases in familiar industries, they were looking for further areas where the technology is applicable and can offer unique benefits to new customers. The contest, which was led by the research department, was running on an existing crowdsourcing platform that already provided a community to answer the question. The global contest was open for any interested participant to join and contribute. The platform offered interactive elements to engage the participants and to co-create, such as the possibility to view, comment, evaluate, and like other participants' contributions. Throughout the six-week challenge, about 400 use cases were submitted by 100 participants. The participants as well as experts from the host company commented on the submissions more than 1,000 times and gave over 820 evaluations. The best 11 submissions were awarded monetary prizes and were considered for potential implementation.

**Example Case - Internal Contest in the Banking Industry**
This internal contest was conducted by a large bank operating in several countries. The goal of running the contest was to find promising ideas and underlying consumer needs in six selected focus areas. Aside from looking for new business opportunities, the bank was also looking for engaged employees who could help to bring the ideas to life after a selection phase. The contest was open to all employees within the different regions and hosted on a platform that was specifically created to run the challenge. The possibilities for interaction were similar to the ones described for the external contest. In total, 765 ideas were submitted by about 3,600 participants in 6 weeks. They were commented on over 3,300 times and liked more than 13,000 times. Furthermore, 268 participants applied to further work on the submitted ideas. The employees providing the best submissions and applications were invited to join a workshop, where they could continue to work on the ideas and pitch them to the management for a chance to further develop them.

For an even better understanding, Table 2 summarizes the most notable differentiators of the internal and external crowdsourcing initiatives we analyzed. It indicates which activities and objectives are more likely to be achieved with a certain initiative.

**Table 2.** Comparison of showcased internal and external open innovation platforms

|  | Internal | External |
|---|---|---|
| Type and structure | Administrative format, focusing on structure and problem statement | Serving as ideation & marketing channel, focusing on brand representation and gamification |
| Objectives | Building an innovational culture, starting a change movement, identifying promising talents, connecting the right dots, leverage existing knowledge within the organization | Integrating the customer and understanding their needs, generating creative solutions and ideas, getting different insights and perspectives on ideas, winning new customers, creating brand awareness |
| Use cases | Internal and production processes where internal background knowledge is useful | New operating fields and industries, beyond the current knowledge and expertise |
| Participants | Employees from different departments | Experts, customers, topic-interested people, innovators, citizens |
| Efforts | Closed social media platform, working hours of the employees | Open social media platform, Incentives for winners, and working hours of the project team |

## 4 Findings and Discussion

The findings of our research are manifold, as the mass of data and insights from over 200 organizations, 70 initiatives, and 10 cases brought more answers and scientific patterns than just those we aim to highlight within this paper. In the following, we focus on our initial research questions with some details and insights aside. This focus also helps to derive clear and selected managerial implications for practical use. Furthermore, we concentrate within our insights and discussion on the major and reoccurring patterns of the analyzed organizations rather than explaining all of them, which would here break the mold.

### 4.1 Key Components for Successful Internal Crowdsourcing Campaigns

Our research shows that several factors influence the success of an internal crowdsourcing campaign. We structure them into strategic and operational factors. Figure 1 summarizes our findings on both levels to create a successful campaign.

On a strategic level, it is important to have upper management (C-level) support for the initiative. As a large part of or even the entire organization is invited to contribute to the campaign, it is essential to have management buy-in. This helps to communicate to the organization that participation is wanted and to avoid the impression that participation on such platforms is only for people who do not have any other important work to do. Communicating top-down through hierarchical structures allows managers on different levels to articulate the importance of taking part in the campaign. Having employees who believe in a culture of collaboration and co-creation is very helpful in this process and should be backed by the management's real effort to turn the results of the campaigns into new products, services, or processes. Successful implementations should always be communicated back to the community or employees. Topics that are unlikely to be implemented and do not yield timely results may stifle the future success of similar campaigns. Depending on the organization it is also important to include other stakeholders such as the workers' council which may have the power to block such initiatives.

On the operational level, the platform forms the basis of the internal crowdsourcing initiative. While our findings do not suggest that technical details of the platform are a decisive success factor, we find that accessibility is still important. Ideally, every employee can access the campaign without much effort - for example, by connecting the platform to the active directory. Blue-collar workers may need another way to participate. Aside from the platform being accessible, the topic also needs to be accessible to the target audience. Ideally, everyone who is invited should in theory be capable of grasping the topic and potentially contribute. Incentives further play an important role in the contest. While prizes may be one way of incentivizing participants, the interaction on the platform can also be a motivating factor. Active community management consisting of providing feedback on the contributions and collaborating on improving them is crucial and valued highly by the participants. Thinking beyond a single campaign, a success factor that came up over and over again in our research is the importance of creating success cases. Therefore, it is important to start campaigns that lead to successful implementations – ideally in the short term. Achieving this requires embedding internal crowdsourcing in existing innovation processes. In addition to having an interface to the corresponding innovation process, it is even more important to include the people responsible for implementation as early as possible. They can, for example, act as experts or coaches on the platform and vote on the contribution in the selection process. This helps them to become owners of the contributions early on and to mitigate the effects of the 'not-invented-here' syndrome.

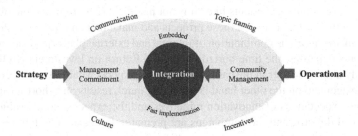

**Fig. 1.** Components of an internal successful crowdsourcing contest

## 4.2 Reasons for the Use of Either Internal or External Crowdsourcing

Our data shows that companies, which use social media crowdsourcing platforms strategically to include internal *and* external stakeholders for generating ideas, creating new business models, and (further) developing concepts and services as well as testing prototypes, belong to a minority. This result still surprises as Open Innovation and crowdsourcing have been part of most organizations' agenda for around a decade now and external crowdsourcing initiatives, as well as the evolution of internal idea processes, have been executed individually as well as shared and promoted through best practices, case studies, keynotes, and articles alike. Therefore, one might assume falsely that the ambidexterity of crowdsourcing (internal and external) is part of most organizations' DNA by now.

Our research shows several reasons why internal and external crowdsourcing are rarely used in parallel, highlighting the most striking deterrents as follows:

- **Different structure:** As shown within the case studies, even though internal and external crowdsourcing use similar mechanics, technology, and methodologies, the set-up, process, needed stakeholders, and communication channels usually differ. Internal crowdsourcing needs a tremendous number of interfaces to other departments and usually approval from the works council or HR due to employee data. "Initiating an open innovation platform is largely about structures, software, and processes", an interviewee confirmed. External crowdsourcing initiatives on the other hand are mainly driven by external consulting firms and intermediaries, thereby avoiding many organizational and structural boundaries. A simple switch from internal to external (or vice versa) is therefore not simple or applicable. The framework must be adjusted accordingly, which means certain time and financial investments.
- **Different objectives:** Both internal and external initiatives search for innovative ideas, but the use of internal and external platforms depends strongly on the topic framing. Internal platforms rely specifically on the know-how, background knowledge, and experience of their employees to improve e.g., organizational or manufacturing processes. External crowdsourcing platforms with the inclusion of customers, experts, and people interested in the topic have a different objective. They are largely used to open new fields of application or generate and discuss ideas about product features, improvements, and technologies based on the communities' experiences and opinions. This is backed up by statements like "it is not just the target group but the objectives in general that differs between those projects and make them hardly copiable".
- **'Lack' of success:** The combination of internal and external platforms leads to higher efforts and expenses, the time horizon related to Return on Investment (ROI) which is usually already longer in the case of innovation projects would extend accordingly. The management on the other hand is expecting quick results and short-term effects. The high expectations of innovation initiatives and the expected added value cannot be reached directly, and the campaigns are prematurely declared as failures. Future budgets and management buy-in are getting harder to assemble and eventually a potential expansion from internal to external crowdsourcing or vice versa (as originally planned) is then no longer considered. One of our interviewees confirmed this, by stating that "to be successful you need to start with building an innovation culture where everyone can develop freely, and failure is not immediately associated with the cancellation of innovation initiatives".
- **Missing capabilities & resources:** Another reason for starting with either an internal or an external open innovation platform is the lack of capabilities and resources. In

most cases, a central innovation-focused department is responsible for those types of initiatives but usually, they are not sufficiently staffed to do both at once. An interviewee stated: "Building an (additional) external platform would take 6–12 months. Processes, procedures, objectives, and target groups would first have to be defined. We would have the skills and know-how, but our capacity is tied up". Simply put, different stakeholders, new methodologies, and unknown terrain raise the fear of uncontrollable workloads and a scarcity of resources for other projects as well as additional spending on uncertain results.

- **Coherent external satellites & internal red tape:** The differences in process and frame, as well as the use of external contractors regarding external crowdsourcing, has different consequences that lead to a coherent division of both initiatives in execution. Even though the external service providers must be paid, the organizational part of that process is way leaner as you simply create an external satellite. However, this means that ideas generated externally have then to be brought into the organization eventually. This often fails as the responsible departments are not willing to accept outside ideas without affective connections, the 'not-invented-here-syndrome' [27], or because of the missing organizational link to connect those ideas to the internal innovation stage-gate process. One interviewee criticized that "after an idea has been generated, 3–5 years can pass before it is implemented due to our red tape. During this time, a lot can happen and those involved lose the motivation to continue being active. Faster, visible results would lead to more acceptance and, above all, benefits for the customer".
- **Use of traditional CIP & opacity:** We want to point out again that many organizations do have a certain internal ideation process. Most of the time this is limited to continuous improvement - not internal crowdsourcing campaigns through social media platforms as defined for this research. Their process of opening and including other departments, integrating further gamification mechanics, or iteratively changing the used platform, even from offline idea boxes to a self-made forum, is sometimes creeping and already a disruptive step for them. However, this process is hard to analyze or categorize and hence a central limitation to our research. But it is obvious that many companies are opaque regarding their approach on how to foster innovation internally and are keen on protecting their IP as well as processes at all costs. They still fear opening to a bigger and external crowd either due to their non-open innovation culture, their traditional industry, or competitive markets and fear of loss of IP. Therefore, many companies alone due to industry or culture already fail to implement internal or external crowdsourcing structures, due not only to their protective and traditional markets, but also to their non-open strategy and culture.

Thus, our qualitative data shows that most organizations focus on external crowdsourcing *or* internal crowdsourcing contests for creating new ideas. Furthermore, even if organizations have used both scenarios it usually hasn't been simultaneously. They start with one approach as a pilot or sometimes even proceed several years before switching to either external or internal initiatives, usually without driving both.

At this stage, we want to share and trigger additional interesting insights apart from the major research questions. The use of external crowdsourcing as pilot projects outnumbers that of internal campaigns [15], even though we have found that the success rate for the implementation of internally sourced ideas is usually higher. On the one hand, this is due to internal experts, even from different departments, having a broad experience and know-how about the market. Their ideas suit the market needs and circumstances and can therefore be transferred more easily into solutions. On the other hand, many organizations have not yet found the right approach on how to integrate and implement ideas from customers or external experts within their own stage-gate process by also including the responsible stakeholders like R&D. Either way, it is also crucial to have the right participants in a sufficient number. Interestingly many organizations are more successful in activating their own employees than external experts. We found reasons for the difficulties of recruiting participants for external contests to inlcude the lack of a sophisticated incentivization system, its few communication channels, its loose customer base, or an unprofessional recruitment strategy.

### 4.3 Internal Initiatives as a Potential Starting Point to Accelerate External Efforts

When companies and organizations decide to start with crowdsourcing and choose an internal innovation platform for this purpose, the reason usually is that they see the internal variant as more protected and can thus approach it slowly. This is especially true for traditional industries such as B2B, pharmaceuticals, or insurance, whereas more innovation-driven industries such as FMCG or automotive look consciously for the touchpoint with end customers and rather rely on external platforms and their potentials, such as strong marketing effects. In many cases, this initial experience and presuming success is necessary to persuade the decision-makers to invest in external innovation platforms as well. Apart from this long-term buy-in, other crucial factors might lead to an acceleration of external efforts through an initial internal set-up.

First, the process of setting up crowdsourcing platforms and initiatives is the basis for future success. That means building capabilities on crowdsourcing in general, but also on certain crowdsourcing subtopics like topic framing, feedback management, community management, communication management, or incentives to motivate users in the social media world, as well as stakeholder management. This know-how can then be transferred to external platforms (for many organizations that means leaving the comfort zone of their more protected terrain). In addition, the possibilities of gamification can already be tested internally before they are applied externally in a meaningful way. These include the duration of the competition, prizes, or evaluation processes (pitch, voting) alike. Another aspect worth looking at is that internal crowdsourcing ideas tend to be implemented more often, as stated before, because they are e.g. incremental rather than disruptive and therefore easier to implement. At the same time, there is also an established process for how the ideas are further exploited. In this context, the long-term integration of internal experts from R&D as well as from other relevant departments seems necessary as our data shows that the companies most successful regarding crowdsourcing integrated those stakeholders from the kick-off or at least via both the community management and feedback management. Methods of communication with users should be practiced as poor communication can be a source of frustration of external users if these users feel they are not treated or handled professionally (time of response for ideas, positive attitude, non-destructive improvement philosophy, etc.). As soon as a vivid communication and interaction is established, internal experts also start to co-create with the community and no longer view the ideas as transactional goods from external users. This helps to lower the barrier of the 'not-invented-here' syndrome. At last, we found that a smart funneling of internal contest topic and framing helps to pre-evaluate potential topics with an external crowd. The internal pre-filtering, evaluation, and feedback through a preceding internal ideation session can lead to prioritized topics adequate for external experts or users. This ensures that the external crowd receives a very specific question that they can then work on with their creative outside perspective and disruptive ideas.

## 5  Further Research and Managerial Implications

In this paper we have summarized some major answers and insights regarding the leading research questions about 1) the success factors of internal crowdsourcing, 2) the various and in-depth evidence on why organizations and managers alike usually do not mix those approaches or drive them simultaneously, and 3) the potential ramp-up of external efforts through internal crowdsourcing. Furthermore, we have detected that many organizations, as well as scientific research, lack a true understanding and data about the nexus and different dimensions of internal crowdsourcing and their coherences regarding external initiatives. Therefore, we see this paper more as a starting point for going beyond the qualitative data of our sample and backing the findings to answer further questions about the usage, duration, needed skill sets, and interaction of internal crowdsourcing projects – also in the scope of upcoming technologies. Here further data and the eruption of our mentioned limitations towards more quantitative (and majorly long-term) data highlighting the project's outcomes in the long run ("innovation as part of a marathon, not a sprint" as an interviewee mentioned) will be very interesting and helpful for sustainable findings. The discussion and insights were heavily focused and, as stated before, still showing tremendous potential for sharing them in more detail. Lastly, as those insights can be used by practitioners and managers to improve their open innovation strategy through social media influenced crowdsourcing, it would be an organic step to transfer our research outcome into hands-on and broad guidelines or a manual for practitioners. Consequently, and as a final outlook, we would like to conclude this paper with a quick overview and sneak-peak of managerial implications to improve crowdsourcing strategies for organizations.

**Separate CIP and Internal Crowdsourcing Efforts:** As our theoretical background and definition have shown, CIP and internal crowdsourcing are different approaches with different processes, methodologies, required capabilities, as well as technology. Many companies believe that they are using internal crowdsourcing when they use their CIP on a new technology or platform. This misunderstanding and lack of differentiation lead to a creeping process from CIP into a semi-open crowdsourcing approach without much dynamic, gamification, and interaction and in most cases then to a non-successful evaluation of those efforts. What we have seen across the successful cases is a clear commitment to internal crowdsourcing separated and clearly distinguished from a still existing CIP targeting efficiency and incremental innovation. Furthermore, the decision gates, the innovation funnel, as well as the responsible managers, are divided and a mix of those two internal processes are strictly avoided.

**Bridge Internal Gaps at an Early Stage:** In addition to getting the upper management on board, it is necessary during the conception phase to build a stakeholder map. One of the main reasons for crowdsourcing initiatives to be categorized as failures is due to internal barriers, inefficiency, or refusal of ideas or processes, rather than due to bad ideas or the output itself. One outstanding issue is still a 'not-invented-here' mindset from the people in charge of the execution or the enhancement of the crowdsourced input. Our interviewees repeatedly stated that "ideas from outside are not ones to implement directly. They are mere parts of a different universe that must be adopted in our system for implementation. A gold nugget is possible but rather hard to find in those initiatives. Therefore, our R&D needs an early bonding with those ideas for quality as well as for effective reasons". It makes sense to include the responsible individuals for potential implementation of the ideas already in the conception phase and by selecting them as members of the core expert team to provide feedback, evaluate, and finally select the ideas they should implement. Getting a direct communication channel between the internal experts on the chosen topic for the crowdsourcing contest and the internal or external users is key to change their minds about a more open, but not competitive, approach. Finally, organizations should focus on teamwork, especially by also including departments or stakeholders who are regarded as critics or innovation objectors. Excluding them may only postpone issues to a later stage in the innovation process, where it might be even more expansive or delicate to stop or proceed. This feeling "of being heard", rather than facing them with cemented guidelines, leads overall to a more fruitful and cooperative surrounding.

**Target Internal and External Crowdsourcing in Parallel:** Our data has shown that there are multidimensional reasons why organizations are not using internal and external crowdsourcing simultaneously. However, those insights exclude reasons for a missing sense of driving both. It is simply very hard to push both on a professional and sustainable level. On the contrary, when asking the decision-makers, they overall support the idea of an omnichannel crowdsourcing strategy and build a vision around it, but most often they fail to implement it. As important learnings from those few organizations with an established dual crowdsourcing program, we can share the importance of a similar process and central team with the needed capabilities for driving both approaches. Secondly, when external service providers are contracted, which they are in most cases, their approach should be integrated or coordinated with that of the organization, in order to form a common process. They should not build external stand-alone systems where only the final selection of ideas is considered for integration into the organization. This shared process leads to further synergies for internal resources and the ongoing innovation funneling. Moreover, a dual program does not need to be implemented right from the beginning, as organizations profit from starting with one approach to pilot the method, build capabilities, and share the learnings. Based on the initial experience from either internal or external initiatives, a plan combining both approaches can be derived. This is important to clarify the intentions of a long-term strategy with the board or responsible decision-makers and to manage the appropriate expectations for this iterative approach. This approach should help to mitigate the dominant belief of a direct ROI through disruptive and incremental ideas being implemented starting with the results of the first campaign. It may take running up to three campaigns until the capabilities, knowledge, exchange, and culture for a sustainable crowdsourcing program are established. This time is also needed to experiment to adjust the methodologies to the processes and internal frameworks. Crowdsourcing programs have huge potential – internal, external, or both together- but need time to be set-up appropriately. The buy-in from the board and top management is important from the get-go to sustain that pressure but is also required to convince the needed stakeholders (e.g., communication, R&D, innovation) and with them the potential critics. Here, it is wise to combine the buy-in with certain responsibilities for the board members (e.g., jury members for selecting the most promising ideas through pitches or by conducting workshops or face-to-face talks), in order to authentically spread the Open Innovation culture and to add layers to your online-offline approach to market and accelerate your campaigns (next to onsite ideation workshops for generating ideas for the online platform, etc.).

# References

1. Malhotra, A., Majchrzak, A., Kesebi, L., Looram, S.: Developing innovative solutions through internal crowdsourcing. MIT Sloan Manag. Rev. **58**(4), 73 (2017)
2. Zuchowski, O., Posegga, O., Schlagwein, D., Fischbach, K.: Internal crowdsourcing: conceptual framework, structured review, and research agenda. J. Inf. Technol. **31**(2), 166–184 (2016)
3. Bhuiyan, N., Baghel, A.: An overview of continuous improvement: from the past to the present. Manag. Decis. **43**(5), 761–771 (2005)
4. Erickson, L.B., Trauth, E.M., Petrick, I.: Getting inside your employees' heads: navigating barriers to internal-crowdsourcing for product and service innovation (2012)
5. Baskerville, R.L., Wood-Harper, A.T.: A critical perspective on action research as a method for information systems research. J. Inf. Technol. **11**(3), 235–246 (1996). https://doi.org/10.1080/026839696345289
6. Boudreau, K.J., Lakhani, K.R.: Using the crowd as an innovation partner. Harv. Bus. Rev. **91**(4), 60–69, 140 (2013)
7. Füller, J., Mühlbacher, H., Matzler, K., Jawecki, G.: Consumer empowerment through internet-based co-creation. J. Manag. Inf. Syst. **26**(3), 71–102 (2009)
8. Koch, G., Rapp, M., Kröger, N.: Harnessing the innovation potential of citizens: how open innovation can be used to co-develop political strategies. In: Pfeffermann, Nicole, Minshall, Tim, Mortara, Letizia (eds.) Strategy and Communication for Innovation, pp. 63–83. Springer, Heidelberg (2013). https://doi.org/10.1007/978-3-642-41479-4_5
9. Brunswicker, S., Chesbrough, H.: The adoption of open innovation in large firms: practices, measures, and risks a survey of large firms examines how firms approach open innovation strategically and manage knowledge flows at the project level. Res. Manag. **61**(1), 35–45 (2018)
10. Howe, J.: The rise of crowdsourcing. Wired Mag. **14**(6), 1–4 (2006)
11. Ghezzi, A., Gabelloni, D., Martini, A., Natalicchio, A.: Crowdsourcing: a review and suggestions for future research. Int. J. Manag. Rev. **20**(2), 343–363 (2018)
12. Zheng, H., Li, D., Hou, W.: Task design, motivation, and participation in crowdsourcing contests. Int. J. Electron. Commer. **15**(4), 57–88 (2011)
13. Lakhani, K.R., Wolf, R.G.: Why hackers do what they do: understanding motivation and effort in free/open source software projects (2003)

14. Hutter, K., Hautz, J., Füller, J., Mueller, J., Matzler, K.: Communitition: the tension between competition and collaboration in community-based design contests. Creat. Innov. Manag. **20**(1), 3–21 (2011)
15. Rapp, M., Kröger, N., Scheerer, S.: Roles on corporate and public innovation communities: understanding personas to reach new frontiers. In: Meiselwitz, Gabriele (ed.) HCII 2020. LNCS, vol. 12194, pp. 95–109. Springer, Cham (2020). https://doi.org/10.1007/978-3-030-49570-1_8
16. Bullinger, A.C., Moeslein, K.M.: Innovation contests-where are we? In: AMCIS, p. 28 (2010)
17. Zynga, A., Diener, K., Ihl, C., Lüttgens, D., Piller, F., Scherb, B.: Making open innovation stick: a study of open innovation implementation in 756 global organizations: a large study of international companies shows that distinct routines and organizational structures differentiate organizations that succeed with open inn. Res. Manag. **61**(4), 16–25 (2018)
18. de Melo, J.C.F., Salerno, M.S., Freitas, J.S., Bagno, R.B., Brasil, V.C.: From open innovation projects to open innovation project management capabilities: a process-based approach. Int. J. Proj. Manag. **38**(5), 278–290 (2020)
19. Neagoe, L.N., Klein, V.M.: Employee suggestion system (Kaizen Teian) the bottom-up approach for productivity improvement. Control **10**(3), 26–27 (2009)
20. Pohlisch, J.: Managing the crowd: a literature review of empirical studies on internal crowdsourcing. In: Ulbrich, H., Wedel, M., Dienel, H.L. (eds.) Internal Crowdsourcing in Companies. Contributions to Management Science, Springer, Cham (2021). https://doi.org/10.1007/978-3-030-52881-2_3
21. Knop, N., Durward, D., Blohm, I.: How to design an internal crowdsourcing system? (2017)
22. Gallus, J., Jung, O., Lakhani, K.R.: Recognition Incentives for internal crowdsourcing: a field experiment at NASA. Harvard Business School Technology & Operations Management Unit Working Paper, no. 20-059 (2020)
23. Benbya, H., Leidner, D.: Harnessing employee innovation in internal crowdsourcing platforms: lessons from Allianz UK (2016)
24. Zhu, H., Sick, N., Leker, J.: How to use crowdsourcing for innovation? A comparative case study of internal and external idea sourcing in the chemical industry. In: 2016 Portland International Conference on Management of Engineering and Technology (PICMET), pp. 887–901 (2016)
25. Simula, H., Vuori, M.: Benefits and barriers of crowdsourcing in B2B firms: generating ideas with internal and external crowds. Int. J. Innov. Manag. **16**(06), 1240011 (2012)
26. Eisenhardt, K.M.: Building theories from case study research. Acad. Manag. Rev. **14**(4), 532–550 (1989)
27. Antons, D., Declerck, M., Diener, K., Koch, I., Piller, F.T.: Assessing the not-invented-here syndrome: development and validation of implicit and explicit measurements. J. Organ. Behav. **38**(8), 1227–1245 (2017)

# The Need for New Education Platforms that Support Inclusive Social Learning: A Case Study of Online and Hybrid K-12 Learning Experience During the COVID-19 Pandemic

Robyn Rice[✉]

STEMD2 R&D Group, Center on Disability Studies, University of Hawaii at Manoa, Honolulu, HI, USA
rice2@hawaii.edu

**Abstract.** The COVID-19 pandemic had a profound impact on education in the 2020–2021 school year. Teachers who were educated and trained for teaching in a face-to-face classroom had to learn to teach online or in hybrid environments with little preparation or training. This paper explores the experiences of K-12 teachers who were teaching in online and hybrid classrooms due to the COVID-19 Pandemic. The participants in this case study consisted of two groups of teachers. The first group of teachers consisted of 12 teachers in Hawai'i who were taking the professional development course that introduced them to the Authentic Social Learning Model (ASLM). The second group of teachers consisted of 5 teachers in Arizona who have been using the ASLM for a minimum of 3 years. The ASLM is based on social learning which is an application of the theory of connectivism. The purpose of this paper is to explore how teachers used the G Suite for Education (GSE) to implement the ASLM in online and hybrid classrooms during the COVID-19 pandemic and to recommend new education platforms that support inclusive social learning. Teachers in the case study indicated that implementing the ASLM resulted in students who were more engaged and motivated. The results indicated that social learning, which is the basis of the ASLM, was the most difficult aspect to implement in online and hybrid classes. Based on the results of this case study, this paper presents recommendations for new technology platforms that would allow teachers to easily implement social learning in K-12 online and hybrid classrooms.

**Keywords:** K-12 online · K-12 hybrid education · G suite for education · Google · Connectivism · Social learning · COVID-19 · Inclusive education

## 1 Introduction

The COVID-19 pandemic had a profound impact on education worldwide. During the COVID-19 pandemic, the only thing that seemed constant in education is change. In the United States, educators had to transition their curriculum to be suitable for online or hybrid learning. Teachers found themselves teaching in completely new ways using new

© Springer Nature Switzerland AG 2021
F. F.-H. Nah and K. Siau (Eds.): HCII 2021, LNCS 12783, pp. 515–527, 2021.
https://doi.org/10.1007/978-3-030-77750-0_33

technologies they may not have been familiar with before. Teachers who were educated and trained for teaching in a face-to-face classroom had to learn to teach online or in hybrid environments with little preparation or training. While educators were familiar with the standards for quality teaching in a face-to-face environment, little research was available on quality education in virtual settings (Nelson and Murakami 2020). Rice (2018) stated that most K-12 educational settings are still traditional teacher-centered classrooms in brick-and-mortar settings. The COVID-19 pandemic quickly changed K-12 classes from brick-and-mortar to online and hybrid settings. School districts were making and changing plans daily (Brelsford et al. 2020). Teachers were tasked with trying to find a way to teach their students in an ever-changing and highly unprecedented situation. Teachers worked hard to adapt their face-to-face lessons to online and hybrid teaching. But most teachers lacked the training to provide the rigorous instruction in their online or hybrid classes that they were providing before the pandemic (Anderson 2020). Despite the added pressure and technology requirements, teachers found ways to continue educating their students during the COVID-19 pandemic. The teachers in this case study utilized our Authentic Social Learning Model (ASLM) to create inclusive online and hybrid classrooms.

## 1.1 Our Authentic Social Learning Model (ASLM)

This case study involves a group of teachers who were participating in a professional development class during the transition to online and hybrid teaching. These teachers were attending a training entitled "Authentic Social Learning: An Inclusive Teaching Model to Support Diverse Learners in Hawai'i". The training course introduced the teachers to our ASLM. Our ASLM was designed as a model for inclusive 21st-century teaching using authentic social learning. This model has been used for several years by teachers in Arizona and was modified and conceptualized for the Ne'epapa Ka Hana Professional Development Series offered in Hawai'i. Our ASLM combines the pedagogical strategies for connectivism, inclusive teaching, authentic learning, and formative assessment (see Fig. 1). The result of this combination is an authentic social learning model for K-12 classrooms that could be adapted to online and hybrid classes. The ASLM professional development training provided teachers with a model for online and hybrid teaching and resources for implementing the model.

Our ASLM is a research-based model for inclusive education that was developed for the Ne'epapa Ka Hana Professional Development Series offered by the Center for Disability Studies in Hawai'i. The purpose of our ASLM is to increase inclusion and improve student achievement through social learning in K-12 classrooms. The model is based on social learning which is an application of the theory of connectivism. Connectivism is a learning theory developed by George Siemens that states that learning occurs through a system of network connections (Siemens 2005). These network connections can be social networks, such as peer groups in a classroom, or technology networks (Siemens 2005). Social learning uses the theory of connectivism to leverage the social nature of students for educational purposes.

Our ASLM utilizes social learning strategies to create an inclusive classroom environment. These strategies, known as our ASLM strategies were derived from the interaction analysis model presented by Gunawardena et al. (1997), the four stages of online

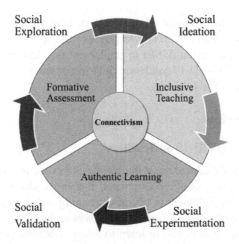

**Fig. 1.** Authentic Social Learning Model (ASLM)

learning by Downes (2010), and the 5E Instructional Model by Bybee (2006). The four ASLM strategies are social exploration, social ideation, social experimentation, and social validation. Abhari (2017) developed our ASLM strategies to operationalize the principles of connectivism: agency, openness, connectivity, and diversity. Our ASLM strategies are a systematic approach that students use to solve authentic problems or challenges. Social exploration allows students to understand why they need to learn. During social exploration, students work as a team to research a challenge and discover the background of the problem and previously proposed solutions. Social ideation helps the students understand what they need to learn. During social ideation, students work together to develop original ideas to solve their problems or challenges. Using social experimentation, the students discover how to learn. During social experimentation, the students test, reject, or refine the solutions they developed during social ideation to develop their final solution. Through social validation, the students understand how to improve their learning. Social validation is the opportunity for students to share their ideas with community members, local experts, or other outside individuals to obtain feedback.

This case study explored a group of 12 teachers in Hawai'i who were being trained on our ASLM during the summer and fall of the 2020–2021 school year. In addition to the teachers participating in the PD, this case study also includes 5 teachers in Arizona who had been using our ASLM for three or more years. Many school districts, like those in this case study, have strategic plans that involved increasing the technology available to students over the next several years. Suddenly these school districts, like many around the country, had to find a way to provide technology to every student in a very short time. At the same time, students had to learn to access and use technology resources for all of their classes and assignments. Unfortunately, the quick integration of technology meant that many teachers and students were not prepared or properly trained on many of the programs they would be using, including Google Suite for Education (GSE). GSE is a free cloud-based service provided by Google that can help integrate and simplify classroom technology (Bray 2016). One of the GSE, Google Classroom, functions as a learning management system (LMS) to help teachers organize and manage their classrooms (Johns et al. 2017). The purpose of this paper is to explore how teachers used the G Suite for Education (GSE) to implement our ASLM in online and hybrid classrooms during the COVID-19 pandemic and to recommend new education platforms that support inclusive social learning.

## 2    Literature Review

### 2.1    The Impact of COVID-19 on Teachers

A large majority of K-12 educators in the United States are trained and teach in face-to-face classrooms. Girelli et al. (2020) stated that most educators view face-to-face instruction as an essential element in effective teaching and student motivation. Due to the COVID-19 pandemic, face-to-face teaching was replaced, literally overnight, with distance learning and teachers had to learn to adapt. Teachers viewed online learning as a response to an emergency, and not as a sustainable replacement for face-to-face teaching (Girelli et al. 2020). Not only were teachers required to change their instructional model, they suddenly had to implement technology into their teaching with little or no proper training (Brelsford et al. 2020). Educators who had been reluctant to implement technology in their classrooms no longer had the choice to continue without technology.

Despite the negative impact of the COVID-19 pandemic on teachers, there have been some benefits. Teachers who had grown comfortable with their teaching practices had to be more innovative and rethink how they approached education. Reimers and Schleicher (2020) reported that the pandemic has resulted in the introduction of new technologies and innovations in the classroom. Teachers have experimented with new strategies, learning tools, and evaluation practices in the hopes of engaging their online and hybrid classes (Girelli et al. 2020). The new skills gained by teachers will not only benefit their students during the pandemic but will continue to benefit them when they return to in-person learning (Girelli et al. 2020). Despite the positive impact, these sudden and abrupt changes had a severe impact on the stress levels of educators.

Teachers were overwhelmed with the pressure of learning to teach in online and hybrid settings and learning to use a variety of technology tools that they may not have been familiar with before the pandemic. Girelli et al. (2020) stated that "COVID-19 has increased teacher workload without sufficient professional development or resources to meet their needs" (p. 54). While resources were provided by lawmakers and administrators, the policymakers often did not have an understanding of the needs of the educators, so they were provided with ineffective resources or insufficient training (Girelli et al. 2020). Educators had to attempt to find ways to adapt state and federal curriculum standards to online and hybrid environments (Anderson 2020). The added workload and lack of training often cut into the teachers' personal and family time (Brelsford et al. 2020). Teachers found themselves working well past school hours to try to plan lessons that are designed for in-person learning but had to be adapted to online or hybrid settings.

### 2.2    The Impact of COVID-19 on Students

Changes in education, whether positive or negative, ultimately impact the end-users of educational policies and practices, the students. The COVID-19 pandemic has drastically changed the way students attend school and has impacted their academic progress as well as their social-emotional progress. Some positive results of the changes that have resulted from the pandemic are higher parent involvement in their children's education and increased autonomy of students (Reimers and Schleicher 2020). However, these positive effects have been overshadowed by concerns regarding the continuation of educational resources through available technology and the students' emotional health.

There has been significant concern regarding accessibility and online access for remote students and those with lower SES. Rather than implementing a standardized approach to the pandemic, each district was given the freedom to choose how to continue education during the pandemic (Anderson 2020). Many districts implemented online and hybrid models that utilized a video conference platform for students and teachers to meet. These online learning and hybrid models offered students and teachers the opportunity to meet, but most teachers do not consider it sufficient to meet the needs of their students (Girelli et al. 2020). Anderson (2020) stated that students from middle and lower-income homes are showing higher rates of academic regression, resulting in a widening of the educational achievement gap. These students often have unstable internet and may have difficulty connecting to online classes.

The students who have been most affected by the COVID-19 pandemic are those with special needs. Like regular education teachers, special education teachers were not provided with specific training for teaching online or hybrid classes. Special education teachers did not have time or additional support to implement specialized instruction to meet the academic and social needs of their students in online and hybrid classes (Brelsford et al. 2020). Girelli et al. (2020) stated that the shift to remote learning has been especially difficult for students with special needs. Students with special needs may not have had the skills or resources required to access their distance learning classes and has resulted in a greater learning gap.

## 2.3  G Suite for Education (GSE)

When the COVID-19 pandemic caused a major shift to educational practice in the United States, it became immediately apparent that many school districts were not prepared for an online learning platform. An international study conducted by Reimers and Schleicher (2020) indicated that the highest priority, and also the greatest challenge, for education was ensuring the continuity of academic learning for students. In the same study, about 75% of principals in the United States reported that teachers had the technical and pedagogical skills to integrate digital technology, though it was only about 55% for disadvantaged schools (Reimers and Schleicher 2020). Only slightly more than three-fourths of the principals surveyed in the United States felt that they had an effective online learning platform available for their students (Reimers and Schleicher 2020). Many K-12 schools turned to the G Suite for Education tools for their learning platform.

The G Suite for Education is a cloud-based set of free technology tools offered by Google to educators to facilitate and manage student learning. GSE includes tools to transform teaching by incorporating the 21st-century skills of creating, collaborating, critical thinking, and information sharing (Johns et al. 2017). GSE includes Google Classroom, which is a platform that teachers can use to manage how the classroom is organized and run, and stores all of the class assignments in one place, thus functioning as a Learning Management System (LMS) (Johns et al. 2017). Google Classroom is also integrated with many other educational tools offered to schools (De Vynck and Bergen 2020). Google Classroom also provides access to a video conferencing platform to hold classes called Google Meet. According to De Vynck and Bergen (2020), the active users of GSE doubled from the beginning of March to the end of March 2020 as schools moved to online platforms due to the COVID-19 pandemic.

As schools shifted to online and hybrid learning using GSE, there were some concerns with accessibility, safety, and security. Some students quickly adapted to online learning platforms while others struggled to navigate the technology needed for virtual learning (Anderson 2020). The greatest strength of GSE is that it can be used for collaboration, but this function could easily be misused by students (Bray 2016). At the beginning of the pandemic, educators who were using Google Meet could be kicked out of the class by the students, so GSE had to quickly update their software as these issues were discovered (De Vynck and Bergen 2020). GSE continues to be updated and implemented in schools worldwide with over 100 million users as of March 2020 (De Vynck and Bergen 2020).

## 3  Methodology

Our ASLM, like most educational models, was originally designed for in-person learning. However, during the COVID-19 pandemic, teachers in this case study implemented the model with the goal of increasing engagement and inclusion in online and hybrid classrooms using GSE. The participants in this case study consisted of two groups of teachers. The first group of teachers consisted of 12 teachers in Hawai'i who were taking the professional development course entitled "Authentic Social Learning: An Inclusive Teaching Model to Support Diverse Learners in Hawai'i" during the beginning of the 2020–2021 school year. The course was offered through the Ne'epapa Ka Hana Professional Development Series in Hawai'i. The second group of teachers consisted of 5 teachers in Arizona who have been using our ASLM for a minimum of 3 years. Both groups of teachers implemented our ASLM in their online and hybrid classes at the beginning of the 2020–2021 school year. The teachers in this case study had varying degrees of experience and expertise with GSE, though they had all had some previous experience with Google Classroom.

As a requirement for completion of the professional development course, the 12 Hawai'i teachers had to submit a portfolio consisting of ASLM lesson plans and course reflections. The portfolio submissions were reviewed for data about the implementation of our ASLM in their online and hybrid courses and the use of GSE in that implementation. The 5 Arizona teachers responded to a questionnaire via Google Forms that asked about their experiences implementing our ASLM in online and hybrid classrooms using GSE. The data from the portfolios and questionnaires were analyzed using structural coding and pattern coding.

## 4  Data Analysis

The purpose of this case study is to explore how teachers used the G Suite for Education (GSE) to implement our ASLM in online and hybrid classrooms during the COVID-19 pandemic and to recommend new education platforms that support inclusive social learning. The teachers implemented lessons and projects that utilized our ASLM during the fall of 2020. The portfolios of the 12 Hawai'i teachers and the questionnaires for the 5 Arizona teachers were analyzed using thematic coding. First, the data were analyzed with structural coding for references to how they used GSE to implement our ASLM. Pattern coding was used to organize the structural codes into themes. The themes that developed from the data analysis were how GSE was used in the switch to online and hybrid learning, and how GSE was used for each of our ASLM components: authentic learning, social learning, inclusive teaching, and formative assessment.

# 5  Discussion

## 5.1  The Switch to Online and Hybrid Learning Using GSE

Teachers in this case study felt that their technology integration timeline was drastically advanced due to the COVID-19 pandemic. Whereas many teachers were slow or reluctant to implement technology before the pandemic and often used computers just to have their students' research topics, they suddenly had to use computers for everything. One teacher stated that she was "100% online and that I would need to find ways to engage my students in a different way, one that tested my technological skills". The teachers quickly learned new platforms to engage their students. Many of the teachers had used Google Classroom before this case study, but they were not using it as an LMS. That changed during the pandemic. Teachers began to rely on Google Classroom as their LMS to keep themselves and their students organized. Teachers also reported that they used Google Jamboard, Google Slides, and Google Meets as platforms to engage their students.

The teachers in this case study reported that they had to find ways to reevaluate their traditional lessons to engage their online and hybrid students. One participant stated that "with distance learning, the need to innovate instruction strategies play a vital role in making sure that every student succeeds." Other teachers reported that the pandemic offered an opportunity to try something new that they would not have done otherwise. One of the common strategies that teachers used to engage their classes during online and hybrid learning was the use of flipped classrooms. The teachers would provide lessons for students to watch during asynchronous instructional time and use synchronous class time for hands-on lessons and social learning. The teachers used breakout rooms during synchronous instructional time to build relationships between peers and between the teacher and students.

Teachers were not the only ones who had to adapt to the rapid infusion of technology. The switch to online and hybrid learning was a big change for the students. The teachers reported that students had to learn to use a variety of technology tools very quickly. One teacher reported that she had several students who did not turn in an assignment. When she met with the students and asked why the work was not done, the student admitted that they did not know how to create the Google Slides that were required for the assignment. Some of the students struggled at the beginning and took a while to adapt, but the teachers reported that the students were getting much better as time went on. Teachers reported that their students found new ways to communicate with them and with one another, specifically citing breakout room discussions, Gmail conversations, and communicating in Google Docs.

The teachers in this case study reported that using Google Classroom as an LMS made the switch to online and hybrid learning easier. Because the teachers and students had some experience with Google Classroom, the transition was smoother because the students were familiar with the Google Classroom platform. The teachers transitioned to using Google Classroom as their LMS to provide a consistent location for all of their assignments, class meeting, and communication. The major advantage reported by the teachers was that the students could access their classwork and meeting from any computer or location. Some of the teachers in this case study even used Google Classroom and Google Meets to teach students who were in person and at home simultaneously. The teachers used Gmail and Google calendars that are integrated with Google Classroom to help the students stay organized so they would meet deadlines and attend class when required.

Even with GSE available to make the switch to online and hybrid learning easier, there were still some areas that the teachers found difficult to overcome. The teachers reported engagement as a major barrier to educating students online. The teachers stated that online settings provided students with a sense of anonymity that did not exist before. Every teacher in the case study reported that students were reluctant to turn on their cameras and participate in class. The teachers stated that it was much more difficult to build strong relationships with their students. The teachers also stated that it was more time consuming to take attendance. While the teachers worked to overcome these obstacles, they still had difficulty engaging students online to the same degree they could engage them in-person. Teachers reported difficulty using the breakout rooms in Google Meets and stated that whole class discussions were difficult in Google Meets. When the teachers tried to engage the students in whole-class discussions, it was awkward with students speaking over each other when they would unmute themselves.

## 5.2   Implementing Our ASLM with GSE

The teachers in this case study were implementing our ASLM, a model for inclusive teaching using authentic social learning. The model is based on social learning which is an application of the theory of connectivism. To implement this model, teachers designed lessons and projects that incorporated the components of our ASLM: authentic learning, social learning, inclusive teaching strategies, and formative assessment. Our ASLM utilizes our ASLM strategies to integrate the components into one pedagogical approach, but for data analysis for this study, the components were reported separately.

**Authentic Learning.** Teachers in this study reported that implementing authentic learning improved the engagement and motivation of their students. One teacher stated that her students were more engaged and willing to participate in online classes when the activities were hands-on and connected to the real world. Another teacher reported that she used asynchronous, individual time to have the students explore or research the concepts at home and then meet with teammates to share their ideas during synchronous class time. The teachers found that the students were more likely to involve their family members in the learning process during authentic learning tasks. Teachers were able to develop tasks and problems that used materials or items found around the students' homes. However, this also presented a problem when students didn't have a particular material at home. One participant stated that it was important to be cognizant of students' home situations during online learning.

Teachers in this case study reported that GSE was useful for implementing authentic learning in their online and hybrid classes. Teachers used Google Jamboard for students to brainstorm ideas during synchronous instruction. The students used the comments section of Google Classroom to share ideas and ask questions. One teacher reported using Google Slides to create a choice board so the students could pick which task they wanted to complete. A math teacher had students use Google Forms to collect data from their classmates that they used in a graphing assignment.

**Social Learning.** Social learning is the basis of our ASLM and was also the most difficult to implement in online and hybrid classes. At first, teachers did not think they would be able to incorporate social learning or collaboration in online classes. Despite the struggle, teachers found ways to implement social learning. One teacher stated that "COVID forced me to look into ways to keep collaboration alive by getting more comfortable with technology". This case study found that the students missed social interactions with their peers during quarantine and were excited to connect and work with their peers. Several teachers reported that their students were more focused and on task during small group meetings than they were during large class meetings.

The teachers used various tools from GSE to find innovative ways to implement social learning. The main tools that were used were small group meetings in Google Meets. Some teachers used breakout rooms while others preferred to open a Google Meet for each group. One teacher used Google Classroom to post open-ended discussion questions that the students could respond to and reply to their classmate's posts, creating a whole class discussion. The students used shared Google Docs or Gmail to collaborate on their assignments. Other teachers reported that students used the chat function in Google Meets to connect with their classmates.

Although teachers were able to find ways to encourage social learning using GSE, they ran into some challenges. Some of the teachers reported that their schools would not allow them to use breakout rooms. When students are placed in breakout rooms, they are not monitored by a teacher at all times, creating safety and security concerns. To overcome this, some of the teachers would open multiple Google Meets with a group in each Meet. However, the teachers reported that volume was an issue when multiple meets were open; they could monitor the students but could not talk to them. Overall, trying to find ways to monitor social learning networks was the most difficult part of implementing our ASLM in online and hybrid classes.

**Inclusive Teaching.** The teachers in this case study reported that GSE and their new technology integration skills acquired due to the COVID-19 pandemic switch to online learning allowed them to provide more options for their students to increase inclusion. The teachers in this study reported providing lessons to their students in multiple formats. The teachers used a variety of online videos and print options to teach concepts. One participant in this study reported that using online resources and GSE inspired them to provide their students with more options to demonstrate their learning. In their in-person classroom, the students are given a worksheet or similar assignment, but in their online classes, the students could choose a variety of formats to show their understanding.

Online and hybrid teaching had some positive impacts on high needs students. Some teachers in this study recorded their live lessons in Google Meets and posted those lessons on Google Classroom. This allowed students who were absent or had connectivity issues to access the lesson later. One teacher stated that the recorded lessons helped her students with special needs because they could go back and watch the lesson again to gain a better understanding. The teacher explained that this is not something students can do during in-person class sessions. One of the participants co-taught a class with a special education teacher. The students who needed specialized instruction were able to get it without fear of being singled out in class. The participant stated that the special education teacher was able to bring the students into breakout rooms for small group instruction without the other students being aware that specialized instruction was taking place like they are in an in-person setting.

Although the teachers in the case study worked to find ways to increase inclusion in their online and hybrid classes, it only worked for the students who chose to attend class and participate. The results from this case study were consistent with the results reported in the research regarding vulnerable populations of students. One teacher of high needs students stated, "unfortunately, distance learning is less than ideal for the population I teach. It is too easy for them not to log on or even if they do log on not to be present. We have been finding that many students do not want to turn on their cameras or say things orally". Many of the students attended the class meetings but did not participate, and some students did not attend classes at all. Using the strategies from our ASLM helped engage and motivate students, but could only work if the students logged on to class.

**Formative Assessment.** Formative assessment is embedded into our ASLM to help students achieve mastery. The teachers use formative assessment to provide feedback for the students and to differentiate instruction and assignments to meet individual student needs. The teachers in this case study indicated that using GSE made embedding formative assessment easier and more diverse. One teacher reported that her formative assessments were previously always the same, but using GSE she was able to diversify the types of assessments she gave her students. Teachers used formative assessment more frequently during online and hybrid learning because it was easier to do quick checks with the technology resources available to them. Some of the methods reported by the teachers included the emoticons and thumbs up tools in Google Meets for a quick check of understanding, Google Jamboard for question responses, and polls in Google Meets for visual displays of understanding. For more in-depth formative assessments, teachers used the comment function in Google Docs to ask questions and provide feedback for the students. One teacher stated that using the shared Google Docs provided valuable insight into the students' level of understanding.

The results of this case study indicated that GSE provided tools for the teacher to provide real-time feedback for their students. The teachers used the private comments in Google Classroom to provide feedback on assignments. One teacher stated that after providing the feedback her students used it to revise and resubmit the assignments until they achieved mastery. This teacher reported that the feedback and revision were especially valuable for the students with special needs and was not something that she had previously done during in-person learning. Some of the teachers scheduled small group meetings in Google Meets for feedback or differentiation based on the formative assessments. One participant stated that the students enjoyed the opportunity to meet with the teacher individually or in small groups to receive feedback.

# 6  Recommendations

Our ASLM is grounded in social learning, which is based on the theory of connectivism that states that people learn using networks of individuals or technology. The literature on the benefits of social learning in K-12 classrooms is abundant (Alzain 2019; Lin et al. 2015). However, this case study has shown that these strategies were difficult to implement in online and hybrid classes during COVID-19. This may partially account for the research that shows that student growth is suffering, particularly in students with special needs.

Although the COVID-19 pandemic will not be permanent, there is some indication that online and hybrid models in K-12 education are not going away even after students can return to school in-person. Based on the results of this case study, this paper presents recommendations for GSE or other educational technology providers for new technology platforms that would allow teachers to easily implement social learning in K-12 online and hybrid classrooms.

## 6.1  The Need for a Platform that Allows Students to Interact During Asynchronous Learning

Asynchronous learning is a concept that is new to most K-12 teachers and students and was introduced during the COVID-19 pandemic. There is a lot of literature on the detrimental effects of the COVID-19 pandemic on the social-emotional well-being of students. Students need social interaction with their peers, and they need to access their social networks to enhance their learning during asynchronous instruction. While Google Classroom provides the students with the ability to post comments in the stream, it is not organized into threads and leads to a disorganized Google Classroom that can be confusing for students who are just trying to find their assignments. The recommendation based on this case study is that K-12 educational technology providers create a secure platform where students could interact and chat when they are not in class during synchronous instruction. The platform should be locked to only allow access to the students in that particular class. The platform should include an academic section that allows students to post questions about assignments and allow their classmates to comment on their posts. The platform should also include a social-emotional section where students can post school-appropriate comments and respond to one another in a conversational format to promote social interaction. The platform would be monitored by the teacher to ensure that the conversations are appropriate. The teacher could also interact with the students to help with relationship-building. It is recommended that the platform organize the topics into threads so students can easily find and participate in different conversations.

## 6.2 The Need for a Platform that Allows Teachers to Monitor Small Group Sessions

The teachers in this case study found that implementing social learning during online and hybrid classes was possible using GSE, but it was difficult. The case study results also indicated that social learning was not a viable option during asynchronous learning times using GSE. Due to safety and security concerns, students were not able to start their own Google Meets, so could only meet with their groups during synchronous learning. However, some of the schools where the teachers taught would not allow the teachers to use breakout rooms due to security concerns. This further limited the students' ability to meet with their networks and utilize social learning strategies. Essentially, the students could only use their social networks for learning during their own time which meant they did not have access to the teacher and the teacher was unable to assist the students or provide feedback. The teachers in this case study found ways to implement social learning with our ASLM in their online or hybrid classes, but they reported that it was less than ideal.

There are some aspects of GSE that allow for limited social learning. Google Meets has an option for breakout rooms, but these rooms do not allow the teachers to monitor all of the rooms at the same time. Students in breakout rooms are unattended until the teacher enters that room, leaving all the other rooms unattended. K-12 teachers need a platform that would allow them to monitor the breakout rooms in the same way they can monitor individuals in a Google Meets or other video conferencing system. In an in-person environment, the teacher moves from group to group, meeting with the students, asking questions, and providing feedback. These interactions are the key to inclusive environments and student success. The recommendation based on this case study is that GSE or other K-12 educational technology providers create a platform that would mimic this in an online setting. The teacher should be able to monitor all the breakout rooms but needs to have the ability to mute and unmute rooms to speak to that particular group of students without disturbing the other groups.

## 7 Conclusion

The purpose of this case study was to explore how teachers used the G Suite for Education to implement our ASLM in online and hybrid classrooms during the COVID-19 pandemic and to recommend new education platforms that support inclusive social learning. Our ASLM was designed to promote inclusive teaching and increase student engagement and achievement. Though our ASLM was originally created for use in in-person classrooms, teachers were able to use GSE to implement our ASLM in their online and hybrid classrooms during the 2020–2021 school year with positive results. Teachers in the case study indicated that implementing our ASLM resulted in students who were more engaged and motivated. The results indicated that the students enjoyed the social interactions embedded in our ASLM strategies. However, the teachers in this case study found that implementing social learning during online and hybrid classes was possible using GSE, but it was difficult. This paper presented recommendations for educational platforms for K-12 education that would improve the ability of students to learn and interact through social networks.

# References

Abhari, K.: A connectivist approach to meeting the needs of diverse learners: the role of social technologies. In: Teaching, Colleges & Community Worldwide Conference, Honolulu, HI (2017). https://www.researchgate.net/profile/Kaveh_Abhari/publication/314554159

Alzain, H.A.: The role of social networks in supporting collaborative e-learning based on connectivism theory among students of PNU. Turk. Online. j. Distance Educ. **20**(2), 46–63 (2019). https://doi.org/10.17718/tojde.557736

Anderson, T.C.: Academics achievement gap nutritional health: the impact of coronavirus on education. Delta Kappa Gamma Bull. **87**(1), 14–17 (2020). https://libguides.gcu.edu

Bray, M.: Going google: privacy considerations in a connected world. Knowl. Quest **44**(4), 36–41 (2016)

Brelsford, S.N., et al.: Keeping the bus moving while maintaining social distance in a COVID-19 world. Int. Stud. Educ. Adm. (Commonwealth Council for Educational Administration Management (CCEAM)) **48**(2), 12–20 (2020). cceam.net

Bybee, R.: Enhancing science teaching and student learning: a BSCS perspective. In: Proceeding of Research Conference (2006). acer.edu.au

De Vynck, G., Bergen, M.: Google classroom users doubled as quarantines spread (2020). https://www.bloombergquint.com/

Downes, S.: What is democracy in education? (2010). http://halfanhour.blogspot.com/2010/10/what-is-democracy-in-education.html

Girelli, C., Bevilacqua, A., Acquaro, D.: COVID-19 what have we learned from Italy's education system lockdown? Int. Stud. Educ. Adm. (Commonwealth Council for Educational Administration Management (CCEAM)), **48**(3), 51–58 (2020). cceam.net

Gunawardena, C., Lowe, C., Anderson, T.: Analysis of a global online debate and the development of an interaction analysis model for examining social construction of knowledge in computer conferencing. J. Educ. Comput. Res. **17**(4), 397–431 (1997). https://doi.org/10.2190/7MQV-X9UJ-C7Q3-NRAG

Johns, K., Troncale, J., Trucks, C., Calhoun, C., Alvidrez, M.: Cool tools for school: twenty first century tools for student engagement. Delta Kappa Gamma Bull. **84**(1), 53–58 (2017). https://libguides.gcu.edu

Lin, J.W., Huang, H.H., Chuang, Y.S.: The impacts of network centrality and self-regulation on an e-learning environment with the support of social network awareness. Br. J. Edu. Technol. **46**(1), 32–44 (2015). https://doi.org/10.1111/bjet.12120

Nelson, M., Murakami, E.: Special education students in public high schools during COVID-19 in the USA. Int. Stud. Educ. Adm. (Commonwealth Council for Educational Administration Management (CCEAM)), **48**(3), 109–115 (2020). cceam.net

Reimers, F.M., Schleicher, A.: A framework to guide an education response to the COVID-19 pandemic of 2020. OECD **14**, 1–40 (2020). https://oecd.dam-broadcast.com/

Rice, R.: Implementing connectivist teaching strategies in traditional k-12 classrooms. In: Nah, F.-H., Xiao, B.S. (eds.) HCIBGO 2018. LNCS, vol. 10923, pp. 645–655. Springer, Cham (2018). https://doi.org/10.1007/978-3-319-91716-0_51

Siemens, G.: Connectivism: a learning theory for the digital age. Int. J. Instr. Technol. Distance Learn. **2**(1), 3–10 (2005). http://www.itdl.org

# Enterprise Social Media Use in Classroom Team Project: A Mixed-Methods Exploration of the Effects of Affordances on Team Productivity and Use

Wietske Van Osch[1,2]([⊠]), Leticia Cherchiglia[2], Elisavet Averkiadi[2], and Yuyang Liang[1,2]

[1] Department of Information Technology, HEC Montréal, Montréal, Canada
vanosch@hec.ca
[2] Department of Media and Information, Michigan State University, East Lansing, USA
{leticia,averkiad,liangyuy}@msu.edu

**Abstract.** This paper explores the adoption of a group-based Enterprise Social Media (ESM) tool (i.e., Microsoft Teams) in the context of a mid-sized undergraduate course in Information and Technology Management (ITM), thereby providing insights into the use and design of tools for group-based learning settings. The study used a mixed-methods approach—interviews, surveys, and server-side (i.e., objective) data—to investigate the effects of three core ESM affordances (i.e., editability, persistence, and visibility) on students' perceptions of ESM functionality and efficiency, and in turn, on ESM-enabled perceived team productivity as well as the students' level of system usage. Through leveraging a combination of qualitative and quantitative (both unobtrusive and self-reported) data, this paper aims to provide insights into the use of ESMs in group-based classrooms which is a theme of great importance given the need for high-quality online education experiences, especially during the current pandemic.

**Keywords:** Enterprise Social Media · Educational settings · Group-based learning · Mixed-methods · Affordances

## 1 Introduction

In recent years, there has been a rapid growth in Enterprise Social Media (ESM), which are web-based platforms adopted by organizations to improve internal communication, collaboration, interaction, and different aspects of workflow between coworkers (Leonardi et al. 2013). ESM are designed to be more multi-functional than traditional office tools (e.g., email) or even group-based communication tools (e.g., Slack) since not only are such functionalities included in ESMs, but they also provide novel features more aligned with social media (e.g., group creation, social networking, blogging); moreover, unlike previous forms of computer-mediated communication, ESMs allows users to broadcast messages within the organization and have all activities recorded to be

© Springer Nature Switzerland AG 2021
F. F.-H. Nah and K. Siau (Eds.): HCII 2021, LNCS 12783, pp. 528–546, 2021.
https://doi.org/10.1007/978-3-030-77750-0_34

accessed at any time (Chin et al. 2019; Leonardi et al. 2013; Van Osch et al. 2015). These unique ESM affordances, specifically in terms of making content and connections more visible, and allowing content to be persistent (i.e., remain available and accessible), help explain the transformative impact of ESMs in organizations.

Pandemics such as COVID-19 (which forced organizations, including schools and universities, to rapidly shift to an online-only modus operandi) will increase the popularity of ESMs in both organizational and educational settings. When considering online learning contexts, ESMs can become suitable and preferable tools of choice especially when considering settings where group work can benefit substantially from ESM's unique affordances designed to facilitate collaboration and knowledge sharing (Rice et al. 2017; Treem and Leonardi 2013).

In order to maximize the effectiveness of group-based learning, educators should consider not only factors leveraging team cognition, accountability, and classroom collaboration (He et al. 2007; Scott et al. 2016; Smart and Csapo 2003), but also choose ESM platforms which are specially tailored to fulfill project-related purposes, such as Microsoft Teams[1]. Microsoft Teams is a fitting tool for educational contexts because it allows the creation of a virtual learning environment through the quick transition from conversations to content creation (Martin and Tapp 2019). From both a design and an educational point of view, it is important to explore the affordances that Microsoft Teams has to offer, but more generally, how to improve ESMs to better fit group-based educational settings.

Therefore, the primary goal of this paper is to investigate the use and design of a group-based ESM (i.e., Microsoft Teams) as a collaboration system in learning settings. In order to do so, this paper aims to answer three overarching research questions: 1) if students' perceptions of ESM affordances affect their ESM interaction perceptions (RQ1); if these users' ESM interaction perceptions affect their perceptions of the ESM impact on team productivity and level of usage (RQ2); and if there are ESM-specific (here, Microsoft Teams) features which could be redesigned for improvement when considering their use in educational settings (RQ3). Based on findings from data collected from a mid-size undergraduate I.T. project management course - including surveys, appreciative interviews, and server-side (i.e., objective) usage data related to content creation within Microsoft Teams – we propose a model connecting ESM affordances, user perceptions of their interactions with the ESM, and the impact of the latter on perceived team productivity and actual ESM usage.

Results suggest that Microsoft Teams affordances can indeed positively impact perceptions of ESM functionality, ESM efficiency, and team productivity. Surprisingly, we found a negative impact of ESM interaction perceptions on the users' actual level of ESM usage, which seems to be largely explained by students' preferences for more familiar tools, but also reveal areas where Microsoft Teams could be improved to support the specified context of use, which will be explored in detail in this paper. Beyond implications for research in terms of extending ESM studies to the educational realm, our findings also lead to recommended improvements in ESM design to facilitate team communication, reinforcing the importance of user experience design.

---

[1] https://www.microsoft.com/en-us/microsoft-365/microsoft-teams.

## 2 Literature Review

### 2.1 Collaboration Systems for Learning Settings

Virtual collaboration is an integral part of online learning settings, and group-based learning can yield more effective experiences given the increased frequency of communications and higher levels of participation, accountability, and decision making (Smart and Csapo 2003), especially when dealing with complex projects involving high degrees of technical knowledge such as when managing I.T. projects (He et al. 2007). The adoption of an ESM in the classroom can help with the formation of team cognition and positive learning outcomes as ESMs have the potential to become "a persistent, private community that contains both time-bound, formal class groups in addition to open learning spaces that allow for community members to interact with each other without direction from a teacher, and yet the possibility for teaching presence to exist on some occasions" (Scott et al. 2016).

One ESM that has a great potential in educational contexts rooted in group-based settings is Microsoft Teams, a digital teamwork hub focused on team collaboration. Microsoft Teams offers communication functionalities (e.g., persistent chat, video calls, messaging capabilities) along with usage of the Office suite (e.g., Word, Excel, Power-Point, OneNote) in a web-based integrated solution. Since its launch in 2017, Microsoft Teams has achieved 75 million daily active users, and it is now available in 53 languages across 181 markets (NTT Ltd. 2020; Warren 2020). The pandemic was responsible for an overall increase of 70% in Microsoft Teams user base (Warren 2020) as well as the expansion of the ESM to educational markets, including the development of new features to better assist online classes (Moorhead 2020).

Microsoft Teams allows collaborative learning to be enacted around peer interaction (mediated or not by the instructor) which has the potential to boost team productivity in educational contexts. While the connection between usage of Microsoft Teams and increased productivity is well-known in organizational settings, we wonder how the ESM will be perceived by and impact students in educational settings. Research focusing specifically on the use of Microsoft Teams in classrooms is still very novel and mostly centered around a descriptive pedagogical approach (Martin and Tapp 2019; Poston et al. 2020; Triyason et al. 2020), rather than investigating the measurable connections between variables such as ESM affordances, students' perceptions of the ESM tool, and usage outcomes, thus underscoring the importance of this study.

### 2.2 ESM Affordances

ESM affordances are unique and can have positive impacts in organizational settings; according to Treem and Leonardi (2013), core ESM affordances include: 1) association (i.e., connections are established from known people/information in order to find new people/information), 2) visibility (i.e., information is visible to other users), 3) persistence (i.e., past information is accessible and stored in a permanent fashion), and 4) editability (i.e., files are created collaboratively and/or edited after they have been created). Although alternative classifications have been suggested offering variations on these four affordances, the above-mentioned framework is the most widely cited at the time of this manuscript's preparation and the one used to guide our model development.

Due to their affordances, ESMs have been adopted and utilized in organizational settings in order to improve workplace processes such as social capital formation, boundary work, attention allocation, and social analytics (Leonardi and Vaast 2017; Van Osch et al. 2015). As ESMs' primary goal is to encourage collaboration and communication within the organization, these affordances are usually part of ESMs' inherent design making ESMs extremely useful tools to facilitate team dynamics. ESM research to date has focused largely on the visibility affordance, with limited research exploring the effects of the other affordances (Brzozowski 2009; DiMicco et al. 2008). Furthermore, as aforementioned, the exploration of the effects of ESM affordances in an educational context represents a novel avenue of investigation using an affordance lens.

### 2.3 ESM Interaction Perceptions and Performance and Usage Outcomes

Specific ESMs' affordances have been studied in terms of their impact on communication and collaboration, knowledge transfer, improved job performance and efficiency, among other factors. ESMs can be especially useful when workers need to share complex and/or domain-specific knowledge (Pee 2018) and ESMs can promote workers' creative performance (Sun et al. 2020), enhance communication and collaboration processes leading to improved workers' efficiency (Kane et al. 2014; Leonardi 2014) and contribute to innovation in the workplace (Ali et al. 2015).

As mentioned before, literature exploring the use of Microsoft Teams in classroom settings is still in its infancy, but there are reasons to believe that ESM affordances can yield positive outcomes similar to those observed in organizational settings. It is important to note that, given the educational context of this particular study featuring only closed networks within the ESM (i.e., student groups using Microsoft Teams), the affordance of association (which highlights the active networking component of ESM) was neither relevant nor applicable. The other three affordances (visibility, persistence, and editability) are relevant because the highly collaborative nature of the group work performed in Microsoft Teams for the course (e.g., editing files together, discussing assignments) will most definitely trigger peer interaction and knowledge transfer.

Specifically, *visibility* enables users to effortlessly access information or browse content shared by others in the organization (Treem and Leonardi 2013) and without hindrance (Alanah et al. 2009). As a result, visibility should not only contribute to perceptions of efficiency—as it will be easier and faster to find and retrieve information—but also to perceptions of functionality, by making it more convenient to access required knowledge and information and improving one's ability to accomplish tasks that require access to information provided by others (Treem and Leonardi 2013), thus contributing positively to perceptions of functionality.

Similarly, *persistence* makes all information and content permanently recorded and allows users to use and reuse it in the future, thus further reinforcing the ability of users to access information freely and easily as initially enabled by the visibility affordance of ESM (Treem and Leonardi 2013). Furthermore, persistence of information provides users with greater choice to deal with problems encountered during their course of work or projects (Treem and Leonardi 2013). Therefore, persistence not only increases efficiency, but should also positively affect perceptions of functionality, by making it more convenient to access required knowledge and information once shared without having to ask others again to repost or reshare such information and thus improving one's ability to accomplish tasks.

Finally, *editability* allows users to freely modify or revise content created by themselves or by others. Hence, it gives users the ability to improve or correct content. Furthermore, this high level of editorial control enables users to strategically edit or adapt content based on specific problem situations. Therefore, not only can projects be performed more efficiently by allowing users to collectively edit and improve materials, but also can contribute to positive perceptions of functionality by improving the usefulness and quality of generated content.

Hence, we propose the following hypotheses:

- **H1:** ESM affordances of a) editability, b) persistence, and c) visibility will lead to more favorable interaction perceptions vis-à-vis ESM functionality.
- **H2:** ESM affordances of a) editability, b) persistence, and c) visibility will lead to more favorable interaction perceptions vis-à-vis ESM efficiency.

In turn, the ability to successfully accomplish tasks using the ESM (i.e., functionality) and to do so efficiently should have a positive effect on teams' perceptions of the ESM's role in aiding the team to be productive and enhance their performance (i.e., the impact of ESM on performance). Furthermore, more favorable initial perceptions of ESM functionality and efficiency should yield greater overall usage of the system, as measured upon the conclusion of the project by the volume of total content created. Thus, the following hypotheses are proposed:

- **H3:** ESM perceived functionality will lead to (a) more favorable perceptions of ESM's impact on performance, and to (b) greater level of usage.
- **H4:** ESM perceived efficiency will lead to (a) more favorable perceptions of ESM's impact on performance, and to (b) greater level of usage.

The conceptual model in Fig. 1 summarizes the constructs used in our study and our hypotheses:

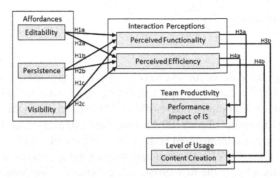

**Fig. 1.** Conceptual model

## 3 Study Context

This study was carried out at a large midwestern university, in the context of a capstone I.T. project management course attended by 87 students majoring in various areas (e.g., business-related: Finance, Supply Chain Management; technology-related: Media, Computer Science).

As a capstone project course, students participate in groups so as to further develop students' project management, teamwork, and communication skills, among others. Student teams were to complete a 10-week real-world I.T. project management challenge in partnership with local companies or organizations (e.g., non-profits or university labs). At the beginning of the course, 17 different I.T. projects were assigned to 17 teams, each comprising either four or five student members, based on project requirements, students' skills and interests. The primary point-of-contact within each project-sponsoring organization was known by student teams as "their client".

In order to support students' learning, ensure the use of proper project management tools and processes as well as monitor teams' progress in the real-world project, members of the instructional team (i.e., two instructors and two teaching assistants) were assigned to mentor and oversee specific projects. The mentor was known to the student team as their "project director" (one director per project; each director oversaw either four or five project teams).

The primary project management tool chosen to be used in the course was Microsoft Teams (free access was provided by the university). Specific team spaces (or channels) were created for each project (restricted to team members and their project director), in addition to one general course space (used for messages from the instructional team to all students enrolled in the course). Team spaces had mandatory uses such as communication with project directors, submission of a weekly project status to project directors, and organization of team files. Furthermore, optional uses of team spaces included within-team communication and file sharing with the client.

It is important to note that Microsoft has a version of Microsoft Teams tailored specifically toward education (Teams for Education), which showcases different features from the regular version. However, since Microsoft Teams was only meant to be used in the course as a place for mentoring and group interaction, the regular ESM version was used instead of Teams for Education.

# 4  Mixed Methods

## 4.1  Design

Two rounds of voluntary online surveys were conducted to provide insights into how student teams collaborate, what drives such collaboration, and what is the role of Microsoft Teams in this context. Participants were offered 1% extra credit in the course and were entered in a raffle for one out of six $100 Amazon gift cards as an incentive to participate.

The first survey was administered at the start of the project, which preceded by two weeks the onset of the COVID-19 pandemic that forced all classroom interactions to become online-only. Hence, the first survey reflects students' perceptions at the beginning of their project (consisting of both in-person/online classroom interactions), while the second survey reflects perceptions at the end of the project (based on online-only classroom interactions). This allows us to explore whether the mandated virtual interactions impacted the nature and level of Microsoft Teams usage. In addition to collecting self-reported data via online surveys, we also extracted basic server-side (i.e., objective) data from Microsoft Teams in order to measure actual—as opposed to self-reported— usage level. Instructor access to server-side data was restricted to the amount of content created in teams' message boards, hence, no other server-side data could be extracted.

For the qualitative portion of this study, seven appreciative interviews were conducted to gain further insights regarding the use of ESMs in a classroom setting, specifically Microsoft Teams, as well as students' perceptions of group work, team collaboration, and team productivity. The appreciative interviewing method was chosen as it allows an exploration of organizational and technological ESM aspects, as well as individuals' positive changes and constructive feedback related to the use and design of ESMs (Avital et al. 2009; Schultze and Avital 2011). Participants were offered $50 Amazon gift cards on a first come first served basis, as an incentive to participate.

Originally, interviews were planned to be conducted in-person, but due to COVID-19, interviews were conducted virtually via Zoom, an online video communications tool. Two interviewers were present in each interview; one member facilitated the interview while the other one took notes and focused on probing when needed. Interviews were conducted following a semi-structured script to ensure that interviews were conducted uniformly. All interviews were voice recorded via Zoom and transcribed with the aid of a paid online audio to text transcription service called Scribie. Interviews ranged from 45 min to one hour.

## 4.2  Participants

From the 87 students taking the I.T. capstone course, a sample of 62 students volunteered to participate in the study by completing the surveys. The sample included students from 16 different projects, categorized as: market/UX research (5), website (4), social media/SEO (3), database (2), or video (2). Most participants (71%) identified as male (female: 29%), and the age of participants ranged from 20 to 29 years old (M = 21.87 years). Most participants (76%) were domestic students (international: 24%), and participants' ethnicity was distributed as follows: White/Caucasian (56%), Asian (35%), Hispanic/Latino (5%), Black/African American (3%). Most participants were seniors (87% vs. 13% for juniors) and business-related majors (77% vs. 23% for technology-related).

For the qualitative portion of this study, seven students (a sub-sample of the quantitative sample) were interviewed – see Table 1 below for a summary of participants' information (note: all names are pseudonyms).

**Table 1.** Qualitative data: summary of participants' information

| Name | Team Id | Position | Gender |
|------|---------|----------|--------|
| Edwin | Database1 | Security Engineer | Male |
| Keith | SocialMedia1 | Project Manager | Female |
| Tammy | SocialMedia1 | SEO Campaign Director | Male |
| Liam | SEO1 | Project Manager | Male |
| Sarah | Research1 | Project Manager | Female |
| Jacob | Video1 | Project Manager | Male |
| Dalton | Research2 | Project Designer | Male |

## 4.3 Measures

The survey included self-report measures that were adopted and adapted from existing research as summarized in Table 2. Although the table only reports the Cronbach's alpha ($\alpha$) and convergent validity (AVE), all constructs in the model displayed adequate reliability as well as convergent and discriminant validity per an examination of loadings, cross-loadings, Cronbach's alpha, Composite Reliability, Fornell-Larcker test, and latent variable correlations. The last variable included in our research model was extracted from Microsoft Teams thus statistics are not available and therefore not reported.

The interview protocol started out by asking students to describe their project and to think of a positive collaboration experience they had with their team, in line with the appreciative interviewing method. After this opportunity for a positive reflection on teamwork, interviewees were asked questions related to Microsoft Teams use cases and affordances, their perception of its impact on team productivity, and the level of its usage.

**Table 2.** Variables and variable statistics

| Variable | Example item | α | AVE |
|---|---|---|---|
| Editability (Rice et al. 2017) | "Microsoft Teams allows me to edit others' information after they have posted it" | 0.86 | 0.77 |
| Persistence (Rice et al. 2017) | "Microsoft Teams allows my information or comments to stay available after I post them" | 0.92 | 0.93 |
| Visibility (Rice et al. 2017) | "Microsoft Teams allows me to see other people's answers to other people's questions" | 0.89 | 0.81 |
| Perceived Functionality (Mithas et al. 2006) | "Please rate the usefulness of the services provided on Microsoft Teams" | 0.86 | 0.88 |
| Perceived Efficiency (Bruni 2004) | "Using Microsoft Teams is fast" | 0.95 | 0.87 |
| Performance Impact of IS (Goodhue 1995) | "Microsoft Teams has a large, positive impact on my productivity in the team" | 0.94 | 0.95 |
| Content Creation [Microsoft Teams' data] | # of messages posted by each individual on their teams' message board | N/A | N/A |

# 5  Results

## 5.1  Quantitative Model Findings

Overall, our results suggest that two affordances (namely persistence and visibility) had significant positive effects on perceptions of Microsoft Teams in terms of its functionality (H1b and H1c supported) and efficiency (H2b and H2c supported). The affordance of editability only showed a positive effect on perceptions of functionality (H1a supported), but not on perceptions of efficiency (H2a not supported). In turn, perceptions of functionality and efficiency had a significant positive effect on perceptions of team productivity as a result of Microsoft Teams (i.e., performance impact of IS – H3a and H3b supported). Furthermore, the paths from the perceptions of the interaction with Microsoft Teams (functionality and efficiency) to objective usage levels (in terms of content creation) were both significant, however, whereas the path from functionality was positive (H4a supported), the one for efficiency was negative (H4b not supported). See Table 3 for detailed statistical information related to these results.

It is worth mentioning that pre-post comparison analysis between all variables of interest were performed to assess if there was any significant impact due to the required transition to a fully virtual modus of operandi due to COVID-19, but no significant paths were found. Therefore, rather than focusing on whether there was a change in students' perceptions due to the pandemic, our findings are generalizable and reflect students' perceptions at large. Our quantitative findings will be further discussed in the discussion section together with findings from the qualitative data (interviews).

**Table 3.** Significant path model results

| Path | Coeff | S.E | R2 |
|---|---|---|---|
| Editability > Perceived Functionality | 0.26** | 0.10 | 0.48 |
| Persistence > Perceived Functionality | 0.23* | 0.10 | |
| Visibility > Perceived Functionality | 0.32*** | 0.09 | |
| Persistence > Perceived Efficiency | 0.44*** | 0.11 | 0.42 |
| Visibility > Perceived Efficiency | 0.22* | 0.10 | |
| Perceived Functionality > Content Creation | 0.31** | 0.12 | 0.07 |
| Perceived Efficiency > Content Creation | −0.34** | 0.12 | |
| Perceived Functionality > Performance Impact of IS | 0.63*** | 0.08 | 0.59 |
| Perceived Efficiency > Performance Impact of IS | 0.18* | 0.08 | |

## 5.2 Qualitative Findings: Microsoft Teams Affordances and Interaction Perceptions

Interview findings support survey findings and underscore that users of Microsoft Teams recognize the affordances of visibility, persistence, and editability, as illustrated by the example quotes in Table 4 below.

Additionally, interviews provided detail by highlighting optimal use-cases for the ESM. For example, interviewees reported that Microsoft Teams is best suited for team projects (57%; n = 4) and quick communication settings (43%; n = 3) given its ease of use related to file sharing/editing and messaging features - see Table 5. One interviewee (Keith) even mentioned class settings as being an optimal use for the ESM: "*I think the message boards, allowing everyone to be able to see a message, to keep up-to-date with what's going on in a class setting, that's really helpful*". In contrast, interviewees considered Microsoft Teams not optimized for social media (29%; n = 2), heavy storage setting (29%; n = 2), and video communication (29%; n = 2); these perceptions were consequent of using an ESM in an educational setting composed of closed networks yet lacking social networking features, experienced issues when uploading large files (e.g., Sarah: "*it like pretty much just shut down the whole app*") and when performing video calls (e.g., Keith: "*I prefer Zoom just because it allows everyone to be up on the screen at the same time, on Microsoft Teams you can only see four people at a time. I've also noticed some lagging*").

In regard to perceived efficiency (H2), overall, interviewees deemed Microsoft Teams effective due to features such as built-in communication tools (e.g., tagging/direct mentions, video, chat) and file organization/storage – see Table 6. For example, Liam said that "*I think it's pretty effective that the instructors can have messages with everyone to*

**Table 4.** Qualitative data: Microsoft Teams affordances

|  | Name |
|---|---|
| Participant's quotes: visibility | |
| *"If we want to update each other, we just put a message on the message board allowing everyone to see it"* | Keith |
| *"It's easy to have a posting and tag the whole team, you can tag individual members to look at certain stuff"* | Sarah |
| *"If someone is working on Microsoft Teams, I'm gonna get that notification"* | Liam |
| Participant's quotes: persistence | |
| *"you could open up Microsoft Teams when you want to reply to that message"* | Jacob |
| *"(a team member) was taking some notes so now we have that chat, it has the time stamp on it"* | Devon |
| *"when I'm on my phone, I can just click the files tab and pull up anything"* | Edwin |
| Participant's quotes: editability | |
| *"If you needed to edit a document really fast, you could easily make that change"* | Sarah |
| *"It's just really easy to upload, edit and work on things all at the same time"* | Liam |
| *"We use a lot of the files 'cause it allows you to work on files at the same time"* | Keith |

let everyone know what's going on, but they can also send you individual messages, or messages to your whole group. They can also see anything that you upload immediately", and Keith said that *"It's allowed us to basically stay in touch, and just all have access to the same information at the same time, and just basically be able to store everything that we're working on, so we don't have to worry about sending it"*. Interestingly, some of these features are identical to those mentioned by others as not ideal, highlighting that the experiences may be highly dependent on the individual's user experience.

However, most interviewees mentioned that the user interface should be improved in order to make it more effective in team project settings. For example, Dalton highlighted design issues with both the ability to make calls (*"I know there's the Call function, but with like Discord it's a one-click thing, and [on Teams] it's on the tab of our specific project or whatever"*) and to get notifications (*"I'm just gonna compare it to GroupMe. It's easy to see notification settings and I think it's better formulated, to where the messages are a little more cleanly played, whereas if I open up my Microsoft Teams chat, I see a bunch of stuff that isn't really applying to me"*), Tammy mentioned visual design issues with the file system (*"I don't really like the organization or how they look [files system]"*), and Edwin brought up that *"archiving and searching through old messages is typically really difficult"*. Other interviewees mentioned formatting issues/glitches (e.g., Tammy: *"I have had issues with trying to edit names and move files to folders, it's hard to do"*) and connectivity issues (e.g., Sarah: *"I had a lot of instances where it would just crash on me a lot when I'd been uploading things on it. And a lot of the team members had similar experiences with that"*). Although it is unclear if these issues were only isolated cases or not (which might help explain the lack of significant path connecting

**Table 5.** Qualitative data: Microsoft Teams use cases

|  | # Mentions (%) |
|---|---|
| *Featured used in Microsoft Teams* | |
| File sharing | 4 (57%) |
| Chat | 3 (43%) |
| File editing | 3 (43%) |
| Message board | 3 (43%) |
| File storage/organization | 2 (29%) |
| Video calls | 2 (29%) |
| *Use-cases Microsoft Teams is best suited for (i.e., features viewed as positive)* | |
| Team projects | 4 (57%) |
| Quick communication setting | 3 (43%) |
| Highly collaborative setting | 2 (29%) |
| Workplace/professional setting | 2 (29%) |
| Class setting | 1 (14%) |
| *Use-cases Microsoft Teams is not suited for (i.e., features viewed as negative)* | |
| Heavy storage setting | 2 (29%) |
| Social media | 2 (29%) |
| Video communication | 2 (29%) |
| E-commerce | 1 (14%) |

editability with perceived efficiency as in H2a), interviews provide valuable insights into the perception of efficiency or lack of efficiency in Microsoft Teams.

### 5.3 Qualitative Findings: Microsoft Teams Impact on Team Productivity and Microsoft Teams Level of Usage

Supporting the quantitative findings related to H3, Microsoft Teams was perceived as a tool able to foster team productivity by most interviewees based on its perceived functionality and efficiency (71%; n = 5). Interviewees mentioned the fact that Microsoft Teams can be considered an *"all-encompassing collaboration platform"* (Edwin) since it seamlessly integrates traditional office programs in one single collaborative space, easy to be accessed by the whole group during their classroom project, as pointed out by Keith: *"you can edit Word documents together, Excel documents. We've used OneNote once or twice, PowerPoint for all of our weekly memos we use. I think two of our team members actually built the Gantt Chart off of Microsoft Teams"*. Such features helped to increase team organization, collaboration, and productivity, as mentioned by a couple of different interviewees; for example: Sarah said that *"it helped us to collaborate more 'cause it was all just like a central location where all of our documents were, so we didn't have to look at several different emails"* and Liam said that *"It's just so easy to*

**Table 6.** Qualitative Data: Microsoft Teams effectiveness

|                                              | # Mentions (%) |
|----------------------------------------------|----------------|
| *What makes Microsoft Teams effective*       |                |
| Built-in communication tools                 | 3 (43%)        |
| File organization/storage                    | 2 (29%)        |
| OS/device/platform independent               | 1 (14%)        |
| File editing via Microsoft Office            | 1 (14%)        |
| Project coordination/collaboration tools     | 1 (14%)        |
| User-friendly                                | 1 (14%)        |
| *Features that could make it more effective* |                |
| Improved user-interface                      | 5 (71%)        |
| Fixed formatting issues/glitches             | 2 (29%)        |
| Less connectivity issues                     | 2 (29%)        |
| Assign roles to team members                 | 1 (14%)        |
| Improved adding members functionality        | 1 (14%)        |
| Pinning messages to message board            | 1 (14%)        |
| Video chat function while editing files      | 1 (14%)        |

work on things together. I can't think of a better platform that I've used so far to work on things with people".

Casting a light into the contradictory quantitative findings for H4 related to ESM level of usage, it seems that although Microsoft Teams was the primary communication tool used when interacting with project directors, the ESM was not frequently or primarily used for team communication, and teams preferred to use the ESM only in desktop mode (see Table 7).

Additionally, as the project progressed requiring more complex team collaborations, and as communication became solely online due to the pandemic, some project managers realized they should have enforced the use of Microsoft Teams for team communication and group work since the beginning. When asked what they would do differently if they could start over, Jacob said *"I would definitely use Microsoft Teams more. I think it would've been great for communicating with our team rather than doing a group message"*, and Liam said *"We probably would have taken advantage of Microsoft Teams a little bit more at the start when we first were introduced to it at the beginning of the semester. We were like, oh, (…) we'll just use Google Docs or something else. But then we realized its potential and the things that you could do with Microsoft Teams"*.

**Table 7.** Qualitative Data: Microsoft Teams level of usage

|  | # Mentions (%) |
|---|---|
| *Frequent team communication on Microsoft Teams* | |
| No | 4 (57%) |
| Uncertain | 2 (29%) |
| Yes | 1 (14%) |
| *Team preference for Microsoft Teams platform use* | |
| Only desktop | 3 (43%) |
| Both desktop and mobile app | 2 (29%) |
| Unsure/did not answer | 2 (29%) |
| *Primary communication tools used* | |
| With the Project Director | |
| Microsoft Teams | 7 (100%) |
| Email; Zoom | 1 (14%) |
| With the Client | |
| Email | 6 (86%) |
| Zoom/Skype/WebEx | 5 (71%) |
| With team members | |
| GroupMe/iMessage | 6 (86%) |
| Zoom | 5 (71%) |

# 6  Discussion

This study, via a mixed-method approach, aimed to explore the effects of ESM affordances on perceptions of functionality and efficiency, and in turn on perceptions of the performance impact of ESM and actual ESM usage. We constructed a model rooted in our expectations that ESM affordances will lead to greater interaction perceptions (H1, H2), which in turn will positively affect team productivity and level of usage of the ESM (H3, H4). Our research model was validated using quantitative analyses of survey data and qualitative interviews served to add depth and explain the quantitative results.

Overall, our findings suggest that Microsoft Teams contains three core affordances of ESMs, namely editability, persistence, and visibility, allowing the ESM to serve its intended goal of assisting team projects by enhancing collaboration primality via file sharing/editing and messaging features. Still, we saw differences between the impact of such affordances on ESM interaction perceptions. It seems that persistence and visibility tend to have positive effects on users' perceptions of Microsoft Teams as a functional, useful, easy to use, and efficient tool. After all, being able to store, access and see information posted by members and their peers in an efficient and reliable way is a pivotal part of teamwork. Both affordances are also extremely important in classroom settings when considering instructor-to-students' announcements in message boards or tagging/notifying specific students/their teams in order to bring attention to specific matters.

Unexpectedly, the affordance of editability was only significantly and positively connected to Microsoft Teams' perceived functionality (i.e., not to perceived efficiency), perhaps because even though editing is possible and perceived as a useful functionality, some students more than others might have experienced issues when editing files collaboratively (e.g., connectivity or formatting glitches, system crash when uploading large files, difficulty of searching though old messages, non-intuitive file system organization and appearance), thereby undermining the anticipated effect on perceived efficiency.

Regardless, participants interaction perceptions of functionality and efficiency were both positively connected with team productivity, a finding strongly supported by interviews. It seems that ESM tools, such as Microsoft Teams, can indeed boost team performance, given, for example: 1) their ability to serve as a central shared hub thus saving teams' time in storing, organizing, and searching for files; 2) the integration with applications (such as Microsoft Office) facilitating the usage of editing tools collaboratively; and 3) availability of built-in communication tools.

Ironically though, based on our findings it seems that students' teams did not take full advantage of such communication tools for team communication. Because the only mandatory use of Microsoft Teams was for turning in weekly course deliverables, organizing team files, and interacting with their project directors, instead of learning how to use the ESM to facilitate team communication, students preferred to use tools they were already familiar with such as GroupMe/iMessage (messaging) or Zoom (video). Such finding is consistence with findings in organizational settings (Van Osch et al. 2015). It seems that given the plethora of competing tools providing solutions for team communication, teams do not utilize the ESM built-in chat/video feature but rather conform to their own preferences by choosing tools the team is already comfortable with, or tools that were specifically designed to afford seamless/optimal communication thus perceived as more efficient than the novel ESM and associated with lower switching costs.

This observation might be even stronger in educational settings given the younger user sample (i.e., undergraduate generation Z students) who seems to be more likely to value communication tools (even in educational settings) which are mobile-based, popular, and afford quick-exchange of messages (McGrath 2019). Based on our interviews, it seems that many teams preferred to use the desktop version of Microsoft Teams (as opposed to the mobile version), making the ESM not as pervasive and easily available as other messaging tools. The reasons behind such decision are unknown thus one limitation of this study, but perhaps students wanted to keep the classroom environment separated from their personal lives, or they thought that installing the Microsoft Teams app on their phones was too invasive.

Still, our model suggests that although perceived functionality is indeed positively connected with level of usage (measured by content creation in Microsoft Teams), perceived efficiency was actually negatively connected with such measure. Perhaps this is due to the fact that interviews highlighted issues with editability, which although not confirmed by survey data might have led to more negative perceptions of efficiency, which in turn undermined the level of usage. Moreover, content creation was objectively measured based on numbers of posts and replies posted on the message board, which does not account for messages exchanged privately via chats between the team, which is another limitation of this study. Future studies should further explore the role of team communication in team productivity and collaboration, invest in using more ESM server-side (objective) data (such as private group chats data) as objective measures supporting findings from self-reported data, explore differences between team/individual knowledge building and how the ESM can facilitate or hinder those learning processes.

Our theoretical contributions are related to the impact that ESM affordances have on users' interaction perceptions, and the impact of users' interaction perceptions on team and system outcomes. By applying traditional organizational-based constructs in the context of group-based online learning, we aim to contribute to the growing body of literature exploring the use of social information systems in educational settings, a promising opportunity to create a better understanding of the impact of ESMs affordances and their effects in novel contexts.

From a strategic and practical point of view, our findings revealed several challenges for the use of Microsoft Teams, and perhaps ESM at large, in educational settings, which can be a starting point for designers in improving the design of such tools to provide better support for educational contexts.

### 6.1 Challenge 1

As the demand for online education grows, collaborative tools such as ESMs should strive to provide seamless experiences for multiple-user access to files and messages. In Microsoft Teams, it seems that both file editing/organization and messaging features could be improved as issues occurred when team members were trying to synchronously collaborate in editing files, upload files into the team shared space (especially for larger files), and search content in old messages. In group-based educational context, such features are of the upmost importance otherwise group collaboration (and therefore learning) will most likely be negatively affected.

### 6.2 Challenge 2

Microsoft Teams (and other group-based ESMs) should improve its visual design in order to increase ease of use, user familiarity, and intuitiveness. After all, it seems that in Microsoft Teams some functionalities are not particularly visually appealing, reinforcing existing research that emphasized the importance of aesthetics and hedonic considerations in user experience and which has shown that 'unpleasant' design will lead to low levels of system use and continued use (Coursaris and Van Osch 2016). Perhaps the ability to customize the platform/app by allowing the customization of the design theme of the interface (e.g., color palettes or object metaphors) would provide users with an experience better tailored to their liking.

### 6.3 Challenge 3

Microsoft Teams appears to have an issue with learnability; i.e., students did not want to bother learning something new as the user experience was significantly different from what they were accustomed to from other software, which seems partially related to the fact that some features are hidden or take extra steps/clicks to be accessed, thus undermining their use. Hence, a clearer and more intuitive understanding of all available features is needed, thus both decreasing the learning curve associated with using the ESM and increasing efficiency. Perhaps the ability to customize the platform/app by allowing the customization or prioritization of features based on use preferences could help overcome some of the issues with learnability.

### 6.4  Challenge 4

Team communication is a complex study topic which should be further studied since providing students with choices for team communication, although a traditional practice in educational settings, might be a setback when instructors are utilizing an ESM which already provides communication features. Given the choice, students will fall upon familiar tools therefore undermining the full potential for team collaboration through the ESM. However, some identified design issues with Microsoft Teams such as lack of specific video features and connectivity unreliability could have prevented an efficient team communication via the ESM since the beginning of the project no matter what. Interestingly, recently Microsoft has fixed one video issue mentioned by our participants (i.e., only having four video call participants in the screen at a time), which received positive feedback, reinforcing the significance of our findings.

Finally, beyond implications for the design of ESM tools to improve their usage in educational settings, the findings also point to a challenge that will be increasingly pertinent for organizations today, which is how to get users to adopt and use voluntary tools. As usage of ESM tools in organizations is typically not mandated, this problem seems to be particularly likely in regard to such tools. For many organizations, ESM tools were implemented given their platform functionality and thus their potential to act as an umbrella tool where all kinds of mediated activities and communications can co-occur therewith allowing to break down knowledge silos (Van Osch et al. 2015; 2018). However, in an era where people are increasingly allowed to bring their own devices to work (BYOD) and/or install software of their choice on corporate devices, the tendency of users to stick to what they are familiar with or prefer could pose real challenges for a high rate of adoption among employees and in turn, significant challenges from a knowledge management and intellectual property perspective (Van Osch et al. 2015).

## 7  Concluding Remarks

ESMs and other collaborative platforms have been experiencing a drastic growth recently in order to facilitate the high demand for online learning and team collaboration tools. Even though such tools have the potential of bringing educational benefits in group-based settings, some improvements in design features are much needed to enable users with a full boost in team communication and productivity. Through a mixed-methods approach, our findings explore the uses and design of Microsoft Teams for educational contexts. We expect that this paper can provide insights for educators faced with the choice for an ESM tool best-suited for group-based classroom settings, as well as designers interested in adapting ESMs to educational contexts, a promising avenue for market expansion.

**Acknowledgements.** This material is based in part upon work supported by the National Science Foundation under Grant Number IIS-1749018. Any opinions, findings, and conclusions or recommendations expressed in this material are those of the author(s) and do not necessarily reflect the views of the National Science Foundation.

# References

Alanah, D., John, M., Dawn, O., Deepak, K., Ilze, Z.: Avatars, people, and virtual worlds: foundations for research in metaverse. J. Assoc. Inf. Syst. **10**(2), 90–117 (2009)

Ali, H., Nevo, D., Wade, M.: Linking dimensions of social media use to job performance: the role of social capital. J. Strat. Inf. Syst. **24**(2), 65–89 (2015)

Avital, M., Boland, R.J., Lyytinen, K.: Introduction to designing information and organizations with a positive lens. Inf. Organ. **19**(3), 153–161 (2009)

Bruni, S.: The role of instant messaging on task performance and level of arousal. Massachusetts Institute of Technology, Term Project, mas, 630 (2004)

Brzozowski, M.J.: WaterCooler. In: Proceedings of the ACM 2009 International Conference on Supporting Group Work - GROUP 2009 (2009). https://doi.org/10.1145/1531674.1531706

Chin, P.Y., Evans, N., Liu, C.Z., Choo, K.K.R.: Understanding factors influencing employees' consumptive and contributive use of enterprise social networks. Inf. Syst. Front. **22**, 1357–1376 (2020)

Coursaris, C.K., Van Osch, W.: A Cognitive-Affective Model of Perceived User Satisfaction (CAMPUS): the complementary effects and interdependence of usability and aesthetics in IS design. Inf. Manag. **53**(2), 252–264 (2016)

DiMicco, J.M., Millen, D.R., Geyer, W., Dugan, C.: Research on the use of social software in the workplace. In: Conference Proceedings on Computer Supported Collaborative Work, pp. 8–12 (2008)

Goodhue, D.L.: Understanding user evaluations of information systems. Manag. Sci. **41**(12), 1827–1844 (1995)

He, J., Butler, B.S., King, W.R.: Team cognition: development and evolution in software project teams. J. Manag. Inf. Syst. **24**(2), 261–292 (2007)

Kane, G., Alavi, M., Labianca, G.J., Borgatti, S.: What's different about social media networks? A framework and research agenda. MIS Q. **38**(1), 275–304 (2014)

Leonardi, P.M., Huysman, M., Steinfield, C.W.: Enterprise social media: definition, history, and prospects for the study of social technologies in organizations. J. Comput.-Mediat. Commun. **19**, 1–19 (2013)

Leonardi, P.M.: Social media, knowledge sharing, and innovation: toward a theory of communication visibility. Inf. Syst. Res. **25**(4), 796–816 (2014)

Leonardi, P.M., Vaast, E.: Social media and their affordances for organizing: a review and agenda for research. Acad. Manag. Ann. **11**(1), 150–188 (2017)

Martin, L., Tapp, D.: Teaching with teams: an introduction to teaching an undergraduate law module using Microsoft Teams. Innov. Pract. High. Educ. **3**(3), 1–9 (2019)

McGrath, M.K.: How to understand Gen Z communication patterns. Rave Mobile Safety (2019). https://www.ravemobilesafety.com/blog/how-to-understand-gen-z-communication-patterns

Mithas, S., Narayan, R., Krishnan, M.S.: Designing web sites for customer loyalty across business domains: a multilevel analysis. J. Manag. Inf. Syst. **23**, 97–127 (2006)

Moorhead, P.: Microsoft Strengthens Its Education Offering With New Microsoft Teams Features. Forbes (2020). https://www.forbes.com/sites/moorinsights/2020/06/22/microsoft-strengths-its-education-offering-with-new-microsoft-teams-features/#60058d005336

NTT Ltd., Cloud Communications Division: 20 Things to Know about Microsoft Teams for 2020. Arkadin (2020). https://www.arkadin.com/sites/default/files/A4_20_things_to_know_about_Teams_2020.pdf

Pee, L.G.: Affordances for sharing domain-specific and complex knowledge on enterprise social media. Int. J. Inf. Manag. **43**, 25–37 (2018)

Poston, J., Apostel, S., Richardson, K.: Using Microsoft teams to enhance engagement and learning with any class: it's fun and easy. In: Pedagogicon Conference Proceedings 6 (2020)

Rice, R.E., Evans, S.K., Pearce, K.E., Sivunen, A., Vitak, J., Treem, J.W.: Organizational media affordances: operationalization and associations with media use. Hum. Commun. Res. **67**, 106–130 (2017)

Schultze, U., Avital, M.: Designing interviews to generate rich data for information systems research. Inf. Organ. **21**(1), 1–16 (2011)

Scott, K.S., Sorokti, K.H., Merrell, J.D.: Learning "beyond the classroom" within an enterprise social network system. Internet High. Educ. **29**, 75–90 (2016)

Smart, K.L., Csapo, N.: Team-based learning: promoting classroom collaboration. Issues Inf. Syst. **4**(1), 316–322 (2003)

Sun, Y., Wang, C., Jeyaraj, A.: Enterprise social media affordances as enablers of knowledge transfer and creative performance: an empirical study. Telemat. Inform. **51**, 101402 (2020)

Treem, J.W., Leonardi, P.M.: Social media use in organizations: exploring the affordances of visibility, editability, persistence, and association. Ann. Int. Commun. Assoc. **36**(1), 143–189 (2013)

Triyason, T., Tassanaviboon, A., Kanthamanon, P.: Hybrid classroom: designing for the new normal after COVID-19 pandemic. In: Proceedings of the 11th International Conference on Advances in Information Technology, pp. 1–8, July 2020

Van Osch, W., Steinfield, C.W.: Strategic visibility in enterprise social media: implications for network formation and boundary spanning. J. Manag. Inf. Syst. **35**(2), 647–682 (2018)

Van Osch, W., Steinfield, C.W., Balogh, B.A.: Enterprise social media: challenges and opportunities for organizational communication and collaboration. In: 48th Hawaii International Conference on System Sciences, pp. 763–77 (2015)

Warren, T.: Microsoft Teams jumps 70 percent to 75 million daily active users. The Verge (2020). https://www.theverge.com/2020/4/29/21241972/microsoft-teams-75-million-daily-active-users-stats

# Digital Transformation and Artificial Intelligence

# Toward a Theory of Digital Mindfulness: A Case of Smartphone-Based Self-monitoring

Kaveh Abhari[1]([⊠]) [iD], Melissa Klase[1], Farzan Koobchehr[2], Fernando Olivares[1], Michael Pesavento[1], Luis Sosa[1], and Isaac Vaghefi[3]

[1] San Diego State University, San Diego, CA, USA
Kabhari@sdsu.edu
[2] University of California, Irvine, Irvine, CA, USA
[3] Pace University, New York, NY, USA

**Abstract.** 'Digital mindfulness' refers to the mindful use of digital technologies, such as smartphones. Despite being a topic of significant interest among researchers and practitioners, there is limited empirical evidence about digital mindfulness in existing HCI literature. This ongoing gap in empirical support led to speculation that digital mindfulness might be an academic fad lacking theoretical rigor. As a response, this study is an attempt to investigate digital mindfulness and uncover the mechanism(s) underlying the mindful use of digital technology in the context of smartphones. Specifically, this study argues that 'self-monitoring' is an important dimension of digital mindfulness that can be objectively defined, systematically measured, and practically supported by digital tools and technologies. Moreover, adding nuance to smartphone-enabled self-monitoring literature, this paper sheds light on the role of digital mindfulness in the enhancement of productivity as well. This in turn paves the way for theorizing the concept of digital mindfulness specifically within an HCI context.

**Keywords:** Digital mindfulness · Self-monitoring · Smartphone · Productivity · Perceived possibility · Perceived agency · Perceived value

## 1 Introduction

Mindfulness is defined as the cultivation of conscious awareness and attention on a moment-to-moment basis [1]. The incorporation of mindfulness practices is known to decrease specific mental health conditions associated with addiction such as anxiety [2]. An undeniable element of mindfulness practice is the self-monitoring of behavior, feelings, or sensations, since it allows individuals to pay attention to what is occurring in the present moment. This quality aids efforts to cultivate awareness in responding to the internal or external stimuli. Hence, mindfulness is considered as an effective mechanism to curb addictive behaviors [3].

In the context of this study, we posit that digital mindfulness can protect smartphone users from overuse and its negative consequences while also helping them cultivate more productive and meaningful smartphone use habits. To this end, the purpose of this study

© Springer Nature Switzerland AG 2021
F. F.-H. Nah and K. Siau (Eds.): HCII 2021, LNCS 12783, pp. 549–561, 2021.
https://doi.org/10.1007/978-3-030-77750-0_35

is to understand how the smartphone itself can help with digital mindfulness—i.e., the implementation of mindfulness strategies via a digital medium. This study is an attempt to understand how smartphones can be used as a self-monitoring tool to bring awareness to unregulated smartphone use and ultimately aid individuals in using their smartphones more productively.

## 2   Research Background

Theories of technology addiction stem from prior research regarding behavioral addiction, which has similar behavioral patterns and biological causations to substance addiction [4]. Addictive behaviors are often experienced subjectively as a 'loss of control' [5] and typically characterized by instant gratification, often coupled with delayed effects [6]. In the last two decades, psychology researchers looked at the additional characteristics of technology addiction. For example, past research proposed active use of technology could present potential for addiction, specifically focusing on user "enjoyment" as a driver of habituation and "hedonistic" usage [7, 8].

Given the current social and technological climate, especially during the COVID-19 pandemic, young adults may become increasingly obsessed with technology use, including and especially smartphones [9]. More so, the excessive use of some smartphone applications such as social media can significantly contribute to severe mental and psychological health challenges [10, 11]. Hence, understanding technology addiction and offering practical solutions are critical to young adults' mental health and emotional well-being.

### 2.1   Smartphone Use

The ubiquity of smartphones in every-day life can rightly be attributed to their enormous functional capacity to simplify life for users, as smartphones provide an essential "any time, any place" access into the entire world wide web of knowledge [12]. However, there is a downside to this expansive reach [13]. Smartphone use, much like other habitual behaviors, substances, and experiences, can be extremely addictive, leading to negative mental health outcomes as a result [14]. Given its significant rise over the past years, smartphone addiction has led to problems with social interactions, school and work interference, and impulse control disorders [15, 16]. Research has also illustrated that smartphone addiction is associated with sleep disturbance, anxiety, and depressive symptoms [17], and therefore merits academic attention to assuage these potential mental health issues [18].

While this study aims to reduce addictive behavior and increase productive smartphone usage, these concepts are not defined by this study as being mutually exclusive conditions of smartphone use, nor are they considered opposites. Instead, we take the view that these categories of usage may in fact coincide, with overuse being a symptom of productive smartphone use. However, as this study focuses specifically on smartphone use in young adults, we frame this study as having behavior modification potential, and not direct, interventive motivations. That said, despite their potentially negative overuse, smartphones can play a significant role in enhancing productivity among young adults

[19]. For example, while smartphones can negatively impact students' academic performance if they are used obsessively [20], their mindful use can provide benefits from increased social capacity to educational engagement to improved mental health [21–23]. Thus, smartphones present unparalleled networking and productivity options while simultaneously threatening to eclipse users' judgement and demand focus and time from them. We argue that scholarship regarding self-monitoring and mindfulness practices can provide theoretical context for strategies that can be employed to mitigate these risks.

### 2.2  Self-monitoring and Mindfulness

Self-monitoring is a low-intensity, secondary preventative strategy for altering one's behavior [24]. Self-monitoring is based on the idea that when people keep records of their behaviors—for example, in the form of diary or checklist—they become aware of gains and deficits of their action, which helps them act more mindfully the next time they are tempted to repeat that behavior [25]. The capacity to self-monitor is contingent upon several factors. "High self-monitors" can observe their behavior objectively, adapting to their environment faster than low self-monitors, and show higher extroversion, agreeableness, and communication skills [26, 27]. High self-monitors also tend to be more principled in their interaction, as there is a high correspondence between their emotions, attitudes, and behavior. Besides this, they tend to be authentic and sincere in their behavior, possessing a higher level of self-esteem and locus of control [28].

Self-monitoring has proved to be beneficial in various contexts, from increasing attention span in students, to accelerating the recovery period for medical patients, and even reducing sedentary behaviors in adults [29]. Moreover, self-monitoring can positively impact behavior, learning productivity, and ultimately improve academic performance in students [30]. For example, students who used standardized diaries as a self-monitoring tool to support self-regulatory behavior shown improvements in learning outcomes [31]. Research has also revealed that self-monitoring can help smartphone users decrease their addictive usage [32].

## 3  Hypotheses

The concept of self-monitoring as a mindfulness strategy is well established, with over 30 years of clinical research documenting its potential [33]. However, many conditions must be met to increase the success of this strategy. To date, several studies have been conducted to demonstrate the effectiveness of technology in recording and enhancing the implementation of self-monitoring behavior [34]. For the purposes of this study we identified three antecedent factors [35] for self-monitoring—*perceived possibility, perceived agency* and *perceived value*—based on integrated behavioral theory and health benefit models in a technology-enabled environment [36]. In our research context, technology is to be used as the main enabler of self-monitoring—since smartphone use is a technology-enabled environment—and therefore, we modeled this investigation on perceived self-monitoring possibility. Self-efficacy predicates perceived self-monitoring agency, and its importance has been well-established in academic literature. The integrated behavioral model, like other behavior models, recognizes value expectation as the main driver of behavior—in this case, self-monitoring [37, 38].

### 3.1 Perceived Possibility of Smartphone Self-monitoring

Previous studies have demonstrated the impacts of technology-based self-monitoring on students [39–41]. Bedesem used smartphones as a functional tool to facilitate students' self-monitoring and showed that normal on-task behavior increased from 45% to 71% due to the intervention [39]. Numerous mobile applications have been developed to bring awareness to users about their smartphone use [40]. The purpose of these applications has primarily been for mental health improvement, which is well-supported by cognitive behavioral therapy literature [41, 42]. Some of the intervention mechanisms for mediating smartphone overuse in these applications are screen-time monitoring, screen locking, nudging, and repeated encouragement. This type of intervention has been successful in addressing smart phone addiction when users are receptive to it [43]. Therefore, the functions of these intervention technologies are important to achieve a behavior change—not necessarily a reduction use but mindful use [44, 45]. These technologies enable users to cultivate awareness in responding to the amount of smartphone use and its positive or negative consequences. We argue that the user perception of self-monitoring possibilities enabled by technology—either as default smartphone capability or enabled by third-party app—is one of the antecedents to the mindful use of smartphone. Therefore, we propose the following hypothesis:

*H1: The more positive the user perception of self-monitoring possibility enabled by smartphone, the higher the likelihood of smartphone use self-monitoring.*

### 3.2 Perceived Value of Smartphone Self-monitoring

The role of intention in self-regulation of behavior has received due focus among behavioral researchers [46]. Studies show that intentions are a key determinant of behavioral change and goal attainment [47] across contexts. For example, the self-monitoring of intention-formation is key to controlling blood sugar in diabetes patients [48]. Moreover, research has shown that intention to self-monitor is a predictor of behavior. This is demonstrated in the intention to self-monitor an increase in physical activity among general population, as it is a good predictor of that behavioral change [49]. Self-monitoring and implementation intention (which are highly related) appear to be promising predictor of behavior change as well [50]. Many studies demonstrate the effectiveness of mindfulness intention on behavior change. A mindfulness intention approach (i.e. the intention to be actively aware of a given behavior), suggests enhanced attention to present experiences, which leads to an increase in self-monitoring and self-controlling one's behavior [51, 52]. Therefore, we assert:

*H2: The more positive the user perception of self-monitoring value enabled by smartphone, the higher the likelihood of smartphone use self-monitoring.*

### 3.3 Perceived Agency of Smartphone Self-monitoring

Self-efficacy manifested in form of perceived agency is the third driver of self-monitoring studied here [53]. We define the perceived agency as one's confidence in own ability to carry an goal-oriented action [54]. Having self-efficacy is an essential component of self-monitoring, as it is more likely for a person with high self-efficacy to complete a task or achieve a goal [44, 55]. Many studies show the relationship between self-efficacy and positive behavior change. Prior research has shown that self-efficacy enables more commitment toward goals, especially the ones that are hard to attain [53, 56]. For example, addiction literature showed that addicts with higher self-efficacy are confident in their ability to resist the urge and are less likely to relapse [57–59]. Therefore, we contend that:

*H3: The more positive the user perception of self-monitoring agency enabled by smartphone, the higher the likelihood of smartphone use self-monitoring.*

### 3.4 Perceived Productivity After Smartphone Self-monitoring

Self-monitoring also helps with enhancing progress and performance [58], enabling greater self-evaluation and facilitates a comparison of one's self-judgments of present performance to one's goal [60]. Studies suggest that self-evaluation, combined with self-efficacy through goal systems, leads to positive results [61]. In this sense, self-monitoring increase the accountability and self-esteem in students and improve academic performance [62].

Various studies have discussed the negative effects of smartphone addiction on productivity, mental health and academic performance [63]. For example, Felisoni and Godoi demonstrated that on average every 100 min spent using a smartphone per day leads to 6.3 points of reduction in students' position in school rankings [64]. Data has also shown that excessive use of technology has negative effects on students' sleep patterns, concentration, and mental health [65]. Therefore, it is expected that self-monitoring can enhance user productivity by enabling the user to be mindful about the utility of time. Based on a study conducted by Rock and Thead, it is apparent that strategic self-monitoring can have significant impacts on academic engagement, accuracy and productivity [66]. Students who practiced intentional self-monitoring reported higher academic interest and generally exceeded baseline conditions, comparing appropriately to intervention effects. Self-monitoring not only encourages a better use of time but also directs more mindful action [66]. In the context of this study, the self-monitoring of smartphone use is not directly translated to less use, but rather mindful (i.e., productive) use. Therefore, we hypothesize that:

*H4: The higher the implementation of (smartphone use) self-monitoring, the higher the user perceived productivity.*

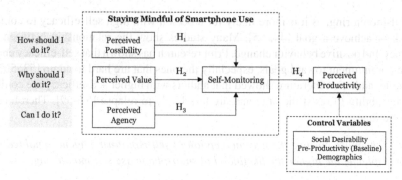

**Fig. 1.** Theoretical model: staying mindful of smartphone use

# 4 Methodology

To test our theoretical model (Fig. 1), we designed an intervention and tracked user behavior longitudinally through a survey on self-monitored smartphone usage among college students. We focused on college students since research has shown that younger generations are more susceptible to smartphone addiction than older generations due to earlier exposure to the technology [67]. More so, the rate of smartphone addiction, smartphone-related mental health issues such as depression and anxiety, and physical problems linked to smartphone over-use are also higher among the younger generations [68]. Thus, we collected data from three state universities in New York, California, and Hawaii, where we asked students to download our application, *Space*, to monitor their phone and application usage anonymously.

We conducted the study in four interrelated phases to measure, validate, and demonstrate potentially problematic smartphone usage. We asked participants to complete a questionnaire at the beginning and end of the first week; at the end of the second week; and at the end of the third week of having *Space* installed. We leveraged this process to identify and analyze the antecedents and outcomes associated with smartphone use. We measured self-monitoring as well as baseline variables such as pre-intervention productivity and social desirability, among others. The data was collected with several demographic categories establishing participant gender, school year, and smartphone operating system. However, for the ease of matching responses, we assigned a random ID to each participant and asked them to use the same ID to submit all four surveys.

In the first phase of data gathering, we asked participants to install the *Space* app, answering a set of pretest questions on their smartphone usage. Then, we instructed participants to upload a screenshot of the app installed on their smartphone as initial confirmation of their usage of the app. The second phase of data collection came at the end of the first week, when we instructed participants to complete a short survey and upload two screenshots of their "dashboard" in the *Space* app, displaying their mobile usage for the past week. In the third phase (at the end of the second week), we told participants to follow the same procedure as phase 2 (i.e., uploading screenshots of the dashboard). In the fourth and final phase, we instructed students to complete a short survey and upload two ultimate screenshots of their dashboard. We also asked the participants to submit the screenshot of the app's weekly report to ensure they had used the app as instructed. The participants who failed to submit this evidence or used the app for five or less days during a week were removed from the dataset.

Our study adopts instrument items from previous studies and adjusts them for the context of this investigation [69–73]. Our final survey included five first-order reflective constructs: perceived productivity, self-monitoring, perceived possibility, perceived value, perceived agency and demographics. We employed the Partial Least Squares (PLS) modeling technique to assess the measurement and structural models of our research model (Fig. 1).

## 5 Results

Of the 469 participants initially gathered, we removed 138 responses due to the respondents' lack of participation or incomplete data, leaving a final sample of 331 usable responses for analysis. The survey sampled both male (59%) and female (41%) students, with an average age of 22 years old. Most participants were pursuing a business degree: Freshman (1%), Sophomore (31%), Junior (50%) and Senior (18%). To ensure that we captured reliable data on self-monitoring behavior, by the end of the study, we asked the participants to self-report how much they achieved the smartphone usage goal that you set at the beginning of each week. About 14% reported 'Fully achieved', 21% 'Mostly achieved', 21% 'Half achieved', 27% 'Mostly not achieved', 17% 'Not achieved at all'. We also asked how frequently they checked their smartphone usage in the Space app during the last 7 days. In total, 45% of participants reported they used the app to monitor their screen time more than once during a day.

After the initial screening, we validated the measurement instrument. The evaluation of reflective constructs involved testing construct reliability (item reliability and internal consistency), construct factorability, and construct validity (discrimination validity). Based on our analysis, all the loadings of measurement items exceeded 0.7, showing acceptable item reliability. Cronbach's alpha and the composite reliability of all the constructs are higher than 0.7, indicating adequate internal consistency among the items measuring each construct (Table 1).

All Average Variance Extracted (AVE) values are higher than 0.50, which evidences adequate convergent validity. Further, all the pathological VIFs resulting from the full collinearity test were lower than 5. Additionally, the loading of each indicator on its own construct was higher than its loading on other constructs, indicating discriminant validity. As shown in Table 2, the AVE of each reflective construct was also higher than the construct's highest squared correlation with any other construct. The HTMT (Heterotrait–Monotrait) ratio of correlations values was also below 0.90, verifying discriminant validity [74].

Our hypotheses were tested using controlled effects of factors that may impact smartphone addiction; namely: demographics, social desirability, and pre-productivity (baseline value). To test the model, we first examined the significance of the direct effect of the antecedents on self-monitoring. The results of data analysis show that positive perception of perceived possibility positively affects self-monitoring (H1: $\beta = 0.33, p < 0.001$). The model reveals that perceived value has a positive impact on self-monitoring (H2: $\beta = 0.20, p < 0.001$). Higher perceived agency is also associated with higher self-monitoring (H3: $\beta = 0.23, p < 0.001$). Lastly, increase in self-monitoring has a positive

**Table 1.** Construct reliability and validity

| Construct | α | CR | AVE |
|---|---|---|---|
| Perceived agency | 0.90 | 0.93 | 0.78 |
| Perceived value | 0.81 | 0.88 | 0.64 |
| Perceived possibility | 0.88 | 0.91 | 0.67 |
| Self-monitoring | 0.83 | 0.89 | 0.67 |
| Perceived productivity | 0.90 | 0.93 | 0.71 |

**Table 2.** Discriminant validity*

| Construct | PAG | PVL | PPS | SMN | PPR |
|---|---|---|---|---|---|
| Perceived agency | **0.88** | | | | |
| Perceived value | 0.45 | **0.80** | | | |
| Perceived possibility | 0.45 | 0.64 | **0.82** | | |
| Self-monitoring | 0.46 | 0.50 | 0.55 | **0.82** | |
| Perceived productivity | 0.46 | 0.29 | 0.32 | 0.39 | **0.85** |

*The diagonal elements are the square root of the shared variance between the constructs and their measures.

effect on perceived productivity (H4: $\beta = 0.30$, $p < 0.001$). As a result, the findings support hypothesis H1, H2, H3, and H4. The three antecedents account for 38% of variance in self-monitoring and self-monitoring accounts for 32% of variance in individual perceived productivity (Table 3).

**Table 3.** Path coefficients and Significance*

| Hypothesis | β | t | $R^2$ | $Q^2$ |
|---|---|---|---|---|
| H1: Perceived possibility → Self-monitoring | 0.33 | 5.42* | 0.38 | 0.24 |
| H2: Perceived Value → Self-monitoring | 0.20 | 3.24* | | |
| H3: perceived Agency → Self-monitoring | 0.23 | 4.12 | | |
| H4: Self-monitoring → Perceived Productivity | 0.30 | 5.45* | 0.32 | 0.21 |

*$p < 0.001$

The findings also revealed the significant but small indirect effect of the antecedents on perceived productivity ($p < 0.001$). The indirect effect of perceived possibility on perceived productivity ($\beta = 0.13$, $p < 0.001$) was more dominant than perceived value ($\beta = 0.07$, $p < 0.005$) and perceived agency ($\beta = 0.08$, $p < 0.001$).

# 6    Discussion and Conclusion

This study was an attempt to uncover a possible mechanism underlying the mindful use of digital technology in the context of smartphone use. Our study focused on self-monitoring as the cornerstone of digital mindfulness and identified its antecedent (perceived possibility, value and agency of self-monitoring) and outcomes (perceived productivity). Our study revealed that the perceived possibility of self-monitoring when enabled by technology (a smartphone app in the context of this study) is the main predictor of smartphone use self-monitoring. Our results also showed perceive value and perceived agency also have positive relationships with self-monitoring, which supported prior findings [25, 75, 76]. Furthermore, results of this study showed that when users are committed to self-monitor their smartphone usage, they are more likely to perceived higher-productivity as a result—further supporting established research on this topic [77].

Given this relationship, it is apparent that interventive self-monitoring techniques enabled by smartphones themselves have potential to effectively change behaviors for smartphone users, which in turn could improve their productivity. This study is significant not only for its verification of previous research in a new context, but also because of its implications for implementing self-monitoring technologies. For example, the positive relationship between monitored smartphone usage and productivity suggests that the first step to increasing productivity is tracking the amount of time users spend using their smartphone and present it to them in a meaningful way. This supports mobile operating system developers' decision to provide screen time report as a default system capability (e.g., Apple provides such report since iOS 11 released in 2018). Moreover, this study recommends developing more advanced smartphone tracking applications beyond the default features to encourage self-monitoring. Likewise, this study provides a more comprehensive understanding of self-monitoring drivers. Therefore, the results can be used to inform the design of more effective self-monitoring interventions that promote user agencies and expected values of self-monitoring along with the features and functionalities.

We believe that the right combination of self-monitoring technology and behavioral intervention can be implemented in both personal and social settings to enhance mindful use of smartphones. As more digital natives are entering the workforce, the contributions offered by this study derive greater importance for management staff across industries. Our findings present considerable opportunity for employers to design contextualized intervention that can help employees with self-monitoring and ultimately enhance their productivity and mental health, two values at the forefront of many firms' concerns today.

This study also presents opportunities for continued scholarship on smartphone addiction and may open new avenues for research. For example, future research can extend the principles established in this study to investigate other potential drivers that impact self-monitoring (such as users' motivations, goals, and capabilities). The use of technologies and mobile applications can further be investigated by analyzing different factors such as user perception of usefulness, accuracy, and data privacy. Considering contextual factors would also offer new research avenues, such as how the quality of smartphone usage differs based on the usage context and user demographics and how these understandings can help them spend time more productively on their smartphones. Further, this study focuses on sample groups that skew predominantly young and educated. Controlling (or manipulating) for demographic factors in future sample selection could yield differing results. Lastly, in theorizing digital mindfulness with some practical implications, alternative or variant mindfulness strategies ought to be considered in future studies. Future research can investigate the right balance between self-monitoring technology and behavioral intervention, including goal setting, positive and negative reinforcement, reflection, or self-enactment.

# References

1. Allen, N.B., Chambers, R., Knight, W.: Mindfulness-based psychotherapies: a review of conceptual foundations: empirical evidence and practical considerations. Aust. N. Z. J. Psychiatry **40**, 285–294 (2006)
2. Witkiewitz, K., Bowen, S., Harrop, E.N., Douglas, H., Enkema, M., Sedgwick, C.: Mindfulness-based treatment to prevent addictive behavior relapse: theoretical models and hypothesized mechanisms of change. Subst. Use Misuse **49**, 513–524 (2014)
3. Black, D.S.: Mindfulness-based interventions: an antidote to suffering in the context of substance use, misuse, and addiction. Subst. Use Misuse **49**, 487–491 (2014)
4. Kurniasanti, K.S., Assandi, P., Ismail, R.I., Nasrun, M.W.S., Wiguna, T.: Internet addiction: a new addiction? Med. J. Indones. **28**, 82–91 (2019)
5. Lyvers, M.: "Loss of control" in alcoholism and drug addiction: a neuroscientific interpretation. Exp. Clin. Psychopharmacol. **8**, 225–249 (2000)
6. Kuss, D.J., Billieux, J.: Technological addictions: conceptualisation, measurement, etiology and treatment. Addict. Behav. **64**, 231–233 (2017)
7. Turel, O., Serenko, A., Bontis, N.: User acceptance of hedonic digital artifacts: a theory of consumption values perspective. Inf. Manag. **47**, 53–59 (2010)
8. Kuss, D.J., Kanjo, E., Crook-Rumsey, M., Kibowski, F., Wang, G.Y., Sumich, A.: Problematic mobile phone use and addiction across generations: the roles of psychopathological symptoms and smartphone use. J. Technol. Behav. Sci **3**(3), 141–149 (2018). https://doi.org/10.1007/s41347-017-0041-3
9. Jiang, Q., Li, Y.: Factors affecting smartphone dependency among the young in China. Asian J. Commun. **28**, 508–525 (2018)
10. Andreassen, C.S.: Online social network site addiction: a comprehensive review. Curr. Addict. Rep. **2**, 175–184 (2015)
11. Park, N., Lee, H.: Social implications of smartphone use: Korean college students' smartphone use and psychological well-being. Cyberpsychol. Behav. Soc. Netw. **15**, 491–497 (2012)
12. Jones, R., Boulos, M.N.K., Wheeler, S., Tavares, C.: How smartphones are changing the face of mobile and participatory healthcare: an overview, with example from eCAALYX. Biomed. Eng. Online **10**(1), 24 (2011)
13. Lee, Y.K., Chang, C.T., Lin, Y., Cheng, Z.H.: The dark side of smartphone usage: psychological traits, compulsive behavior and technostress. Comput. Hum. Behav. **31**, 373–383 (2014)
14. Mosalanejad, L., Nikbakht, G., Abdollahifrad, S., Kalani, N.: The prevalence of smartphone addiction and its relationship with personality traits, loneliness and daily stress of students in Jahrom University of medical sciences in 2014: a cross-sectional analytical study. J. Res. Med. Dent. Sci. **7**, 131–136 (2019)
15. Panova, T., Carbonell, X.: Is smartphone addiction really an addiction? J. Behav. Addict. **7**, 252–259 (2018)

16. Mok, J.-Y., et al.: Latent class analysis on internet and smartphone addiction in college students. Neuropsychiatr. Dis. Treat. **10**, 817–828 (2014)
17. Lemola, S., Perkinson-Gloor, N., Brand, S., Dewald-Kaufmann, J.F., Grob, A.: Adolescents' electronic media use at night, sleep disturbance, and depressive symptoms in the smartphone age. J. Youth Adolesc. **44**(2), 405–418 (2014). https://doi.org/10.1007/s10964-014-0176-x
18. Cho, J.: Roles of smartphone app use in improving social capital and reducing social isolation. Cyberpsychol. Behav. Soc. Netw. **8**, 350–355 (2015)
19. Morphitou, R.N.: The use of smartphones among students in relation to their education and social life. In: Proceedings of 2014 International Conference on Interactive Mobile Communication Technologies and Learning, IMCL 2014 (2015)
20. Giunchiglia, F., Zeni, M., Gobbi, E., Bignotti, E., Bison, I.: Mobile social media usage and academic performance. Comput. Hum. Behav. **82**, 177–185 (2018)
21. Sarwar, M., Soomro, T.R.: Impact of smartphones on society. Eur. J. Sci. Res. **98**, 216–226 (2013)
22. Kalkbrenner, J., Mccampbell, A.: The advent of smartphones: a study on the effect of handheld electronics on personal and professional productivity. J. Appl. Glob. Res. **4**, 1–9 (2011)
23. Narli, N.: Life, connectivity and integration of Syrian refugees in Turkey: surviving through a smartphone. Quest. Commun. **33**, 269–286 (2018)
24. Gunstone, C.: Self-monitoring. Br. J. Gen. Pract. **63**, 182–183 (2013)
25. Schwarzer, R., Antoniuk, A., Gholami, M.: A brief intervention changing oral self-care self-efficacy and self-monitoring. Br. J. Health Psychol. **20**, 56–67 (2015)
26. Mill, J.: High and low self-monitoring individuals: their decoding skills and empathic expression. J. Pers. **52**, 372–388 (1984)
27. Pillow, D.R., Hale, W.J., Crabtree, M.A., Hinojosa, T.L.: Exploring the relations between self-monitoring, authenticity, and well-being. Personality Individ. Differ. **116**, 393–398 (2017)
28. Day, D.V., Schleicher, D.J.: Self-monitoring at work: a motive-based perspective. J. Pers. **74**, 685–714 (2006)
29. Compernolle, S., et al.: Effectiveness of interventions using self-monitoring to reduce sedentary behavior in adults: a systematic review and meta-analysis. Int. J. Behav. Nutr. Phys. Act. **16**, 1–16 (2019)
30. Ghanizadeh, A.: The interplay between reflective thinking, critical thinking, self-monitoring, and academic achievement in higher education. High. Educ. **74**, 101–114 (2017)
31. Schmitz, B., Perels, F.: Self-monitoring of self-regulation during math homework behaviour using standardized diaries. Metacogn. Learn. **6**, 255–273 (2011)
32. Palokangas, L.: Nudging problematic smartphone use to a lower level. Theseus.fi (2016)
33. Bruhn, A.L., Vogelgesang, K., Schabilion, K., Waller, L.N., Fernando, J.: "I don't like being good!" changing behavior with technology-based self-monitoring. J. Spec. Educ. Technol. **30**, 133–144 (2015)
34. Bruhn, A.L., Vogelgesang, K., Fernando, J., Lugo, W.: Using data to individualize a multi-component, technology-based self-monitoring intervention. J. Spec. Educ. Technol. **31**, 64–76 (2016)
35. Miltenberger, R.G.: Behavior Modification: Principles and Procedures: Principles and Procedures. Cengage Learning, Boston (2011)
36. Glanz, K., Rimer, B.K., Viswanath, K.: Health Behavior Theory Research and Practice, 5th edn. Wiley, New York (2015)
37. Lin, H.C., Chang, C.M.: What motivates health information exchange in social media? The roles of the social cognitive theory and perceived interactivity. Inf. Manag. **55**, 771–780 (2018)
38. Johnson, R.E., Lin, S.-H., Lee, H.W.: Self-control as the fuel for effective self-regulation at work: antecedents consequences and boundary conditions of employee self-control. In: Advances in Motivation Science, pp. 87–128 (2018)

39. Bedesem, P.L.: Using cell phone technology for self-monitoring procedures in inclusive settings. J. Spec. Educ. Technol. **27**, 33–46 (2012)

40. Howells, A., Ivtzan, I., Eiroa-Orosa, F.J.: Putting the 'app' in happiness: a randomised controlled trial of a smartphone-based mindfulness intervention to enhance wellbeing. J. Happiness Stud. **17**(1), 163–185 (2014). https://doi.org/10.1007/s10902-014-9589-1

41. Bakker, D., Rickard, N.: Engagement in mobile phone app for self-monitoring of emotional wellbeing predicts changes in mental health: MoodPrism. J. Affect. Disord. **227**, 432–442 (2018)

42. Chan, S., Torous, J., Hinton, L., Yellowlees, P.: Towards a framework for evaluating mobile mental health apps. Telemed. e-Health **21**, 1038–1041 (2015)

43. Lee, H., Ahn, H., Choi, S., Choi, W.: The SAMS: smartphone addiction management system and verification. J. Med. Syst. **38**(1), 1 (2014). https://doi.org/10.1007/s10916-013-0001-1

44. Klasnja, P., Consolvo, S., Pratt, W.: How to evaluate technologies for health behavior change in HCI research. In: Proceedings of the SIGCHI Conference on Human Factors in Computing Systems, pp. 3063–3072 (2011)

45. Lubans, D.R., Smith, J.J., Skinner, G., Morgan, P.J.: Development and implementation of a smartphone application to promote physical activity and reduce screen time in adolescent boys. Front. Public Heal. **2**, 42 (2014)

46. Bandura, A., Simon, K.M.: The role of proximal intentions in self regulation of refractory behavior. Cognit. Ther. Res. **1**, 177–193 (1977)

47. Webb, T.L., Sheeran, P.: Does changing behavioral intentions engender behavior change? A meta-analysis of the experimental evidence. Psychol. Bull. **132**, 249 (2006)

48. Conner, M., Norman, P.: The role of social cognition in health behaviours. In: Predicting Health Behaviour: Research and Practice with Social Cognition Models (1996)

49. Godin, G., Conner, M.: Intention-behavior relationship based on epidemiologic indices: an application to physical activity. Am. J. Heal. Promot. **22**, 180–182 (2008)

50. Mairs, L., Mullan, B.: Self-monitoring vs. implementation intentions: a comparison of behaviour change techniques to improve sleep hygiene and sleep outcomes in students. Int. J. Behav. Med. **22**(5), 635–644 (2015). https://doi.org/10.1007/s12529-015-9467-1

51. Shapiro, S.L., Carlson, L.E., Astin, J.A., Freedman, B.: Mechanisms of mindfulness. J. Clin. Psychol. **62**, 373–386 (2006)

52. Chatzisarantis, N.L.D., Hagger, M.S.: Mindfulness and the intention-behavior relationship within the theory of planned behavior. Pers. Soc. Psychol. Bull. **33**, 663–676 (2007)

53. Bandura, A.: Social cognitive theory: an agentic perspective. Annu. Rev. Psychol. **52**, 1–26 (2001)

54. Carberry, A.R., Gerber, E.M., Martin, C.K.: Measuring the innovation self-efficacy of engineers. Int. J. Eng. Educ. **34**, 590–598 (2018)

55. Williams, P.A., Jenkins, J.L., Valacich, J.S., Byrd, M.D.: Measuring actual behaviors in HCI research – a call to action and an example. AIS Trans. Hum. Comput. Interact. **9**, 339–352 (2017)

56. Bandura, A.: Human agency in social cognitive theory the nature and locus of human agency. Am. Psychol. **44**, 1175 (1989)

57. Gulliver, S.B., Hughes, J.R., Solomon, L.J., Dey, A.N.: An investigation of self-efficacy, partner support and daily stresses as predictors of relapse to smoking in self-quitters. Addiction **90**, 767–772 (1995)

58. Schunk, D.H.: Self-efficacy for reading and writing: influence of modeling, goal setting, and self-evaluation. Read. Writ. Q. **19**, 159–172 (2003)

59. Tang, M.Y., Smith, D.M., Mc Sharry, J., Hann, M., French, D.P.: Behavior change techniques associated with changes in postintervention and maintained changes in self-efficacy for physical activity: a systematic review with meta-analysis. Ann. Behav. Med. **53**, 801–815 (2019)

60. Schunk, D.H.: Goal and self evaluative influences during children's cognitive skill learning. Am. Educ. Res. J. **33**, 359–382 (1996)
61. Bandura, A., Cervone, D.: Self evaluative and self efficacy mechanisms governing the motivational effects of goal systems. J. Pers. Soc. Psychol. **45**, 1017 (1983)
62. van der Bij, T., Geijsel, F.P., ten Dam, G.T.M.: Improving the quality of education through self-evaluation in Dutch secondary schools. Stud. Educ. Eval. **49**, 42–50 (2016)
63. Samaha, M., Hawi, N.S.: Relationships among smartphone addiction, stress, academic performance, and satisfaction with life. Comput. Hum. Behav. **57**, 321–325 (2016)
64. Felisoni, D.D., Godoi, A.S.: Cell phone usage and academic performance: an experiment. Comput. Educ. **117**, 175–187 (2018)
65. Wang, R., et al.: StudentLife: assessing mental health academic performance and behavioral trends of college students using smartphones. In: Proceedings of the 2014 ACM International Joint Conference on Pervasive and Ubiquitous Computing (2014)
66. Rock, M.L.: Use of strategic self-monitoring to enhance academic engagement productivity and accuracy of students with and without exceptionalities. J. Posit. Behav. Interv. **7**(1), 3–17 (2005)
67. Wang, H.Y., Sigerson, L., Cheng, C.: Digital nativity and information technology addiction: age cohort versus individual difference approaches. Comput. Hum. Behav. **90**, 1–9 (2019)
68. Matar Boumosleh, J., Jaalouk, D.: Depression, anxiety, and smartphone addiction in university students - a cross sectional study. PLoS ONE **12**, e0182239 (2017)
69. Rockmann, R., Gewald, H.: Activity tracking affordances: identification and instrument development. In: Proceedings of the 22nd Pacific Asia Conference on Information Systems (2018)
70. Gökçearslan, Ş, Mumcu, F.K., Haşlaman, T., Çevik, Y.D.: Modelling smartphone addiction: the role of smartphone usage, self-regulation, general self-efficacy and cyberloafing in university students. Comput. Hum. Behav. **63**, 639–649 (2016)
71. Houghton, J.D., Neck, C.P.: The revised self-leadership questionnaire: testing a hierarchical factor structure for self-leadership. J. Manag. Psychol. **17**, 672–691 (2002)
72. Zhang, S., Zhao, L., Lu, Y., Yang, J.: Do you get tired of socializing? An empirical explanation of discontinuous usage behaviour in social network services. Inf. Manag. **53**, 904–914 (2016)
73. Miller, J.S., Cardy, R.L.: Self-monitoring and performance appraisal: rating outcomes in project teams. J. Organ. Behav. **21**, 609–626 (2000)
74. Henseler, J., Ringle, C.M., Sarstedt, M.: A new criterion for assessing discriminant validity in variance-based structural equation modeling. J. Acad. Mark. Sci. **43**(1), 115–135 (2014). https://doi.org/10.1007/s11747-014-0403-8
75. Shapiro, S.L., Schwartz, G.E.: The role of intention in self regulation toward intentional systemic mindfulness. Handb. Self. Regul. **2000**, 253–273 (2011)
76. Rickard, N., Arjmand, H.-A., Bakker, D., Seabrook, E.: Development of a mobile phone app to support self monitoring of emotional well-being: a mental health digital innovation. JMIR Mental Health **3**, e49 (2016)
77. Duke, É., Montag, C.: Smartphone addiction, daily interruptions and self-reported productivity. Addict. Behav. Rep. **6**, 90–95 (2017)

# Haptic Interaction for VR: Use-Cases for Learning and UX, Using the Example of the BMBF Project SmartHands

Oliver Gast[✉], Alina Makhkamova, Dirk Werth, and Mareike Funk

AWS-Institut Für Digitale Produkte Und Prozesse gGmbH, 66123 Saarbrücken, Germany
{oliver.gast,alina.makhkamova,dirk.werth,
mareike.funk}@aws-institut.de

**Abstract.** VR is becoming increasingly popular and is developing from a niche market to a mass market currently experiencing thriving. Highly developed technology at affordable prices and a spectrum of applications ranging from gaming to learning to e-business are shaping the VR landscape in 2021. There are attempts to address many human senses through software and hardware to make the scenarios even more realistic. The integration of haptics is becoming the focus of current trends and developments. This paper attempts to do justice to this trend and looks at haptic interaction from different angles. Besides a brief excursus to the development of haptic devices, we will also discuss physiological grounds to grasp better the possibilities offered by integrating the sense of touch. Also, practical examples from the BMBF project SmartHands will illustrate how and when haptic feedback in the form of haptic gloves can be usefully integrated into a VR learning application. We will also attempt to build a direct bridge to application-oriented e-business by outlining promising use cases to embed haptic feedback in e-commerce.

**Keywords:** Virtual reality · Haptics · User experience · e-business

## 1 Introduction

The depiction of immersive virtual worlds is becoming increasingly popular – the VR representation applies not only to games but also to e-business and education and training. The worlds become more and more detailed, and the achieved immersion and interaction comes closer to the real world. We can already address several senses to enhance the user experience in VR. However, it is still not so common to replicate the sense of touch, although it can be crucial to the sense of presence and development of psychomotor skills.

Therefore, the project SmartHands is researching learning methods integrating VR and haptic devices in the field of manual medicine, i.e., the training of physiotherapists. In manual therapy, the sense of touch is naturally essential, and in training, a great deal of repetitive practice is required until the correct hand movements are mastered. Particularly in the current situation with the Corona pandemic, practicing on real patients

F. F.-H. Nah and K. Siau (Eds.): HCII 2021, LNCS 12783, pp. 562–577, 2021.
https://doi.org/10.1007/978-3-030-77750-0_36

is challenging. Therefore, a digital learning environment can be conducive. Addressing the sense of touch is vital for two reasons.

On the one hand, the haptics could directly affect the perceived user experience and thus the acceptance of the application. On the other hand, it enables learning scenarios previously only available with real training partners/patients. The embedding of the sense of touch in VR worlds is by no means a pure "nice-to-have" requirement to make the application "more attractive." The haptic input and feedback are a self-contained form of interaction in its own right: the interaction can solely occur in this channel. However, the integration of haptic feedback in VR can lead to a significant advance not only in the context of medical education. In e-business and especially in e-commerce, haptic feedback can also generate added value for the user, which is also directly relevant to the companies' success. For example, the lack of haptic feedback in e-commerce is still a significant driver of high return rates.

## 2  Virtual Reality

Historically, the foundations of VR and AR were grounded by Ivan Sutherland in the 1960s (Dörner et al. 2019). He invented "The Ultimate Display" (Sutherland 1965), a kind of precursor of the later PC, and in 1968 the Head-Mounted Display System, which can be seen as the first AR system, as it already had a see-through property (Sutherland 1968). However, the term AR was first coined in the early 1990s by a pilot project in which information was faded-into the visual field of Boeing workers to facilitate the relocation of aircraft cables (Caudell and Mizell 1992). In the late 1980s, the term Virtual Reality (VR) was first used by Jaron Lanier (Dörner et al. 2019). A few years later, in the early 1990s, research made enormous progress in that it was now possible to create projection-based images (Dörner et al. 2019). For example, the University of Illinois developed the CAVE (Cave Automatic Virtual Environment), a room-scale virtual environment with four screens (Dörner et al. 2019). Since the release of the Oculus Rift data goggles in 2013, VR has experienced a real boom, which resulted in the Playstation VR, etc., for example (Dörner et al. 2019).

### 2.1  The Difference Between VR and AR

Virtual reality (VR) can be defined in different ways in the literature; however, we can find some similarities: For example, technically, in VR, a multisensory presentation of 3D content occurs while the user's body movements are tracked (Dörner et al. 2019). Tracking the user within the 3D environment allows, for example, to change the user's perspective as soon as the user moves their head (ibid.). These actions are also interactive, meaning that they receive sensory feedback matching their actions. One of the essential characteristics is that the user's perception of the real environment in VR is entirely replaced by the perception of a virtual environment (Azuma 1997). In this context, metaphors are of great importance, as they convey to users that virtual objects behave as users know them from the real world, allowing them to interact naturally with virtual objects (Dörner et al. 2019).

In contrast to VR, AR extends the user's perception of the real environment with virtual content (Azuma 1997). AR systems can be characterized as follows according to Azuma (ibid.): AR systems are a combination of virtuality and reality that interact in real-time and in which the virtual content is displayed in 3D. Users thus perceive the virtual content and the real environment simultaneously (Azuma 1997; Dörner et al. 2019). Since the virtual content behaves like real ones, it seems that the virtual content has a fixed place within the users' reality (Dörner et al. 2019). In this context, the virtual content aims to appeal to users' senses in such a way that, in extreme cases, it is no longer possible for them to distinguish between virtual and real sensory impressions (ibid.).

However, besides some similarities, such as an egocentric perspective, multimodal presentation, or even real-time simulation and interaction, there are also other differences between VR and AR (Dörner et al. 2019). E.g., VR is mostly used indoors, while AR is more mobile and is also used outdoors (Dörner et al. 2019). Due to currently still prevailing technical restrictions, haptic feedback, especially with haptic gloves, can be predominantly integrated into VR.

## 2.2 Immersion, Presence and UX

Immersion, presence, and user experience, three factors that influence each other, are considered essential factors in VR applications development. Immersion and presence describe the degree to which a user can be absorbed (cf. Frank 2020) in the virtual world and thus receive it as real. The term immersion is often used as an umbrella term for both immersion and presence. But in the scientific community, the term immersion usually describes the system's specific technical properties such as resolution, viewing angle, optics, and interactivity. It also means the degree to which a system can engage users in the experience (Jerald 2015). These are all objective factors that can be easily quantified for measurement (cf. Gerth and Kruse 2020, pp. 146–147).

Presence, by contrast, refers to mental and subjective aspects (Dörner et al. 2019). Presence means the feeling of "being there" within the virtually created environment (Dörner et al. 2019). It can be seen, for example, in the way users react within the VR application as if it were the real world (Dörner et al. 2019).

Presence is further composed of place illusion, plausibility illusion, and involvement (Dörner et al. 2019). Place illusion refers to the user having the feeling of being in the place represented in virtual reality (Slater 2009). Plausibility Illusion refers to the perception of virtual reality events as if they were actually happening (Slater 2009), especially events that are not initiated by the user but affect them (Dörner et al. 2019). Involvement refers to the user's interest or attention in the virtual environment (Witmer and Singer 1998). Involvement and plausibility are influenced by the content of virtual reality (Dörner et al. 2019). It could be that a user feels part of the virtual world but is bored, which indicates a strong place illusion but low involvement (Dörner et al. 2019).

In its technical meaning, the degree of immersion strongly influences the user's possibilities to also experience VR mentally, in the sense of presence. Both factors together also have a substantial effect on the degree of user experience of the system. Immersion corresponds to the usability, as an element of the user experience, of the application (cf. Bodendörfer 2016). On the other hand, presence is in exchange with the

UX elements that address the psychological area, such as emotions, expectations, and experiences (cf. Bodendörfer 2016).

Thus, both factors address different user experience elements and complement each other in their impact on the UX. To acheive a high user experience, there should be a certain degree of immersion and presence, and both must be implemented in a balanced manner.

### 2.3 The Role of the Senses in Immersive Systems

To enable a high level of immersion and, consequently, a strong presence and user experience, VR users' sensory impressions must be addressed by several (the more, the better) output devices (Dörner et al. 2019). According to Slater and Wilbur (1997), output devices should isolate the user as completely as possible from the real world, and thus not only limit the user's view but also wholly surround the user, appeal to as many senses as possible, and provide as realistic representation as possible. The focus of previous VR developments was predominantly on the visual component, i.e., the sense of "seeing," flanked by the sound (sense of "hearing") matching the graphic design. This was mostly justified by the lack of technical possibilities to address other senses so that they have a positive effect on presence and UX. Following the "Uncanny Valley Effect", it can be assumed that an unrealistic integration of the senses can even lead to a reduction in presence and UX.

Accelerated by the rapid digitization and the increasing spread of VR, research on the integration of other senses, such as tasting and smelling, has also emerged. However, it can be stated that related projects such as Feelreal (https://feelreal.com/) on smelling in VR or studies by the University of Tokyo (Niijima and Ogawa 2016) on tasting in VR are not yet really suitable for the masses. The sense of touch as the largest sensory organ of humans, on the other hand, can already look back on about 30 years of development. Due to the challenges listed above, innovations in this area were for a long time seen at best as a supplement to the preferred senses, but not as equivalent. The development of marketable haptic gloves, in particular, has rekindled the topic of haptics and made research and development aware of the enormous relevance of the human sense of touch.

## 3   The Sense of Touch

To illustrate how important the sense of touch is in the senses' structure, especially in virtual worlds in VR, it is worth taking a closer look at the sense of touch, specifically from a physiological perspective.

A look at the receptors involved and the number of different possible stimulating qualities reveals how complex the human sense of touch is. The receptors are located not only in the skin, as a non-professional might assume, and in muscles, tendons, joints, connective tissue, and even hair (cf. Grunwald 2017). The possible stimuli are expressed primarily in pressure, stretching, and vibration, which is also highly relevant in haptic devices. However, the number of different receptors and their density in the body illustrates the importance and sensitivity of tactile sense. In direct comparison to the other senses, the sense of touch is the most sensitive, with up to 700–900 million

(Grunwald 2017) touch-relevant receptors in the human body. As the sense with the second most receptors, the sense of sight only has approximately 126 million receptors (per eye) in comparison (Grunwald 2017).

Not all touch-relevant receptors can be addressed in the context of haptic devices. To identify which ones are relevant, one must consider the functions of the tactile system. These can be divided into the exteroception, the proprioception, and the interoception (cf. Grunwald 2012). The first function, in particular, plays a decisive role when it comes to integrating haptic feedback into virtual worlds. The exteroceptive part of the sense of touch makes use of the receptors located at the interface of the entire body (skin, hair). These are used to detect physical environmental properties and their changes actively and passively (hard/soft, rough/smooth, warm/cold, etc.). Here one can differentiate between tactile and haptic perception (Grunwald 2006) in its narrower sense.

Tactile perception describes the passive sensitivity to touch. The perceiving subject does not move actively (Grunwald 2006). In this context, the human body - the skin - is differently sensitive to touch in different body regions. This can be measured, for example, using the so-called two-point threshold. This is the distance at which two pressure stimuli are perceived as only one stimulus at one point (Grunwald 2006). For example, the two-point threshold at a particularly touch-sensitive location, such as the inside of the index finger, is about 2 mm (Kern 2009), while the two-point threshold on the back only begins at about 50 mm (Birbaumer and Schmidt 1999).

On the other hand, haptic perception describes perception through movement activities, i.e., in contrast to tactile perception, it is actively driven by the perceiving subject. As a further contrast, we can say that haptic thresholds, as active tactile perception, are more significant than tactile thresholds, which are only relevant in experimental situations. The active threshold in active exploration is 1 $\mu$m (Grunwald and Müller 2017). Considering that the beginning of an adhesive tape is about 41 $\mu$m "thick," this threshold value concretely means that humans can actively sense even the most minimal structural differences in fabrics.

Both types of perception serve as a basis for distinguishing haptic devices, especially haptic gloves.

# 4   Development of Haptic Devices

Despite its importance for UX in virtual worlds and human-computer interaction, the extensive lack of the haptic component is well known to researchers and developers. For a long time, however, the technical capabilities were the bottleneck for overall end-user-ready development. However, rapid digitization increasingly changed this, and in the area of VR in particular, the growing economic influence of the gaming industry also served as an accelerator for development.

In the course of the last 30 years of development, various directions of haptic feedback development emerged.

One can identify three main directions, which are also suitable for the selective classification of haptic devices (cf. Wang et al. 2019):

- Desktop haptic
- Surface haptic
- Wearable haptic

Desktop and surface haptics primarily address 2D and 3D applications with lower immersion, while wearable haptics has relevance specifically and almost exclusively in highly immersive virtual worlds (VR). Although recent developments are predominantly in wearable haptics, it can be stated that all three areas still play a role in certain use cases.

### 4.1 Desktop Haptics

Desktop haptic devices are also referred to as "end effector displays" (Grimm et al. 2019, p.215). The basis of these devices is typically the combination of a multi-jointed robotic arm with an input-output device, usually in the form of a pen, which is attached to a tabletop for use, for example (hence the name) (Wang et al. 2019).

The user interacts directly with the pen and controls virtual tools, such as a scalpel, while the robotic arm tracks movements, and haptic feedback is provided to the user via force feedback (Wang et al. 2019). Desktop haptics is widely used in virtual assisted medicine, especially within surgery (Wang et al. 2019). A widely used representative of this class of devices is the Phantom Omni (Grimm et al. 2019).

### 4.2 Surface Haptics

Surface haptic devices are predominantly based on touch displays of different sizes. In contrast to the desktop haptics class devices, where physical contacts between the user and virtual objects only occur indirectly via the input-output stylus, the surface haptics class's devices aim to simulate direct interaction between the user's fingers and the virtual objects (Wang et al. 2019). For example, users should feel the contour of an image displayed on a cell phone (Wang et al. 2019). The most common form of feedback used here is vibration, or vibrotactile feedback, which can already be found in most smartphones (Wang et al. 2019). The feedback granularity ranges from very general vibration, which the user cannot assign to a specific position on the display, to vibration feedback which can be discriminated with near pixel accuracy.

Pressure-sensitive mats, e.g., in the form of loungers (Laak et al. 2018) or entire floors (Fraunhofer IFF 2021), also belong to the class of surface haptics but are not very well represented. It must be added here, however, that the focus of these mats is on detecting pressure and less on generating haptic feedback.

### 4.3 Wearable Haptics

Although wearable haptics is the most recent and current category in terms of feedback in virtual worlds, the first developments took place as early as 1987 with the "Data Glove" a glove that could collect finger data using optical fibers on the top of the hand (Dörner et al. 2019). Wearable haptics refers to all haptic feedback devices that the user can "put on." These range from full-body suits, such as the Tesla Suit (https://teslasuit.io/), which allows stimulation of different body regions using haptic feedback, to haptic gloves, which can be worn either individually or in pairs. Compared to desktop haptics, haptic gloves, for example, offer users the possibility to manipulate virtual objects directly and intuitively with their own hands (Wang et al. 2019). Especially the latter group of haptic gloves is fascinating in the context of VR.

On the one hand, there is a surge in development and innovation in this sector particularly, as the gloves can be applied in many different industries, such as medicine, rehabilitation, education, gaming, or e-business (cf. Wang et al. 2019). As a result, the processing, prices, and availability of the devices are becoming increasingly suitable for a mass consumer market. On the other hand, haptic gloves do not exclusively enable the generation of haptic feedback. They can also serve as an alternative and innovative interaction modality (not least due to their system-immanent finger tracking). This is particularly important in the SmartHands project with its target group of physiotherapists, as hands are essential in diagnostics and therapy. Virtualization of the training can only be implemented in a demand-oriented manner if both the active (interaction) and the passive functions (receiving haptic feedback) of the hands can be represented in VR.

Haptic gloves can be divided according to the type of feedback. For example, there are gloves with tactile feedback, with force feedback, and gloves based on a combination of both (Cf. Grimm et al. 2019). In gloves with tactile feedback, such as the glove from Cynteract (https://www.cynteract.com/), the feedback is implemented via vibration, mostly through so-called actuators. Depending on the technology used, it is possible to stimulate even the fingers and hands' smallest areas with pinpoint accuracy. Force feedback gloves, the gloves from Senseglove (https://www.senseglove.com/), make it possible to feel resistances of different strengths, such as those that occur when grasping, pressing, and lifting objects, by incorporating small exoskeletons (cf. Grimm et al. 2019).

To achieve the highest possible immersion, tactile and force feedback can be combined in one glove, as is the case with the Haptx glove (https://haptx.com/), for example.

## 5  State-of-the-Art of Haptic Gloves

To have a better overview and based on the project's goals illustrated below, this section of work provides a selective overview of commercially available haptic gloves. This form of devices is highly demanded and, at the same time, the most complex in terms of development (Perret and Vander Poorten 2018), and, thus, the most relevant for e-commerce and e-business. We summarized the essential information about some of the commercial gloves in Table 1.

There are several classifications of the gloves. E.g., Perret and Vander Poorten (2018) propose distinction based on the form between traditional gloves (made of some flexible fabric which fits contours of the hand), thimbles (have contact with the hand only on the fingertips), and exoskeletons (structures that one wears over the hand with the transmission of forces to the fingers). However, it somehow aligns with the types of feedback provided: exoskeletons rely on force feedback, whereas thimbles mostly on the tactile.

**Table 1.** Comparison of haptic gloves.

| Category | Cynteract | Sensorial XR (former AvatarVR) | VRgluv | SenseGlove | SenseGlove Nova | HaptX |
|---|---|---|---|---|---|---|
| Feedback | Vibrotactile | Vibrotactile | Force Feedback, Palm vibration | Force & vibration | Force & vibrotactile | Force & tactile (microfluidic) |
| Resolution | n/a | 10 low latency vibrotactile actuators, 1024 vibration intensity levels | 10 lbs. (45N) on each finger | 9lbs.(40N) per finger | 4 passive force feedback modules delivering a max. force of 4.5 lbs. (20N) | 40 lbs. (175 N) per hand, 130 points of feedback per hand |
| Hand tracking DoF | Flexion, extension, and spreading of fingers, the hand, and, to some extent, the arm | All the degrees of freedom gathered by 7 9-AXIS IMUs (2 in the thumb, 1 in the back of the hand, 1 in the rest of the fingers), absolute and local rotations, and positions | 3 DoF fingers incl. lateral movement, 5 DoF thumb, 28 DoF total | Total 24 DoF per hand | 5 DoF per finger, 9-axis absolute orientation sensor in the wrist | 6DoF per finger, 30 DoF total |
| Wireless | No | Yes, via Bluetooth | Yes, via Bluetooth | Yes, with the use of an additional Wireless Kit | Yes, via Bluetooth | No, external console |
| Weight | n/a | n/a | n/a | 300g each | n/a | 450g |
| Published price | Starting from ca. €1000 per pair[a] | Starting from 1500€ per pair[b] | n/a | Starting from €2.999,00 per pair[c] | Starting from 4.499,00$[d] | n/a |

*The information in the table is based on openly published information.*
[a] https://cynteract.com/de/faq.
[b] https://sensorialxr.com/product/sensorial-xr-pair-2/
[c] https://www.senseglove.com/product/developers-kit/
[d] https://www.senseglove.com/product/nova/

Force feedback interfaces were the earliest ones. They usually weigh more and are bulkier, as they typically need to be grounded to the desk or ground, and recently, to the hand's back. This type of glove focuses on providing sensations of weight, inertia, and collision with virtual objects. Devices with tactile feedback give the feeling from the surface: roughness, slippage, sometimes temperature.

Cynteract (https://www.cynteract.com/) gloves were developed with a particular focus on medical use, i.e., rehabilitation use cases. A young German company's product represents traditional gloves made of fabric, available in three sizes (S, M, and L).

Sensorial XR (https://sensorialxr.com/) is also looks like a pair of traditional gloves, but compared to Cynteract, it is possible to use them wirelessly. They are made from antibacterial & fireproof lycra. As Cynteract, Sensorial XR provides vibrotactile feedback.

VRgluv (https://www.vrgluv.com/) focuses on the active force feedback, although they do not look like an exoskeleton.

The same applies to SenseGlove Nova, an updated version of SenseGlove produced in the form of an exoskeleton (https://www.senseglove.com/).

HaptX provides probably the bulkiest equipment (the gloves per se, and they are also tethered to a backpack module) and the most realistic haptic experience, at the expense of microfluidic technology. The gloves provide a combination of tactile and dynamic force feedback.

Nonetheless, it seems that the majority of providers decided on the manufacturing of haptic gloves, looking more or less to resemble gloves in their general understanding. Probably, this is affected by the ease of use and pleasant view factors. Gloves are comfortable to put on and less customization with straps needed. This, however, does not solve the problem with hands of different sizes. Still, not all of the companies provide their products in various sizes.

An interesting question in times of pandemic is the question of hygiene, e.g. disinfection of such devices. While it is easy to disinfect plastic and exoskeletons (for example, SenseGlove made out of ABS), it is not so straightforward when the device consists predominately out of fabric. This also includes the issue of sweat.

A particular question is the usability of those devices. The research highlights the importance of usability throughout the whole product development process. Usability is sometimes defined as "ease of use," but this does not say a lot about the interface itself, especially its measurability. A better definition would be the ability to be used effectively, efficiently, and enjoyable for tasks that need specific tools within a given environment (Falcão and Soares 2012). Though, best to our knowledge, there is a lack of works aiming directly to compare the devices' usability. We believe that for widespread wearable haptics, the devices should provide all kinds of haptic sensations, less rely on unnatural ones, like vibration, and generally comply with the human's senses characteristics.

The haptic devices should also be intended for long wear without threatening comfort. There is an issue of the so-called gorilla-arm effect (Hincapié-Ramos 2014), which significantly complicates the widespread use of haptic gloves. The hands are prone to fatigue and feeling of heaviness due to mid-air interactions. At the expense of the extra weight, the use of gloves can accelerate the onset of this effect.

Usually, haptic devices such as wearable ones are being used to enhance the UI, e.g., to feel feedback from a button, and are typical for entertainment and game scenarios. However, as we can demonstrate in the next sections, they provide more excellent value for training and e-business.

# 6   The Project SmartHands

The project SmartHands aims to integrate innovative media for the domain of healthcare learning. The enabling technological framework for the project is a learning management system. Serving as a unifying platform and as a single point of access, it brings together all the learning actors, technologies, and content. The project's other technical base is the utilization of virtual & mixed reality head-mounted displays and haptic devices.

The project consists of several scenarios; in this paper, we will focus specifically on the virtual reality simulator for practicing case-based learning.

The primary learning audience are those who continue professional education in manual medicine, e.g., further qualification of physiotherapists. Conventionally, the learning in medical domains takes the form of apprenticeship. The student traditionally learns over a range of presentations during study years and practices predominately with peers and lab sessions. Considering the barriers to that (lack of teaching and tutoring resources, COVID-associated restrictions), we try to integrate alternatives to traditional skills development methods. We propose to support the learning with a head-mounted VR system, enabling the learner to train without a partner, with the help of haptics-enabling gloves.

A distinct part of this project is virtual reality and haptic devices in introducing them into the curriculum. We aim to tackle the problems of the lack of teaching staff, the lack of a personalized approach to each student, the lack of practice, especially in a pandemic environment, and to show that these technologies can stimulate the development of professional and methodological skills, as well as the self-reflection of the learners.

An integral part of this domain is the sense of touch, applied pressure, and psychomotor skills. Consider, for example, palpation, a physical examination technique. It is used for localization of body landmarks, for evaluation of dysfunctions, for mastering treatment techniques. The palpation task is complex and requires various types of knowledge, perceptual and motor skills, and practical experience (Aubin 2014; Ulrich 2012). Moreover, palpation skills and associated diagnostic findings affect the accuracy of clinical reasoning (Esteves 2011), the processes of thinking and decision making in the patient-centered care, which quintessence is autonomous clinical practice, including the social interaction and interplay of declarative and procedural knowledge (Higgs et al. 2008). Having the goal to recognize if there is a somatic dysfunction (asymmetry, restriction of movement, stiffness, and texture abnormalities), this diagnostic procedure is an engagement in information evaluation provided by senses. Also, this domain's medical professionals heavily rely on manipulations of various types, e.g., joint mobilization techniques, a sequence of movements that are applied to joints or muscles to restore optimal mobility and reduce pain.

Clinical reasoning usually is defined as a context-dependent way of thinking and decision making to guide practice (Higgs et al. 2008). As it is usually embedded in the construction of narratives and makes sense of many variables, its development involves a solution similar to real-world problems, sometimes with simulators allowing that. That is the main reasoning behind our VR solution. The final system should enable the learners to see patients, engage in clinical reasoning, make therapeutic hypotheses, collect anamneses and administer/perform interventions.

A significant challenge in this project is a reality-approximate simulation of a patient. Here, the users (doctors and medical students) should engage in problem-solving by communicating and interacting with the virtual patient. The simulation will be designed to improve learners' effectiveness by running a case scenario in a safe environment. The communication between the patient and the learner will be done in a game-like manner via selection from a set of questions and answers. At the end of the run, the learner will be given prompts to engage in self-reflection and to request feedback on actions and decisions made.

As hands and psychomotor manual skills are an essential component of manual medicine education, we also have set a goal to transfer this into the virtual world. Depending on the learners' experience, there will be the possibility to adjust the gameplay's difficulty and the concurrent feedback.

While the hands and sensations from them, beyond the shadow of a doubt, are the critical elements in the way the therapists perceive patients, it is also an interesting question how much the visual information contributes to diagnosis and clinical reasoning. In the medical communities, it is believed, a good practitioner can identify the source of the problem at the exact moment a patient walks into the office: based on the subtle cues from the pose, the pace, the stride, etc. The visual information from the tissues can also affect the diagnosis: e.g., stiffness, redness, and asymmetry can be inferred visually. This question certainly needs further investigation. We believe that the visual information can be the key to higher presence when the haptic information is scarce or shallow.

Current advances in the hardware and graphics provide quite a good representation of medical procedures in VR, however, there is a significant gap in the haptic technologies' integration. A considerable amount of work in this direction in healthcare domains has been done for surgical simulations. The simulators for that domain particular and not easily transferable to other fields. E.g., the surgeons rely on haptic feedback from tools like a scalpel. In our case, on the contrary, the therapist uses hands primarily, but also sometimes the whole body (e.g., to put an entire weight, to lift extremities, or for the leverage). The users should also be provided with the believable reconstruction of body tissues to palpate and administer/perform interventions.

In the project, we are currently using SenseGlove and considering its potentials as a force feedback source. It is an interesting question if the force feedback will be enough to provide adequate feedback for palpation and treatment, or the users won't be able to disconnect from the absence of the usual cues like smoothness and temperature of the skin, etc. If the force feedback is not enough, we will proceed to other options of a combination of force and tactile feedback types.

To summarize the challenges and outline the directions of the future work:

- To what extent can the visual information substitute or augment the haptic information. Specifically, is it possible to achieve the goals of the project with the low-budget state-of-the-art devices? Will it be feasible to use only force feedback or tactile information necessary for that specific use-case and impact the sense of presence, learnability, and ability to diagnose and treat patients in the domain of manual medicine?
- How critical are the haptics and the sense of weight for shoulders and overall smooth experience and presence?
- Is it possible to discriminate body tissues and create a reality-similar touch to a human body?
- Which interaction techniques do come to the fore in this regard?

The answers to these questions in the future will determine the success of the project and overall user experience, as well as have implications for the research community and e-business.

## 7  Implication for e-business

The integration of haptic feedback in VR enables creation of virtual worlds that correspond even more closely to their real-world counterparts. It is precisely the possibility of a previously unrealizable real-world representation that also opens up new e-business opportunities. With the increasing spread of VR glasses and the rapid development and spread trend of haptic glasses, the consideration of B2C e-commerce and its pain points is becoming interesting.

One pain point is undeniable here: the avoidance of returns. After all, lowering the returns rate in e-commerce would be a win-win situation for both customers and retailers. A recent survey by elaboratum GmbH (2020) on frustration factors in e-commerce puts a customer-unfriendly returns process in third place among the top 10 frustration factors for online customers. In 2018, 490 million items were returned in Germany, according to a study by the University of Bamberg (Asdecker 2019). Apart from the fact that retailers do not have the items available for resale during the returns process, in the vast majority of cases, they also have to bear the costs of returns (if not factored into the mixed calculation). This is particularly sensitive for business sectors with a high returns rate, such as the fashion sector with up to 30% (Statista 2019) or also the furniture sector, whose items incur additional return costs (shipping delivery) due to their size. The advantages of falling return rates then seem immense.

The following use cases show how the integration of haptic feedback can help reduce return rates:

- Use Case 1: Virtual trial living

Jasmin, a customer, wants to buy a new real wood closet for her bedroom to match her existing furniture. To do this, she tries out the latest VR Haptic app from her furniture store. After recording her bedroom furnishings on her smartphone and importing them into the app, she selects the item she wants in the store and clicks to have it appear in her virtual bedroom. With VR glasses' help, she can now look around the bedroom and see whether the new closet does fit visually into her bedroom. Besides, she can virtually run her hand over the wardrobe's surface using a haptic glove and thus feel and experience the structure of the article in addition to its appearance. She thus grasps the complete "look and feel" (as an essential factor of the user experience) and is now sure that the wardrobe suits her. A return will not be necessary.

- Use Case 2: Virtual dressing room

The customer Tom wants to buy a new suit for his sister's wedding. Like most of his purchases, this special occasion item will be purchased online. To do this, he tries out his fashion store's new VR Haptic app. After the app measures his body, he can enter the virtual fitting room with VR glasses' help. Here he has the choice of all available suits, and with one click, he sees himself in the chosen suit in a virtual mirror. He can now quickly check the look and fit of the suit. Besides, he can use a haptic glove to check the texture of the suit's fabric virtually. To do this, he runs his hand over the suit's surface and pulls lightly on the material. In this way, he captures the complete "look and feel" (as an essential factor of the user experience) and is now sure that the suit is the right one. A return will not be necessary.

Both use cases have in common that articles can be realistically felt and experienced with the help of haptic feedback. For a long time, the lack of haptics, the inability to touch an item, was a significant difference between off- and online retail and a driver for returns. In the future, this gap can be closed by integrating VR and haptic feedback into store structures.

## 8  Conclusion

It can be stated that the consideration of haptic feedback in virtual worlds has a positive effect on the degree of immersion and presence and, as a consequence, on the level of user experience perceived by the user. However, implementing haptic feedback does not per se lead to a better experience. The following factors should be considered:

- Use Case
- Haptic function
- Multi-modality

The UX achieved as an aggregate of immersion and presence is highly dependent on the use case at hand and the technology used for this purpose. Initially, we must clarify the question which functions the haptics will take on. Should it only be an addition to round off the scenario or represent a modality of its own, integral to the setting? Furthermore, it must be determined how fine-grained haptic feedback should be generated to correspond to the original real-world scenario. If haptic feedback serves as a modality, even small deviations from user expectations (cf. expectation conformity) will be perceived as active interference with the interaction. In the learning context, the expectations towards such accuracy will also be significantly higher than, for example, in the gaming context. Taking SmartHands as an example: if it is not possible to experience the forces and resistances during the virtual learning of a grip technique in the same way as the learner would experience them during a real treatment, the desired learning success will fail to materialize. The success will depend not only on the learning process itself but also on the possibility to have haptic sensations from the virtual patient.

This example also shows the influence of the selected technology on the UX. When deciding whether to use a tactile or a force feedback glove, the use case must also be taken into account. In the SmartHands example above, a force feedback glove is mandatory because the focus is on resistances and pressures. With a tactile glove, it would only be possible to determine the correct position of cartilage, for example, but not properties such as size and hardness. Ideally, one should use techniques that allow both tactile and force feedback.

But even if the choice of technology, the granularity of the feedback, and the technical implementation are tailored to the use case, it is still essential that the haptic component corresponds with other modalities and elements. In particular, the visuals must match the haptic feedback to enable positive effects on UX. For example, it is not enough that the user can feel the resistance when squeezing a virtual tennis ball, the visual representation of the ball must correspond to this.

Concerning the outlined use cases for e-business, the listed factors are also relevant. Because haptic feedback is still a little-discussed topic, especially in B2C e-commerce, it can be assumed that the user or better the customer will be willing to tolerate more "teething troubles" for the time being. This means that, in terms of agile, iterative development, products can also be rolled out initially at MVP status. This means that they reach the customer earlier. However, it must also be clear that success in terms of reducing the return rate correlates with the accuracy of the haptic feedback and is therefore likely to be even lower in MVP status.

Despite all the positive developments, the integration of haptic feedback in virtual worlds is not yet a game-changer in immersion, presence, and UX. However, this is less due to this new modality per se than to the devices' current technical possibilities and development. We hope that the development will continue to progress as rapidly as it currently does in the area of haptic gloves. In particular, work must be done on the feedback's sensitivity to enable the sensing of different materials, different temperatures, or weights of objects. Initial research and products such as the ThermoReal process from the company Tegway (http://tegway.co/tegway/) for haptic feedback of temperatures give rise to hope and provide a glimpse of what may be possible.

**Acknowledgments.** The results of this work were supported by the Bundesministerium für Bildung und Forschung within the project "SmartHands" which was funded under the project reference 01PG20006.

# References

Aubin, A., Gagnon, K., Morin, C.: The seven-step palpation method: a proposal to improve palpation skills. Int. j. Osteopath. Med. **17**(1), 66–72 (2014)

Asdecker, B.: Praeventives retourenmanagement und ruecksendegebuehren - neue studienergebnisse [Pressemeldung] (2019). http://www.retourenforschung.de/info-praeventives-retourenm anagement-und-ruecksendegebuehren---neue-studienergebnisse.html

Azuma, R.T.: A survey of augmented reality. Presence: Teleoperators and Virtual Environ, vol. **6**(4), 355–385 (1997). https://doi.org/10.1162/pres.1997.6.4.355

Birbaumer, N., Schmidt, R.F.: Somatosensorik, nozizeption, schmerz. In: Biologische Psychologie, pp. 326–371. Springer, Berlin, Heidelberg (1999). https://doi.org/10.1007/978-3-662-06097-1_16

Bloom, B.S., Engelhard, M.D., Furst, E.J., Hill, W.H., Krathwohl, D.R.: Taxonomy of Educational Objectives, Handbook I: The Cognitive Domain. Longmans, New York (1956)

Bodendörfer, X.: Virtual Reality und UX – wann das Eintauchen in eine andere Welt das Benutzererlebnis behindern kann. Usabilityblog. https://www.usabilityblog.de/virtual-reality-und-ux-wann-das-eintauchen-in-eine-andere-welt-das-benutzererlebnis-behindern-kann/

Caudell, T., Mizell, D.W.: Augmented reality: an application of heads-up display technology to manual manufacturing processes. Proc. Twenty-Fifth Hawaii Int. Conf. Syst. Sci. **2**, 659–669 (1992)

Dörner, R., Broll, W., Jung, B., Grimm, P., Göbel, M.: Einführung in virtual und augmented reality. In: Dörner, R., Broll, W., Grimm, P., Jung, B. (eds.) Virtual und Augmented Reality (VR/AR), pp. 1–42. Springer, Heidelberg (2019). https://doi.org/10.1007/978-3-662-58861-1_1

elaboratum GmbH. Das E-Commerce-Frustbarometer. elaboratum (2020). https://www.elabor atum.de/news/ecommerce-frustbarometer-2020-elaboratum-trusted-shops/

Esteves, J.E.: Diagnostic Palpitation in Osteopathic Medicine: A Putative Neurocognitive Model of Expertise (Doctoral dissertation, Oxford Brookes University) (2011)

Falcão, C.S., Soares, M.: Ergonomics, usability and virtual reality: a review applied to consumer product. In: Falcão, C.S., Soares, M., (ets) Advances in Usability Evaluation Part II, pp. 297–306 (2012)

Frank, T.B.: Erstellung und anwendung von 360°-Videos. In: Orsolits, H., Lackner, M. (ets) Virtual Reality und Augmented Reality in der Digitalen Produktion, pp. 263–273. Springer Fachmedien, Wiesbaden (2020). https://doi.org/10.1007/978-3-658-29009-2_13

Fraunhofer, I.F.F.: Taktile Sensorsysteme in drucksensitiven Fußbodenbelägen (2021). https://www.iff.fraunhofer.de/de/geschaeftsbereiche/robotersysteme/taktile-sensorsysteme-drucksensitive-fussbodenbelaege.html

Gerth, S., Kruse, R.: VR/AR-Technologien im Schulungseinsatz für Industrieanwendungen. In: Orsolits, H., Lackner, M. (ets) Virtual Reality und Augmented Reality in der Digitalen Produktion, pp. 143–179. Springer, Fachmedien, Wiesbaden (2020). https://doi.org/10.1007/978-3-658-29009-2_8

Grimm, P., Broll, W., Herold, R., Reiners, D., Cruz-Neira, C.: VR/AR-Ausgabegeräte. In: Dörner, R., Broll, W., Grimm, P., Jung, B.: (ets) Virtual und Augmented Reality (VR/AR): Grundlagen und Methoden der Virtuellen und Augmentierten Realität, pp. 163–217. Springer, Berlin, Heidelberg (2019). https://doi.org/10.1007/978-3-662-58861-1_5

Grunwald, M., Müller, S.: Wissenschaftliche grundlagen der palpation. In: Mayer, J., Standen, C. (ets) Lehrbuch Osteopathische Medizin. 1. Auflage, pp. 251–265. Urban & Fischer Verlag/Elsevier GmbH. (2017)

Grunwald, M.: Homo Hapticus. Warum Wir Ohne Tastsinn Nicht Leben Können. München, Droemer-Verlag (2017)

Grunwald, M.: Haptik: der handgreiflich-körperliche zugang des menschen zur welt und zu sich selbst. In: Schmitz, T.H. (et.) Werkzeug-Denkzeug, pp. 95–125. Transcript Verlag (2012)

Grunwald, M.: Der Tastsinn im griff der technikwissenschaften? herausforderungen und grenzen aktueller haptikforschung. Internet-Zeitschrift des Leibniz-Instituts für interdisziplinäre Studien e. V. (LIFIS). (2009)

Higgs, J., Jones, M.A., Loftus, S., Christensen, N.: Clinical reasoning in the health professions E-book. Elsevier Health Sciences (2008)

Hincapié-Ramos, J.D., Guo, X., Moghadasian, P., Irani, P.: Consumed endurance: a metric to quantify arm fatigue of mid-air interactions. In: Proceedings of the SIGCHI Conference on Human Factors in Computing Systems, pp. 1063–1072 (2014)

Jerald, J.: The VR book: human-centered design for virtual reality. Morgan & Claypool (2015)

Kern, T.A.: Biologische grundlagen haptischer wahrnehmung. In: Kern, T.A. (et.) Entwicklung Haptischer Geräte: Ein Einstieg für Ingenieure, pp. 39–64. Springer, Berlin, Heidelberg (2009). https://doi.org/10.1007/978-3-540-87644-1_3

Laak, M., Müller, K., Ebert, A.: Die drucksensitive liege: eine intuitive eingabemethode für VR applikationen. In: Dachselt, R., Weber, G. (ets) Mensch und Computer 2018 - Tagungsband. Bonn: Gesellschaft für Informatik e.V. (2018). https://doi.org/10.18420/muc2018-mci-0399

Moreno, R., Mayer, R.: Interactive multimodal learning environments. Educ. Psychol. Rev. 19(3), 309–326 (2007)

Niijima, A., Ogawa, T.: Study on control method of virtual food texture by electrical muscle stimulation. In: Proceedings of the 29th Annual Symposium on User Interface Software and Technology, pp. 199–200 (2016). https://doi.org/10.1145/2984751.2984768

Perret, J., Poorten, E.V.: Touching virtual reality: a review of haptic gloves. In: Proceedings of 16th International Confernce on New Actuators, 270–274 (2018)

Slater, M, Wilbur, S.: A Framework for immersive virtual environments (FIVE): speculations on the role of presence in virtual environments. Presence: Teleoperators Virtual Environ. 6, 603–616 (1997)

Slater, M.: Place illusion and plausibility can lead to realistic behaviour in immersive virtual environments. Philos. Trans. r. Soc. Lon. b, Biol. Sci. **364**(1535), 3549–3557 (2009). https://doi.org/10.1098/rstb.2009.0138

Statista: Online bestellte produkte welcher kategorie haben sie in den vergangenen zwölf Monaten zurückgesendet? (2019). https://de.statista.com/statistik/daten/studie/655805/umfrage/retoure-online-bestellter-ware-nach-produktkategorien/

Sutherland, I.E.: The ultimate display. In: Proceedings of the IFIP Congress, 506–508 (1965)

Sutherland, I.E.: A head-mounted three dimensional display. Proceedings of the December 9–11 1968. Fall Joint Computer Conference, Part I, pp. 757–764. https://doi.org/10.1145/1476589.1476686

Ullrich, S., Kuhlen, T.: Haptic palpation for medical simulation in virtual environments. IEEE Trans. Visual Comput. Graphics **18**(4), 617–625 (2012)

Wang, D., Guo, Y., Liu, S., Zhang, Y., Xu, W., Xiao, J.: Haptic display for virtual reality: progress and challenges. Virtual Reality Intell. Hardware **1**(2), 136–162 (2019). https://doi.org/10.3724/sp.j.2096-5796.2019.0008

Witmer, B.G., Singer, M.J.: Measuring presence in virtual environments: a presence questionnaire. Presence: Teleoperators Virtual Environ. **7**(3), 225–240 (1998). https://doi.org/10.1162/105474698565686

# Leveraging Artificial Intelligence in Medicine Compliance Check

Guoping Jia[1], Wei Zhu[2]([⊠]), JinJun Tang[3], and Wenping Zhang[1]

[1] School of Information, Renmin University of China,
Beijing 100872, People's Republic of China
[2] Beijing RayooTech Co., Ltd., Beijing 100000, People's Republic of China
zhuwei@rayootech.com
[3] Taikang Pension Co., Ltd., Beijing 100000, People's Republic of China

**Abstract.** This paper aims to utilize AI technology to solve the challenge of medicine compliance check. More specifically, we propose a Logic-BERT model to estimate whether certain medicine can be used in specific situations of a patient based on electronic medical record. We design a sentence level architecture that distill the text content by segmentation, selection and recombination to solve the length limitation of bidirectional encoder representations from transformers (BERT). We also apply data augmentation integrating logic rules to enhance the performance of our proposed model. Experiments based on real data have verified the effectiveness of our model.

**Keywords:** Artificial intelligence · BERT · Medicine overuse · Logic rules

## 1 Introduction

The usage of medicine is a critical issue in treatment. Regulators have made strict and detailed regulations to guide and restrict the usage of medicines. However, the situation is still far from optimism. Misuse and improper-use of medicine happen frequently in real practice. Various reasons, such as lack of experience, misjudge of condition, or brokerage of a certain medicine, may contribute to this situation. Thus, there is a serious call for a more effective medicine compliance check method to guarantee the usage of a medicine in a treatment meet the criterions.

Medicine compliance check is a very difficult task in real practice, given complexity of the situations in real treatment. Regulators mainly rely manual checks to detect medicine improper-use. Some recent systems employ simple rules and shallow text mining techniques (e.g., string match) as assistant to conduct medicine improper-use detection. The drawbacks of these systems are obvious. The efficiency is rather low while the cost is relatively high. Considering the amount of the data (e.g., case reports) that need to be checked every day, current systems cannot meet the basic requirement in medicine compliance check. In this paper, we leverage artificial intelligence (AI) technology to conduct medicine compliance check. More specifically, we incorporate the latest deep learning techniques to mine electronic medical record (EMR) and determine

© Springer Nature Switzerland AG 2021
F. F.-H. Nah and K. Siau (Eds.): HCII 2021, LNCS 12783, pp. 578–587, 2021.
https://doi.org/10.1007/978-3-030-77750-0_37

whether the usage of certain medicine meets the specification according to patients' physical situation and treatment history.

In our research, we utilize the latest bidirectional encoder representations from transformers (BERT) framework to construct our system. The effectiveness of BERT [1] in complex text mining tasks has been proved by previous research. Despite the effectiveness, BERT has an obvious weakness that it is incapable of processing long texts due to its quadratically increasing memory and time consumption. In our design, we propose a sentence level architecture that distill the text content by segmentation, selection and recombination to solve this problem. The superiority of deep learning in various tasks relies heavily on the abundance of labeled training data. It is well known that expressions in EMR are extremely concise, leaving little redundant information (e.g., term co-occurrence) for algorithms to learn. Moreover, although the total records of EMR are extremely large, the labeled data are relatively few, especially considering the varieties of medicines and diseases. In our design, we adopt data enhancement techniques to alleviate these problems.

The contributions of our research are threefold: (1) We design a deep learning model to mine the electronic medical record (EMR) to conduct medicine compliance check; (2) We propose a sentence level architecture that distill the text content by segmentation, selection and recombination to solve the length limitation of BERT; (3) We develop a data enhancement model to increase the data usage efficiency.

The rest of the paper are organized as follows. In Sect. 2, we review and summarize the related literatures that close to our research. In Sect. 3, we describe the details of our model design. The experiments are shown in Sect. 4. We make the conclusion of this research and clarify the future direction in Sect. 5.

## 2 Literature Review

### 2.1 Existing Work on Medicine Compliance Check

Previous works have paid a long attention to medical overtreatment and have made some achievements. There are two main directions in medical overtreatment study: one is the analysis of the overall phenomenon of medical overtreatment in the field of medical insurance [2–4], and other studies are about medical overtreatment of specific diseases (including the Necessity analysis of some common examination methods for a specific disease) [5–7]. However, these studies are mainly focused on the medicine knowledge exploration. The combination of artificial intelligence is rare to see. This fact is largely due to the particularity of medical data. Most of the medical data is in free text format. The data is complex and has a wide range of sources, which contains many proper nouns [8]. It has high requirements for semantic understanding, which is beyond the capability of traditional neural network based electronic medical records processing methods [9]. The traditional unidirectional language model cannot extract patient's information well, and easy to miss and misjudge.

### 2.2 Bidirectional Encoder Representations from Transformers (BERT)

It has long been noticed that pre-training could enhance the performance of deep learning significantly [10]. Following research also verified the effectiveness of language model pre-training for natural language processing (NLP) tasks [11–13]. Strategies for incorporating pre-trained language representations to NLP tasks can be summarized into two streams: features-based [12] and fine-tuning [13]. In feature-based approaches, pre-trained representations are embedded in task-specific architectures as additional features. A typical example is Embeddings from Language Models (ELMo) [12]. In fine-tuning approaches, the power of pre-trained language representations are transferred by minimal task-specific parameters and the enhancement is achieved by the simple parameter fine-tuning process. A typical example is Generative Pre-trained Transformer (OpenAI GPT) [13]. The unidirectional design of these models limits the flexibility of the architectures in pre-training. To deal with this weakness, Google AI language lab proposed the Bidirectional Encoder Representations from Transformers (BERT). BERT utilized a "masked language model" to overcome the unidirectionality constraint [1]. Given a sequence of input, the masked language model masks some randomly selected tokens, then uses information of the left, including both left and right context, to predict these masked tokens. It could significant enrich the information learnt by pre-training. BERT's impressive high performance has made it widely used in various language processing tasks, such as sequential recommendation [14], dialogue state tracking [15] and answer selection [16]. Some attempts also have been made to utilize BERT to solve health care related problem [17, 18].

### 2.3 Long Text Challenge of BERT

Despite these impressive advantages of BERT, it also has some flaws in current version. One of the most obvious flaws that limits its application is real practice is the restriction of the text length. Since the memory consumption will exponentially increase when the length of input embedding increases, max position embedding is usually limited to 512 in practice [1]. Even though, it still surpass the capacity of common GPUs [19]. In this case, when a long sequence is fed, it will be broken into small fragments that no longer than 512. Apparently, it breaks the long dependence among terms, which finally decrease the performance. Considering the high frequency of long sequence in real setting (e.g., EMR in our study) and the importance of long dependence in NLP, this length restriction will be serious challenge both researchers and practitioners need to face. Some successful attempts have been made since BERT was proposed.

One simplest way to address this problem is slicing the text by a sliding window [20] or simplifying transformers. A long text can be divided to many small pieces. BERT can process these pieces individually and summarized them as result. Although sliding window is easy to achieve, it has a terrible performance on long-term attention. If the key fragments which influence the result greatly cannot always in a same window, this model will hardly get a right result. This method sacrifices the possibility that the distant tokens "pay attention" to each other, which becomes the bottleneck for BERT to show its efficacy in complex tasks. Some researchers [21, 22] tried to use different way to integrate information from different window, such as max-pooling and mean-pooling. However, these models are still weak in long-term memory. Some other methods pay attention to simplify transformers [23, 24], but most of them have not yet applied to BERT.

As the sliding window method cannot solve long-term attention problem, Zhang [25] combined the BERT with multi-channel LSTM. This method increases the consideration of the relevance between different fragments. Even if the key sentence is not in a same small fragment, it can be identified and extracted. However, such methods do not consider the importance difference among divisions of fragments. Simply using the longest processing length of BERT for division does not provide a good understanding of semantics. The interpretability of the model remains to be enhanced.

According to the characteristics of human working memory, Ding [26] proposed the cognize long texts model (CogLTX). It identifies key sentences by training a judge model, concatenates them for reasoning, and enables multi-step reasoning via rehearsal and decay. This model greatly improves the ability to understand and expand semantics, but if the key sentence is not selected in the first round, it will not enter the final model calculation, and the correct answer cannot be selected. The subsequent BERT model cannot extract full text information. At the same time, due to the particularity of the question answering model, there are initial problems that can calculate the similarity. For some unsupervised initial training, the initial key sentence can only be calculated according to the word frequency weight. The experiments on various datasets proved the superiority than other methods. Moreover, the scenario we involve is similar to the situation they intended to solve. For instance, in EMR not all sentences are equally important. Experts need to identify some relevant important sentences, then make decisions based on them. As a result, we take CogLTX as the foundation for our model design. We borrow the idea of their model and make adjustments and improvements on it.

## 2.4 Data Enhancement

Deep learning provides a powerful mechanism for learning patterns from massive data. It has shown new levels performance on many tasks, such as machine translation [27], image classification [28], text classification [29], document summarization [30], and so forth. Despite the impressive advances, the widely used deep learning methods have a serious limitation. The high predictive accuracy heavily relies on large amounts of labeled data. The quality and quantity of data determine their performance. When the labeled dataset is not sufficient enough, the deep leaning models will either suffer the problem of under-fitting or over-fitting, which finally limits the generalization and accuracy. In fact, when we are dealing with real problems, there is rarely enough available label data. Preparing a large annotated dataset is very time-consuming. In many cases, only professional experts can provide reliable suggestions for labels. Considering the rareness of professional experts, it is almost impossible to obtain enough no say sufficient labeled data. For instance, only experienced doctors could make reliable judgment based on EMR in our medicine compliance check.

To solve this dilemma, data augment techniques was proposed. The data augment technique was firstly used in the field of image classification [31]. Given its obvious performance enhancement capability, especially when lack of labelled data, it was soon introduced into language processing and many variants were proposed. Widely used data argument methods in language models include back translation with different language [32], easy data augmentation (EDA) [33], deep learning [34], contextual augmentation [35] etc. The EDA method, is simple and effective, consists of four simple but powerful operations: synonym replacement, random insertion, random swap, and random deletion. Besides, EDA demonstrates particularly strong results for smaller datasets.

## 3  Model Design

### 3.1  Design of Logic-BERT

The maximum length limit in BERT naturally reminds us the limited of human memory. When we make a decision, we utilize some key information instead of all information we have learned. Then the problem shifts to how to select and make best use of accessible knowledge. In this paper, we propose a Logic-BERT model to select the key sentences and make use of key sentences to solve downstream tasks. Our model can be decomposed into four steps as shown in Fig. 1.

In the first step, raw medical long texts are segmented into short sentences. These short sentences should meet two conditions: shorter than a threshold $SL_{max}$ (e.g., $SL_{max} = 10$) and containing relative competed meaning (e.g., a meaningful phrase). Generally, punctuations could do the job. In some special cases, such as extremely long sentences, additional helps (e.g., conjunctions and phrase mining techniques) are needed.

In the second step, short sentences obtained from the first step are filtered and key sentences are identified. In our specific task, only limited key sentence determine the result of the medicine compliance check. Most of these sentences are redundancy or noises. On one hand, these sentences will increase the burden of computation; on the other hands the noises brought by these sentences will reduce the classification performance. Thus, filter and selection is necessary and important. In our model, we use the score from the self-attention as the criterions of the key sentence selection. Intuitively, these selected key sentences could be combined into a much shorter text with most significant information for the medicine compliance check.

In the third step, selected key sentences in the second step are recombined into texts. The reason we recombine these key sentences is to achieve certain dependence during learning. To achieve optimal performance, dynamic recombination is utilized. That is key sentences with highest scored are selected with priority. The score of the left key sentences will be updated accordingly during each iteration.

In the fourth step, the recombined texts are fed into BERT to carry binary classification task. The classification results in this step is the final results for the medicine compliance check.

By segmentation and recombination, we solve the problem of the length limitation of BERT. In next section, we try to incorporate logic rules and data augmentation to alleviate the challenge brought by lack of labelled data.

### 3.2  Data Augmentation with Logic Rules

The scenario like medicine compliance check has specific preconditions, which usually exist as series of rules. In human based checking, the process is extremely straightforward—if the situation satisfies certain preconditions, then given corresponding labels. Although it suffers the problem of low efficiency and recall, the human based approach

## Logic-BERT

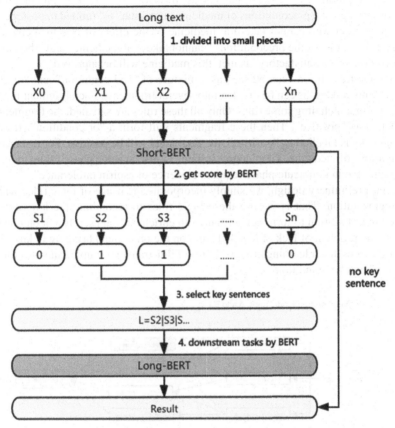

**Fig. 1.** The Logic-BERT illustration for text classification. The long text $x$ is broken into blocks $[X1...Xn]$. In the second step, $X2$ and $X3$ get a high score which means they are key sentences. Then the long-BERT classify the new long text $L$ which consists $X2$ and $X3$. If the short-BERT cannot get a sentence has high score, this long text will be directly classified.

could reach pretty good performance (e.g. precision). It would be great loss if these specific preconditions are omitted. Thus, in our design, we aim to allow deep learning algorithms to learn both from labelled examples and predefined rules.

Given a set of rules, the situations can be classified into three categories: "and condition", "or condition" and "joint condition".

In "and condition", a case will be labelled as "positive" (i.e. pass the check in out scenario) only if all preconditions are met. For instance, the preconditions of a medicine named "Argatroban Injection" is "limited to diagnosis of acute cerebral infarction and signs of motor nerve palsy and medication within 48 h after onset". There are three preconditions: "acute cerebral infarction", "signs of motor nerve palsy" and "medication within 48 h after onset". Only all of these three preconditions are met, the case will be labelled as "positive (pass)".

In "or condition", a case will be labelled as "positive" if one of these preconditions is met. For instance, the preconditions of medicine "Dynastat" is "limited to postoperative analgesia patient who cannot take oral medicine or the effect of oral medicine is not satisfactory". If one of the preconditions "cannot take oral medicine" and "the effect of oral medicine is not satisfactory" is met, this medicine will be approved.

The "joint condition" can be seen as a mixture of "and condition" and "or condition". The preconditions can be divided into several fragments. Each fragment is a "and condition" that including some rules. Only all these rules are satisfied, the fragment will be labelled as "positive". Then these fragments will form a "or condition". If one of the fragments is labelled as "positive", the final label will be positive. For instance, the preconditions of medicine "Clopidogrel sulfate" is "use in acute phase for no more than 12 months; use in non-acute phase requires evidence of aspirin intolerance".

In our preliminary design, we simply incorporate the usage of logic rules with the data augmentation. That is we use these logic rules to recombine the key sentences selected in last section to form new instances to enrich our data set. It will on one hand alleviate the problem of lack of labelled data; on the other hand bringing in knowledge from logic rules in our learning process. Figure 2 illustrate two simple examples for "and condition" and "or condition".

**Data arguementation { logic rules: A and B }**

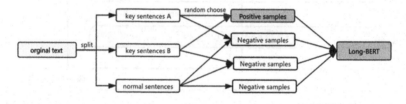

**Data arguementation { logic rules: A or B }**

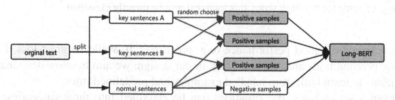

**Fig. 2.** Illustration of data augmentation. When we prepare training dataset of Long-BERT, we simulate the result of Short-BERT by random choose sentences. When the medicine limitation is to meet the condition A and condition B at the same time, splitting the original text data and obtain a lot of short sentences. Some of them can meet the condition A or condition B, and the other cannot meet any condition named normal sentences. These short sentences generate many new labeled samples for Long-BERT.

# 4  Experiment

To verify the effectiveness of our proposed model, we conduct experiment on a real dataset. In our preliminary test, the dataset contains 1511 positive (pass) instances and 1490 negative (fail) instances. The label of these instances are offered by a group of experienced doctors. The mechanism of deep learning and traditional machine learning techniques are quite different. The performance of traditional machine learning techniques, such as support vector machine, decision tree and logistic regression, relies heavily on the richness of feature set which need to be predefined manually. Deep learning, as representative learning models, could learn directly from the raw data. Thus, it is nonsense to compare our deep learning based model with traditional algorithms. In our experiments, we choose Long Short Term Memory (LSTM), short BERT, and long BERT as baselines.

The short BERT is original BERT with only limited text fed into the model [1]. In fact, we use commas, periods and semicolons to divide the original sentences to small pieces. The longest fragment is 77 characters. The long BERT uses the sliding window methods follow Wang et al.'s [20] approach. The results are summarized in Table 1.

**Table 1.** The results comparison of various models

| Model | Positive instances | | | Negative instances | | | |
|---|---|---|---|---|---|---|---|
| | Precision | Recall | F1-Score | Precision | Recall | F1-Score | Overall accuracy |
| LSTM | 0.862 | 0.902 | 0.882 | 0.883 | 0.873 | 0.878 | 0.875 |
| Short BERT | 0.852 | 0.848 | 0.850 | 0.869 | 0.811 | 0.839 | 0.858 |
| Long BERT | 0.901 | 0.923 | 0.912 | 0.915 | 0.940 | 0.927 | 0.904 |
| Logic BERT | 0.957 | 0.945 | 0.951 | 0.970 | 0.960 | 0.965 | 0.962 |

From Table 1, we can observe that our proposed logic BERT could improve the performance both in positive instances and negative instances. It verifies that our proposed model could make better use of knowledge embedded in the training dataset.

# 5  Conclusion and Future Work

In this paper, we propose an artificial intelligent model to conduct medicine compliance check. The advanced pre-training model BERT is adopted to automatically classify the check results based on electronic medical record. To overcome the length limitation of BERT, we propose a sentence level architecture that distill the text content by segmentation, selection and recombination. Furthermore, we also introduce data augmentation mechanism to enrich our dataset. Logic rules are also incorporated during the data augmentation process. Experiments based on a real dataset verify the effectiveness of our proposed model.

In this preliminary attempt, we only make shallow use of logic rules. We believe these logic rules could play more important roles in the learning and classification process. In the future work, we would try to make better use of these logic rules.

# References

1. Devlin, J., Chang, M.W., Lee, K., et al.: BERT: Pre-training of deep bidirectional transformers for language understanding. arXiv preprint arXiv:1810.04805 (2018)
2. Armstrong, N.: Overdiagnosis and overtreatment as a quality problem: insights from healthcare improvement research. BMJ Qual. Saf. **27**(7), 571–575 (2018)
3. Lyu, H., Xu, T., Brotman, D., et al.: Overtreatment in the United States. PLoS One, 12(9). e0181970 (2017)
4. Lenzer, J.: Experts consider how to tackle overtreatment in US healthcare (2012)
5. Heijnsdijk, E.A.M., der Kinderen, A., Wever, E.M., et al.: Overdetection, overtreatment and costs in prostate-specific antigen screening for prostate cancer. Br. J. Cancer **101**(11), 1833–1838 (2009)
6. McCoy, R.G., Van Houten, H.K., Ross, J.S., et al.: HbA1c overtesting and overtreatment among US adults with controlled type 2 diabetes, 2001–13: observational population based study. BMJ **351**, h6138 (2015)
7. Orish, V.N., Ansong, J.Y., Onyeabor, O.S., et al.: Overdiagnosis and overtreatment of malaria in children in a secondary healthcare centre in Sekondi-Takoradi. Ghana. Trop. Doc. **46**(4), 191–198 (2016)
8. Sun, W., Cai, Z., Li, Y., et al.: Data processing and text mining technologies on electronic medical records: a review. J. Healthc. Eng. (2018)
9. Zhou, X., Han, H., Chankai, I., et al.: Approaches to text mining for clinical medical records. In: Proceedings of the 2006 ACM Symposium on Applied Computing, pp. 235–239 (2006)
10. Erhan, D., Courville, A., Bengio, Y., et al.: Why does unsupervised pre-training help deep learning? In: Proceedings of the Thirteenth International Conference on artificial Intelligence and Statistics. JMLR Workshop and Conference Proceedings, pp. 201–208 (2010)
11. Dai, A.M., Le, Q.V.: Semi-supervised sequence learning. arXiv preprint arXiv:1511.01432 (2015)
12. Peters, M E., Neumann, M., Iyyer, M., et al.: Deep contextualized word representations. arXiv preprint arXiv:1802.05365 (2018)
13. Radford, A., Narasimhan, K., Salimans, T., et al.: Improving language understanding with unsupervised learning (2018)
14. Sun, F., Liu, J., Wu, J., Pei, C., Lin, X., Ou, W., Jiang, P.: BERT4Rec: sequential recommendation with bidirectional encoder representations from transformer. In: Proceedings of the 28th ACM International Conference on Information and Knowledge Management, pp. 1441–1450 (2019)
15. Chao, G.L., Lane, I.: BERT-DST: scalable end-to-end dialogue state tracking with bidirectional encoder representations from transformer. arXiv preprint arXiv:1907.03040 (2019)
16. Laskar, M.T.R., Hoque, E., Huang, J.X.: Utilizing bidirectional encoder representations from transformers for answer selection. arXiv preprint arXiv:2011.07208 (2020)
17. Li, F., Jin, Y., Liu, W., Rawat, B.P.S., Cai, P., Yu, H.: Fine-tuning bidirectional encoder representations from transformers (BERT)–based models on large-scale electronic health record notes: an empirical study. JMIR Med. Inf. **7**(3), e14830 (2019)
18. Xu, D., Gopale, M., Zhang, J., Brown, K., Begoli, E., Bethard, S.: Unified medical language system resources improve sieve-based generation and Bidirectional encoder representations from transformers (BERT)–based ranking for concept normalization. J. Am. Med. Inform. Assoc. **27**(10), 1510–1519 (2020)

19. Ding, M., Zhou, C., Yang, H., Tang, J.: CogLTX: Applying BERT to long texts. advances in neural information processing systems, vol. 33 (2020)
20. Wang, Z., Ng, P., Ma, X., Nallapati, R., Xiang, B.: Multi-passage BERT: a globally normalized bert model for open-domain question answering. arXiv preprint arXiv:1908.08167 (2019)
21. Wang, W., Yan, M., Wu, C.: Multi-granularity hierarchical attention fusion networks for reading comprehension and question answering. arXiv preprint arXiv:1811.11934 (2018)
22. Pappagari, R., Zelasko, P., Villalba, J., Carmiel, Y., Dehak, N.: Hierarchical Transformers for Long Document Classification. In 2019 IEEE Automatic Speech Recognition and Understanding Workshop (ASRU) (pp. 838–844). IEEE(2019).
23. Rae, J.W., Potapenko, A., Jayakumar, S.M., Lillicrap, T.P.: Compressive transformers for long-range sequence modelling. arXiv preprint arXiv:1911.05507 (2019)
24. Qiu, J., Ma, H., Levy, O., Yih, S.W.T., Wang, S., Tang, J.: Blockwise self-attention for long document understanding. arXiv preprint arXiv:1911.02972 (2019)
25. Zhang, R., Wei, Z., Shi, Y., Chen, Y.: BERT-AL: BERT for arbitrarily long document understanding (2019)
26. Ding, M., Zhou, C., Yang, H., Tang, J.: CogLTX: applying BERT to long texts. advances in neural information processing systems, vol. 33 (2020)
27. Sutskever, I., Vinyals, O., Le, Q.V.: Sequence to sequence learning with neural networks. Adv. Neural. Inf. Process. Syst. 27, 3104–3112 (2014)
28. Krizhevsky, A., Sutskever, I., Hinton, G.E.: Imagenet classification with deep convolutional neural networks. Commun. ACM 60(6), 84–90 (2017)
29. Socher, R., Perelygin, A., Wu, J., Chuang, J., Manning, C. D., Ng, A. Y., Potts, C.: Recursive deep models for semantic compositionality over a sentiment treebank. In Proceedings of the 2013 conference on empirical methods in natural language processing, pp. 1631–1642(2013).
30. Wang, D., Liu, P., Zheng, Y., Qiu, X., Huang, X.: Heterogeneous graph neural networks for extractive document summarization. arXiv preprint arXiv:2004.12393 (2020)
31. Perez, L., Wang, J.: The effectiveness of data augmentation in image classification using deep learning. arXiv preprint arXiv:1712.04621 (2017)
32. Xie, Q., Dai, Z., Hovy, E., Luong, M.T., Le, Q.V.: Unsupervised data augmentation for consistency training. arXiv preprint arXiv:1904.12848 (2019)
33. Wei, J., Zou, K.: Eda: Easy data augmentation techniques for boosting performance on text classification tasks. arXiv preprint arXiv:1901.11196 (2019)
34. Anaby-Tavor, A., Carmeli, B., Goldbraich, E., Kantor, A., Kour, G., Shlomov, S., et al.: Not enough data? Deep Learning to the Rescue! (2019)
35. Kobayashi, S.: Contextual augmentation: data augmentation by words with paradigmatic relations. arXiv preprint arXiv:1805.06201 (2018)

# Privacy, Ethics, Trust, and UX Challenges as Reflected in Google's People and AI Guidebook

Dan McAran(✉)

Estateably Inc., Toronto, Canada
dmcaran@estateably.com

**Abstract.** Google's People and AI Guidebook (Guidebook) was accessed online and an analysis performed of text associated with privacy, ethics, trust, usability, user experience, and intuitive interaction. Significant privacy, ethical, and trust issues related to the management of training data, AI human-like interfaces, and feedback were identified. In addition, novel components of UX design related to AI were revealed: (1) deciding if AI adds unique value, (2) assessing the need for automation vs. augmentation, (3) designing & evaluating the reward function, (4) considering precision & recall tradeoffs, and (5) monitoring negative impacts of the product's decisions. The analysis presented in this paper also reveals greatly increased complexity and a dynamic process in assessing/providing usability/user experience/intuitive interaction; preliminary novel measurement items are proposed. Future research could seek to develop new or modify existing instruments for measuring privacy, usability, user experience, and intuitive interaction of AI technology and the integration of the novel concepts with current concepts. A design-based approach may also be indicated.

**Keywords:** Privacy · Ethics · Trust · User experience · Intuitive interaction · Google · AI

## 1 Introduction

While there have been references to the Google People & AI Guidebook (Guidebook) [1] in the human-computer interaction literature [2–4], most notably in the paper *Seven HCI Grand Challenges* [5], as far as can be determined there has been no thematic analysis of the Guidebook [1]. The method used was to review the text of the Guidebook, consistent with grounded theory [6], to develop themes. There is a strong focus in this paper on privacy, ethical and trust issues with specific concerns identified relating to training data, AI like human interfaces, and feedback provided by the user. Additionally, there has been an attempt to outline novel salient issues related to human computer interaction and AI. There is no representation that the analysis or presentation is complete, the paper seeks only to be representative.

A key precept of the Guidebook is "Take time to critically consider how introducing AI to your product might improve, or regress, your user experience" [1, p. 4]; it is

© Springer Nature Switzerland AG 2021
F. F.-H. Nah and K. Siau (Eds.): HCII 2021, LNCS 12783, pp. 588–599, 2021.
https://doi.org/10.1007/978-3-030-77750-0_38

hoped this paper will contribute to this injunction, with an emphasis on privacy and related issues, providing a basis to extend research into the design of human computer interaction, usability, user experience, and intuitive interaction in regards to AI systems; some preliminary novel measurement items are provided.

The remainder of this paper is organized as follows. Section 2 presents a brief review of the literature; Sect. 3 presents the method used; Sect. 4 is the results; Sect. 5 is the discussion; Sect. 6 outlines limitations of and future research; Sect. 7 is the conclusion.

## 2 Literature

Ethics, privacy and security is identified as one of the seven grand challenges in the keynote *Seven HCI Grand Challenges* paper [5]. "Ethics, privacy, trust and security have always been important concerns in relation to technology, acquiring yet new dimensions in the context of technologically augmented and intelligent environments" [5, p. 1239].

Because privacy, ethics, and trust are identified together in this paper and because they are closely related, these issues are investigated together. It is important to understand the nature of privacy, Kizza provides a definition which mirrors a number of the issues identified in this paper, particularly in regards to training data and feedback:

> Privacy can be defined as "a human value consisting of a set of rights including solitude, the right to be alone without disturbances; anonymity, the right to have no public personal identity; intimacy, the right not to be monitored; and reserve, the right to control one's personal information, including the dissemination methods of that information" [7, p. 303] as cited in [5, p. 1240-1241].

Existing measurement instruments for usability, user experience, and intuitive interaction design do not contain items for privacy, ethics, security, and trust. Interestingly, trust has been found to be important in technology adoption particularly in relation to online shopping [8]. In the traditional UX framework an AI system would be evaluated in terms of usability, user experience and intuitive interaction. The usability of the AI system would be evaluated in terms of effectiveness, efficiency, and satisfaction [9]. User experience would be assessed in regards to (1) attractiveness, (2) ease to learn and understand, (3) efficiency. (4) dependability, (5) stimulation, and (6) novelty [10]. The ISO definition of user experience also does not mention privacy, ethics, or trust [9]. The intuitive interaction would be assessed in terms of (1) familiarity, (2) ease of use, (3) feedback/feedforward mechanisms, (4) error tolerance, and (5) goal achievement [11]. A novel finding of this paper is that as a result of AI, usability, user experience, and intuitive interaction becomes a dynamic process.

The Guidebook provides practical guidelines for optimal user experience with AI. Some of the content of the Guidebook has been already been described in the academic literature. In an ACM paper [12], in which all but one of the co-authors are employees of Microsoft corporation, design guidelines have been proposed for AI which mirror elements extracted from the analysis of the Guidebook. In this ACM paper, a key point is made:

> *AI-infused systems* can violate established usability guidelines of traditional user interface design. For example, the principle of consistency advocates for minimizing unexpected changes with a consistent interface appearance and predictable

behaviors. However, many AI components are inherently inconsistent due to poorly understood, probabilistic behaviors based on nuances of tasks and settings, and because they change via learning over time [12, p. 2].

The above underlies a key premise of this paper, not only usability specifically mentioned in the above quote, but also user experience and intuitive interaction evolves as part of the dynamic process inherent to AI – this leads to the conclusion that we need a new way of measuring usability, user experience, and intuitive interaction in AI systems which can be postulated as an additional challenge to the *Seven HCI Grand Challenges* [5].

Hassnzahl [13] has advocated for design in human computer interaction "The experience approach to designing interactive products, thus, starts from the assumption that if we want to design for experience, we have to put them [the experiences] first, that is, before the products" (p. 2–3). The proposal for the design of usability, user experience, and intuitive interaction in the AI context can be seen as an extension of this insight.

## 3   Method

The Guidebook [1] was accessed online and reviewed three times. A textual analysis was performed using a method consistent with the grounded theory of Corbin and Strauss [6]. Matrix analysis was also used [14]. Miles & Huberman comment: "Think, *display*, and invent formats that will serve you best" [14, p. 240, emphasis in the original]. In this paper matrices are used to identify and comment on key extracted text from the Guidebook in a manner consistent with the creation of memos in grounded theory [6]. This resulted in the creation of three tables (1) Extracted Text Relating to Privacy, Ethics, and Trust, (2) New Conceptual Elements Related to Usability, User Experience, and Intuitive Interaction, and (3) Proposed Measurement Items. After reflection it was decided to group privacy, ethics, and trust findings together in Table 1. This was done because of the close relation of privacy and ethics appearing in the *Seven HCI Grand Challenges* [5]. Trust was included because of its close relation to privacy and ethics which can be seen in the following quotation.

In summary, trust is hard to come by, and requires initial trust formation and continuous trust development, not only through transparency, but also through usability, collaboration and communication, data security and privacy, as well as goal congruence [5, p 1243].

The methodology was limited primarily in regards to scope; only the most salient results were identified. In regards to Table 3 – Proposed Measurement Items – the approach provides some salient candidates for novel measurement items, numerous additional measurement items could be developed, perhaps of greater significance, than the measurement items presented here.

It would not be possible to suggest that theoretical saturation as prescribed by Corbin and Strauss [6] has been achieved. A reflective approach was used in the sense of Schön [15], potentially mitigating this concern.

# 4 Results

Distinct issues related to privacy, ethics, and trust were identified in regards to training data, AI like human interfaces, and feedback provided by the user: these are summarized in Table 1. The analysis of the text revealed novel aspects of AI not presently identified with usability, user experience, and intuitive interaction: these are summarized in Table 2. Finally, additional measurement items were identified for potential inclusion in existing usability, user experience, and intuitive interaction instruments; these are described in Table 3. Because of space limitations only salient results are reported.

Table 1 below includes both privacy, ethics, and trust issues. As previously described, these are listed together as they are closely related. Also included in Table 1 are related potential new measurement items.

**Table 1.** Extracted text relating to privacy, ethics, and trust

| Section | Relevant text | Comments |
|---------|---------------|----------|
| **Data collection + evaluation**<br>Manage privacy & security | "What limits exist around user consent for data use? When collecting data, a best practice, and a legal requirement in many countries, is to give users as much control as possible…You may need to provide users the ability to opt out or delete their account." [1, p. 23] | This would suggest new measurement items: (1) Was the training data collected with optimal privacy considerations? (2) Were the individuals providing the data permitted to opt out or delete their account? |
| **Data collection + evaluation**<br>Manage privacy & security | "Is there a risk of inadvertently revealing user data? What would the consequences be? … if an AI assistant reminds the user to take medication through a home smart speaker, this could partially reveal private medical data" [1, p. 23] | This would suggest a new measurement item: Has a risk assessment been made of the consequences if personal data was revealed? |
| **Data collection + evaluation**<br>Commit to fairness | "Data is collected in the real world, from humans, and reflects their personal experiences and biases—and these patterns can be implicitly identified and amplified by the ML model" [1, p. 25] | This would suggest a new measurement item: Has an evaluation been made related to human bias in the selection of training data? |
| **Data collection + evaluation**<br>Use data that applies to different groups of users | "Your training data should reflect the diversity and cultural context of the people who will use it" [1, p. 26] | This would suggest a new measurement item: Does the training data reflect the diversity and cultural context of the eventual user base? |
| **Data Collection + Evaluation**<br>Source your data responsibly | "Once you've identified the type of training data you need, you will figure out how and where to get it. Make sure that whatever you decide, you have permission to use this data and the infrastructure to keep it safe" [1, p. 28] | This would suggest a new measurement item: Have steps been taken to ensure the security of the data? |
| **Data collection + evaluation**<br>Protect personally identifiable information | "No matter what data you're using, it's possible that it could contain personally identifiable information" [1, p. 30] | This would suggest a new measurement item: Have steps been taken to ensure protection of personally identifiable information? |
| **Data collection + evaluation**<br>Ensure rater pool diversity | "Think about the perspectives and potential biases of the people in your [rater] pool…In some cases, providing raters with training to make them aware of unconscious bias has been effective in reducing biases" [1, p. 32] | This would suggest a new measurement item: Have steps been taken to minimize rater pool biases? |
| **Mental models**<br>Account for user expectations of human-like interaction | "When users confuse an AI with a human being, they can sometimes disclose more information than they would otherwise, or rely on the system more than they should…Specifically, your messages should make it extremely clear that the product is not a human, in a way that's accessible to all users regardless of age, technical literacy, education level or physical ability" [1, p. 54] | There can be issues related to the disclosure of personal information to a chatbot interface. This would suggest the measurement item: "Is the AI chatbot interface clearly identified as not human?" |

*(continued)*

**Table 1.** (*continued*)

| Section | Relevant text | Comments |
|---|---|---|
| **Explainability + trust**<br>Articulate data sources | "… say you're installing an AI-driven navigation app, and you click to accept all terms and conditions, which includes the ability for the navigation app to access data from your calendar app…Later, the navigation app alerts you to leave your home in 5 min…If you didn't read, realize, or remember that you allowed the navigation app to access to your appointment information, then this could be very surprising" [1, p. 65] | This privacy issue results because the user was not explicitly advised that this data was being collected. This can be remedied by ensuring the user click specific accepting check boxes, prominently identified as relating to privacy issues, when accepting the terms and conditions |
| **Explainability & trust**<br>Help users calibrate their trust | "Help users calibrate their trust…based on system explanations, the user should know when to trust the system's predictions and when to apply their own judgement" [1, p. 61] | Trust is a new concept to usability/user experience/intuitive interaction. This would suggest a new measurement item: Does the user know when to trust the system? |
| **Explainability + trust**<br>Help users calibrate their trust | "…you could become suspicious of the app's data sources; or, you could over-trust that it has complete access to all your schedule information. Neither of these outcomes are the right level of trust… In fact, regulations in some countries may require such specific, contextual explanations and data controls" [1, p. 62] | This relates privacy concerns to trust indicating that to gain the trust of the user privacy concerns must be clearly addressed |
| **Explainability + trust**<br>Help users calibrate their trust | "Whenever possible, the AI system should explain the following aspects about data use:<br>**Scope.** Show an overview of the data being collected …and which aspects of their data are being used for what purpose<br>**Reach.** Explain whether the system is personalized to one user or device, or if it is using aggregated data across all users<br>**Removal.** Tell users whether they can remove or reset some of the data being used" [1, p. 63] | The section indicates key information should be communicated to the user to respect their privacy including:<br>1. The scope of data collected<br>2. The degree to which the system is personalized to the user<br>3. How the user's personal data can be removed from the system |
| **Feedback + control**<br>Align feedback with model improvement | "…it's important to let users know what information is being collected, what it's for, and how its use benefits them" [1, p. 83] | There are additional privacy issues related to the collection of feedback |
| **Feedback + control**<br>Align feedback with model improvement | "Implicit feedback is data about user behavior and interactions from your product logs…Often, this happens as part of regular product usage … you should let users know you're collecting it, and get their permission up front…In particular, you should allow users to opt out of certain aspects of sharing implicit feedback—like having their behavior logged—and this should be included in your terms of service" [1, p. 83] | There is a need to disclose gathering of implicit feedback in the terms of service and the user should be able to opt out |

The use of AI will result in new concepts being introduced in usability, user experience, and intuitive interaction. Also included in Table 2 are potential new measurement items salient to these concepts.

Preliminary novel measurement items for usability, user experience, and intuitive interaction are proposed in Table 3. This is an only illustrative of the process that might be undertaken to generate new measurement items that could then be evaluated based on recommended procedures [16].

**Table 2.** New conceptual elements related to usability, user experience, and intuitive interaction

| Section/concept | Relevant text | Commentary |
|---|---|---|
| **User needs +** <br> **defining success** <br> Decide if AI adds unique value | "Once you identify the aspect you want to improve, you'll need to determine which of the possible solutions require AI, which are meaningfully enhanced by AI, and which solutions don't benefit from AI or are even degraded by it" [1, p. 4] | A novel issue with AI is the value proposition. This would suggest a new measurement item: Does AI add unique value? |
| **User needs +** <br> **defining success** <br> Assess automation vs. augmentation | "…evaluate the different ways AI can solve the problem and help users accomplish their goals. One large consideration is if you should use AI to automate a task or to augment a person's ability to do that task themselves" [1, p. 7] | A novel issue with AI is whether to automate or use augmentation. This would suggest a new measurement item: Is AI best used to automate or augment? |
| **User Needs +** <br> **Defining Success** <br> Design & evaluate the reward function | "Any AI model you build or incorporate into your product is guided by a reward function… This is a mathematical formula, or set of formulas, that the AI model uses to determine "right" vs. "wrong" predictions. It determines the action or behavior your system will try to optimize for, and will be a major driver of the final user experience" [1, p. 11] | A novel issue with AI is to assess the suitability of the reward function. This would suggest a new measurement item: Has careful consideration been given to the effect of false positives & false negatives in the reward function? |
| **User needs + defining success** <br> Consider precision & recall tradeoffs | "Precision and recall are the terms that describe the breadth and depth of results that your AI provides to users, and the types of errors that users see. Precision refers to the proportion of true positives correctly categorized out of all the true and false positives. Recall refers to the proportion of true positives correctly categorized out of all the true positives and false negatives" [1, p. 13] | A novel issue with AI is the trade-off between precision and recall. This would suggest a new measurement item: Has careful consideration been given to the relative importance of precision and recall in AI results? |
| **User needs + defining success** <br> Assess inclusivity <br> Account for negative impact | "You'll want to make sure your reward function produces a great experience for all of your users…As AI moves into higher stakes applications and use-cases, it becomes even more important to plan for and monitor negative impacts of your product's decisions" [1, p. 15–16] | New measurement items could be developed around these themes. There are close connections to correct design of the reward function and ethical concerns inclusive of fairness and inclusiveness |
| **Feedback + control** <br> Weigh situational stakes & error risk | "In some situations, AI errors and failure are inconvenient, but in others, they could have severe consequences…errors in AI-suggested email responses have very different stakes than errors related to autonomous vehicle handling" [1, p. 106] | Situational stakes & error risk is a new concept to usability/user experience/intuitive interaction. This would suggest a new measurement item: Does the system correctly weigh situational stakes & error risk? |
| **Feedback + control** <br> Provide paths forward from failure | "Your primary goal in these fail states should be to prevent undue harm to the user and help them move forward with their task" [1, p. 114] | This would suggest new measurement items: (1) Does the system provide a path forward after failure? (2) Does the system prevent undue harm after failure? |

**Table 3.** Proposed measurement items

| Section/concept | Relevant text | New measurement item |
|---|---|---|
| **Mental models**<br>Fail gracefully | "The first time the system fails to meet expectations, the user will likely be disappointed. However, if the mental model includes the idea that the system learns over time…then failure…becomes an opportunity to establish the feedback relationship" [1, p. 51] | This would be a new measurement item related to error management: Does the system explain that when it fails it learns over time through feedback? |
| **Explainability & trust**<br>Understanding | "In some cases, there may be no explicit, comprehensive explanation for the output of a complex algorithm…In other cases, the reasoning behind a prediction may be knowable, but difficult to explain to users in terms they will understand" [1, p. 61] | This would be a new measurement item: Can the user understand the system? |
| **Explainability & trust**<br>Confidence levels | "If, when, and how the system calculates and shows confidence levels can be critical in informing the user's decision making and calibrating their trust" [1, p. 61] | This would suggest a new measurement item:<br>Does the system correctly display confidence levels? |
| **Explainability & trust**<br>Articulate data sources | "Every AI prediction is based on data, so data sources have to be part of your explanations" [1, p. 62] | This would suggest a new measurement item:<br>Does the system use data sources as part of its explanations? |
| **Feedback + control**<br>Easy to understand | "The question and answer choices you provide in explicit feedback should be easy for users to understand" [1, p. 85] | This would suggest a new measurement item:<br>Is the explicit feedback mechanism easy for users to understand? |
| **Feedback + control**<br>Adaptability | "For AI-driven products, there's an essential balance between automation and user control. Your product won't be perfect for every user, every time, so allow users to adapt the output to their needs, edit it, or turn it off" [1, p. 94] | This would be a new measurement item: Can the user adapt the output? |
| **Feedback + control**<br>Balance control & automation | "When first introducing your AI, consider allowing users to test it out or turn it off. Once you've clearly explained the benefits, respect their decision not to use the feature." [1, p. 104] | This would be a new measurement item: Can the user turnoff an AI feature? |
| **Feedback + control**<br>Failstates | "Your system can't provide the right answer, or any answer at all due to inherent limitations to the system. These could be true negatives: the ML is correct in discerning that there's no available output for a given input, but according to users, there should be" [1, p. 104] | This would be a new measurement item: Has the user been informed about the system's limitations? |

# 5   Discussion

This discussion is limited to highlighting the most significant observations that can be made from the textual analysis. There are additional insights that can be identified in the Guidebook but because of the limited scope and length of this paper they are not identified here. One notable example is "One of the most exciting opportunities for AI is being able to help people make better decisions more often. The best AI-human partnerships enable better decisions than either party could make on their own" [1, p. 73]. This would appear to be a new type of human computer interaction beyond usability, user experience, and intuitive interaction, which might be identified as Human Computer Cognitive Enhancement.

The results section has analyzed the text of the Guidebook in terms of three issues, (1) privacy, ethical, and trust issues (which are closely related), (2) novel concepts specific to AI that do not appear in standard UX instruments, (3) new measurement items that emerge out of the context of AI that could be integrated into existing UX instruments.

In Table 1 - Extracted Text Relating to Privacy, Ethics, and Trust - the most salient finding is that privacy, ethics, and trust are closely related such that they should be considered as one integrated entity. There is also a close association of privacy to security; security is necessary but not sufficient to protect privacy. In the analysis of the Guidebook three foci related to privacy, ethics, and trust emerged; (1) training data, (2) AI human-like interfaces, and (3) feedback. One approach to these related issues would be the creation of a combined instrument containing measurement items on privacy, ethics, and trust component factors. Another possible approach would be the addition of a privacy subscale to existing usability/user experience/intuitive interaction instruments.

In Table 2 - New Conceptual Elements Related to Usability, User Experience, and Intuitive Interaction – the concepts described in this table are outside of the scope of existing UX instruments. This would suggest a new UX instrument be created which specifically addresses these concerns. As already mentioned, this could be preliminary identified as the Human Computer Cognitive Enhancement instrument. In the comments section of Table 2 possible measurement items for such an instrument are provided: two examples of such items are: Does AI add unique value?, Is AI best used to automate or augment?

In Table 3 – Proposed Measurement Items – it is conceivable that existing UX instruments could be modified using the measurement items proposed in this table to become more suitable for AI applications, Again, what has been presented here is only indicative of how this may generally proceed, established procedures [16] would need be followed in regards to instrument measurement item validation. Notably a degree of triangulation, providing general support, for the novel usability/user experience/intuitive interaction measurement items proposed in this paper is found in the ACM paper [12] *Guidelines for Human-AI Interaction paper* primarily authored by individuals associated with Microsoft. Table 4 below presents some of the corresponding text.

The remainder of the discussion section focusses on the unique challenges of AI and on the need for design in all aspects of AI related to human-computer interaction. The use of human-like interfaces like Cortana, Alexa, or Siri which are characterized as chatbots and "defined as tools that allow us to pursue a certain goal through a natural language dialogue with a machine, either text-based or voice-based [17. p. 36]. As outlined in

**Table 4.** New measurement items as compared to *Guidelines for Human-AI Interaction* [12]

| Section/concept | Proposed measurement item | Concept from *guidelines for human-AI interaction* paper [12] |
|---|---|---|
| **Mental models** Fail gracefully | Does the system explain the that when it fails it learns over time through feedback? | **Support efficient correction.** Make it easy to edit, refine, or recover when the AI system is wrong [12, p. 3] |
| **Explainability & trust** Understanding | Can the user understand the system? | **Make clear what the system can do.** Help the user understand what the AI system is capable of doing. [12, p. 3] |
| **Explainability & trust** Confidence Levels | Does the system correctly display confidence levels? | **Make clear how well the system can do what it can do.** Help the user understand how often the AI system may make mistakes [12, p. 3] |
| **Explainability & trust** Articulate data sources | Does the system use data sources as part of explanations? | **Make clear why the system did what it did.** Enable the user to access an explanation of why the AI system behaved as it did. [12, p. 3] |
| **Feedback + control** Easy to Understand | Is the explicit feedback mechanism easy for users to understand? | **Encourage granular feedback.** Enable the user to provide feedback indicating their preferences during regular interaction with the AI system |
| **Feedback + control** Adaptability | Can the user adapt the output? | **Learn from user behavior.** Personalize the user's experience by learning from their actions over time. [12, p. 3] |
| **Feedback + control** Balance control & automation | Can the user turnoff an AI feature? | **Support efficient dismissal.** Make it easy to dismiss or ignore undesired AI system services. [12, p. 3] |
| **Feedback + control** failstates | Has the user been informed about the system's limitations? | **Make clear what the system can do.** Help the user understand what the AI system is capable of doing. [12, p. 3] |

the Guidebook such chatbot interfaces can interfere with the mental models related to the AI technology, distorting the user interaction with the AI, particularly in relation to issues of trust.

An example of such distortion would be issues related to the disclosure of personal information to a chatbot interface. Google recommends that the user be clearly informed that the interface is not human, suggesting a novel measurement item in any related instrument relating to an AI chatbot "Is the AI chatbox interface clearly identified as not human?". The Guidebook specifically notes, "This topic is the subject of ongoing research, and these considerations are just a first step" [1, p. 54], indicating a need for academic research.

Intuitive interaction is defined by Blackler as "applying existing knowledge in order to use an interface or product easily and quickly, often without consciously realizing exactly where that knowledge came from" [11, p. ix]. Intuitive interaction is important in relation to AI. In the Guidebook this is highlighted, "Examples can help users understand surprising AI results, or intuit why the AI might have behaved the way it did. These explanations rely on human intelligence to analyze the examples and decide how much to trust the classification." [1, p. 70]. The use of examples is a form of metaphor, a key component of intuitive interaction [11]. Adaptability is a component of intuitive interaction [18]. These factors indicate that the additional research of intuitive interaction in relation to AI systems is warranted.

There is a strong focus in AI on design, "The User Needs + Defining Success chapter illustrates how to design and evaluate the reward, function, which the AI uses to optimize its output" [1, p 109]. As previously outlined, this corresponds to call for experience design made by Hassnzahl [13]. This is also emphasized in the *Seven HCI Grand Challenges* paper "In conclusion, a new code of ethics needs to be established, pursued in three directions: ethics by design, in design, and for design (Dignam, 2018). In this new code, user privacy should be further shielded," [5, p 1244]. As Simon notes "Everyone designs who devises courses of action aimed at changing existing situations into preferred ones" [19, p. 111]. In summary, AI is designed, but design also must be extended to privacy, ethical issues, usability, user experience, and intuitive interaction related to AI.

Given the current limited content of the ISO definition of usability a new expanded definition specific to AI applications may be indicated inclusive of a privacy, ethics, and trust components. Optimally, usability/user experience/intuitive interactions would benefit from a design process.

## 6 Limitations and Future Work

In this paper only a high-level overview of the potential changes to privacy, ethics, trust, usability, user experience, and intuitive interaction relating to the emergence of AI technology has been outlined. This limitation was amplified by the decision to report only the most salient results because of the space limitations. Further, there was no check on the textual and tabular analysis of the author who was the sole researcher. This paper is limited to the AI technology as represented in the Guidebook; this may not be representative of AI technology in general.

Future work specifically related to privacy could include the development of a privacy subscale that could be added to existing usability/user experience/intuitive interaction instruments. Future work could review additional emerging AI guidelines from other AI technology providers with a view to identify additional factors and dynamics related to AI technology that have not been identified in this paper and that can be related to usability, user experience, and intuitive interaction design. As briefly mentioned in this paper privacy, usability, user experience, and intuitive interaction are now dynamic processes that would be open to design, future research could both identify and conceptualize design related elements and provide normative standards.

## 7 Conclusion

This research has found significant privacy, ethics and trust issues in relation to training data, AI human-like interfaces, and feedback processes found in AI systems. In addition, novel components of UX design related to AI have been identified which could indicate the need for a novel UX instrument specific to AI. Preliminary relevant measurement items are proposed that could potentially be integrated into existing UX instruments. A design process for human computer interaction with AI is proposed. Future research is indicated in relation to the privacy, ethics, and trust issues identified in regards to AI with a view to including measurement items and also a privacy subscale into new or existing instruments measuring usability, user experience, intuitive interaction. Modification of existing instruments may be indicated for privacy, ethic and trust factors specific to AI. Privacy issues related to AI continue as a "Grand Challenge" to Human-Computer interaction [5].

# References

1. Google: PAIR. People + AI Guidebook. Published May 8. https://pair.withgoogle.com/gui debook. Accessed 21 Jan 2021
2. Bhatia, A., Gupta, M., Gupta, A., Singhal, N.: AICA: Artificial intelligence conversation assistant. In: Companion Publication of the 2020 ACM Designing Interactive Systems Conference (DIS 2020 Companion). Association for Computing Machinery, New York, pp. 569–573 (2020)
3. Wallach, D.P., Flohr, L.A., Kaltenhauser, A.: Beyond the buzzwords: on the perspective of AI in UX and vice versa. In: Degen, H., Reinerman-Jones, L. (eds) Artificial Intelligence in HCI. HCII 2020. Lecture Notes in Computer Science, vol. 12217. Springer, Cham (2020). https://doi.org/10.1007/978-3-030-50334-5_10
4. Heier, J., Willmann, J., Wendland, K.: Design intelligence - pitfalls and challenges when designing ai algorithms in B2B factory automation. In: Degen, H., Reinerman-Jones, L. (eds.) HCII 2020. LNCS, vol. 12217, pp. 288–297. Springer, Cham (2020). https://doi.org/10.1007/978-3-030-50334-5_19
5. Stephanidis, C., Salvendy, G., et al.: Seven HCI Grand Challenges. Int J. Hum. Comput. Interact. 35(14), 1229–1269 (2019)
6. Corbin, J., Strauss, A.: Basics of Qualitative Research. Sage, Los Angeles (2008)
7. Kizza, J.M.: Ethical and social issues in the information age, 6th edn. Springer, Cham (2017). https://doi.org/10.1007/978-3-319-70712-9
8. Benbasat, I., Barki, H.: Quo Vadis, TAM? J. Assoc. Inf. Syst. 8(4), 211–218 (2007)
9. ISO 9241–210:2019: ISO. International organization for standardization. https://www.iso.org/standard/77520.html. Accessed 21 Jan 2021
10. User Experience Questionnaire (UEQ): UEQ. www.ueq-online.org. Accessed 21 Jan 2021
11. Blackler, A. (ed.): Intuitive Interaction: Research and Application. CRC Press, Boca Raton (2018)
12. Amershi, S., et al.: Guidelines for Human-AI interaction. In: CHI Conference on Human Factors in Computing Systems Proceedings (CHI 2019), 4–9 May 2019, Glasgow, Scotland UK. ACM, New York, p. 13 (2019)
13. Hassenzahl, M.: Experience design: technology for all the right reasons. Synth. Lect. Hum.-Centered Inf. 3(1), 1–95 (2010)
14. Miles, M.B., Huberman, A.M.: Qualitative Data Analysis, 2nd edn. Sage, Thousand Oaks (1994)
15. Schön, D.A.: The reflective practitioner: how professionals think in action. Basic Books, New York (1983)
16. MacKenzie, S.B., Podsakoff, P.M., Podsakoff, N.P.: Construct measurement and validation procedures in MIS and behavioral research: integrating new and existing techniques. MIS Q. 35(2), 293–334 (2011)
17. Müller, L., Mattke, J., Maier, C., Weitzel, T., Graser, H.: Chatbot acceptance: a latent profile analysis on individuals' trust in conversational agents. In: SIGMIS-CPR 2019 - Proceedings of the 2019 Computers and People Research Conference, pp. 35–42. Nashville, TN (2019)

18. McAran, D.: Development of the technology acceptance intuitive interaction model. In: Black-ler, A. (ed.) Intuitive Interaction: Research and Application, pp. 129–150. CRC Press, Boca Raton (2018)
19. Simon, H.A.: The Sciences of the Artificial, 3rd edn. The MIT Press, Cambridge Mass (1996)

# An Experiment on the Impact of Information on the Trust in Artificial Intelligence

Julien Meyer[✉] ⓘD and David Remisch

Ryerson University, Toronto, ON, Canada
Julien.meyer@ryerson.ca

**Abstract.** Artificial intelligence (AI) has made considerable progress in a variety of fields and is suggested to do as well or better than many experts, creating great expectations about its potential to improve decision-making. While much progress has been made in refining the accuracy of algorithms, much remains to determine on how these algorithms will influence decision-makers, especially in life or death decisions such as in medicine. In such fields, human experts will remain for the foreseeable future the ultimate decision-makers. Literature suggests that reliance on algorithms by decision-makers may be influenced by the accuracy of algorithm and by the information on how the algorithm reached its conclusions.

The objective of this paper is to determine the propensity to influence pathologists' decision-making using algorithmic expertise and information on AI algorithm accuracy and model interpretability. To test our hypotheses, we will conduct an online, quasi-experimental survey study with 120 respondent pathologists. Each participant will provided with a series of prostate cancer samples and asked to assess the Gleason grade. Our hypothesis is that increasing the level of information will lead to increased reliance in automated systems. This research will provide insight into trust in AI: first, the extent to which pathologists trust AI advice; second, the extent to which each type of information contributes to trust.

**Keywords:** Artificial intelligence · Pathology · Trust · Reliance

## 1 Introduction

### 1.1 Background

The COVID-19 pandemic has revealed the need to provide testing capacities that are scalable and can substitute for human resources until it is safe to meet with patients in-person. In the last few years, artificial intelligence has made great strides in the field of pathology, however, these types of findings are limited by their inability to generalize beyond a traditional laboratory setting.

Computers have been used for a long time in clinical practice to support image analysis [1]. However, such tools only analyze information and there are still very few commercial AI-driven software tools available yet for pathology [2, 3]. The limited use of AI in the field of pathology is about to change quickly. In the last few years, artificial intelligence has made great strides and multiple papers have tested algorithms

© Springer Nature Switzerland AG 2021
F. F.-H. Nah and K. Siau (Eds.): HCII 2021, LNCS 12783, pp. 600–607, 2021.
https://doi.org/10.1007/978-3-030-77750-0_39

that achieved significant performances in accuracy [4]. As a consequence, eighty percent of pathologists anticipate that AI will be introduced into their pathology laboratories within the coming decade [5].

The implementation of AI systems into medical practice will require pathologists, solution providers and healthcare organizations to overcome significant challenges [6, 7], which have thwarted many promising medical technological innovations in the past [8]. And beyond implementation, research within the field needs to establish whether the alleged performance of algorithms will translate into better clinical decisions and better health outcomes for patients and, furthermore, under what conditions these changes would be most effective [6].

Decision makers (pathologists) will play a key role in this translation into health outcomes. Many AI studies compare AI algorithms to pathologists, who are blinded to the algorithm's results, often reaching accuracy rates very similar or better than pathologists. But when these systems will be implemented, pathologists and AI systems are unlikely to be competing or blinded to each other. For the foreseeable future, pathologists are expected to retain the final say as to whether to rely on algorithms' conclusions or not [9]. As a result, algorithms are likely to be used as tools that augment pathologists' skills rather than substitute them [6, 10]. This corresponds to a level of only 3 or 4 on Parasuraman et al.'s scale of autonomy of human interaction with automation (10 being a fully autonomous system) [2].

As a consequence, and for the foreseeable future, the impact of AI on clinical decisions and health outcomes will be mediated by the behavior of pathologists and their reliance on AI expertise. Experiments suggest that AI does indeed influence pathologists' decisions and improve clinical outcomes [9], and a survey suggests that 73.3% of pathologists are interested or excited about integrating AI [5]. However, there is also a societal skepticism towards AI for vital decisions related to healthcare [8, 11] and pathologists may distrust AI expert advice and decide not to rely on it, which could slow down the adoption of these tools [8, 11, 12]. Moreover, surveys and opinion papers reflect an abstract opinion towards "AI", which is often a loaded and fantasized word and it is yet to be determined whether such beliefs translate into avoidant behaviors. Pathologists may express optimism towards the role and impact of AI, but the question remains whether they will rely on it to make decisions that are critical to their work and the welfare of their patients.

While not all decision-makers will rely on AI, we anticipate that a significantwill. Therefore, we posit that:

- H1: The presence of AI recommendations will influence decisions

Second, while automated aids are introduced with the expressed goal of reducing human error, several studies showed that that their use does not automatically lead to human error reduction, but instead often bring new types of errors, which may be summarized under the labels of complacency (overreliance, that is, non-vigilance about machine states) and bias ("tendency to ascribe greater power and authority to automated aids than to other sources of advice.") [13] When decision aids are imperfect, automation bias drives both omission, which "occur when operators do not take an appropriate action, despite non automated indications of problems because they were not informed on an imminent system failure or problem by an automated decision aid", [14] and commission errors "that occur when people incorrectly follow an automated directive or recommendation, because they do not verify it against other available information, or in spite of contraindications from other sources of information of which they are aware." [14] Both complacency and bias are observed for either novices and expert machine operators, and cannot be attributed to lack of knowledge or skill [13].

For instance, in an experiment, [14] automated aids enhanced performance in a multi-task environment when the aid provided accurate feedback but when the aid provided inaccurate feedback (e.g. it missed a system event), participants in the non-automated condition performed much better than participants in the automated condition on these same events.

People may blindly trust technology and that complacency may induce excessive reliance on decision support systems [15]. Physicians have also been proved to rely on beliefs rather than actual data when provided with AI advice [16]. As a consequence, we posit that:

H2: Participants will make more wrong decisions with wrong AI recommendations than without.

Beyond the effect of the presence of AI recommendations, a mature stream of research has investigated the antecedents of reliance on automated systems, to which artificial intelligence systems belong [17, 18]. This stream of research highlights that trust in the automated system is a key determinant of reliance and use of the system - "People tend to rely on automation they trust and tend to reject automation they do not" [18]. Decision makers may be more likely to rely on AI when the task is complex 10,17, since it helps process information and problem solve.17 But decision makers may struggle to switch from concrete data to objective data provided by the automatized machines. Zuboff identified a "crisis of trust" meaning the lack of trust of operators in automatized machines is driven by two main factors.18 First, the lack of intellective skills to understand the significance of data, which were removed from the action context while they used to rely on data related to their direct experience in the action-centered world. Second, the ambiguity of action i.e. the feeling about the real effects using the machine. Therefore, operators expressed a feeling of "losing touch with reality" and important contextual information.

Experience and knowledge about AI play a role in building that trust. Information about performance is the key factor in generating trust in machines but real conditions testing may not be available for new or updated systems where real conditions cannot be replicated in a lab. Other kinds of information have been shown to influence decision-makers' trust. In this study, we focus on two key pieces of information: the accuracy of the AI and the transparency about its inner working and logic.

## 1.2    Algorithm Accuracy

Research suggests that information about performance is the key factor in generating trust in machines [19]. Specifically, providing confidence level helps users adjust their level of trust towards a decision aid system [17]. Disclosing accuracy rate estimates with predictions of AI tools may thus help pathologists build trust in the tools' results [11]. As a result, we posit that:

H3: pathologists will rely more on an AI associated with higher accuracy.

### 1.3 Model Interpretability

Researchers and surveys of decision-makers suggest that even highly accurate algorithms could face adoption challenges if AI remains a black box [20]. The opacity of AI tools and their "black box" nature may thus impede adoption [11]. *Model interpretability* (or explainability) means, for the user, the ability to understand how the algorithm works and how it reaches its conclusions [6]. Multiple studies have confirmed that transparent automation systems are associated with greater trust [17, 18] and lack of interpretability in AI conclusions is a primary concern when implementing AI technology [15]. It has been argued that machines should be as comprehensible and transparent as possible [21], to the extent that more simple systems may lead to more trust and reliance than more efficient but more complex systems [18]. As a consequence, we posit:

H4: pathologists will rely more on an AI associated with more model interpretability

Finally, we posit that model interpretability and algorithm accuracy have a cumulative effect. Therefore:

H5a: pathologists will rely more on an AI associated with more model interpretability and algorithm accuracy than on an AI associated with model interpretability alone
H5b: pathologists will rely more on an AI associated with more model interpretability and algorithm accuracy than on an AI associated with algorithm accuracy alone

In this study, we investigate the hypotheses above to answer the following research question: to what extent does AI model interpretability and decision accuracy influence reliance on AI by pathologists? To test these hypotheses, we will conduct an online survey of pathologists who will assess the Gleason grade for a series of prostate images.

## 2 Methodology

In this study, we focus on pathologists, some of the most highly trained professionals, performing a decision that is routine but also critical to patient outcomes: assessing prostate cancers.

A review of the pathological tasks was conducted to identify an adequate task meeting the following requirements: 1) can be completed by most pathologists via an online survey 2) shows potential for improvements in future applications of AI; 3) is ambiguous enough so that variance between pathologists can be expected; 4) is an important task with significant clinical implications; 5) can be performed quickly. The Gleason grading system was identified as an assessment that a large proportion of pathologists are familiar with; it is performed relatively quickly and it often defines key outcomes that lead to important clinical decisions for patients with prostate cancer diagnoses. Furthermore, previous pathologist assessments of prostate cancer have shown significant heterogeneity with low-moderate agreement scores, ranging from 47%–70% [22] suggesting an opportunity for the implementation of machine learning tools to improve accuracy.

An online experiment will be developed via the online survey platform, QualtricsTM. 120 participants will be recruited from medical associations and social media groups to review a series of biopsy sample images and assess the Gleason grade of prostate biopsy samples. Eligible participants will include practicing or retired pathologists as well as pathology students, residents and fellows with adequate knowledge to assign a Gleason Grade. The research team.

Prostate biopsy samples will be provided by The Radboud University Medical Center and Karolinska Institutet as part of the 2020 Prostate cANcer graDe Assessment (PANDA) Challenge, which made public around 11,000 whole-slide images to explore the potential of automated deep learning systems in pathology [29]. Samples from both datasets were scored by 3 experienced pathologists with a subspecialty in urological pathology to determine the consensus Gleason scores used for the study [30]. For the study, the AI advice will be expressed as a result of algorithmic processes, but these scores were based on these predetermined ground truths. By using deception, it is possible to measure reliance on AI advice based on decision accuracy, which will be computed as the number of cases where respondents made the same decision as the true score. Respondents will be told that recommendations come from an algorithm.

Transparency will be operationalized as a brief summary in lay terms of the steps followed by the algorithm model to reach its conclusion. These functional steps were extracted from previous studies of automated Gleason grading tools [4, 23] and revised by a team of researchers to improve readability and ensure that it is accessible to most pathologists. The algorithm accuracy will be expressed as the accuracy rate (70%) relative to typical pathologist agreement (61%) based on a previously developed experimental deep learning system (DLS) used for whole-slide image Gleason scoring [22, 24]. Participants will be instructed to review the prostate sample image and read any additional information provided before recording their own clinical decision.

The research design is a 2×2 between subjects, quasi-experimental design, as illustrated in Table 1 below.

**Table 1.** Experimental conditions

|  | No model interpretability | Model interpretability |
|---|---|---|
| System accuracy | **Condition 2.** Accuracy No interpretability | **Condition 4.** Both accuracy and interpretability |
| No system accuracy | **Condition 1.** Neither accuracy nor interpretability | **Condition 3.** No accuracy interpretability |

All participants will answer 6 questions without any aid in order to assess their performance. For the remaining 6 questions, participants will be assigned to one of the four conditions:

Condition 1: Participants will received a Gleason grade recommendation that they will be told comes from an "AI" system, with no further information.

Condition 2: Participants will received a Gleason grade recommendation that they will be told comes from an "AI" system. They will be provided with a rate of accuracy for the AI system, which will be compelling compared to typical human error rates.

Condition 3: Participants will received a Gleason grade recommendation that they will be told comes from an "AI" system. They will be provided with information to provide transparency on how the AI proceeded to reach its recommendation.

Condition 4: Participants will received a Gleason grade recommendation that they will be told comes from an "AI" system. They will be provided with both the accuracy rate and the transparency information.

There will be 30 respondents per condition.

Within each image batch will consist of three samples from Groups 2 and 3 and one sample from Group 1, 4 or 5. Grades 2 and 3 require additional analysis of proportions of patterns 3 and 4 [25], which represent the most common cancer grades according to previous studies [26]. The order of the items within each batch will also be randomized.

Finally, in all conditions, some of the expert advice provided will be "correct" and some will be "incorrect". The correctness will be determined based on well established pre coded training databases.

Upon completing the Gleason grading questions, the participants will fill out a follow-up questionnaire and standard demographics form measuring age, gender, location, type of organization where they work, position and discipline. Level of trust in AI advice, perceived efficacy of diagnostic AI tools and overall confidence in assessing Gleason Grades will be measured on a 5-point likert scale. Upon completing the survey, all participants will receive a debrief form explaining the use of deception and a summary of their answers to allow for constructive reflection.

One of the key challenges in this project will be the recruitment of pathologists to act as respondents. Pathologists are a relatively small population of busy, highly paid professionals who, like other physicians, often get solicited to participate in research studies. To improve our chances of recruiting enough respondents, all included participants will receive a $20 gift card.

## 3  Conclusions

This study is a step towards understanding the impact of AI on professionals' decision. AI holds promises of giant progress but for critical decisions, its impact will be mediated by professionals. Beyond healthcare, this project could lead to applications with professionals and organizations interested in developing AI tools. These findings will help assess reliance on AI and some factors leading to reliance that could be applicate to various settings. It is crucial to focus on the interaction between operators and systems in healthcare and in non-medical contexts to help organizations achieve the full potential of AI.

It is also important to acknowledge the role and responsibility of humans and to put the human back in the center of decision-making. For all its potential and "intelligence",

AI remains a tool that will be put in the hands of professionals. Taking these professionals into account and ensuring that they are in the position to take the best decisions, rather than stacking them in competition with AI, should be fundamental to practitioners, developers, implementers and regulators alike.

# References

1. Niazi, M.K.K., Parwani, A.V., Gurcan, M.N.: Digital pathology and artificial intelligence. Lancet Oncol. **20**, e253–e261 (2019). https://doi.org/10.1016/S1470-2045(19)30154-8
2. Parasuraman, R., Sheridan, T.B., Wickens, C.D.: A model for types and levels of human interaction with automation. IEEE Trans. Syst. Man Cybern. Part A Syst. Humans. **30**, 286–297 (2000). https://doi.org/10.1109/3468.844354
3. Tizhoosh, H.R., Pantanowitz, L.: Artificial intelligence and digital pathology: challenges and opportunities. J. Pathol. Inform. **9**, 38 (2018). https://doi.org/10.4103/jpi.jpi_53_18
4. Chang, H.Y., et al.: Artificial intelligence in pathology. J. Pathol. Transl. Med. **53**, 1–12 (2019). https://doi.org/10.4132/jptm.2018.12.16
5. Sarwar, S., et al.: Physician perspectives on integration of artificial intelligence into diagnostic pathology. Npj Digit. Med. **2**, 28 (2019). https://doi.org/10.1038/s41746-019-0106-0
6. He, J., Baxter, S.L., Xu, J., Xu, J., Zhou, X., Zhang, K.: The practical implementation of artificial intelligence technologies in medicine. Nat Med. **25**, 30–36 (2019). https://doi.org/10.1038/s41591-018-0307-0
7. Houssami, N., Kirkpatrick-Jones, G., Noguchi, N., Lee, C.I.: Artificial Intelligence (AI) for the early detection of breast cancer: a scoping review to assess AI's potential in breast screening practice. Expert Rev Med Devices **16**, 351–362 (2019). https://doi.org/10.1080/17434440.2019.1610387
8. Vourgidis, I., Mafuma, S.J., Wilson, P., Carter, J., Cosma, G.: Medical expert systems – a study of trust and acceptance by healthcare stakeholders. In: Lotfi, A., Bouchachia, H., Gegov, A., Langensiepen, C., McGinnity, M. (eds.) UKCI 2018. AISC, vol. 840, pp. 108–119. Springer, Cham (2019). https://doi.org/10.1007/978-3-319-97982-3_9
9. Tschandl, P., et al.: Human–computer collaboration for skin cancer recognition. Nat. Med. pp. 1–6 (2020). https://doi.org/10.1038/s41591-020-0942-0
10. Holzinger, A., Malle, B., et al.: Towards the augmented pathologist: challenges of explainable-ai in digital pathology. ArXiv Preprint https://arxiv.org/1712.06657. (2017)
11. Colling, R., et al.: Artificial intelligence in digital pathology: a roadmap to routine use in clinical practice. J Pathol. **249**, 143–150 (2019). https://doi.org/10.1002/path.5310
12. Parkes, A.: The effect of individual and task characteristics on decision aid reliance. Behav. Inf. Technol. **36**, 165–177 (2017). https://doi.org/10.1080/0144929X.2016.1209242
13. Parasuraman, R., Manzey, D.H.: Complacency and bias in human use of automation: an attentional integration. Hum. Factors **52**, 381–410 (2010)
14. Skitka, L.J., Mosier, K.L., Burdick, M.: Does automation bias decision-making? Int. J. Hum Comput Stud. **51**, 991–1006 (1999)
15. Gretton, C.: Trust and transparency in machine learning-based clinical decision support. In: Zhou, J., Chen, F. (eds.) Human and Machine Learning. HIS, pp. 279–292. Springer, Cham (2018). https://doi.org/10.1007/978-3-319-90403-0_14
16. Jussupow, E., Spohrer, K., Heinzl, A., Gawlitza, J.: Augmenting medical diagnosis decisions? An Investigation Into Physicians' Decision Making Process with Artificial Intelligence, Information Systems Research: ISR. (2020) tba
17. Hoff, K.A., Bashir, M.: Trust in automation: Integrating empirical evidence on factors that influence trust. Hum. Factors **57**, 407–434 (2015)

18. Lee, J.D., See, K.A.: Trust in automation: designing for appropriate reliance. Hum. Factors **46**, 50–80 (2004)
19. Hancock, P.A., Billings, D.R., Schaefer, K.E., Chen, J.Y., De Visser, E.J., Parasuraman, R.: A meta-analysis of factors affecting trust in human-robot interaction. Hum. Factors **53**, 517–527 (2011)
20. Bera, K., Schalper, K.A., Rimm, D.L., Velcheti, V., Madabhushi, A.: Artificial intelligence in digital pathology - new tools for diagnosis and precision oncology. Nat. Rev. Clin. Oncol. (2019). https://doi.org/10.1038/s41571-019-0252-y
21. Patrzyk, P.M., Link, D., Marewski, J.N.: Human-like machines: transparency and comprehensibility [Commentary], Behav. Brain Sci. 40 (2017)
22. Nagpal, K., et al.: Development and validation of a deep learning algorithm for improving Gleason scoring of prostate cancer. Npj Digit. Med. **2**, 1 (2019). https://doi.org/10.1038/s41746-019-0112-2
23. Arvaniti, E., et al.: Author correction: automated gleason grading of prostate cancer tissue microarrays via deep learning. Sci Rep. **9**, 7668 (2019). https://doi.org/10.1038/s41598-019-43989-8
24. Bulten, W.: Epithelium segmentation using deep learning in H&E-stained prostate specimens with immunohistochemistry as reference standard. Sci Rep. **9**, 864 (2019). https://doi.org/10.1038/s41598-018-37257-4
25. Samaratunga, H.: The prognostic significance of the 2014 International Society of Urological Pathology (ISUP) grading system for prostate cancer. Pathology **47**, 515–519 (2015)
26. Epstein, J.I., Allsbrook, W.C., Jr., Amin, M.B., Egevad, L.L.: Committee, The 2005 International Society of Urological Pathology (ISUP) consensus conference on Gleason grading of prostatic carcinoma. Am. J. Surg. Pathol. **29**, 1228–1242 (2005)

# Empirical Research as a Challenge in Day-to-Day Teaching During the Pandemic of 2020/21 - Practical Solutions

Christina Miclau[✉], Annebeth Demaeght, and Andrea Müller

Hochschule Offenburg – University of Applied Sciences, Badstrasse 24, 77652 Offenburg, Germany
christina.miclau@hs-offenburg.de

**Abstract.** Due to the pandemic of 2020, many teaching and research institutions are confronted with extraordinary working conditions. In order to enable empirical data collection under these special circumstances, teachers and scientists need to respond flexibly and new concepts need to be developed. This paper deals with the challenges that arise in day-to-day teaching and provides different approaches to meet these challenges. It covers quantitative surveys, remote UX-testing methods as an alternative to eye tracking studies in the lab, as well as face-to-face user experience testings under strict hygiene measures.

**Keywords:** Empirical research · Quantitative marketing research · User experience test · Online studies · Challenges during pandemic 2020

## 1 Relevance

Providing the customer with the best offers, the best platform or the best type of communication is key to success. The identification of their needs is essential within this context. In order to create the optimal framework for the customers, it is important to fully understand their specific behavior and needs. Who are my customers? What do they want and what do they expect from me as a provider? What is the best way to get in touch with them and how can they find their way along my platforms? These are the central questions that need to be addressed.

Surveys, interviews or user experience (UX) testings enable us to find answers to these questions. But what could we do if we can no longer talk to our customers in person and the usual UX testings are no longer possible?

Empirical data collection must not be neglected in times of contact restrictions during the corona pandemic of 2020/21. Customers continue to evolve, understanding of wishes and personalized user interaction remain essential. In addition, the importance of online presence increased dramatically, which is why an investigation of the user experience has now become even more important.

The critical challenge we had to cope with as professors and teachers at Offenburg University was a large number of marketing students who were faced with the challenge

F. F.-H. Nah and K. Siau (Eds.): HCII 2021, LNCS 12783, pp. 608–618, 2021.
https://doi.org/10.1007/978-3-030-77750-0_40

of continuing their work and projects, so research could not remain a deadlock. This paper presents practical examples of data collection in the framework of surveys and UX testings to master health critical situations.

## 2  Quantitative Marketing Research – A Case Study

As part of the lectures "Quantitative Methods in Marketing" and "Consumer Behavior and Marketing Research", students of the bachelor's program in business administration conducted a quantitative online survey during the summer term of 2020, a time period which was in many ways highly affected by the Corona virus.

The marketing research project took place in cooperation with an industry partner who was in the process of developing a new product and wanted to use market re-search techniques to achieve a better understanding of consumer preference structures.

The project enabled the students to gain practical insights into the systematic phases of the marketing research process (see Fig. 1) [2], even under strict conditions. The individual phases of the project with further information on how the students adjusted to the Covid 19-guidelines are described in more detail below.

**Fig. 1.**  Phases of the marketing research process based on Meffert et al. [2]

**Phase 1: Briefing and Problem Definition**
The clear formulation of the marketing problem is an important prerequisite for determining the data collection requirements [2]. Therefore, the project started with a briefing by the decision makers of the cooperating company on the objectives and requirements of the study. In order to avoid physical contact, the meeting was held in a videoconference using the software Zoom.

The marketing problem was determined in reference to new product development plans of the industry partner. The company's main objective was to determine consumer preferences for a variety of product alternatives which differed in terms of:

- price
- benefits for the consumer
- benefits for the environment (for each sold product a contribution would be made to an ecological project e. g. tree planting, ocean plastics cleanup or local environmental protection measurements).

The central question was: "Which product attributes influence the preference of potential buyers the most? Is it the price, the consumer benefits or the contribution to environmental projects?"

In addition, the question arose as to whether intergenerational preference differences occur: "Do Generation Z (up to 20 years), Generation Y (20–40 years), and the 'Silver Surfer' generation (50+) evaluate product features differently?".

With the defined research questions at hand the following stages of planning and designing data collection started.

**Phase 2: Data Collection**
In the second phase of a marketing research process data needs to be collected in order to find an answer to the central research questions. The researchers determine which tools of secondary or primary research are suitable, conceptualize the research design and gather data.

**Research Method:** In order to answer the central research questions, a survey was conducted in the target group (primary research). The students decided to use an online survey as a method for data collection rather than a personal interview. This method has the advantage of being implemented at low cost, allowing respondents to be contacted quickly, achieving a high reach, and enabling automated data compilation [2]. In view of the Corona situation another advantage is that these surveys can be conducted without direct contact. However, this has the consequence that the response situation could not be controlled.

After reviewing a wide range of online questionnaire tools, it was decided to use the software LimeSurvey [1] for conducting the survey. LimeSurvey is a free online survey application which makes it possible to develop and publish online surveys without programming knowledge. The tool offers a comprehensive package of functions that also meet scientific requirements. A particular advantage is that data privacy can be guaranteed since the software and the surveys are provided on your own server.

**Research Design:** During the survey design the students dealt with different types of scales and question formulations. The survey comprised a total of 15 questions, five of which were about the participants' general interests, environmental awareness and media consumption, one ranking question about the product variants and nine questions about the socio-demographic features of the respondents.

The ranking question had the highest priority for the central research objective. The participants were asked to rank eight product variants which were specified by the characteristics of different attributes, combined in various ways. Due to a confidentiality agreement details on the product cannot be shared but Table 1 shows an exemplary overview of the product variants and their specifications:

The participants were asked to sort the variants per drag and drop in a ranking according to their preferences, with the highest-ranking item at the top.

**Research Scope:** The cooperating company provided an e-mail address database of approximately 180,000 e-mail addresses of people belonging to the target group. The e-mail addresses were segmented into three groups according to their age: Generation Z (up to 20 years), Generation Y (20–40 years) and 'Silver Surfer' (50+). The specifications of the product characteristics in the ranking question were formulated differently for the various generations (Z, Y and Silver Surfer), all other questions were the same for all groups.

**Table 1.** An exemplary overview of the product variants and their specifications

|  | Specifications | | |
|---|---|---|---|
|  | Price | Consumer benefit | Environmental benefit |
| Product variant 1 | 10 € | Benefit X | Planting a tree |
| Product variant 2 | 15 € | Benefit X | Planting a tree |
| Product variant 3 | 10 € | Benefit Y | Planting a tree |
| Product variant 4 | 15 € | Benefit Y | Planting a tree |
| Product variant 5 | 10 € | Benefit X | Ocean cleanup |
| Product variant 6 | 15 € | Benefit X | Ocean cleanup |
| Product variant 7 | 10 € | Benefit Y | Ocean cleanup |
| Product variant 8 | 15 € | Benefit Y | Ocean cleanup |

The mailing of the invitation to participate was managed by the industry partner. Students provided the subject line, the text and the link to the survey. To achieve the highest possible response rate a prize was raffled among the respondents.

A total of 2066 people took part in the survey, 201 of whom belonged to the "Generation Z" age group, 275 to the "Generation Y" age group and 1590 to the "Silver Surfer" age group.

**Phase 3: Data Analysis**
The results of the survey were analyzed using the SPSS statistical and analysis software. For this purpose, the data was first exported from LimeSurvey and imported into SPSS. During this process it was noted that the results of the ranking question were mapped differently in LimeSurvey than in SPSS: In SPSS, the product variants are mapped as variables and the assigned values correspond to the rank number whereas in LimeSurvey the rank number is mapped as a variable. Therefore, an intermediate step was necessary before the data could be analyzed with a conjoint analysis.

Conjoint analyses are primarily used in the market launch of products. Its most important goal is to determine the influence of individual product characteristics on the emergence of an overall preference in order to better assess buyers' preferences for alternative product concepts [3].

As described above, a controlled set of potential products was shown to the participants in the ranking question. A conjoint analysis was used to determine how the individual elements making up the product (in this case: price, consumer benefit and environmental benefit) are evaluated by the consumer.

The data analysis showed that the price was the attribute with the highest influence on consumer preferences.

**Phase 4: Communication**
In the final phase, the students prepared the results and presented them to the decision

makers of the cooperation company within a video conference. The students interpreted the figures and used them to draw up valuable recommendations for upcoming decisions.

**Conclusion:**  Students were perfectly able to gain practical empirical research experience with primary marketing research methods via online teaching. The large e-mail address database of the industry partner, as well as the survey software LimeSurvey, and the analysis tool SPSS enabled the collection and analysis of relevant marketing data, as well as the creation of decision-oriented recommendations.

## 3   User Experience Testing by Using Customer Experience Tracking

In addition to extensive surveys, empirical studies in the field of user experience were also realized. At the beginning of the contact restrictions, no testing could take place in the Customer Experience Tracking Laboratory of the Offenburg University, which is why all studies were conducted online until the laboratory was reopened. The challenge was to replace common modules such as eye tracking in a meaningful way in order to guarantee the preservation of nearly equivalent data. For this reason, we used our proven Customer Experience method, which includes a number of additional modules that provide information besides the eye tracking data and, in general, the interaction with a digital application. These are measurement tools such as facial expression analysis, Think Aloud and qualitative questionnaires as well as other options like mouse tracking [4, 5].

The Customer Experience Tracking (CXT) procedure (see Fig. 2) is a multi-stage, modular and scalable procedure for investigating the usability of interactive systems, applications and products, which was developed at the Offenburg University. [4] It is based on the measurement procedure for user experience, but differs from common ways of procedure implementation. Although the components heuristic evaluation, usability test and questionnaire form the basis for the measurement procedure, the approach changes in the selection of the used methods. Significant in the composition is the orientation and thus the focus of the procedure on the emotions triggered by the various stimuli [6].

As a result of many previous investigations of applications in e-commerce using the CXT method, it has been validated and can be safely used for the optimization of applications of any kind. In doing so, the CXT laboratory uses various survey methods, such as eye tracking, facial expression analysis, Think Aloud and questionnaires and data entry reports to develop targeted recommendations for action [4].

**Kick off Meeting:**  Fundamental for the kick off meeting is the specification of the research objectives, which includes the definition of the problem, the research framework and the target group. The first meeting provides communication and an essential basis and starting point for a goal-oriented investigation [7].

**Expert Evaluation:**  Expert evaluation is the first step in the analysis of an interactive system, application or product. During the expert evaluation, weak points or irritations are identified and potential factors are explored that could influence the user experience negatively [4].

**Fig. 2.** CXT procedure

**Preparation of the Testing:** Following the expert evaluation, the upcoming testing has to be planned and organized. This includes the selection and preparation of the CXT modules (see Fig. 3), the definition of the tasks, i.e. the tasks that a participant has to perform in the course of the testing and which are developed on the basis of the expert evaluation, and the acquisition of the participants, which is oriented toward the target group [4, 7].

**Testing, Analysis and Presentation of Results:** As soon as the preparation of the testing has been completed and the appointments have been made, the testing can be carried out. During this time, the participant is observed by the test leader, which ensures that issues can be addressed. After the testing has been completed, the data is evaluated and analyzed and made available to the client as documentation and recommendations for action as part of the presentation of the results [4].

As mentioned above the following modules or measuring instruments can be used as part of the CXT procedure.

**Eye Tracking:** In the context of the CXT, eye tracking is considered the central measuring instrument for determining irritations and user behavior. The eye tracking system enables the measurement of the gaze course by means of four cameras and infrared technology. As a result, it is not necessary to wire the persons to the technology, so that the measurement can run unnoticed and motionless. Eye movements are recorded in real time in the form of fixation points and saccades as well as changes in pupil diameter, which is an additional indicator of emotional activation [4].

**Facial Expression Analysis:** Facial expressions are considered an essential instrument for the expression of emotions and attitudes and occur simultaneously with emotion [8].

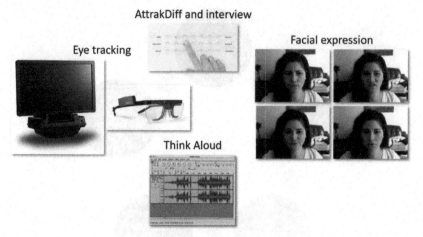

**Fig. 3.** CXT modules

Due to the 43 muscles in the human face, an exact and versatile reproduction of the emotions is possible [9] - an expression of emotions.

By means of a webcam, the participants can be recorded and the data subsequently analyzed and evaluated, independently and unnoticed by the participant [10]. During the recording and analysis, the six basic emotions according to EKMAN, joy, anger, disgust, surprise, fear and sadness [11], are recognized and assigned with the help of EmFACS, EKMAN's classification. EmFACS is a modification of the scheme for classification called FACS, with the difference in the number of expressions in the face (action units) used for analysis [12] (Fig. 4).

**Fig. 4.** Basic emotions in facial expression analysis (Ekman/Friesen, 1977)

**Think Aloud:** Important for studies using the CXT method is the "thinking aloud" of the participants, who are supposed to actively comment on the tasks while completing them. The method can be divided into two types - the Retrospective Think Aloud (RTA), where the questioning and the comments take place after the completion of the execution, i.e. retrospectively, and the Concurrent Think Aloud (CTA), which takes place during the investigation and is mainly used for user experience testings. The advantage of the concurrent variant is the recording of natural behavior and the expression of irritation at the time of occurrence [13].

**Questionnaire and Interview:** In order to capture a holistic view of the customer experience and the user experience, the questionnaire and interview serve to capture the expectations and emotions of the participants before and after use. In the analysis phase, the results are then compared, allowing to identify differences that can be attributed to the usage and experience with the product. In addition to specifically created questionnaires, the online platform AttrakDiff is used for this purpose. AttrakDiff is an online tool (INTERFACE DESIGN GmbH) and was developed for interactive applications to investigate the perceived pragmatic, hedonic quality and attractiveness [14].

### 3.1   User Experience Testings Performed Online

Due to the Corona pandemic, the CXT lab at Offenburg University of Applied Sciences was forced to close. Already planned UX studies could no longer take place on site, so the testings were conducted online, in our case via Zoom. Cancelling the studies altogether was out of the question due to the need for research. Final papers, study projects and lectures are fundamental to ensure the educational purposes.

As a result of the decision to conduct user experience testings online, both the CXT process and the available modules were considered closely. Important for ensuring a beneficial examination, the focus had to be slightly shifted.

The CXT procedure itself was not adapted; only the expert evaluation became more prominent. Since bias effects and other types of influence were now more likely as a result of the online implementation, the system had to be checked for irritations by the students themselves with a high standard of accuracy. Depending on the research objective, expert evaluation may nevertheless play a lesser role and only serve as a basis for creating the tasks and orientation. In this case it is essential to obtain beneficial results.

Furthermore, not all modules can be used in online testing. Eye tracking and the facial expression analysis via software have to be used locally, so that the choice of the correct modules and their adaptation is decisive.

Therefore, essential for online testings, besides expert evaluation, is the information that is verbally communicated by the participant. Think Aloud also provides significant insights into the participant's thoughts, feelings and opinions while offline. In addition, the focus of this type of research is on the interview. During the interview additional insights are gained, details are collected, and behavior and feelings are explored in detail.

Within an interview, moreover, information can be obtained that provides information about the gaze pattern and thus the perception of the test object. Of course, no definitive statements can be made, but specific questions allow a rough assessment of the gaze behavior. At the beginning of an interview it can be helpful to ask what the person remembers (information about memories or what was noticed always immediately after testing), in order to determine what was "seen". On the other hand, it is also possible to ask directly about certain images, functions, buttons or the like, if they are relevant to the research objective, in order to check their perception and thus positioning.

In addition, the analysis of facial expressions can be used to capture emotions. Here it is necessary to switch on the camera of the test person and in the best case to have the permission to record the testing in order to do a following analysis as accurate as possible. It should be noted that the quality of the analysis in this case may be more difficult and depends significantly on the quality of the camera images. In addition, a briefing of the investigator, in this case students, is an essential requirement. We conducted a brief "training" in advance on the most important and significant action units to guarantee the effectiveness of the investigation.

One aspect that needs modification, and is essential in UX testings that involve recording video and audio, is to clarify and ensure consent and privacy. In offline testings, a privacy statement is presented to the participant prior to the testing, which is then signed by the participant. In online testings, we decided to send privacy statements to test persons as part of the appointment clarification process and ask for written confirmation in order to have the students' assurance. Moreover, participants are asked for consent again at the beginning of the Zoom meeting and asked to repeat their consent after the recording has been started. Thus, both written and verbal data have been recorded. The recordings can also be saved on the student's own computer and used for analysis and evaluation.

### 3.2 User Experience Testings Performed Offline During a Pandemic

In the summer of 2020, we were given the permission to open the UX Lab at Offenburg University. This required compliance with current hygiene regulations, which is why the organization and implementation of testings was adjusted. In contrast to online testing, all modules of the CXT laboratory can be used without restrictions.

First and foremost, the disinfection of hands and any surfaces must be assured. Here, in addition to a disinfection dispenser at the building entrance, a possibility for disinfection is provided before entering the room. To ensure that these are also utilized, the test person is picked up by the laboratory staff. Between each participant, the objects touched (mouse, back of chair and keyboard, if applicable) and the table surface are disinfected.

Additionally, testing sessions are now scheduled with longer time intervals so that test subjects do not cross paths, the room is aired properly, and, as in our case, the keyboard is exchanged. This requires scheduling generous time buffers between appointments and means a comparatively slower pace of testing.

To ensure increased safety and also due to current regulations, the wearing of a mouth-nose protection is mandatory. For the protection of the testing supervisor (student), this protection is not removed during the testing. In addition, the test leader accompanies the testing in the same room, but at a distance of 2–3 m from the participant and only with an open window to ensure air circulation.

After the test, it is no longer possible to analyze and evaluate the data on site, which is why the data is exported immediately afterwards and passed on to the student. For a correct evaluation, a specific briefing of the student is already carried out in advance, in which the criteria, process steps and advices to be followed are given.

To sum up, although the current situation has made the organization of a test more extensive and the scheduling more detailed, it has not made its implementation impossible. Despite minor restrictions, such as the wearing of a mouth-nose protection or the indispensable disinfection, no disadvantages affecting the previous examinations have been identified.

## 4  Final Evaluation and Recommendation

The pandemic teaching situation has challenged all of us. It has been important for Offenburg University to ensure its practical research workshops and teaching can continue, which is why it was mandatory to adapt quickly to the new framework conditions.

Indeed, many hurdles arise for students and staff, such as the fact that not all students have a computer with a camera and microphone, or that there is a poor internet connection and thus an insecure basis for online examinations and lectures. However, reliable technical solutions were found so that final papers, student projects, and research papers are successfully submitted.

The findings show that surveys can be conducted online using suitable tools such as LimeSurvey and that effective data collection is achievable in order to overcome health critical situations where no physical contact is possible. Moreover, even UX testing can be implemented with minor modifications, so that studies can also be performed alternatively online in the future, of course always depending on the research objective. Applying this research procedure with specific technical and methodical modifications, projects can be realized, which in other cases had to be rejected e.g. due to lack of capacity or wide distances between research object and researcher.

In conclusion, the pandemic has put us as a lab in a predicament, but we have discovered and made use of new innovative ways for us to maintain research and teaching ongoing.

## References

1. Limesurvey GmbH./LimeSurvey: An Open Source survey tool/LimeSurvey GmbH, Hamburg, Germany (n.d.). http://www.limesurvey.org
2. Meffert, H., Burmann, C., Kirchgeorg, M.: Marketing. Grundlagen marktorientierter Unternehmensführung; Konzepte - Instrumente - Praxis-beispiele. 10., vollst. überarb. und erw. Aufl. pp. 98, 159, Gabler, Wiesbaden (2008). https://doi.org/10.1007/978-3-658-21196-7
3. Raab, G., Unger, A., Unger, F.: Methoden der Marketing-Forschung. Grundlagen und Praxisbeispiele. 3., überarbeitete und erweiterte Auflage, p. 324, Springer Gabler, Wiesbaden (2018).https://doi.org/10.1007/978-3-658-14881-2_1
4. Mueller, A., Gast, O.: Customer experience tracking – online-kunden conversionwirksame erlebnisse bieten durch gezieltes emotions-management. In: Keuper, F. et al. (Pub.): Daten-Management und Daten-Services – Next Level, Berlin 2014, p. 333 (2014)
5. Miclau, C., Gast, O., Hertel, J., Wittmann, A., Hornecker, A., Mueller, A.: Avoiding mistakes in medical high-tech treatments and E-Commerce applications – a salutary UX-research innovation. In: Nah, F.H., Siau, K. (eds.) HCII 2019. LNCS, vol. 11588, pp. 306–322. Springer, Cham (2019). https://doi.org/10.1007/978-3-030-22335-9_21

6. Thüring, M., Mahlke, S.: Usability, aesthetics and emotions in human–technology interaction. Int. J. Psychol. **42**(4), 253 (2007). https://doi.org/10.1080/00207590701396674

7. Ziegler, M.: Marktforschung. In: Baur, N., Blasius, J. (eds.) Handbuch Methoden der empirischen Sozialforschung, pp. 183–193. Springer, Wiesbaden (2014). https://doi.org/10.1007/978-3-531-18939-0_10

8. Argyle, M.: Körpersprache et Kommunikation. Nonverbaler Ausdruck und soziale Interaktion. 10., überarb. Neuaufl. Paderborn: Junfermann (Fachbuch Non-verbale Kommunikation), p. 155 (2013)

9. Matschnig, M.: Körpersprache verstehen. 5., überarbeitete Aufl. Offenbach [Germany]: GABAL (30 Minuten), p. 59 (2012)

10. Noldus: FaceReader: Project Analysis Module (n.d.). http://www.noldus.com/facereader/project-analysis-module

11. Ekman, P., Friesen, W.: Manual for the Facial Action Coding System. Palo Alto, Santa Clara (1977)

12. Paul Ekman Group: Facial Action Coding System (FACS) FAQ - Paul Ekman Group (n.d.). http://www.paulekman.com/facs-faq/

13. Jo, M.Y., Stautmeister, A.: Don't make me Think Aloud! – Lautes Denken mit Eye-Tracking auf dem Prüfstand. In: Henning Brau und et al. (Hg.): Usability Professionals 2011. Stuttgart, p. 177 (2011)

14. Hassenzahl, M., Burmester, M., Koller, F.: AttrakDiff: ein fragebogen zur messung wahrgenommener hedonischer und pragmatischer qualität. In: Jürgen Ziegler und Gerd Szwillus (Hg.): Mensch & Computer 2003. Interaktion in Bewegung. Wiesbaden: Vieweg+Teubner Verlag (Berichte des German Chapter of the ACM, 57), p. 79 (2003)

# Designing the Empathetic Research IoT Network (ERIN) Chatbot for Mental Health Resources

Brandon Persons, Prateek Jain[✉], Christopher Chagnon, and Soussan Djamasbi

Worcester Polytechnic Institute, Worcester, USA
{bdpersons,pjain,cjchagnon,djamasbi}@wpi.edu

**Abstract.** Grounded in the user experience driven innovation (UXDI) framework, we designed and developed a chatbot, ERIN, to help college students with finding resources about sensitive issues such as mental health and Title IX. ERIN was designed to be accessed via different devices. Throughout the design process, the analysis of user interviews suggested that the service experience of the chatbot and its adoption may strongly be influenced by the medium through which it is accessed. To test this possibility, we conducted an experiment comparing user reactions to the chatbot using two different devices: laptop and smart phone. The preliminary results showed that user experience of the chatbot was almost significantly better in the mobile group and people in that group were almost significantly more likely to adopt the chatbot. These results and their implications are discussed.

**Keywords:** Empathetic chatbot · Chatbot adoption · Chatbot design · Chatbot medium

## 1 Introduction

Conversational user interfaces (UI) such as chatbots are becoming increasingly popular because they offer users an intuitive way to interact with often a large ecosystem of smart and connected technologies [4]. Human-chatbot interaction allows users to complete a task (e.g., complete a form or request for a service) as if they were talking to a human actor [19]. More and more companies across industries (e.g., Royal Bank of Scotland, Disney, and Domino's to name a few) utilize chatbots to provide a more engaging and interactive service experiences for their customers [19].

Chatbots can be particularly useful when users seek anonymity. Users feel more comfortable sharing personal issues (such as sexual harassment) with a chatbot because they feel embarrassed and ashamed, or fear judgement from people [13, 14]. Users, especially teenagers, believe that bots will not reveal their secrets when shared [14]. In such circumstances, empathetic conversational UIs allow users to interact with chatbots by accessing the needed resources or information without having to face another person. Hence, these chatbots can provide users with the anonymity and privacy they desire.

Using the user experience driven innovation (UXDI) framework [8], in this study, we designed and developed such a chatbot. Our chatbot, ERIN, is designed to help college

© Springer Nature Switzerland AG 2021
F. F.-H. Nah and K. Siau (Eds.): HCII 2021, LNCS 12783, pp. 619–629, 2021.
https://doi.org/10.1007/978-3-030-77750-0_41

students to find resources about sensitive issues such as mental health and Title IX [21]. The latter often leads to experiencing serious mental health issues such as anxiety and depression, which form the top two mental health illnesses in American young adults. If not properly addressed anxiety and depression can lead to serious health concerns such as suicidal thoughts or actions. In the US, suicide is the second leading cause of death among young adults [17].

Because mental health issues and Title IX cases have been increasing across all college campuses in United States [22], a chatbot like ERIN could serve as a useful tool for Student Development and Counselling Centers in universities to expand their reach and serve a broader population of students [20].

In this paper, we discuss ERIN's iterative design process based on UXDI framework [8]. One main objective of this project is to explore the influence of medium on ERIN's user experience (UX). People tend to prefer to use desktop and laptop computers to communicate confidential information but for short messaging services they tend to prefer mobile technologies (e.g. mobile phones and tablets) [5]. The ERIN chatbot uses a conversational UI to communicate typically short sensitive information. Hence it is important to investigate user reactions to this chatbot when accessed via laptop and mobile phones. Another objective of the study is to examine whether and how users' reactions to the chatbot could impact their intention to adopt it.

## 2  Background

Using chatbots to provide information about available mental health resources offers the opportunity to respond to many people who seek help simultaneously anytime they need help [7]. For such chatbots, it is essential to use natural empathetic (human-like) conversational scripts to communicate with their users [15, 19]. The empathetic design of such a chatbot can reduce the possibility of aggravating a user's already existing heightened negative emotions. While reducing cognitive effort is generally an accepted design principal, a recent eye tracking study shows that minimizing cognitive effort can particularly be important for decision tools that deal with sensitive and emotion-laden issues. For example, reduced cognitive effort (operationalized as improved navigation experience) resulted in significantly better engagement (improved fixation to visit ratios) with the provided online material [9]. Although humans are naturally better than machines in exhibiting empathy when sensitive issues are communicated, machines are typically better in satisfying users' need for anonymity. Fear of embarrassment and being judged by others when sharing sensitive information often lead to a great need for anonymity [13, 14]. Therefore, it is important for a chatbot that provides sensitive information (e.g. mental health resources and/or resources for victims of sexual harassment) to offer its users both empathy and anonymity [18].

To design and develop our empathetic chatbot, we used the UX driven innovation (UXDI) framework, which highlights the centrality of UX in designing novel products and services [8]. This framework requires a development project to start by gaining a deep understating about the target users and their needs. We achieved this objective by developing proto and research-based personas [12]. Personas refer to vivid representations of user groups revealing their explicit and tacit needs. Personas are used by the development team to discuss design issues, set design priorities, and make informed design decisions. Proto-persona development is a process in which the key stakeholders of the design process brainstorm the needs, goals, frustrations, and other critical aspects of the users. Proto-personas are then often verified using research-based personas to detect gaps and or identify further opportunities for innovation [12].

The UXDI framework also requires an iterative process for developing and testing prototypes to improve the UX of a product/service. Ultimately, the goal of any innovation is to achieve market success, i.e., achieving target users' acceptance and adoption of the product/service [8].

One of the most prominent models to evaluate adoption behavior of a product is the Technology Acceptance Model (TAM) [6]. According to TAM, a user's technology acceptance behavior (BI) is influenced by the degree to which the user finds the technology easy to use and useful. A recent study [11] suggests that BI may also be impacted by the perception of task effort indirectly through its impact on users' perception of usability. Therefore, we will use these two models to explore adoption behavior for the chatbot in our study. Type of device (medium) may also have an impact on adoption behavior as people tend to favor different types of devices to perform different types of activities. For example, research shows that desktop and laptop is typically preferred for sharing confidential information while tablet and smartphone is often preferred for short messaging [5]. Therefore, we will also explore to see whether device type (laptop vs. mobile phone) has an impact on user experience of ERIN.

## 3   Designing and Developing ERIN Chatbot

### 3.1   Step 1: Key Informant Interviews

Using the UXDI framework [8], interviews with two key informants were conducted to identify and assess the need for a chatbot that can provide resources for sensitive issues, such as sexual harassment, gender discrimination, and/or mental health issues for college students. These interviews revealed that developing such a chatbot would be useful to students (especially undergraduate students) because it can cue a stronger sense of anonymity and privacy. The interviews also emphasized the need for an empathetic look and feel for the UI. This is because ERIN is intended to be used for addressing sensitive issues and hence its users are likely to experience heightened negative emotions when they are interacting with the chatbot.

The interviews with key informants also provided insight for developing proto personas, which are essential in designing successful products and services [8, 12].

The conversational scripts for this chatbot were initially developed using training manuals for Student Support Network program at a North Eastern university. These scripts, which were designed to address the need of the developed personas, were then reviewed and refined by an expert, a counselor who provides mental health services for university students [20]. Figure 1 provides the snapshot of the initial prototype that was developed based on key informant interviews.

**Fig. 1.** Look and Feel of Chatbot 1.0.0 Design

### 3.2   Step 2: User Study

The insight obtained from key informant interviews were tested via user interviews with 15 undergraduate students. Open-ended questions were used to verify user needs and preferences. The analysis of these open-ended questions verified the developed personas and confirmed students' need and preference for a chatbot that can anonymously and privately provide them with information/resources for handling sensitive cases.

Unstructured user interviews were also used to solicit user feedback and reactions to the chatbot design in Fig. 1. User interviews revealed preference for an intuitive chatbot interface, a UI similar to those in text messaging applications. User interviews also revealed preference for simple (minimalistic) and clean design for ERIN. Participants seemed to find the light blue (pastel) colors to provide a calming and welcoming look and feel for the chatbot.

Next, each participant was given 4 different scenarios randomly selected from a predefined set of 8 scenarios outlining a stressful situation such as experiencing anxiety and depression due to receiving a bad grade. The scenarios were developed based on key informant reflecting top major issues for which students seek consoling at universities.

After reading the scenario, participants were asked to assume that they have discovered a chatbot provided by their university to help them find resources for dealing with stressful situations. Showing them the prototype design in Fig. 1, the participants were instructed to walk the experimenter through the conversation that they would have with the chatbot and the responses they would expect to receive back from the chatbot. This think-out-loud methodology not only provided feedback about user expectations of the chatbot but also provided user utterances which were used to improve human-chatbot interaction.

### 3.3   Step 3: Prototype Implementation

Feedback and preferences captured from user interviews were used to design the next version of the chatbot, which incorporated design decisions (e.g., larger font size, foreground/background contrast, a more pronounced border design and chatbot icon) to reduce cognitive effort and improve visual appeal (Fig. 2).

To implement the chatbot we used the single page application (SPA) and Node.js framework. This allowed an implementation infrastructure that was quick in response

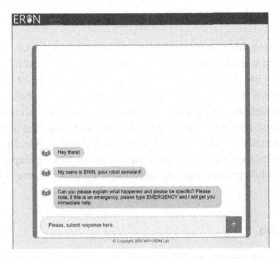

**Fig. 2.** Look and Feel of Chatbot 1.0.1 Design

time and scalable for accommodating growth. We used two main libraries to develop the chatbot: conversational-form and node-nlp. The conversational form allowed for a simple integration of a chatbot user interface (UI) by taking an HTML form and converting it into a text message style conversational UI. It also allowed to easily modify the HTML form to include conditionals (e.g. true false statements) and facilitated the ability to dynamically add responses to the chatbot (e.g., by using the flowCallback function) which was necessary for continual update/development of the chatbot.

Interpreting user utterances was facilitated by using a library named 'node-nlp', which converts user utterances into intents in order to match to the resource entities. This library utilizes a Natural Language Generation Manger (NLGM) to take a keyword library (intents) to generate a resource entity (answer) and calculate the Levenshtein distance between a substring of the utterance and a string in the keyword library to find the smallest distance [16]. Using the NLGM functionality allowed for the keyword library to be developed through the creation of a manager document for each keyword. The keywords were gathered through rich user interviews, as well as synthetically using pre-defined similar word databases and Google Trend statistics. Upon completion of the NLGM, a user utterance was passed to the keyword library to develop a confidence score (0 to 1) from the Levenshtein distance [16]. The intent with the highest confidence score would return its resource entity from the NLGM.

## 4   Exploring UX and Adoption Behavior

Interviews provided an opportunity to gather rich information about users. The analysis of interviews suggested that chatbot experience maybe influenced by medium because many users expressed a preference for a chatbot UI that resembles text messaging UI of mobile phones. To test this possibility and to gain a better understanding of what factors could affect chatbot experience and adoption, we developed another user study. The study design and preliminary results are discussed in the following sections.

## 4.1  Method

It is important to note that this is an ongoing project. For this paper, we report the preliminary results that was obtained by the first set of data, gathered by recruiting twelve undergraduate students to participate in an exploratory between-subject design experiment. All participants were provided with 2 scenarios, which as before were randomly selected from a predefined set of 8 major scenarios. Participants were asked to read the scenario and then use the chatbot to address the situation described in the scenario. Participants were randomly assigned to two groups: laptop and mobile. In the former group participants accessed the chatbot via their laptop, in the latter group they accessed the chatbot via their mobile phones. Participants completed a set of surveys after completing the task.

## 4.2  Measurements

To measure users' experience of the chatbot, we employed the widely used system usability scale (SUS) [2]. SUS is a 10-item Likert scale with standardized scores that range between 0 and 100. Higher SUS scores indicate better user experience. SUS scores larger or equal to 85 are considered to represent excellent experience [3]. Because of its UI's resemblance to those of text messaging apps, we anticipated a better SUS score in the mobile group.

We also used the MUX survey [24] to measure mobile user experience. Because our experience has shown that people tend to consider laptops and mobile phones both as portable devices, we did not anticipate significant differences in MUX score between the two groups.

Perceived task effort (PTE), which refers to experience of task difficulty was measured on a 5-point Likert scale [23]. Higher PTE scores in our study represented lower task difficulty. Because the chatbot UI was similar to text messing apps, we expected to see a more favorable ratings for PTE in the mobile group.

For adoption behavior we measured behavioral intention (BI) to use the chatbot [10]. Because a previous study shows that SUS can impact BI [11] and because we expected better SUS ratings in the mobile group, we expected people in the mobile group to provide better BI ratings. Similarly, we expected more favorable ratings for perceived ease of use (PEOU) and usefulness (PU) [1] in the mobile group.

## 4.3  Results

In order to interact with ERIN, participants formed their own wording to interact with and solicit a response from the chatbot. It is important to note that chatbot responses to user inputs were 100% accurate and context sensitive (i.e. the chatbot provided the correct resource for the specified situation). This was not only verified by experimenter (observation) but also was revealed through user feedback and self-reported measures used in the study. These results provided support for ERIN's effectives in interpreting user utterances and providing them with correct support.

We assessed possible differences in user reactions between the two groups by comparing their self-reported measures through a series of t-tests. The results showed that average SUS score in the laptop group were in the "good" range (79.58), the same scores in the mobile group were in the "excellent" range (91.67) [3]. The difference in SUS scores between the two groups was almost significant ($p = 0.07$).

We did not find significant differences ($p = 0.78$) in MUX scores between the two groups. MUX scores in both groups were in the above average range (4.33 and 4.44 out of 5). These scores indicated, as we expected, that participants considered both devices to be portable, providing similar mobile experiences.

Our results did not show that PTE was experienced differently in the two groups. The average PTEs in both groups indicated that participants were able to complete the task easily; the rating in both groups were in the above average range (4.28 and 4.39 out of 5) indicating that participants in both groups experienced little to no difficulty to complete the task.

The comparison of the BI scores revealed a more favorable adoption behavior in the mobile group (with mean of 4.00 on a 5-point scale indicating that ratings were in the above average range) compared to the laptop group (with mean of 2.67 indicating ratings in the lower range of the 5-point scale), this difference was also almost significant ($p = 0.06$). PEOU, and PU ratings in both groups were in the above average range (3.83 and 4.44 for PEOU, 4.28 and 4.83 for PU on a 5-point scale) indicting that users in both groups found the application easy to use and useful. While the differences between the two groups for these variables were not significant, as shown in Table 1, participants rated these two variables more favorably in the mobile phone group. These results together show an almost significantly better user experience (SUS score) and more favorable adoption behavior (BI score) in the mobile phone group.

**Table 1.** t-test comparing user reactions

| Mean (SD) | Laptop | Mobile | p-value |
|-----------|--------|--------|---------|
| SUS | 79.58(10.54) | 91.67(10.45) | $p = 0.07$ |
| MUX | 4.33(0.35) | 4.42(0.60) | $p = 0.78$ |
| BI | 2.67(1.23) | 4.00(0.89) | $p = 0.06$ |
| PTE | 4.28(0.39) | 4.39(0.49) | $p = 0.67$ |
| PEOU | 3.83(0.72) | 4.44(0.46) | $p = 0.11$ |
| PU | 4.28(0.71) | 4.83(0.41) | $p = 0.13$ |

To gain a deeper understanding of user experience and adoption behavior in our study, we looked at the relationship between perceived task effort, SUS scores, and behavioral intention. A recent study [11] suggests that BI is impacted by PTE indirectly through its impact on SUS. To test this possibility, we used regression analysis (Table 2).

Consistent with the argument put forward by Jain et al. [11], our results showed that the impact of PTE on BI was mediated by SUS. Table 2 shows that SUS had a strong significant ($p = 0.00$) impact on BI; 54% of variation in BI was explained by the SUS score. Similarly, perceived task effort (PTE) had a strong significant impact ($p = 0.00$)

**Table 2.** Analysis for UX-BI model

| Relationship | Values |
|---|---|
| PTE –> SUS | Adj $R^2$ = 0.62, t-Stat = 4.39, B = 22.5, p = 0.00 |
| SUS –> BI | Adj $R^2$ = 0.54, t-Stat = 3.70, B = 0.08, p = 0.00 |
| PTE –> BI | Adj $R^2$ = 0.17, t-Stat = 1.81, B = 1.44, p = 0.10 |

on user experience; 62% or variance in SUS was explained by PTE. Like the results obtained by Jain et al., 2020. we did not find a significant direct relationship between PTE and BI.

Behavioral intention is known to be influenced by ease of use and usefulness of a technology. Hence, the next logical step in our exploratory analysis was to estimate TAM (Table 3).

**Table 3.** Analysis for TAM

| Relationship | Values |
|---|---|
| PEOU –> BI | Adj $R^2$ = 0.17, t-Stat = 1.80, B = 22.5, p = 0.10 |
| PU –> BI | Adj $R^2$ = 0.25, t-Stat = 2.14, B = 22.5, p = 0.06 |
| PEOU –> PU | Adj $R^2$ = 0.79, t-Stat = 6.53, B = 0.85, p = 0.00 |

The results of this model estimation showed only a strong significant positive relationship between PEOU and PU with 79% of variance in PU explained by PEOU. The results, however, did not show a significant relationship between PEOU and BI. The results showed only a marginally significant relationship (p = 0.06) between PU and BI. These results show that the UX-BI model (Table 2) provided a stronger predicting power than TAM (Table 3) for behavioral intention of the chatbot in our study.

Because PTE impacted BI, indirectly in the UX-BI model, we conducted an exploratory analysis to see if PTE had any impact on PEOU and PU. The relationship between PTE and PEOU, and between PTE and PU are displayed in Table 4. These results show that PTE had a marginally significant effect on PEOU (p = 0.07). While the results show a significant relationship between PTE and PU (p = 0.04) once the impact of PEOU on PU was taken into consideration, this relationship became non-significant. These results provide further support that behavioral intention for ERIN in our study was best explained with the UX-BI model estimated in Table 2.

### 4.4 Discussion

In this study, we used the UXDI framework to design and develop a chatbot to help students find relevant resources for dealing with sensitive and emotionally laden cases such as mental health and Title IX issues. The insight gathered by rich user interviews

**Table 4.** PTE and TAM constructs

| Relationship | Values |
| --- | --- |
| PTE –> PEOU | Adj $R^2$ = 0.22, t-Stat = 2.02, B = 0.83, p = 0.07 |
| PTE –> PU | Adj $R^2$ = 0.31, t-Stat = 2.41, B = 0.89, p = 0.04 |

indicated that the medium with which the chatbot is accessed may have an impact on its user experience and as such may influence its adoption. We tested this possibility via an experiment.

The preliminary results of this experiment showed that, as we expected, participants found both laptops and mobile devices to serve as portable mediums for technology usage. The result also confirmed our expectation by showing that SUS and BI scores in the mobile groups were rated almost significantly better (p = 0.07 and p = 0.06 respectively). We found that ratings for PTE, PEOU, and PU were all in above average range in both groups, the ratings were slightly better (although not significantly better) in the mobile group.

While PTE scores showed favorable ratings for task effort via laptop and mobile phone (with no significant differences between the two groups) regression analysis suggested that task effort may have had a significant influence on chatbot experience, which in turn may have significantly impacted behavioral intention to use the chatbot.

The results showing that the relationship between SUS and BI was stronger than the relationship between PU and BI, confirm the role of UX in technology adoption [11] and suggest that UX-BI may serve as a useful model for predicting chatbot adoption. Obviously, these are only preliminary results and they must be verified with larger datasets and extensive future studies.

From a theoretical point of view, the UX-BI model discussed in this study, according to the UXDI framework, refers to a dynamic phenomenon, a phenomenon that is carefully developed in the design world but can reveal its full potential only after it is released in the usage world [8]. UX driven innovations raise people expectations of technology. Raised user expectations demand technology development to go beyond satisfying utilitarian attributes. People demand novel delightful user experiences with the release of every new product [8]. Technologies that have the potential to learn from and/or adopt to user needs, such as the chatbot developed in this study, can provide continual context sensitive data artifacts, which can be used to develop and refine UX-BI focused predictive models [8].

From a practical point of view, this study developed a chatbot that can assist students in finding help for sensitive issues. This chatbot is not only helpful to students but also is beneficial to universities. By providing relevant information in real-time to students, universities can improve the health and wellness of their communities.

### 4.5 Limitations and Future Research

As a preliminary investigation, the sample size was low in this study. Increasing the number of participants in future studies can help to overcome this shortcoming. Despite low sample size, our preliminary results showed that user experience and behavioral intention was almost significantly better in the mobile group. This finding, captured with a low sample size, not only suggests a possible impact of medium on chatbot experience and adoption behavior but also indicates that such impact is likely to be large. Similarly, despite low sample size the significant relationships between task effort, user experience, and behavioral intention in our study suggest that these association are strong. Future studies are needed to test these possibilities.

As in any experiment, the generalizability of our study results is limited to the task and setting. In this study, the task required participants to responded to two scenarios, which were randomly selected from a pool of top issues that students typically suffered from. Expanding the number and type of scenarios presented to each participant can strengthen and refine the results.

We tested user reactions to only two devices. Future studies are needed to expand this investigation to other devices such as desktops and tablets.

# References

1. Adipat, B., Zhang, D., Zhou, L.: The effects of tree-view based presentation adaptation on mobile web browsing. MIS Q. 99–121 (2011)
2. Albert, W., Tullis, T.: Measuring the user experience: collecting, analyzing, and presenting usability metrics. Newnes (2013)
3. Bangor, A., Kortum, P., Miller, J.: Determining what individual SUS scores mean: adding an adjective rating scale. J. Usability Stud. **4**, 114–123 (2009)
4. Brandtzaeg, P., Følstad, A.: Why people use chatbots. In: Kompatsiaris, I., et al. (eds.) INSCI 2017. LNCS, vol. 10673, pp. 377–392. Springer, Cham (2017). https://doi.org/10.1007/978-3-319-70284-1_30
5. Bröhl, C., Rasche, P., Jablonski, J., Theis, S., Wille, M., Mertens, A.: Desktop PC, tablet PC, or smartphone? An analysis of use preferences in daily activities for different technology generations of a worldwide sample. In: Zhou, J., Salvendy, G. (eds.) ITAP 2018. LNCS, vol. 10926, pp. 3–20. Springer, Cham (2018). https://doi.org/10.1007/978-3-319-92034-4_1
6. Davis, F.D., Bagozzi, R.P., Warshaw, P.R.: User acceptance of computer technology: a comparison of two theoretical models. Manag. Sci. **35**, 982–1003 (1989)
7. De Gennaro, M., Krumhuber, E.G., Lucas, G.: Effectiveness of an empathic chatbot in combating adverse effects of social exclusion on mood. Front. Psychol. **10**, 3061 (2020)
8. Djamasbi, S., Strong, D.: User experience-driven innovation – theory and practice: introduction to special issue. AIS Trans. Hum.-Comput. Interact. **11**, 208–214 (2019). https://doi.org/10.17705/1thci.00120
9. Djamasbi, S., Tulu, B., Norouzi Nia, J., Aberdale, A., Lee, C., Muehlschlegel, S.: Using eye tracking to assess the navigation efficacy of a medical proxy decision tool. In: Schmorrow, D.D., Fidopiastis, C.M. (eds.) HCII 2019. LNCS (LNAI), vol. 11580, pp. 143–152. Springer, Cham (2019). https://doi.org/10.1007/978-3-030-22419-6_11
10. Hong, S.-J., Tam, K.Y.: Understanding the adoption of multipurpose information appliances: the case of mobile data services. Inf. Syst. Res. **17**, 162–179 (2006)
11. Jain, P., Djamasbi, S., Hall-Phillips, A.: The impact of feedback design on cognitive effort, usability, and technology use. In: Americas Conference on Information Systems (AMCIS) (2020)
12. Jain, P., Djamasbi, S., Wyatt, J.: Creating value with proto-research persona development. In: Nah, F.F.-H., Siau, K. (eds.) HCII 2019. LNCS, vol. 11589, pp. 72–82. Springer, Cham (2019). https://doi.org/10.1007/978-3-030-22338-0_6

13. Kim, J., Kim, Y., Kim, B., Yun, S., Kim, M., Lee, J.: Can a machine tend to teenagers' emotional needs? A study with conversational agents. In: Extended Abstracts of the 2018 CHI Conference on Human Factors in Computing Systems, pp. 1–6 (2018)
14. Lee, Y.-C., Yamashita, N., Huang, Y., Fu, W.: "I Hear You, I Feel You": encouraging deep self-disclosure through a chatbot. In: Proceedings of the 2020 CHI Conference on Human Factors in Computing Systems, pp. 1–12 (2020)
15. Lin, Z., et al.: CAiRE: an end-to-end empathetic chatbot. In: AAAI, pp. 13622–13623 (2020)
16. Miller, F.P., Vandome, A.F., McBrewster, J.: Levenshtein distance: information theory, computer science, string (computer science), string metric, damerau? Levenshtein distance, spell checker, hamming distance (2009)
17. NAMI. https://nami.org/mhstats
18. Park, H., Lee, J.: Can a conversational agent lower sexual violence victims' burden of self-disclosure? In: Extended Abstracts of the 2020 CHI Conference on Human Factors in Computing Systems, pp. 1–8 (2020)
19. Park, M., Aiken, M., Salvador, L.: How do humans interact with chatbots? An analysis of transcripts. Int. J. Manag. Inf. Technol. **14**, 3338–3350 (2019)
20. Persons, B.: Empathetic Conversational Agent Assisting with Title IX Cases and Digital Counseling. User Experience and Decision-Making Lab, vol. IQP. Worcester Polytechnic Institute (2020)
21. U.S. Department of Education. https://www2.ed.gov/about/offices/list/ocr/docs/tix_dis.html
22. U.S. Department of Education. https://www2.ed.gov/about/offices/list/ocr/docs/investigations/open-investigations/tix.html
23. Wang, B.: Interactive decision aids for consumer decision making in e-commerce: the influence of perceived strategy restrictiveness. MIS Q. **33**(2), 293–320 (2009). https://doi.org/10.2307/20650293
24. Wilson, E.V., Djamasbi, S.: Measuring mobile user experience instruments for research and practice. Commun. Assoc. Inf. Syst. **44**, 8 (2019)

# The Effect of Hubert Dreyfus's Epistemological Assumption on the Philosophy of Artificial Intelligence

Bo-chiuan Su and Batnasan Luvaanjalba[✉]

Department of Information Management, National Dong Hwa University, Hualien, Taiwan
bsu@gms.ndhu.edu.tw

**Abstract.** Hubert Dreyfus is one of the professionals who has done some research on epistemology in the field of artificial intelligence research. He made an epistemological assumption in the field of artificial intelligence. As artificial intelligence develops, it becomes more connected to the field of knowledge. In the field of knowledge, the more you will connect with the field of philosophy that emphasizes knowledge. In this paper, we examines the epistemological assumption in the philosophy of artificial intelligence and attempts to identify some key questions. The purpose of this paper is to provide a close, detailed analysis of the frequency, nature, and depth of visible use in an epistemological assumption and artificial intelligence of Hubert Dreyfus's early works "What computers can't do". This research investigates the trend as the consequences of the epistemology assumption concerns and experiment of epistemology assumption experience are analyzed. The results show that contrary to initial expectations, the epistemology assumption related works in question are relatively little used by AI scholars in journal articles, and where they are used, such use is often only vague, brief, or in passing. The need to intensify human-centred research in artificial intelligence research is clear from Hubert Dreyfus's epistemological assumption. Furthermore, in order to develop artificial intelligence, it is necessary to develop brain function and physical body interaction together.

**Keywords:** Artificial intelligence · Human-computer interaction · Philosophy · Epistemology

## 1 Introduction

The field of artificial intelligence (AI) research has been developing since 1956. Since then, artificial intelligence has been actively searching for what components to have and what exactly to study. Artificial intelligence's researchers and other related professionals have always focused on improving their knowledge of what they are studying. Philosophy is one of the most important fields for updating and improving knowledge. For this reason, some researchers have linked the study of artificial intelligence to philosophy.

This is because philosophy helps redefine some of the concepts in the field. As a result, the field of philosophy itself is being renewed as rich. On the other hand, an

© Springer Nature Switzerland AG 2021
F. F.-H. Nah and K. Siau (Eds.): HCII 2021, LNCS 12783, pp. 630–644, 2021.
https://doi.org/10.1007/978-3-030-77750-0_42

interest in philosophical questions always helps artificial intelligence researchers to see their work in a bigger picture. The field of philosophy is a unique field that seeks to understand a wide range of concepts. Such coherent research can be very beneficial in both areas. Researchers also recognize the importance of such mutualistic research. In such a mutualistic way, artificial intelligence has been linked to epistemology, a branch of philosophy, and has been effective in both fields.

Additionally, artificial intelligence approaches create epistemological boundaries between research groups, which further clarify the nature of research and other complexities. Novel approaches in AI such as critical realism and phronesis defy such restrictive epistemological categories. These restrictive categories become epistemology matters, and they play a role in research. Its critical role is realised only when it is conceived to be closely related to all the other philosophical fields such as metaphysics, axiology, and rationality.

The topic of this research article is Hubert Dreyfus's epistemological assumption in philosophy of artificial intelligence. Hubert Lederer Dreyfus (1929–2017) was an American philosopher and professor of philosophy at the University of California, Berkeley. His main interests included existentialism, phenomenology and the philosophy of both psychology and literature, as well as the philosophical implications of artificial intelligence.

Hubert Dreyfus has been a critic of artificial intelligence research since the 1960s. In a series of papers and books, including Alchemy and AI (1965), What Computers Can't Do (1972; 1979; 1992) and Mind over Machine (1986), he presented a pessimistic assessment of AI's progress and a critique of the philosophical foundations of the field. He was one of the first scientists to emphasize the development of human-centred artificial intelligence. He wrote "What Computers Can't Do: The Limits of Artificial Intelligence", 1972.

In this work, he speculative four assumptions:

1. *A biological assumption* that on some level of operation usually supposed to be that of the neurons the brain processes information in discrete operations by way of some biological equivalent of on/off switches.
2. *A psychological assumption* that the mind can be viewed as a device operating on bits of information according to formal rules. Thus, in psychology, the computer serves as a model of the mind as conceived of by empiricists such as Hume (with the bits as atomic impressions) and idealists such as Kant (with the program providing the rules). Both empiricists and idealists have prepared the ground for this model of thinking as data processing a third-person process in which the involvement of the "processor" plays no essential role.
3. *An epistemological assumption* that all knowledge can be formalized, that is, that whatever can be understood can be expressed in terms of logical relations, more exactly in terms of Boolean functions, the logical calculus which governs the way the bits are related according to rules.
4. Finally, since all information fed into digital computers must be in bits, the computer model of the mind presupposes that all relevant information about the world, everything essential to the production of intelligent behavior, must in principle be analyzable as a set of situation-free determinate elements. This is *the ontological*

*assumption* that what there is, is a set of facts each logically independent of all the others [1].

One of those is the epistemological assumption. In his work, the epistemological assumption is explained in two parts. The first is: A Mistaken Argument from the Success of Physics.

The second is: A Mistaken Argument from the Success of Modern Linguistics. He emphasized the difference between human and artificial intelligence.

The academic significance of this article is that it asks questions about "What computers can't do" and answers them in a specific order. This article consists of a brief professional biography, abstract, introduction, literature review, discussion, methodology, results, conclusions, and references.

## 2  Literature Review

In writing a literature review, we focused on two things.

1. The views of Hubert Dreyfus in the philosophy of artificial intelligence.
2. The epistemological assumption's effect of Hubert Dreyfus in the philosophy of artificial intelligence.

### 2.1  The Views of Hubert Dreyfus in the Philosophy of Artificial Intelligence

In recent years, artificial intelligence (AI) has progressed from an emergent concept to an increasingly common function in philosophy sector.

How to effectively use people's minds is an AI issue. It is very much related. Philosophers are trying to create new knowledge. Consequently, the production of knowledge is based on people's thoughts and interests.

An example is the production of knowledge-based AI. Philosophers therefore propose their ideas to change their minds and preach their ideas. This is to say that you need the philosophy of AI to arrive at the contents of the field, to describe how knowledge is developed and advanced, how knowledge is justified and/or validated, and how traditional questions of philosophy may be manifest within the field.

It's important to relate new knowledge into artificial intelligence. Dreyfus just cared about that. He believed that the human mind and knowledge depended primarily on unconscious processes rather than conscious symbols. Therefore, it has been proven that unconscious abilities can never be fully mastered by formal rules.

This critique is based on the understanding of the philosophers Heidegger and Merleo-Pontius. In the first wave of artificial intelligence research, attempts were made to express reality, use high-level formal symbols, and reduce intelligence to symbolism. When his idea was first introduced in the mid-1960s, few people supported it. By the 1980s, however, many of his prospects had been discovered by researchers in the fields of robotics and new communications. It is called "sub-symbolic" because it emphasizes the high-level signs of early artificial intelligence research.

In the 21st century, a statistical approach to machine learning mimics the unconscious process of perceiving, noticing, and making quick conclusions about brain defects.

These methods are very successful and are currently widely used in industry and research.

Historian and AI researcher Daniel Crevier writes: "time has proven the accuracy and perceptiveness of some of Dreyfus's comments [2].

Indeed, his assumption brought the right direction to the philosophy of artificial intelligence. So, Dreyfus said in 2007, I figure I won and it's over—they've given up (Quoted in Fearn, 2007). In order to theorize artificial non-human intelligence while remaining true to Dreyfusian intuitions, it is therefore necessary to expand Dreyfus's analysis [3].

Daniel Susser's proposal highlights many of the correct features of Hubert Dreyfus's assumption. My goal in what follows is to show how we might begin to do that, and to offer some thoughts on what expanding the analysis means, theoretically and practically, for future artificial intelligence research [3].

Let's find out now from his very interesting findings.

In order to do so, I attempt to bring Dreyfus's work into conversation with the work of Mark Bickhard, whose "interactivist" theory of cognition resembles Dreyfus's theory of skillful coping in crucial ways... Instead of being framed in terms of human intelligence and human bodies, Bickhard's account is framed in terms of physical systems generally. And thus it offers a way of extracting from Dreyfus's picture the basic features of bodies, common to all intelligent, embodied beings [3].

Another way to gain an understanding of Dreyfus's views is to read together Dreyfus's theory of skilful coping and Bihard's cognitive interactive theory.

The crux of Dreyfus's argument is that contrary to formalist desires, (1) meaning is inherently context-dependent, and (2) context-dependence in principle can't be formalized, because contexts are inherently indeterminate. Therefore, categorizing these issues and conducting research in a specific context is another opportunity to further explore that research.

Because there are so many issues like this, the most important thing is to understand the nature of the person behind it. However, philosophers such as H. Dreyfus believe that AI cannot understand human language because it cannot understand the context in which language is used [4].

Therefore, categorizing these issues and conducting research in a specific context is another opportunity to further explore that research. This problem, known in linguistics and AI research as the "Frame Problem," is at bottom a matter of determining relevance.

"Framing" something means determining the appropriate context within which to understand it, and doing that amounts to determining what is and isn't relevant to its meaning [3]. The importance of the dependencies, which can be considered important, becomes clearer than the exclusion of the exceptions.

At each moment and in every situation the body guides our sense of what is relevant, he claims, and it does so in three ways. The first has to do with brain architecture:

The possible responses to a given input must be constrained by [...] this innate structure [which] accounts for phenomena such as the perceptual constants that are given from the start by the perceptual system as if they had always already been learned [5].

The brain, that is, acting as a transducer of sensory information intrinsically limits, by virtue of its physical architecture, the possible ways a situation can be perceived. We see only a certain part of the light spectrum, hear only certain wavelengths of sound, and the brain, though flexible, combines and interprets such sensory input in a relatively stable manner. The second way Dreyfus calls "body-dependent order of presentation".

This describes how the physical structure of the body delimits the possible ways one might act in or interact with a given situation, and thus determines the range of possible ways one might understand it [3]. All of this reminds us of the need to balance Dreyfus's study of the relationship between the physical body and the brain.

In sum, on Dreyfus's account the body anchors us at the center of a perspective; it opens up a world. And it does so in three ways: first, by acting as a sensorial sieve, limiting at the outset what about the physical world can be perceived; second, by structuring the immediate environment around possibilities for action; and third, by pre-reflectively orienting movement toward the optimal relationship to (and understanding of) a given situation or some object in view. In other words, the body is what makes it possible to discover at any given moment that certain parts of the world are relevant to our interests or that they aren't, indeed to have interests at all. Our bodies embed us in a world of meaningful relations, make those relations matter to us, enable us to understand them (and ourselves in relation to them), and guide our activities in and through them [3].

## 2.2 The Effect of Hubert Dreyfus's Epistemological Assumption on the Philosophy of Artificial Intelligence

All knowledge can be formalized. This has to do with the problem of epistemology, or the study of knowledge. Dreyfus argues that this assumption cannot be justified because much of human knowledge is not symbolic.

Epistemology is 'a way of understanding and explaining how we know what we know [6]. Also, Epistemology is also 'concerned with providing a philosophical grounding for deciding what kinds of knowledge are possible and how we can ensure that they are both adequate and legitimate [6].

To prove this philosophical direction, we do some research and make some assumptions. Although human performance might not be explainable by supposing that people are actually following heuristic rules in a sequence of unconscious operations, intelligent behavior may still be formalizable in terms of such rules and thus reproduced by machine. This is the epistemological assumption [1].

Let's take a closer look at the epistemological assumption. The epistemological assumption involves two claims: (a) that all nonarbitrary behavior can be formalized, and (b) that the formalism can be used to reproduce the behavior in question. In this chapter we shall criticize claim (a) by showing that it is an unjustified generalization from physical science, and claim (b) by trying to show that a theory of competence cannot be a theory of performance: that unlike the technological application of the laws of physics to produce physical phenomena, a timeless, contextless theory of competence cannot be used to reproduce the moment-to the Epistemological Assumption moment involved behavior required for human performance; that indeed there cannot be a theory of human performance. If this argument is convincing, the epistemological assumption, in the form in which it seems to support AI, turns out to be untenable, and, correctly understood, argues against the possibility of AI, rather than guaranteeing its success [1].

The epistemological assumption is that all activity (either by animate or inanimate objects) can be formalized in the form of predictive rules or laws.

Claim (a), that all non-arbitrary behavior can be formalized, is not an axiom. It rather expresses a certain conception of understanding which is deeply rooted in our culture but may nonetheless turn out to be mistaken. We must now turn to the empirical arguments which can be given in support of such a hypothesis. It should also be clear by now that no empirical arguments from the success of AI are acceptable, since it is precisely the interpretation, and, above all, the possibility of significant extension of the meager results such as Bobrow's which is in question.

Since two areas of successful formalization physics and linguistics seem to support the epistemological assumption, we shall have to study both these areas. In physics we indeed find a formalism which describes behavior (for example, the planets circling the sun), but we shall see that this sort of formalism can be of no help to those working in AI. In linguistics we shall find, on the other hand, a formalism which is relevant to work in AI, and which argues for the assumption that all non-arbitrary behavior can be formalized, but we will find that this formalism which expresses the competence of the speaker that is, what he is able to accomplish cannot enable one to use a computer to reproduce his performance that is, his accomplishment [1].

It's because of the epistemological assumption that workers in the field argue that intelligence is the same as formal rule-following, and it's because of the ontological one that they argue that human knowledge consists entirely of internal representations of reality.

A digital computer is a machine which operates according to the sort of criteria Plato once assumed could be used to understand any orderly behavior. This machine, as defined by Minsky, who bases his definition on that of Turing, is a "rule-obeying mechanism." As Turing puts it:

The... computer is supposed to be following fixed rules.... It is the duty of the control to see that these instructions are obeyed correctly and in the right order. The control is so constructed that this necessarily happens." So the machine in question is a restricted but very fundamental sort of mechanism. It operates on determinate, unambiguous bits of data, according to strict rules which apply unequivocally to these data. The claim is made that this sort of machine a Turing machine which expresses the essence of a digital computer can, in principle, do anything that human beings can do that it has, in principle, only those limitations shared by man [1].

On the basis of these two assumptions, workers in the field claim that cognition is the manipulation of internal symbols by internal rules, and that, therefore, human behaviour is, to a large extent, context free.

Daniel Crevier writes: "Time has proven the accuracy and perceptiveness of some of Dreyfus's comments. Had he formulated them less aggressively, constructive actions they suggested might have been taken much earlier [2].

The press reported these predictions in glowing reports of the imminent arrival of machine intelligence. Dreyfus felt that this optimism was totally unwarranted.

He believed that they were based on false assumptions about the nature of human intelligence.

Thus, given enough memory and time, any computer even such a special sort of analogue computer could be simulated on a digital machine. In general, by accepting the fundamental assumptions that the nervous system is part of the physical world and that all physical processes can be described in a mathematical formalism which can in turn be manipulated by a digital computer, one can arrive at the strong claim that the behavior which results from human "information processing," whether directly formalizable or not, can always be indirectly reproduced on a digital machine [1].

We all know that because the nervous system is a physical process, mathematical formalism cannot replace the nervous system. These predictions were based on the success of an "information processing" model of the mind, articulated by Newell and Simon in their physical symbol systems hypothesis, and later expanded into a philosophical position known as computationalism by philosophers such as Jerry Fodor and Hilary Putnam [7].

The information processing model is not about imitating the human mental process, but about finding and harmonizing its nature. Believing that they had successfully simulated the essential process of human thought with simple programs, it seemed a short step to producing fully intelligent machines. However, Dreyfus argued that philosophy, especially 20th-century philosophy, had discovered serious problems with this information processing viewpoint. The mind, according to modern philosophy, is nothing like a digital computer [3].

There is a difference between processing information with a digital computer and processing information in the human brain. Abundant data, real-time and historical, are easily accessible through AI devices [8]. New knowledge is the use of past databases for the future [9].

The human mind depends on what symbol is used. Much depends on where, when and how the symbol is used. Hubert Dreyfus is one of the scientists who has been serious about the development and direction of artificial intelligence since its inception. Although he criticized AI, his criticism was not a denial of AI at all.

But there was criticism that we need to focus on proper development. At the time, he began to criticize artificial intelligence as an alchemy because it was raised by overly optimistic scientists. In order for any science to develop properly and in the right direction, it is important for leading scientists to participate and share their criticisms.

In this way, science will be able to correct its mistakes and develop better. That's exactly what Dreyfus feels. He made the mistake of thinking that the AI industry should be developed properly, not developed. Those who fall back on the epistemological assumption have realized that their formalism, as a theory of competence, need not be a theory of human performance, but they have not freed themselves sufficiently from Plato to see that a theory of competence may not be adequate as a theory of machine performance either.

The idea here is that formalism is a code of behavior, not an original behavior. Therefore, it is important to continue to carefully study the empirical evidence. There is no point in just following the rules. Much depends on who develops the rules and for what reason.

This is presumably Turing's generalization of Wittgenstein's argument that it is impossible to supply normative rules which prescribe in advance the correct use of a word in all situations. Turing's "refutation" is to make a distinction between "rules of conduct" and "laws of behavior" and then to assert that "we cannot so easily convince ourselves of the absence of complete laws of behavior as of complete rules of conduct." Now as an answer to the Wittgensteinian claim, this is well taken [10].

For Wittgenstein, the word must have a definite meaning. Turing is in effect arguing that although we cannot formulate the normative rules for the correct application of a particular predicate, this does not show that we cannot formulate the rules which describe how, in fact, a particular individual applies such a predicate [10].

The clearer the meaning of the word, the more important it is. In other words, while Turing is ready to admit that it may in principle be impossible to provide a set of rules describing what a person should do in every circumstance, he holds there is no reason to doubt that one could in principle discover a set of rules describing what he would do. But why does this supposition seem so self-evident that the burden of proof is on those who call it into question? Why should we have to "convince ourselves of the absence of complete laws of behavior" rather than of their presence? Here we are face to face again with the epistemological assumption. It is important to try to root out what lends this assumption its implied a priori plausibility [10].

The more ambiguous a word is, the more confusing it is. This is uncertainty. It is important to be clear in word, behavior, and action. To begin with, "laws of behavior" is ambiguous. In one sense human behavior is certainly lawful, if lawful simply means orderly. But the assumption that the laws in question are the sort that could be embodied in a computer program or some equivalent formalism is a different and much stronger claim, in need of further justification [10].

If human behavior is orderly, then we need a law that can penetrate the depths of that order and unravel its secrets. The idea that any description of behavior can be formalized in a way appropriate to computer programming leads workers in the field of artificial intelligence to overlook this question. It is assumed that, in principle at least, human behavior can be represented by a set of independent propositions describing the inputs to the organism, correlated with a set of propositions describing its output [10].

When programming a behavioral process for a computer program, someone should always consider whether one fully understands the nature of the behavior. The clearest statement of this assumption can be found in James Culbertson's move from the assertion that one could build a robot using only flip/flops to the claim that in theory at least it could therefore reproduce all human behavior. Using suitable receptors and effectors we can connect them together via central cells.

If we could get enough central cells and if they were small enough and if each cell had enough end bulbs and if we could put enough bulbs at each synapse and if we had time enough to assemble them, then we could construct robots to satisfy any given input output specification, i.e., we could construct robots that would behave in any way we desired under any environmental circumstances. There would be no difficulty in constructing a robot with behavioral properties just like John Jones or Henry Smith or in constructing a robot with any desired behavioral improvements over Jones and Smith [10].

Even though they think so, we still don't know the secret behind the cells. Or put more baldly: Since [these complete robots] can, in principle, satisfy any given input output specifications, they can do any prescribed things under any prescribed circumstances— ingeniously solve problems, compose symphonies, create works of art and literature and engineering, and pursue any goals [10].

We already know that such robots can work under human control. But we always doubt whether we can think like a human being. Thus, given enough memory and time, any computer—even such a special sort of analogue computer—could be simulated on digital machine [10].

When simulating an analogue computer on a digital machine, keep in mind that the nervous system is an integral part of the physical world. In general, by accepting the fundamental assumptions that the nervous system is part of the physical world and that all physical processes can be described in a mathematical formalism which can in turn be manipulated by a digital computer, one can arrive at the strong claim that the behavior which results from human "information processing," whether directly formalizable or not, can always be indirectly reproduced on a digital machine. This claim may well account for the formalist's smugness, but what in fact is justified by the fundamental truth that every form of "information processing" (even those which in practice can only be carried out on an "analogue computer") must in principle be simulable on a digital computer? [10].

This is not as easy as the formalists believe. We have seen it does not prove the mentalist claim that, even when a human being is unaware of using discrete operations in processing information, he must nonetheless be unconsciously following a set of instructions. Does it justify the epistemological assumption that all nonarbitrary behavior can be formalized? [10].

Someone will have to remember to follow the instructions when processing the information. One must delimit what can count as information processing in a computer. A digital computer solving the equations describing an analogue information processing device and thus simulating its function is not thereby simulating its "information processing." It is not processing the information which is processed by the simulated analogue, but entirely different information concerning the physical or chemical properties of the analogue [10].

The ability to process all information digitally is currently limited.

Thus the strong claim that every form of information can be processed by a digital computer is misleading. One can only show that for any given type of information a digital computer can in principle be programmed to simulate a device which can process that information. Thus understood as motion—as the input and output of physical signals— human behavior is presumably completely lawful in the sense the formalists require [10].

Because human behavior is a complex process, it is important not only to define it by analogical calculations but also to go beyond the physical process.If the laws of physical activity related to the human brain are not well understood, it will be difficult to understand the functioning of the human body and other control systems.

There is a special kind of impossibility involved in any attempt to simulate the brain as a physical system. The enormous calculations necessary may be precluded by the very laws of physics and information theory such calculations pre suppose. Yet workers in the field of AI from Turing to Minsky seem to take refuge in this confusion between physical laws and information processing rules to convince themselves that there is reason to suppose that human behavior can be formalized; That the burden of proof is on those who claim that "there are processes… which simply cannot be described in a formal language but which can nevertheless be carried out, e.g., by minds [10].

Therefore, it is important to study the physical systems of the brain in relation to the information processing process. Once we have set straight the equivocation between physical laws and information processing rules, what argument remains that human behavior, at what AI workers have called "the information processing level," can be described in terms of strict rules? [10].

This is more effective than simply copying and coding simulated behaviors that have nothing to do with the physical system of the human body. If no argument based on the success of physics is relevant to the success of AI, because AI is concerned with formalizing human behavior not physical motion, the only hope is to turn to areas of the behavioral sciences themselves.

Galileo was able to found modern physics by abstracting from many of the properties and relations of Aristotelian physics and finding that the mathematical relations which remained were sufficient to describe the motion of objects. What would be needed to justify the formalists' optimism would be a Galileo of the mind who, by making the right abstractions, could find a formalism which would be sufficient to describe human behavior [10].

The advantages of formalism can be asserted as a result of abstraction, but the disadvantages can also be revealed.John McCarthy expresses this longing for a rapprochement between physics and the behavioral sciences: Although formalized theories have been devised to express the most important fields of mathematics and some progress has been made in formalizing certain empirical sciences, there is at present no formal theory in which one can express the kind of means ends analys is used in ordinary life.

Our approach to the artificial intelligence problem requires a formal theory. Recently such a breakthrough has occurred. Chomsky and the transformational linguists have found that by abstracting from human performance—the use of particular sentences on particular occasions—they can formalize what remains, that is, the human ability to recognize grammatically well formed sentences and to reject ill formed ones. That is, they can provide a formal theory of much of linguistic competence [10].

If linguistic competence can be provided by formal theory, that competence will be the subject of research related to the functioning of the human body. This has its advantages. This success is a major source of encouragement for those in AI who are committed to the view that human behavior can be formalized without reduction to the physical level, for such success tends to confirm at least the first half of the epistemological hypothesis.

A segment of orderly behavior which at first seems non rule like turns out to be describable in terms of complex rules, rules of the sort which can be processed directly by a digital computer (directly—that is, without passing by way of a physical description of the motions of the vocal cords of a speaker or the physiochemical processes taking place in his brain).But such a formalization only provides justification for half the epistemological hypothesis.

Linguistic competence is not what AI workers wish to formalize. If machines are to communicate in natural language, their programs must not only incorporate the rules of grammar; they must also contain rules of linguistic performance. In other words, what was omitted in order to be able to formalize syntactic theory—the fact that people are able to use their language—is just what must also be formalized.

The question whether the epistemological hypothesis is justified thus comes down to the test case: is there reason to suppose that there can be a formal theory of what linguists call pragmatics? There are two reasons to believe that such a generalization of syntactic theory is impossible: (1) An argument of principle: for there to be a formal theory of pragmatics, one would have to have a theory of all human knowledge; but this may well be impossible. (2) A descriptive objection: not all linguistic behavior is rule like. We recognize some linguistic expressions as odd—as breaking the rules—and yet we are able to understand them [10].

Assuming that there must be a theory of all knowledge, the theory of all things in physics will somehow relate to it. If this is the case, it will be even more important to uncover the unified nature of the problem, to make some changes in the process of studying everything separately and piece by piece.

The question whether the epistemological hypothesis is justified thus comes down to the test case: is there reason to suppose that there can be a formal theory of what linguists call pragmatics? There are two reasons to believe that such a generalization of syntactic theory is impossible: (1) An argument of principle (to which we shall turn in the next chapter): for there to be a formal theory of pragmatics, one would have to have a theory of all human knowledge; but this may well be impossible. (2) A descriptive objection (to which we shall now turn): not all linguistic behavior is rule like. We recognize some linguistic expressions as odd—as breaking the rules—and yet we are able to understand them.

There are cases in which a native speaker recognizes that a certain linguistic usage is odd and yet is able to understand it—for example, the phrase "The idea is in the pen" is clear in a situation in which we are discussing promising authors; but a machine at this point, with rules for what size physical objects can be in pig pens, playpens, and fountain pens, would not be able to go on. Since an idea is not a physical object, the machine could only deny that it could be in the pen or at best make an arbitrary stab at interpretation. The listener's understanding, on the other hand, is far from arbitrary [10].

It is difficult to see logically how rules can be formulated. Therefore, the more balanced the development of one branch of linguistics, the more it is beneficial for the development of both.

Any value depends on the data. Therefore, in order to apply the rule, it is necessary to minimize the ambiguity as much as possible. If language as a whole is a calculation, it should consist of strict rules. Since there are no such strict rules, there is no better solution than to study language in relation to the functioning of the human brain.

It is a question of whether there can be rules even describing what speakers in fact do. To have a complete theory of what speakers are able to do, one must not only have grammatical and semantic rules but further rules which would enable a person or a machine to recognize the context in which the rules must be applied.

Thus there must be rules for recognizing the situation, the intentions of the speakers, and so forth. But if the theory then requires further rules in order to explain how these rules are applied, as the pure intellectualist viewpoint would suggest, we are in an infinite regress. Since we do manage to use language, this regress cannot be a problem for human beings. If AI is to be possible, it must also not be a problem for machines [10].

We should never confuse the rules of how to use language with the rules of how to connect language with artificial intelligence. The rules we use in our language are processes based on ready-made brain activity. As for artificial intelligence, it needs rules and a detailed scheme of brain activity.

It cannot survive because it cannot cope with that particular situation. Therefore, when the rules are not completely clear, there will always be ambiguities and uncertainties related to the rules. This may be an idea that a more realistic answer can be obtained by relying on specific sub-explanations in addition to well-designed data to generate clear rules.

A full refutation of the epistemological assumption would require an argument that the world cannot be analyzed in terms of context free data. Then, since the assumption that there are basic unambiguous elements is the only way to save the epistemological assumption from the regress of rules, the formalist, caught between the impossibility of always having rules for the application of rules and the impossibility of finding ultimate unambiguous data, would have to abandon the epistemological assumption altogether [10].

## 3   Methodology

Artificial intelligence approaches create epistemological boundaries between research groups, which further clarify the nature of research and other complexities. Novel approaches in AI such as critical realism and phronesis defy such restrictive epistemological categories. These restrictive categories become epistemology matters, it plays a role in research. Its critical role is realised only when it is conceived to be closely related to all the other philosophical fields such as metaphysics, axiology, and rationality.

For how can one study something, when the essence of metaphysics of what to study is as yet underdetermined? How can one be sure of the knowledge surrounding AI strategy, for example, if both "AI" and "strategy" can take different forms depending on who is researching, which articles are relied on, and how they are conceived?

It is in these situations that philosophy offers solutions and alternatives. The relationships between philosophy and methods are not as contrived or mechanical as is commonly viewed in AI. Epistemology implies theoretical perspectives which in turn dictates a particular research method. Notwithstanding the political, economic and sociological demands that researchers face, starting with a focus on the metaphysics of the problem, coupled with clear research questions, and judicious use of epistemological choices, will best serve the researcher.

**Design/Methodology/Approach** – The study involved conducting extensive full-text searches in a large number of electronically available LIS journal databases to find citations of Hubert Dreyfus's works, then examining each citing article and each individual citation to evaluate the nature and depth of each use.

**Findings** – Contrary to initial expectations, the epistemology assumption related works in question are relatively little used by scholars in journal articles, and where they are used, such use is often only vague, brief, or in passing. A total of 40 scientific articles related to this topic were collected and 10 of them were selected and used. Also, Hubert, L. Dreyfus, What Computers Can't Do: The Limits of Artificial Intelligence, published in 1972, and Hubert L. Dreyfus, What Computers Still Can't Do: A Critique of Artificial Reason (1992) a version was also used.

**Research Limitations/Implications** – This study is limited to specific articles. Other research methods, such as report analysis, social media analysis, and scholarly interviews, may reveal patterns of use and influence that are not seen in journal articles.

**Originality/Value** – This study's intensive, in-depth study of quality as well as quantity of citations challenges some existing assumptions regarding citation analysis and the sociology of citation practices.

**Research Design and Data Analysis** – In this paper, we analyzed the data collection of the epistemological assumption.

## 4   Results

- The reason Hubert Dreyfus analyzed the epistemological hypothesis was to clarify the boundaries of cognition. Because he did research on what computers can't do and what they can do. This research paper seeks to identify the limitations of what computers can do. It has become clear that computers cannot completely replace human thinking.
- In order to develop artificial intelligence, it is necessary to develop brain function and physical body interaction together.
- It is more important to develop and direct the activities of human-centred robots than to promote robots beyond the human mind.
- The need to intensify human-centred research in artificial intelligence research is clear from Hubert Dreyfus's epistemological assumption.

## 5   Discussion

Artificial intelligence research is developing more and more year by year and month by month. As it develops, it becomes narrower and narrower. It is developing in connection with many industries. The field between artificial intelligence and philosophy is very interesting and very successful. I hope that researchers will pay more attention to this connection in the future.

We wish researchers were more interested in artificial intelligence and epistemology. Epistemology is a unique branch of philosophy that can be developed in any field at any time. Hubert Dreyfus's philosophy of artificial intelligence is also very interesting. Some of his seemingly pessimistic arguments at the time contributed to a new perspective on the philosophy of artificial intelligence and a new level of correction. So why not look back and study the work of this researcher in accordance with their respective fields? For example, a biologist may study biological assumption in accordance with his or her speciality. Psychologists can also study psychological assumption. Philosophers and physicists can study epistemological assumption and ontological assumption.

## 6 Conclusions

The development of technology is an example of how artificial intelligence uses the differences and controls of human thoughts to direct their thoughts to their own goals. Moreover, thanks to this opportunity, it is becoming a source of change in the interests of society, their minds and knowledge. In particular, the goal of this century is to create knowledge using new technologies, and in return to share that knowledge and take advantage of it.

The set of documents collected in this issue is intended to illustrate some of the significance and significance of philosophical work in artificial intelligence. They should be studied from a variety of philosophical perspectives and provide an important basis for current and future research.

When studying the prospects for the creation of non-human artificial intelligence, it is necessary to take an interest in the views of Hubert Dreyfus. Because Dreyfus's work is human-centred. Dreyfus believes that the body is the foundation of the mind. Therefore, in order to develop a human-centred artificial intelligence, he emphasizes the study of the physical body in relation to each other.

Hubert Dreyfus's work on the philosophy of the mind proved that the body is the foundation of all aspects of intelligent life. Thus, Dreyfus warned about the validity of pure algorithms and formalist fantasies of the mind without the body. Furthermore, Dreyfus's phenomenological work argues that the creation of the human artificial intelligence requires the human body to replicate, socialize, integrate into human daily life, and gradually develop its capabilities in a way that is evolving.

It is hoped that a brief introduction to the philosophical possibilities in artificial intelligence will inspire the flow of research to define artificial intelligence research as a key reference area for the study of new and emerging technologies.

## References

1. Dreyfus, H.L.: What Computers Can't Do: The Limits of Artificial Intelligence, pp. 101–118. Harper and Row Publishers (1972)
2. Crevier, D.: AI: The Tumultuous History of the Search for Artificial Intelligence, p. 125. Basic Books, New York (1993)
3. Susser, D.: Artificial intelligence and the body: Dreyfus, Bickhard, and the future of AI. In: Müller, V. (ed.) Philosophy and Theory of Artificial Intelligence. Studies in Applied Philosophy, Epistemology and Rational Ethics, vol. 5, pp. 277–287. Springer, Heidelberg (2013). https://doi.org/10.1007/978-3-642-31674-6_21

4. Dreyfus, H.L.: What Computers Can't Do of Artificial Reason, p. 19. Harper & Row Publishers (1975)
5. Dreyfus, H.L., Dreyfus, S.: Mind Over Machine: The Power of Human Intuition and Expertise in the Era of the Computer, p. 236. Free Press, New York (1986)
6. Crotty, M.: The Foundations of Social Research: Meaning and Perspectives in the Research Process, 3rd edn, vol. 10, p. 256. Sage Publications, London (2003)
7. Horst, S.: The computational theory of mind. In: Zalta, E.N. (ed.) The Stanford Encyclopedia of Philosophy (2005)
8. Kastrinos, N.: Towards a new knowledge system - targeted scenario. European Commission Directorate-General for Research and Innovation Directorate A Policy Development and Coordination, no. 19, pp. 1–30 (2018)
9. Ghassib, H.: A Theory of the Knowledge Industry. The Princess Sumaya University for Technology (PSUT), pp. 1–15 (2013)
10. Dreyfus, H.L.: What Computers Still Can't Do : A Critique of Artificial Reason. MLA (Modern Language Association) The MIT Press, APA (American Psychological Association), p. 354 (1992)

# Human-Robot Interactions Design for Interview Process: Needs-Affordances-Features Perspective

Karenina Nicoli H. Zaballa(✉), Lance Dean Cameron(✉),
and Adrianna Skyler Lugo(✉)

Artificial Intelligence Lab, San Diego State University, San Diego 92182, USA
lcameron@sdsu.edu

**Abstract.** Human robot interaction (HRI) offers potential in fulfilling the social needs of humans specifically, in the context of an interview setting. While human robot interaction has proven potentials to provide relatively measurable outcomes in experimentation, applications in real life are limited mainly due to primitive HRI design and implementation. Research in HRI is thus the necessary first step to the diffusion of robots and robotic technologies into social life. This study presents the results a case study on HRI design for a formal interview process. The findings are presented in a framework that elucidates the key expected robot affordances—action possibilities afforded by a humanoid robot—and their relationships with humans in the interactive interview context. This framework development has been informed by the Needs-Affordances-Features perspective.

**Keywords:** Human robot interaction · Robots · Interview · Needs-affordances-features perspective

## 1 Introduction

Human-robot interaction presents an opportunity to extend the use of robots in everyday life. These robots could help interview humans in settings where questions are repetitive and therefore may cause humans to tire, be annoyed, and most dangerously, be biased. In this study, we evaluate the degree to which a robot could help a human in performing formal and systematic interviews. In this context, the robot is given a set of questions to ask an individual and could have prescribed parameters regarding the answers they are given back. We discuss a set of features that can make these verbal and non-verbal interactions more trustworthy and comfortable, allowing the robot to complete its assigned task. Lastly, to identify the affordances, we evaluate how this set of features can satisfy the needs associated with the interview process. The list of affordances can help future researchers with HRI design and evaluation for interviewing and other interactive experiences. Moreover, the methodology presented here can be used to examine HRI in different contexts or environments.

© Springer Nature Switzerland AG 2021
F. F.-H. Nah and K. Siau (Eds.): HCII 2021, LNCS 12783, pp. 645–655, 2021.
https://doi.org/10.1007/978-3-030-77750-0_43

## 2 Background

Since robots have been introduced to the manufacturing industry, the interest in designing settings wherein robots and humans can work and communicate side-by-side grew. Hence, the field of human-robot interaction (HRI) was born. To separate this idea from human-computer interaction, HRI has a physical embodiment or casing that interacts with humans, and this shell is what constrains as well as focuses the capabilities of the robot.

Bartneck, et.al. Explains, HRI is a "multidisciplinary field of study that involves designing and creating robotic hardware and software, analyze human behavior when interacting with robots in different social contexts, the design of the environments that involve said interactions, and the subject matter expertise of the field of application" [2]. Because of this multi-faceted approach as well as the evolution of actuators, sensors, and software, robots not only became increasingly instrumental in industry and commerce, but in communication and gaining the trust of humans as well. Such social robots are further explained below.

### 2.1 Social Robot

The idea of a social robot was born during the industrial robot was created in the 1950's: the Unimate [12]. Initially, controlled by humans, they became partially and eventually fully autonomous because their ability to execute and react to human commands and non-verbal behavior evoked a semblance of social presence among humans. The two factors that determine human-robot engagement are a focal point or a "face" to look at and determine responsiveness from, and the ability to respond behaviorally. The robot's exterior does not need to look human, but there does need to be a focal point [18] by which humans can anthropomorphize the robot with. This can be achieved physically or behaviorally. Physically, facial features or a semblance of them can be fashioned as in the Kismet robot, a "neck-and-face" combination that could mimic and simulate emotion [12]. Kismet has enlarged eyes, nose, and mouth but does not look human. Another non-humanoid robot that has a physical focal point is the Paro robot, that comes in the form of a seal, so it has eyes as the focal point, but also has tactile sensors as input, so it can respond to physical touch. Other examples of physical focal points are humanoid robots, such as the SoftBank's NAO Robot, Pepper, and Sophia.

What is noteworthy is that such focal points can also present themselves by the way that the robots respond to human social cues. For example, the Keepon robot is composed of two spheres placed on top of each other. Its ability to "bob" up and down and bend side to side in response to music or human movement indicated a clear focal point on its upper sphere [2]. However, it cannot convey emotions since it has no facial features. Equally important, it is robots' responsiveness to human behavioral cues. To dissect this responsiveness further, we must understand the sequence of events. To start, the robot must be able to recognize and process any visual, audio, or tactile input from the human. This human input will then have to be analyzed by the robot, much like a function, and then deliver an output that is recognizable and sensible to the human. What is key is that the human understands this output. In an interview setting, this loop must happen as smoothly as possible. The software for this responsiveness to human social cues has been present since the conception of chatbots and even automatic call distributor systems. Over time, the responses become more fluid to the point where it is almost human-like. The combined focal point and behavioral response to its environment make a social presence that undeniably allows humans affordability depending on the robots' design [2, 5, 18].

## 2.2 Social Robot

The Needs-Affordances-Features Perspective asserts that robot features must allow affordances that satisfy human needs in HRI. To understand this, we explore general robot advantages over humans that make working with them convenient. Because robots are good at repetitive tasks, they do not tire or complain, making consistency and reliability their salient advantages. Because of this reliability, their outcomes can be measured, making experimentation easier. In addition, robots are programmable. Their constraints can be defined. What they can learn and absorb as input can be controlled. For example, there are studies that are done in healthcare, there are settings in which certain words or gestures that are natural to most humans can be psychologically triggering for patients. Robots can bypass having to deal with self-control issues like most humans would. Another example would be humans can program how autonomous they would like the robot to be. Depending on how the robot is designed, all their features can be calibrated accordingly for their function. The same control can be said about what pool of knowledge the robot is connected to. A good example is Alexa or Google Home. The convenience of having the information on hand is priceless.

## 2.3 Human Context in HRI

The factor that will contribute the most variability to HRI experimentation is habitus which encompasses the "full social experience and context of practices" and therefore unique to every human [8]. This also cannot be controlled by anyone in the study except for the human actor. For example, people may have had experiences prior to the experiment that shape their natural predisposition to robots or technology in general. Some may choose to engage with the robots gladly and others may not choose to at all. Because of the nature of habitus, affordance is not enough to account for all results of experimentation. Instead, both habitus (context) and affordance (action possibility) paint the results of the experiment together [8]. In addition, since habitus introduces so much variability, it is important for studies to factor in habitus to help standardize practice. In truth, the human experience cannot fully be captured, but the field can come close to it by including it in future studies.

## 3 Case Study

### 3.1 Robot as an Interviewer

We propose to use SoftBank's Pepper robot to conduct an interview with human participants, measuring the human interviewee's perception of the affordances provided by

Pepper that facilitate the interview. Pepper was designed as a service robot to assist in home and business settings, making it well suited for communication research in HRI. Pepper robot has 20 degrees of freedom between its 17 joints. These include Pepper's head, shoulders, elbows, wrists, hands, hips, knee, and base plate. These allow Pepper to move gracefully and express a range of gestures and other non-verbal communication. An array of microphones allows Pepper to speak via built-in speakers. Pepper was intentionally designed to not appear male or female to avoid the consequences of anthropomorphizing human gender [2]. This also applies to Pepper's voice, which is intentionally androgenous.

Pepper is also equipped with several cameras for eye tracking and navigation. Andrist [1], found that well timed gaze aversion can make a robot conversational partner appear thoughtful. Eye tracking helps Pepper to respond to human gaze behavior further enriching the nonverbal communication channel. An LED screen located on the chest can provide an additional communication avenue [1], provides a more complete review of Pepper's features and capabilities.

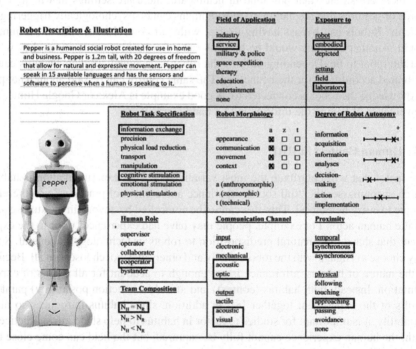

**Fig. 1.** The Taxonomy of Pepper as defined by Onnasch and Roesler [18]

Figure 1 implements Onnasch's [18] taxonomy for classifying HRI using Pepper in our proposed case study. Although the primary field of application is in service, the interview scenario could be applicable in police, therapy, and education as well. In our proposed interview, Pepper will be 2 m from the human participant in a laboratory setting. Pepper is an embodied, anthropomorphic robot with a high degree of information acquisition and information analysis robot autonomy. For our case study, Pepper will have low decision-making autonomy and will be used as a puppet for a human operator to operate out of sight of the interviewee. Pepper will have a medium degree of action implementation autonomy in this case study. Even though a human will be coordinating verbal responses, Pepper will still use built-in gaze management and natural movement settings. The single human participant will be a cooperator in this case study, working with Pepper to complete the interview.

### 3.2 'Needs' Associated with the Interview Process

Karahanna [16] devised a Needs-Affordances-Features framework that sought to discover how social media features provide affordances that satisfy human psychological needs. We seek to utilize this same framework to codify the needs, affordances, and features associated with a human-robot interview. During an interview, human participants have a set of relatively stable needs that - if fulfilled - will facilitate the interview process. Self Determination Theory [3] states that humans have three basic psychological needs: competency, relatedness, and autonomy. In an interview scenario competency and relatedness offer the best opportunities for psychological need fulfillment.

Competency refers to the innate desire to have some level of mastery or proficiency towards accomplishing a task. In a novel interview situation like a robot-conducted interview, a human who is confident in their competency interacting with other humans may not feel that same confidence when speaking to a robot interviewer. This new situation allows a human to build competency with human-robot interaction, satisfying their need. This could take the form of competency in communicating clearly with the robot and understanding the robot's communication (verbal and non-verbal) towards the robot. Part of satisfying the human need for competency in the interaction is having a robot interviewer that can execute the tasks they were designed for well.

Relatedness presents another psychological need that can be satisfied in an interview scenario. Relatedness at its most basic level refers to the need for humans to interact with others. At this basic level, a positive interactive experience during an interview can constitute satisfaction of this need. Interaction between a robot interviewer and a human interviewee is primarily verbal and non-verbal, physical interaction is optional. Pepper has microphones for listening, speakers to verbally communicate, and various nonverbal communication features – making Pepper a good candidate for an interview robot.

### 3.3 Key Affordances

The essential affordances that can be provided by a robot interviewer in an HRI interview scenario are interactivity, communication, and sourcing. Reviewing existing literature on affordances in HRI, HCI, and communication research shows varied definitions of affordances, with some efforts to arrive at an essential definition [6]. Evans [6], provides criteria for determining if a proposed affordance is in fact an affordance. The first of these criteria requires the proposed affordance is neither the object itself nor a feature of the object providing the affordance. The second requires that the affordance is not an outcome, affordances should invite outcomes. The third criterion is that the proposed affordance has a variable range.

Interactivity affordances refer to the degree human actions will prompt robot reactions [15]. In an HRI interview where the robot is conducting the interview, this will constitute both verbal and nonverbal cues that features of a robot interviewer can afford. Interactivity is not a feature, but rather an affordance provided by a collection of features. Interactivity is also not an outcome, but an affordance that allows for the outcome of interaction. Interactivity can vary in degree from highly responsive and to a more subdued responsiveness. This is largely influenced by the capability and limitations of robot features. For example, a robot interviewer could have a low or high threshold for responding to a human interviewee fixing their gaze on something. However, the variable nature of the interactivity affordances is due to the context of the interaction. Interaction context includes the environment the interview takes place in as well as the habitus of the human interviewee [8]. When the interactivity affordances are adequately presented via enabling robot features, the psychological need for relatedness will motivate the human interviewee to act on interactivity affordances they perceive.

Communication affordances refer to affordances that enable various verbal and nonverbal communications with humans. The communication affordances are not features of a robot interviewer, but the possibilities that are perceived by humans for verbal and non-verbal communication. A robot's face is a feature of the robot that affords verbal communication if paired with other features like audio output and chatbot software. Many affordances in HRI exist in this "web of mediators" where different pieces of technology together provide different affordances than alone [14]. Communication affordances are not the outcome of communication, but the combined perceived potential of several robot features to enable communication. Both verbal and non-verbal communication affordances have variable ranges due to the relational nature of HRI. Different humans will perceive different possible communication actions due to their combined experience, temperament, and capabilities. The psychological needs for relatedness and competency will motivate the human to act on perceived communication affordances.

Sourcing affordances enable human interviewees to both provide and request information or resources. In an HRI interview context this could include both physical sourcing for documents and informational sourcing during questioning. Sourcing affordances are separate from the features that create them. The features that allow a robot to direct a line of questioning towards a human with appropriate language and timing are not affordances, but they do enable the affordance to be perceived. Sourcing affordances are not the outcome of sourcing information and resources, but rather the combined perceived potential for sourcing to or from a robot interviewer. Due to the same relational nature of HRI and subjective habits of individual humans, sourcing affordances have variability in the degree they are perceived and acted on. The psychological need for competency will motivate humans to act on sourcing affordances.

## 4 Discussion

### 4.1 Theoretical Contribution

Experimentation of features should move the future study with the needs and affordances in mind. We have discussed two needs which are competency and relatedness. First, because we know that competency is one of the needs robot interviewers can fulfill, we need to explore ways by which humans feel that they can master interaction with the robot. Maybe prior training before meeting with a robot detailing how exactly to engage can help. Additionally, robotic features that increase familiarity to natural interactions, such as incorporating more human-like responsiveness to behavioral cues can help. In addition, we can experiment on the robot-to-human ratio in the interview setting [18]. Much like how the self-checkout lines in the grocery stores, one dedicated employee is assigned to help sort out issues in the self-checkout machines in case anything goes wrong with the transactions. Similarly, we can find out differences in affect when there are more humans than robots, equal number of humans and robots, and more robots than humans [18]. What we must realize here is that the robot and human interviewee are collaborators in defining successful interviews, meaning they share a common goal and are dependent on each other for the achievement of said goal [18]. Due to the idea of habitus [8], responses can vary, as mentioned. In addition, having humanoid morphology can contribute to higher perception of a more natural communication such as speech and human mimicry in conversation [18].

Next, we can experiment on the relatedness need that robot interviewers fulfill. We have discussed about how responsiveness helps in helping humans better perceive robots. Part of this response to behavioral and verbal cues is their ability to be mobile or mimic human response. We can experiment with this mimicry by conducting experiments where we vary the degrees by which the robot can be mobile. For instance, we can have one where the robot just speaks and does not move anything else. In another we can have a robot that is totally fluid in movement in response to humans. In addition, any variables in tone and language and ability to make the interaction a positive one. Here is where emotion detection and analysis counts. Because if robots can recognize and analyze emotions better, then they can respond accordingly and maintain the positivity of the interaction. They can for example be programmed not to say any trigger words for patients with post-traumatic stress disorder or autism spectrum disorder.

Affordances are elusive because they are a collection of features that allow the human to interact with the robot as opposed to one specific feature that has a single goal. Knowing this, we now explore how we can experiment with interactivity, communication, and sourcing. For interactivity, we can explore limiting or expanding features that relate to mimicry, like the number of axes of mobility or the tone of voice that the robot responds with. For instance, think about a robot asking for a boarding pass and travel documents in an airport versus a robot asking for latest symptoms from a patient in a medical setting. There is an urgency that must be conveyed in the first scenario and sensitivity when asking for patient health information in the latter. Next, we have communication which allows humans to interact with each other verbally and non-verbally. Here we can play with input sensors, like infrared, auditory, visual input devices. To add, we can experiment with the engines that process these inputs. This is where machine learning techniques, software for emotion detection, sentiment analysis, and natural language processing, can be explored. In addition, we have output mechanisms, such as speakers, facial features like blinking, and a plethora of facial expressions to play around with. Moreover, the mechanisms by which we can make communication easier for example, multilingual capabilities and additional output devices like screens can supplement communicative affordances. As mentioned, Pepper can speak fifteen languages and has a screen on its chest that can supplement any auditory and visual response, like a diagram or a photo. Last is sourcing, which allows human interviewees to provide and request for information. Aside from input, processing, and output devices that can be improved, studies that can be done by experimenting on the number of input and output devices. For example, if the robot has requested for a piece of information but has numerous modes of input. It may appear confusing to the user and will not contribute to mastery. Think of a bill-to-coin changer machine, as opposed to an ATM with a keypad, slots for deposit slips, and various other buttons to facilitate the transaction. Affordances are, after all, supposed to help humans perceive action possibilities. In this case, experimenting with the number of input and output devices may or may not contribute to information overload rather than helping with humans' day-to-day activity. As we can see, both affordances and satisfaction of needs can be explored accordingly.

## 4.2 Practical Implications

Designers trying to build a robot that fulfills interview functions can use key interview needs and affordances identified here to inform their design choice and feature selection. Some examples of the robot types that would benefit from these are: receptionist robots, robots in healthcare specifically for the elderly and psychotherapy, robots for learning, and robots for security in travel ports and border patrol offices.

Receptionist robots can be designed to interview incoming clients in a business setting. In many instances, they were also used for navigational purposes so that they can direct clients to the specific room they are having a meeting in. There is a short interview in the beginning to ask the client for what they need. In such cases, it is more helpful to have extra communicative features since humans need more information from the robot, for example, Pepper's monitor can show more information while she is speaking [2, 22].

Robots in healthcare can serve as medical intake assistants and socially assistive robots or SAR's [2]. As medical receptionists, they can interview the incoming patient with a standard questionnaire [2, 4]. A study with a humanoid NAO robot was found to need studies that deal with increasing the robot's social presence [2]. To delve into the idea of robots in this setting, we understand that doctors in medical settings are stretched too thin between patients. In addition, they, like a lot of medical personnel, have arduously long shifts that have an undeniable effect on their well-being and their mood. Such factors can negatively impact significant exchanges with their patients. In this setup, robots can help by being the information-givers regarding extended questions of a lab result. That way, any extra information they need can be addressed for however the patient needs, and the doctors can tend to their other patients or appointments. More of this information dissemination will be discussed in robots for education below. Another aspect that robots in healthcare can contribute is in providing personal assistance for the elderly, such as helping them with "pre-clinic and tele-clinic appointments at home," as well as providing them with companionship, which then reduces costs and improves their psychological well-being [2]. These interviews may take a more conversational approach wherein the robot must remember certain input from the elderly to build trust and provide information. Extra features to be explored include assessment of consciousness and improved conversational abilities. This situation is where we can experiment with the communication and sourcing affordances we have discussed, specifically tone of voice and choice of words.

Robots for education can provide one-on-one education [2]. For enhanced teaching, Pepper, as mentioned, has a monitor on her chest to show different diagrams [23]. Increased studies on the robots' behavioral responses may contribute to students' learning. As in other scenarios, the robot can go over any clarifications that the student may need at the pace of the student, which in a normal classroom setting, may cause delay in other pupils' learning or frustration on the part of the educator. Communication, interactivity, and sourcing affordances can be enhanced in this context.

Last, we discuss robots for security in travel ports and border patrol offices. These round-the-clock high stress environments are the prime reason that robots can help in interview scenarios. Humans can tire, complain, and be biased. Since robots do not fatigue or do not complain, they can produce the personalized interviews that these situations require. To add, since robots are programmable and therefore can produce relatively predictable outcomes, their efficacy can be measured. For instance, robots have been considered for deception detection in deceptive interviews and mock crime [5]. The affordances to explore in design would be communication, interactivity, and sourcing.

In summary, the contexts above can be used to explore distinct features that can increase affordability and help further ease the human needs of competency and relatedness. As we can observe, each of the interview settings have overlapping affordances and corresponding features that can be improved on.

## 5  Conclusion and Future Research Avenues

We have established key affordances to be provided by interview robots. After establishing the key affordances that a robot interviewer can provide in an interview, further research on what robot features and combinations of features specifically provide these affordances is warranted. Affordances are unanimously defined as being shaped by the context and environment they take place in [8]. Therefore, the effect that varying interview scenarios and contexts have on perceived affordances should be studied. In addition, the reverse interview situation where a social robot is interviewed or questioned by a human should be examined. The affordances desired and features required for a question-answering social robot may differ from those of a question-asking robot. Identifying both sets of features will allow for a better understanding of the possible constraints and synergies of features that will allow for a truly versatile generation of social robots that can provide a full range of affordances.

## References

1. Andrist, S., Tan, X.Z., Gleicher, M., Mutlu, B.: Conversational gaze aversion for humanlike robots. In: Proceedings of the 2014 ACM/IEEE International Conference on Human-Robot Interaction, pp. 25–32. University of Wisconsin-Madison Department of Computer Sciences (2014). https://doi.org/10.1145/2559636.2559666

2. Bartneck, C., Belpaeme, T., Eyssel, F., Kanda, T., Keijsers, M., Šabanović, S.: Human-Robot Interaction: An Introduction. Cambridge University Press, Cambridge (2019)

3. Deci, E., Vallerand, R., Pelletier, L., Ryan, R.: Motivation and education: the self-determination perspective. Educ. Psychol. 26(3–4), 325–346 (1991). https://doi.org/10.1080/00461520.1991.9653137

4. Edwards, A., Omilion-Hodges, L., Edwards, C.: How do patients in a medical interview perceive a robot versus human physician? In: Proceedings of the Companion of the 2017 ACM/IEEE International Conference on Human-Robot Interaction, HRI 2017, Vienna, Austria, pp. 109–110. Companion (2017)

5. Elkins, A., Gupte, A., Cameron, L.: Humanoid Robots as Interviewers for Automated Credibility Assessment. Artificial Intelligence Lab. San Diego State University, USA (2018)

6. Evans, S.K., Pearce, K.E., Vitak, J., Treem, J.W.: Explicating affordances: a conceptual framework for understanding affordances in communication research. J. Comput.-Mediat. Commun. 22(1), 35–52 (2016)

7. Fallon, M., et al.: An architecture for online affordance-based perception and whole-body planning. J. Field Robot. 32(2), 229–254 (2015). https://doi.org/10.21236/ada602904

8. Fayard, A.-L., Weeks, J.: Affordances for practice. Inf. Organ. 24(4), 236–249 (2014). https://doi.org/10.1016/j.infoandorg.2014.10.001

9. Fox, J., Gambino, A.: Relationship development with humanoid social robots: applying interpersonal theories to human/robot interaction. Cyberpsychol. Behav. Soc. Netw. 1–5 (2021). https://doi.org/10.1089/cyber.2020.0181

10. Ghazali, A.S., Ham, J., Barakova, E., Markopoulos, P.: Assessing the effect of persuasive robots interactive social cues on users' psychological reactance, liking, trusting beliefs and compliance. Adv. Robot. 33(7–8), 325–337 (2019). https://doi.org/10.1080/01691864.2019.1589570

11. Hancock, P.A., Billings, D.R., Schaefer, K.E., Chen, J.Y., de Visser, E.J., Parasuraman, R.: A meta-analysis of factors affecting trust in human-robot interaction. Hum. Factors: J. Hum. Factors Ergon. Soc. 53(5), 517–527 (2011). https://doi.org/10.1177/0018720811417254

12. Harris, J., Sharlin, E.: Exploring the affect of abstract motion in social human-robot interaction. RO-MAN (2011). https://doi.org/10.1109/roman.2011.6005254

13. Jamone, L., et al.: Affordances in psychology, neuroscience, and robotics: a survey. IEEE Trans. Cogn. Dev. Syst. 4–25 (2018). https://doi.org/10.1109/tcds.2016.2594134

14. Kahn, P.H., et al.: Will people keep the secret of a humanoid robot? In: Proceedings of the Tenth Annual ACM/IEEE International Conference on Human-Robot Interaction, HRI 2015, Portland, Oregon, pp. 173–180 (2015)

15. Kaptelinin, V., Nardi, B.: Affordances in HCI: toward a mediated action perspective. In: Proceedings on Human Factors in Computing Systems, CHI 2012, Austin, Texas, pp. 967–975 (2012)

16. Karahanna, E., Xin Xu, S., Xu, Y., Zhang, N.: The needs–affordances–features perspective for the use of social media. MIS Q. 42(3), 737–756 (2018). https://doi.org/10.25300/MISQ/2018/11492

17. Khan, A.N., Ihalage, A., Ma, Y., Liu, B., Liu, Y., et al.: Deep learning framework for subject-independent emotion detection using wireless signals. PLOS ONE 16(2), 1–16 (2021). https://doi.org/10.1371/journal.pone.0242946

18. Onnasch, L., Roesler, E.: A taxonomy to structure and analyze human–robot interaction. Int. J. Soc. Robot. (2020). https://doi.org/10.1007/s12369-020-00666-5

19. Onyeulo, E.B., Gandhi, V.: What makes a social robot good at interacting with humans? Information 11(43), 1–13 (2020). https://doi.org/10.3390/info11010043

20. Ötting, S.K., Masjutin, L., Steil, J.J., Maier, G.W.: Let's work together: a meta-analysis on robot design features that enable successful human–robot (2020)

21. Interaction at Work. Hum. Factors: J. Hum. Factors Ergon. Soc. 1–24 (2020). https://doi.org/10.1177/0018720820966433
22. Pandey, A.K., Alami, R.: Affordance graph: a framework to encode perspective taking and effort based affordances for day-to-day human-robot interaction. In: IEEE/RSJ International Conference on Intelligent Robots and Systems 2013, IROS, Tokyo, Japan, pp. 2180–2187 (2013). https://doi.org/10.1109/iros.2013.6696661
23. Pandey, A.K., Gelin, R.: Pepper: the first machine of its kind a mass-produced sociable humanoid. In: IEEE/RSJ International Conference on Intelligent Robots and Systems 2013, IROS, Tokyo, Japan, pp. 2180–2187 (2018). https://doi.org/10.1109/iros.2013.6696661
24. Shu, T., Ryoo, M.S., Zhu, S.-C.: Learning social affordance for human-robot interaction. In: 25th International Joint Conference on Artificial Intelligence, IJCAI 2016, New York, pp. 3454–3461 (2016)
25. Vallverdú, J., Trovato, G.: Emotional affordances for human–robot interaction. Adapt. Behav. 24(5), 320–334 (2016). https://doi.org/10.1177/1059712316668238
26. Vallverdú, J., Trovato, G., Jamone, L.: Allocentric emotional affordances in HRI: the multimodal binding. Multimodal Technol. Interact. 2(78), 1–20 (2018). https://doi.org/10.20944/preprints201808.0312.v1
27. Wang, S.M., Cheng, W.M.: Design thinking for developing a case-based reasoning emotion-sensing robot for interactive interview. In: Symposium on Emerging Research from Asia and on Asian Contexts and Cultures, CHI 2020, Hawaii, pp. 13–16 (2020). https://doi.org/10.1145/3391203.3391205
28. Zheng, J., Jarvenpaa, S.L.: (PDF) [Internet]: Thinking Technology as Human: Affordances, Technology Features, and Egocentric Biases in Technology Anthropomorphism. ResearchGate (2020). https://www.researchgate.net/publication/347484661_Thinking_Technology_as_Human_Affordances_Technology_Features_and_Egocentric_Biases_in_Technology_Anthropomorphism. Accessed 21 Feb 2021

# Author Index

Printed in the United States
by Baker & Taylor Publisher Services